Contemporary Authors®

ISSN 0010-7468

Contemporary Authors®

A Bio-Bibliographical Guide to
Current Writers in Fiction, General Nonfiction,
Poetry, Journalism, Drama, Motion Pictures,
Television, and Other Fields

volume 207

GALE®

THOMSON
GALE

Detroit • New York • San Diego • San Francisco • Cleveland • New Haven, Conn. • Waterville, Maine • London • Munich

Contemporary Authors, Vol. 207

Project Editor
Scot Peacock

Editorial
Katy Balcer, Sara Constantakis, Anna Marie Dahn, Alana Joli Foster, Natalie Fulkerson, Arlene M. Johnson, Michelle Kazensky, Julie Keppen, Jennifer Kilian, Joshua Kondek, Lisa Kumar, Thomas McMahon, Jenai A. Mynatt, Judith L. Pyko, Mary Ruby, Lemma Shomali, Susan Strickland, Anita Sundaresan, Maikue Vang, Tracey Watson, Denay L. Wilding, Thomas Wiloch, Emiene Shija Wright

Research
Tamara C. Nott, Sarah Genik, Nicodemus Ford, Michelle Campbell

Permissions
Lori Hines

Imaging and Multimedia
Dean Dauphinais, Robert Duncan, Leitha Etheridge-Sims, Mary K. Grimes, Lezlie Light, Dan Newell, David G. Oblender, Christine O'Bryan, Kelly A. Quin, Luke Rademacher

Composition and Electronic Capture
Carolyn A. Roney

Manufacturing
Stacy L. Melson

LIBRARY OF CONGRESS CATALOG CARD NUMBER 62-52046

ISBN 0-7876-5200-8
ISSN 0010-7468

Printed in the United States of America
10 9 8 7 6 5 4 3 2 1

Contents

Indexing note: All *Contemporary Authors* entries are indexed in the *Contemporary Authors* cumulative index, which is published separately and distributed twice a year.

As always, the most recent Contemporary Authors cumulative index continues to be the user's guide to the location of an individual author's listing.

Preface

Contemporary Authors (*CA*) provides information on approximately 100,000 writers in a wide range of media, including:

- Current writers of fiction, nonfiction, poetry, and drama whose works have been issued by commercial publishers, risk publishers, or university presses (authors whose books have been published only by known vanity or author-subsidized firms are ordinarily not included)

- Prominent print and broadcast journalists, editors, photojournalists, syndicated cartoonists, graphic novelists, screenwriters, television scriptwriters, and other media people

- Notable international authors

- Literary greats of the early twentieth century whose works are popular in today's high school and college curriculums and continue to elicit critical attention

A *CA* listing entails no charge or obligation. Authors are included on the basis of the above criteria and their interest to *CA* users. Sources of potential listees include trade periodicals, publishers' catalogs, librarians, and other users of the series.

How to Get the Most out of *CA*: Use the Index

The key to locating an author's most recent entry is the *CA* cumulative index, which is published separately and distributed twice a year. It provides access to *all* entries in *CA* and *Contemporary Authors New Revision Series* (*CANR*). Always consult the latest index to find an author's most recent entry.

For the convenience of users, the *CA* cumulative index also includes references to all entries in these Gale literary series: *Authors and Artists for Young Adults, Authors in the News, Bestsellers, Black Literature Criticism, Black Literature Criticism Supplement, Black Writers, Children's Literature Review, Concise Dictionary of American Literary Biography, Concise Dictionary of British Literary Biography, Contemporary Authors Autobiography Series, Contemporary Authors Bibliographical Series, Contemporary Dramatists, Contemporary Literary Criticism, Contemporary Novelists, Contemporary Poets, Contemporary Popular Writers, Contemporary Southern Writers, Contemporary Women Poets, Dictionary of Literary Biography, Dictionary of Literary Biography Documentary Series, Dictionary of Literary Biography Yearbook, DISCovering Authors, DISCovering Authors: British, DISCovering Authors: Canadian, DISCovering Authors: Modules* (including modules for Dramatists, Most-Studied Authors, Multicultural Authors, Novelists, Poets, and Popular/ Genre Authors), *DISCovering Authors 3.0, Drama Criticism, Drama for Students, Feminist Writers, Hispanic Literature Criticism, Hispanic Writers, Junior DISCovering Authors, Major Authors and Illustrators for Children and Young Adults, Major 20th-Century Writers, Native North American Literature, Novels for Students, Poetry Criticism, Poetry for Students, Short Stories for Students, Short Story Criticism, Something about the Author, Something about the Author Autobiography Series, St. James Guide to Children's Writers, St. James Guide to Crime & Mystery Writers, St. James Guide to Fantasy Writers, St. James Guide to Horror, Ghost & Gothic Writers, St. James Guide to Science Fiction Writers, St. James Guide to Young Adult Writers, Twentieth-Century Literary Criticism, 20th Century Romance and Historical Writers, World Literature Criticism,* and *Yesterday's Authors of Books for Children.*

A Sample Index Entry:

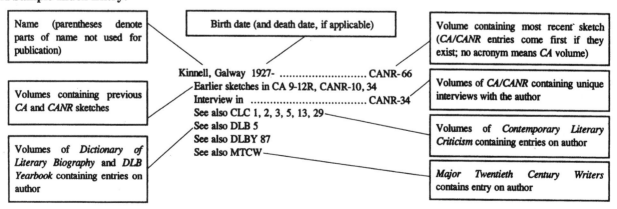

How Are Entries Compiled?

The editors make every effort to secure new information directly from the authors; listees' responses to our questionnaires and query letters provide most of the information featured in *CA*. For deceased writers, or those who fail to reply to requests for data, we consult other reliable biographical sources, such as those indexed in Gale's *Biography and Genealogy Master Index,* and bibliographical sources, including *National Union Catalog, LC MARC,* and *British National Bibliography.* Further details come from published interviews, feature stories, and book reviews, as well as information supplied by the authors' publishers and agents.

An asterisk (*) at the end of a sketch indicates that the listing has been compiled from secondary sources believed to be reliable but has not been personally verified for this edition by the author sketched.

What Kinds of Information Does An Entry Provide?

Sketches in *CA* contain the following biographical and bibliographical information:

- **Entry heading:** the most complete form of author's name, plus any pseudonyms or name variations used for writing

- **Personal information:** author's date and place of birth, family data, ethnicity, educational background, political and religious affiliations, and hobbies and leisure interests

- **Addresses:** author's home, office, or agent's addresses, plus e-mail and fax numbers, as available

- **Career summary:** name of employer, position, and dates held for each career post; resume of other vocational achievements; military service

- **Membership information:** professional, civic, and other association memberships and any official posts held

- **Awards and honors:** military and civic citations, major prizes and nominations, fellowships, grants, and honorary degrees

- **Writings:** a comprehensive, chronological list of titles, publishers, dates of original publication and revised editions, and production information for plays, television scripts, and screenplays

- **Adaptations:** a list of films, plays, and other media which have been adapted from the author's work

- **Work in progress:** current or planned projects, with dates of completion and/or publication, and expected publisher, when known

- **Sidelights:** a biographical portrait of the author's development; information about the critical reception of the author's works; revealing comments, often by the author, on personal interests, aspirations, motivations, and thoughts on writing

- **Interview:** a one-on-one discussion with authors conducted especially for *CA*, offering insight into authors' thoughts about their craft

- **Autobiographical essay:** an original essay written by noted authors for *CA*, a forum in which writers may present themselves, on their own terms, to their audience

- **Photographs:** portraits and personal photographs of notable authors

- **Biographical and critical sources:** a list of books and periodicals in which additional information on an author's life and/or writings appears

- **Obituary Notices** in *CA* provide date and place of birth as well as death information about authors whose full-length sketches appeared in the series before their deaths. The entries also summarize the authors' careers and writings and list other sources of biographical and death information.

Related Titles in the *CA* Series

Contemporary Authors Autobiography Series complements *CA* original and revised volumes with specially commissioned autobiographical essays by important current authors, illustrated with personal photographs they provide. Common topics include their motivations for writing, the people and experiences that shaped their careers, the rewards they derive from their work, and their impressions of the current literary scene.

Contemporary Authors Bibliographical Series surveys writings by and about important American authors since World War II. Each volume concentrates on a specific genre and features approximately ten writers; entries list works written by and about the author and contain a bibliographical essay discussing the merits and deficiencies of major critical and scholarly studies in detail.

Available in Electronic Formats

GaleNet. *CA* is available on a subscription basis through GaleNet, an online information resource that features an easy-to-use end-user interface, powerful search capabilities, and ease of access through the World-Wide Web. For more information, call 1-800-877-GALE.

Licensing. *CA* is available for licensing. The complete database is provided in a fielded format and is deliverable on such media as disk, CD-ROM, or tape. For more information, contact Gale's Business Development Group at 1-800-877-GALE, or visit us on our website at www.galegroup.com/bizdev.

Suggestions Are Welcome

The editors welcome comments and suggestions from users on any aspect of the *CA* series. If readers would like to recommend authors for inclusion in future volumes of the series, they are cordially invited to write the Editors at *Contemporary Authors*, Gale Group, 27500 Drake Rd., Farmington Hills, MI 48331-3535; or call at 1-248-699-4253; or fax at 1-248-699-8054.

Contemporary Authors Product Advisory Board

The editors of *Contemporary Authors* are dedicated to maintaining a high standard of excellence by publishing comprehensive, accurate, and highly readable entries on a wide array of writers. In addition to the quality of the content, the editors take pride in the graphic design of the series, which is intended to be orderly yet inviting, allowing readers to utilize the pages of *CA* easily and with efficiency. Despite the longevity of the *CA* print series, and the success of its format, we are mindful that the vitality of a literary reference product is dependent on its ability to serve its users over time. As literature, and attitudes about literature, constantly evolve, so do the reference needs of students, teachers, scholars, journalists, researchers, and book club members. To be certain that we continue to keep pace with the expectations of our customers, the editors of *CA* listen carefully to their comments regarding the value, utility, and quality of the series. Librarians, who have firsthand knowledge of the needs of library users, are a valuable resource for us. The *Contemporary Authors* Product Advisory Board, made up of school, public, and academic librarians, is a forum to promote focused feedback about *CA* on a regular basis. The seven-member advisory board includes the following individuals, whom the editors wish to thank for sharing their expertise:

- **Anne M. Christensen,** Librarian II, Phoenix Public Library, Phoenix, Arizona.

- **Barbara C. Chumard,** Reference/Adult Services Librarian, Middletown Thrall Library, Middletown, New York.

- **Eva M. Davis,** Youth Department Manager, Ann Arbor District Library, Ann Arbor, Michigan.

- **Adam Janowski, Jr.,** Library Media Specialist, Naples High School Library Media Center, Naples, Florida.

- **Robert Reginald,** Head of Technical Services and Collection Development, California State University, San Bernadino, California.

- **Katharine E. Rubin,** Head of Information and Reference Division, New Orleans Public Library, New Orleans, Louisiana.

- **Barbara A. Wencl,** Media Specialist, Como Park High School, St. Paul, Minnesota.

International Advisory Board

Well-represented among the 100,000 author entries published in *Contemporary Authors* are sketches on notable writers from many non-English-speaking countries. The primary criteria for inclusion of such authors has traditionally been the publication of at least one title in English, either as an original work or as a translation. However, the editors of *Contemporary Authors* came to observe that many important international writers were being overlooked due to a strict adherence to our inclusion criteria. In addition, writers who were publishing in languages other than English were not being covered in the traditional sources we used for identifying new listees. Intent on increasing our coverage of international authors, including those who write only in their native language and have not been translated into English, the editors enlisted the aid of a board of advisors, each of whom is an expert on the literature of a particular country or region. Among the countries we focused attention on are Mexico, Puerto Rico, Germany, Luxembourg, Belgium, the Netherlands, Norway, Sweden, Denmark, Finland, Taiwan, Singapore, Spain, Italy, South Africa, Israel, and Japan, as well as England, Scotland, Wales, Ireland, Australia, and New Zealand. The sixteen-member advisory board includes the following individuals, whom the editors wish to thank for sharing their expertise:

- **Lowell A. Bangerter,** Professor of German, University of Wyoming, Laramie, Wyoming.

- **Nancy E. Berg,** Associate Professor of Hebrew and Comparative Literature, Washington University, St. Louis, Missouri.

- **Frances Devlin-Glass,** Associate Professor, School of Literary and Communication Studies, Deakin University, Burwood, Victoria, Australia.

- **David William Foster,** Regent's Professor of Spanish, Interdisciplinary Humanities, and Women's Studies, Arizona State University, Tempe, Arizona.

- **Hosea Hirata,** Director of the Japanese Program, Associate Professor of Japanese, Tufts University, Medford, Massachusetts.

- **Jack Kolbert,** Professor Emeritus of French Literature, Susquehanna University, Selinsgrove, Pennsylvania.

- **Mark Libin,** Professor, University of Manitoba, Winnipeg, Manitoba, Canada.

- **C. S. Lim,** Professor, University of Malaya, Kuala Lumpur, Malaysia.

- **Eloy E. Merino,** Assistant Professor of Spanish, Northern Illinois University, DeKalb, Illinois.

- **Linda M. Rodríguez Guglielmoni,** Associate Professor, University of Puerto Rico—Mayagüez, Puerto Rico.

- **Sven Hakon Rossel,** Professor and Chair of Scandinavian Studies, University of Vienna, Vienna, Austria.

- **Steven R. Serafin,** Director, Writing Center, Hunter College of the City University of New York, New York City.

- **David Smyth,** Lecturer in Thai, School of Oriental and African Studies, University of London, England.

- **Ismail S. Talib,** Senior Lecturer, Department of English Language and Literature, National University of Singapore, Singapore.

- **Dionisio Viscarri,** Assistant Professor, Ohio State University, Columbus, Ohio.

- **Mark Williams,** Associate Professor, English Department, University of Canterbury, Christchurch, New Zealand.

CA Numbering System and Volume Update Chart

Occasionally questions arise about the *CA* numbering system and which volumes, if any, can be discarded. Despite numbers like " 29-32R," " 97-100" and "206," the entire *CA* print series consists of only 250 physical volumes with the publication of *CA* Volume 207. The following charts note changes in the numbering system and cover design, and indicate which volumes are essential for the most complete, up-to-date coverage.

CA **First Revision**	• 1-4R through 41-44R (11 books) *Cover:* Brown with black and gold trim. There will be no further First Revision volumes because revised entries are now being handled exclusively through the more efficient *New Revision Series* mentioned below.
CA **Original Volumes**	• 45-48 through 97-100 (14 books) *Cover:* Brown with black and gold trim. 101 through 207 (107 books) *Cover:* Blue and black with orange bands. The same as previous *CA* original volumes but with a new, simplified numbering system and new cover design.
CA **Permanent Series**	• *CAP*-1 and *CAP*-2 (2 books) *Cover:* Brown with red and gold trim. There will be no further Permanent Series volumes because revised entries are now being handled exclusively through the more efficient *New Revision Series* mentioned below.
CA **New Revision Series**	• CANR-1 through CANR-116 (116 books) *Cover:* Blue and black with green bands. Includes only sketches requiring significant changes; **sketches are taken from any previously published CA, CAP, or CANR volume.**

If You Have:	You May Discard:
CA First Revision Volumes 1-4R through 41-44R and *CA Permanent Series* Volumes 1 and 2	*CA* Original Volumes 1, 2, 3, 4 Volumes 5-6 through 41-44
CA Original Volumes 45-48 through 97-100 and 101 through 207	**NONE:** These volumes will not be superseded by corresponding revised volumes. Individual entries from these and all other volumes appearing in the left column of this chart may be revised and included in the various volumes of the *New Revision Series*.
CA New Revision Series Volumes *CANR*-1 through *CANR*-116	**NONE:** The *New Revision Series* does not replace any single volume of *CA*. Instead, volumes of *CANR* include entries from many previous *CA* series volumes. All *New Revision Series* volumes must be retained for full coverage.

A Sampling of Authors and Media People Featured in This Volume

Dan Chaon

An instructor at Oberlin College, Chaon is the author of two short story collections, *Fitting Ends and Other Stories* and *Among the Missing.* Chaon's tales often take place on a bleak Midwestern landscape, with the action shifting from small towns to the big city. In *Among the Missing,* which was a National Book Award finalist, the stories explore the idea of what it means to be absent on either a physical or a psychological level, or both. Chaon is the recipient of the Raymond Carver Memorial Award, the A. B. Guthrie, Jr. Short Fiction Award, and a Notable Book Award from the American Library Association.

Nora Kelly

Kelly has written a number of well-received mysteries, and reviewers have complimented her flair for creating intelligent, fully developed characters. Her first book, *In the Shadow of King's,* introduces readers to super sleuth Gillian Adams, a history professor who travels back and forth between the Pacific Northwest and the United Kingdom, much like the author herself. Other titles by Kelly include *My Sister's Keeper, Bad Chemistry, Old Wounds,* and *Hot Pursuit.*

Laurie R. King

King's unconventional take on the mystery genre has led to the development of two popular series characters: Mary Russell, the detective wife of Sherlock Holmes, and Kate Martinelli, a San Francisco policewoman. Through a number of books featuring each protagonist, King has formed their characters—and those of their cohorts—while consistently crafting tense thrillers, many with religious themes. A recipient of the Edgar Allan Poe Award and the Nero Wolfe Award, King is also author of an autobiographical essay included in this volume of *CA.*

Kenneth Kraft

A professor and author, Kraft is considered to be at the forefront of contemporary Buddhist thought. He has written extensively on Buddhism, including the "greening" of Buddhism—the use of Buddhist doctrines and practices to foster ecological awareness and integrity. He has also written authoritatively on Zen's relationship to language. His works include the editorship of *Zen: Tradition and Transition,* which collects original essays by eleven contemporary Zen scholars and masters, and *Eloquent Zen: Daito and Early Japanese Zen,* a study of the medieval Japanese Rinzai Zen master Daito Kokushi (also known as Myocho).

Bruno Maddox

Born to a British literary family, Maddox is a former *Spy* magazine editor and the author of the novel *My Little Blue Dress,* which purports to be a memoir of an old woman in New York who was born at the turn of the century. The memoir is written by "Bruno Maddox," a twenty-something hack writer who takes care of the woman but spends as much time talking about the hip Manhattan scene and his own hangups as he does telling her story—most of which he invents himself. Critics were generally favorable toward *My Little Blue Dress,* though some questioned the loosely structured narrative.

Marcia Millman

As a professor of sociology, Millman specializes in family dynamics, social psychology, deviance and conformity, social interaction, occupations and professions, and the study of popular representations and narratives of social life. She has written a number of books and is coeditor, with Rosabeth Moss Kanter, of *Another Voice: Feminist Perspectives on Social Life and Social Science.* Millman is also the author of *Warm Hearts and Cold Cash: The Intimate Dynamics of Families and Money* and *The Seven Stories of Love: And How to Choose Your Happy Ending.*

Samrat Upadhyay

With his first collection of short stories, *Arresting God in Kathmandu,* Upadhyay gained notice as a skilled commentator on the universal human condition and as the first Nepali author writing in English to be published in the West. Critics were impressed by the subtle manner with which he presents the troubles of ordinary people who live in a place perceived to be extraordinary by outsiders. A recipient of the Whiting Award in 2001, Upadhyay is also the author of the 2003 novel *The Guru of Love.*

Andrew Spurgeon Nash Young (A. S. "Doc" Young)

Young, who wrote as A. S. "Doc" Young, was a top editor and sportswriter, beginning in the 1940s, who also covered the social issues, politics, entertainment, and business of the black community. Young contributed to the major African-American and general interest publications of the day and was one of the first black members of the Baseball Writers Association of America. *Great Negro Baseball Stars, and How They Made the Major Leagues,* Young's first book, is a history of black athletes who had become major league players during the six years prior to the book's 1953 publication.

Acknowledgments

Grateful acknowledgment is made to those publishers, photographers, and artists whose work appear with these authors' essays. Following is a list of the copyright holders who have granted us permission to reproduce material in this volume of *CA*. Every effort has been made to trace copyright, but if omissions have been made, please let us know.

Photographs/Art

Eavan Boland: All photos reproduced by permission of the author, except as noted: O'Connell Bridge in Dublin, Ireland, spanning the River Liffey, by R. Humphrey, © Hulton Archive/Getty Images. Reproduced by permission.

Laurie R. King: All photos reproduced by permission of the author, except as noted: portrait of King (jacket and glasses), © Seth Affoumado, courtesy of Bantam Dell Publishing Group. Reproduced by permission.

Larry Niven: All photos reproduced by permission of the author.

A

ALBO, Mike 1969-

PERSONAL: Born May 22, 1969, in Dayton, OH; son of Charles (an entrepreneur), and Gail (a homemaker) Albo. *Education:* University of Virginia, B.A. (English), 1991; Columbia University School of the Arts, Writing Division, M.F.A., 1996.

ADDRESSES: Agent—c/o HarperCollins, 10 East 53rd St., New York, NY 10022. *E-mail*—virginia@inch. com.

CAREER: Writer, dancer, performance artist.

MEMBER: Member and founder, Dazzle Dancers, a performance dance troupe, New York, NY.

AWARDS, HONORS: Essay contest winner, *Washington Post,* 1987.

WRITINGS:

(With Graham Willoughby) *I'm SO Relaxed: A Flippy Radio Play,* produced at Independent Art Here, New York, NY, May 28-29, 1999.
Sex-o-theque (two-act play), first produced , Austin, TX, November, 1999; New York, NY, May-June, 2000; .
Hornito: My Lie Life, HarperCollins (New York, NY), 2000.

Contributor of columns, reviews and, short stories to magazines and online publications, including *Out, Word, Salon.com, Mademoiselle, Boston Phoenix, Village Voice, Nerve.com,* and *New York.*

WORK IN PROGRESS: Three Women in Indecision, a play going into production in January 2003.

SIDELIGHTS: Mike Albo was born in Dayton, Ohio, and spent much of his life growing up in the Washington, DC suburb of Springfield, Virginia, while his father served in the military. Albo pursued his interest in writing as an undergraduate at the University of Virginia at Charlottesville and as a graduate student at the Columbia University School of the Arts.

Although much of his life as an adolescent was conventional, Albo clearly did not fit the mold in one crucial respect: he was gay and he knew it from an early age. In an interview with Kurt B. Reighley of *Seattle Weekly,* Albo discussed his motivation for writing his first novel, *Hornito: My Lie Life,* a fictionalized account of growing up gay in suburbia in the 1970s and 1980s. "I wanted to talk about the gay childhood and these feelings that masculinity was learned in me. I'm glad I'm the way I am, but I definitely had to learn to run like a boy. If we lived in a completely different culture, like the Hopi Indians, I'd be one of those gay guys who lives in their own tepees. I would have been appreciated in a different way. But in our weird, stratified culture, I had to learn certain signals to be a guy."

Albo explained in an interview with CZ Lee for *GayWired.com,* that *Hornito* is a "story of a gay guy trying to figure out how to survive the emotionally twisted existence that is America: slogans, television, mowed suburban lawns, displayed desire, polluted love." Richard LeBlonté, reviewing *Hornito* for *PlanetOut.com,* began by saying, "Oh, sigh. Not another young man's tale of confused coming out, frustrated libido, and existential angst. But wait: the writing is vivid, sharp, and smart."

Hornito takes place in both the East Village, the gay mecca for New York City, and a suburban high school much like the one in which the author spent his early youth. In a review for the *New York Times,* Catherine Texier talked about the story and its grim realities. "As outsiders often are, both the author and the character are sharp and mordant observers of the cruel pecking order of social interaction. The parallel between high school and the East Village gay scene is particularly resonant. Whether as a teenager or a grown-up, Mike is forever trying to climb the social ladder and belong to the coolest clique, while yearning for an impossible kind of love. In his world, hairstyle is character, and his attempts to fit in are both hilarious and poignant," she noted. Albo's character in *Hornito* has an older brother who constantly berates him for being a sissy and terrifies him with claims such as "Abraham Lincoln's head is floating in your closet." Instead of a career in dancing, which Mike desperately wants to pursue, he enrolls in a soccer league. Instead of choosing to play the flute, he decides to play the trombone because it is a more masculine instrument, according to the monitors he carries with him in his head. In her review for the *Book Review Revue,* Emily Hall pointed out one of the most interesting facets of the published work: "Not judging a book by its cover is strictly a pre-postmodern concept; these days you can learn a lot about a book before you even open it. The cover of performance artist Mike Albo's debut novel, *Hornito,* contains a pair of stacked black-and-white photographs, one of a volcano, one of the bulge in a pair of briefs; silver holographic foil; and a subtitle: *My Lie Life.* What you might deduce is that this is a story about desire, set in the '70s, somewhere between memoir and fiction. And you would be right."

The dictionary definition of "hornito" is "beehive-like mound built from molten lava." Albo clearly used the word as a symbolic reference to the eruption of his life. A *Publishers Weekly* reviewer wrote: "The brilliance of Albo's cynical nostalgia may be lost on those who neither came of age in the New Wave '80s nor participated in the urban retro trends of the '90s; this

writer's formidable gift for humor and self-flagellating satire transcends the limits of a generation-X audience."

Albo told *CA* that what he liked most about the novel was writing it. "I became a part of the book. My whole mode of expression is very emotional, almost too emotional. And I feel, in a way, when I finished that book, that it is a living extension of myself -almost like a weird spellbook or something. Totally Harry Potter." He also added "I have this heartfelt, psychotic need to connect with people and feel every wavelength. I think I am someone who wants to communicate, and whatever form I can take to connect with people I use. I get sort of sad when people consider me only a gay writer. That happens a lot. I think to myself—'why do people insist on shelving and typecasting people?' I read *Red Badge of Courage, Song of Solomon,* and other works by people who had wholly different lives. I would hope others could do the same. The whole act of expression is to bring people together to tell stories, to create that jingly feeling that we matter as humans. Is that fruitcakey or what?"

While Albo sees himself primarily as a writer, he is also a well-known performance artist and monologist who writes his own work and has performed throughout the United States and Canada and as far away as London. He performs with the dance company he founded, the Dazzle Dancers.

Albo's original performances have included the much-lauded two-act play *Sex-o-theque,* performed in New York City in the spring of 2000; *Unitard,* with Nora Burns and David Ilku, performed at Fez in New York City in 2001-2002; *Please Everything Burst,* performed as full-length solos at the Soho Theater in London, May-June, 2001, and at PS 122 in New York City, April, 2000; and *Spray,* a full-length solo performed at PS 122, January-February, 1999, at Center Stage in Baltimore, October, 1999, and at the Philadelphia Fringe Festival, September, 2001. He has also written radio plays, including *Takeout Tax,* performed on NPR's *Anthem,* November, 1998, as well as live at The Moth at Lansky Lounge, New York City, in September, 1998. A *New York* magazine contributor noted that "Albo is living the freelancer's typically disjointed life. When he's not dispensing advice as *Out* magazine's love columnist, the 31-year-old Albo consults with a professional astrologer to write, 'Horoscopes from the Lavender Planet' for the Webzine *Word.*"

Albo told *CA,* "I am still trying to figure out ways to articulate why I perform and write at the same time. I think I am trying to make these words seem as honest and true and funny as possible. When I am performing my writing, I often 'see' the words while I am saying them. It's almost like the script and the life become the same thing. I see no difference between the word and the life." He also noted that "there is nothing better than getting those occasional e-mails or whatever from young people who read me in their suburban grid and felt a little freer because of my book."

BIOGRAPHICAL AND CRITICAL SOURCES:

BOOKS

Albo, Mike. *Hornito: My Lie Life,* HarperCollins (New York, NY), 2000.

PERIODICALS

Back Stage, April 14, 2000, Jane Hogan, review of *Please Everything Burst,* p. 51.
Entertainment Weekly, October 20, 2000, review of *Hornito: My Lie Life,* p. 72.
Lambda Book Report, November, 2000, Brian Perrin, review of *Hornito,* p. 18.
New York, June 26, 2000, Logan Hill, review of *Sex-o-theque,* p. 167.
New York Times, December 31, 2000, Catherine Texier, "Avenue A or Bust," p. 10.
Publishers Weekly, September 11, 2000, review of *Hornito,* p. 68.
Seattle Weekly, December 14, 2000, Kurt B. Reighley, "Two Ears and a Tale."

OTHER

Book Review Revue, http://www.thestranger.com/ (January 18, 2001), Emily Hall, review of *Hornito.*
Gaywired.com, http://www.gaywired.com (October 9, 2001), CZ Lee, "Mike Albo: Dazzle Dancer, Dazzling Author."
Mike Albo Web site, http://www.mikealbo.com (February 3, 2002).
OFFOFFOFF.com, http://www.offoffoff.com (September 13, 2001), Robin Eisgrau, "Comics' Trip.
PlanetOut, http://www.planetout.com (September 13, 2001), Richard Labonté, review of *Hornito.*

Performances include monologues and group performances, including *Brooklyn Tour Guides,* radio improvisation with Sharon Glassman, "The Next Big Thing" on WNYC, June, 2000.

* * *

ALLGOR, Catherine 1958-

PERSONAL: Born November 26, 1958, in Trenton, NJ; daughter of Clifford and Mary Allgor; married Jonathan Lipman, June, 1996 (divorced, December, 2001). *Education:* Bucks County Community College, A.A., 1978; attended North Carolina School of the Arts, 1979-81; Mount Holyoke College, A.B. (summa cum laude), 1992; Yale University, M.A., 1994, M.Phil. (with distinction), 1995, Ph.D. (with distinction), 1998.

ADDRESSES: Home—3 Winter St., No. 3, Salem, MA 01970. *Office*—Department of History, University of California—Riverside, Riverside, CA 92521-0204. *Agent*—Christy Fletcher, Carlisle and Co., 24 East 64th St., New York, NY 10021. *E-mail*—catherine. allgor@ucr.edu.

CAREER: Actress, historian, and educator. Professional actress, 1986-93; Plimouth Plantation, Plymouth, MA, living history interpreter and research assistant, 1991; Simmons College, Boston, MA, assistant professor of history, 1998-2001; University of California—Riverside, assistant professor of history, 2001—, fellow of Center for Ideas and Society, 2002-03. Decatur House Museum, member of board of directors of interpretive planning committee, 2000—; Massachusetts Historical Society, editor of "Louisa Catherine Johnson Adams Papers," 2000-02; workshop presenter; public speaker. Teacher of acting, voice, speech, and pantomime at colleges, theater companies, and camps, 1978-90; Bucks County Community College, teacher, 1988-90; Princeton Repertory Company, member of board of directors, performer, and producer, 1988-90.

MEMBER: American Historical Association, Society for Historians of the Early Republic, Actors's Equity Association, Phi Beta Kappa.

AWARDS, HONORS: Quarterly Paper Prize, Association of Living History Farms and Agricultural Museums, 1991; Webb-Smith Essay Competition winner,

University of Texas—Arlington, 1998; grants from Simmons College, 1999 and 2000; Lerner-Scott Prize for best dissertation in U.S. Women's History, Organization of American Historians, 1999; James H. Broussard First Book Prize, Society for Historians of the Early American Republic, 2000; Annual Book Award, Northeast Popular Culture/American Culture Association, 2000; fellow of Radcliffe Institute for Advanced Study, 2000-03.

WRITINGS:

Parlor Politics: In Which the Ladies of Washington Help Build a City and a Government, University Press of Virginia (Charlottesville, VA), 2000.

Adaptor, *A Christmas Carol* (stage play; based on the novel by Charles Dickens), produced in Princeton, NJ, by Princeton Repertory Company. Contributor to books, including *Women and the Unstable State in Nineteenth-Century America,* edited by Alison M. Parker and Stephanie Cole, Texas A & M University Press, 2000; *The Presidential Companion: Readings on the Political Significance of First Ladies,* edited by Robert P. Watson and Anthony J. Eksterowicz, Northern Illinois University Press, 2002; and *Created Capitals: Congress Moves to Washington, D.C.,* edited by Kenneth Bowling, Ohio University Press (Athens, OH), 2003. Contributor of articles and reviews to periodicals, including *Washington History* and *Diplomatic History.* Member of editorial board, *White House Studies,* 2000—.

WORK IN PROGRESS: Last of the Founders: Dolley Madison and the Creation of the American Nation, publication by Henry Holt (New York, NY) expected in 2005.

BIOGRAPHICAL AND CRITICAL SOURCES:

PERIODICALS

American Historical Review, February, 2002, Jean Baker, review of *Parlor Politics: In Which the Ladies of Washington Help Build a City and a Government,* p. 190.
American History, August, 2001, Jennifer Barger, review of *Parlor Politics,* p. 69.

Choice, June, 2001, P. D. Travis, review of *Parlor Politics,* p. 1851.
History: Review of New Books, spring, 2001, Elizabeth E. Dunn, review of *Parlor Politics,* p. 109.
Journal of American History, December, 2001, Mary Beth Norton, review of *Parlor Politics,* p. 1058.
Journal of Southern History, August, 2002, Charlene M. Boyer Lewis, review of *Parlor Politics,* p. 688.
Journal of the Early Republic, fall, 2001, Cynthia A. Kierner, review of *Parlor Politics,* p. 523.
New York Review of Books, March 29, 2001, Gordon S. Wood, review of *Parlor Politics,* p. 17.
Publishers Weekly, November 27, 2000, review of *Parlor Politics,* p. 66.
Virginia Magazine of History and Biography, winter, 2001, Pamela Tyler, review of *Parlor Politics,* p. 99.
Wall Street Journal, December 26, 2000, Alan Pell Crawford, review of *Parlor Politics,* p. A9.
White House Studies, summer, 2001, R. Sam Garrett, review of *Parlor Politics,* p. 433.
William and Mary Quarterly, July, 2001, Elizabeth R. Varon, review of *Parlor Politics,* p. 764.

*   *   *

ALLMAN, Barbara 1950-

PERSONAL: Born August 7, 1950, in Detroit, MI; daughter of Robert (a sales manager) and Mary (a homemaker) DeFazio; married John Allman (a health care consultant). *Education:* Attended Michigan State University, 1968-70; Oakland University, B.A. (elementary education), 1972, M.A. (teaching), 1978. *Hobbies and other interests:* Singing in a choral group, reading with children at a local elementary school.

ADDRESSES: Home—P.O. Box 1088, Jacksonville, OR 97530. *E-mail*—b.a.reader@barbaraallman.com.

CAREER: Jim Thorpe Elementary School, Sterling Heights, MI, teacher, 1972-78; Warren Consolidated Schools, Warren, MI, language arts consultant, 1979-82; Frank Schaffer Publications, Torrance, CA, editor, 1984-93; freelance writer, 1993—. Member of the board of directors, Friends of the Jacksonville Library, 2002.

MEMBER: International Reading Association, National Council for the Social Studies, Society of Children's

Book Writers and Illustrators, Authors Guild, Music Educators National Conference.

WRITINGS:

Teddy Bear, Strong and Healthy, illustrated by Sue Ryono, Frank Schaffer Publications (Palos Verdes Estates, CA), 1985.

Letter and Number Reversals: Grades K-3, illustrated by Marlene Albright, Frank Schaffer Publications (Palos Verdes Estates, CA), 1987.

Maps, Charts and Graphs: Grades 1-2, Frank Schaffer Publications (Palos Verdes Estates, CA), 1988.

Reading Puzzles and Games: Grades 1-2, illustrated by Marlene McAuley, Frank Schaffer Publications (Palos Verdes Estates, CA), 1988.

Reading Puzzles and Games: Duplicating Masters, illustrated by Marlene McAuley, Frank Schaffer Publications (Palos Verdes Estates, CA), 1988.

Famous Black Americans: Grades 1-2, illustrated by Mark Mason, Frank Schaffer Publications (Torrance, CA), 1988.

Prefixes, illustrated by Mark Mason, Frank Schaffer Publications (Torrance, CA), 1988.

Reading and Writing Spanish, illustrated by Sue Ryono, Frank Schaffer Publications (Torrance, CA), 1989.

(With Marsha Elyn Jurca and Peggy Haynes) *Children's Authors and Illustrators,,* Frank Schaffer Publications (Torrance, CA), Volume 1, 1991, Volumes 2-3, 1992.

Create with Clay, Instructional Fair (Grand Rapids, MI), 1996.

Create with Paint, Instructional Fair (Grand Rapids, MI), 1996.

Bible Story Activities, Grace Publications (Torrance, CA), 1996.

Create with Puppets and Props, Instructional Fair (Grand Rapids, MI), 1996.

Consonants, Frank Schaffer Publications (Torrance, CA), 1996.

Vowels, Frank Schaffer Publications (Torrance, CA), 1996.

Blends, Digraphs and More, Frank Schaffer Publications (Torrance, CA), 1996.

Test-taking Skills: Grade 3, Frank Schaffer Publications (Torrance, CA), 1996.

Her Piano Sang: A Story about Clara Schumann, illustrated by Shelly O. Haas, Carolrhoda Books (Minneapolis, MN), 1997.

Choral Reading: Grade 1, Frank Schaffer Publications (Torrance, CA), 1997.

My First Story tp Read: Grade 1, Frank Schaffer Publications (Torrance, CA), 1997.

(Reteller) Robert Louis Stevenson, *Treasure Island,* illustrated by Tani Brooks Johnson, Frank Schaffer Publications (Torrance, CA), 1997.

Social Studies Made Simple, Frank Schaffer Publications (Torrance, CA), 1997.

Developing Character When It Counts, Grades K-1: A Program for Teaching Character in the Classroom, Frank Schaffer, Publications (Torrance, CA), 1999.

Developing Character When It Counts, Grades 2-3: A Program for Teaching Character in the Classroom, Frank Schaffer Publications (Torrance, CA), 1999.

Language Arts Puzzles and Games: A Workbook for Ages 4-6, illustrated by Larry Nolte, Lowell House (Los Angeles, CA), 1999.

A World in Focus: A Unique Text for Social Studies: Central and South America, Blackbirch Press (Woodbridge, CT), 2000.

Dance of the Swan: A Story about Anna Pavlova, illustrated by Shelly O. Haas, Carolrhoda Books (Minneapolis, MN), 2001.

Alphabet, Grade k-1, Frank Schaffer Publications (Torrance, CA), 2002.

Colors, Grade K, Frank Schaffer Publications (Torrance, CA), 2002.

Numbers, Grade K, Frank Schaffer Publications (Torrance, CA), 2002.

Shapes, Grade K, Frank Schaffer Publications (Torrance, CA), 2002.

Following Directions, Grade K, Frank Schaffer Publications (Torrance, CA), 2002.

Following Directions, Grade 1, Frank Schaffer Publications (Torrance, CA), 2002.

Sight Word Comprehension, Grade K, Frank Schaffer Publications (Torrance, CA), 2002.

Sight Word Comprehension, Grade 1, Frank Schaffer Publications (Torrance, CA), 2002.

Editor of *Schooldays,* 1984-93; contributor to *Chicken Soup for the Kid's Soul,* Health Communications (Deerfield Beach, FL), 1998, *Let's Play and Learn,* Instructional Fair (Grand Rapids, MI), 1999, and *Dance Teacher,* Lifestyle Ventures (New York, NY), 2002.

SIDELIGHTS: Barbara Allman told *CA:* "I am a freelance writer specializing in educational materials and nonfiction for children. My first career was as an elementary teacher and reading consultant in schools in Michigan. I moved to Los Angeles in 1983 and became the editor of *Schooldays,* a magazine of creative ideas for elementary teachers.

"I have written two biographies for middle-grade readers—*Dance of the Swan: A Story about Anna Pavlova* and *Her Piano Sang: A Story about Clara Schumann.* I am currently working on two more. *Her Piano Sang* was selected by the Library of Congress to be published in Braille. I believe biographies make good reading for children because the genre can help children discover what's important in life. The more children learn about people of worth and achievement, the better they come to know themselves. In reading about the lives of people who have made a difference, children come to understand their own potential.

"I have also authored more than seventy teacher's guides, student texts, and activity books, including a supplemental social studies text for fifth grade, *A World in Focus: Central and South America.* My short story titled, 'Grandpa's Bees,' appears in the best-selling book, *Chicken Soup for the Kid's Soul.*

"In writing biographies, I am able to combine three of my main interests: education, writing, and the arts. *Dance of the Swan* tells the story of Anna Pavlova, considered by many to be the greatest ballet dancer ever to grace a stage. With the zeal of a missionary, Pavlova, the petite Russian ballerina, introduced the soaring beauty of classical dance to people the world over.

"As an eight-year-old piano student, I was fascinated by the stories of composers in my piano book. I read every composer's biography I could find in the children's room of the East Detroit Public Library and wondered why there were no biographies written about women composers. Later in life, when I discovered that there *still* were no biographies of women composers written for children, I wrote one about Clara Schumann—*Her Piano Sang.*"

Allman's early interest in the piano came from her mother, whose piano-playing saved her sanity when the clamor of seven children (Allman is the oldest) became too much. "[Taking piano lessons] was my idea because my mom played the piano. I always

thought that was the greatest thing," Allman told Elisabeth Deffner in the Irvine, California *Independent.* An early interest in biographies also set the stage for Allman's own first biography, *Her Piano Sang.* In this biography for middle-grade readers, Allman brings into focus the life and times of Clara (Wieck) Schumann, whose musical genius—she was performing as a virtuoso at the age of nine—found expression despite the strictures of an overbearing father, a mentally ill husband, and the tasks of running and supporting a household. In addition, the conventions of the era demanded that she give up her career upon marriage, which Schumann refused to do. Critics noted that though more is known about Clara Schumann's husband, composer Robert Schumann, "it is refreshing to read about the Schumanns from Clara's perspective," remarked Mollie Bynum in *School Library Journal.* A contributor to *Kirkus Reviews* dubbed *Her Piano Sang* "a fine introduction to a strong, disciplined artist."

Classical music is the common thread connecting *Her Piano Sang* and *Dance of the Swan,* Allman's second biography for young people. In this biography of the famous Russian ballerina of the nineteenth century—some claim, the most famous ballerina of all time—Allman focuses on the ethereal woman's determination to bring ballet to the four corners of the earth. Writing in *School Library Journal,* Carol Schene called *Dance of the Swan* "clearly written and upbeat," and predicted that "this sensitive portrayal will inspire young readers."

BIOGRAPHICAL AND CRITICAL SOURCES:

PERIODICALS

Horn Book Guide, fall, 2001, review of *Dance of the Swan: A Story about Anna Pavlova.*
Independent (Irvine, CA), July 18, 1997, Elisabeth Deffner, "Mary De Fazio and Barbara Allman: Mom Inspired Daughter's Writing," pp. 2, 11.
Jacksonville Review Monthly (Jacksonville, OR), October-November, 2001, "Local Author Writes Biography of World-renowned Ballerina," p. 13.
Kirkus Reviews, December 1, 1996, review of *Her Piano Sang: A Story about Clara Schumann.*
School Library Journal, January, 1997, Mollie Bynum, review of *Her Piano Sang;* July, 2001, Carol Schene, review of *Dance of the Swan.*

OTHER

Barbara Allman Web site, http://www.barbaraallman. com (January 29, 2002).

*   *   *

AMMI, Ben
   See BEN AMMI

*   *   *

ANKERBERG, John (F.) 1945-

PERSONAL: Born December 10, 1945, in Chicago, IL; son of Floyd Ankerberg (an evangelist minister); married wife, Darlene, 1970; children: Michelle. *Education:* University of Illinois, B.A. (with honors), 1972; Trinity Evangelistic Divinity School, Deerfield, IL, M.A. (church history and history of Christian thought; with honors), M.Div. (with honors), 1973; Luther Rice Seminary, doctor of ministry, 1991.

ADDRESSES: Office—Ankerberg Theological Research Institute, P.O. Box 8977, Chattanooga, TN 37414-0977.

CAREER: Ordained Baptist minister. Willow Creek Community Church, founding member, until 1976; evangelist minister, 1976—. Ankerberg Theological Research Institute, Chattanooga, TN, president, founder, and producer of *The John Ankerberg Show.* Host of *Roundtable* (Christian television talk show), Kansas City, MO, 1982-83, and *The John Ankerberg Show,* 1983—. Founding member, Committee on Evangelical Unity in the Gospel, Glendale Heights, IL; member of board of directors, National Religious Broadcasters; member of advisory board, Pro-Life Majority Coalition, Chattanooga, TN; member of the board of reference for Christian Film and Television Commission, Institute for Religious Research, and Christian Service Brigade; advisor to International Committee of Reference of New Life 2000.

AWARDS, HONORS: Genesis Award, 1984, and National Religious Broadcasters Award, for television producer of the year, 1992, both for *The John Ankerberg Show.*

WRITINGS:

WITH JOHN WELDON

Is the Theory of Evolution Supported or Disproved by Today's Scientific Facts?, John Ankerberg Evangelistic Association (Chattanooga, TN), 1987.
Astrology: Do the Heavens Rule Our Destiny?, Harvest House Publishers (Eugene, OR), 1989.
The Facts on False Teachings in the Church, Harvest House Publishers (Eugene, OR), 1989.
The Case for Jesus the Messiah: Incredible Prophecies That Prove God Exists, Ankerberg Theological Research Institute (Chattanooga, TN), 1989.
The Facts on the Masonic Lodge, Harvest House (Eugene, OR), 1989.
The Facts on "The Last Temptation of Christ," Harvest House (Eugene, OR), 1989.
The Facts on Spirit Guides, Harvest House (Eugene, OR), 1989.
The Facts on the New Age Movement, Harvest House (Eugene, OR), 1989.
The Facts on the Jehovah's Witnesses, Harvest House (Eugene, OR), 1989.
The Facts on Astrology, Harvest House (Eugene, OR), 1989.
Christianity and the Secret Teachings of the Masonic Lodge, John Ankerberg Evangelistic Association (Chattanooga, TN), 1989, expanded edition published as *The Secret Teachings of the Masonic Lodge: A Christian Perspective,,* Moody Press (Chicago, IL), 1990.
When Does Life Begin? and Thirty-nine Other Tough Questions about Abortion, Wolgemuth & Hyatt (Brentwood, TN), 1990.
Do the Resurrection Accounts Conflict? And What Proof Is There That Jesus Rose from the Dead?, Ankerberg Theological Research Institute (Chattanooga, TN), 1990.
Can You Trust Your Doctor?: The Complete Guide to New Age Medicine and Its Threat to Your Family, Wolgemuth & Hyatt (Brentwood, TN), 1991.
Cult Watch, Harvest House Publishers (Eugene, OR), 1991.
One World: Bible Prophecy and the New World Order, Moody Press (Chicago, IL), 1991.
Rock Music's Powerful Message, Ankerberg Theological Research Institute (Chattanooga, TN), 1991.
The Facts on the Mormon Church, Harvest House (Eugene, OR), 1991.

The Facts on Islam, Harvest House (Eugene, OR), 1991.

The Facts on Hinduism, Harvest House (Eugene, OR), 1991.

The Facts on the Occult, Harvest House (Eugene, OR), 1991.

The Facts on Holistic Health and the New Medicine, Harvest House (Eugene, OR), 1991.

Everything You Ever Wanted to Know about Mormonism: The Truth about the Mormon Church, Harvest House Publishers (Eugene, OR), 1992, published as *Behind the Mask of Mormonism,* Harvest House Publishers (Eugene, OR), 1992.

The Facts on Rock Music, Harvest House (Eugene, OR), 1992.

The Facts on UFOs and Other Supernatural Phenomena, Harvest House (Eugene, OR), 1992.

The Facts on Life after Death, Harvest House (Eugene, OR), 1992.

The Facts on Sex Education, Harvest House (Eugene, OR), 1993.

The Facts on Jesus the Messiah, Harvest House (Eugene, OR), 1993.

The Facts on the Faith Movement, Harvest House (Eugene, OR), 1993.

The Facts on Roman Catholicism, Harvest House (Eugene, OR), 1993.

The Facts on Creation vs. Evolution, Harvest House (Eugene, OR), 1993.

The Facts on Mind Sciences, Harvest House (Eugene, OR), 1993.

The Coming Darkness, foreword by Walter Martin, Harvest House Publishers (Eugene, OR), 1993.

(With Craig Branch) *Thieves of Innocence: Protecting Our Children from New Age Teachings and Occult Practices,* Harvest House Publishers (Eugene, OR), 1993.

The Myth That Homosexuality Is Due to Biological or Genetic Causes, Ankerberg Theological Research Institute (Chattanooga, TN), 1993.

A Parent's Handbook for Identifying New Age Beliefs, Psychotherapeutic Techniques, and Occult Practices in Public School Curriculums, Ankerberg Theological Research Institute (Chattanooga, TN), 1993.

The Myth of Safe Sex: The Devastating Consequences of Violating God's Plan, Moody Press (Chicago, IL), 1993.

Protestants and Catholics: Do They Now Agree?, Ankerberg Theological Research Institute (Chattanooga, TN), 1994.

The Facts on Self-Esteem, Psychology, and the Recovery Movement, Harvest House (Eugene, OR), 1995.

The Facts on Homosexuality, Harvest House (Eugene, OR), 1995.

The Facts on Angels, Harvest House (Eugene, OR), 1995.

The Facts on Abortion, Harvest House (Eugene, OR), 1995.

Encyclopedia of New Age Beliefs, Harvest House Publishers (Eugene, OR), 1996.

Knowing the Truth about the Resurrection, Harvest House Publishers (Eugene, OR), 1996.

Knowing the Truth about Jesus the Messiah, Harvest House Publishers (Eugene, OR), 1996.

Knowing the Truth about the Trinity, Harvest House Publishers (Eugene, OR), 1996.

The Facts on the King James Only Debate, Harvest House (Eugene, OR), 1996.

The Facts on Near-Death Experiences, Harvest House (Eugene, OR), 1996.

The Facts on Halloween, Harvest House (Eugene, OR), 1996.

The Facts on Psychic Readings, Harvest House (Eugene, OR), 1997.

The Facts on the Jesus Seminar, Harvest House (Eugene, OR), 1997.

Knowing the Truth about Salvation, Harvest House Publishers (Eugene, OR), 1997.

Knowing the Truth about Eternal Security, Harvest House Publishers (Eugene, OR), 1997.

Knowing the Truth about the Reliability of the Bible, Harvest House Publishers (Eugene, OR), 1997.

Ready with an Answer for the Tough Questions about God, Harvest House Publishers (Eugene, OR), 1997.

Darwin's Leap of Faith, Harvest House Publishers (Eugene, OR), 1998.

Encyclopedia of Cults and New Religions: Jehovah's Witnesses, Mormonism, Mind Sciences, Baha'i, Zen, Unitarianism, Harvest House Publishers (Eugene, OR), 1999.

Fast Facts on Defending Your Faith, Harvest House Publishers (Eugene, OR), 2002.

Fast Facts on Islam, Harvest House Publishers (Eugene, OR), 2002.

What Do Mormons Really Believe?, Harvest House Publishers (Eugene, OR), 2002.

OTHER

Coauthor of several booklets, including "The Anker Series," a series of booklets refuting various non-Christian religious denominations and sects, Harvest House Publishers (Eugene, OR).

*   *   *

ARMOUR, Peter (James) 1940-2002

OBITUARY NOTICE—See index for *CA* sketch: Born November 19, 1940, in Fleetwood, Lancashire, England; died of cancer June 18, 2002, in London, England. Educator and author. Armour was best known as a scholar and interpreter of Italian literature, particularly the writings of the medieval poet Dante Alighieri. Through his early studies at the Pontifical Gregorian University in Rome, Armour acquired a thorough understanding of medieval theology, philosophy, and political thought. Subsequent study at the universities of Manchester and Leicester led to a doctorate in Italian and a career as a university professor, most recently as the chair of Italian studies at the Royal Holloway College of the University of London, where he also served as associate director of the Institute for Romance Studies. Alexander is chiefly remembered for his incisive and cogent interpretations of Dante, as reflected in his books *The Door of Purgatory: A Study of Multiple Symbolism in Dante's "Purgatorio"* and *Dante's Griffin and the History of the World: A Study of the Earthly Paradise ("Purgatorio," Cantos XXIX-XXXIII)*. Alexander once told *CA* that he was fascinated by the multiple layers of meaning within Dante's writing, and it was his tenacious quest to unravel the complexities and perceived inconsistencies in Dante's *Commedia,* and especially the *Purgatorio,* that he gained the respect of scholars and critics. Armour remained active even in his later years, and was a visiting professor at the University of Virginia as late as 1998. At the time of his death he was reportedly studying the intellectual origins of the sculpture and poetry of Michelangelo.

OBITUARIES AND OTHER SOURCES:

PERIODICALS

Guardian (London, England), July 11, 2002, obituary by Jane E. Everson, p. 20.
Independent (London, England), July 16, 2002, obituary by Mark Davie, p. 16.
Times (London, England), July 5, 2002, p. 34.

ARMYTAGE, R.
See WATSON, Rosamund Marriott

*   *   *

AZICRI, Max 1934-

PERSONAL: Born February 24, 1934, in Havana, Cuba; immigrated to the United States, 1960; naturalized U.S. citizen; son of Leon (in business) and Fanny (a homemaker; maiden name, Levy) Azicri; married Elisa Gosoff (deceased); married, April 14, 1973; wife's name Nicolette (a painter); children: Fanny Azicri Kerbel, David L., Danielle S. *Ethnicity:* "Caucasian." *Education:* Havana Institute, B.A., 1952; attended Havana School of Journalism, 1956, and Havana University, 1959; University of Southern California, M.A., 1968, Ph.D., 1975. *Politics:* Democrat. *Religion:* Jewish. *Hobbies and other interests:* Reading, music, travel.

ADDRESSES: Home—4000 Ridgewood Dr., Erie, PA 16506. *Office*—Department of Political Science and Criminal Justice, Edinboro University, Edinboro, PA 16444; fax: 814-732-2118. *E-mail*—mazicri@edinboro.edu; and max0224@msn.com.

CAREER: Journalist and author. *Diario Nacional,* Havana, Cuba, reporter, 1955; *Excelsior,* Havana, Cuba, reporter, 1956-57; Cuban Treasury Department, official, 1959-60; *Avance,* Miami, FL, South American correspondent, 1960-61; high school teacher in Temple City, CA, 1965-69; Edinboro University, Edinboro, PA, professor of political science, 1969—. *Military service:* U.S. Army, Cuban Unit, 1963.

MEMBER: Latin American Studies Association.

AWARDS, HONORS: Distinguished Faculty Award, Commonwealth of Pennsylvania Department of Education, 1983.

WRITINGS:

Cuba: Politics, Economics, and Society, Pinter Publisher (London, England), 1988.
Cuba Today and Tomorrow: Reinventing Socialism, University Press of Florida (Gainesville, FL), 2000.

Contributor of more than 100 articles to journals and newspapers in the United States and abroad.

WORK IN PROGRESS: Editing and writing an introductory chapter for *Cuban Socialism in a New Century: Adversity, Survival, and Renewal,* with others, for University Press of Florida (Gainesville, FL); research on Caribbean migration and globalized identities.

SIDELIGHTS: Max Azicri told *CA*: "Having experienced the Cuban revolution as a young man in my country of birth, and having studied it since arriving in the United States in late 1960, it has become a subject that has taken most of my intellectual and academic attention. During the time I lived in South America I could experience the hemispheric impact that such a small island was exerting.

"By extension, the subject of social change, more specifically revolutionary change, caught my interest and became the object of my attention in the 1980s in Nicaragua. The worldwide changes in the late 1980s and throughout the 1990s originated in Europe with the fall of the Soviet Union and the Soviet bloc and brought a new dimension to my study: how could Cuba survive while the USSR and socialist Europe have vanished? My second book on Cuba looks deeply into this subject. In my work in progress, the issue is Cuba's changes and adaptations to a new century while still enduring the enmity of the United States, more specifically the George W. Bush administration and Cuban-American southern Florida."

B

BALCAVAGE, Dynise 1965-

PERSONAL: Born March 14, 1965, in Shenandoah, PA. *Education:* Kutztown University, B.F.A., 1986; Arcadia University, M.A., 1995. *Hobbies and other interests:* Fiber arts, traveling, exercising, gardening.

ADDRESSES: Home—Philadelphia, PA. *Office*—c/o Author Mail, Chelsea House Publishers, 1974 Sproul Rd., Ste. 400, Bromall, PA 19008. *E-mail*—dyniseb@ yahoo.com.

CAREER: Freelance writer and editor, teacher of writing. Arcadia University, Glenside, PA, publicity associate and assistant editor, 1992-94, assistant director, College Relations, 1997-98; Chestnut Hill Health-Care, Philadelphia, PA, associate director, marketing and public relations, and acting director, 1999-2000; editor, Pariscape.com, and freelance editorial consultant, 2000—.

MEMBER: People for the Ethical Treatment of Animals.

WRITINGS:

Express (play), performed at Arcadia University, 1994.
Ludwig van Beethoven, Composer, Chelsea House (New York, NY), 1996.
Steroids, Chelsea House (Philadelphia, PA), 2000.
The Great Chicago Fire, Chelsea House (Philadelphia, PA), 2000.

The Federal Bureau of Investigation, Chelsea House (Philadelphia, PA), 2000.
Janis Joplin, Chelsea House (Philadelphia, PA), 2001.
Saudi Arabia, Gareth Stevens Publishers (Milwaukee, WI), 2001.
Philip Sheridan: Union General, Chelsea House (Philadelphia, PA), 2001.
Gabrielle Reece, Chelsea House (Philadelphia, PA), 2001.
Iowa, Children's Press, (New York, NY), 2002.
Welcome to Saudi Arabia, Gareth Stevens Publishers (Milwaukee, WI), 2002.
Culture Shock! Syria, revised second edition, Times Publishing, Inc. (Singapore, Malaysia), 2002.
Iraq, Gareth Stevens Publishers (Milwaukee, WI), 2003.

Contributor to periodicals, including *Georgia Review, Desktop Publishers Journal, Publish, Dynamic Graphics, Spin-Off, Imprint, Counselor,* and *Vitalcast.com.*

WORK IN PROGRESS: A book of poetry.

SIDELIGHTS: Dynise Balcavage told *CA:* "When I was a little girl, I spent hours writing and illustrating my own books. I remember impressing my mother with one 'novel' I wrote at age ten. I called it *Disaster 1980,* and it was chock full of your usual Armageddonesque light fare—hurricanes, tornadoes, earthquakes, floods, droughts, and tidal waves all happening simultaneously. Although I still think the title was good, as you can imagine, the 'book' was poorly written (and illustrated!)—but it didn't matter. I *loved* and *needed* to write. In fact, I've kept a diary since the age of six.

"Not surprisingly, after studying ballet in New York and teaching dance, I ended up working in public relations and marketing. I was happy even when composing advertising copy and press releases, but I especially enjoyed writing magazine articles. Uncovering each individual's unique story and motivation made me feel like an archeologist of tales. While working full time in the public relations office and attending graduate school in English at Arcadia University, I began writing books for young readers and magazine articles on the side.

"In 2000, I 'moved up' and took a position heading a busy public relations and marketing office in a hospital. After attending far too many meetings and feeling jealous whenever I assigned an article or piece of copy to someone else, I realized the job was not for me—I desperately missed writing. Since I had amassed a wealth of contacts from my years of part-time freelancing, I decided to leave the hospital to become a full-time freelance writer, despite the advice of friends and family. Yes, it was a huge risk, but not an uncalculated one. Following my gut instinct has always taken me to the happiest places, and as it turned out, this was no exception.

"I have been a full-time freelance writer and editor for three years now, and I have not looked back. I love the variety and the challenges. I enjoy the solitude of working in my office, but at the same time, I enjoy the camaraderie and collaboration that comes with consulting for various businesses in Philadelphia, nationally, and internationally. I concentrate mainly on magazine work, publishing, and advertising, but I usually complete one or two creative writing projects, mainly for my own fulfillment. No matter which way you slice it, I adore the fact that my work days revolves around words.

"When people hear that I work full-time out of my home office, they often say things like, 'I guess you can sleep until 11:00.' When you think about it, though, if I don't work, I don't get paid—just like any person who has a regular, nine-to-five job. Luckily, I am extremely disciplined. I'm at my desk by 8:00 or 8:30, and I usually work straight through until about 4:00. I keep a notebook in my purse, in the same way that an artist keeps a sketchbook, and I jot down ideas and descriptions while they are fresh (otherwise, I would forget them).

"Although I usually juggle several projects a day—writing an article, for example, working on a book, and developing a marketing plan for a local business—I try never to write and edit on the same day. These two activities use different parts of your brain. After writing something, you need to give the work some space, and then go back and revise it with a sense of objectivity. Hemingway said, 'Sometimes, you have to kill your darlings,' but it's harder to cut them when you've only just written them.

"Why do I write for children? I grew up in a very small coal mining town in Pennsylvania—there were ninety-two in my graduating class—and I felt cut off from the energy and beat of the world. I could not wait to grow up, move to the city, and travel! As a kid, especially if you are creative or intellectually curious, you can feel quite powerless and limited by your surroundings or familial circumstances. Reading, for me, was like taking a free trip to other places and into other people's minds. Books empower children by helping them to escape and to see the possibility and inspiration in life.

"One of my favorite quotes deals with the Buddhist concept of the beginners' mind. 'In the beginner's mind there are many possibilities, but in the expert's mind there are few' (Suzuki). I teach writing, and although I see a lot of talented writers, I also come across many beginners who consider themselves experts and are impatient about getting published. The fact is that we *all* know how to write; we all, of course, learned how to write in school. But being able to type or to form letters with a pencil does *not* make you a writer. It can take a long time for a beginner to understand this. Writing *every* day, on the other hand, seeking out and observing new experiences with an open mind, and being brutally honest with yourself will eventually lead to better writing—and to finding your own voice."

*   *   *

BALINT, Christine 1975-

PERSONAL: Born August 5, 1975, in Melbourne, Australia. *Education:* Melbourne University, Australia, B.A. (with honors), 1997, doctoral study, 2000-03.

ADDRESSES: Agent—Bryson Agency Australia, P.O. Box 226, Flinders Lane PO, Melbourne 8009, Australia.

CAREER: School of Creative Arts, Melbourne University, Melbourne, Australia, instructor in creative writing, 1999—.

AWARDS, HONORS: Finalist, Vogel Literary Award for *The Salt Letters,*1998; editorial fellowship and mentorship fellowship, Varuna Writers' Centre, 1998; cited as one of Australia's Best Young Novelists, *Sydney Morning Herald,* 1999.

WRITINGS:

The Salt Letters, Allen & Unwin (St. Leonards, New South Wales, Australia), 1999, Norton (New York, NY), 2001.

The Salt Letters has been translated into Italian and German

ADAPTATIONS: The Salt Letters was produced for ABC Radio, Australia, 2000.

WORK IN PROGRESS: A second novel set in the nineteenth century, a fictionalized account of the life of a Shakespearean actress.

SIDELIGHTS: Christine Balint began writing at the age of six, publishing stories in her elementary school newsletter. While still a teenager, she published several poems, and won awards for her short stories. Full-fledged success came in her early twenties, when Balint's first novel, *The Salt Letters,* was put on the short list for the Australian Vogel Literary Award in 1998. After her success in Australia, a major American publisher, W. W. Norton, picked up *The Salt Letters* to be published in the United States. This was a notable achievement for a story that began as Balint's undergraduate honors thesis at the University of Melbourne. As Mark Rozzo wrote in the *Los Angeles Times,* Balint's book has is "tempered by the kind of delicate observations you can't learn in school."

The Salt Letters tells the story of Sarah, a young Englishwoman in the nineteenth century forced to leave home for Australia. The book chronicles her sea voyage, including the horrific living conditions she endures as well as her memories of the life she leaves behind. In particular, Sarah thinks about her relationship with her cousin Richard, and the readers slowly learns that he is the reason for her flight. Balint's story focuses on the details of Sarah's existence aboard the ship: traveling in the quarters designated for unmarried women, she is under the control of the Matron who ensures their proper behavior. Filth, disease, extreme weather, and lice make their days unbearable, while the livestock on board roams freely through their cabins. The story shifts between dream, memory, and reality.

Nora Krug, reviewing *The Salt Letters* for the *New York Times,* described Balint's style as one that "relies heavily on allegory and magic realism." As Balint acknowledged in an interview for Allen & Unwin, Gabriel García Marquéz, the Colombian master of magic realism, has been an influence on her work. Commenting in *Booklist* on Balint's use of imagery, Carol Haggas called the novel "a work of haunting beauty," while Rozzo, writing in the *Los Angeles Times,* said her writing is "seductively impressionistic." Some reviewers, however, suggested that the style of *The Salt Letters* is overdone: *Library Journal* contributor Elizabeth C. Stewart called, the writing "at times indulgently self-conscious." Krug also wrote, "while these devices allow her to showcase her elegant prose style, at times they feel forced and distracting," though she concluded that such moments "do not overshadow the power of Balint's brief but affecting novel."

BIOGRAPHICAL AND CRITICAL SOURCES:

PERIODICALS

Booklist, May 15, 2001, Carol Haggas, review of *The Salt Letters,* p. 1729.
Library Journal, May 15, 2001, Elizabeth C. Stewart, review of *The Salt Letters,* p. 160.
Los Angeles Times Book Review, July 15, 2001, Mark Rozzo, review of *The Salt Letters,* p. 10.
New York Times Book Review, August 26, 2001, Nora Krug, "Below Decks," p. 14.

OTHER

Allen & Unwin Web site, http://allenandunwin.com/ (October 6, 2001), interview with Christine Balint.
Bryson Agency Web site, http://www.bryson.com/ (October 6, 2001), short biography of Christine Balint.

BARROWCLIFFE, Mark 1964-

PERSONAL: Born 1964, in Coventry, England. *Education:* Attended University of Sussex, 1984-87.

ADDRESSES: Home—London, England. *Agent*—c/o Author Mail, Hodder Headline, 338 Euston Road, London NW1 3BH, England.

CAREER: Financial Times, London, England, subeditor, 1994; also worked as conference planner.

WRITINGS:

Girlfriend 44, Headline (London, England), 2000, St. Martin's (New York, NY), 2001.
Infidelity for First-time Fathers, Headline (London, England), 2001.

Also author of columns and articles for *The Big Issue.*

SIDELIGHTS: Mark Barrowcliffe worked for many years as a journalist and stand-up comedian before he wrote his first novel, *Girlfriend 44.* The work was written at the prompting of a literary agent who read one of Barrowcliffe's articles in *The Big Issue,* a magazine for which he was writing. The result was *Girlfriend 44,* a comedic look into the behavior of the single male, represented in the book by Harry Chesshyre and his roommate Gerard. Although Harry has been searching for the woman of his dreams for many years, none seem to meet his impossible qualifications, among them "hair that looks as if blonde and brunette had put their heads together and come up with a better colour." Into his life comes Alice, a woman over whom a friend has recently committed suicide. Convinced she is the perfection they seek, Gerard and Harry each embark on a quest to win her affections.

New York Post reviewer Theresa O'Rourke commented that "The book's dialogue is fast-paced and cheeky and never loses steam, and the engrossing climax is a jaw-dropper."

Barrowcliffe followed his best-selling debut novel with *Infidelity for First-time Fathers,* which a reviewer for the London *Times* described as a comic look at the "c-

risis in modern masculinity." As he struggles between his sense of responsibility towards his now-pregnant fiancé and his new mistress, Dag, the thirty-something hero of this novel, "in between all the gags . . . can hit you with a profound insight into such topics as male friendship, what makes for moral behaviour, or ageing," noted the *Times* critic.

BIOGRAPHICAL AND CRITICAL SOURCES:

PERIODICALS

Guardian, June 13, 2001, "Father's Daze."
New York Post, January 14, 2001, Theresa O'Rourke, review of *Girlfriend 44.*
Publishers Weekly, December 18, 2000, review of *Girlfriend 44,* p. 56.
Times (London, England), July 28, 2001, review of *Infidelity for First-time Fathers.*

OTHER

Street Smart Chicago, http://newcitychicago.com/ (January 25, 2001), Joshua Fisher, "Boyfriend in a Coma."*

* * *

BARTIROMO, Maria Sara 1967-

PERSONAL: Born September 11, 1967, in Brooklyn, NY; daughter of Vincent and Josephine Bartiromo; married Jonathan Steinberg (a business executive), 1999. *Education:* New York University, B.A. (journalism and economics), 1989, certification in screenwriting, 1990.

ADDRESSES: Home—New York, NY. *Office*—c/o CNBC New York, 2200 Fletcher Ave., Fort Lee, NJ 07024-5005.

CAREER: News correspondent and investment writer. *Investment Magazine,* New York, NY, freelance columnist, 1991; CNN Business News, New York, NY, producer, 1989-93; *Barry Farber Show,* New York, NY, associate producer, 1989-93; CNBC, New

York, NY, correspondent, 1993-97, financial anchor, beginning 1997, anchor for *Market Week,* beginning 2000. Contributor of articles to periodicals, including *Individual Investor* and *Ticker.*

MEMBER: New York Financial Writers Association.

AWARDS, HONORS: Excellence in Broadcast Journalism Award, Coalition of Italo-American Associations, 1997; nominated for a Cable ACE Award for her three-part series on the Internet and its implications for investors.

WRITINGS:

(With Catherine Fredman) *Use the News: How to Separate Noise from the Investment Nuggets and Make Money in Any Economy,* HarperCollins (New York, NY), 2001.

SIDELIGHTS: Television news correspondent Maria Bartiromo, known for being the first journalist to report live from the floor of the New York Stock Exchange while trading was taking place, published her debut book in 2001. Titled *Use the News: How to Separate Noise from the Investment Nuggets and Make Money in Any Economy* and co-written by Catherine Fredman, the work is meant to help readers navigate through the many pitfalls of investing in the stock market.

Bartiromo has worked for CNBC since 1993, and by 1998 *USA Weekend Magazine* writer Jeffrey Zaslow claimed she was "fast becoming the most famous face in business news." In 1997 the cable network was so impressed with Bartiromo's abilities that it gave her a show of her own to host called *Business Center.* "She's an excellent financial news journalist," CNBC boss Bruno Cohen told K. C. Baker in an interview for Knight-Ridder/Tribune News Service. "She has excellent sources. And the audience responds to her extremely well." It was her live reports from the floor of the New York Stock Exchange that established her as a prominent figure in the world of financial news. In a *Harris Online* interview, Bartiromo discussed how that experience helped hone her ability to make recommendations to viewers about which stocks to buy and which ones to stay away from. "Often, a story

will break or there will be a very large crowd of people standing around one of the posts down on the floor, and it's obvious that somebody knows something because there is all this buying interest in one stock down on the floor," she said. "It's sort of finding out what is happening and going with it as it's happening."

Bartiromo also used her firsthand knowledge from being on the floor of the Exchange while writing her book. According to her interview with writer Joshua Kennon, Bartiromo decided to write the book to help the average person wade through the avalanche of conflicting information about investment in the press and on television and the Internet. "The concept for the book came from my realizing that there's been an explosion of financial information and we are in information overload," she told Kennon, who called her "one of the most influential and trusted journalists in the world." How to locate useful investment information on the Internet and when to trust market professionals, and when not to, are just some of the tips Bartiromo gives readers.

Most literary critics lauded *Use the News.* "Written in an intelligent, warm style, this is a book that today's stock investors will want to read and study," wrote Susan C. Awe in *Library Journal.* Reviewing the book for *Booklist,* Eileen Hardy felt that it was "easy to read" and "a primer for the average individual investor to choose the news to use in making investments." A *Publishers Weekly* contributor praised the book's "friendly, hands-on style."

BIOGRAPHICAL AND CRITICAL SOURCES:

PERIODICALS

Book, July, 2001, review of *Use the News: How to Separate the Noise from the Investment Nuggets and Make Money in Any Economy,* p. 27.
Booklist, May 15, 2001, Eileen Hardy, review of *Use the News,* p. 1716.
Investment News, April 24, 2000, Valerie Block, "How Sweet It Is!: A Star Rises at CNBC," p. 32.
Knight-Ridder/Tribune News Service, June 10, 1999, K. C. Baker, "CNBC Is Sweet on 'Money Honey' Maria Bartiromo," p. K4059.
Library Journal, May 15, 2001, Susan C. Awe, review of *Use the News,* p. 136.

Newsweek, June 2, 1997, Leslie Kaufman, "Business Beautiful: CNBC's Bartiromo Makes Financial News Fun," p. 50.

Publishers Weekly, April 23, 2001, review of *Use the News,* p. 56.

USA Weekend Magazine, January 23-25, 1998, Jeffrey Zaslow, "Straight Talk."

OTHER

Maria Sara Bartiromo's Web site, http://www.bartiromo.com (March 15, 2002).

Investing for Beginners, http://beginnersinvest.about.com/ (March 15, 2002), Joshua Kennon, "One on One: Maria Bartiromo."

Harris Online, http://www.harrisonline.com/ (March 15, 2002), interview with Maria Bartiromo.*

*   *   *

BARTON, Beverly

PERSONAL: Born in Tuscumbia, AL; married; children: son, daughter. *Education:* Attended University of North Alabama (Florence, AL).

ADDRESSES: Office—PO Box 1024, Tuscumbia, AL 35674. *E-mail*—beverly@beverlybarton.com.

CAREER: Romance writer.

MEMBER: Romance Writers of America.

AWARDS, HONORS: Romantic Times Career Achievement Award for Series Romantic Adventures, 1998; Georgia Romance Writers (GRW) Award, for *Sugar Hill,* 1992, and for *Gabriel Hawk's Lady,* 1998; GRW Maggie Award finalist, for *This Side of Heaven,* 1992, and for *The Tender Trap,* 1997, for *Roarke's Wife,* 1997, and for *Keeping Safe,* 1999; National Readers' Choice Award, for *Paladin's Woman,* 1993, for *Lover and Deceiver,* 1994, and for *Gabriel Hawk's Lady,* 1998; Puget Sound Romance Readers' Award, for *Cameron,* 1993; Laurel Wreath Award, for *The Outcast,* 1995; Star Rider Studio Author of the Year award, 1996; Romance Writers of America (RWA) Rita Award finalist, for *This Side of Heaven,* 1992; *Romance Times*

Reviewers' Choice nominee, for *This Side of Heaven,* 1992, for *Emily and the Stranger,* 1998, and for *Gabriel Hawk's Lady,* 1998; Holt Medallion award finalist, for *Gabriel Hawk's Lady,* 1998; Colorado Award of Excellence, for *The Outcast,* 1995, and for *Guarding Jennie,* 1996; Desert Rose Golden Quill award finalist, for *A Man Like Morgan Kane,* 1997.

WRITINGS:

"THE PROTECTORS" SERIES

Yankee Lover, Harlequin Press (Don Mills, Ontario, Canada), 1990.

Lucky in Love, Harlequin Press (Don Mills, Ontario, Canada), 1991.

Out of Danger, Harlequin Press (Don Mills, Ontario, CA), 1991.

Sugar Hill, Harlequin Press (Don Mills, Ontario, Canada), 1992.

Talk of the Town, Harlequin Press (Don Mills, Ontario, Canada), 1992.

This Side of Heaven, Harlequin Press (Don Mills, Ontario, Canada), 1992.

The Wanderer, Harlequin Press (Don Mills, Ontario, Canada), 1993.

Cameron, Harlequin Press (Don Mills, Ontario, Canada), 1993.

Paladin's Woman, Harlequin Press (Don Mills, Ontario, Canada), 1993.

The Mother of My Child, Harlequin Press (Don Mills, Ontario, Canada), 1994.

Lover and Deceiver, Harlequin Press (Don Mills, Ontario, Canada), 1994.

Nothing but Trouble, Harlequin Press (Don Mills, Ontario, Canada), 1994.

The Outcast, Harlequin Press (Don Mills, Ontario, Canada), 1995.

Defending His Own, Harlequin Press (Don Mills, Ontario, Canada), 1995.

Guarding Jennie, Harlequin Press (Don Mills, Ontario, Canada), 1996.

Blackwood's Woman, Harlequin Press (Don Mills, Ontario, Canada), 1996.

Flower Girls, Harlequin Press (Don Mills, Ontario, Canada), 1996.

The Tender Trap, Harlequin Press (Don Mills, Ontario, Canada), 1997.

A Child of Her Own, Harlequin Press (Don Mills, Ontario, Canada), 1997.

Roarke's Wife, Harlequin Press (Don Mills, Ontario, Canada), 1997.

A Man Like Morgan Kane, Harlequin Press (Don Mills, Ontario, Canada), 1997.

Gabriel Hawk's Lady, Harlequin Press (Don Mills, Ontario, Canada), 1998.

Emily and the Stranger, Harlequin Press (Don Mills, Ontario, Canada), 1998.

Lone Wolf's Lady, Harlequin Press (Don Mills, Ontario, Canada), 1998.

Keeping Annie Safe, Harlequin Press (Don Mills, Ontario, Canada), 1999.

3-2-1 Married, Harlequin Press (Don Mills, Ontario, Canada), 1999.

Murdock's Last Stand, Harlequin Press (Don Mills, Ontario, Canada), 2000.

Egan Cassidy's Kid, Harlequin Press (Don Mills, Ontario, Canada), 2000.

Her Secret Weapon, Harlequin Press (Don Mills, Ontario, Canada), 2000.

Navajo's Woman, Harlequin Press (Don Mills, Ontario, Canada), 2001.

Whitelaw's Wedding, Harlequin Press (Don Mills, Ontario, Canada), 2001.

Sweet Caroline's Keeper, Harlequin Press (Don Mills, Ontario, Canada), 2001.

Jack's Christmas Mission, Harlequin Press (Don Mills, Ontario, Canada), 2001.

The Fifth Victim, in press. *The Protectors: The Early Years,* (includes *Guarding Jeannie, Blackwood's Woman,* and *Roarke's Wife*), in press. *Grace under Fire,* in press.

"THE PROTECTORS" SERIES; UNDER ZEBRA ROMANTIC SUSPENSE IMPRINT

After Dark, Kensington Publishing (New York, NY), 2000.

Every Move She Makes, Kensington Publishing (New York, NY), 2001.

What She Doesn't Know, Kensington Publishing (New York, NY), 2002.

SIDELIGHTS: Beverly Barton wrote her first book when she was only nine-years old. As a daughter of the South and a sixth-generation Alabamian, she wrote a story that she has described as "a little southern girl's poor imitation of *Gone with the Wind.*" From the time her grandfather gave her a copy of *The Beauty and the Beast* when she was a very young child, Barton's romantic imagination began to unfold.

Born in Tuscumbia, Alabama, Barton was raised there and in Chattanooga, Tennessee. She lost her mother at a young age and was raised by her grandmother, surrounded by a large extended family steeped in the traditions of the South. Also an early devotee of movies, Barton had begun by the age of seven to rewrite films she saw in the theater and on television to give the stories a happy ending. Throughout high school and into her college years Barton wrote everything from short stories to television scripts to poetry and novels.

Barton did not graduate from college; instead she dropped out to marry the man she has called "the love of my life" and became a military wife. She and her husband have raised two children, a son and a daughter, and have lived in the same house for over twenty-five years. Barton cherishes her life as a wife and mother, noting that every age and stage of her children's development have been precious to her. During her years of full-time mothering she continued to read and go to movies faithfully. In her mid-thirties, when her children were teenagers, Barton decided it was time to write again, primarily as a hobby at first. But before she turned forty Barton realized that it was time to make writing her career.

Barton sold her first book in 1989, and it was released as *Yankee Desire.* The story was set in Tuscumbia during the town's annual Helen Keller Festival. Since her debut, Barton had written more than thirty-five romance novels by the spring of 2002.

When Barton's novel *Every Move She Makes* was published in 2001, a *Publishers Weekly* critic noted that "the novel's sizzling sexual chemistry and high suspense will satisfy sunbathers longing for sultry poolside reading." The critic also noted that romances set in the South were in high demand—a fact that must suit Barton well.

"I was raised by a very old-fashioned 'steel magnolia' grandmother who taught me that it was poor manners to brag on yourself and that it was a task better left to others," Barton noted on her Web site, "I've found that in this business—being a professional writer—it's essential to promote yourself. So, I hired a brilliant web designer to produce a Web site for me that would reflect my personal tastes. And here I am, despite my 'southern belle' upbringing, doing a little braggin', a little self-promotion, and hoping that you'll like my books, my Web site, and me." Barton caters to her reading audience by keeping her Web site updated regularly, with seasonal notes and news of her upcoming books.

Joining Romance Writers of America around the time she returned to writing, Barton also helped found the Heart of Dixie chapter in Alabama and remains active in that organization.

Barton says in her biography on *eHarlequin.com,* she "has had it all, just not all at the same time." With her husband of over thirty years, she also believes, it is always necessary to find time to keep romance alive. She offers that she does so "by never taking each other for granted. We always kiss hello and good-bye. We also take romantic, 'time-alone' vacations a couple of times a year."

Barton has become one of the Harlequin's most successful romance writers and is continuing to enjoy success as well with her books written for the Zebra Romantic Suspense imprint, published by Kensington. In addition to living a life of romance, she advises other would-be writers to "read, read, read! Write, write, write! And never give up!" Her intention "to write until the day I die" and "to never disappoint my readers" is likely to please her readers for decades to come.

BIOGRAPHICAL AND CRITICAL SOURCES:

PERIODICALS

Publishers Weekly, July 23, 2001, review of *Every Move She Makes,* p. 55.

OTHER

All about Romance, http://www.likesbooks.com (May 18, 1999), Ellen Micheletti, "Beverly Barton: Southern Towns and Bad Boys."

Beverly Barton Web site, http://www.beverlybarton. com (March, 2002).
BookBrowser, http://www.bookbrowser.com (September 25, 2001), Harriet Klausner, review of *Every Move She Makes.*
Harlequin Enterprises, http://www.eharlequin.com (March 5, 2002), "Beverly Barton."
Likesbooks, http://www.likesbooks.com/ "Beverly Barton: Southern Towns and Bad Boys," (October 6, 2001).
Romance Reader Web site, http://www. theromancereader.com/ (October 6, 2001), Thea Davis, review of *Emily and the Stranger.*
Romantic Times Web site, www.romantictimes.com/ (October 6, 2001), reviews of *Emily and the Stranger, A Child of Her Own, After Dark,* and *Every Move She Makes.*
Silhouette Intimate Moments, http://www. intimatemomentsauthors.com/ (October 6, 2001), review of *Every Move She Makes,* .
Word Weaving, http://www.wordweaaving.com (March 6, 2002), "Beverly Barton."*

* * *

BECKETT, Wendy 1930-
   (Sister Wendy)

PERSONAL: Born February 25, 1930, in Johannesburg, South Africa; immigrated to Edinburgh, Scotland. *Education:* St. Anne's College, Oxford, 1950-53 (congratulatory first in literature); attended Liverpool teachers' college, 1953. *Religion:* Roman Catholic. *Hobbies and other interests:* Prayer, solitude.

ADDRESSES: Agent—Toby Eady Associates, Ltd., Third Floor, 9 Orme Court, London W2 4RL, England; fax: 020-7792-0879.

CAREER: Sisters of Notre Dame, England, nun, beginning 1945, became reverend mother, then Consecrated Virgin and entered contemplative life, 1970; teacher in South Africa, 1954-69; British Broadcasting Corporation (BBC), London, England, host of television series *Sister Wendy Beckett's Odyssey,* 1992, *Sister Wendy's Grand Tour,* 1994, *Sister Wendy's Story of Painting,* 1997, and *Sister Wendy's A Collection,* 2002; host of *Sister Wendy's American Collection* (television program), WGBH, 2001. Judge of *National Catholic Reporter* competition to find the best likeness of Jesus, 2000.

WRITINGS:

Contemporary Women Artists, Universe Books (New York, NY), 1988.

Peggy Glanville-Hicks (biography), Angus & Robertson (Pymble, New South Wales, Australia), 1992.

The Gaze of Love: Meditations on Art and Spiritual Transformation, HarperSanFrancisco (San Francisco, CA), 1993.

The Mystical Now: Art and the Sacred, Universe (New York, NY), 1993.

The Story of Painting: The Essential Guide to the History of Western Art, British National Gallery of Art/Dorling Kindersley (New York, NY), 1994.

A Child's Book of Prayer in Art (for children), Dorling Kindersley (New York, NY), 1995.

The Mystery of Love: Saints in Art through the Centuries, HarperSanFrancisco (San Francisco, CA), 1996.

(With George Pattison) *Pains of Glass: The Story of the Passion from King's College Chapel, Cambridge,* Parkwest Publications (New York, NY), 1996.

Sister Wendy's Grand Tour: Discovering Europe's Great Art, Stewart, Tabori & Chang (New York, NY), 1996.

The Duke and the Peasant: Life in the Middle Ages (for children), Prestel (New York, NY), 1997.

Sister Wendy's Story of Christmas, Prestel (New York, NY), 1997.

Max Beckmann and the Self, Prestel (New York, NY), 1997.

Sister Wendy's Book of Meditations, Dorling Kindersley (New York, NY), 1998.

Sister Wendy's Book of Saints, Dorling Kindersley (New York, NY), 1998.

Sister Wendy's Nativity (young adult book), HarperCollins (New York, NY), 1998.

Sister Wendy's Odyssey: A Journey of Artistic Discovery, BBC Books (London, England), 1993, Stewart, Tabori & Chang (New York, NY), 1998.

(With David Torkington) *Inner Life: A Fellow Traveler's Guide to Prayer,* Alba House, 1998.

Sister Wendy's Book of Muses, Harry N. Abrams (New York, NY), 1999.

Dan Paulos: In the Midst of Chaos, Peace, Ignatius Press (San Francisco, CA), 1999.

My Favorite Things: Seventy-five Works of Art from around the World, Harry N. Abrams (New York, NY), 1999.

(With Patricia Wright) *Sister Wendy's 1,000 Masterpieces,* Dorling Kindersley (New York, NY), 1999.

Sister Wendy's American Collection, HarperCollins (New York, NY), 2000.

(With Patricia Wright) *Sister Wendy's American Masterpieces: Sister Wendy Beckett's Selection of the Greatest American Paintings,* Dorling Kindersley (New York, NY), 2001.

(With Patricia Wright) *Sister Wendy's Impressionist Masterpieces: Sister Wendy Beckett's Selection of the Greatest Impressionist Paintings,* Dorling Kindersley (New York, NY), 2001.

"MEDITATION" SERIES

Meditations on Joy, Dorling Kindersley (London, England), 1995.

Meditations on Love, Dorling Kindersley (London, England), 1995.

Meditations on Peace, Dorling Kindersley (London, England), 1995.

Meditations on Silence, Dorling Kindersley (London, England), 1995.

Translated the writings of John, Abbot of Ford, *Sermons on the Final Verses of the Song of Songs,* Cistercian Publications, Inc., numerous volumes, 1977-1984.

SIDELIGHTS: Despite the avalanche of books published by Sister Wendy Beckett since 1988, writing receives only a small portion of the nun's energy. The major focus of her life as a nun is in contemplative devotion to God, which makes it all the more surprising that during the 1990s a large portion of her time was spent as an art critic for the British Broadcasting Corporation. Familiar to viewers of public television in the United States beginning in 1997, Sister Wendy is known, particularly in Great Britain, despite—or perhaps because of—her simple warmth and honest thoughts when expounding upon a particular piece of art. Wearing the full habit of a traditional nun also helps impress her image upon viewers. The unusual combination of Sister Wendy's life of solitude in a trailer parked at a convent and her very public, near-celebrity status seems odd, yet her vibrant personality and love of all God's creation somehow brings the two worlds together.

Born in 1930, Beckett entered a Catholic convent at the age of sixteen, earned her novitiate, and then went on to study at St. Anne's College, Oxford. Although she returned to her native South Africa to teach in the 1960s, recurring epileptic seizures forced her to return to England. There, in 1970, she began to live the contemplative life, making her home in a trailer on the grounds of a Carmelite monastery in England. It was while living the studious life that she developed her interest and knowledge of art.

When Sister Wendy was fifty-eight years old she wrote her first book, her authorial efforts intended to help raise money for the Carmelite Order of nuns on whose property her trailer sits. The book, *Contemporary Women Artists,* contains photographs of paintings, drawings, and sculptures, all created by women. Sister Wendy's commentary, appearing on the page opposite from the art, allows readers to study the image while reading her comments. A *Publishers Weekly* reviewer pointed out that the book's theme seems to be the vast diversity of contemporary art. Reaction to *Contemporary Women Artists* varied, but was positive overall. M. M. Doherty, writing for *Choice,* found weaknesses in Sister Wendy's discussion of women's art as well as in the book's overall scholarship, observing that the book didn't include any writings on women in the bibliography. "Although fresh and informative," Doherty explained, "the writing cannot atone for Beckett's failure to footnote even direct quotations or her admission that she quotes sources she has omitted from the minimal artist bibliographies in the appendix." A *Booklist* reviewer, on the other hand, praised the book, commenting that Sister Wendy's "meditations on contemporary women's artwork force . . . the reader, too, to look deeply and carefully at the spiritual essence of art."

Reviewed less positively was Sister Wendy's second effort, a biography titled *Peggy Glanville-Hicks.* The work is an informal account of Glanville-Hicks, who appointed Beckett her "official biographer" before her death. As Thomas Shapcott reported in the *Australian Book Review,* "The most attractive aspects of this book lie precisely in this informal approach. . . . [but] it is sloppy and frequently inaccurate; it tackles issues far outside of the author's field of competence—including music, where time and again she is way out of her depth; and it is decidedly muddled in its chronology and its emphases."

Sister Wendy returned to her strong suit—art—in her next book, *The Gaze of Love.* The 1993 volume brings together images of twentieth-century art with the inten-

tion of illuminating the spiritual aspects of the work. "The range of these works is astonishing, and the author's readiness to take on themes of violence, passion, sexuality, terror and beauty and relate them to grand themes of the spiritual life is impressive," commented a *Christian Century* reviewer. Sister Wendy's *The Mystical Now* addresses similar themes. *Publishers Weekly* reported, "This volume is a wonderful odyssey through a neglected domain of modern art, its exploration of the spiritual or sacred. Beckett's uncanny communion with the inner meanings of these paintings and sculptures opens readers to art's transformative potential." Becket's writings on art came to the attention of BBC producer Nicholas Rossiter, who was then in search of a host for an art program based in London's National Gallery of Art. Through her work for the BBC, Sister Wendy quickly became a household name and her books were soon in great demand.

In her most comprehensive work, Sister Wendy took on the ambitious task of presenting centuries of art in *The Story of Painting: The Essential Guide to the History of Western Art.* Published in association with the U.S. National Gallery of Art, the volume offers an art timeline and interesting sidebars, and highlights thirty paintings drawn from different eras. "More personal than scholarly, this is a very engaging overview of painting through history, and the author's obvious love of art shines through," wrote Jane Van Wiemokly in *Voice of Youth Advocates.* Mark Herring, reporting in *American Reference Books Annual,* praised the book: "This is a garden of visual delights, a panopticon of panoramas, a pastiche of paintings, a soon-to-be-best-selling coffee-table book. But the paintings are only half the story. Beckett's scholarly yet highly readable account adds immeasurably to this volume's worth."

Moving to a younger audience—specifically early to middle elementary children—Sister Wendy published *A Child's Book of Prayer in Art,* which is a series of fifteen paintings matched with a particular virtue such as listening, selflessness, love, and understanding. The oversized layout includes a reproduction of the painting, a simple prayer, and a paragraph explaining the spiritual significance of the work. Noting that the Sister "takes us into her meaning derived from the canvas in a few well-chosen words," Terence Copley added in the *Times Education Supplement* that "children are not patronized in the process." Patricia Lothrop Green, reviewing the work in the *School Library Journal,* praised *A Child's Book of Prayer in Art* and maintained that "No one could reasonably object either to the sterling qualities showcased, or to the lovely reproductions." Shelley Townsend-Hudson concluded in *Booklist:* "With appeal to older as well as middle readers, this is a remarkable book, not only for its innate spirituality and wisdom, but also for its harmonious partnership of great art and astute interpretation." Also aimed at a younger audience, Beckett's *The Duke and the Peasant: Life in the Middle Ages* features Jean duc de Berry's calendar paintings from the *Book of Hours.*

Some of Beckett's books, particularly *Sister Wendy's Grand Tour: Discovering Europe's Great Art* and *Sister Wendy's Odyssey: A Journey of Artistic Discovery,* are companion pieces to her BBC television series. *Sister Wendy's Grand Tour* is a sampling of the paintings she reviewed while on tour in ten continental European cities. Four to ten works from each city are accompanied by a one-page overview of their region. While limiting itself to six cities in Great Britain, *Sister Wendy's Odyssey* features a similar layout. Both volumes are especially suited for those looking for general knowledge on art. "The way she explains their superlativeness is a refreshing trip back to what these paintings are about," praised Gilbert Taylor in *Booklist.* "Sure the good sister is subjective, but her honest wonderment is certain to affect all who read her book (and see the TV show) and perhaps improve their sensitivity to great art."

A few of Beckett's books contain a narrower focus. *Sister Wendy's Book of Saints* examines thirty-five saints. The work provides color illustrations of the saints drawn from sources in Italian library manuscripts, biographical information such as how each became a saint, and an explanation of the art work. "A born storyteller, Sr. Wendy intelligently introduces such issues as separation of church and state and the status of women," commended Anna Donnelly in *Library Journal.* Reviewer Kieran Egan was less enthusiastic in her *Journal of Adolescent and Adult Literacy* review. Beckett "is excellent at drawing attention to an expression, stance, or some other feature of the illustrations one might easily miss. None of it is profoundly insightful, nor is intended to be, but it is the kind of intelligent guidance that helps one to see more. . . . The problem is," Egan continued, "that Sister Wendy doesn't deal with the elements of these stories adequately to help the modern reader understand them."

Among Beckett's more topical works is *Sister Wendy's Book of Nativity,* which examines images from illuminated manuscripts in the Italian State Library and the Vatican Library that are specific to the birth and life of Christ. "Her commentary is both revealing and inspirational, and it is offered in the trademark Sister Wendy fashion," noted an *Artline, Etc.* reviewer. "Her religious beliefs are held separate from her criticism, so that readers are enlightened artistically and allowed to draw their own spiritual conclusions."

Among the most recent books by Sister Wendy are her top-picks in different categories of paintings: *My Favorite Things: Seventy-five Works of Art from around the World; Sister Wendy's 1,000 Masterpieces; Sister Wendy's American Collection; Sister Wendy's Impressionist Masterpieces: Sister Wendy Beckett's Selection of the Greatest Impressionist Paintings;* and *Sister Wendy's American Masterpieces: Sister Wendy Beckett's Selection of the Greatest American Paintings.* For readers and viewers who are fond of Beckett's style, the variety of her coverage is welcomed.

While Beckett has gained a popular following, she has also gained detractors. "Predictably, Sister Wendy's fame has bred contempt, mostly among established critics," noted Marshall Sella in the *New York Times Magazine.* "They regard her as a kind of art-world Ross Perot: an interloper, mesmerizing in her anecdotes and colorful in her speech, with a vast following to boot." Sister Wendy confessed that the criticism hurts her feelings, telling interviewer Lucy Kellaway of the *Financial Times,* "People have said the programmes are anodyne: my manner is theatrical but the matter is very dull—which was not very nice to hear. . . . If you don't feel hurt you are not human. Read the gospels. Jesus was deeply hurt." Yet she continues to hold her ground, asserting that average people need simple explanations so as to draw them into, rather than away from, the love of art.

What no critic can dispute is the joy with which Sister Wendy approaches her subject. Said the author to Elaine Liner of the *Boston Herald,* "In art it's very clear that this human being has been privileged to look, as it were, into the divine depths and bring something back of that to us."

BIOGRAPHICAL AND CRITICAL SOURCES:

BOOKS

Newsmakers 1998, Gale (Detroit, MI), 1998.

PERIODICALS

America, November 4, 1995, Michael Downey, review of *The Gaze of Love: Meditations on Art and Spiritual Transformation,* p. 34; November 11, 1998, Emilie Griffin, review of *Sister Wendy's Book of Meditations,* p. 31.

American Reference Books Annual, 1995, Mark Y. Herring, review of *The Story of Painting: The Essential Guide to the History of Western Art,* p. 443.

Australian Book Review, June, 1992, Thomas Shapcott, "Melody Missing," p. 27.

Booklist, January 15, 1989, review of *Contemporary Women Artists,* p. 828; September 1, 1995, Shelley Townsend-Hudson, review of *A Child's Book of Prayer in Art,* p. 58; November 1, 1996, Gilbert Taylor, review of *Sister Wendy's Grand Tour: Discovering Europe's Great Art,* p. 471; January 1, 2000, Bonnie Smothers, review of *My Favorite Things: Seventy-five Works of Art from around the World,* p. 856.

Boston Herald, September 6, 1997, Elaine Liner, "Nun Gives PBS a New *Masterpiece Theater,*" p. 18.

Catholic Library World, June, 1999, Gretchen Fox, review of *Sister Wendy's Nativity,* p. 49.

Choice, April, 1989, M. M. Doherty, review of *Contemporary Women Artists,* p. 1317; March, 1998, J. M. Curtis, review of *Max Beckmann and the Self,* p. 1180.

Christian Century, November 23, 1994, review of *The Gaze of Love,* p. 1139.

Financial Times, July 6, 1996, Lucy Kellaway, "Lovely Food Is a Gift from God," p. 3.

Guardian, June 26, 1996, Joanna Moorehead, "Inside Story: Habitual Change," p. 6.

Independent (London, England), June 22, 1996, John Walsh, "John Walsh Meets Sister Wendy Beckett: Art Critic, Trekkie, and the Nation's Favourite Nun," p. 10.

Journal of Adolescent and Adult Literacy, May, 1999, Kieran Egan, review of *Sister Wendy's Book of Saints,* p. 685.

Library Journal, November 15, 1994, Daniel J. Lombardo, review of *The Story of Painting,* p. 64; February 15, 1997, Anne Marie Lane, review of *Sister Wendy's Grand Tour,* p. 130; May 15, 1998, Anna M. Donnelly, review of *Sister Wendy's Book of Saints,* p. 90; October 15, 1999, Eric Bryant, review of *My Favorite Things,* p. 65.

New York Times, September 1, 1997, Alan Riding, "She May Not Get out Much, but She Does Know a Lot about Art," pp. C11-20.

New York Times Magazine, January 26, 1997, Marshall Sella, "'You Have a Cold Heart, Degas!,'" pp. 154-157.

Publishers Weekly, November 25, 1988, review of *Contemporary Women Artists,* p. 59; July 26, 1993, review of *The Mystical Now,* p. 52; October 5, 1998, review of *Sister Wendy's Odyssey: A Journey of Artistic Discovery,* p. 75; November 8, 1999, review of *My Favorite Things,* p. 61.

Quill & Quire, September, 1997, Susan Hughes, "Essence of Tree," p. 20.

Reference & Research Book News, February, 1998, review of *Max Beckmann and the Self,* p. 126.

Review for Religious, November, 1999, review of *Sister Wendy's Nativity,* p. 661.

School Arts, May, 2002, Kent Anderson, review of *Sister Wendy's American Masterpieces,* p. 60.

School Librarian, August, 1995, Janet Sims, review of *A Child's Book of Prayer in Art,* p. 111.

School Library Journal, June, 1989, Jenni Elliott, review of *Contemporary Women Artists,* p. 134; August, 1995, Patricia Lothrop Green, review of *A Child's Book of Prayer in Art,* p. 132; June, 1998, Pam Johnson, review of *Sister Wendy's Book of Saints,* p. 178.

Times Educational Supplement, April 14, 1995, Terence Copley, review of *A Child's Book of Prayer in Art,* p. 26.

Voice of Youth Advocates, March, 1995, Jane Van Wiemokly, review of *The Story of Painting,* pp. 59-60; October, 1998, Gloria Grover, review of *Sister Wendy's Book of Saints,* p. 302.

Wilson Library Bulletin, January, 1995, Cathi Dunn MacRae, "The Young Adult Perplex," pp. 121-123.

OTHER

Artline, Etc., http://www.vaxxine.com/artline/ (December 21, 1998), review of *Sister Wendy's Nativity.*

CBC Infoculture, http://www.infoculture.cbc.ca/ (August 20, 1999), "Sister Wendy Judges Jesus."*

* * *

BEIGBEDER, Frederic 1965-

PERSONAL: Born September 21, 1965; son of an employment counselor and a literary translator; divorced; children: Chlöe.

ADDRESSES: Agent—Editions Dargaud, 15/27 rue Moussorgski, Paris 75 018, France. *E-mail*—fredbeig@ club-internet.fr.

CAREER: Literary critic and novelist. Formerly worked in advertising. Founder and editor of periodicals *Genereaux,* 1992—, *Deluxe,* 1994—, and *NRV,* 1996—.

WRITINGS:

Mémoires d'un jeune homme derange, Editions La Table Rond (Paris France), 1990.
Vacances dans le coma, Editions Grasset (Paris, France), 1994.
L'amour dure trois ans, Editions Grasset (Paris, France), 1997.
Nouvelles sous ecstasy, Edition Gallimard (Paris France), 1999.
99 francs, Editions Grasset (Paris, France), 2000.
14,99 euros, Editions Grasset (Paris, France), 2001.
Dernier inventaire avant liquidation, Editions Grasset (Paris, France), 2001.
Barbie, Editions Assouline (Paris, France), 2001.
(With Philippe Bertrand) *Rester Normal,* Editions Dargaud (Paris, France), 2002.

Contributor of reviews to periodicals.

SIDELIGHTS: By the age of thirty-five, Frederic Beigbeder had published five novels, started four magazines and become "l'enfant terrible" of the French advertising world. From a privileged upbringing in the Neuilly section of Paris, Beigbeder graduated from prestigious schools and immediately set out to become a fixture of the Paris nightclub scene. A self-proclaimed dandy and literary snob, he organized soirees at a private club, chez Castel, for the in-crowd for ten years. This led him to ten years in the advertising business and, beginning in 1997, with Thierry Ardisson, he held court on the literary and cultural goings on of France nightly on prime time television.

He is the founder and editor of three magazines, *Genereux* in 1992, *Deluxe* in 1994 and *NRV,* a literary review in 1996. Beigbeder's range as a literary critic also encompasses reviews and critiques for such diverse magazines as *Lire, Paris Match, Elle, Le Figaro Literaire* and *Techni art.* He also is a contributor to *Masque et la Plume,* a literary radio program.

The French advertising world was a rich pool of talent in the 1980s, and the most talented players attained rock star status. Beigbeder, along with film director Jean Jacques Beineix and musician and multi-media artist Jean Paul Goude, were considered the crème de la crème. This is the world Beigbeder ruthlessly dissects in his novel *99 francs.*

99 Francs is a thinly disguised roman à clef that apparently cost him his high-paying job at the multinational ad agency, Young & Rubicam. From the beginning of the book, the narrator claims that "I am writing the book to get fired." Beigbeder's premise is clear: everything and everybody is for sale. "In my profession, no one wants you to be happy, because happy people don't consume," the narrator tells us. He argues that advertising is a perversion of democracy. Bruce Crumley, reviewing the book for *Time International,* wrote that "Whether or not he wins one of the prestigious awards soon to be doled out during France's literary high season, Frederic Beigbeder has already secured first prize for audacity with his novel, *99 francs,* a hyperbolic savaging of the author's own profession, advertising."

Beigbeder's other novels are no less controversial: in his 1997 book, *L'amour dure trois ans,* he develops his theory that love cannot exist for more than three years. His *Nouvelles sous ecstasy* is an ode to drugs, especially the nightclub drug, ecstasy.

In the tradition of the urbane and cynical cultural arbiters of the twentieth century, Beigbeder's iconoclastic novels and biting reviews have won him a cult following in France.

BIOGRAPHICAL AND CRITICAL SOURCES:

PERIODICALS

AdAgeGlobal, December, 2000, Lawrence J. Spear, review of *99 francs,* p. 10.
Economist, June 30, 2001, review of *Dernier inventaire avant liquidation,* p. 10.
Time International, October 2, 2000, Bruce Crumley, review of *99 francs,* p. 86.

BELL, James Scott 1954-

PERSONAL: Born August 10, 1954, in Los Angeles, CA; married; wife's name Cindy; *Education:* University of California—Santa Barbara, B.A., 1976; University of Southern California Law Center, J.D. (cum laude), 1984.

ADDRESSES: Office—James Scott Bell, P.O. Box 705, Woodland Hills, CA 91365. *Agent*—Broadman & Holman Publishers,127 Ninth Avenue North, Nashville, TN 37234. *E-mail*—JSB@jamesscottbell.com.

CAREER: Lawyer and writer. Adjunct professor of writing and screenwriting at Learning Tree University, and Masters College, 1995; Created curriculum for Writers Digest School Online Fiction Courses, "Creating Dynamic Characters" and "Writing Effective Dialog." Commentator on legal matters for radio and television, including appearances on *Good Morning America* and CBS radio.

MEMBER: California Bar Association.

AWARDS, HONORS: Order of the Coif; American Board of Trial Advocates Award for Excellence; Hale Moot Court Honors Program; Christy Award for Excellence in Christian Fiction, 2001.

WRITINGS:

The Darwin Conspiracy, Broadman and Holmes (Nashville, TN), 1995.
Circumstantial Evidence, Broadman and Holmes (Nashville, TN), 1997.
Final Witness, Broadman and Holmes (Nashville, TN), 1999.
Blind Justice, Broadman and Holmes (Nashville, TN), 2000.
The Nephilim Seed, Broadman and Holmes (Nashville, TN), 2001.
Deadlock, Zondervan (Grand Rapids, MI), 2002.

"SHANNON" SERIES

(With Traci Peterson) *City of Angels,* Broadman and Holmes (Nashville, TN), 2001.
(With Traci Peterson) *Angels Flight,* Broadman and Holmes (Nashville, TN), 2001.

(With Traci Peterson) *Angels of Mercy,* Broadman and Holmes (Nashville, TN), 2002.
A Greater Glory, Bethany House (Minneapolis, MN), 2003.

OTHER

Also author of *Bell's Compendium on Search and Seizure, Bell's Motion Manual, Bell's Bugging Book, Bell's Points and Authorities, Successful Closing Argument Techniques, Top Courtroom Performance, Guerrilla Trial Tactics,* and *Trial Weapons,* all for Courtroom Compendiums (Woodland Hills, CA).

Editor of monthly newspapers *Trial Excellence,* and *California DUI Report.* Contributing editor to *Writers Digest Magazine,* 2002. Contributing writer for *Teachers in Focus* and *Writers Digest* magazines and short stories for *Multnomah Quarterly.* Columnist for *Christian Communicator,* 1995-98.

SIDELIGHTS: James Scott Bell is an author of both contemporary thrillers and historical suspense novels. A former trial lawyer since 1995, he has written and lectured full time. Bell is the author of over 300 articles and several books for the legal profession, but his fiction focuses on suspense, faith and the struggle of people to find meaning in their lives. Bell told *CA,* "Each of my novels, in one way or another, offers a defense of the Christian faith. The best writing both moves us and makes us think—it changes us and that's what I try to do with my fiction."

Bell became a Christian in high school. After college, he spent several years as an actor in New York and Hollywood before becoming a lawyer. He practiced in a civil litigation in a large firm before opening his own solo practice in 1985. Bell told *CA,* "I wasn't happy about spending so much time away from my young family, so I opened my own office, associating with my father, who is also a lawyer." During this period he began legal writing. *Bell's Compendium on Search and Seizure,* his first book, became the best selling treatise on the subject and has been used by lawyers and judges in many prominent trials, including the O. J. Simpson murder case. His expertise has led to appearances on *Good Morning America* and CBS radio as a legal expert commentator.

Using his legal background, Bell has written three thrillers and most recently has tackled the topic of bioethics in *The Nephilim Seed.* "In my writing," Bell told *CA*, "I want to champion the Kingdom of God—to help people to see that it is emotionally and intellectually the most fulfilling vision of how to live."

BIOGRAPHICAL AND CRITICAL SOURCES:

PERIODICALS

Booklist, June 1, 2001, John Mort, review of *The Nephilim Seed*, p. 1844; March 1, 2001, John Mort, review of *City of Angels*, p. 1228; March 1, 2000, John Mort, review of *Blind Justice*, p. 1196.
Publishers Weekly, April 9, 2001, review of *The Nephilim Seed*, p. 52.*

*   *   *

BELLACERA, Carole

PERSONAL: Born in Hot Springs, AR; married Frank Bellacera; children: two. *Education:* Prince George's Community College, Largo, MD. *Hobbies and other interests:* Downhill skiing.

ADDRESSES: Agent—c/o Forge Books, 175 Fifth Ave., New York, NY 10010. *E-mail*—Carole@Bellacera.com.

CAREER: Medical technician, librarian, executive secretary, and Congressional receptionist. *Military service:* U.S. Air Force, medical technician, served in United States and Europe.

AWARDS, HONORS: Austin Heart of Film Competition finalist, 1995, grand prize, Great American Script Search, 1995, New Horizons first place winner, screenplay category, Houston Writers Conference, 1997, RITA Award nominee for Best Romantic Suspense and Best First Book, 2000, and Volusia County Laurel Wreath Award, 2000, all for *Border Crossings;* Holt Medallion finalist, Best Mainstream Novel, 2001, for *Spotlight;* Bookseller's Best Awards finalist, 2001, for *Spotlight.*

WRITINGS:

Border Crossings, Forge Books (New York, NY), 1999.
Spotlight, Forge Books (New York, NY), 2000.
East of the Sun, West of the Moon, Forge Books (New York, NY), 2001.

Understudy, in press.

Also author of *Velma and Louie*, a comedic screenplay, and several short stories appearing in publications including *Family, Star*, the *Washington Post*, and *Woman's World*, and in anthologies including *Chocolate for a Woman's Heart* and *Chicken Soup for a Couple's Soul.*

WORK IN PROGRESS: She is currently working on a book called *Tango's Edge*, a novel about a Russian ice dancer who defects to America with the help of the heroine, and American ice dancer.

SIDELIGHTS: Carole Bellacera started her writing career with short stories, beginning with a story inspired by a chance meeting with the late British Princess Diana Spencer while serving in the Air Force. She published that story, "The Day Princess Di Spoke to Me," in a military magazine, and began to pursue her dream of publishing a novel. Her first novel, *Border Crossings*, actually began as an award-winning screenplay. Set in Northern Ireland, it tells the story of Kathy O'Faolain, who is unwittingly drawn into political turmoil when her husband, a professor of Irish history, decides to join Sinn Fein, part of the IRA. Writing about her book for *Amazon.com*, Bellacera said, "I hope readers of *Border Crossings* will come away with a better understanding of the Troubles in Northern Ireland, as seen through the eyes of an American woman, desperate to hold onto her love for her husband, yet afraid for their very lives." Critics responded to Bellacera's portrayal of Kathy's sadness and fear. Writing for *Booklist*, Margaret Flanagan called *Border Crossings* a "riveting psychological thriller." A reviewer for *Publishers Weekly* suggested that in *Border Crossings* Bellacera tended to depict the political strife in Ireland "through a misty, romantic lens," concluding that "she is more successful when describing the domestic, sexual and parental relationships to which her homey prose is better suited." In focusing on the feelings of Kathy, said Susan Gene Clifford in *Booklist*, Bellacera created "a powerful and deeply moving story of terror, death, hope, and love."

Bellacera's next book, *Spotlight*, similarly addresses the Troubles in Ireland. It is a love story between Devin, an Irish rock star whose brother died on Bloody Sunday, and Fonda, a photojournalist for the music magazine *Spotlight*, who joins Devin on tour to write a book about him and his band. Obstacles the lovers face include Devin's wife Caitlyn, an active member of the IRA who is now in prison, and the cultural divide between political activism of Devin and the naiveté of Fonda. *Spotlight* is also a political thriller, implicating the unwitting Devin in a plot to buy arms for the IRA, a group to which Devin, a pacifist, is strongly opposed.

Critical response to the book was mixed. Writing for *Booklist*, Patty Englemann called *Spotlight* "riveting and romantic suspense," though she suggested that the book might best suit the young adult market. A reviewer for *Publishers Weekly* wrote, "the overstuffed plot bursts its seams toward the end, and Bellacera's dialogue tends to the mawkish," while a critic in *Kirkus Reviews* suggested that the combination of a "bodice-ripper" and a political thriller "doesn't quite work." Romance readers were more enthusiastic, however. Jennifer L. Schendel, reviewing *Spotlight* for *All about Romance Web site,* said the novel is for "anyone who enjoys an interesting story with engaging characters and an intricate plot," saying that Devin and Fonda were "interesting people that I enjoyed spending time with, and will miss." On the Web site *Romance and Friends,* Kathy Boswell called the novel "a page turner from the very first page."

In Bellacera's third book, *East of the Sun, West of the Moon,* the author leaves behind the Irish setting to focus on the intimate struggles of an American family. The book's heroine, Leigh Fallon, discovers that her congressman husband is having an affair with his administrative assistant. Leigh uses her husband's lapse as an excuse to give in to her feelings for Erik, a Norwegian college student living with the Fallons for year. She returns to Norway with Erik, allowing her husband to turn her grown children against her and finding that further troubles lie ahead. Critics found the novel compelling and relevant. A reviewer for *Publishers Weekly* said that the theme of balancing family responsibilities with personal needs "should resonate with readers, many of whom are confronted with the same question on a daily basis," and concluded that the novel is "written with . . . assurance." Boswell of *Romance and Friends* called *East of the Sun* "powerful and moving," and a "must read," and John Charles wrote in *Booklist* that "Bellacera handles her book's complex subject matter beautifully," with an authentic depiction of Leigh's experiences.

BIOGRAPHICAL AND CRITICAL SOURCES:

PERIODICALS

Booklist, May 15, 1999, Margaret Flanagan, review of *Border Crossings,* p. 1666; June 1, 2000, Patty Englemann, review of *Spotlight,* p. 1851; August 2001, John Charles, review of *East of the Sun, West of the Moon,* p. 2100.

Kirkus Reviews, May 15, 2000, review of *Spotlight,* p. 648.

Library Journal, March 15, 1999, Susan Gene Clifford, review of *Border Crossings,* p. 108.

Publishers Weekly, March 29, 1999, review of *Border Crossings,* p. 91; May 29, 2000, review of *Spotlight,* p. 50; July 30, 2001, review of *East of the Sun, West of the Moon,* p. 64.

OTHER

All about Romance, http://www.likesbooks.com/ (October 6, 2001), Jennifer L. Schendel, review of *Spotlight.*

Amazon.com, http://www/amazon.com (March 15, 2003), interview with Carole Bellacera.

Carole Bellacera Home Page, http://www.bellacera. com/ (October 6, 2001)

Harriet Klausner's Review Archive, http:// harrietklausner.wwwi.com/ (October 6, 2001), reviews of *East of the Sun, West of the Moon,* and *Spotlight.*

Romance Fiction, http://romancefiction.about.com/ (July 2, 2001).

Romance and Friends, http://www.geocities.com/ romancebooks.geo/ (October 6, 2001), Kathy Boswell, reviews of Carole Bellacera's novels.

Romantic Times, http://www.romantictimes.com/ (October 6, 2001), Jill M. Smith, reviews of *Border Crossings* and *East of the Sun, West of the Moon.**

*　　*　　*

BEN AMMI 1939-
(Ben Ammi Ben-Israel)

PERSONAL: Original name, Ben Carter; born 1939 (some sources say 1940), in Chicago, IL; married four times; children: fifteen.

ADDRESSES: Office—Public Relations Department, World African Hebrew Israelite Community, P.O. Box 465, Dimona, Israel 86000.

CAREER: World African Hebrew Israelite Community (also known as Original Hebrew Israelite Nation and African Hebrew Israelites of Jerusalem), Dimona,

Israel, founder and leader, c. 1967—. Worked as a bus driver in Chicago, IL, and as a foundry worker, between 1960 and 1966.

WRITINGS:

"RESURRECTION SERIES"

God, the Black Man, and Truth, Communicators Press (Chicago, IL), 1982.

The Messiah and the End of This World, Communicators Press (Washington, DC), 1991.

God and the Law of Relativity, Communicators Press (Washington, DC), 1991.

Everlasting Life: From Thought to Reality, Communicators Press (Washington, DC), 1994.

(As Ben Ammi Ben-Israel) *Yeshua the Hebrew Messiah or Jesus the Christian Christ,* Communicators Press (Washington, DC), 1996.

An Imitation of Life: Redefining What Constitutes True Life and Living in the New World, Communicators Press (Washington, DC), 1999.

BIOGRAPHICAL AND CRITICAL SOURCES:

BOOKS

Ben Yehuda, Shaleak, *Black Hebrew Israelites from America to the Promised Land,* Vantage Press (New York, NY), 1975.

Contemporary Black Biography, Volume 11, Gale (Detroit, MI), 1996.

Religious Leaders of America,, Gale (Detroit, MI), 1999.

PERIODICALS

Chicago Tribune, August 14, 1986, p. 12; September 11, 1986, p. 23; September 14, 1990, p. 1.

Guardian, September 10, 1998, Julian Borger, "Let My People Go, Too," p. T8.

OTHER

African Hebrew Israelites of Jerusalem, http://www.kingdomofyah.com/ (February 8, 2003).*

BENEDICT, Elinor Divine 1931-

PERSONAL: Born June 4, 1931, in Chattanooga, TN; daughter of Thomas McCallie and Mary Hills (Faxon) Divine; married Samuel Sollie Benedict, October 3, 1953; children: Samuel, Jonathan, Kathleen. *Education:* Duke University, B.A. (English), 1953; Wright State University, M.A. (English), 1977; Vermont College, M.F.A. (writing), 1983. *Politics:* Democrat. *Religion:* Presbyterian. *Hobbies and other interests:* Birding, traveling.

ADDRESSES: Home—8627 South Lakeside T.5 Dr., Rapid River, MI 49878-9528.

CAREER: Poet, writer, journalist, editor, college instructor. Times Publications, Kettering, OH, staff writer, 1968-76; Centerville, OH, public schools, public information consultant, 1976; Bay de Noc Community College, Escanaba, MI, part-time instructor, 1977-86; *Passages North* literary magazine, Escanaba, MI, founding editor, 1979-89. William Bonifas Fine Arts Center, Escanaba, MI, secretary of the board of directors, 1985-86, vice president, 1986-87; member of Commission on Art in Public Places, Detroit, MI, 1987-91; member of the arts project panel, Michigan Council for the Arts, Detroit, MI, 1987-91.

MEMBER: Society for Study of Midwestern Literature, Associated Writing Programs.

AWARDS, HONORS: Fiction Prize, *Mademoiselle* magazine, 1953; Wright State University fellow, 1976; Creative Artist Award, Michigan Council for the Arts, 1985; Coordinating Council of Literary Magazines grantee, 1987; May Swenson Poetry Award, 2000.

WRITINGS:

POETRY

(With others) *A Bridge to China,* Hardwood Books (Plattsburgh, NY), 1983.

The Green Heart (chapbook), Illinois State University Press (Normal, IL), 1994.

Chinavision (chapbook), March Street Press (Greensboro, NC), 1995.

The Tree between Us (chapbook), March Street Press (Greensboro, NC), 1997.
All That Divides Us, Utah State University Press (Logan, UT), 2000.

OTHER

(Editor) *Passages North Anthology: A Decade of Good Writing,* Milkweed Editions (Minneapolis, MN), 1990.

SIDELIGHTS: Elinor Divine Benedict was born and raised in Chattanooga, Tennessee, but has spent most of her adult life in the north woods of Michigan. As a college student in 1953, Benedict won *Mademoiselle* magazine's coveted fiction prize, a benchmark for many aspiring young women writers in mid-twentieth-century America. She has combined a career in writing with raising a family, teaching, volunteering on various community arts committees, and serving as a founding editor for one of the Midwest's most prestigious literary magazines, *Passages North.*

When Benedict was awarded the May Swenson Poetry Award in 2000 for her collection *All That Divides Us,* she revealed an old family story to a reading audience who could relate to her memories as a mature woman. The collection grew out of the tale of one of her aunts, who in the 1930s left the Benedict family "to marry a Chinaman" and subsequently remained away from the family until she came home to die. Benedict told Amazon.com that, although she's not Chinese herself, "I'm part of a bigger story about China and the United States of America. In *All That Divides Us,* my version of the story is personal and internal, revealing through poetry how the mysterious figure of Grace Divine Liu, my beloved father's only sister, of whom he often said I reminded him, haunted my growing-up and made me fiercely aware of the gulfs and tensions between two families, two cultures."

In her foreword to the collection, Swenson Award judge Maxine Kumin noted that the story "unspools" as Benedict describes the experience of having a 'rebel aunt' in China. "As the poems' author, I appreciate Kumin's imagery of 'unspooling'; for it often seemed to me that the story itself, as it was happening over the years, was weaving a significant corner of some vast and cryptic tapestry. From China to our small

house in Tennessee came exotic gifts and news of floods, famine, world war, civil war, and cultural revolution. To us, those years meant the Depression, World War II, and finally the Cold War, when the McCarthy era made having relatives in 'Red China' suspect and perhaps even dangerous. Then the cultural revolution brought new fears. As the tapestry grew, I became almost obsessed with 'Aunt Grace,' who seemed a doppelganger, a double of sorts, as a distant reflection of my father's love," Kumin recalled.

Benedict's Aunt Grace returned home to the United States in 1974 when cultural relations between the two nations were enjoying a thaw. In 1980 Benedict and her daughter traveled to China to meet her half-Chinese cousins and to attend a memorial for her aunt in the Hall of Revolutionary Martyrs. Two more visits in 1993 and 1995 helped the poet connect not only to her aunt and the life she had lived but to bridge the cultural gap brought about within the family by her aunt's decision as a young woman. The story of Grace was also written in prose form by two of Benedict's cousins, the American Eleanor Cooper and the half-Chinese William Liu, and published by Black Belt Press in 1999.

Benedict has also produced five chapbooks of poetry, in addition to her work as founding editor of *Passages North* literary magazine and as editor of the *Passages North* anthology published in 1990. She encourages the writing of others as well through her involvement with the Bay de Noc Writers' Conferences in Michigan.

BIOGRAPHICAL AND CRITICAL SOURCES:

PERIODICALS

American Poet, winter, 2000-01, review of *All That Divides Us,* p. 41.
Booklist, October 1, 1990, Pat Monaghan, review of *Passages North Anthology,* p. 247.
Village Voice Literary Supplement, October, 1990, p. 20.

OTHER

Utah State University Press Web site, http://www.usu.edu/ (September 13, 2001), May Swenson, "All That Divides Us."*.

BEN-ISRAEL, Ben Ammi
    See BEN AMMI

*   *   *

BERG, Dave
    See BERG, David

*   *   *

BERG, David 1920-2002
    (Dave Berg)

OBITUARY NOTICE—See index for *CA* sketch: Born June 12, 1920, in Brooklyn, NY; died of cancer May 16, 2002, in Marina del Rey, CA. Cartoonist and author. Berg is best remembered for his contributions to *MAD* magazine, especially for his "The Lighter Side Of . . ." comic strip. A talented artist from a young age, Berg began his formal art education at the age of twelve when he took classes at the Pratt Institute; while in high school he studied at the Cooper Union Art School in New York. His first job as a comic-strip artist came when, at the age of twenty, he inked backgrounds for "The Spirit" newspaper comic feature, and he later worked on "Death Patrol" and "Uncle Sam" comic books. During World War II Berg was a war correspondent, covering news in Guam, Iwo Jima, Saipan, and, after the war, Japan. When he returned to the United States he was given a job working for Stan Lee at Timely Comics—the predecessor of Marvel—and Archie Comics. He joined the staff at *MAD* in 1955, drawn to the magazine's satirical bent, and his "The Lighter Side Of . . ." debuted in 1961. The comic strip became notable for its satires of human behavior and often featured Berg himself as the character Roger Kaputnik. Berg continued to draw his strip until his death, and his last work was published in the September, 2002 issue of *MAD*. In addition to this, Berg published a number of collections of his cartoons in such books as *MAD's Dave Berg Looks at People* (1966) and *MAD's Dave Berg Looks at You* (1982). Actively involved in Little League organizations, the Girl Scouts, and in the B'nai B'rith, where he was a former president of the Marina del Rey branch, Berg also published two humorous looks at religion: *My Friend GOD* (1972) and *Roger Kaputnik and GOD* (1974).

OBITUARIES AND OTHER SOURCES:

BOOKS

Who's Who in America, 55th edition, Marquis (New Providence, NJ), 2001.

PERIODICALS

Los Angeles Times, May 24, 2002, p. B16.
New York Times, May 25, 2002, p. A28.
Washington Post, May 25, 2002, p. B6.

*   *   *

BERGEL, Colin J. 1963-

PERSONAL: Born August 30, 1963, in Detroit, MI; married, 1988; wife's name, Joyce (a registered nurse); children: Ian, Kayla, Emily. *Education:* Ferris State University, B.A.

ADDRESSES: Home—2095 West Fox Farm Rd., Manistee, MI 49660. *Agent*—EDCO Publishing, 2648 Lapeer Rd., Auburn Hills, MI 48326. *E-mail*—cjbergel@ chartermi.net.

CAREER: Sea captain and author. U.S. Merchant Marine, third mate, advancing to captain, for Oglebay Norton Co., 1988—. Freelance writer.

AWARDS, HONORS: Michigan Historical Society Merit Award, and Great Lakes Book Award finalist, both 2001, both for *Mail by the Pail.*

WRITINGS:

Mail by the Pail, illustrated by Mark Koenig, Wayne State University Press (Detroit, MI), 2000.
Michigan L.A.P.S. Great Lakes Unit, Colin Bergel's Journal, EDCO Publishing (Auburn Hills, MI), 2002.

WORK IN PROGRESS: A sequel to *Mail by the Pail;* other children's books.

SIDELIGHTS: Colin J. Bergel is a Michigan-based author whose full-time job is as a member of the Merchant Marine, the branch of the U.S. military that pilots commercial ships. His first published book, *Mail by the Pail,* focuses on what he knows best: life as a sailor working on one of the freighters that carries heavy building materials and other goods to the many cities and towns located along the shores of the Great Lakes.

In *Mail by the Pail,* a young girl named Mary decides to send her father a birthday card. While for many children such a task would be simple—just handing a card to Dad during breakfast—Mary has a far greater challenge. Her father works as a sailor on a lake freighter and spends weeks at a time away from home. To reach him, Mary's birthday card must travel to a central post office in Detroit, Michigan, be transferred to a mailboat, and then be hoisted aboard her father's freighter in a metal pail tied to a rope. Readers follow the path of Mary's birthday card as it makes its way to its destination, and learn a little bit about what life is like for sailors and their families along the way.

Bergel told *CA:* "Originally *Mail by the Pail* was not written for the public. I was missing my children after sailing on a freighter for six weeks. After passing the mailboat and not receiving mail, I was wishing for a letter from home. I decided to write a story for my children to show them where I worked away from home. It took a number of years to find a publisher for this book as it was unique. After finding a publisher, it took another two and a half years to become reality." When Bergel is not working as a freighter captain, he speaks to groups of children and adults about his writing and his experiences sailing the Great Lakes region.

*　　*　　*

BLAKELY, Mike 1958-

PERSONAL: Born 1958, in Wharton County, TX; son of James "Doc" Blakely (a rancher, musician, and humorist). *Education:* University of Texas at Austin, B.A. (journalism), 1984.

ADDRESSES: Home—P.O. Box 1818, Marble Falls, TX 78654. *Agent*—c/o Tom Doherty Associates, 175 Fifth Ave., New York, NY 10010. *E-mail*—mike@www.mikeblakely.com.

CAREER: Writer, songwriter, musician, humorist. Member of "The Swing Riders Show," and Ghost Council (band). *Military service:* U.S. Air Force, 1977-81.

MEMBER: Western Writers of America (president, 1998-2000), Ozark Creative Writers.

AWARDS, HONORS: Spur Award finalist for Best Novel of the West, Western Writers of America, 1994, for *Shortgrass Song,* 1998, for *Comanche Dawn.*

WRITINGS:

FICTION

The Glory Trail: A Magnificent Epic of Texas, Harper Paperbacks (New York, NY), 1990.
Baron of the Sacramentos, National Book Network, October 1991.
The Snowy Range Gang, Forge/Tor Books (New York, NY), 1991.
Shortgrass Song, Forge/Tor Books (New York, NY), 1994.
More Wild Camp Tales, Republic of Texas Press (Plano, TX), 1995.
Too Long at the Dance, Forge/Tor Books (New York, NY), 1996.
Comanche Dawn, Forge/Tor Books (New York, NY), 1998.
Spanish Blood, Forge/Tor Books (New York, NY), 1997.
Dead Reckoning, Forge/Tor Books (New York, NY), 1997.
Vendetta Gold, Forge/Tor Books (New York, NY), 1998.
Summer of Pearls, Forge/Tor Books (New York, NY), 2000.
Moon Medicine, Forge/Tor Books (New York, NY), 2001.

NONFICTION

(Editor, with Mary Elizabeth Sue Goldman) *Forever Texas: Texas History, the Way Those Who Lived It Wrote It,* Forge (New York, NY), 2000.

Also wrote a self-syndicated column, "Lone Star Legacy," on Texas history and folklore, 1985-88; contributor to various magazines, including *Texas Highways, The Cattleman, Sports Afield, Sporting Classics, American West, Texas Sportsman, Texas Fish and Game, Ultra,* and *Western Horseman.*

WORK IN PROGRESS: Sequel to *Moon Medicine,* set in Fort Adobe, Texas.

SIDELIGHTS: Mike Blakely is more than simply a writer whose novels have made him a household word among devotees of the western novel—he is almost an entire industry promoting the Old West, as well as his beloved home state of Texas. Blakely is also a musician, songwriter, and speaker who takes endless pleasure in his first love, horses, and who shares this love with his audiences around the world. Describing himself to Steven Law in an interview published for *Readwest.com,* Blakely described the childhood passion that carried him into his career as both a writer and a musician. "My earliest memory in life," Blakely recalled, "was a horse standing in a field. Thanks to the lifestyle my parents chose, I grew up in the country and learned to ride horses, work cattle, and also how to hunt and fish and appreciate the great outdoors." He spent his childhood growing up in a Texas ranching family, that included a musician father who influenced his own love of music, and traveling to a dozen countries in Central America and Europe by the time he was fourteen.

Blakely grew up in Wharton County, Texas. By his own admission, he was not the best student. Following his graduation from high school, he spent four years in the U.S. Air Force. When his mother told him that his former high school English teacher had told her that she thought he should consider a career in writing, he was inspired to use his GI Bill benefits to attend the University of Texas at Austin. Even before graduation, Blakely's class assignments were being published in local and regional magazines. By 1985 he was producing a self-syndicated column on Texas history and folklore in honor of the Texas Sesquicentennial, "Lone Star Legacy," which he published in Texas newspapers for three years. As he continued to write not only magazine articles but songs, Blakely established a home in the Texas hill country near the town of Marble Falls.

Blakely discusses his full-fledged entry into the world of westerns on his Web site. "The great western writer, Elmer Kelton, was a friend of my father's," Blakely

writes, "and he recommended that I join Western Writers of America. I joined in 1992 and went to the convention—it was in Jackson, Wyoming, that year. At the convention, I met Bob Gleason, editor-in-chief of Tor/Forge Books. I also met Tom Doherty, the founder of the company. We hit it off, and Forge Books ended up offering me a contract for several novels. So, my career began to take shape, and I got more involved with the inner workings of Western Writers of America."

Shortgrass Song, set from 1860 to 1884, tells the story of a drifting cowboy musician, Caleb Holcomb, who "brought music to lonely places, told stories to voice-starved ears." In a review for *Library Journal,* James B. Hemesath wrote that Blakely "delivers an oft-told tale of the Old West, but this particular family saga proves more than ordinary due to strong, vivid writing." *Roundup* reviewer, Doris R. Meredith, said that the book is "a philosophical message disguised as a pleasant read for a winter day."

Comanche Dawn, also a finalist for the Spur Award, tells the story of the birth of the Comanche Nation. Budd Arthur wrote in *Booklist* that not only is the book "a heartfelt expression of the author's love of horses, [but] this fine novel also offers a detailed study of life among those Blakely considers to have been the greatest horsemen of all time." Blakely drew on his extensive research into the history of the early Plains Indians to write this story. Longer than the average western novel at 413 pages, *Comanche Dawn,* according to a review in *Publishers Weekly,* "reads briskly, despite its length and is leavened with much Comanche lore."

Blakely received praise for two of his earliest novels from Sister Avila, writing reviews for *Library Journal.* She wrote that *Baron of the Sacramentos* is "not a traditional Western, although it starts like one." The hero of the story, Bart Young, "is *not* cast in a heroic mold . . ." Sister Avila said. "His rise and fall make a suspenseful tale, full of violent action involving treachery, brutality, even murder, and very unpleasant people, some being mere caricatures." She concluded her brief review by saying that this novel is "perhaps for readers who like novels off the beaten path." In her review of *The Snowy Range Gang,* Sister Avila noted that the book has "a tattered old plot" that is "transformed by the author's skill into an exciting, suspenseful novel with well-fleshed characters and several surprises."

Blakely's novel *Moon Medicine,* published in 2001, continues the story of a character he introduced in his novel *Too Long at the Dance,* published in 1996 and considered the sequel to *Shortgrass Song.* The character Honore Greenwood, given the nickname Plenty Man by the Comanche Indians, is introduced at the end of *Too Long at the Dance,* and *Moon Medicine* is the first book in what Blakely envisions as a series of "Plenty Man" adventures. A *Publishers Weekly* contributor noted that Greenwood is "like a spirited western Forrest Gump with a high IQ." Greenwood tells his story at the age of ninety-nine in 1927, the *Publishers Weekly* writer noted, "with arrogant good humor and the honesty of an old man who delights in admitting that 'Even in my youth I was a marvelous liar.'"

Blakely told Law that his early inspirations among writers was the western storyteller J. Frank Dobie, as well as novelists Ernest Hemingway and John Steinbeck.

In addition to his writing, Blakely is a prolific songwriter and a western performer who often appears with his father, Dr. James "Doc" Blakely, a musician and humorist. The two have traveled throughout the United States and taken their tour as far away as Australia, performing western music as "The Swing Riders Theatre Show." In 1995 Blakely cowrote a song in Nashville with John Arthur Martinez and Alex Harvey that he described to Law as "a fun Tex-Mex song called 'Seguro Que Hell Yes!'" Tejano accordion player Flaco Jimenez recorded the song and won a Grammy for his entire album, which included Blakely's song. Blakely has his own band, Ghost Town Council, which toured in Italy and Switzerland in the late 1990s.

Still living in his one-room cabin on his horse ranch, the "Who Knows," near Marble Falls, Texas, Blakely gives visitors to his Web site, www.mikeblakely.com, regular updates on all facets of his creative life.

BIOGRAPHICAL AND CRITICAL SOURCES:

PERIODICALS

Booklist, February 15, 1996, Wes Lukowsky, review of *Too Long at the Dance,* p. 989; August, 1998, Budd Arthur, review of *Comanche Dawn,* p. 1958.

Library Journal, September 1, 1991, Sister Avila, review of *Baron of the Sacramentos,* p. 227; February 15, 1992, Sister Avila, review of *The Snowy Range Gang,* p. 195; November 15, 1994, James B. Hemesath, review of *Shortgrass Song,* p. 86.

Publishers Weekly, September 13, 1991, review of *Baron of the Sacramentos,* p. 61; February 10, 1992, review of *The Snowy Range Gang,* p. 72; October 31, 1994, review of *Shortgrass Song,* p. 45; September 14, 1998, review of *Comanche Dawn,* p. 47; August 14, 2000, review of *Summer of Pearls,* p. 329; July 30, 2001, review of *Moon Medicine,* p. 60.

Roundup, March, 1995, Doris R. Meredith, review of *Shortgrass Song,* p. 27; April, 1996, Doris R. Meredith, review of *Wild Camp Tales,* p. 21; December, 1996, Doris R. Meredith, review of *Spanish Blood,* p. 24; October, 2000, Doris R. Meredith, review of *Summer of Pearls,* p. 32.

Roundup Quarterly, fall, 1990, review of *The Glory Trail: A Magnificent Epic of Texas,* p. 43.

School Library Journal, May, 2001, Pamela B. Rearden, review of *Summer of Pearls,* p. 175.

Voice of Youth Advocates, December, 2000, Julie Wilde, review of *Summer of Pearls,* p. 344.

OTHER

Mike Blakely Web site, http://www.mikeblakely.com/ (March, 2002).

Readwest.com, http://www.readwest.com (March, 2002), Steven Law, "A Conversation with Mike Blakely."

*   *   *

BLYTON, Carey 1932-2002

OBITUARY NOTICE—See index for *CA* sketch: Born March 14, 1932, in Beckenham, Kent, England; died of cancer July 13, 2002, in Woodbridge, Suffolk, England. Educator, music editor and arranger, and composer. Blyton's music may be more easily recognizable to people than his name. One of his most popular compositions was the children's song "Bananas in Pyjamas," which was broadcast widely on children's television programs throughout Australia and eventually England. The song, which Blyton reportedly created as a bedtime singalong for his son, was published in *Bananas in Pyjamas: A Book of Nonsense Songs and Nonsense Poems for Children.* In addition to his accomplishments as a composer for film and television, including some episodes of the popular British series *Doctor Who,* Blyton was also a serious musician whose formal compositions ranged from the whimsical orchestral work "Overture: The Hobbit" to the children's composition "Dracula!" to "In the Spice Markets of Zanzibar," the last a work for brass instruments published in 1999. Blyton's career involved him in many segments of the music business. On the scholarly side, he served as a professor of harmony, counterpoint, and orchestration at London's Trinity College of Music in the 1960s, and later as a visiting professor of composition for film, television, and radio at the Guildhall School of Music and Drama. On the business side, he worked as a music arranger and editor for various publishers, notably Mills Music and the London-based firm of Faber and Faber.

OBITUARIES AND OTHER SOURCES:

PERIODICALS

Independent (London, England), July 25, 2002, p. 18.
Times (London, England), July 17, 2002, p. 31.

* * *

BOBER, P(hyllis) P(ray) 1920-2002

OBITUARY NOTICE—See index for *CA* sketch: Born December 2, 2002, in Portland, ME; died May 30, 2002, in Ardmore, PA. Educator, art historian, and author. Bober was a scholar most noted for her work on "The Census of Classical Works Known to the Renaissance," a forty-year project that resulted in a standard resource for academics; she was also renowned for her knowledge of ancient and medieval cuisine. Bober received her B.A. from Wellesley College in 1941 and her Ph.D. in 1946 from New York University. After completing her doctoral studies she embarked on a long academic career. Beginning as an instructor and lecturer in art at Wellesley, she moved on to New York University in 1949 and the Massachusetts Institute of Technology in 1951. She then returned to New York University in 1953, where she

taught for the next twenty years. Bober's last years as an academic were spent at Bryn Mawr College, where she became the Leslie Clark Professor of the Humanities in 1988 before retiring in 1991; she also served as dean of Bryn Mawr's College Graduate School of Arts and Sciences. Bober's interest in the history of art encompassed many topics, ranging from Roman sculpture to Renaissance architecture. She was also fascinated by the types of foods people prepared and ate through the centuries, and on that subject she published *Art, Culture, and Cuisine: Ancient and Medieval Gastronomy* (1999). She was also the coauthor of *Renaissance Artists and Antique Sculpture* (1986) and the author of *Drawings after the Antique by Amico Aspertini: Sketchbooks in the British Museum* (1957).

OBITUARIES AND OTHER SOURCES:

BOOKS

Who's Who in America, 55th edition, Marquis (New Providence, NJ), 2001.

PERIODICALS

New York Times, June 15, 2002, p. A27.

* * *

BOLAND, Eavan (Aisling) 1944-

PERSONAL: Born September 24, 1944, in Dublin, Ireland; daughter of Frederick (a diplomat) and Frances (a painter; maiden name, Kelly) Boland; married Kevin Casey (a novelist), 1969; children: two daughters. *Education:* Trinity College, Dublin, B.A., 1966.

ADDRESSES: Home—Dundrum, Ireland. *Office*—Department of English, Stanford University, 450 Serra Mall, Stanford, CA 94305. *E-mail*—boland@stanford.edu.

CAREER: Trinity College, Dublin, Ireland, lecturer; School of Irish Studies, Dublin, lecturer; Stanford University, Stanford, CA, Bella Mabury and Eloise Mabury Knapp Professor in Humanities and director

Eavan Boland

of creative writing program. Has taught at University College, Dublin, at Bowdoin College, Brunswick, ME, at the University of Utah, and as Hurst Professor at Washington University, St. Louis, 1993. Participated in the University of Iowa International Writing Program, 1979.

MEMBER: Irish Academy of Letters.

AWARDS, HONORS: Irish Arts Council Macauley fellowship, 1967, for *New Territory;* Poetry Book Society Choice, 1987, for *The Journey,* 1990, for *Outside History,* and 1994, for *In a Time of Violence;* Irish American Cultural Award, 1983; Lannan Award for Poetry, 1994; Irish American Literary Award, 1994; Bucknell Medal of Merit, 2000; *Against Love Poetry* was selected by the *New York Times* as a notable book, 2001; Corrington Medal for Literary Excellence, Centenary College, 2002; Frederick Nims Memorial Prize, *Poetry,* 2002, and Smartt Family Prize, *Yale Review,* for poems in *Against Love Poetry.* Honorary degrees from University College, Dublin, 1997; Strathclyde University, 1997; Colby College, 1998; and Holy Cross College, 2000.

WRITINGS:

POETRY

23 Poems, Gallagher (Dublin, Ireland), 1962.
Autumn Essay, Gallagher (Dublin, Ireland), 1963.

New Territory, Allen Figgis & Co. (Dublin, Ireland), 1967.
The War Horse, Gollancz (London, England), 1975.
In Her Own Image, Arlen House (Dublin, Ireland), 1980.
Introducing Eavan Boland, Ontario Review Press (New York, NY), 1981.
Night Feed, M. Boyars (Boston, MA), 1982.
The Journey, Deerfield Press (Deerfield, MA), 1983.
The Journey and Other Poems, Carcanet Press (Manchester, England), 1987.
Selected Poems, Carcanet Press (Manchester, England), 1989.
Outside History: Selected Poems, 1980-1990, Norton (New York, NY), 1990.
In a Time of Violence, Norton (New York, NY), 1994.
A Dozen Lips, Attic Press (Dublin, Ireland), 1994.
A Christmas Chalice, State University of New York at Buffalo (Buffalo, NY), 1994.
Collected Poems, Carcanet Press (Manchester, England), 1995, published as *An Origin Like Water: Collected Poems, 1967-1987,* Norton (New York, NY), 1996.
Anna Liffey, Poetry Ireland (Dublin, Ireland), 1997.
Limitations, Center for the Book Arts (New York, NY), 2000.
Against Love Poetry, Norton (New York, NY), 2001.
Journey with Two Maps: An Anthology, Carcanet Press (Manchester, England), 2002.

Work represented in anthologies, including *The Observer Arvon Poetry Collection,* Guardian Newspapers (London, England), 1994; *Penguin Modern Poets,* Penguin (London, England), 1995; *To Persephone,* Wesleyan University Press with the New England Foundation for the Arts (Hanover, NH), 1996; *The Norton Anthology of Poetry,* edited by Margaret Ferguson, Mary Jo Salter, and Jon Stallworthy, Norton, 1998; *American's Favorite Poems,* edited by Robert Pinsky and Maggie Dietz, Norton, 1999; *The Norton Anthology of English Literature,* edited by M. H. Abrams and Stephen Greenblatt, Norton, 1999; *The Body Electric: America's Best Poetry from the American Poetry Review,* edited by Stephen Berg, David Bonanno, and Arthur Vogelsang, Norton, 2000; *The Longman Anthology of Women's Literature,* edited by Mary K. Deshazer, Longman, 2000; *The Norton Introduction to Literature,* eighth edition, edited by J. Paul Hunter, Alison Booth, and Kelly J. Mays, Norton, 2001; and *The Longman Anthology of British Literature: The Twentieth Cenbury,* edited by David Damrosch, Addison-Wesley Longman, 2002; and *Faber*

Anthology of Irish Verse, Penguin Anthology of Irish Verse, Pan Anthology of Irish Verse, and *Sphere Anthology of Irish Verse.*

OTHER

(With Michael MacLiammoir) *W. B. Yeats and His World,* Thames & Hudson (London, England), 1971, Thames & Hudson (New York, NY), 1986.

The Emigrant Irish, The British Council (London, England), 1986.

A Kind of Scar: The Woman Poet in a National Tradition, Attic Press (Dublin, Ireland), 1989.

(With Aileen MacKeogh and Brian P. Kennedy) *House,* Dublin Project (Dublin, Ireland), 1991.

Gods Make Their Own Importance: The Authority of the Poet in Our Time, Society Productions (London, England), 1994.

Object Lessons: The Life of the Woman and the Poet in Our Time, Norton (New York, NY), 1995.

(With Harriet Levin) *The Christmas Show,* Beacon Press (Boston, MA), 1997.

(Editor, with John Hollander) *Committed to Memory: 100 Best Poems to Memorize,* Riverhead Books (New York, NY), 1997.

The Lost Land, W. W. Norton & Company (New York, NY), 1998.

(Editor, with Mark Strand) *The Making of a Poem: A Norton Anthology of Poetic Forms,* Norton (New York, NY), 2000.

(Editor, with J. D. McClatchy), *Horace, the Odes,* Princeton University Press (Princeton, NJ), 2002.

Regular contributor to *Irish Times.* Contributor to *Irish Press, Spectator, American Poetry Review,* and *Soundings.*

SIDELIGHTS: Over the course of a career that began in the early 1960s, when she was a young wife in Dublin, Eavan Boland has emerged as one of the foremost female voices in Irish literature. Describing those formative years in an interview with Jody Allen Randolph in *Colby Quarterly* (later included on the Web site of her publisher, Carcanet Press), Boland said, "I began that time watching milk being taken in metal churns, on horse and cart, towards the city center. And I ended it as a married woman, in a flat on Raglan Road, watching this ghostly figure of a man walking on the moon. I suppose I began the decade in a city which Joyce would have recognized, and ended it in one that would have bewildered him."

During this time, Boland honed an appreciation for the ordinary in life, an appreciation reflected in the title of her 2001 collection, *Against Love Poetry.* "So much of European love poetry," she told Alice Quinn of the *New Yorker* online, "is court poetry, coming out of the glamorous traditions of the court. . . . Love poetry, from the troubadours on, is traditionally about that romantic lyric moment. There's little about the ordinariness of love." Seeking a poetry that would express the beauty of the plain things that make up most people's existences, she found that she would have to create it for herself. It is "dailiness," as Boland called it, that reviewers often find, and praise, in Boland's poetry. Frank Allen, in a *Library Journal* review of *Against Love Poetry,* wrote, "This volume . . . dramatizes conflicts between marriage and freedom ('what is hidden in / this ordinary, aging human love')."

Certainly, "conflicts between marriage and freedom" is a feminist theme, and though Boland has been described as a feminist, her approach is not an overtly political one. Perhaps this is because she is not content, as a poet, to uphold one view of things to the exclusion of all others: hers is a voice, in the words of Melanie Rehak in the *New York Times Book Review,* "that is by now famous for its unwavering feminism as well as its devotion to both the joys of domesticity and her native Ireland."

Acknowledgement for Boland's work has been long in coming, but as Randolph noted, that recognition has arrived, and in a big way. Irish students wishing to graduate from secondary school must undergo a series of examinations for what is called the "leaving certificate." The writings of great national poets such as Seamus Heaney are a mandatory part of the leaving exam, and since 1999, would-be graduates are required to undergo examinations in Boland's work as well.

AUTOBIOGRAPHICAL ESSAY:

Eavan Boland contributed the following autobiographical essay to *CA:*

Writing the Place

I

I was born south of a river. And since this fragment of autobiography is partly about place and influence, I will begin there. Begin, that is, with the sweet-natured, untidy, swerving river Liffey, which rises on the southeast slopes of Kippure and flows west through Wicklow and Kildare.

When I am far away from it, as I often am now, I like to imagine its progress as it travels the fifty or so miles of its course. I imagine it receiving tributaries, picking up willow branches, absorbing the darkness of cormorant wings. The last nine miles take it through the old river neighborhoods of Lucan and Palmerston. Only then does it gather itself under the bridges that were built around its existence—the Carlisle Bridge, the Halfpenny Bridge. Every day, all day, its waters renew the old compact. Every day, all day the memories of Viking steel and rebel fire and commerce and romance and drownings and dances are reenacted.

I begin with the Liffey because a river is not a place: it is a maker of places. Without the river there would be no city. Every day, turning its narrow circle, endlessly absorbing and re-absorbing the shapes and reflections of the city, it mirrors what it created. With the river, the city every day has to throw itself again into those surfaces, those depths, those reflections which have served as the source of all its fictions.

This piece is about the making of a place. It is about my need to locate myself in my life and find a language to follow that location. But place and influence are only part of my subject. There is more.

When I was young it seemed to me that the visible life of the poet and the hidden life of the woman were almost magnetically opposed. I wanted to bring them together but I hardly knew how. I wanted to put the life I lived as a woman into the words I used as a poet but this also proved surprisingly difficult. Now I know that the construction of a poetic self is a complex, difficult business—made up of almost equal parts of history and resistance. This essay is about a journey: part of it through the physical terrain of my life in Ireland—at first the city and then the suburbs. More of it through the shadows and doubts and discoveries by which a poetic self is made.

*

I was born in Dublin, hardly a mile from the main bridge over the Liffey. But my early memories of the river are almost nonexistent. My childhood was fractured by travel. I left Dublin at five and came back when I was fourteen.

When I came back it took me a long time to adjust. If I learned anything in that painful process it is that connections to place are not to be taken for granted. And yet most people do just that. For most people the place they live in is a place arranged around their childhood. The streets they walk on, the buildings they go to work in, the cityscapes they see in their adult life are always relenting into the hot afternoons and ice cream cones, the Sunday picnics, and sweet twilights of another existence.

But I lacked that other existence. I was bitterly conscious of it. And my teenage years were full of the pain of that lack. When I walked through the city I felt strange, as though it were a relative who refused to recognize me. Because I had not been a child there, it was almost impossible to find the necessary clues to becoming an adult in that environment.

For a year or so after I returned almost everything, from the shop fronts to the street signs, was an essay in the unfamiliar. It was hard to find places of connection. But there were a few. One of them was just to the side of O'Connell Bridge. On summer evenings and weekends I would stop there on my way back to the flat I shared with my sisters. There was always something to delay me. The color of the water, for instance. It had a murky, khaki, sinuous appearance unlike any other water. And at the side of the bridge, a flight of narrow steps went down to the water. The steps themselves were dungeon-colored and slippery with moss. Almost always beside them two or three swans, self-possessed and beginning to gleam in the onset of the twilight.

When I look back now I wonder why it was there, in the middle of the city, that I first felt connected to the place I was born. There were, after all, other places. The leafy quiet of Stephen's Green. The long tunnel of poplar leaves over the canal. Or the blue, low mountains. Any or all of them might have offered a start in rebuilding my sense of my own origin.

And if alternate places were not enough, there was always the alternate reality of the moment. This was a new era in Dublin. The early sixties, with its static of new communications, easier travel, the first whispers of European commerce, was coming to the edges of the old and insular town. It was a time of foreign cars, American books, clothes from England. The deep rhythm and insular self-confidence of an almost forgotten margin was being disrupted. Ireland was on the threshold of becoming a modern state. I could have connected myself to that moment and by so doing have joined myself to its excitement and promise.

But I didn't. I stayed in my own thorny world of exclusions. Occasionally, on weekends away from boarding school, or summer nights after the cinema, I would walk by myself. And whatever fragile moments of belonging there were, whatever small impulses of connection I had, were by the river. I would stand there or put my elbows on the bridge. When I look back the image and the time become one: it is always twilight, the eerie late brightness of a European summer stretches far out over the Custom House and into the horizon. I am that girl leaning on the white self-important granite of the bridge. Out towards the water, towards the ships, towards the barges and masts and traffic of a port city, is the skyline of Dublin.

When I think back, if I am accurate, the image broadens into something less than ideal: I see the grimy light of late July. I see the ugliness of neon and smell the fat welcome of chip shops along the quays. I hear the nonstop jangling of bicycle bells. I see my own girlhood, as awkward as my teenage body. I see my mind, so placeless and lost in its lumpy understandings and half-realized instincts.

But accuracy is not autobiography. "The actual journey may have been different," wrote Henry Adams, "but the actual journey has no interest for education. The memory was all that mattered" (*The Education of Henry Adams,* 1918). And in that spirit I can go back to rescue the girl, who has nothing to do this particular evening. And the way I rescue her is by making her see what she could never have seen then: by making her see what I can see now.

I will lay the later meaning over the earlier one—that endless franchise of autobiography—and say that she is there at the river for a reason. She there because in some way the river can tell her not what she has lost—there are enough places in the city for that—but what she can regain.

Because of my childhood outside Ireland, I lacked the dialect of belonging which merges a place and a person, and allows one to speak for the other. I would

The O'Connell Bridge on the River Liffey, where the author "first felt connected to the place I was born"

never regain it. But the river whispered to me: What if I could start again? What if there was some place which began with me, which I could name and create and associate with my life? A place which could never refuse to recognize me, as the Dublin I was born into appeared to.

This fragment is about such a place. A small neighborhood to which I came in my twenties. A place I stumbled on. Most autobiography begins with the place of birth, the years of childhood, the time of growth. There is a value, a solid chronology in those details. But this fragment begins midpoint. And there's a reason for it. I wanted to write about my beginnings—but the beginning of my spirit, not my body.

Nothing would have seemed less likely when I first came to the suburb. It was just a dark, half-built road, with a few streetlamps and a thick surrounding of trees. A road, moreover, that was scarcely distinguishable from all the other new house construction that was going on all over the city. Just another neighborhood, or so I thought, made by the secular exigencies of mortgages and marriages. And yet out of those compromises-and the place itself was one of them—

came without warning a visionary world of ritual, repeated actions, children, neighbors, summer mornings and thick, icy December nights. So that even today I am not sure what part of it was actual, and what part imagined. What part I found by writing about it. What part I wrote about because I was found there. So that even today I hardly know how to answer the question: What element of a daily life is comparable to the small beginnings of water, high in the hills, brown with peat?

I could so easily have missed it. Inexperienced, anxious to belong to the apparent center of Dublin life, I was a stiff-necked, awkward young woman, caught in the derivative excitements of my own time. It was a different world then. In many ways, Dublin was still shadowed by its nineteenth-century existence as a garrison town. The compass of existence was smaller, neater, less ambitious. A ten-minute bus journey here, a ten-minute taxi ride there, and the compass was complete. The were far fewer shops. Even the central streets still kept the solemn store fronts of necessity rather than the consumer theatre that came later. Tobacco. Spectacles. Surgical instruments. Bedding. There was no denying that Dublin, despite being a capital city, was also still a town.

And no denying either that Dublin was and is one of the most jeweled and beautiful cities on earth. Caught on one side by water, rinsed in winter by the ocean-fogs of the Irish sea, above it are the hills whose woods kept back the English, trapped them in dense foliage and wild ambushes for centuries. "Few cities are more fortunate than Dublin in the beauty of their environs" wrote a nineteenth-century traveler (*Scenery and Antiquities of Ireland,* 1840).

By the time I came to it as a student, it was a very different place. Change, rebellion, independence, an intense and passionate conversation about Irishness had provided it with an inward turmoil at odds with the shabby colonial grace those older travelers had counted on. It was now a literary city. A location of resistance. A place where the small miracle of national transformation had taken place. Even though I felt an outsider still, at the edges of the sort of belonging I saw all around me, I was proud to come from the city. Proud of its hierarchies of drama and malice and poetry and late-night talk. Its superb, self-confident, self-centeredness.

While I was a student I lived in a flat on Morehampton Road. I was near enough to Trinity on one side, and to my parents house on the other. A short bus journey brought me into college. The flat was at the top of an old narrow house. Everything in it seemed neutral, shabby, not—mine. In the three or four years I lived there, I never put a poster on a wall or a photograph on a shelf. I folded the thick green sheets around the comfortable, sagging bed and slept there. That was all. I had no sense of homecoming, no attachment to the rooms themselves. In the morning, I looked out on the trees of the road, and felt myself shaped by the sloping attic roof. I was young, callow, unable to think for myself, unsure how to behave.

When I came out of Front Gate in the evening time there was no need to go back to the flat. I rarely had far to go for company or talk. A few hundred yards from the gate of the old university, Grafton Street began. In cold, murky twilights the whole array of the street and the side streets constituted a haven of steamed windows and soft, inviting lights. Cafes and pubs and teatime conversations would be already in full swing. Any of them could be joined just by sitting still, ordering a cheese sandwich, listening to the vivid and continuous talk that seemed to come into the air already shaped by the blue perfume of cigarette smoke. Sitting there, my sandwich in my hand, I felt less callow. Looking around me, I could see that these people belonged. They were part of an intense adventure. Surely, if I sat there long enough, the belonging would come to me also: like a contagion.

Instead, without meaning to, I began to notice something about the conversation itself. When the arguments died down, there was a chatter. A static of prejudices, beliefs, jokes, ribaldry, assumptions, superiorities. The lexicon of a malicious and self-regarding city.

What did I begin to see? It was there, just hiding in the talk, just visible in gestures or asides. A sort of disdain. A pushing away. A disregard for anything that looked like the ordinary life of ordinary people. At first it was hard to recognize it, clothed as it was in throwaway details and scornful references. In neighborhoods. In the descriptions of bus routes. In the pitying account of unfathomable places people had to leave and return to in order to sustain the passionate and fascinating life at the center.

And then the names. Names I began to hear now, some for the first time, listening to the edge of dismissal with which they were spoken. Rathgar. Terenure.

Rathmines. Clontarf. Rathfarnham. Places, it was understood, that people went to under duress, that they left with relief. Where the old structures of generations, meals, money, and a general bookless darkness still held sway. Those neighborhoods of worthy brick and windows whose lights died before midnight. And that was not all. Here in this brilliant center it was to be understood that those were the places where dreams died also.

That disdain by the center for the margin was something I absorbed. Without even being much aware of it, by the time my university years were over, I was letter perfect. There in those rooms, at those tables, I learned a lesson I would never forget about the prescriptive power of cultural centers.

Yet the men and women—but far less women than men—who gathered in the evening and talked in that way, had less hold on the world than most. Less money. Less job security. Less of a future. They were students, poets, writers, journalists. And yet their talk was furious with a self-conscious sense of superiority. Banks opened and closed around them. Schools and shops and legislatures went about their daily life. But their business was to clothe themselves in every conversation in the powers and freedoms which make up the toxic offerings of a capital city. To speak with the language of passion and argument, and then turn it around to disdain that life which was regulated around their unruly existences.

By the time I left university, married, and went to look at some new houses in a suburb a few miles outside the city, I was primed to regret what I would find there. I was suspicious of the conventional life. We might buy a house there. We might even live there. But our real lives were to be elsewhere. The life of imagination learned in the small hours, watching the curl of blue smoke could not be transferred here. I understood all too well that this was a new life. That I was about to join those people I had heard spoken of with pity: those who put their bodies at the edge of the city but brought their souls—like animals to a watering-hole at dusk—back into the lighted center.

*

Dundrum is a rough translation of three words—The Fort on the Ridge. In the eleventh century it became, like so many other Dublin townlands, part of the Nor-

man fortifications of the city. The castles that were built—and Dundrum had one of them—stood as a line of defense against the raids of the Wicklow clans who marauded in at night to attack the new invaders.

By the nineteenth century, the small Norman township had become a sober village. It appears briefly in advertisements in 1820 promoting the excellence of goat's milk and styling itself as a spa resort offering a rest cure near the mountains. In 1813 a morning newspaper carried the notice for Meadowbrook House, on a street just around the corner from the house we would buy: "The second whey season having commenced, Ladies and Gentlemen are respectively informed that there are a few vacancies in the house" (Weston St. John Joyce, *The Neighborhood of Dublin,* 1939).

By the end of the nineteenth century the village was acquiring other things as well, putting on the darkness as well as the light of that prosperous century. Behind the main street was a private asylum, a large house hidden by leafy trees. Elsewhere, life was more normal. The grocery shops sold smoked bacon and homemade butter. Two small tributaries, the Swan and the Tinnehy, flowed together at the edge of the village and with enough force to power a paper mill that made bank notes. Mill cottages were set down at the edges of the water. More importantly, above the shops, asylums, houses and cottages ran the Harcourt Street Line, a train service that was gone by the time we got there.

Until the nineteen fifties, Dundrum must have continued in that way, looking like so many other neighborhoods a few miles from Dublin. A mixture, like so many others, of graceful seclusion and hard, practical daily life. A long main street. Some shops. The shadows and leaves of poplars and rowans and mulberries shielding it from any appearance of busyness or stress. A quiet, forgotten neighborhood.

But already a noise was beginning, just out of earshot. The noise of a new Ireland. New plans, new strategies, an ending of economic protectionism, a stimulus for foreign exports—all those were just the beginning. The impetus for a new, ambitious economy was gathering speed. It began slowly. The exodus from the land to Dublin. The ending of economic tariffs against imports. The decision, above all, to build houses.

Houses and more houses. All these were part of it. And there, at the end of the long process of decision and change, lay the small village of Dundrum, lying in the easy light and shadow of its old peace and seclusion. Who would have noticed the men with their quadrants and maps and notebooks?

And somewhere, in that vast process of change and restatement, our lives got included. We came to Dundrum, as we saw it, at the start of our marriage and in search of our home. In fact, without knowing it, we were part of a tidal shift, a blurring of the old lines between town and country. Old distinctions were being erased. And we, who felt so particular, so individual in our quest for our lives were simply part of the erasure.

When I came to Dundrum I was in my middle twenties. I had published one book of poetry. I had an uneasy sense of being trapped in the conventions of my first practices as a poet. But it was unformed, a feeling to be brushed away. I had learned the way of writing a poem which was around me. I knew—or thought I did—how to put a poem together. And yet I had no sense of where to go. I had no exact sense of where I was.

I received no instruction, no help from my first, bewildered weeks in the neighborhood. We had arrived in December. It was the second year of our marriage. The days had a beautiful wintry cast to them, the light filtering shyly into our north facing and empty kitchen. Everything was new. My husband, Kevin, a novelist, worked by day in an advertising agency. I had time to look around our new home. To hear the strange echoey acoustics of the bare floorboards. To see how bare the white walls were.

We were exactly four miles from Grafton Street. Already now, with twilight falling, I knew that the lights would be going on. The steam, the smoke, the conversation, the gathering noise would all be arraying itself into a steady, drumming festivity. That sound of voices, greetings, the small ringing and clinking of glass.

I had done nothing more than leave one neighborhood and come to another. But for me the change was decisive and seemed, at first, ominous. I had left a world of books, of talk, of effortless superiority. I had come to this place where the values were entirely different. In the rumors put about in literary conversation it was The Swamp of Ordinariness. The place where dreams died. And yet, it seemed to me, I would have to live on the terms of this place. I would have to shop, and drive, and gather things for the house. In that I would be the same as all the hundreds of women around me doing the same thing. By the time I came to this neighborhood I had almost persuaded myself that the life lived here—with its routines, its necessities—was indeed anti-imaginative.

There is very little to excuse my own perceptions. All I can say is that I believed, as so many women of my generation had been taught to believe, that in order to achieve my own sense of things I would have to pick my way carefully against the common routes of a woman's life, like someone lifting her skirts to avoid being splashed by rain in a gutter. I had inherited or absorbed—it was a toxic article of faith—that a woman's life needed to be separated from the life of the mind or the ambitions of an art, for fear that both would be compromised. It was only later, looking back, that I understood just how much of my belief in myself a young women poet owed to my sense that I was exempt from an ordinary woman's life.

One of the first things I noticed about our new home was the silence. Complete silence. For a few hours during the day it would be broken by the desolate chugging of concrete mixers. After twilight it returned. The distances were bare. The back garden was muddy, icy. The trees, where they were planted at all, looked puny and unbountiful. A few hedges straggled across bleak driveways.

Our house faced the Dublin mountains. At night I would come out and stand in an almost rural darkness, looking with wonder and unease at what was around me. There were flat roofed houses in front of us. Our top windows looked clear to the foothills. To Kippure, that is. At night the cars were small, star-shaped moving lights, descending towards the city and home.

But the silence was more than physical. This terrain of dailyness was not a subject I had found in Irish poetry. Poetry—or so I had learned at college—was a high art. It needed high subjects. Wars. Love affairs. Death. These were certainly the approved subjects in Irish poetry. But a baby at night, a washing machine, a woman's day—these were not. And so all around me, in this suburb, was a life which lay outside the poem I had learned to write.

If I were to bring that life into my poems, then I would have to change: not just the poems but the self engaged in writing them. My idea of the poet would have to widen to include the fact that I was living the life of a woman.

That life surprised me: The golden, foggy windows of other houses seen in the pre-dawn when I got up to feed my first baby. The jagged breath of a neighbour going home in the frost. Or the first smoke from a chimney saying the time for peat fires had come. The truth was that these images, repeated over and over, wore away at my inward picture of a poet's self. It was no longer a portrait of a tough and polished core, made rigid with the responsibility of ordained inheritance. It was something different—solving and dissolving itself in the images of this place. Year after year, those images drew me into an imaginative empathy with the lives being lived around me. Year after year that empathy wore down the angry individuality that I and so many other impressionable young writers had been persuaded was the necessary accoutrement for the true artist.

I was writing the place. The place in turn was redirecting that writing. I was beginning to understand that a shift in my way of being a poet had an intimate and charged connection to this apparently everyday world. The place was a sign of the life I lived. Gravity, they say, can bend starlight. If the poem was starlight, then this place with its shrubs, its bicycles, its orange beaker thrown in the grass was gravity.

Place and poetry. I would come to know that writing a place can also involve—as it did here—breaking a silence. But for an external silence to be broken it must first of all be broken within. And for that to happen, barriers would have to break also. I would have to try to understand how a poem comes to be written in its own time. I would have to decipher, at a rational and clear level, the complicated connections between worlds and languages which I had stumbled into.

And so I found that the place I had come to live was becoming the poem I wanted to write. The distance I had come—from city to suburb—was emblematic of other, far more elusive distances. In order to travel them I would have to understand them.

Evolving as poet, wife, and mother in the suburban village of Dundrum

What does a place mean to a poem? When I drew the curtains in Dundrum in the morning everything seemed modest, normal, and ordinary. Quiet streets except for the clanking electric cart of the milkman or the sound of a car reversing out of a driveway.

But the ordinary has complex roots. The conflict between a literary city and an obscure suburb, between metropolitan life and neighborly existence, between a sense of being at the center and an unease at being on the margin—all this went deeper than I knew. It was not just a rift between two Irish cultures, although it was that also. As time went on, I came to believe that all these differences were part of a greater one: the difference—the vast distance—between the past and history.

History, I began to see, was just the official version of the past. But it was also, paradoxically, a version which could suppress it. In the case of Ireland, history was eloquent, compelling, memorable. After the dark centuries of oppression and humiliation, Irish history, according to its contemporary script, was a vibrant story of heroes.

The past was something else. The Irish past, in particular, was certainly not a story of heroes. It was a territory of whispers, shadows, silences. It was unwritten lives and lost annals. It was those who were thrown into Famine graves, who died in the workhouse, who took ship for America. Their stories did not belong in a narrative of heroes. And so they entered that silence which is the past.

Women, especially in Ireland, belonged to the past. Their stories were lost there. In my own case, that difference between the past and history was a charged and personal thing. In coming to this suburb, in some strange and emblematic way, I felt that I had moved from one to the other.

And with all those tensions, there was something more. The poem of the Irish canon was heroic, bardic, male. It went with the history. It had been relentlessly public and political throughout the nineteenth century and into the twentieth.

It had also been a strange mix of eloquence and unresponsiveness. The nineteenth century was a dark time for Ireland. It had been split at the root by the Famine of 1846. The sordid darknesses of fever and starvation, of the workhouse and the emigrant ship defined those years and had profound consequences for the rest of the century. Grim stories of women gnawing at their own children's flesh, of children being left on the steps of the workhouse while their parents fled on the Atlantic route—these rumors were a fever all their own. And yet not a whisper, not a reference to that reality comes into the poetry of that part of the nineteenth century. It seemed that the public reality could only exist if it erased the private one.

I was uneasy with that tradition. I did not see my name in it. I instinctively understood that if I tried to write that poem I would never see my name there. As time went on, I became more and more interested in exploring a different relation between the private and public poem. In this neighborhood of ritual and dailyness, the private was a sovereign realm. But it was also a borderland from which the public world could be seen more clearly. There was an irony in this. Neighborhoods like this had been held up to me as a young poet as places of compromise and oppression. In fact I was discovering that a margin can also be a vantage point.

II

And here I will stop and change direction: if autobiography and history were one and the same, this essay

could take its time. But they are not. The self is created in moments; the historic narrative is assembled in solid stretches. Maybe both are a myth, but I will go with the first here and not the second. I need a mechanism to show how the place changed, and how I changed with the place. And so instead of a settled narrative—which would deceive by its symmetry—I have chosen four poems, written over more than twenty years.

My account of writing them will let me swerve and turn, and make time move forward faster than it ever could in an ordinary narrative. It will also be more conscious, more analytical than I could be at the time. Poems are written in the moment, without the benefit of the understandings they themselves give to hindsight. And yet describing how I wrote these poems will let me serve the purposes of autobiography—which are revelatory—rather than the logic of history, which is linear.

If the self is created in moments, it is also sustained by questions. I hope that the story of how I came to write these poems will help to clarify the relation between the poem and the place, between the local and the wider horizon, between the past and history.

Often it was only after I wrote the poem that I understood the questions I had asked in it. And, by so doing, I found new questions with which to write new poems. Therefore the poems I have chosen to go forward with here are not the most finished: they are simply the most questioning.

*

I remember the first poem I wrote in that suburb. It was called "The War Horse." In one sense its true point of reference was the eroding civilian killings in the North of Ireland. That violence had begun a year or so before we moved into our house. Now it was a chronic, inescapable part of life. Every day someone was killed or maimed. Every evening news came in of a bomb going off in Belfast, or a man shot on his own doorstep in front of his children.

Belfast was ninety miles away from our quiet neighborhood. We were out of earshot of the gunfire and the explosions. But the violence not only took lives; it also poisoned speech. The toxin seeped towards us, as it did towards everyone. There was no getting away. It was in the air of the island.

The poem was no more able to escape this than I was. But it was a private view of the turmoil, not a public one. In that sense, it also recorded my first, bewildered weeks in the neighborhood. I moved through the bare rooms, the unpacked crates, the books still piled up in corners, in a dream of newness. The twilights seemed to come earlier and more suddenly than in the middle of the city. We faced a huge stand of old spruce trees which seemed to traffic in the quick darkness of the evening. When they began to blacken I knew the last light was going.

One night, at teatime, I was alone in the house and standing in the front room. It was almost completely bare of furniture. The living room was uncarpeted, an echoing chamber of sound and newness. When six o' clock came the small black-and-white television at one end of it began chanting its chorus-like accounts of danger and injury.

I heard a sound at the front door. Even in a few weeks, I had become sensitive to the rhythms of sound and silence. I was used to the cars swishing and pushing through the half-laid roads to this driveway or the other. But this noise was different. Not a knock at the door. But something at the door.

I opened it. There, hardly six inches from me, was a horse. A large, dapple-grey horse. One hoof up on the doorstep. His big head as low as my waist and swinging like a huge hinge of surprise and distress. I was astonished and, for a moment, disoriented. It was a strange sight: this gleaming, displaced animal. Behind the startled head the lights on the Dublin hills stretched away. And all around us both, the half-finished houses, the half-built lives to which neither of us could relate.

It was a traveler's horse. They were a familiar sight all over these neighborhoods, where the tinkers—or, as they are now called, travelers—made their camps and tethered their animals. Obviously, our houses had built on their old grazing lands. Now here in the twilight this dispossessed animal had come back looking for a world which no longer existed.

A moment or so passed as I looked at it, unsure what to do. Then the horse swung back and away, pulling its hoof away from granite with a flinty bang. In a single clumsy movement, it clattered onto the road, was caught by the street-light, and made its way off into the darkness.

I wrote the poem slowly, adding and revising couplets as I went along. I wanted it to reflect associations, intuitions which were crowding in on me. On the one hand, this new neighborhood. On the other, this animal out of its element. Above both, the shadows gathering around our country and our consciences. As I wrote, the sound of the hooves was my starting point: somehow, it made incarnate this strange engagement between the age-old animal vitality and the fragile, compromised lives of this place and time.

In this poem, I intended the horse as an emblem of a wider menace. Perhaps to imply an intention suggests more of a consciousness than I really had. The truth is, it was also a real horse. Destructive in a down-to-earth, reflexive and practical way. Seeking for its old life, it injured our new ones. Small crocuses, hedge saplings, daffodil bulbs lay in its wake. The new garden beds had no resistance to offer to its hooves.

I remember that first evening, when it swung away from our door, I watched its sheer force and bulk turning and moving on out to the road. That was not the moment when the poem became inevitable. But it was, nonetheless, a moment of surprise and unease. This off-kilter encounter between the old and the new city, between the animal life and the self-conscious desire to make a neighbourhood went with a strange temporary mood of loneliness. I had lost my bearings. In a way, my sense of being adrift went with something larger: the island itself was adrift, caught in those first years of violence into its own spiral of hate and re-enactment.

None of that was clear at the time. But the writing of the poem marked that confusion for me, and by marking it, led me to something clearer. There are always poems which point forward not back. Which tell you where to go next. This was one of them. There was something about the horse and its casual vandalism which stirred and disturbed me. But it also opened a window for me. If the horse represented, at least for a moment, the dangerous life beyond the suburb, it was also true that the suburb—however flawed my concept of it—allowed me for the first time to feel a communal threat rather than an individual one, to say *we*

The War Horse: ". . . Writing about my own doorstep, my own windowsill . . . [and] this ghost of tribal anger"

in a poem. It allowed me to begin, in the most faltering way, to explore that crucial distance between the *I* and the *we* which determines the truth and force of the political poem. When finally the horse, the gardens, the current violence melded to make a single image—of an outside force threatening the small new world of this neighborhood—I knew I had made a start in measuring that distance.

"The War Horse" became the title poem of my second collection (1975). It gave me a glimpse of the energies involved in the political poem. But for all that I still felt uneasy and confused. When I had finished it I was no nearer resolving the unease. Nor was I satisfied. I was in my middle twenties then. I was still uncertain as to how to assemble parts of the poem. On the one hand, by writing about my own doorstep, my own windowsill, I had broken through a superstition. I had taken the details of the place—the curtains, the windows, the street—and claimed them for the poem I was writing. On the other hand, I was still unsure as to where to locate myself in a poem: from which place exactly to throw my voice.

In the end, "The War Horse" was not so much about violence as about its effects: about the entry into our settled lives of this ghost of tribal anger, which roamed our speech and our homes. Like everyone else in Ireland, I had been a bystander at the violence. I had felt what was happening. I had understood the waste and loss as a citizen. But as a poet I had not known how to imagine it.

Now, unexpectedly, a private world to which I had come—doubtfully, reluctantly—had allowed me access to a public one. I had found a way to envision the neighborly violence of Irish history, not through any central role in it, but simply by acknowledging the private world of my own neighborhood.

For the first time I had a glimpse that the place where I lived and the life I lived there—if I wrote them both carefully and rigorously—could be sources of a new understanding. The poem was not satisfactory. But it was a beginning.

The horse returned for two or three evenings. Then he was gone. He took with him an inference of lost grazing grounds and an earlier, more rural version of where we now lived. But he remained in my mind as an emblem. As an emblem he continued to enlighten me. So much so that a year or so later I mentioned him to an eminent Irish sculptor, Oisin Kelly. In some way I was wistful about the sheer power of that presence and hopeful of recovering a visual image that I could keep. At first Oisin Kelly was noncommittal. A week or so later he sent me a note, saying he had finished an image of the horse, taken from the poem.

I went to collect the blocky wood sculpture on a February evening. It was a night of cold, driving rain. But the horse glowed in front of me on Oisin Kelly's table. Its strength was recovered for me by the blind tilt of the head and the eyeless wooden face. I have kept that sculpture to remind me of exemplary public statement: of how realities can heal inside their expression. Of how the original menace of the horse was resolved by the eloquence of the wood and the sculptor's imagination.

*

Years passed. The suburb grew and changed. The building had long finished. The trees put on inches with the children. Saplings all, they lengthened and strengthened over summers which seemed to contest the Irish reputation for grayness and dullness.

Essentially, the suburb was just two long, well-built roads. In the morning we followed one or the other out onto main thoroughfares which led to a changing Ireland. My old city of soot and iron, of sleepy habits and a slow pace was stirring and spreading. The decades of the seventies and eighties saw it pushing out from the center to the neighborhoods my friends had once disdained. But they—and we—were no longer outlandish boundaries. We were now the city limits.

As the country changed, the literature changed as well. Unlike new buildings or businesses, these were subtle shifts; hard to measure, difficult to register. Like every other Irish writer, I was part of them. A different Ireland was coming to the edge of the short story, the poem, the play—challenging the old conventions. A new population—less rural, more educated and more European—was reading that literature. The old subject matter, with its potent fusion of history and memory and heroism, was being overwritten.

It was a time of change. New plays revealed a gritty, less ideal Ireland. New poems were no longer so indebted to the old cadences and ideals of the Irish Revival. In my generation women, who had been the objects of the Irish poem, began at last to be its authors.

But I was restless. I lived the daily, rushed life of a housewife and mother. For a few afternoons every week I taught classes nearer to the center of the city. Sometimes when I drove home, after an hour of teaching Yeats's poems, my mind would divide into a sort of Janus-faced meditation: As I turned the car through the traffic of Ballsbridge, Clonskeagh, Goatstown I saw everywhere the signs of irreversible change. At the same time, like a fragment of melody, I could hear Yeats's line in my head: *Out of Ireland have we come.* As I turned up the Taney Road, ready to reenter the small fastness of Dundrum, I wondered what that line meant in this fast-moving, shape-shifting time. And how both these things—the old rhetoric of the Irish poem and the new life of an Irish woman—could meet in the poem I wanted to write.

It was difficult. When I was young I had learned to write a lyric poem which was of little use to me now. Now, on a summer evening, as I sat down with my notebook, I knew that I wanted to unwrite that poem.

The problem lay not just in subject matter but stance. The bardic tradition, with its complex and powerful inheritance, had been shaped by and for the male Irish poet. It kept at its center codes of obligation which went back into a history of audience and interest I could not claim. Its space echoed with memories of national loss and public histories.

I could not live or write in that space. To start with, that inheritance had made no provision for me. There was no room there to include a poet like myself whose life and writing was so at odds with the public, bardic poem. I could not see myself in that tradition. If anything, I saw myself in a silence, a void. But slowly, surely, I was beginning to elect my own tradition, my own subject matter: I felt it around me in the powerful shadows and silences of women like me who had come to their place in life, as I had come to this neighborhood, committed to the rituals of love and the hardships of unrelenting dailyness. And I saw something else as well. That generations of such women in Ireland had lived, whether they knew it or not, with a startling deprivation: their names, lives, actions, perceptions were not recorded in the Irish poem.

I felt that deprivation. It guided me, angered me, drove me towards the poems I wanted to write. It forced me to think about the relation of a devalued subject matter to the Irish poem. My life was involved with detail, with routine, with the domestic. And the domestic, especially, was devalued in the Irish poetic tradition, and in the wider society also. It was seen as a realm of necessity, not of art. But for me, for those very reasons, the domestic poem—with its codes of a hidden life—represented an exciting freedom. I was sure that if it were written with care and truth, its private perspective could be a critique of the exclusions of a bardic poetic tradition.

And so it was that this second poem came to be written. I associate it now with the time and place of its writing. It was high summer. There was a rare, golden burnish to the days. My children were small and I was beginning to see the life I lived as not just valuable but also available at last to my poems. When I see myself in a photograph with them now I can remember the grace of those days.

On long, eerily bright summer evenings it seemed as if the light would never go behind the Dublin mountains. Gradually it did. Then the trees darkened.

The windows brightened. And for less than an hour there was a rare human season, when women went out to collect their small children, recognizing them in the distance by their hair or their T-shirts.

I wanted to write a poem in which the visionary color of that less-than-an-hour event could be stated. I called it "This Moment" (from *In A Time of Violence,* 1994). My own sense of the light, of the hour, of the changing weather of my body and of the body it had made—above all, of the reunion between the two—became a short, abrupt series of statements.

The poem was not long. Just fifteen lines in fact. The staccato of language I aimed for represented the surreal and fragmented moment I found myself in. It was the hour of twilight. But also the time when the boundaries between the solid and the spatial seemed to shimmer and dissolve. I could describe the neighbourhood, the darkening tree, the sudden, buttery light of a neighbour's window. What I wanted was to suggest that moment when the child's return to the mother is almost indivisible from the moth, the starlight and the rind on the apple mysteriously growing stronger and sweeter.

A short poem is often the most difficult to write. In this case, there were other difficulties: in some ways, language is the least visionary of artistic instruments. The paint which skids from the brush to make a sky or the quick daub of a tree, or the musical riff which suggests loss or exaltation—they seem better suited to it, at least to me. But I had lived the small, exact vision of that moment: the reunion with a small child at dusk. And I was stubborn in wanting the poem to relive it.

Later I believed it was this lyric, above all, which allowed me to unwrite the one I had learned. Why? First of all, because I could make a claim there for an actual, lived moment. More than that, it insisted that the life I lived was as capable of transformation as the old life of high purpose and high subjects which had filled the Irish poem till then.

*

A new Ireland. An old literature. For more than a decade I had been caught in my own life, raising children, doing my own work, feeling myself growing older. The raw surroundings of our first bleak winter were almost forgotten. Now, on summer afternoons, the trees were so thick that we could no longer see the hills.

But this was no pastoral. To start with, the violence continued. Every day television and radio beamed their pictures and sounds of hate into our quiet corner of the island. It was as if an old fault of the earth was always breaking open under a smooth surface, throwing its cruel breath of fire here and there. Sometimes, after hearing of an atrocity, or a killing, or a false move in the peace process, I would look out the window. The roofs stretched away to the foothills. The blues and greens of the mountains dissolved into the rain-heavy skies over Wicklow. It could hardly have been more peaceful.

The reality was different. There was not an inch of land seen from my window which was not implicated in the sorrows and compromises of Irish history. When I had first come here I had felt the rawness and newness of the neighborhood. Now I felt its age and the poignance of its existence above the old wolf-haunted woodlands of south Dublin. Increasingly, I felt the powerful upward pressure of that past on the surfaces of our present.

It was not a new preoccupation for me. Just as the horse had been an emblem of contemporary disruption, now, as I grew older, the unsettled past became more real. But their source was the same. The more I wrote myself into the local, the more the local widened into a meshing of themes which mirrored my own questions.

One evening I drove from Dundrum into the neighborhood of Balally. It was a drive of ten minutes, no more. I was there to see something wonderful and strange. And yet what greeted me was a nondescript rise of grass about thirty meters long. To one side was a small house. Further down was a semicircle of older cottages. On the grass itself was an unkempt mountain ash. To look at it was nothing more than a neighborly scene. And yet this slight incline was rich with the tensions and meanings of the past.

During the thirteenth century Dublin had become the Pale: a castellated, armed space to protect the capital from the incursions of the wild Irish beyond the city limits. Between 1488 and 1494 an earthen rampart, four meters high, had been made part of those defenses. Undoubtedly, the ambitious building had been prompted by the 1429 Pale Statue of Henry VI—an opening shot in the attempt to subdue Ireland—which offered a building subsidy of ten pounds, a large sum then, to those who undertook the defense of the city limits.

It was a poignant thought: the idea of a neighborhood, similar to my own in its dailyness and ordinariness, concealing this sign of history and resistance. The idea of a ditch built to drive back the native speech and unsuppressed Irishness of a people on the wrong side of it suddenly a compelling thought. And yet here, in the late light, the survivors of those hatreds played on the grass, which was all that was left of them.

I was moved by the sight. For all that I had lived here, I had never escaped the meanings and menaces of my own origins. The suburb was a shelter; it was not a cloister. The abrasion of Irishness was always there, from the horse to this small length of grass. I had redirected the conflicts of my youth, but I had not banished them. The poem I began to write was called "The Mother Tongue" (from *The Lost Land,* 1998). The first line was written that very evening. I began with a narrative of the pale ditch itself: the way it was dug and drained and used to defend the old, emerging city of Dublin—my city after all—from the threat of the unknown.

Something about this theme described the moment I was in: my sense of how place could establish its present, but never disestablish the past. Our neighbourhood was a sign of a new Ireland. But the old one, with its wounds and memories, kept intruding.

The fact was that the place I had come to had led, in a circular way, back to all the issues and concerns I had had when I was a young poet. Where did I belong? What part had poetry in Irish history? What were the obligations of a poet in the making and un-making of a nation? And what had this plain dailyness to do with the power of a compelling history?

Twenty years separated my first sight of the horse, stumbling into our fragile world, and this old stretch of grass. But the dilemmas felt as fresh and painful as ever.

*

If I stand in my front garden and look southwest to the Dublin hills, I can see the slopes of Kippure and

Site of trace remains of the Pale ditch in Ballaly, Dublin, where "survivors of those old hatreds played on in the grass"

the Sally Gap. Hidden in that blue, far-fetched distance is the source of the Liffey. It rises as a small trickle of water, surrounded by ling and heather and tinted by peaty soil. Its headwaters gather speed and purpose on those slopes. Eventually the river comes to the city it defined and continues to define. And so, in describing how I came to write the fourth poem here, which is about the river, I have come full circle.

The poem is called "Anna Liffey" (from *In a Time of Violence,* 1994). Of all the poems here, it is the one that felt most natural to write. According to fable, *Life* was the legendary wife of a tribal Irish chief. She asked that the river be named for her. And so the river took a woman's name. But it was more than that.

I wrote the poem in my late forties, during the months of a long, cold Irish spring. As March gave way to April, as the days lengthened, a delicate and clement light began to arrive. In the early afternoons, I would stand in the open doorway of our house and look directly across at Kippure.

On clear days it was a view of connected blues and greens, softened by humid light. When the colors took on a staring clearness I would know that rain was imminent.

The poem felt like statement of intent: I had come to this neighborhood in my early twenties. I had feared the isolation it would bring; the way it seemed to signal the end of my inclusion in a literary and metropolitan life. Now it was my point of connection with the world.

My children had come here as infants and had grown up in these gardens and along these roads. More than that, the suburb had acted as a variable in my sense of reality: at once the physical and metaphysical meeting point of my different worlds of poetry and womanhood. Here I had been able to connect them, as I might never have done if I had remained at the so-called center of a literary life. Here I had come to understand that the distance between the visible life of the poet and the hidden life of the woman was a register of tensions and resistances in the culture itself: in its history, in its literature. And that to explore that distance, as I had been forced to do, was the only way I could have opened a dialogue with my own literary inheritance.

I had, after all, lived the ordinary, daily life of a woman in this house, in these rooms. I had got up at 4 a.m. to feed my first daughter. And when I had seen other lighted windows at that hour, I had known I was not alone: that this adventure belonged to others as well. I had backed my car out of the drive, morning after morning, noticing the new height of a neighbor's child, the new roof on a neighbor's garage. By writing the place as well as living my life there it had become for me a location of ordinary detail and extraordinary renewal. It was not so much that the life I had lived here had fitted my sense of being a poet. It had transformed it.

In the year I wrote "Anna Liffey" I would stand in my doorway looking at the hills, conscious of the journey I had made in this place. But conscious also that I wanted the poem to be as close as possible to the reality of what I had become—an ageing woman.

The connection between the poem and my own ageing was central. One of the reasons my relation to my own country and its poetry had been so difficult—I was sure of this—was because of the way women were represented in Irish literature. The heroic writing of the nineteenth century had often fused images of nationhood and womanhood. The national and feminine stylized one another in a suffocating way. In ballads, in stories, in poems, Ireland appeared again and again as a young woman. Or, in a more stylized way,

The author at her home

as an old woman needing the strength of her sons to fight for her. She was the Shan Van Vocht. Or Dark Rosaleen. Or Cathleen ni Houlihan.

I recognized the power of nineteenth-century Irish poetry. I understood its struggle with a lost language and a garrison culture. But as time went on, I had less and less patience with these fictions. It seemed to me a strange transposition that the women of the Irish past—hard pressed and suffering—should appear in their own literature in this utterly unrepresentative way. I thought of a letter I had seen, framed and hung on the wall, in the Famine Museum in Strokestown. It was written by a woman who had emigrated to America in the second year of the famine. She was writing now to the land agent on the estate where she had been a tenant, asking him to recover her children from the workhouse where she had left them.

Her story is incomplete and unknowable. But her letter is a message from a circle of hell. And yet how was it that the queens, the sibyls, the oracular women who represented Ireland in poems and novels did not represent her? In fact, the opposite. The relentless attempt to feminize the national had all but erased her reality.

I was an ageing woman, my children growing older, my sense of life was altered and deepened by that. Writing "Anna Liffey" allowed me to intrude on the old, heroic themes of Irish poetry. It allowed me to mark my own life as an ageing, unperfect woman, caught in the dailyness of this time and place, feeling the limits of the body and the strains of the mind. In writing counter to Irish poetry's old tendency to idealize women—to confuse the national with the feminine—I felt I had opened a new dialogue, and on my own terms.

In fact, it seemed to me more and more important that I would be in my poems as I was in my life—caught in time and not exempt from it. "Anna Liffey" was driven by that purpose. It was also a small cartography of my journey until that moment—from city to suburb and back. Above all, it reflected my own longing to write a poem that would show the flawed and actual life of a woman in her time.

BIOGRAPHICAL AND CRITICAL SOURCES:

BOOKS

Adams, Henry, *The Education of Henry Adams*, introduction by Edmund Morris, Random House (New York, NY), 1999.

Boland, Eavan, *In a Time of Violence*, Norton (New York, NY), 1995.

Boland, Eavan, *An Origin like Water*, Norton (New York, NY), 1997.

Contemporary Literary Criticism, Gale (Detroit, MI), Volume 40, 1986, Volume 67, 1992.

Coyne, J. Stirling and N. P. Willis, *Scenery and Antiquitites of Ireland*, Virtue (London, England), 1840.

Dictionary of Literary Biography, Volume 40: *Poets of Great Britain and Ireland since 1960*, Gale (Detroit, MI), 1985.

Haberstroh, Patricia Boyle, *Women Creating Women: Contemporary Irish Women Poets*, Syracuse University Press (Syracuse, NY), 1996.

Joyce, Weston St. John, *The Neighborhood of Dublin*, M. H. Gill & Son (Dublin, Ireland), 1939.

Yeats, W. B., *Collected Poems of W. B. Yeats*, Macmillan (London, England), 1936.

PERIODICALS

American Poetry Review, September, 1999, review of *The Lost Land*, p. 7.

Bloomsbury Review, March, 1998, review of *Object Lessons*, p. 22.

Booklist, March 15, 1994, p. 1322; February 15, 1996, p. 983; October 15, 1998, review of *The Lost Land*, p. 389; March 15, 1999, review of *The Lost Land*, p. 1276.

Commonweal, November 4, 1988, p. 595.

Entertainment Weekly, January 15, 1999, review of *The Lost Land*, p. 58.

Hudson Review, August, 1999, review of *The Lost Land*, p. 507.

Kirkus Reviews, October 15, 1998, review of *The Lost Land*, p. 1492.

Irish Literary Supplement, fall, 1994, p. 23; fall, 1995, p. 8; spring, 1996, p. 30; spring 1999, review of *The Lost Land*, p. 15.

Library Journal, November 15, 1990, p. 74; March 1, 1994, p. 90; July, 2001, Frank Allen, review of *Against Love Poetry*, pp. 94-95.

Nation, June 6, 1994, p. 798; April 24, 1995, p. 564.

New Statesman & Society, January 26, 1996, p. 40.

New York Review of Books, May 26, 1994, p. 25.

New York Times Book Review, April 21, 1991, p. 40; November 4, 2001, Melanie Rehak, "Map of Love."

Poetry, July, 1990, p. 236; October, 1994, p. 41; February, 1998, review of *An Origin Like Water*, p. 282.

Publishers Weekly, October 26, 1990, p. 62; December 18, 1995, p. 51; August 31, 1998, review of *The Lost Land*, p. 69.

Southern Review, spring, 1999, review of *The Lost Land*, p. 387.

Times Literary Supplement, August 5, 1994, p. 19; September 8, 1995, p. 28; December 10, 1999, review of *The Lost Land*, p. 23.

Women's Review of Books, September, 1995, p. 7; April, 1999, review of *The Lost Land*, p. 17.

Yale Review, July, 1999, review of *The Lost Land*, p. 167.

OTHER

Academy of American Poets Web Site, http://www.
poets.org/ (September 18, 2001), "Eavan Boland."

Carcanet Press Web site, http://www.carcanet.co.uk/
(October 16, 2002), Jody Allen Randolph, "A
Backward Look: An Interview with Eavan
Boland."

Skoool.ie Interactive Learning, http://www.skoool.ie/
(October 16, 2002), "Eavan Boland."

New Yorker Web site, http://www.newyorker.com/
(October 29, 2001), Alice Quinn, "Q&A: The Sto-
icisms of Love" (interview with Eavan Boland).

*　　*　　*

BOONE, Jack W. 1922-

PERSONAL: Born September 8, 1922, in Montgomery,
AL; married Anne (a homemaker), April 14, 1946;
children: James W. *Education:* University of California, 1945. *Politics:* "Independent." *Hobbies and other
interests:* Golf.

ADDRESSES: Home—971 East Callaway Road, Marietta, GA 30060. *E-mail*—jabo@mindspring.com.

CAREER: Novelist. Marietta, GA, self-employed,
CEO, 1953-85; writer, 1985—. Former on the board
of directors of five companies; held director post at
Salvation Army and Kiwanis. *Military service:* U.S.
Army, 1941-45; became captain; earned Silver Star
and Purple Heart.

MEMBER: Georgia Writers Association, Kiwanis.

WRITINGS:

CRIME FICTION

A Plan to Kill, Grafco Productions, 1986.
Doc Rogers, Grafco Productions, 1988.
The Eagle Society, Grafco Productions, 1989.
Billy Box, Grafco Productions, 1991.

The Estonia System, Grafco Productions, 1993.
The Rebel, Grafco Productions, 1995.

Also author of short stories, other crime fiction novels,
and several works of nonfiction.

WORK IN PROGRESS: Two untitled crime-fiction
novels, a book of short stories, numerous essays,
newsletters, and a stage play due for production in
2003.

SIDELIGHTS: Jack W. Boone told *CA:* "I write every
day, usually seven days a week unless promotional
activities intrude. My working hours are usually in the
morning until noon. I rewrite in the afternoons and
evenings."

*　　*　　*

BRADLEY, Joseph (C., Jr.) 1945-

PERSONAL: Born December 15, 1945, in Madison,
WI; son of Joseph C. (an artist) and Josephine (Ratner)
Bradley; married Irina Krivtsova, December 10, 1975
(marriage ended August 8, 1989); married Christine
Ruane (a professor), May 24, 1992. *Education:*
University of Wisconsin, B.A., 1968; Harvard Univer-
sity, M.A., 1971, Ph.D., 1978.

ADDRESSES: Home—5508 East 104th St., Tulsa, OK
74137. *Office*—Department of History, University of
Tulsa, Tulsa, OK 74104; fax: 918-631-6057. *E-mail*—
joseph-bradley@utulsa.edu.

CAREER: Educator and historian. Boston University,
Boston, MA, visiting assistant professor, 1977-78;
University of Tulsa, Tulsa, OK, assistant professor,
1979-86, associate professor, 1986-91, professor of
history, 1991—, department chair, 1998—. University
of London, visiting fellow at London School of
Slavonic and East European Studies, 1983; Moscow
State University, exchange fellow, 1983-84; Columbia
University, visiting scholar at Harriman Institute, 1986;
Harvard University, Weatherhead visiting fellow at
Russian Research Center, 1985, visiting fellow, 1992;
Ohio State University, visiting associate professor,

1987-88; Georgetown University, visiting associate professor, 1989-90; guest lecturer at other institutions, including University of Texas—Austin, University of Warwick, University of California—Berkeley, Purdue University, Ohio State University, and University of Kansas. Tulsa-Zelenograd Sister Cities Association, member of board of directors.

MEMBER: American Historical Association, American Association for the Advancement of Slavic Studies, Phi Beta Kappa, Phi Kappa Phi, Phi Alpha Theta.

AWARDS, HONORS: Fulbright fellow in the USSR, 1972-73; grants from National Endowment for the Humanities, 1981, 1987, and 1993, and National Council for Soviet and East European Research, 1993-94.

WRITINGS:

(Editor) *The Soviet Aluminum Industry,* Delphic Associates (Falls Church, VA), 1983.
Muzhik and Muscovite: Urbanization in Late Imperial Russia, University of California Press (Berkeley, CA), 1985.
Guns for the Tsar: American Technology and the Small-Arms Industry in Nineteenth-Century Russia, Northern Illinois University Press (DeKalb, IL), 1990.
(Editor, with others, and contributor) *AHA Guide to Historical Literature,* Volume 2, Oxford University Press (New York, NY), 1995.

Contributor to books, including *The City in Late Imperial Russia,* edited by Michael Hamm, Indiana University Press (Bloomington, IN), 1986; *Between Tsar and People: Educated Society and the Quest for Public Identity in Late Imperial Russia,* edited by Samuel Kassow and James West, [Princeton, NJ], 1991; *Reform in Russian and Soviet History,* edited by Theodore Taranovski, Cambridge University Press (New York, NY); and *Merchant Moscow: Images of a Vanished Bourgeoisie,* edited by James L. West and Iurii A. Petrov, Princeton University Press (Princeton, NJ), 1998. Contributor of articles and reviews to periodicals, including *Russian Review, Russian History, Slavonic and East European Review,* and *Journal of Urban History.* Editor, *Kritika,* 1971-72; coeditor, *Russian Studies in History,* 1993—.

WORK IN PROGRESS: Research for *Voluntary Associations and the Formation of Civil Society in Russia, 1750-1930.*

BIOGRAPHICAL AND CRITICAL SOURCES:

PERIODICALS

American Historical Review, April, 1987, Diane P. Koenker, review of *Muzhik and Muscovite: Urbanization in Late Imperial Russia,* p. 458.
Annals of the American Academy of Political and Social Science, March, 1987, David Hecht, review of *Muzhik and Muscovite,* p. 218.
Journal of Interdisciplinary History, summer, 1987, Laura Engelstein, review of *Muzhik and Muscovite,* p. 174.
Journal of Modern History, September, 1987, Paul M. Hohenberg, review of *Muzhik and Muscovite,* p. 648.
Journal of Social History, winter, 1989, Adele Lindenmeyr, review of *Guns for the Tsar: American Technology and the Small-Arms Industry in Nineteenth-Century Russia,* p. 428.
Library Journal, November 15, 1990, John Yurechko, review of *Guns for the Tsar,* p. 80.

*   *   *

BRANLEY, Franklyn M(ansfield) 1915-2002

OBITUARY NOTICE—See index for *CA* sketch: Born June 5, 1915, in New Rochelle, NY; died May 5, 2002, in Brunswick, ME. Educator and author. Branley was an innovative educator who became one of the first to teach science to elementary school children, and he was a prolific author of over 140 books explaining scientific concepts to young people. He received his teaching license from the New Paltz Normal School (now the State University of New York College at New Paltz), a bachelor's degree from New York University in 1942, and his M.A. and Ed.D. from Columbia University in 1948 and 1957 respectively. From 1936 until 1954, Branley was a teacher at various elementary schools in the state of New York. Because science lessons were still new to younger students at the time, Branley worked with other educators to write a pamphlet on how best to teach the subject. This was the first step toward his writing career. He began writing science books for children with Nelson Frederick Beller in the 1940s that taught young students how to perform simple experiments. Branley joined Jersey State Teachers College (now Jersey City State College), where he was a science professor from 1954 to 1956, but it was his work as director of educational services at the American Museum of Natural History's Hayden Planetarium that sparked his interest in astronomy and space exploration. What followed was a series of books on astronomy, including the multi-volume "Exploring Our Universe," "Mysteries of the Universe," and "Voyage into Space" series. Branley remained at the planetarium, becoming its astronomer in 1963 and chairman of the planetarium in 1968 before retiring in 1972. In addition to his series on astronomy, he authored many other science books explaining a wide variety of concepts to young readers; he also wrote and edited college textbooks. Many of Branley's books received awards as outstanding science books, and in 1970 he was named New Jersey's Children's Book Writer of the Year.

OBITUARIES AND OTHER SOURCES:

BOOKS

Something about the Author Autobiography Series, Volume 16, Gale (Detroit, MI), 1993, pp. 17-32.

PERIODICALS

New York Times, May 9, 2002, p. A29.

*   *   *

BRAOUDE, Patrick

PERSONAL: Married to Guila Braoude (a film director and actor).

ADDRESSES: Agent—c/o UGC FOX Distribution, 2 av. Montaigne, 75 008 Paris, France.

CAREER: Actor, director, producer, screenwriter.

Film appearances include *Femmes de personne,* European Classics Video, 1984; *Until September,* 1984; *Je hais les acteurs,* Galaxy International, 1986; *Sale destin,* 1987; *L'ete en pente douce,* Prima Film, 1987; *L'oeil au beur noir,* 1987; *Génial, mes parents divorcent!,* 1991; *Neuf mois,* 1994; *Grossesse nerveuse,* 1994; *Dis-moi oui . . .* 1995; *Drole de conception,* Lauren Film, 1996; *Amour et confusions,* NTV-PROFIT, 1997; *Que la lumiere soit,* AFMD, 1998; *Quasimodo d'el Paris,* Bac Films, 1999; *Je veux tout,* United International Pictures, 1999; *Deuxième vie,* UGC-Fox Distribution, 2000; *And Now . . . Ladies and Gentlemen,* 2002; *Carpe dans le baignoire,* 2003.

Film work includes (director) *Génial, mes parents divorcent!,* 1991; (assistant director) *Neuf mois,* 1994; (director) *Amour et confusions,* NTV-PROFIT, 1997; (executive producer) *Je veux tout,* United International Pictures, 1999; (producer and director) *Deuxième vie,* UGC-Fox Distribution, 2000.

Television appearances include (miniseries) *David Lansky,* 1989; (movies) *Roitelet,* Deux flics a Belleville, 1988; *La guerre des prives,* 1992.

WRITINGS:

SCREENPLAYS

Amour et confusions, NTV-PROFIT, 1997.
Deuxième vie, UGC-Fox Distribution, 2000.

Also author of *Black Mic Mac,* 1986; *Un pere et passe,* 1987; *L'oeil au beur noir,* 1987; *Génial, mes parents divorcent!,* 1991; *Neuf mois,* 1994; *Splitsville,* 1998.

ADAPTATIONS: Amour et confusions and *Neuf mois* were remade as English-language films under the titles *Love and Confusion* and *Nine Months* respectively.

SIDELIGHTS: Reviewing *Nine Months,* an American remake of French writer and director Patrick Braoude's *Neuf mois,* Eleanor Ringel in the *Atlanta Constitution* called the American version "the cinematic equivalent of turning perfectly aged Roquefort into Cheez Whiz." The original, she maintained, "is a stunningly truthful, totally hilarious, and ultimately touching look at the tensions and changes wrought on men, as well as women, by impending parenthood."

Parents, children, and families are also at the center of *Génial, mes parents divorcent!,* whose title means "Oh, great, my parents are getting a divorce!" Protagonist

Julien is a sixth-grader shaken up by his parents' decision to end their marriage. He finds strength in the company of others, however, as he discovers, half the members of his class at school have divorced parents as well.

Braoude used a larger existential canvas to play out his original screenplay, *Deuxième vie.* The story begins on a day in 1982, when thirty-two-year-old protagonist Vincent is confronted by a number of decisions, which he attempts to sort out while recovering from the semi-final loss of the French team in the World Cup.

A car accident acts as a linchpin for a dramatic twist of fate. Vincent slams into a column, only to be saved by an airbag. Gradually he comes to the realization that it is 1998, and he is forty-eight years old. France has just won the World Cup, but he has more pressing matters to consider: for instance, how he came to have two teenage children, who are sitting in the back seat of the car, and how he came to marry their mother—a woman he met briefly on that day in 1982, when he was engaged to someone else. Most of all, Vincent must confront the tyrannical, though financially successful, figure he has become.

BIOGRAPHICAL AND CRITICAL SOURCES:

BOOKS

Contemporary Theatre, Film, and Television, Gale (Detroit, MI), Volume 34, 2001.

PERIODICALS

Atlanta Constitution, July 12, 1995, Eleanor Ringel, review of *Nine Months,* p. B9.
Variety, April 22, 1991, review of *Génial, mes parents divorcent!,* p. 52; February 28, 1994, Lisa Nesselson, review of *Neuf mois,* p. 73; March 24, 1997, Stephen O'Shea, review of *Love and Confusion,* p. 37.*

*   *   *

BRISON, Susan J.

PERSONAL: Married; husband's name, Tom; children: one son. *Education:* University of Toronto, Ph.D., 1987.

ADDRESSES: Home—Academy Road, P.O. Box 177, Thetford, VT, 05074. *Office*—Department of Philosophy, Dartmouth College, P.O. Box 5612, Hanover, NH 03755. *E-mail*—susan.brison@dartmouth.edu.

CAREER: Dartmouth College, Hanover, NH, assistant associate professor of philosophy, 1985—; visiting professor at Tufts University, New York University, and Princeton University. Panelist, women's rights conferences, 1999-2000.

AWARDS, HONORS: Mellon Fellow, New York University, 1988-89; National Endowment for the Humanities fellow, Institute for Advanced Study, 1997-98; one of ten best philosophy articles of 1998, *Philosopher's Annual,* for "The Autonomy Defense of Free Speech."

WRITINGS:

(Editor, with Walter Sinnott-Armstrong) *Contemporary Perspectives on Constitutional Interpretation,* Westview Press (Boulder, CO), 1993.
Aftermath: Violence and the Remaking of a Self, Princeton University Press (Princeton, NJ), 2001.
Speech, Harm, and Conflicts of Right, Princeton University Press (Princeton, NJ), 2001.

Contributor to books, including *On Feminist Ethics and Politics, Cambridge Companion to Simone de Beauvoir, Feminists Rethink the Self, Relational Autonomy, Feminist Perspectives on Autonomy,* and *Agency and the Social Self;* contributor to journals and other periodicals, including *Legal Theory, Nomos, Ethics, Chronicle of Higher Education, Guardian, New York Times, La Stampa, Les Temps Modernes,* and the Web site *ArtsAndLettersDaily.com.*

SIDELIGHTS: Susan J. Brison was on a morning walk in rural southern France when she was grabbed from behind, brutally beaten, sexually assaulted, strangled into unconsciousness, and left for dead. In *Aftermath: Violence and the Remaking of a Self,* she tells of how she survived this horrible experience, and reached healing and acceptance.

Brison, an academician long accustomed to abstract views of life, had to re-evaluate her perception of human nature. Her world was shattered, and *Aftermath* follows more than a decade of self-analysis and retraining.

Although the book is a personal narrative of recovery, Brison's philosophy training helps her dig deeper, stretch intellectually, and analyze topics such as memory and truth, identity and self, the importance of autonomy even within community, and what she feels is society's role in victimizing women. Weaving personal experience with larger philosophical questions, she demonstrates how philosophy falls far short, at times, in grasping life's realities.

A *Publishers Weekly* reviewer praised the book as "an intellectually stimulating read, even as she successfully avoids the academic tone that could be off-putting to a wider audience." Jo Ann Beard of *O, The Oprah Magazine* called *Aftermath* "a testament to endurance and, ultimately to survival." Feminist author Catharine MacKinnon hailed Brison's work as groundbreaking. "By facing what follows from traumatic abuse without blinking, by refusing to forget that the world can never be as it was, Susan Brison's shatteringly insightful *Aftermath* reconstructs philosophy as she reinvents survival."

BIOGRAPHICAL AND CRITICAL SOURCES:

PERIODICALS

Booklist, December 15, 2001, Vanessa Bush, review of *Aftermath: Violence and the Remaking of a Self,* p. 686.
Ethics, July, 1995, review of *Contemporary Perspectives on Constitutional Interpretation,* p. 977.
Globe and Mail, June 22, 2002, Martin Levin, "Rape and Narrative," p. D12.
Kirkus Reviews, November 1, 2001, review of *Aftermath,* p. 1527.
O, The Oprah Magazine, January, 2002, Jo Ann Beard, "Stronger in the Broken Places: In Aftermath, Susan Brison Tells the True Story of Her Harrowing Assault and Extraordinary Struggle Back to Wholeness," p. 103.
Publishers Weekly, November 19, 2001, review of *Aftermath,* p. 57.
Women's Review of Books, April, 2002, Mimi Wesson, "Mind over Matter."

OTHER

Dartmouth College Web site, http://www.dartmouth.edu/ (May 27, 2002).
University Press of Kansas Web site, http://www.kansaspress.ku.edu/ (May 27, 2002), review of *On Feminist Ethics and Politics.*

Princeton University Web site, http://www.pup.princeton.edu/ (May 27, 2002), reviews of *Aftermath.*

*   *   *

BROADUS, Calvin
See SNOOP DOGGY DOGG

*   *   *

BROWN, James Nathaniel
See BROWN, Jim

*   *   *

BROWN, Jane 1938-

PERSONAL: Born December 6, 1938, in Winchester, England; divorced; children: Nicholas, Philip.

ADDRESSES: Agent—Caradoc King, A.P. Watt, Ltd., 20 John St., London WC1N 2DR, England.

CAREER: Author, landscape historian.

WRITINGS:

(Editor, with Timothy Cochrane) *Landscape Design for the Middle East,* The Landscape Institute, (Forest Grove, OR), 1978.
The Everywhere Landscape, Wildwood House (London, England), 1982.
Vita's Other World: A Gardening Biography of V. Sackville-West, Viking (New York, NY), 1985.
The English Garden in Our Time: From Gertrude Jekyll to Geoffrey Jellicoe, Antique Collectors Club (Woodbridge, Suffolk, England), 1986, revised edition published as *The English Garden through the Twentieth Century,* 1999.
Lanning Roper and His Gardens, Rizzoli (New York, NY), 1987.
The Art and Architecture of the English Gardens: The Garden from the Collection of the Royal British Architects, 1607 to the Present Day, Rizzoli (New York, NY), 1989.

Fulbrook: A House You Will Love to Live In: The Sketchbook, Letters, Specification of Works and Accounts for a House by Edwin Lutyens, 1896-1899, Libanus Press (Marlborough, Wiltshire, England), 1989.

Sissinghurst: Portrait of a Garden, Abrams (New York, NY), 1990.

Gardens of a Golden Afternoon: The Story of a Partnership: Edwin Lutyens & Gertrude Jekyll, Penguin Books (New York, NY), 1994.

Beatrix: The Gardening Life of Beatrix Jones Farrand, 1872-1959, Viking (New York, NY), 1995.

A Garden and Three Houses, Antique Collectors Club (Woodbridge, Suffolk, England), 1999.

The Pursuit of Paradise: A Social History of Gardens and Gardening, HarperCollins (London, England), 1999.

Spirits of Place: Five Famous Lives in Their Landscape, Viking (New York, NY), 2001.

WORK IN PROGRESS: Currently writing a social history of rhododendrons, to be published by HarperCollins in 2004. Also working on a history of the gardens of Buckingham Palace, and a biography of Henrietta St. John (1700-1756), a poet and landscape gardener.

SIDELIGHTS: Jane Brown is a landscape historian who has created a subgenre of landscape biographies. She explores the lives of people through the connections they created to their surroundings. In her book, *Spirits of Place: Five Famous Lives in Their Landscape,* Brown shows how her chosen subjects, Virginia Woolf, E. M. Forster, Rupert Brooke, Carrington and L. P. Hartley, connected to their particular English landscapes and how they made these places their inspiration. This theme is exposed through short biographies of the artists filled with interesting tidbits of gossip and local color. Brown also insists that eventual exile from these havens in rural England provided her subjects' creative drives. As Lindsay Duguid commented in the *Times Literary Supplement,* "The overall impression is of a timeless landscape dotted with clever, eccentric Englishmen and beautiful women." Brown ends the book with a plea for a conservation effort for these literary and geographical sites.

In *The Modern Garden,* Brown traces the history of the garden in the twentieth century. She describes hundreds of gardens from the works of such famous Modernists as Isamu Noguchi, Walter Gropius, Geoffrey Jellicoe, and Dan Kiley. She pays special attention to Gueverkian's garden at Hyeres, France, Ludwig Gerns' work in Germany, Arne Jacobson's garden at St. Catherine's College, England, Noguchi's California Scenario, Dan Kiley's Miller House in Indiana and Walter Gropius's home garden in Massachusetts. The primary departure of the modern garden is the employment of materials such as metals, plastics, glass, synthetic fabrics and solar panels that had never before been used in gardens. Brown shows how the modern impulse manifested in the garden is a quest for harmony between the natural and the man-made world and an expression of how we perceive our physical spaces.

In *Gardens of a Golden Afternoon: The Story of a Partnership: Edwin Lutyens and Gertrude Jekyll,* Brown studies the successful collaboration of English architect Edwin Lutyens and landscapist Gertrude Jekyll; he designed the houses, and she designed the gardens. As a reviewer for the *Washington Post Book World* noted, "It was a brilliant partnership which produced some of England's most delightful domestic architecture. Working in the twentieth century, Lutyen harked back to earlier times with his Tudor rooflines and chimneys, half-timbered walls, and square bay windows. Jekyll softened the stone walls with her romantic gardens—perennial borders riotous with color, vines climbing over gates, ferns blurring the lines between garden and wood."

Brown considers the Dumbarton Oaks in Washington D.C. one of the most successful gardens of the twentieth century. In her biography, *Beatrix: The Gardening Life of Beatrix Jones Farrand, 1872-1959,* Brown follows Farrand's career, showing that although she was part of a privileged circle and was able to extensively tour the greatest European gardens (she was a niece of Edith Wharton and a close friend of Henry James), she went on to create an American style of her own.

Nigel Nicholson, Vita Sackville-West's son, provided Brown with photographs and correspondence from his mother's private collection. From this, Brown wrote *Vita's Other World: A Gardening Biography of V. Sackville-West,* contending that although Sackville-West won prizes for her fiction and poetry, her garden [at Sissinghurst Castle] ensures her lasting fame. "Brown conveys a feeling of intimacy with her subject, someone whose more flamboyant activities have hitherto created a sacred monster in the popular imagination," wrote Diana Saville in the *Spectator.*

Brown's biography of Lanning Roper, *Lanning Roper and His Gardens,* describes the masterpiece gardens of the expatriate American landscapist, including Chartwell, Churchill's home, Lord Snowdon's bower garden in Kensington, and his work for Prince Sadruddin Aga Khan at the Château Bellrive near Geneva. Mary Keen, writing in the *Spectator,* commented that "Jane Brown has done a thorough and timely job on researching his [Roper's] gardens before they disappear, which ought to prove invaluable when the moment comes to think about his work more objectively."

In *The Everywhere Landscape,* Brown takes a hard look at conservation theories and finds them wanting. Landscape, she says, is not something only to be enjoyed on a Sunday outing and preserved as our idea of pristine nature. It is something with which we live and which is always around us. Moreover, it is our principal source of food and fuel. Brown contends that it is man in partnership with nature, and not nature alone, that should create intelligent landscapes for funccitional as well as pleasurable, educational and recreational environments. Brown's call-to-arms for local conservation is sounded further in *A Garden and Three Houses.* The author records the trials of Peter Aldington, a forward-thinking architect who chose to design his houses in the 1960s in harmony with his wooded lot by cutting no existing trees at all. A noble idea, but, at the time, British officialdom blocked him at every turn. Now, thirty years later, the gardens are mature, and the Aldington projects are celebrated as some of the best village housing design in Europe.

According to Brown, "We seem to have lost the need for and the knack of pleasure in gardens both public and private." *The Pursuit of Paradise: A Social History of Gardens and Gardening* is a cultural history of these gardens. She sees garden history evolving away from the grand monuments of the past toward an understanding of why we garden and how we enjoy our works. Montagu Don, in his review for the *Observer,* wrote "Jane Brown writes with a rare combination of academic rigour and a sure, personal style. She is learned, opinionated, disrespectful and generous, and, while she established herself as a serious writer with *Vita's Other World* and *The Gardens of a Golden Afternoon,* with *The Pursuit of Pleasure* she has made

a genuinely important contribution, not just to understanding the gardens of the past, but to how we might get the most pleasure from the gardens of the future."

BIOGRAPHICAL AND CRITICAL SOURCES:

BOOKS

Brown, Jane, *Beatrix: The Gardening Life of Beatrix Jones Farrand, 1872-1959,* Viking (New York, NY), 1995.
Brown, Jane, *Gardens of a Golden Afternoon: The Story of a Partnership: Edwin Lutyens and Gertrude Jekyll,* Penguin Books (New York, NY), 1994.
Brown, Jane, *Lanning Roper and His Gardens,* Rizzoli (New York, NY), 1987.
Brown, Jane, *Spirits of Place: Five Famous Lives in Their Landscape,* Viking (New York NY), 2001.
Brown, Jane, *The Pursuit of Paradise: A Social History of Gardens and Gardening,* HarperCollins (London, England), 1999.
Brown, Jane, *Vita's Other World: A Gardening Biography of V. Sackville-West,* Viking (New York, NY), 1985.

PERIODICALS

Architects' Journal, June 10, 1999, review of *A Garden and Three Houses,* p. 70.
Architectural Review, February, 1997, Margaret Richardson, review of *Gardens of a Golden Afternoon: The Story of a Partnership: Edwin Lutyens and Gertrude Jekyll,* p. 89.
Booklist, September 1, 1990, John Brosnahan, review of *Sissinghurst: Portrait of a Garden,* p. 16; January 1, 1995, George Cohen, review of *Beatrix: The Gardening Life of Beatrix Jones Farrand, 1872-1959,* pp. 790-791.
British Book News, September, 1982, Allen Layne, review of *Gardens of a Golden Afternoon: The Story of a Partnership: Edwin Lutyens and Gertrude Jekyll,* p. 564.
Building Design, January 12, 2001, review of *The Modern Garden,* p. 26.
Choice, October, 1995, K. T. Settlemyer, review of *Beatrix: The Gardening Life of Beatrix Jones Farrand, 1872-1959,* p. 319; February, 1990, D. Stillman, review of *The Art and Architecture of English Gardens,* p. 941.

Contemporary Review, September, 1996, Annabella Cloudsley, review of *Gardens of a Golden Afternoon: The Story of a partnership: Edwin Lutyens & Gertrude Jekyll,* p. 185.

Horticulture, June, 2000, J. Robert Ostergaard, review of *A Garden and Three Houses,* p. 68; April, 1995, review of *Beatrix: The Gardening Life of Beatrix Jones Farrand, 1872-1959,* pp. 81-83.

Kirkus Review, October 1, 1996, review of *Lutyens and the Edwardians: An English Architect and His Clients,* p. 1437.

Library Journal, January 1, 1983, Daniel S. Kalb, review of *Gardens of a Golden Afternoon: the story of a partnership: Edwin Lutyens and Gertrude Jekyll,* p. 43; May 1, 2001, Paula Frosch, *The Modern Garden,* p. 21.

Los Angeles Times Book Review, November 30, 1996, Barbara Saltman, review of *Vita's Other World: A Gardening Biography of V. Sackville-West,* p. 7; December 10, 1989, Sam Kaplan, review of *The Art and Architecture of English Gardens,* p. 7; May 12, 1991, review of *Eminent Gardeners: Some People of Influence and Their Gardens,* p. 6.

New York Times Book Review, Allen Lacey, review of *Lanning Roper and His Gardens,* p. 14.

Observer (London, England), September 12, 1999, Mantagu Don, review of *The Pursuit of Paradise,* p. 11.

Publishers Weekly, May 15, 1987, review of *Lanning Roper and His Gardens,* p. 278.

Punch, June 30, 1982, Mary Anne Bonney, review of *The Everywhere Landscape,* p. 1073.

Spectator, December 23, 1989, George Clive, "From Archways to Cabbages," p. 71; November 20, 1999, Rosanna James, review of *The Pursuit of Paradise,* p. 56; May 18, 1996, Jane Ripley, review of *Lutyens and the Edwardians: An English Architect and His Clients,* p. 41; November 2, 1985. Mary Keen, review of *Vita's Other World: A Gardening Biography of V. Sackville-West,* p. 33; June 20, 1987, Mary Green, review of *Lanning Roper and His Gardens,* p. 24.

Sunday Telegraph (London, England), May 13, 2001, Anne Chisholm, review of *Spirits of Place: Five Famous Lives in Their English Landscape.*

Times Literary Supplement, November 26, 1982, John Buxton, review of *Gardens of a Golden Afternoon: The Story of a Partnership: Edwin Lutyens and Gertrude Jekyll,* p. 1321; November 1, 1985, Diana Saville, review of *Vita's Other World: A Gardening Biography of V. Sackville-West,* p. 1244; February 2, 1990, Christopher Ridgway,

The Art and Architecture of English Gardens, p. 128; December 28, 1990, Alexander Urquart, review of *Eminent Gardeners: Some People of Influence and Their Gardens,* pp. 61, 408; November 26, 1999. Alexander Urquart, review of *The Pursuit of Paradise,* p. 14; June 22, 2001, Lindsay Duguid, review of *Spirits of Place,* p. 27.

Wall Street Journal, December 15, 2000, Mac Griswold, review of *The Modern Garden,* p. W10.

Washington Post Book World, April 7, 1991, review of *Eminent Gardeners: Some People of Influence and Their Gardens,* p. 13; May 2, 1999, review of *Vita's Other World: A Gardening Biography of V. Sackville-West,* p. 6; March 2, 1986, review of *Gardens of a Golden Afternoon: The Story of a Partnership: Edwin Lutyens and Gertrude Jekyll,* p. 13.

*   *   *

BROWN, Jim 1936-

PERSONAL: Born James Nathaniel Brown, February 17, 1936, in St. Simons Island, GA; son of Swinton (a professional boxer) and Theresa (a housekeeper) Brown; married, wife's name Sue, 1959 (divorced, 1972); married second wife, Monique; children: (first marriage) Kim and Kevin (twins), Jim, Jr., another child. *Education:* Attended Syracuse University.

ADDRESSES: Agent—Sterling Winters Company, 2040 Avenue of the Stars, fourth floor, Los Angeles, CA 90067.

CAREER: Athlete, actor, producer, and writer. Played football with Cleveland Browns, 1957-65.

Film appearances include *Rio Conchos,* Twentieth Century-Fox, 1964; *The Dirty Dozen,* Metro-Goldwyn-Mayer, 1967; *Operation Dirty Dozen,* 1967; *The Mercenaries,* Metro-Goldwyn-Mayer, 1968; *Ice Station Zebra,* Filmways, 1968; *The Split,* Metro-Goldwyn-Mayer, 1968; *The Man Who Makes the Difference,* 1968; *100 Rifles,* 1969; *Riot,* Paramount, 1969; *Kenner,* Metro-Goldwyn-Mayer, 1969; . . . *Tick* . . . *Tick* . . . *Tick* . . . , Metro-Goldwyn-Mayer, 1970; *The Grasshopper,* National General, 1970; *El Condor,*

National General, 1970; *The Phynx,* Warner Bros., 1970; *Ein Kafer geht aufs,* 1971; *Sam's Song,* Cannon, 1971; *Slaughter,* American International, 1972; *Black Gunn,* Columbia, 1972; *Slaughter's Big Rip-off,* American International, 1973; *The Slams,* Metro-Goldwyn-Mayer, 1973; *I Escaped from Devil's Island,* United Artists, 1973; *Three the Hard Way,* Allied Artists, 1974; *Take a Hard Ride,* Twentieth Century-Fox, 1975; *Adios Amigo,* Atlas, 1976; *Mean Johnny Barrows,* Atlas, 1976; *Kid Vengeance,* Cannon, 1977; *Fingers,* Brut, 1978; *Pacific Inferno,* VCL, 1979; *One Down, Two to Go,* Almi, 1983; *Abducted,* Inter Pictures Releasing/Modern Cinema Marketing, 1986; *The Running Man,* TriStar, 1987; *I'm Gonna Git You Sucka,* Metro-Goldwyn-Mayer/United Artists, 1988; *L.A. Heat,* Raedon Entertainment Group, 1989; *Crack House,* Twenty-first Century Releasing, 1989; *Twisted Justice,* Borde Releasing Corp., 1990; *The Divine Enforcer,* 1991; *Original Gangstas,* Orion, 1996; *Mars Attacks!,* Warner Bros., 1996; *He Got Game,* Buena Vista, 1998; *Small Soldiers,* DreamWorks Distribution L.L.C., 1998; *Any Given Sunday,* Warner Bros., 1999; *Jim Brown All American,* 2002. Film work includes (producer) *Pacific Inferno,* VCL, 1979; (executive producer) *Richard Pryor Here and Now,* Columbia, 1983.

Television appearances include (series) *NFL on CBS,* CBS, 1977; *Dynamic Duos,* NBC, 1978. Television movies include *Lady Blue,* ABC, 1985; (specials) *Black Champions,* PBS, 1986; *Hammer, Slammer, and Slade,* 1990; *The Record Breakers of Sport,* HBO, 1990; *The Nineteenth Annual Black Filmmakers Hall of Fame,* 1992; *In This Corner . . . Boxing's Historic Battles,* HBO, 1994; *Fields of Fire: Sports in the '60s,* HBO, 1995; *The NFL at Seventy-Five: An All-Star Celebration,* ABC, 1995; *Celebrate the Dream: Fifty Years of Ebony,* ABC, 1996; *The Journey of the African-American Athlete,* HBO, 1996; *Unitas,* HBO, 1999; *Ali-Frazier I: One Nation . . . Indivisible,* HBO, 2000; *Bill Russell: My Life My Way,* HBO, 2000; *George Foreman: Blow by Blow,* HBO, 2000. Appearances on episodic TV include "Cops and Robbers," *I Spy,* 1967; "End of the Line," *Police Story,* 1977; "Roller Disco: Parts 1 & 2," *CHiPs,* 1979; "High Times," *CHiPs,* 1983; "Knight of the Drones," *Knight Rider,* 1984; "Quarterback Sneak," *The A-Team,* 1986; "Whose Trash Is It Anyway?," *Highway to Heaven,* 1988; "Living Single Undercover," *Living Single,* 1997; *Between Brothers,* UPN, 1997; "Kung Fools," *Between Brothers,* UPN, 1998; "You Can Pick Your Friends . . .," *Arli$$,* HBO, 2000. Also appeared on *The Flip Wilson Show.* Work as television producer includes (movies) *The Magnificent Magical Magnet of Santa Mesa,* 1977.

AWARDS, HONORS: Jim Thorpe Trophy, 1958, 1965; Player of the Year, 1958, 1963, 1965; Named to NFL Pro Bowl, 1958-65; Hickoc Belt Athlete of Year, 1964; All-American Award, 1956; NFL Hall of Fame, 1971; Named best football player of the twentieth century, *Sports Illustrated;* Appointed by California Assembly Speaker Willie L. Brown, Jr., to the Commission on the Status of African American Males, 1994.

WRITINGS:

(With Myron Cope) *Off My Chest,* Doubleday (Garden City, NY), 1964.
(With Steve Delsohn) *Out of Bounds,* Kensington (New York, NY), 1989.

SIDELIGHTS: Widely regarded as one of the most outstanding athletes in the history of football, Jim Brown in 1963 established a league record for rushing: 1,883 yards. Yet after less than a decade (1957-65) with the Cleveland Browns, he left football behind, retiring from the sport at age twenty-nine to embark on a second career in film. The latter was concentrated primarily in the late 1960s and early 1970s, when, as Brown later recalled in his autobiography *Out of Bounds,* Hollywood was prepared to give unprecedented opportunities to black actors. After that time, he maintained, the fervor for social change in entertainment died down, and with it, his career.

Thereafter Brown devoted himself bringing about economic and social progress within the black community. Just as he had elicited controversy with his early retirement from football and film roles that made him the first black star cast in a romantic lead opposite a white woman (Raquel Welch in 1969's *One Hundred Rifles*), now he raised even further discussion by association with radical figures. Brown even called Nation of Islam leader Louis Farrakhan a friend in *Out of Bounds,* yet his message could not easily be summed up in political terms: much of what he preached was a gospel of self-reliance and rejection of government aid that comported well with the laissez-faire philosophy of the Republican Party. Nor, in his writing, is there any hint of the racial animosity that has long characterized Farrakhan and other African

American militants: while calling for social change, Brown clearly did not feel any aversion toward whites as people. Yet much of Brown's positive message has been obscured by still another controversial aspect of his life and career: his violence toward women, a tendency that became the focal point of a scandalous incident in the late 1960s, and which in the early 2000s earned him a jail sentence on abuse charges.

Despite the many varied aspects of his life, the focal point of *Out of Bounds*—which he wrote, he said, because he was not happy with his first autobiography, *Off My Chest,* published a quarter-century earlier—is something people were not as comfortable discussing back in 1964: sex. In a typical passage from the 1989 book, Brown writes that he likes physically small women, but "I don't mean mousy small. I mean tight. Petite. Delicate. No excess. Thin legs, nice butt. . . small. When I get into the bedroom, I don't want to see anything that's big like me."

For this reason, he maintains, he was one of the few heterosexual American men in 1969 who did not find the voluptuous Welch attractive. Yet, as he explains in *Out of Bonds,* in filming a sex scene all of that changed: "Her bosoms were exposed, I was kissing her and holding her and . . . she became incredibly sexy to me." He stuck his tongue in her ear, but during a break she asked him not to do it again, which made him laugh. Then, tantalizingly, he adds that "I did stay away from Raquel's ear, even when we dated, though that's another story." On a more serious note, in the book Brown also discussed men's ideas of manhood, and the differing ways that athletes and actors approximate those ideals, as well as the failure of Hollywood to produce realistic portrayals of black characters.

BIOGRAPHICAL AND CRITICAL SOURCES:

BOOKS

Brown, Jim, with Myron Cope, *Off My Chest,* Doubleday (Garden City, NY), 1964.

Brown, Jim, with Steve Delsohn, *Out of Bounds,* Kensington (New York, NY), 1989.

Contemporary Black Biography, Gale (Detroit, MI), volume 11, 1996.

Contemporary Theatre, Film, and Television, Volume 35, Gale (Detroit, MI), 2001.

Haley, Alex, and Murray Fisher, *The Playboy Interviews,* Ballantine (New York, NY), 1993.

Lace, William W., *Top Ten Football Rushers,* Enslow Publishers (Hillside, NJ), 1994.

Newsmakers 1993, Gale (Detroit, MI), 1993.

Prentzas, G. S., *Jim Brown,* Chelsea House (New York, NY), 1995.

St. James Encyclopedia of Popular Culture, St. James Press (Detroit, MI), 2000.

Sullivan, George, *Sports,* Scribner (New York, NY), 1988.

Summerall, Pat; Jim Moskovitz; and Craig Kubey. *Pat Summerall's Sports in America: Thirty-two Celebrated Sports Personalities Talk about Their Most Memorable Moments in and out of the Sports Arena,* HarperCollins (New York, NY), 1996.

PERIODICALS

Atlanta Constitution, October 1, 1989, review of *Out of Bounds,* p. L10.

Ebony, November, 1989, review of *Out of Bounds,* p. 24.

Jet, October 30, 1989, Lou Ransom, review of *Out of Bounds,* pp. 46-50.

New York Times Book Review, November 19, 1989, William C. Rhoden, review of *Out of Bounds,* p. 744.

Washington Post, September 8, 1989, Megan Rosenfeld, review of *Out of Bounds,* p. B1.*

*   *   *

BRUCE, George 1909-2002

OBITUARY NOTICE—See index for *CA* sketch: Born March 10, 1909, in Fraserburgh, Scotland; died July 25, 2002, in Edinburgh, Scotland. Poet, television and radio producer, and educator. Bruce was a prominent figure in the twentieth-century Scottish literary renaissance, composing poems celebrating his Scots heritage while writing on a wide variety of other subjects as well. After receiving his teaching certificate from Aberdeen University in 1933, Bruce taught physical education, English, and history at Dundee High School in Dundee, Scotland during the 1930s and early 1940s. He left teaching in 1946 to join the British Broadcasting Corporation (BBC), where he produced a number of radio and television arts programs, among them *Scottish Life and Letters* and *Arts Review,* and was a copresenter on the program *Counterpoint.* Retiring from his producer's job in 1970, Bruce taught creative writing at the University of Glasgow from 1971 to 1973 and was a visiting professor and writer-in-residence at several other colleges and universities in the United States. His many poetry collections include *Sea Talk* (1944); *The Collected Poems of George Bruce* (1970); *The Red Sky Poems* (1985); *Pursuit: Poems, 1986-1998* (1999), which won the Saltire Scottish Book of the Year; and *Today, Tomorrow: Collected Poems* (2001). Critics often said that some of Bruce's best verse is contained in his later collections.

OBITUARIES AND OTHER SOURCES:

BOOKS

Writers Directory, 16th edition, St. James Press (Detroit, MI), 2001.

PERIODICALS

Scotsman (Edinburgh, Scotland), July 26, 2002, p. 14.
Times (London, England), August 1, 2002.

*   *   *

BRULLE, Robert J.

PERSONAL: Son of Robert Vanden (an aerospace engineer) and Margaret Helen (a homemaker; maiden name, Roth) Brulle; married December 22, 1977; wife's name Mariette A. (marriage ended December 31, 1999); children: Joseph C., Timothy S. *Education:* U.S. Coast Guard Academy, B.S., 1974; New School for Social Research (now New School University), M.A., 1981; University of Michigan, M.S., 1982; George Washington University, Ph.D., 1995.

ADDRESSES: Office—Department of Culture and Communications, Drexel University, 3141 Chestnut St., Philadelphia, PA 19104. *E-mail*—brullerj@drexel.edu.

CAREER: U.S. Coast Guard, career officer, 1974-94, including assignments as operations officer on the cutter *Bramble,* based in Port Huron, MI, 1974-76, affirmative action staff chief for Third Coast Guard District, New York, 1976-77, marine inspector at Marine Inspection Office, New York, 1977-80, policy analyst for Office of Marine Environment and Systems, 1981-86, division chief at Great Lakes Regional Examination Center, 1986-89, research and planning analyst in Office of Personnel and Training, 1989-91, and senior policy analyst for Marine Environmental Protection Division, 1991-94, retiring as lieutenant commander. George Mason University, Fairfax, VA, research associate and lecturer, 1995-96; Drexel University, Philadelphia, PA, assistant professor of sociology and environmental policy, 1997—. Visiting professor at other institutions, including University of Frankfurt and University of Uppsala, both 1996; Northwestern University, guest speaker, 2002; guest on media programs; consultant to National Research Council.

MEMBER: International Sociological Association, American Sociological Association, American Political Science Association, Society of Environmental Journalists, Rural Sociological Society, American Association for the Advancement of Science, Eastern Sociological Association.

AWARDS, HONORS: Military: Two Coast Guard Commendation medals, Coast Guard Achievement Medal, and Humanitarian Service Medal. *Other:* Grants from American Sociological Association, 1994, American Association for the Advancement of Science, 1997, Army Environmental Policy Institute, 1998, and National Science Foundation, 2000.

WRITINGS:

Agency, Democracy, and Nature: U.S. Environmental Movements from a Critical-Theory Perspective, MIT Press (Cambridge, MA), 2000.

Author of government publications related to environmental issues. Contributor to books, including *Social Movements: Critiques, Concepts, Case Studies,* edited by Stanford Lyman, Macmillan Press (New York, NY), 1995; *Toward a Democratic Science: Scientific Narration and Civic Communication,* Yale University Press

(New Haven, CT), 1998; *The Environment and Society Reader,* edited by R. Scott Frey, Allyn & Bacon (Needham Heights, MA), 2001; and *Foundations for Social Change: Critical Perspectives on Philanthropy and Popular Movements,* edited by Daniel Faber and Debra McCarthy, Temple University Press (Philadelphia, PA), in press. Contributor of articles and reviews to periodicals, including *Human Ecology Review, Current Perspectives in Social Problems, Sociological Inquiry,* and *Environmental Politics.*

WORK IN PROGRESS: Where We Live, Work, and Play: A Critical Perspective of the Environmental Justice Movement, with David Pellow.

BIOGRAPHICAL AND CRITICAL SOURCES:

PERIODICALS

Environment, November, 2001, Allan Mazur, review of *Agency, Democracy, and Nature: U.S. Environmental Movements from a Critical-Theory Perspective,* p. 40.

*   *   *

BURNIE, David

PERSONAL: Male.

ADDRESSES: Agent—Dorling Kindersley Ltd., The Penguin Group (UK), 80 Strand, London WC2R ORL, England.

CAREER: Biologist, ranger, and author of nonfiction. Consultant to films and television.

WRITINGS:

Bird, Knopf (New York, NY), 1988.
Tree, Knopf (New York, NY), 1988.
Plant, Knopf (New York, NY), 1989.
Machines and How They Work, Dorling Kindersley Publishing (New York, NY), 1991.
How Nature Works, Readers Digest Association (Pleasantville, NY), 1992.

(With Jill Bailey) *Birds,* Dorling Kindersley Publishing (New York, NY), 1992.
Animals, Simon and Schuster for Young People (New York, NY), 1993.
Seashore, Dorling Kindersley Publishing (New York, NY), 1993.
Life, Dorling Kindersley Publishing (New York, NY), 1993.
Flowers, Dorling Kindersley Publishing (New York, NY), 1993.
Dictionary of Nature, Dorling Kindersley Publishing (New York, NY), 1994.
Animals: How They Work, Sterling Publishing Company (New York, NY), 1994.
(With John Kelly) *Everyday Machines: Amazing Devices We Take for Granted,* Turner Publishing (Atlanta, GA), 1995.
(With Richard Platt) *Apes and Other Hairy Primates,* Dorling Kindersley Publishing (New York, NY), 1995.
101 Nature Experiments, Dorling Kindersley Publishing (New York, NY), 1996.
Insects and Spiders, Time-Life Books (Alexandria, VA), 1997.
Birds and How They Live, Dorling Kindersley Publishing (New York, NY), 1998.
Mammals, Dorling Kindersley Publishing (New York, NY), 1998.
Forest, Dorling Kindersley Publishing (New York, NY), 1998.
Microlife, Dorling Kindersley Publishing (New York, NY), 1998.
Concise Encyclopedia of the Human Body, Dorling Kindersley Publishing (New York, NY), 1998.
Evolution, Time-Life Books (Alexandria, VA), 1999.
Kingfisher Illustrated Animal Encyclopedia, Kingfisher Books (Cornwall, England), 2000.
(Coeditor with Don E. Wilson) *Animal: The Definitive Guide to the World's Wildlife,* Dorling Kindersley Publishing (New York, NY), 2001.
Earth Watch, Dorling Kindersley Publishing (New York, NY), 2001.
Kingfisher Encyclopedia of Dinosaurs, Dorling Kindersley Publishing (New York, NY), 2001.

SIDELIGHTS: David Burnie studied zoology at the University of Bristol. After graduating, he worked as a nature reserve ranger and biologist, and in 1979 began a career writing and editing books on natural sciences. He has written, or contributed to, over seventy-five books and multimedia titles. He has also acted as a consultant and scriptwriter for a number of natural history television programs. Burnie's *Animal,* which he co-edited with Don E. Wilson, was on most journalist's lists for the best of nonfiction and science in 2001. Burnie's editorial style—including careful composition and choice of photographs, clear organization of large amounts of material in an easy-to-use design, made *Animal* an immediate classic in the genre. Burnie and Wilson selected spectacular photographic portraits to bring a vast array of animals vividly to life, with special features on well-known and important animals such as the Galapagos tortoise.

Discussing images in *Animal,* Burnie noted on *Dorling Kindersley Online,* "Together with the project's designers and editors, I was involved in selecting every photo in the book. I can't say how many we looked at altogether, but the total must have run into tens of thousands. It was always exciting when—after weeks of searching—a photo of a particularly rare or elusive species turned up at last."

How Nature Works is also written for upper elementary and middle-school students. Various aspects of natural history are photographed and explained step by step. Diane Nunn, reviewing the book for *School Library Journal,* called *How Nature Works* "a captivating interactive approach to learning that promotes the naturalist's motto, 'Look, learn, and then leave alone'." Burnie's "Eyewitness" series (*Bird, Plant, Tree, Light, Communication, Life, Seashore* and *Matter*) focused on the story of science from the ancient world through current research. Chris Sherman wrote in *Booklist,* "Student struggling in physical science classes will be grateful for the books because their clear explanations and attractive formats make potentially difficult scientific principles comprehensible."

BIOGRAPHICAL AND CRITICAL SOURCES:

PERIODICALS

American Biology Teacher, November, 1994, Michael Emsley, review of *Life,* p. 506; November, 1994, review of *Seashore,* p. 503; June, 1999, Roxanne Price, review of *Mammals,* p. 471.

American Reference Books Annual, 1995, Angela Marie Thor, review of *Dictionary of Nature,* p. 679; 1996, Katherine Margaret Thomas, review of *The Kingfisher First Encyclopedia of Animals,* p. 682.

Appraisal, spring, 1990, Rudolf Schmid, review of *Tree,* p. 13; autumn, 1992, Gertrude Wehking and S. Angela Hoffman, review of *Communication,* pp. 42-43; fall, 1994, Janet Kosky and Kathryn Zeiler, review of *Seashore,* pp. 63-64; fall, 1994, Edward Zilenski, review of *Dictionary of Nature,* pp. 12-13; summer, 1996, Martha Mahoney, review of *Concise Encyclopedia of the Human Body,* p. 6; fall, 1996, Alson Jarvis and Helen Seagraves, review of "Eyewitness" series, p. 75; winter, 1996, Sarah Helman and Marlon Wissink, review of "Eyewitness" series, p. 74-75; fall, 1998, Alison Jarvis and Helen Seagroves, review of *Flowers,* p. 31-32.

Booklist, October 15, 1989, Barbara Elleman, review of *Plant,* p. 448, 454; December 15, 1992, Chris Sherman, review of *Communication,* p. 729; January 15, 1993, Chris Sherman, review of *Light,* p. 894; February, 1993, Janice Del Negro, review of *Bird,* p. 978; August, 1994, review of *The Dictionary of Nature,* p. 2069-2070; November 15, 1994, review of *The Kingfisher Illustrated Animal Encyclopedia,* p. 628; December 1, 1995, Sandy Whiteley, review of *The Concise Encyclopedia of the Human Body,* p. 654; February 15, 2001, review of *The Kingfisher Illustrated Animal Encyclopedia,* p. 1174.

Book Report, March, 1990, Pamela Longbrake, review of *Plant,* p. 52; March, 1992, Liz Hunter, review of *How Nature Works,* p. 54; November, 1994, James Gross, review of *The Dictionary of Nature,* p. 57.

Books for Keeps, May, 1998, John Farndon, review of *Inside Guides Series,* p. 29.

Books for Your Children, autumn, 1988, Pat Thomson, review of *Bird,* p. 30; autumn, 1992, Pat Thomson, review of *How Nature Works,* p. 16.

Childhood Education, winter, 1998, Kathleen Secker, review of *Bird,* p. 118.

Geographical, November, 2001, Lizzie Orcutt, review of *Animal,* p. 81.

Horn Book Guide, spring, 1994, Barbara Barstow, review of *Mammals,* p. 129; fall, 1996, Peter D. Sieruta, review of *Everyday Machines We Take for Granted,* p. 350; Spring 1998, Eric Hinsdale, review of *Insects and Spiders.*

Junior Bookshelf, December, 1988, review of *Tree,* p. 298.

Kirkus Reviews, July 1, 1997, review of *Insects and Spiders,* p. 1027.

Library Journal, November 1, 2001, Deborah Emerson, review of *Animal: The Definitive Visual Guide to the World's Wildlife,* p. 80.

Los Angeles Times Book Review, December 11, 1994, Martin Zimmerman, review of *Seashore,* p. 12.

Magpies, September 1993, Lynn Babbage, review of *Light,* p. 37; September 1993, Malanie Guile, review of *Flowers,* p. 35.

New Scientist, May 23, 1992, Maggie McDonald, review of *How Nature Works,* p. 40.

Publishers Weekly, April 29, 1998, review of *Bird,* p. 76; October 1, 2001, review of *Animal,* p. 47; December 17, 2001, review of *The Kingfisher Illustrated Dinosaur Encyclopedia,* p. 93.

Reading Today, June, 2001, Lynne T. Burke, review of *Ocean Watch,* and *Earth Watch,* p. 32.

School Library Journal, December, 1988, Steve Matthews, review of *Tree,* p. 124; May, 1989, Joy Daentl, review of *Bird,* p. 23; January, 1990, Louise Sherman, review of *Plant,* p. 110; December, 1991, Diane Nunn, review of *How Nature Works,* p. 37; May, 1992, Margaret Hagel, review of *Machines and How They Work,* p. 119; August, 1992, Tina Smith Entwistle, review of *Insects,* p. 150; November, 1992, Steve Englefried, review of *Light,* p. 127; February, 1993, Steve Matthews, review of *Flowers,* p. 96; August, 1994, Jonathan Betz-Zall, review of *Life,* p. 171; November, 1994, Lauren Mayer, review of *The Dictionary of Nature,* p. 134; February, 1995, Danita Nichols, review of *The Kingfisher Illustrated Animal Encyclopedia,* p. 128; February, 1996, Lauren Mayer, review of *The Concise Encyclopedia of the Human Body,* p. 124; September, 2000, Peter Fowler, review of *Reader's Digest Book of Amazing Facts,* p. 112; February, 2001, John Peters, review of *The Kingfisher Illustrated Animal Encyclopedia,* p. 78; June, 2001, Patricia Manning, review of *Earth Watch,* p. 164; February, 2002, Tina Hudak, review of *Animal,* p. 83.

Science Books and Films, January/February, 1989, Theresa Knapp, review of *Bird,* p. 167; May/June, 1990, Yvonne Heather Burry, review of *Plant,* p. 258; October, 1994, Johnes K. Moore, review of *Seashore,* p. 209; December, 1994, Lucia Anderson, review of *Life,* p. 267.

Science Teacher, February, 1989, Ronald Giese, review of *Bird,* p. 74.

Scientific American, December, 1989, Phillip Morrison, review of *Bird,* p. 152.

Teacher Librarian, October, 1999, Jessica Higgs, review of *Forest,* pp. 60-61.

Voice of Youth Advocates, February, 1992, Judy Fink, review of *How Nature Works,* p. 391; February, 1996, Terri Evans, review of *Encyclopedia of the Human Body,* p. 408; September 1999, Jessica Higgs, review of *Forest,* p. 60.

Wilson Library Bulletin, February, 1995, Charlene Strickland, review of *The Kingfisher Illustrated Animal Encyclopedia,* p. 93.

OTHER

Dorling Kindersley Online, http://www.dk.com/ (March 29, 2002), interview with David Burnie.

Kosmoi: Life & Nature, http://kosmoi.com/ (January 8, 2002), review of *Animal.**

C

CANINO, Frank 1939(?)-

PERSONAL: Born c. 1939 in Chicago, IL; son of Peter (a maintenance worker) and Angeline (a homemaker; maiden name, Restivo) Canino. *Ethnicity:* "Italian." *Education:* Loyola University of Chicago, B.S. (with honors), 1960; Catholic University of America, M.A., 1962; attended Université Laval, 1966-67. *Politics:* "Cheerful anarchy." *Religion:* "Ecumenical." *Hobbies and other interests:* Modern poetry, music, opera, art, workout exercises.

ADDRESSES: Home—666 West Ferry St., Unit 30, Buffalo, NY 14222-1625; and 124-680 Queen's Quay W., Toronto, Ontario M5V 2Y9, Canada; fax: 416-260-8516. *E-mail*—fcanino@compuserve.com.

CAREER: Playwright, director, actor, stage manager, and teacher. English teacher at a private academy in New York, 1962-63; St. Francis Xavier University, Antigonish, Nova Scotia, lecturer in acting and communications, 1963-66; freelance theatrical director and teacher in Ontario and eastern provinces of Canada, 1967-69; University of Ottawa, Ottawa, Ontario, associate professor of fine arts, 1969-72; University of Toronto, Scarborough College, Westhill, Ontario, co-artist-in-residence, 1975-76; York University, Downsview, Ontario, lecturer in theater, 1978-79; Centennial College, continuing education teacher, 1986-87; George Brown College, teacher of English and liberal studies, 1988-90, continuing education teacher, 1989-94. Participant in Peter Brook's International Workshop and Ronconi Seminar, both Paris, France, and Grotowski Theater Laboratorium, Wroclaw, Poland, all 1972-73; Pacun Peras Productions, story editor and as-

sociate producer of short films and feature films, 1994-97. Director of plays at theaters in Canada and the United States, including Comus Theater Workshop, Theater Fountainhead, Mermaid Theater, Acadia Playhouse, Neptune Theater, and Arlington Opera Society in Virginia. Has given readings, including appearances in New York City at Lark Theater and LaMama Galleria.

MEMBER: Literary Managers and Dramaturges of the Americas, Playwrights' Union of Canada, Canadian Actors' Equity Association, Association of Canadian Television and Radio Artists, Dramatists Guild, Association of Italian-Canadian Writers.

AWARDS, HONORS: First prize in one-act competition, Ottawa Little Theater, 1994, for *Stand Up!! or Leontyne and Me;* first prizes, Center Theater Ensemble and Hudson River Classics, and finalist, Midwest Theatre Network, all 1998, all for *The Swan Queen and the Radical Faerie;* finalist, Paul Green Playwrights Prize, 1998, and South Carolina Playwrights' Festival, 2000, both for *The Angelina Project;* third price, Chicano Latino Literary contest, 1998, for *The Tango Ladies Dance On;* finalist, Twisted Machismo Festival competition, Wharf Rat Theater, 1999; grants from Toronto Arts Council, 1995 and 1998, and from Canada Council, Tagliere Fund, and Banff Radio Drama Workshop.

WRITINGS:

PLAYS

NightWalking: Ladder Play No. 7 (one-act; produced by Synchronicity Theater Group, New York, NY, 1994), published in *Collages and Bricolages,* 2001.

The Swan Queen Monologue, produced at New Voices Workshop, New York, NY, 1994, at LaMama Galleria, 1997, and at Myriad Arts Festival, 1999.

The Swan Queen in the Lilac Garden (radio play), produced in Banff, Ontario, Canada, at Banff Radio Drama Workshop, 1994.

"A" and "J": Ladder Play No. 4 (one-act), produced in Toronto, Ontario, Canada, at Festival of Original Theater, University of Toronto, 1995.

Wally Loves Claude, Claude Loves Wally (play and television script), produced in a staged reading in Hollywood, CA, at Attic Theater, 1995.

All Dressed Up and Nowhere to Go, produced by Live Sparks Productions, 1995, produced in New York at Expanded Arts, 1997.

Gentlemen, Be Seated (one-act), produced in a workshop at Stephenville Brave New Works, 1995.

Apostrofee Funk: Performance Artist in Spite of Himself (one-act), produced in Toronto, Ontario, Canada, at Summerworks Festival, 1995.

There Goes the Neighbourhood (one-act), published in *CAN: BAIA Newsletter,* 1996.

Everybody Is Sexy for Somebody, produced by Live Sparks Productions, 1995, produced in New York at Theatrix-Shorts Festival, 2000.

The Swan Queen and the Radical Faerie (stage version), produced in New York, NY, at Lark Theater, 1999.

The Morning Vigil, performed in a reading at Shenandoah International Playwrights Retreat, 1999.

China Boy and Gringo (one-act), published in *Lamia Ink! Anthology,* 2000.

The Angelina Project (produced in Los Angeles, CA, at Chance Theater, 2000), Guernica Editions (Tonawanda, NY), 2000.

Other plays include *Up the Canal!* (full-length), commissioned by Theater Ontario Commission; *Lotte and Bert* (full-length), Comus Music Theater Workshop; *The Tango Ladies Dance On* (full-length); and *Stand Up!! or Leontyne and Me: Ladder Play No. 5* (one-act), produced at Toronto Fringe Festival and other venues, including the Festival of Original Theater Cabaret at the University of Toronto. Children's plays include *Afashe,* produced at Ontario Youtheatre, North Bay, Ontario; and *Collage No. 1,* produced at Confederation Centre, Prince Edward Island.

Also translator and adapter of plays, including *No Trifling with Love,* produced at the University of British Columbia, Vancouver; *Spoon River Anthology* and

Age of Darkness, produced at the Asolo Festival, FL; *Collage No. 2,* produced at University of Ottawa, Ottawa, Ontario; *First Canto: Wordflesh,* produced at Carleton University, Montreal, Quebec; and *Wakefield Cycle.* Also author of videotaped dramas, including *As the Worm Turns, Half-Real, Half-Dream,* and *Watch My Show of Hands.*

Author of column "The Square Deal." Contributor to periodicals, including *Toronto Life, Scene Changes,* and *Canadian Theater Review.* Contributing editor for *Arcadian Rag.*

WORK IN PROGRESS: Baby Makes Three, about two gay men who adopt a baby; *The Morning Vigil,* about a young Franciscan seminarian who enters Auschwitz and "fails to be a hero or a saint."

SIDELIGHTS: Though well acquainted with theater through his work as a stage manager, director, and actor, Frank Canino came to playwriting relatively late in his career. He had written and produced several plays in the 1990s when a Toronto producer urged him to read an article about an Italian immigrant in Canada who murdered her abusive husband in 1911. From that research came what is perhaps Canino's best-known work, *The Angelina Project,* which had its debut in 2000. The author, according to Eric Marchese in an online *My Orange County* article, uses the murder case as the basis "for an intriguing mystery that's also part treatise on social issues." The play is set in the present day as well as the past, as an Italian-American woman explores the murder case for her thesis and finds that the patterns of spousal abuse hit closer to home than she had expected. As Canino told *CA,* the protagonist "struggles to rediscover her Italian past while simultaneously trying to be thoroughly modern. As she researches her thesis on the abuse of immigrant women, she stumbles across a family secret which proves that secrets and lies shape your life, even when you don't realize it."

Canino further told *CA:* "'Between two worlds' is the best way of describing my career. Though born in Chicago, I have spent most of my life in Canada. As a dual citizen, I've lived between two cultures long enough to create an aesthetic schizophrenia that informs all my work. My plays are filled with people caught between different ways of living.

"In *The Swan Queen and the Radical Faerie,* a retired ballerina from a very conservative artistic milieu locks horns with a young stepson who challenges all of her values. She loves designer clothes and Brahms. He's an artist and gay activist with AIDS. They can't stand each other, of course. Then she gets cancer, and he gets sick again. Together they smoke pot, go to meditation class, and try to figure out how to live well in the time they have left. It's a comedy under a shadow.

"*The Tango Ladies Dance On* (a collaboration with South American actresses) is about two dancers from widely different social classes who eke out a living in a cheap tango bar. During the course of one evening, the immigrants go through assimilation . . . nostalgia . . . and then serene despair—an experience that I can well attest to as a person with feet firmly planted on both sides of a border.

"Coincidentally, I have worked in four languages: English, French, Spanish, and American Sign Language. If you include my stay at Peter Brook's theater workshop in Paris, you might add Orghast/bird language. At one point I even became fluent enough in German to consider relocating to that country, though I learned it while working at Grotowski's Theater Laboratorium in Poland. This is not to forget the intense six weeks I spent living in Ghana in Africa. It was the turning point of my life, living on no money and absorbing another culture that turned my Catholic/European heritage on its head.

"All this accounts for the wide range of my material in substance and form. It also explains why writing came late in my career, and only after I had spent considerable time as a teacher (from university down to primary grades), a stage manager (in English and French), an actor (commercials to 'movie of the week' to *Tamara* in its Toronto stage premiere before it went on to international fame), and a director (operas to avant-garde, Shakespeare to children's theater). In the first years since I've focused exclusively on writing, I picked up thirty citations for my plays, plus readings and workshops across Canada and the United States. My computer now holds full-length and one-act scripts, films, monologues, revue sketches, song lyrics, and even some award-winning one-minute plays.

"But I don't have a clear philosophy and method of writing. I wake up some mornings with a nucleus of a story in my imagination. It grows and grows all over me—like a second skin that I have to peel off and put together as a script. I really don't have much choice."

BIOGRAPHICAL AND CRITICAL SOURCES:

OTHER

Los Angeles Times CalendarLive, http://www. calendarlive.com/ (June 22, 2001), Mike Boehm, "Live Theater with a Grisly Death at Its Heart."

My Orange County, http://myoc.com/ (June 22, 2001), Eric Marchese, "'Angelina' Probes Brutality, Humanity."

Playwrights' Union of Canada Web site, http://www. puc.ca/ (June 17, 2000).

Shenandoah Playwrights International Web site, http:// www.shenanarts.org/ (August 13, 2001), "SPI Alum Buzz."

*   *   *

CARREY, James Eugene 1962- (Jim Carrey)

PERSONAL: Born January 17, 1962, in Jacksons Point (some sources say Newmarket or Toronto), Ontario, Canada; son of Percy (a musician and accountant) and Kathleen (a homemaker) Carrey; married Melissa Womer (an actress), 1986 (one source says 1987; divorced, 1995); married Lauren Holly (an actress), September 23, 1996 (divorced, July 29, 1997); children: (first marriage) Jane. *Hobbies and other interests:* Alternative rock music, drawing, watching dramatic films, tennis, reading self-help books.

ADDRESSES: Agent—United Talent Agency, 9560 Wilshire Blvd., Fifth Floor, Beverly Hills, CA 90212.

CAREER: Actor, comedian, and writer. Standup comedian, 1979—. Titan Wheels (factory), Toronto, Ontario, Canada, former laborer.

Film appearances include *All In Good Taste,* Manesco Films, 1983; *Copper Mountain,* Rose and Ruby Productions, 1983; *Finders Keepers,* Warner Bros., 1984; *Once Bitten,* Samuel Goldwyn Company, 1985; *Peggy Sue Got Married,* TriStar, 1986; *The Dead Pool,* Warner Bros., 1988; *Pink Cadillac,* Warner Bros., 1989; *Earth Girls Are Easy,* Vestron, 1989; *High Strung,* Summa, 1991; *The Itsy Bitsy Spider,* Paramount, 1992; *Ace Ventura: Pet Detective,* Warner Bros., 1994; *Dumb and Dumber,* New Line Cinema, 1994; *The Mask,* New Line Cinema, 1994; *Ace Ventura: When Nature Calls,* Warner Bros., 1995; *Batman Forever,* Warner Bros., 1995; *The Mask's Revenge,* 1996; *The Cable Guy,* Columbia/TriStar, 1996; *Liar Liar,* Universal, 1997; *Simon Birch,* Buena Vista, 1998; *The Truman Show,* Paramount, 1998; *Man on the Moon,* Universal, 1999; *The Incredible Mr. Limpet,* Warner Bros., 1999; *Me, Myself & Irene,* Twentieth Century-Fox, 2000; *How the Grinch Stole Christmas,* Universal, 2000; *The Majestic,* 2001; *Laughing Out Loud: America's Funniest Comedians,* 2001; *Bruce Almighty,* 2003; *Children of the Dust Bowl,* 2004; *Over the Hedge* (voice only) 2005.

Television appearances include series *The Duck Factory,* NBC, 1984; and *In Living Color,* Fox, 1990-94. Television work includes series' character creator *Ace Ventura: Pet Detective,* CBS and Nickelodeon, 1995. Television appearances include movies *Introducing . . . Janet,* CBC, 1983; *Mike Hammer: Murder Takes All,* CBS, 1989; and *Doing Time on Maple Drive,* Fox, 1992. Television appearances include specials *Jim Carrey: The Un-Natural Act,* Showtime, 1991; *Tom Arnold: The Naked Truth,* HBO, 1991; *The Comedy Store's 20th Birthday,* NBC, 1992; *Comic Relief V,* HBO, 1992; *A Tribute to Sam Kinison,* Fox, 1993; *The Barbara Walters Special,* ABC, 1995; *Comedy Central Spotlight: Jim Carrey,* Comedy Central, 1995; *A Comedy Salute to Andy Kaufman,* NBC, 1995; *Riddle Me This: Why Is Batman Forever?,* ABC, 1995; *Canned Ham: The Cable Guy,* Comedy Central, 1996; *In My Life,* Bravo, 1998; *AFI's 100 Years . . . 100 Stars,* CBS, 1999; *Andy Kaufman's Really Big Show,* Arts and Entertainment, 1999; *AFI's 100 Years, 100 Laughs: America's Funniest Movies,* CBS, 2000; *Canned Ham: Me, Myself & Irene,* Comedy Central, 2000; *America: A Tribute to Heroes,* 2001; *Concert for New York City,* 2001; *Comedy Store: The E! True Hollywood Story,* 2001; and *Hollywood Salutes Nicholas Cage: An American Cinematheque Tribute,* 2002. Also appeared in specials broadcast on MTV.

Appearances on episodic television include "Jerry Lewis Week," *Buffalo Bill,* NBC, 1984; *The Dennis Miller Show,* syndicated, 1992; *The Tonight Show Starring Johnny Carson,* NBC, 1994; "The Mask," *Space Ghost Coast to Coast,* The Cartoon Network, 1994; "Le livre d'histoire," *Space Ghost Coast to Coast,* The Cartoon Network, 1995; *The Life and Death of Sam Kinison: The E! True Hollywood Story,* E! Entertainment Television, 1996; *Saturday Night Live,* NBC, 1996; *The Entertainment Business,* Bravo, 1998; *Oprah,* syndicated, 1998; "Flip," *The Larry Sanders Show,* HBO, 1998; "Rodney Dangerfield: Respect at Last," *Biography,* Arts and Entertainment, 1998; *Larry King Live,* CNN, 1999; and "Nicholas Cage: Wild at Heart," *Biography,* Arts and Entertainment, 1999. Appeared in *The Brady Bunch,* ABC; *Sesame Street,* PBS; and episodes of other series.

Appearances in awards presentation ceremonies include *A Salute to Steven Spielberg,* NBC, 1995; *The 9th Annual American Comedy Awards,* 1995; *The Blockbuster Entertainment Awards,* 1996; *A Salute to Clint Eastwood,* ABC, 1996; *The 68th Annual Academy Awards,* ABC, 1996; *The VH1 1997 Fashion Awards,* VH1, 1997; *The 1998 MTV Movie Awards,* MTV, 1998; *The 24th Annual People's Choice Awards,* 1998; *The 1999 MTV Movie Awards,* MTV, 1999; *The 71st Annual Academy Awards Presentation,* ABC, 1999; *The 2000 MTV Video Music Awards,* MTV, 2000.

AWARDS, HONORS: MTV Movie Award nomination, best comedic performance, 1994, Blockbuster Entertainment Awards, favorite actor—comedy on video, and favorite male newcomer on video, both 1995, all for *Ace Ventura: Pet Detective;* Golden Globe Award nomination, best performance by an actor in a motion picture—comedy/musical, MTV Movie Award nominations, best comedic performance and best dance sequence (with Cameron Diaz), all 1995, for *The Mask;* MTV Movie Awards, best comedic performance and best kiss (with Lauren Holly), and MTV Movie Award nomination (with Jeff Daniels), best on-screen duo, all 1995, for *Dumb and Dumber;* MTV Movie Awards, best male performance and best comedic performance, and MTV Movie Award nomination (with Sophie Okonedo), best kiss, all 1996, for *Ace Ventura: When Nature Calls;* MTV Movie Award nomination, best villain, 1996, for *Batman Forever;* MTV Movie Awards, best comedic performance and best villain, and MTV Movie Award nomination (with Matthew Broderick), best fight, all 1997, for *The Cable Guy;* named one of the "top 100 movie stars of all time," *Empire* magazine, 1997; Showman of the Year Award, 1998; MTV Movie Award, best comedic performance, Blockbuster Entertainment Award, favorite actor—comedy, and Golden Globe Award nomination, best performance by an actor in a motion picture—comedy/

musical, all 1998, for *Liar Liar;* Golden Globe Award, best performance by an actor in a motion picture—drama, MTV Movie Award, best male performance, Saturn Award nomination, Academy of Science Fiction, Horror and Fantasy Films, best actor, American Comedy Award nomination, funniest actor in a motion picture (leading role), Blockbuster Entertainment Award nomination, favorite actor—drama, and Chicago Film Critics Association Award nomination, best actor, all 1999, for *The Truman Show;* American Comedy Award nomination, funniest male guest appearance in a television series, 1999, for "Flip," an episode of *The Larry Sanders Show;* named one of the "100 greatest entertainers," *Entertainment Weekly,* 1999; Boston Society of Film Critics Award, best actor, Toronto Film Critics Association Award runner-up, best male performance, and Online Film Critics Society Award nomination, best actor, all 1999, Golden Globe Award, best performance by an actor in a motion picture—comedy/musical, Screen Actors Guild Award nomination, outstanding performance by a male actor in a leading role, Golden Satellite Award nomination, best performance by an actor in a motion picture, comedy, or musical, MTV Movie Award nomination, best male performance, American Comedy Award nomination, funniest actor in a motion picture (leading role), and Canadian Comedy Award nomination, film—performance male, all 2000, all for *Man on the Moon;* ShoWest Award, National Association of Theatre Owners (NATO), male star of the year, 2000; received a star on the Hollywood Walk of Fame, 2000.

WRITINGS:

Jim Carrey: The Un-Natural Act (teleplay), Showtime, 1991.
(With Jack Bernstein and Tom Shadyac) *Ace Ventura: Pet Detective* (screenplay), Warner Bros., 1994.

Wrote teleplays (with others) for *In Living Color,* Fox, 1990-94. Created material for characters for *Ace Ventura: When Nature Calls,* Warner Bros., 1995, and created character for cartoon series *Ace Ventura: Pet Detective,* CBS and Nickelodeon, 1995. Contributed to the writing of the video *Laughing Out Loud: America's Funniest Comedians,* 2001.

ADAPTATIONS: Ace Ventura: Pet Detective was adapted as a novel by Marc A. Cerasini, Random House (New York, NY), 1995.

SIDELIGHTS: Though he had already attracted attention within the Los Angeles stand-up comedy scene, and had won a national fan base with his role on *In Living Color* (1990-94), comedian Jim Carrey truly emerged as a superstar with *Ace Ventura: Pet Detective* (1994). The screenplay, which he cowrote with Jack Bernstein and director Tom Shadyac, concerns a Florida detective whose job, as the title implies, is to solve crimes involving animals. Malcolm Johnson in the *Hartford Courant* called the story "clearly inspired," and Mal Vincent of the *Virginian-Pilot* predicted that *Ace Ventura* "may well become the successor to 'Pee Wee's Big Adventure' and the original 'Wayne's World' as a comedy movie that is so delightfully offbeat that it can be embraced by everyone across age and hipster levels."

Indeed, the film did spawn a sequel, *Ace Ventura: When Nature Calls,* as well as a TV cartoon series, *Ace Ventura: Pet Detective.* (Carrey created characters for both of these.) But that was only the beginning of the successes to which Carrey's career would rise in the next few years as he became one of Hollywood's most sought-after performers. He had come a long way from his home in Ontario, where, after a happy childhood in which he had enjoyed a reputation—not surprisingly—as the class clown, he worked in a factory to help support his beleaguered family.

Carrey held on to his comic gift and eventually worked his way up through the Toronto stand-up scene before moving to Hollywood. There he underwent a major change in his act, switching from impersonations to the development of original characters. His talent for creating his own comic personae would stand him in good stead on *In Living Color,* where Carrey—the only white male in a mostly African-American ensemble—developed such memorable figures as female bodybuilder Vera de Milo, pyromaniac Fire Marshall Bill, and the dysfunctional Grandpa Jack McGee.

BIOGRAPHICAL AND CRITICAL SOURCES:

BOOKS

Knelman, Martin, *Jim Carrey: The Joker Is Wild,* Firefly (Buffalo, NY), 2000.

Lipschultz, Andy, *How the Grinch Stole Hollywood: The Making of the Movie Starring Jim Carrey as the Grinch,* Random House (New York, NY), 2000.

Newsmakers 1995, Gale (Detroit, MI), 1995.

Siegel, Scott, and Barbara Siegel, *The Jim Carrey Scrapbook,* Carol Publishing Group (Secaucus, NJ), 1995.

PERIODICALS

Hartford Courant (Hartford, CT), February 4, 1994, Malcolm Johnson, review of *Ace Ventura: Pet Detective,* p. B3.

Los Angeles Times, February 4, 1994, Chris Willman, review of *Ace Ventura: Pet Detective,* p. 6.

Seattle Times, November 10, 1995, Doug Thomas, review of *Ace Ventura 2: When Nature Calls,* p. G1.

Virginian-Pilot, February 5, 1994, Mal Vincent, review of *Ace Ventura: Pet Detective,* p. B2.

OTHER

The Jim Carrey Area, http://www.geocities.com/Hollywood/9090/ (October 22, 2002).

Jim Carrey Online, http://www.jimcarreyonline.com/ (October 22, 2002).*

*　　　*　　　*

CARREY, Jim
See CARREY, James Eugene

*　　　*　　　*

CARTER, Ben
See BEN AMMI

*　　　*　　　*

CARTER, Dixie 1939-

PERSONAL: Born May 25, 1939, in McLemoresville, TN; daughter of Halbert Leroy (a retail businessman and realtor) and Virginia (Hillsman) Carter; married Arthur Carter (a businessman), 1967 (divorced, 1977); married George Hearn (an actor), 1977 (divorced, 1979); married Hal Holbrook (an actor and director), May 27, 1984; children: (first marriage) Ginna, Mary-Dixie.

ADDRESSES: Agent—International Creative Management, 8942 Wilshire Blvd., Beverly Hills, CA 90211-1934.

CAREER: Singer and actress on stage, television, and in film.

Stage appearances include *Carousel,* Front Street Theatre, Memphis, TN, 1961; *A Winter's Tale,* New York Shakespeare Festival, 1963; *Pal Joey,* Circle in the Square, New York City, 1976; *Jesse and the Bandit Queen,* New York Shakespeare Festival, 1976; *Fathers and Sons,* New York Shakespeare Festival, 1978; *Taken in Marriage,* 1979; *A Coupla White Chicks Sitting around Talking,* Astor Place Theatre, New York City, 1980; *Buried Inside Extra,* Martinson Hall, Public Theatre, New York City, then Royal Court Theatre, both 1983; *Master Class,* Broadway production, 1997; *A Woman of No Importance,* Shakespeare Theatre, Washington, DC, 1998. Also appeared in *The King and I, Carousel,* and *The Merry Widow,* all at the Lincoln Center for the Performing Arts, New York City; appeared in *Sextet; A Streetcar Named Desire; Oklahoma;* and *Kiss Me Kate.*

Film appearances include *Going Berserk,* 1983; *We Met on the Vineyard,* Menemsha Entertainment, 1999; *Wallowitch & Ross: This Moment,* 1999; and *The Big Day,* 1999.

Television series appearances include *The Edge of Night,* CBS, 1974-76; *On Our Own,* CBS, 1977-78; *Out of the Blue,* 1979; *Filthy Rich,* CBS, 1982-83; *Diff'rent Strokes,* NBC, 1984-85; *Designing Women,* CBS, 1986-93; *Ladies Man,* CBS, 1999-2000; and *Family Law,* CBS, 1999. Also appeared in *The Doctors,* late 1970s. Episodic television appearances include "Hallie," *Bret Maverick,* NBC, 1982; "The Pretty Prisoner," *Best of the West,* 1982; "The Face of Fear," *Quincy,* 1982; "Lilacs, Mr. Maxwell," *The Greatest American Hero,* 1982; *Reading Rainbow,* PBS, 1993; "Fox on the Range," *Crazy Like a Fox,* 1986; *Christy,* 1994; "Murder in the Courthouse," *Diagnosis Murder,* CBS, 1995; "The Mother of All Gwens," *Fired Up,* NBC, 1997; and "Honey, I Shrunk the Turkey," *Fired Up,* NBC, 1997.

Television miniseries appearances include *Gambler V: Playing for Keeps*, CBS, 1994; *Dazzle*, 1995; *Gone in the Night*, CBS, 1996. Television movie appearances include *OHMS*, 1980; *The Killing of Randy Webster*, 1981; and *A Perry Mason Mystery: The Case of the Lethal Lifestyle*, NBC, 1994. Appearances on TV pilots include *Morning Glory, S.C.*, CBS, 1996; and *Ladies Man*, 1999.

Appearances on TV specials include *The 41st Annual Emmy Awards*, 1989; *Macy's Thanksgiving Day Parade*, 1989; *US Magazine—Live at the Emmys!*, 1989; *Bob Hope's 1990 Christmas Show from Bermuda*, NBC, 1990; *The Designing Women Special: Their Finest Hour*, CBS, 1990; *Face to Face with Connie Chung*, 1990; *The 44th Annual Tony Awards*, 1990; *Soap Opera Awards*, 1990; *Circus of the Stars #16*, CBS, 1991; *The 43rd Annual Primetime Emmy Awards Presentation*, 1991; *The Ninth Annual Soap Opera Awards*, 1993; *Cabaret*, 1994; *The Kentucky Derby*, ABC, 1996; *The Walt Disney World Very Merry Christmas Parade*, ABC, 1996; *The 51st Annual Tony Awards*, CBS, 1997; *Southern Living: Our Holiday Memories*, HGTV, 1998; *The Washington Opera Production of "La Rondine,"* PBS, 1999; *The 54th Annual Tony Awards*, CBS, 2000; *The Great American History Quiz: Heroes and Villains*, History Channel, 2000; and *Intimate Portrait: Dixie Carter*, Lifetime, 2001.

Recordings include (albums) *Dixie Carter Sings John Wallowitch Live at the Carlyle*, 1991; (videos) *Dixie Carter's Unworkout*, MCA/Universal, 1992; and *Dixie Carter's Yoga for You: Unworkout II*, MCA/Universal, 1994.

AWARDS, HONORS: Distinguished Achievement Award in Creative and Performing Arts, University of Memphis, 1993.

WRITINGS:

Trying to Get to Heaven: Opinions of a Tennessee Talker, Simon & Schuster (New York, NY), 1996.

Recorded an audio version of *Trying to Get to Heaven: Opinions of a Tennessee Talker*, Simon & Schuster Audio (New York, NY), 1996.

SIDELIGHTS: Though she made a name for herself on television in the 1980s with the television series *Designing Women*, in her book *Trying to Get to Heaven: Opinions of a Tennessee Talker* actress Dixie Carter says almost nothing about the highly successful show in which she starred opposite Delta Burke. Nor is the book an autobiography, though reviewers often approached it as such; rather, as the title indicates, it is a collection of Carter's musings on a variety of subjects, ranging from yoga to gardening, from facelifts to housework, and from religion to table manners.

Carter's name recognition inspired confidence from her publisher, Simon & Schuster, which printed 100,000 hardback copies of the book. She later told the Memphis, Tennessee, *Commercial Appeal*, that she already had the publishing offer before she came up with the subject. The result, written without the aid of a ghostwriter, reads like "a comforting bonding session with your mother," according to Miriam Longino of the *Atlanta Journal-Constitution*. Joanne Kaufman in *People* described it as "a folksy, generally endearing disquisition" on a variety of subjects. Cataloging some of the items of advice offered in the book, Jill Johnson Piper of the *Commercial Appeal* wrote that "Tastelessness on television, fax machines in the bedroom, and wedding guests who wear black"—three things Carter condemns—"are among the many sermonettes represented in *Trying to Get to Heaven*."

The book contains little either about *Designing Women* or the celebrated feud between Burke and creator Linda Bloodworth-Thomason; nor is there the usual dishing of dirt so common in Hollywood celebrity books. Carter is also sparing in discussion of her personal life, including her marriage to actor Hal Holbrook, but she is frank about her facelifts, and discusses her early years in New York's Greenwich Village. Eschewing the strictly autobiographical format, Carter told the *Commercial Appeal*, "I'm not exactly Winston Churchill. I don't see any point in the glut of autobiographies written by people who, frankly, did not win the Second World War."

BIOGRAPHICAL AND CRITICAL SOURCES:

PERIODICALS

Atlanta Journal-Constitution, December 14, 1995, Miriam Longino, review of *Trying to Get to Heaven: Opinions of a Tennessee Talker*, p. G7.

Commercial Appeal (Memphis, TN), December 17, 1995, Jill Johnson Piper, review of *Trying to Get to Heaven,* p. G1.

People Weekly, February 12, 1996, Joanne Kaufman, review of *Trying to Get to Heaven,* p. 35.

Publishers Weekly, November 6, 1995, Genevieve Stuttaford, review of *Trying to Get to Heaven,* p. 77.

USA Today, January 2, 1996, Nanci Hellmich, "Celebrity Weight-Watching: 'Yoga Does It All' for Actress Dixie Carter," p. D6.

OTHER

Cabaret: dixiecarter.com, http://www.dixiecarter.com/ (October 22, 2002).*

*   *   *

CASON, Ann 1942-

PERSONAL: Born May 30, 1942, in Hutchinson, KS; daughter of Clifford Emerson and Mary Lois (Lamont) Adams; married Fred Cason, September 12, 1975 (divorced, 1982); companion of Jack Bodner; children: (with Cason) Eric Winn. *Education:* University of Arizona, B.A., 1964. *Religion:* Buddhist.

ADDRESSES: Home and office—2165 Southwest Main, Portland, OR 97205. *E-mail*—acason@together.net.

CAREER: Home health care professional. Founder and operator of a home-care agency for the aged and dying, Boulder, CO, beginning c. 1970s; Circles of Care (support agency for elders and families), director.

WRITINGS:

Circles of Care: How to Set up Quality Home Care for Our Elders, Shambhala Publications (Boston, MA), 2001.

WORK IN PROGRESS: Changing Places, a memoir "focused on aging."

SIDELIGHTS: Ann Cason told *CA:* "The urge to write came upon me early, but I didn't start until my meditation master, Chogyam Trungpa, told me to write a book about the care of old and dying people. He died in 1987. Within months I sat down and wrote the first draft of *Circles of Care,* which I then called *Entering an Old Person's World.*

"The book was rejected by the first agent and publisher. I rewrote and sent it out again. Thus began a journey that included increasing my understanding of myself and of the discipline required to write. Sitting down to write is learning to trust yourself and not losing heart. In my case it meant getting out of my own way. I wanted so much to convey the art of being human regarding the care and appreciation of the very old without making it philosophical or falling back on jargon. I knew I had to convey practical information, but at the same time I wanted vignettes to open a window into the elder's world. Since the subject could be heavy and ponderous, I wanted the writing to have a light touch."

*   *   *

CHABAL, Patrick (Enri) 1951-

PERSONAL: Born April 29, 1951, in Taroudant, Morocco; immigrated to England, 1977; son of Eric and Josette C. (Mondain) Chabal; married Farzana Shaikh, August 27, 1977; children: Emile. *Education:* Harvard University, B.A. (government), 1972, Columbia University, M.A. (international relations) and certificate in African studies, 1976, M.Phil. (political science), 1977, Cambridge University, England, Ph.D. (African history and politics), 1981.

ADDRESSES: Office—King's College, London, Strand, London WC2R 2LS, England. *E-mail*—patrick.chabal@kcl.ac.uk.

CAREER: Cambridge University, Cambridge, England, research fellow, 1981-83; University of East Anglia, Norwich, England, lecturer, 1983-84; King's College, London, England, lecturer, 1984-90, reader, 1990-94, professor of Lusophone African studies, 1994—, head of Portuguese department, 1990—; Africa Institute, Pretoria, South Africa, research fellow, 1993—. Visiting professor at Instituto Internacional de Estudios Avanzados, Caracas, Venezuela, 1984, École des Hautes Etudes en Sciences Sociales, Paris, France, 1991, Instituto Universitario Orientale, Naples, Italy, 1997, and University of Oporto, 1998; Africa Institute, Pretoria, South Africa, research fellow, 1993—, visiting fellow, 1995. Rockefeller Foundation, Bellagio, Italy, scholar-in-residence, 1991. President, Africa-Europe Group for Interdisciplinary Studies in Social Science and Humanities, 1996—. Advisor to institutions and publications in the United Kingdom, United States, France, Portugal, and Lusophone Africa; lecturer in United Kingdom, Portugal, France, Italy, Germany, United States, Mozambique and other African countries. Contributor to BBC external services.

MEMBER: Africa-Europe Group for Interdisciplinary Studies in Social Sciences and Humanities (president).

AWARDS, HONORS: Gulbenkian Foundation research grants, 1978, 1988; research fellowship, Clare Hall, Cambridge, 1981-83; British Academy research grants, 1986, 1988, 1990, 1995; London University Hayter Research Grant, 1986.

WRITINGS:

NONFICTION

Amilcar Cabral: Revolutionary Leadership and People's War, Cambridge University Press (New York, NY), 1983, second edition, Hurst (London, England), 2001.

(Editor) *Political Domination in Africa: Reflections on the Limits of Power,* Cambridge University Press (Cambridge, England, and New York, NY), 1986.

Power in Africa: An Essay in Political Interpretation, St. Martin's (New York, NY), 1992, reprinted with corrections, 1994.

Vozes Moçambicanas: Literatura e nacionalidade, Vega (Lisbon, Portugal), 1994.

(With others) *The Post-Colonial Literature of Lusophone Africa,* Northwestern University Press (Evanston, IL), 1996.

(With Jean-Pascal Daloz) *Africa Works: Disorder as Political Instrument,* Indiana University Press (Bloomington, IN), 1999.

(With Jean-Pascal Daloz) *L'Afrique est partie! Du désordre comme instrument politique,* Economica (Paris, France), 1999.

A History of Postcolonial Lusophone Africa, Hurst (London, England), 2001.

Contributor to books, including *Guide Constitutionnel et Politique des etats d'Afrique,* Economica (Paris, France), 1984; *Les littératures Africaines de langue Portugaise,* Fondation Calouste Gulbenkian (Paris, France), 1985; *Biographical Dictionary of Marxism,* Greenwood Press (Westport, CT), 1986; *Political Domination in Africa: Reflections on the Limits of Power,* Cambridge University Press, 1986; *Political Leaders of Contemporary Africa South of the Sahara: A Biographical Dictionary,* edited by Harvey Glickman, Greenwood Press (Westport, CT), 1992; *Portuguese, Brazilian and African Studies Presented to Clive Willis on His Retirement,* Aris & Philips, 1995; *Postcolonial Identities in Africa,* edited by Terence Ranger and Richard Werbner, Zed Press (London, England), 1996; *The Encyclopedia of Sub-Saharan Africa,* edited by John Middleton, Scribner's (New York, NY), 1997; and *Rewriting Africa: Toward a Renaissance or Collapse,* edited by Kurimoto Eisei, [Osaka, Japan].

Contributor of numerous articles to periodicals, including *West Africa, African Affairs, Canadian Journal of African Studies, Journal of Commonwealth and Comparative Politics, Cambridge Quarterly, Journal of Southern African Studies, Portuguese Studies, Africa Insight, African Languages and Cultures,* and *Nova Africa.* Co-editor, *Portuguese Studies,* 1984—, and *Politique Africaine,* 1996-99. Member of editorial board, *Nova Africa,* 1995—; member of "Conseil Scientifique," *Lusotopie.*

SIDELIGHTS: Patrick Chabal is a Moroccan-born English author and educator whose works focus on African history and politics. He is a professor of Lusophone African Studies and head of the Department of Portuguese and Brazilian Studies at King's College, London, where he has taught since 1984.

Chabal's first work, *Amilcar Cabral: Revolutionary Leadership and People's War,* published in 1983, is the first biography of African nationalist leader Cabral.

Cabral is widely considered a unique and remarkable leader for his role in the creation of an independence movement in Guinea-Bissau, a Portuguese colony in West Africa. Chabal was the leader of the African Party for the Independence of Portuguese Guinea and Cape Verde (PAIGC), "whose political and military struggles culminated, a few months after his assassination, in the fall of the Portuguese dictatorship and the independence of both colonies," summarized John D. Hargreaves in the *British Book News.*

Critical reaction to the work was largely positive. Paul H. Thomas in *Library Journal* lauded the work, calling it a "fascinating biography." Aaron Segal in *Africa Today,* however, disagreed. Segal felt that *Amilcar Cabral* "works best as an analysis of the movement he founded and the Guinean independence struggle. It is Cabral the man, though, that is missing." Segal concluded, "The definitive biography of Cabral remains to be written." Noting that Chabal was able to draw on a "dazzling array" of sources, including the private papers of Cabral, a *Choice* reviewer called the work "indispensable" for an understanding of Portuguese African history.

Chabal's next work, *Political Domination in Africa: Reflections on the Limits of Power,* is a collection of essays in which he "seeks to restore hallowed concepts from political theory—accountability, representation, and good government—to the discourse on contemporary African politics, while at the same time attending to the distinctive continuities of governance that Africans have inherited from their past," described Michael Bratton in *World Politics.* The collection explores the possibilities of democratic governments emerging in the nations of Africa. Bratton concluded that Chabal "achieves his goal of weaving an approach that is simultaneously philosophical and historical."

Power in Africa: An Essay in Political Interpretation is another interpretive work on politics in Africa. Noting the political crises in Africa—debt problems, widespread corruption, lagging development—Chabal "correctly believes that for too long, analysts have focused on the uniqueness of Africa rather than understanding the process as we do anywhere else in the world," summarized Patrick O'Meara in the *American Political Science Review.*

The work received mixed reviews. Michael Chege in the *Times Literary Supplement* called the work a "brave effort," but faulted it on a number of levels,

concluding: "Overall, the central arguments of the book are not easy to follow because of its opaque, long-winded and often abstract style. . . . But perhaps the greatest disappointment lies in Chabal's failure to deliver, after having promised to expose 'unreconstructed colonialists, racists and conservatives who felt that Africans were congenitally incapable of ruling themselves.'" O'Meara also found fault with the work but was less severe in his assessment, concluding: "While his [Chabal's] analytical framework is based on universal political concepts, in applying them Chabal ultimately emphasizes uniquely African predicaments and responses. Nonetheless, this is an important and provocative study."

Chabal continued his studies of African political culture with the publication of *Africa Works: Disorder as Political Instrument,* co-written with Jean-Pascal Daloz, a French scholar from the Institut d'Etudes Politiques in Bordeaux. *Africa Works* argues that "Africa is making a new political system out of disorder," explained a critic for the *Economist.* The critic found that the book offered "gloomy prognostications but no answers." Gail M. Gerhart in *Foreign Affairs,* however, called *Africa Works* one of the "most stimulating recent analyses of African realpolitik."

BIOGRAPHICAL AND CRITICAL SOURCES:

PERIODICALS

Africa Today, 4th quarter, 1984, Aaron Segal, review of *Amilcar Cabral,* p. 48.
American Political Science Review, September, 1993, Patrick O'Meara, review of *Power in Africa,* pp. 801-802.
British Book News, October, 1983, John D. Hargreaves, review of *Amilcar Cabral,* p. 655.
Choice, November, 1983, review of *Amilcar Cabral,* p. 488; October, 1995, Marion E. Doro, review of *Political Domination in Africa* and *Power in Africa,* pp. 245-257; November, 1999, review of *Africa Works,* p. 610.
Current History, May, 1987, review of *Political Domination in Africa,* p. 221.
Economist, August 7, 1999, review of *Africa Works,* p. 72.
Foreign Affairs, November-December, 1999, Gail M. Gerhart, review of *Africa Works,* p. 139.

Library Journal, June 1, 1983, Paul H. Thomas, review of *Amilcar Cabral,* pp. 1130-1131.

Times Literary Supplement, December 18, 1992, Michael Chege, review of *Power in Africa,* p. 10.

World Politics, April, 1989, Michael Bratton, "Beyond the State: Civil Society and Associational Life in Africa," pp. 407-430.

* * *

CHADWICK, Geoffrey 1950-
(Geoffrey Wall)

PERSONAL: Born July 10, 1950, in Cheshire, England; married; children: three sons, one daughter. *Education:* University of Sussex, B.A., 1972; St. Edmund Hall, Oxford, B.Phil., 1975.

ADDRESSES: Office—Department of English, University of York, YO1 5DD, England.

CAREER: York University, York, England, member of English department; writer.

MEMBER: Society of Authors, Association of University Teachers, Translators Association.

WRITINGS:

UNDER PSEUDONYM GEOFFREY WALL

(Translator) Gustave Flaubert, *Madame Bovary,* Penguin (London, England), 1992.

(Translator) Gustave Flaubert, *Selected Letters,* Penguin (London, England), 1999.

Flaubert: A Life (biography), Faber (London, England), 2001.

Contributor to periodicals, including *Literature and History* and *Cambridge Quarterly.*

SIDELIGHTS: Geoffrey Chadwick is a lecturer and writer whose publications—as Geoffrey Wall—include various works related to French novelist Gustave Flaubert. In 1992 Wall produced a translation of Flaubert's best-known novel, *Madame Bovary,* which constitutes a stylized account of one woman's undoing through her social aspirations. Roger Huss, writing in the *Times Literary Supplement,* noted Wall's success in "rendering Flaubert's meticulous verbal patterning," and he recommended Wall's translation to readers interested in a "lingering . . . reading."

Wall followed his edition of *Madame Bovary* with *Selected Letters,* a collection of Flaubert's correspondence. James Wood, in a *New Republic* critique, noted that Flaubert's letters serve as evidence of the novelist's enduring obsession with *The Temptation of St. Antony,* which he ceased writing in the late 1840s, then resumed and completed in the mid-1870s. "The book, which is written out in the form of a play, is silkily, weightlessly fantastical," Wood contended. "Yet Flaubert's letters reveal that this book was the marriage of his life, and the others were merely affairs."

Wall is also the author of *Flaubert: A Life,* a biography hailed by Maya Slater, in a *Times Literary Supplement* review, as a compelling accompaniment to Flaubert's actual writings. "The best insight into Flaubert . . . is still his work," Slater affirmed. "But this excellent biography brilliantly fleshes out the portrait." Another reviewer, writing in the *Economist,* declared, "Mr. Wall remains focused on the life; yet in doing so he manages to cast a good deal of light on the work." The *Economist* critic described Wall's own writing style as "relentlessly chatty" but added that *Flaubert* is nonetheless "an engaging and perceptive life of one of the defining figures of modern literature."

BIOGRAPHICAL AND CRITICAL SOURCES:

PERIODICALS

Economist, November 10, 2001, "No Larger than Life."

New Republic, January 18, 1999, James Wood, "Half-against Flaubert," p. 37.

Times Literary Supplement, October 22, 1993, Roger Huss, "Flaubert in English," p. 24; October 12, 2001, Maya Slater, "Recluse at Work," pp. 4-5.*

* * *

CHAON, Dan 1964-

PERSONAL: Name is pronounced "Shawn"; born June 11, 1964, in Omaha, NE; son of Earl D. (a construction worker) and Teresa N. (a homemaker; maiden name, Tallmage) Chaon; married Sheila M. Schwartz,

June 4, 1988; children: Philip, Paul. *Education:* Northwestern University, B.A., 1986; Syracuse University, M.A., 1990.

ADDRESSES: Home—2863 Meadowbrook Blvd., Cleveland Heights, OH 44118. *Office*—Oberlin College, 12 Rice Hall, Oberlin, OH 44074. *Agent*—Noah Lukeman, AMG/Renaissance, 140 West 57th St., New York, NY 10019. *E-mail*—chaon@buckeyeweb.com.

CAREER: Educator and writer. Cleveland State University, Cleveland, OH, lecturer, 1990-95, assistant professor, 1998; Ohio University, Athens, OH, assistant professor of English, 1995-97; Oberlin College, Oberlin, OH, visiting writer, 1998-2001, assistant professor, 2001—. Director of Cleveland State University Imagination Conference, 1998-2000.

AWARDS, HONORS: Individual artist grantee, Illinois Arts Council, 1988; Raymond Carver Memorial Award, Syracuse University, 1989; individual artist grantee, Ohio Arts Council, 1995; Fiction award, Chilcote Foundation, 1997; A.B. Guthrie, Jr. Short Fiction Award, 1997-98; Notable Book Award, American Library Association, and National Book Award nominee, both 2001, for *Among the Missing.*

WRITINGS:

Fitting Ends and Other Stories, Triquarterly Books/ Northwestern University Press (Evanston, IL), 1995.
Among the Missing, Ballantine Books (New York, NY), 2001.

Contributor to anthologies, including *Best American Short Stories,* 1996, and *The Pushcart Prize,* 2000 and 2002. Contributor to journals, including *Story, Ploughshares,* and *Triquarterly.*

WORK IN PROGRESS: You Remind Me of Me: A Novel, Ballantine Books, (New York, NY), forthcoming.

SIDELIGHTS: Dan Chaon is the author of two short story collections: *Fitting Ends and Other Stories* and *Among the Missing.* Chaon commented in an essay appearing in *Bold Type:* "A collection of short fiction is

often an odd, hybrid thing. The 'short story' as a species tends to be a solitary and lonely creature, and it often resists being corralled into a pack with its fellows. They are meant to be experienced singly, I've often thought, with a long, silent pause between each one."

A reviewer from *Publishers Weekly* noted that Chaon's pieces in *Fitting Ends and Other Stories* "are deftly written and brilliantly structured." These stories take place in a Midwestern landscape that is flat, broad, and bleak. The action frequently begins in a small town in Nebraska and shifts to Chicago, a big city on a lake. In his *Chicago Tribune* review, Michael Upchurch praised Chaon for his great talent in describing the contrasting regions. Through the characters in his stories, Upchurch noted, Chaon explores the dichotomy between urban and rural life, writing from the point of view "of those who were left behind, not those who got away." His characters, said Upchurch, "rebel against their place of origin," while facing a future that is unknowable, and therefore, frightening. Upchurch also praised Chaon's ability to slip underneath the skin of each character. He noted that although the characters "may not be heroes in the usual sense . . . they make for surprisingly engaging company on the page."

In a *Prairie Schooner* review of *Fitting Ends and Other Stories,* Kate Flaherty described the characters as "typical angst-ridden twenty-somethings of the nineties who inflict pain on others and themselves simply because it's what gives them control." Flaherty later wrote that "Chaon is able to rouse our sympathy for these people" who demonstrate a certain "nobility" in the way in which they handle their misfortunes. Flaherty concluded: "*Fitting Ends* [is] worth the effort; the book may have been more stellar had it been more distilled, but it is rewarding all the same."

In *Among the Missing,* which was a National Book Award finalist, Chaon wrote on the "themes of absence, loss, and recovery," as described by Anson Lang in *Bold Type.* The collection's twelve stories examine the mysterious and complex nature of human relationships. Chaon observed in his *Bold Type* essay that in writing these stories he "wanted to try to get a grip on the odd, ambient, disconcerting experience of negotiating through late twentieth-century America."

In *Among the Missing,* Chaon explores the idea of what it means to be absent on either a physical or a psychological level, or both. One story, "Safety Man," tells of a young wife trying to adjust to the sudden death of her husband. The title story focuses on a family whose car mysteriously lands in a lake with them inside, and the effect that their disappearance has upon the town.

In a *Booklist* review, Donna Seaman commented on Chaon's ability to penetrate "the immensity and mystery floating silently below the surface of everyday life." A reviewer for *Publishers Weekly* called the stories in *Among the Missing* "unsettling, moving, even beautiful." In a *San Francisco Chronicle* assessment, the reviewer commented that Chaon's prose is "straightforward, chiseled with a Hemingwayesque clarity and deceptive simplicity." Beverly Lowry of the *New York Times* wrote: "the stories in *Among the Missing* sneak resolutely up on you." She noted that "most of [Chaon's] book hums with life and wry humor."

Upchurch remarked that "Chaon is a writer to savor and to watch." Chaon, in his *Bold Type* essay, said that through his writing he hopes to "rescue those 'missing' moments in time, to take a snapshot of those fleeting, life-or-death visions, before they vanish back into the haze of daily life."

Chaon told *CA:* "I became a writer by accident. I grew up in a very tiny rural community called Brownson in western Nebraska, and my background wasn't literary at all. Instead, it was I suppose what you would call working class—my father was a construction worker, and my mom was a housewife, neither one had graduated high school. Growing up, I didn't know any adults who read books for pleasure.

"I was extremely lucky, though, in that I encountered a really wonderful teacher, my seventh grade teacher, Mr. Christy. We were given creative writing assignments in his class, and we could read any book we wanted for extra credit. I began to write a lot, and then another important thing happened. In the middle of the school year, Mr. Christy gave an assignment for us to write letters to our favorite author. Mine was Ray Bradbury, and once I'd written the letter I went a little further than the other kids and actually found his address in a directory (it was, ironically, *Contemporary Authors*). I sent my letter off to him, along with some stories I had written, which were pretty slavish imitations of Bradbury's own work. The amazing thing was

that Bradbury actually wrote back to me, praising the stories and offering a critique. Bradbury was full of kindness and hyperbole, and told me that he thought I would soon be published. I was around thirteen, and this is when I decided that I was going to be a writer. I began sending stories out to magazines, being basically too ignorant to know any better, and not quite realizing that the rejection slips I was getting were form letters. By the time I went away to college (at Northwestern University), writing was a habit that I'd gotten into, and I was encouraged by my teachers there as well, including one of my lifelong mentors, Reginald Gibbons, who eventually published my first book, *Fitting Ends and Other Stories,* at Northwestern University Press.

"I recognize now that I was extremely fortunate. I had parents who, however puzzled they were by my weirdness, were tolerant of it, and loving; I stumbled upon encouraging teachers at just the right time in my youth and college years; and, finally, I happened upon a particularly generous spirit in Ray Bradbury, whose kindness put me on a track I might not have had the confidence to pursue otherwise.

"I think one of my main interests as a writer are those moments that are unpackagable, and, conversely, trying to re-mystify the stuff that's been already packaged. I'm not particularly interested in the idea of Truth, or even of 'epiphany' in fiction. Instead, I think the thing I value most is ambiguity, uncertainty, 'mystery,' for lack of a better word. I don't feel like I can stand up on a stage and preach anything convincingly; I'd prefer if the reader and I were standing together on a common ground, both of us puzzling and wondering in the face of these moments that can't be explained."

BIOGRAPHICAL AND CRITICAL SOURCES:

PERIODICALS

Booklist, July, 2001, Donna Seaman, review of *Among the Missing,* p. 1977.
Chicago Tribune, January 28, 1996, Michael Upchurch, "Those Spacey, Midwestern Blues," p. 7.
New York Times, August 5, 2001, Beverly Lowry, review of *Among the Missing.*
Prairie Schooner, fall, 1996, Kate Flaherty, review of *Fitting Ends and Other Stories,* pp. 182-186.

Publishers Weekly, September 25, 1995, review of *Fitting Ends and Other Stories,* p. 53; January 24, 2000, John F. Baker, "Two-Book Deal for Story Whiz," p. 172; June 11, 2001, review of *Among the Missing,* p. 56.

San Francisco Chronicle, July 8, 2001, review of *Among the Missing,* p. 58.

OTHER

Bold Type, http://www.randomhouse.com/boldtype/ (January 8, 2002), Anson Lang, "Dan Chaon"; (June 2, 2002), Dan Chaon, "Author Essay."

HoustonChronicle.com, http://www.chron.com/ (October 19, 2001), excerpt from *Among the Missing.*

*   *   *

CHAPMAN, Matthew 1950-

PERSONAL: Born September 2, 1950, in Cambridge, England; son of Cecil and Clare (Cornford) Chapman; married Denise Teixeira; children: Anna Bella. *Religion:* "Skeptic/Agnostic".

ADDRESSES: Home—New York, NY. *Agent*—c/o Author Mail, Picador USA, 175 Fifth Ave., New York, NY 10010.

CAREER: Director of motion pictures; writer.

MEMBER: Directors Guild of America, Writers Guild of America.

WRITINGS:

SCREENPLAYS

(And director) *Hussy,* Watchgrove, 1979.

(With Blaine Novak; and director) *Strangers Kiss* (adapted from Blaine Novak's story), Orion Classics, 1984.

Slow Burn, Joel Schumacher Productions/Universal, 1986.

(And director) *Heart of Midnight,* Samuel Goldwyn, 1988.

Consenting Adults, 1992.

(With Billy Ray) *Color of Night,* 1994.

What's the Worst That Could Happen? (adapted from Donald Westlake's novel), Metro-Goldwyn-Mayer, 2001.

OTHER

Trials of the Monkey: An Accidental Memoir (nonfiction), Picador (New York, NY), 2001.

SIDELIGHTS: Matthew Chapman is a filmmaker and writer whose various works range from thrillers to comedy and from drama to autobiography. Chapman began his film career in 1979 as writer and director of *Hussy,* a love story about a prostitute and a nightclub worker who find their romance threatened by unstable friends and dangerous associates. Chapman followed *Hussy* with *Strangers Kiss,* a 1983 thriller—which he both wrote, with actor Blaine Novak, and directed—wherein an aspiring filmmaker discovers that life mirrors art as he attempts to obtain funding for a movie about a boxer determined to free his girlfriend, a taxi dancer, from her malicious employer. A *Variety* reviewer noted the film's "sense of fun and mystery." Another work, *Heart of Midnight,* concerns a deranged woman who runs afoul of various fiends, including a drug-dispensing villain posing as a police officer, while trying to renovate a nightclub. The film was described in *Variety* as "a twisted little sadomasochistic outing."

Other films by Chapman include *Consenting Adults,* in which a successful advertising writer is framed for murder by a scheming neighbor, and *Color of Night,* wherein a psychiatrist comes to suspect one of his patients of murder. Stanley Kauffmann, writing in *New Republic,* decried *Consenting Adults,* which Alan J. Pakula directed from Chapman's script, for its "howling flaws," and Richard Schickel, in a *Time* review, similarly dismissed the film as "implausible." But *Color of Night,* which Richard Rush directed from a script by Chapman and Billy Ray, won praise in *New Yorker* as "lively and sneakily intelligent."

Among Chapman's other film credits is *What's the Worst That Could Happen?,* a comedy about a professional thief who endeavors to retrieve a valuable ring taken from him by one of his supposed victims. James Berardinelli, in a *Colossus* appraisal, rejected *What's the Worst That Could Happen?* as "a caper comedy that replaces humor and cleverness with tedium and stupidity." Berardinelli added that the film "has surprisingly little going for it." However, as Chapman told *CA,* the final version of the script was completely different from what he had originally written. The original script "bears little resemblance to the movie, which is indeed tedious and stupid," Chapman commented, and therefore any criticism of the movie is not really a reflection on his work.

Chapman is also the author of *Trials of the Monkey: An Accidental Memoir,* in which he combines accounts of his great-great-grandfather, nineteenth-century evolutionist Charles Darwin, with considerations on the Scopes Monkey Trial (where evolutionary theory triumphed over creationism), as well as more personal reflections. Michael D. Cramer, writing in *Library Journal,* described *Trials of the Monkey* as "an odd but fascinating mix of history, science, religion, travel, and memoir," and Steve Weinberg, in a *Booklist* analysis, deemed Chapman's book "well worth reading." Cramer added that "the writing is excellent," and Weinberg concluded his review by declaring that "Chapman's rapier-like wit is difficult to resist." A *Publishers Weekly* reviewer, meanwhile, praised *Trials of the Monkey* as "an honest, ironic autobiography" and "an absorbing and finely honed journal of courageous, often amusing self-awareness." Still another critic, Tony Gould, wrote in *Spectator* that *Trials of the Monkey* constitutes a "hugely entertaining book." Gould added, "It sets out to tell the story of the Scopes 'Monkey' trial of 1925 . . . and its legacy in latter-day Dayton, Tennessee, and ends up telling the story of the author's life: how a drop-out from a privileged but dysfunctional English family became a highly paid Hollywood scriptwriter."

BIOGRAPHICAL AND CRITICAL SOURCES:

PERIODICALS

Booklist, August, 2001, Steve Weinberg, review of *Trials of the Monkey: An Accidental Memoir,* p. 2080.
Library Journal, September 1, 2001, Michael D. Cramer, review of *Trials of the Monkey,* p. 192.
Publishers Weekly, July 30, 2001, review of *Trials of the Monkey,* p. 70.

New Republic, November 16, 1992, Stanley Kauffmann, review of *Consenting Adults,* p. 28.
New Yorker, September 5, 1984, Terrence Rafferty, "Helter Skelter," pp. 106-107.
Spectator, November 25, 2000, Tony Gould, "Unnerved by Ancestral Voices," pp. 54-55.
Time, October 26, 1992, Richard Schickel, review of *Consenting Adults,* p. 88.
Variety, September 7, 1983, review of *Stranger's Kiss,* p. 17; May 25, 1988, review of *Heart of Midnight,* p. 19.

OTHER

Colossus, http://movie-reviews.colossus.net/ (December 2, 2001).

*   *   *

CHARGAFF, Erwin 1905-2002

OBITUARY NOTICE—See index for *CA* sketch: Born August 11, 1905, in Czernowitz (now Chernivisti), Austria (now Ukraine); died June 20, 2002, in New York, NY. Biochemist, educator, and author. Chargaff will undoubtedly be remembered as one of the pioneering scientists whose research helped to reveal the role of deoxyribonucleic acid (DNA) in heredity. It was Chargaff—already a highly respected scientist—who discovered in the 1940s that all tested DNA contains four chemical groups or bases; and further, that two of the bases always occur in equal amounts as do the other two, though the proportions vary from one organism to another. These findings led other scientists to eventually identify that the equal groups are paired to one another in a double-helix structure and that DNA, not amino acid as previously believed, is responsible for hereditary material. DNA research was only one of Chargaff's projects during a forty-year career. He worked in Berlin and Paris before joining Columbia University in 1935. At Columbia, in addition to research on the biochemistry of blood, plant chromoproteins, and other topics, Chargaff also served as a professor and department chair until 1973, and he lectured at prestigious institutions around the world. Toward the end of his career, it is reported, Chargaff became increasingly alienated from his profession and his colleagues. He was particularly critical of advances in molecular biology that allowed scientists to move genetic material from one living organism to another. Though it was his own research that led to the emerging fields of medical genetics and gene therapy, Chargaff was acutely worried about safety issues as well as about the appropriate application of these technologies. Chargaff's many honors include the Charles Leopold Mayer Prize of the French Academy of Sciences, the Heineken Prize in biochemistry of the Royal Netherlands Academy of Sciences, and the U.S. National Medal of Honor. His writings, in addition to scientific publications, include *Voices in the Labyrinth: Nature, Man, and Science* and *Serious Questions: An ABC of Skeptical Reflections.*

OBITUARIES AND OTHER SOURCES:

BOOKS

Chargaff, Erwin, *Heraclitean Fire: Sketches from a Life before Nature,* Rockefeller University Press (New York, NY), 1978.

PERIODICALS

Guardian (London, England), July 2, 2002, obituary by Pearce Wright, p. 16; July 5, 2002, p. 17.
New York Times, June 30, 2002, obituary by Nicholas Wade, p. A23.

*   *   *

CHAZIN, Suzanne 1961-

PERSONAL: Born April 19, 1961, in New York, NY; married. *Education:* Northwestern University, Medill School of Journalism, B.S., 1982.

ADDRESSES: Agent—Matt Bialer, Trident Media Group, Carnegie Hall Tower, 1521 West 57th St., 16th floor, New York, NY 10019.

CAREER: Novelist, editor, writer, and teacher. New School University, New York, NY, adjunct faculty member. *Reader's Digest,* former senior editor and staff writer.

MEMBER: International Association of Arson Investigators.

WRITINGS:

NOVELS; "GEORGIA SKEEHAN" SERIES

The Fourth Angel, Putnam (New York, NY), 2001.
Flashover, Putnam (New York, NY), 2002.

Contributing writer to newspapers and magazines, including *American Health, New York Times, People, Chicago,* and *Money.*

WORK IN PROGRESS: Third novel in the "Georgia Skeehan" series, to be published in 2003.

SIDELIGHTS: Suzanne Chazin was born in New York City and raised in nearby Tenafly, New Jersey. She received her bachelor's degree from the Medill School of Journalism at Northwestern University in Evanston, Illinois. For over ten years she served as an editor for *Reader's Digest* and submitted articles to other magazines and newspapers, including *Chicago* and the *New York Times.* Chazin also continues to teach college-level writing at the New School University in New York City as an adjunct faculty member.

Chazin's first novel, *The Fourth Angel,* published in 2001, emerged after years of work as a senior editor at *Reader's Digest.* Her experience of being married to a New York City firefighter for over thirteen years gives Chazin an inside view of firehouse culture and firefighting skills that makes this book an even timelier read owing to the tragic events of September 11, 2001, in New York City. The story is based on the twenty actual high-temperature fires that have occurred throughout New York since 1984 and remain unsolved.

Georgia Skeehan is a single mother and a rookie fire marshal who is working diligently to find the cause of a series of high-temperature fires. Letters begin to arrive at the department from someone who calls himself "the Fourth Angel"—a reference to the passage in the Book of Revelations about scorching people with fire. Much to Skeehan's concern and surprise, the letters not only are kept out of the media spotlight but are kept away from the department's investigation team as well. Skeehan still suffers from guilt over not having been able to save her partner from an earlier fire, and she is the focus of some intradepartmental resentment for having been promoted over other more senior members of the investigation squad. That she is the only woman on the investigation squad does not help her cause either. No one will take her seriously when she decides that all of the mysterious fires have been caused by the same arsonist—and that the arsonist is most likely a fellow New York firefighter.

A *Publishers Weekly* contributor noted that Chazin's "gradual revelation of a harrowing event in Georgia's past is convincing," and that her character Skeehan "could prove to be a refreshing new face in the growing legion of female investigators."

In a biographical sketch for *Authors on the Web*, Chazin noted that it took her five years to write her first book. "I was juggling the demands of a baby and a job as a magazine writer, so all of my writing had to be done after the baby went to bed. I wrote from 9:00 p.m. to 1:00 a.m., usually four or five nights a week." It took Chazin more than two years to write the first draft; the next two drafts took another year. In the end she would produce six drafts, and all the rewriting paid off when the manuscript was accepted for publication. Her agent, Mike Bialer, had received three immediate offers and closed the deal in only ten days.

"A lot of research went into my book," Chazin told Cathy Sova in an interview posted online for *The Mystery Reader*. "I was fortunate because my husband is a New York City firefighter, so he was able to help me with the details. But I also interviewed firefighters and fire marshals—male and female, in New York and outside of it—to give the book the gritty sense of reality it needed. I live near Manhattan, so I walked the buildings I was going to write about. I went to arson investigation scenes. I hung out and listened to the men talk. And I used the Internet to find out those random things that could take a day to get answered otherwise."

Chazin's second novel in the "Georgia Skeehan" series, *Flashover,* follows the female fire marshal's attempt to solve another arson-related mystery. This time Georgia must figure out why two doctors have died in "flashover" fires—the overwhelming combustion of a room by simultaneous ignition. Both doctors

worked on a regulatory board that evaluates compensation requests for firefighters injured in the line of duty. Another element in the mystery is the threat of betrayal—when Georgia's best friend Connie Ruiz goes missing, Georgia's boyfriend and supervisor, Mac Marenko, is discovered in Connie's blood-stained apartment, dazed and with no memory of what happened. Politics, greed, and murder all play a part this chilling sequel.

BIOGRAPHICAL AND CRITICAL SOURCES:

PERIODICALS

Booklist, December 15, 2000, David Pitt, review of *The Fourth Angel,* p. 790.
Kirkus Reviews, December 15, 2000, review of *The Fourth Angel,* p. 1702.
People Weekly, March 12, 2001, Christina Cheakalos, review of *The Fourth Angel,* p. 43.
Publishers Weekly, January 8, 2001, review of *The Fourth Angel,* p. 47.
Washington Times, February 11, 2001, Judith Kreiner, review of *The Fourth Angel,* p. 8.

OTHER

Authors on the Web, http://www.authorsontheweb.com/ (October 6, 2001), "Suzanne Chazin."
Fiction Readers' Advisory Reviews, http://www.noblenet.org/ (April 3, 2001), Leane M. Ellis, review of *The Fourth Angel.*
Harriet Klausner's Review Archive, http://harrietklausner.wwwi.com/ (October 6, 2001), review of *The Fourth Angel.*
Mystery Reader, http://www.themysteryreader.com/ (October 6, 2001), "New Faces 32—Suzanne Chazin."*

*   *   *

CITRA, Becky 1954-

PERSONAL: Born June 23, 1954, in Vancouver, British Columbia, Canada; married Larry Citra, July 2, 1988; children: Meghan. *Education:* Attended University of British Columbia; Simon Fraser University, teaching certificate. *Hobbies and other interests:* Horseback riding, gardening, hiking, reading.

ADDRESSES: Home—Box 22, Bridge Lake, British Columbia V0K 1E0, Canada. *E-mail*—ercitra@ hotmail.com.

CAREER: Author and teacher. Elementary school teacher in Hazelton, Port Hardy, Chilliwack, and Bridge Lake, all in British Columbia, Canada, 1976—.

AWARDS, HONORS: Rocky Mountain Book Award, 2002, for *Ellie's New Home.*

WRITINGS:

My Homework Is in the Mail!, illustrated by Karen Harrison, Scholastic (Richmond Hill, Canada), 1995.
School Campout, Scholastic (Richmond Hill, Canada), 1996.
Ellie's New Home, Orca Book Publishers (Custer, WA), 1999.
The Freezing Moon, Orca Book Publishers (Custer, WA), 2001.
Danger at the Landings, Orca Book Publishers (Custer, WA), 2002.
Dog Days, Orca Book Publishers (Custer, WA), 2003.

WORK IN PROGRESS: Research on Native Indians and on Canada in the 1880s.

SIDELIGHTS: Becky Citra told *CA:* "My joy of writing began when I was a child. An avid reader of the Hardy Boys and Nancy Drew, I started scribbling my own mystery series at eleven years old. I took a long break from writing when I became a teacher. However, reading wonderful books out loud everyday to young children in schools inspired me one day to give it a try myself—and I've never looked back. My first books drew on experiences right out of the classroom and I still find my students a great source of material! A fascinating story in a magazine about young children immigrating to Upper Canada in the 1800s sparked my interest to do further research and my series on a pioneer family was born. I enjoy writing historical novels and am planning future books about Native Indians and Vikings! I try to write every day, in between a busy teaching career, and love the initial stages of a story best when everything is new and full of potential. For breaks, I ride my horse on our ranch, garden, hike, and read, read, read."

Citra's early-reader books are praised for plots filled with suspense and lively action, realistic characters, and child-centered narratives. Her first book, *My Homework Is in the Mail!,* recounts the trials and tribulations of Samantha "Sam" Higgins, when her parents move her from urban Vancouver to a farm so far removed from civilization that Sam's school is a correspondence course. "There is much here to interest young readers," remarked Leslie Millar in *Canadian Review of Materials.* "Apprehension about school, moving, and lots of contact with animals will be sure to strike a chord with most youngsters." Sam's mother charges her to find four things she can be grateful for by Thanksgiving, and though Sam devoutly doubts her ability to do this at the start of the book, she comes to appreciate meeting a real cowboy, learning to take care of the farm animals, meeting her eccentric correspondence school teacher in person, and finally making friends. "Citra's writing is tight and graceful, and she definitely knows how kids tick, what pleases them, and what mortifies them," observed Kenneth Oppel in *Quill & Quire.*

Another early reader with a contemporary setting, *School Campout,* was similarly praised for providing a likeable cast of young characters with realistic problems and approaches to solving them. When David's third-grade class plans a camping trip, David is terrified of the possibilities—getting lost, being attacked by a bear—and when he is paired with the new kid, Bradley, who just moved from the city, he knows he will not find any help there. As the trip unfolds, David learns something about the out-of-doors, about his friends, and about himself. Anne Louise Mahoney, who reviewed *School Campout* for *Quill & Quire,* enumerated the book's highlights: "This novel gives seven-to-nine-year-olds a fast-paced read with a familiar situation (school), an element of surprise (the camping adventure), and a happy ending."

With *Ellie's New Home,* Citra published her first historical novel. Compared to Laura Ingalls Wilder's "Little House" books for its focus on the pioneer experience, *Ellie's New Home* has a distinctly Canadian flavor. The story centers on nine-year-old Ellie, who immigrates to Canada from England with her father and younger brother, Max, after her mother's death. When they arrive in Canada, Ellie's father leaves her and her brother with another family while he scouts for a location for their new home. Ellie is left to learn the skills that make pioneer life possible from the friendly, but rough, pioneer family. A sequel, *The Freezing Moon,* depicts Ellie and Max's first winter in Upper Canada on their father's homestead. Pioneer life in winter is hard enough, but when their father fails to return from a hunting trip, Ellie and Max must rely on help from a European woodcutter and the Native Indians whose village is nearby, neither of whom they are certain they can trust. Gillian Richardson, writing in *Resource Links,* found much to admire in *The Freezing Moon,* which "quickly engages the reader in a dramatic first chapter encounter with a bear." Though Citra skillfully maintains a high level of action and suspense, "the characters are convincing," and "vivid details bring the wilderness setting into sharp focus," Richardson maintained. Gwyneth Evans, writing in *Quill & Quire,* noted the similarities between Citra's books and the "Little House" series by Laura Ingalls Wilder, concluding: "While Ellie's family and adventures are not so vividly drawn as Laura's they offer an enjoyably Canadian-flavoured version of the pioneer experience."

BIOGRAPHICAL AND CRITICAL SOURCES:

PERIODICALS

Books in Canada, November, 1995, Phil Hall, review of *My Homework Is in the Mail!,* p. 40.
Quill & Quire, October, 1995, Kenneth Oppel, review of *My Homework Is in the Mail!,* p. 38; November, 1996, Anne Louise Mahoney, review of *School Campout,* p. 48; May, 2001, Gwyneth Evans, review of *The Freezing Moon,* p. 35.
Resource Links, June, 2001, Gillian Richardson, review of *The Freezing Moon,* p. 9.

OTHER

Canadian Review of Materials, www.umanitoba.ca/ cm/ (December 8, 1995), Leslie Millar, review of *My Homework Is in the Mail!*

*   *   *

CLARKE, Jaime 1971-

PERSONAL: Born April 15, 1971, in Kalispell, MT; son of Douglas and Glenda Gilkey (Kelly) Clarke. *Ethnicity:* "White." *Education:* University of Arizona, B.A., 1994; Bennington College, M.F.A., 1997.

ADDRESSES: Agent—Wendy Schmalz, Harold Ober Associates, 425 Madison Ave., New York, NY 10017.

CAREER: Pete's Fish-n-Chips, Tolleson, AZ, night manager, 1987-89; American Continental Corp., Phoenix, AZ, runner, 1989-92; University of Arizona Law Library, Tucson, AZ, in technical services, 1993; William S. Rose, Jr., P.A., Paradise Valley, AZ, legal assistant, 1994; Biltmore Pro Print, Phoenix, AZ, customer service specialist, 1995-97; Harold Ober Associates, New York, NY, assistant to the president, 1997-2000.

MEMBER: National Writer's Union, Burgundy Club.

AWARDS, HONORS: Pushcart Prize nomination, for short story "We're So Famous."

WRITINGS:

We're So Famous, Bloomsbury (New York, NY), 2001.

Also contributor to periodicals, including *Chelsea, Agni, Black Dirt,* and *Mississippi Review.* Founding editor, *Post Road,* 2000—.

WORK IN PROGRESS: Standard Deviation, a short story collection.

SIDELIGHTS: Jaime Clarke's first published novel, *We're So Famous,* made a strong debut with critics who found it a clever satire of the American obsession with celebrity. Clarke's response to a negative review, however, brought the novelist even more attention, which was not entirely welcome. Though his characters appear willing to achieve fame by any means necessary, Clarke has said that he is more interested in the anonymous work of writing.

Clarke grew up in Phoenix and briefly attended Arizona State University, majoring in English before flunking out. He was sidetracked by his work for soon-to-be-famous 1980s developer Charles Keating, through American Continental Corp. Much of his work actually involved taking care of Keating's cars and hanging around the young women with whom Keating surrounded himself. Eventually Clarke returned to school at the University of Arizona, getting a degree in creative writing; he continued to study writing in the M.F.A. program at Bennington College in Vermont.

In pursuit of a literary career, Clarke moved east and began work at Harold Ober Associates, the oldest literary agency in the United States. He wrote a novel, *A Complete Gentleman,* after hours at Ober, attracting the interest of a co-worker who offered to represent the book. The novel was never accepted for publication, and eventually Clarke self-published it through Xlibiris. In the meantime, he worked on expanding one of his earlier short stories, "We're So Famous," to novel length. The book focuses on three teenage girls in the suburbs of Phoenix—Paque, Daisy, and Stella—who are determined to find fame despite their lack of talent. Their band, Masterful Johnson, finds a hit in the song "I'd Kill You If I Thought I Could Get Away With It" after they are unwittingly connected to the murder of a senator's son. Their dreams appear out of reach when their lack of actual musical ability is exposed, but after a series of further misfires they finally achieve the celebrity they seek. The novel is divided into three sections, each told from the perspective of a different girl, and in different genres, including fan letters to their favorite band, 1980s girl group Bananarama. The narrative is heavily laced with pop culture references, especially those involving dead celebrities, which are Stella's obsession.

Responses to the novel varied. Many critics appreciated the satire of a culture where fame, no matter how it is earned, is all that matters and everything is disposable. Writing about the book for the *Village Voice Literary Supplement,* Mike Albo said, "Clarke captures that unsatisfyingly minidonut flavor of entertainment culture—a million cable channels of syndicated shows that are scarily self-organizing." *Entertainment Weekly* reviewer Daniel Fierman wrote, "It's nothing we haven't heard a million times before . . . but, somehow, the satire works, sliding down as silvery and toxic as liquid mercury." Other critics, however, found the book lacking depth, especially in its rendering of the teenage heroines. "None of the girls reveal what lies beneath their superficial desires," wrote Emily White in the *New York Times.* A reviewer for *Publishers Weekly* suggested that although readers under 30 wouldn't be familiar with much of the "'80s arcana,' older readers won't have the patience for the puerile protagonists." Some readers, however, found the girls engaging:

Kelcey Nichols, in a review for *CommunityBookstore. com,* felt "their determination and spunk makes it impossible not to root for them." Clarke himself addressed the fine line he had to walk in creating Paque, Daisy, and Stella. He told Brian Smith, a reporter for the *Phoenix New Times,* "That was the hard part about creating these characters because you want to make them likable. I do like these characters, but what they are after all is empty and shallow."

Generally speaking, reviews for *We're So Famous* were positive, but the *Publishers Weekly* reviewer concluded that the novel's weaknesses outweighed its strength. The anonymous review in an important publishing magazine angered Clarke, who sent the magazine's editor and several other journalists and editors an e-mail offering $1,000 for the name of the reviewer. The bounty put up by Clarke was an immediate source of controversy in the publishing world, as some found him foolish and others brave. Though he later said he regretted that the e-mail made him come off as base and a bully, he maintained the position that reviews should be signed.

A month after *We're So Famous* was published, Clarke announced that he would give fifty percent of his royalties through December 31, 2001, to Literacy Volunteers of Maricopa County (Arizona). He felt moved to do so because going through life without reading seemed impossible to him. "Adults who can't read isn't a problem that this country should have, or anybody should have," he said in the *West Valley View.* "It's hard to believe that there are adults that don't have those fundamentals." Clarke spent the fall of 2001 doing a book tour of the college circuit and planned to return to his Brooklyn home in January 2002 to look for a new job. He told the *Phoenix New Times* that he did not expect the success of his novel to make the aspirations of being a writer any easier, because every time one starts a new book it is like starting all over again. "Being a writer, nobody knows who you are," he said. "That is the funny thing. I am a writer, and that's it."

BIOGRAPHICAL AND CRITICAL SOURCES:

PERIODICALS

Kirkus Reviews, February, 2001, review of *We're So Famous,* p. 125.
New York Times, April 29, 2001, Emily White, review of *We're So Famous.*

Phoenix New Times, June 14, 2001, Brian Smith, "Almost Famous."

Publishers Weekly, February, 2001, review of *We're So Famous,* p. 68.

Voice Literary Supplement, April, 2001, Mike Albo, "Stardom Trek."

OTHER

Community Bookstore, http://www.community bookstore.com/ (August 22, 2001), Kelcey Nichols, review of *We're So Famous.*

University of Arizona Web site, http://uanews.opi. arizona.edu/ (April 2, 2001), Rich Amada, "UA Alum, Jaime Clarke, to Read from His Story *We're So Famous.*"

We're So Famous.com, http://www.weresofamous.com/ (August 22, 2001).

West Valley View, http://www.westvalleyview.com/ (August 22, 2001), Kate Cahill Otto, "Local Author Donates Royalties to Charity."

                    *   *   *

CLAVIR, Miriam (Lisa) 1948-

PERSONAL: Surname is pronounced "*Clay*-vur;" born May 25, 1948, in Toronto, Ontario, Canada; daughter of Leo and Harriet Clavir; married John Donlan, 1995. *Education:* University of Toronto, B.A. (with honors), 1969; Queen's University (Kingston, Ontario, Canada), M.A., 1976; University of Leicester, Ph.D., 1998.

ADDRESSES: Home—Vancouver, British Columbia, Canada. *Office*—Museum of Anthropology, University of British Columbia, 6393 Northwest Marine Dr., Vancouver, British Columbia, Canada V6T 1Z2; fax: 604-822-2974. *E-mail*—clavir@interchange.ubc.ca.

CAREER: Museum conservator and author. Royal Ontario Museum, Toronto, Ontario, Canada, assistant in archaeology and conservation, 1969-72; Parks Canada, National Historic Sites Service, assistant conservator and conservation assistant for the Quebec region of Canada and in Ottawa, Ontario, 1973-80; University of British Columbia, Vancouver, British Columbia, Canada, began as conservator, became senior conserva-

tor at Museum of Anthropology, 1980—. University of Washington, Seattle, member of sessional faculty at Burke Museum, 1999, 2000, 2002.

MEMBER: International Institute for Conservation of Historic and Artistic Works (fellow), International Council of Museums (member of conservation committee), Canadian Association for Conservation, Canadian Association of Professional Conservators, Canadian Museums Association, American Institute for Conservation, British Columbia Museums Association.

WRITINGS:

Preserving What Is Valued: Museums, Conservation, and First Nations, University of British Columbia Press (Vancouver, British Columbia, Canada), 2002.

Contributor to professional journals, including *Native Peoples, Studies in Conservation,* and *New Zealand Museums Journal.*

WORK IN PROGRESS: Working with First Nations communities to define protocols for the care of material heritage in museum collections.

                    *   *   *

CLEMENT, Alison

PERSONAL: Married Chuck Willer (a conservationist); children: Sasha, Charlotte.

ADDRESSES: Home—Western OR. *Agent*—c/o Publicity Director, MacAdam/Cage Publishing, 155 Sansome St., Suite 620, San Francisco, CA 94104. *E-mail*—Pretty@peak.org.

CAREER: Librarian and novelist. Has worked as a waitress and bartender.

WRITINGS:

Pretty Is as Pretty Does, MacAdam/Cage (San Francisco, CA), 2001.

Contributor to various periodicals, including *Sun, High Country News,* and *Alaska Quarterly Review.*

SIDELIGHTS: Alison Clement, an elementary school librarian in Oregon, published her debut novel, *Pretty Is as Pretty Does,* in 2001. Clement's writing had previously appeared in a number of periodicals, including *High Country News* and the *Alaska Quarterly Review.* Before becoming a librarian, Clement held jobs as a waitress and bartender. Much like the protagonist in her novel, she spent some of her formative years in the small Midwestern town where she moved when she was fifteen after spending her childhood in the South.

Labeled "an understated black comedy with an unlikely heroine" by its publisher, MacAdam/Cage, *Pretty Is as Pretty Does* is set in the fictional Illinois farming town of Palmyra. The tale is narrated by the twenty-two-year-old protagonist Lucy Fooshee, the winner of several local beauty pageants, who uses her good looks to attract the men of Palmyra. Lucy, whom a reviewer for *Publishers Weekly* called "vain, selfish, sharp-tongued and obtuse," manipulates a man named Bob Bybee into marrying her. Bob is a farmer from one of the richest families in Palmyra, and the two move into the kind of big home that Lucy, who is from a much poorer family, has always dreamed of. However, it does not take long for her to realize that life with a farmer is not what she expected, and she quickly gets annoyed by many of Bob's crude habits, such as chewing with his mouth open.

Lucy's life takes a big turn when she meets a drifter named Billy Lee at the local café just two weeks after her wedding. Lucy is immediately interested in the handsome Billy, who is working as a handyman for his aunt. The two begin a romance, and Billy awakens in Lucy feelings of love and a sexuality that she has never known before. However, the affair draws the ire of the townspeople, who not only disdain her for her infidelity but also look down on Billy because he is half Native American. And in Palmyra racism runs deep. Despite Lucy's attempts to keep the romance from her husband, Bob ultimately finds out about it and brings it to a swift end. Still, Lucy learns much about herself and life in general, leading reviewer Lynn T. Theodose of the *Boulder Weekly* to characterize the novel as "a story of one woman's liberation through self-discovery." Other critics also praised Clement's depiction of Lucy, including Ann H. Fisher of *Library Journal,* who called her "a fresh, spunky heroine who lights up this first novel." Likewise in *Booklist,* reviewer Elsa Gaztambide labeled Lucy "a

complex character" who "ignites the pages with lusty passages spewed from a volcano of pent-up desire." Finding the book "a very satisfying read," Melanie Danburg of the *Houston Chronicle* added that Clement writes "with ease and inherent humor."

BIOGRAPHICAL AND CRITICAL SOURCES:

PERIODICALS

Booklist, August, 2001, Elsa Gaztambide, review of *Pretty Is as Pretty Does,* p. 2084.
Houston Chronicle, December 16, 2001, Melanie Danburg, "A Heroine Both Laughable and Likable," p. 18.
Library Journal, August, 2001, Ann H. Fisher, review of *Pretty Is as Pretty Does,* p. 159.
Publishers Weekly, July 30, 2001, review of *Pretty Is as Pretty Does,* p. 57.

OTHER

Alison's Self Promotion Page (author's Web site), http://www.alisonclement.org (January 30, 2002).
Boulder Weekly.com, http://www.boulderweekly.com (January 30, 2002), Lynn T. Theodose, review of *Pretty Is as Pretty Does.**

*   *   *

CLOGG, Richard 1939-

PERSONAL: Born 1939; married; wife's name, Mary Jo.

ADDRESSES: Agent—c/o St. Martin's Press, 175 Fifth Ave., New York, NY 10010.

CAREER: Historian and writer. King's College, London, England, former lecturer; University of London, London, England, former professor of modern Balkan history; St. Antony's College, Oxford, Oxford, England, senior research fellow and professor emeritus.

MEMBER: Oxford Balkan Society (senior member, executive committee).

WRITINGS:

A Short History of Greek Literature, Cambridge University Press (Cambridge, England), 1979.

A Short History of Modern Greece, Cambridge University Press (Cambridge, England), 1979.

(With Mary Jo Clogg) *Greece,* ABC-CLIO (Santa Barbara, CA), 1981.

Greece in the 1980s, St. Martin's Press (New York, NY), 1983.

Politics and the Academy: Arnold Toynbee and the Koraes Chair, Frank Cass Publications (London, England), 1986.

Parties and Elections in Greece: The Search for Legitimacy, Duke University Press (Durham, NC), 1988.

A Concise History of Greece, Cambridge University Press (Cambridge, England), 1992.

Anatolica: Studies in the Greek East in the Eighteenth and Nineteenth Centuries, Ashgate Publishing Company (London, England), 1996.

EDITOR

(With George Yannopoulos) *Greece under Military Rule,* Basic Books (New York, NY), 1972.

The Struggle for Greek Independence: Essays to Mark the 150th Anniversary of the Greek War of Independence, Shoestring Press (Nottingham, England), 1973.

The Movement for Greek Independence, 1770-1821: A Collection of Documents, Barnes & Noble (Totowa, NJ), 1976.

Balkan Society in the Age of Greek Independence, Rowman & Littlefield Publishers, Inc. (Lanham, MD), 1981.

Greece, 1981-1989: The Populist Decade, St. Martin's Press (New York, NY), 1993.

The Greek Diaspora in the Twentieth Century, St. Martin's Press (New York, NY), 1999.

Anglo-Greek Attitudes: Studies in History, St. Martin's Press (New York, NY), 2000.

Greece, 1940-1949: Occupation, Resistance, Civil War: A Documentary History, Palgrave Macmillan Ltd. (New York, NY), 2002.

OTHER

(Translator and introduction writer) *Inside the Colonels' Greece,* Chatto and Windus (London, England), 1972.

Clogg is a member of the advisory board for *Synthesis: Review of Modern Greek Studies,* and a member of the editorial board for the *Journal of Modern Greek Studies.*

WORK IN PROGRESS: A Concise History of Romania, for Cambridge University Press (Cambridge, England), scheduled for publication in August 2003.

SIDELIGHTS: Richard Clogg is a historian and writer specializing in Greek and Balkan history. His book *A Short History of Modern Greece* recounts events in Greece from the thirteenth century to 1978. Taki Theodoracopulos, writing in the *Spectator,* wrote that the book offers "not one single new twist or revelation," but he noted that Clogg writes "well and concisely" and "knows Greek history well." A *Choice* reviewer, on the other hand, called *A Short History of Modern Greece* "a splendid book" and found it "lucidly written." Similarly, Steven Runciman reported in the *Times Literary Supplement* that Clogg's book is "written with great clarity."

Clogg's *Politics and the Academy: Arnold Toynbee and the Koraes Chair* relates the establishment of the Koraes Chair of Modern Greek and Byzantine History at King's College, Cambridge in 1918, when it was bestowed onhistorian Arnold Toynbee. Toynbee later resigned after running afoul of the school's Greek donors. "This book is about the political economy of academic freedom," wrote Irving J. Spitzberg, Jr., in the *Journal of Higher Education.* Spitzberg called *Politics and the Academy* "a monograph for historians of university life in Great Britain," adding that the book's message renders it "required reading for the larger community of scholars, faculty leaders, presidents, and especially vice presidents for development." Arthur Engel wrote in *American Historical Review* that Clogg "is explicit in maintaining the parallel dangers today when support for academic programs . . . is declining in Britain and the temptation is strong to seek funding from foreign governments or individuals interested in bolstering the public image of their country." J. S. F. Parker noted in *English Historical Review* that *Politics and the Academy* "tells a complex and painful story with exemplary clarity enlivened by occasional touches of comedy."

Parties and Elections in Greece: The Search for Legitimacy examines Greek politics from the late nineteenth century to the mid-1980s, with emphasis on the most recent decades. In his *Times Literature Supplement* critique, Nigel Clive recommended Clogg's study as "the most up-to-date analysis of all the salient political events [in Greece] since the end of the Second World War. There is nothing to match it in Greek." M. G. Roskin wrote in *Choice* that Clogg's book is "excellent, comprehensive, and up-to-date." The book also includes a "well-written . . . jam-packed first chapter summarizing about a hundred years," observed Betty A. Dobratz in the *American Political Science Review*.

Writing in *Choice*, T. Natsoulas recommended another of Clogg's books, *A Concise History of Greece*, as "an informative introductory political history of modern Greece." C. M. Woodhouse commented in *English Historical Review* that the book is "clear and objective, sympathetic and comprehensive." Further praise came from Kevin Featherstone, who wrote in *West European Politics* that *A Concise History of Greece* is "a well-written guide," and Andrew Mango, who stated in the *Times Literary Supplement* that Clogg's book is "succinct, accurate and graphic." Mango concluded, "Readers who go no further than this concise history will have at their disposal the basic knowledge needed to understand Greece and what made it what it is today."

Clogg has also edited numerous collections of scholarly essays on the history of modern Greece. *Greece under Military Rule*, which he co-edited with George Yannopoulos, appeared five years after military officials assumed control of Greece. In the book, contributors examine various aspects of Greek life under military leaders and analyze developments in Greek politics, education, and the arts. A *Choice* reviewer stated that "all topics are well researched" and called *Greece under Military Rule* "the best book on the subject to date." L. S. Stavrianos wrote in *Nation* that the book "provides much useful data." A *Times Literary Supplement* critic observed that the book constitutes "a brave attempt at a difficult task."

Another collection edited by Clogg, *The Struggle for Greek Independence: Essays to Mark the 150th Anniversary of the Greek War of Independence*, examines various aspects of the 1821 Greek war of independence from Ottoman rule. The volume includes subjects ranging from the Orthodox Church to the development of the Greek state. In *American Historical Review*, Domna Visvizi-Dontas called *The Struggle for Greek Independence* "a collection of well-researched essays

that deserve the attention of scholars of modern Greek history and literature." A *Times Literary Supplement* reviewer, however, found that some of the essays "show little feel for evaluating sources." An *Economist* reviewer, noting that the work contains "a rather mixed bag" of topics, concluded that the book "throws [light] on the complicated social, political and economic origins of the Greek independence movement."

In *The Movement for Greek Independence, 1770-1821: A Collection of Documents*, Clogg presents primary documents related to a turbulent period culminating in Greek independence from Ottoman rule. Donald J. Murphy, in a *Library Journal* review, praised the book as a "fine collection," adding that it "provides needed information on the roots of the Greek independence movement." A *Choice* reviewer, however, found the book "spotty, sometimes exciting and sometimes dull." C. W. Crawley wrote in the *English Historical Review* that *The Movement for Greek Independence* affords readers "helpful as well as lively reading." William St. Clair stated in the *Times Literary Supplement* that Clogg's book "is full of . . . memorable episodes and anecdotes."

Balkan Society in the Age of Greek Independence is a collection of papers on events in the Balkan states of Serbia, Montenegro, Bulgaria, and Romania during the Greek's struggle for freedom in the late eighteenth and early nineteenth centuries. *British Book News* reviewer Ian Scott-Kilvert declared that "the topics are well chosen and most of the papers written in a challenging and stimulating manner." Traian Stoianovich, however, observed in *American Historical Review* that the volume lacks "a conclusion or synthesis, an attempt to relate the papers." Roderic H. Davison, in his *History: Reviews of New Books* analysis, commented on the absence of maps. Davison concluded that *Balkan Society in the Age of Greek Independence* is nonetheless "welcome to scholars of the Balkans."

Greece, 1981-1989: The Populist Decade won praise from *International Affairs* contributor James Pettifer, who called it "a very useful and instructive book." In the *Slavonic and East European Review*, Gerasimos Augustinos noted that the work "provides a useful introduction to public affairs during an intriguing era in Greek history."

Clogg also edited *Anglo-Greek Attitudes: Studies in History*, a collection of essays examining what Michael Llewellyn Smith, writing in the *Times Literary Supple-*

ment, described as "the intense and troubled relationship between Britain and Greece." While commenting that "the title . . . promises more than the book delivers," Smith noted that readers "with a special interest in twentieth-century Greek history will welcome the collection of these essays in handy form."

BIOGRAPHICAL AND CRITICAL SOURCES:

PERIODICALS

American Historical Review, June, 1975, Domna Visvizi-Dontas, review of *The Struggle for Greek Independence,* pp. 686-687; February, 1982, Traian Stoianovich, review of *Balkan Society in the Age of Greek Independence,* pp. 215-216; April, 1988, Arthur Engel, review of *Politics and the Academy,* pp. 420-421.

American Political Science Review, September, 1989, Betty A. Dobratz, review of *Parties and Elections in Greece,* pp. 1050-1051.

British Book News, November, 1981, Ian Scott-Kilvert, review of *Balkan Society in the Age of Greek Independence,* p. 701.

Change, July/August, 1987, Rosemary Park, review of *Politics and the Academy,* p. 53.

Choice, October, 1972, review of *Greece under Military Rule,* pp. 1028-1029; October, 1976, review of *The Movement for Greek Independence, 1770-1821,* p. 1040; November, 1979, review of *A Short History of Modern Greece,* p. 1221; September, 1988, M. G. Roskin, review of *Parties and Elections in Greece,* p. 212; March, 1993, T. Natsoulas, review of *A Concise History of Greece,* p. 1214.

Economist, December 29, 1973, "Deep Divisions," p. 65.

English Historical Review, January, 1978, C. W. Crawley, review of *The Movement for Greek Independence, 1770-1821,* pp. 211-213; April, 1989, J. S. F. Parker, review of *Politics and the Academy,* pp. 539-540; September, 1995, C. M. Woodhouse, review of *A Concise History of Greece,* p. 1010.

History: Reviews of New Books, March, 1982, Roderic H. Davison, review of *Balkan Society in the Age of Greek Independence,* pp. 125-126.

International Affairs, July, 1994, James Pettifer, review of *Greece, 1981-1989,* pp. 577-578.

Journal of Higher Education, November, 1988, Irving J. Spitzberg, Jr., review of *Politics and the Academy,* pp. 692-694.

Library Journal, August, 1976, Donald J. Murphy, review of *The Movement for Greek Independence, 1770-1821,* p. 1630.

Nation, October 22, 1973, L. S. Stavrianos, "The Best Damn Government since Pericles," pp. 405-407.

New York Review of Books, October 8, 1981, Peter Green, "Greece against Itself," p. 35.

Slavonic and East European Review, April, 1995, Gerasimos Augustinos, review of *Greece, 1981-1989,* pp. 366-368.

Spectator, June 30, 1979, Taki Theodoracopulos, "The Greek Experience," pp. 22-23.

Times Literary Supplement, March 9, 1973, "Greece in Darkness," pp. 255-256; February 1, 1974, "A Greece for Greeks," p. 102; September 17, 1976, William St. Clair, "The Founding Fathers," p. 1179; November 23, 1979, Steven Runciman, review of *A Short History of Modern Greece,* p. 5; July 22, 1988, Nigel Clive, "From ERE to PASOK," p. 816; April 30, 1993, Andrew Mango, "From Province to Suburb," p. 24; October 12, 2001, Michael Llewellyn Smith, "Venom and Venizelos," p. 12.

West European Politics, January, 1994, Kevin Featherstone, review of *A Concise History of Greece,* p. 208.

OTHER

Journal of Modern Greek Studies, http://www.press.jhu.edu/ (May 27, 2002), "Editors and Editorial Boards."

Oxford Balkan Society, http://www.balkans.org.uk/ (May 27, 2002), "Executive Committee Members."

St. Antony's College, Oxford Web site, http://www.sant.ox.ac.uk/ (May 27, 2002), "European Studies Centre."

Synthesis: Review of Modern Greek Studies, http://www.hri.org/synthesis/ (May 27, 2002).*

*   *   *

CLOUTS, Sydney 1926-1982

PERSONAL: Born January 10, 1926, in Cape Town, South Africa; died 1982; children: three. *Education:* Attended South African College; University of Cape Town, B.A.

CAREER: Institute of the Study of English, Africa, research fellow, beginning 1969.

AWARDS, HONORS: Ingrid Jonker Prize, 1968; Olive Schreiner Award, 1968.

WRITINGS:

One Life, Purnell (Cape Town, South Africa), 1966.
Sydney Clouts: Collected Poems, David Philip (Cape Town, South Africa), 1984.

Contributor to magazines, including *Contrast, New Coin, Transatlantic Review,* and *Listener.*

SIDELIGHTS:

Although only one of Sydney Clout's books was published during his lifetime, the South African poet continues to be an object of discussion for many literary critics, largely due to his crusade to develop a unique South African language. Born January 10, 1926, in the South African city of Cape Town, Clouts was a white man who once described himself as "not aboriginaly African," but rather "a South African Jewish writer writing in English." In his earliest poetry, Clouts attempted to meld himself, the poet, with the African landscape. By the mid-1950s, however, his verse increasingly turned to the theme of what it meant to be African, with its racial divisions and hostilities. "My country has given me flint for a soul," he wrote in the poem "Roy Kloof," which is about a boy of mixed origin who is filled with confusion about his heritage and his homeland. Other poems, including "The Game," continues this theme. "Flowers are toppling/ the earth burbles blood./ O scholars of Mercy/ interpret the flood!," Clouts wrote.

Clouts wrote the majority of his poetry in the 1950s and 1960s, publishing his first volume, *One Life,* in 1966. The book became the only one published during his lifetime; a compilation of his work, titled *Sydney Clouts: Collected Poems,* was published in 1984, two years after his death.

Despite Clouts' ambitions, many critics felt he never accomplished his goal of becoming a voice for his homeland. In *World Literature Written in English,* critic Stephen Watson wrote: "Clouts failed to achieve what I imagine must have been his dearest wish: to become an African poet. He remains a colonizer poet, one neither of England nor wholly of Africa, occupying a ground so indeterminate that it frequently appears to be groundless. And that was his tragedy." Watson concluded, "He never really discovered a language for his anguish."

While Clouts never achieved the kind of recognition he sought during his lifetime, some more recent critics, including D. R. Beeton, have praised him. "I believe Sydney Clouts to be a truly great poet," Beeton wrote in *Contemporary Poets.* "His quality is immediately apprehended in his crystalline imagery, but it is often best seen in the quieter shades of his perception."

Clouts did receive some critical praise immediately following the publication of *One Life,* and the book earned him several literary honors in 1968, including the Ingrid Jonker Prize and the Olive Schreiner Award. In addition to the two volumes of his work, Clouts' poetry appeared in a number of publications, including *Contrast, New Coin, Transatlantic Review,* and *Listener.* Beginning in 1969, he also worked as a research fellow at the Institute of the Study of English in Africa.

BIOGRAPHICAL AND CRITICAL SOURCES:

BOOKS

Contemporary Poets, 3rd edition, St. James Press (Detroit, MI), 1980.

PERIODICALS

English in Africa, October, 1984; October, 1992, pp. 15-34.
Theoria, May, 1990, Susan Joubert, "The Unresolved Shibboleth: Sydney Clouts and the Problems of an African Poetry," pp. 87-106.
World Literature Written in English, autumn, 1988, Stephen Watson, "Sydney Clouts and the Limits of Romanticism," pp. 210-232.*

CLYDE, Laurel Anne 1946-

PERSONAL: Born February 7, 1946, in Holbrook, Australia. *Education:* University of Sydney, B.A., 1965, Diploma of Education, 1966, M.A., 1973; James Cook University of North Queensland, Ph.D., 1981.

ADDRESSES: Office—Faculty of Social Science, University of Iceland, 101 Reykjavik, Iceland. *E-mail*—anne@hi.is.

CAREER: University of British Columbia, Vancouver, British Columbia, Canada, associate professor, 1991-93; University of Iceland, Department of Library and Information Science, Reykjavik, Iceland, professor, 1993—; University of Western Australia, Graduate School of Management, Crawley, Western Australia, adjunct professor, 1993—. Netweaver, Perth, Western Australia, consultant to business in areas of Web development and Internet training. International Association of School Librarianship, Webmaster.

MEMBER: Fellow of the Library Association (United Kingdom), Associate of the Australian Library Association; Australian Computer Society, International Association of School Librarianship, Records Management Association of Australia.

WRITINGS:

(With D. Joan Joyce) *Computers and School Libraries: An Annotated Bibliography,* Alcuin Library Consultants (Wagga Wagga, Australia), 1986.
Computer Software for School Libraries: A Directory, Alcuin Library Consultants (Wagga Wagga, Australia), 1986.
(With Marjorie Lobban) *Out of the Closet and into the Classroom,* D.W. Thorpe (Melbourne, Australia), 1992.
Computer Applications in Libraries: A Directory of Systems and Software, D.W. Thorpe (Melbourne, Australia), 1993.
An Introduction to the Internet, Lindin Publications (Reykjavik, Iceland), 1995.
School Libraries and the Electronic Community: The Internet Connection, Scarecrow Press (Lanham, MD), 1997.

Managing Infotec in School Library Media Centers, Libraries Unlimited (Englewood, CO), 1999.
The School Library Web Site, Linwood Press, 2002.

WORK IN PROGRESS: Research in quality indicators for school library Web sites.

SIDELIGHTS: Laurel Anne Clyde is an international authority on the use of online information services in the school library. Clyde has made an ongoing study of the evaluation of school library Web sites. As media specialists in school libraries strive to make quality content available, constant changes in technology make their task increasingly difficult. *Managing Infotec in School Library Media Centers* begins with a step-by-step plan on using and managing technology and tech services. The book clearly shows the division of responsibilities, including circulation, acquisition, collection assessment, budgeting and security.

Dividing her time between the University of Iceland and her native Australia, Clyde maintains the necessary global perspective on her topic. In *Booklist,* reviewer Roger Leslie noted that "Media specialists at any stage of technological expertise—from those just beginning to automate a single facility to those managing an extensive network of media centers—will find Clyde's ambitious work clear, authoritative, and ultimately invaluable." Carolyn Giambra, writing in *Teacher Librarian,* said "the author provides the school library media program context so frequently ignored in other technology writing."

BIOGRAPHICAL AND CRITICAL SOURCES:

PERIODICALS

American Libraries, May, 2000, Cathleen Boordon, review of *Managing Infotec in School Library Media Centers,* p. 93.
Booklist, August, 2000, Roger Leslie, review of *Managing Infotec in School Library Media Centers,* p. 2151.
Multimedia Schools, January, 2001, Jean Reese, review of *Managing Infotec in School Library Media Centers,* p. 43.
Teacher Librarian, June, 2000, Carolyn Giambra, review of *Managing Infotec in School Library Media Centers,* p. 43.

COHEN, G(erald) A(llan) 1941-

PERSONAL: Born April 14, 1941, in Montreal, Quebec, Canada; son of Morrie (a dress cutter) and Bella (Lipkin) Cohen; married Margaret Pearce, July 24, 1965 (marriage ended, September, 1996); married Michèle Perrenoud, July 12, 1999; children: (first marriage) Gideon, Miriam, Sarah. *Ethnicity:* "Jewish." *Education:* McGill University, B.A., 1961; Oxford University, B.Phil., 1963. *Hobbies and other interests:* Solitaire, the *Guardian* crossword puzzle, Broadway and Hollywood music, the politics of India, the visual arts.

ADDRESSES: Home—6 Bartlemas Rd., Oxford OX1 4AL, England. *Office*—All Souls' College, Oxford University, Oxford OX1 4AL, England; fax: 44-01865-279-299. *E-mail*—gerald.cohen@all-souls.ox.ac.uk.

CAREER: University College, London, London, England, lecturer, 1963-78, reader in philosophy, 1978-85; Oxford University, Oxford, England, Chichele Professor of Social and Political Theory and fellow of All Souls' College, 1985—.

MEMBER: British Academy (fellow).

AWARDS, HONORS: Isaac Deutscher Memorial Prize, 1979.

WRITINGS:

Karl Marx's Theory of History, Princeton University Press (Princeton, NJ), 1978, expanded edition, 2000.
History, Labour, and Freedom: Themes from Marx, Oxford University Press (Oxford, England), 1988.
Self-Ownership, Freedom, and Equality, Cambridge University Press (Cambridge, England), 1995.
If You're an Egalitarian, How Come You're So Rich?, Harvard University Press (Cambridge, MA), 2000.

BIOGRAPHICAL AND CRITICAL SOURCES:

PERIODICALS

Canadian Journal of Philosophy, December, 1998, Peter Vallentyne, review of *Self-Ownership, Freedom, and Equality,* p. 609.

Dialogue, spring, 2002, Elisabeth Boetzkes, review of *If You're an Egalitarian, How Come You're So Rich?,* p. 386.
Dissent, spring, 2001, George Scialabba, review of *If You're an Egalitarian, How Come You're So Rich?,* p. 115.
Economist, September 23, 2000, review of *If You're an Egalitarian, How Come You're So Rich?,* p. 160.
Ethics, April, 1997, Eric Mack, review of *Self-Ownership, Freedom, and Equality,* p. 517.
Inquiry, December, 1989, William H. Shaw, review of *History, Labour, and Freedom: Themes from Marx,* p. 437.
Mind, October, 2000, Leif Wenar, review of *Self-Ownership, Freedom, and Equality,* p. 869.
New Left Review, January-February, 2001, Jacob Stevens, review of *If You're an Egalitarian, How Come You're So Rich?,* p. 145.
Philosophical Quarterly, October, 2001, Axel Gosseries, review of *If You're an Egalitarian, How Come You're So Rich?,* p. 563.
Philosophy, July, 1997, D. A. Lloyd Thomas, review of *Self-Ownership, Freedom, and Equality,* p. 478.
Political Studies, December, 1990, David McLellan, review of *History, Labour, and Freedom,* p. 756; December, 1997, Vittorio Bufacchi, review of *Self-Ownership, Freedom, and Equality,* p. 963; June, 2001, Saladin Meckled-Garcia, review of *If You're an Egalitarian, How Come You're So Rich?,* p. 341.
Political Theory, May, 1990, Daniel Little, review of *History, Labour, and Freedom,* p. 312; June, 1998, Keith Ansell Pearson, review of *Self-Ownership, Freedom, and Equality,* p. 399.
Review of Radical Political Economics, winter, 1998, Renzo Llorente, review of *Self-Ownership, Freedom, and Equality,* p. 108.
Review of Social Economy, fall, 1997, Tom Mayer, review of *Self-Ownership, Freedom, and Equality,* p. 389.
Theological Studies, June, 1997, Arthur F. McGovern, review of *Self-Ownership, Freedom, and Equality,* p. 382.
Times Higher Education Supplement, January 12, 2001, John Dunn, review of *If You're an Egalitarian, How Come You're So Rich?,* p. 469.
Times Literary Supplement, July 21, 1989, David McLellan, review of *History, Labour, and Freedom,* p. 809; June 23, 2000, Thomas Nagel, review of *If You're an Egalitarian, How Come You're So Rich?,* p. 5.

COLE-WHITTAKER, Terry 1939-

PERSONAL: Born 1939, in Los Angeles, CA; married John Cole (divorced); married John Whittaker (divorced); married Michael Peterson (divorced); married Leonard Radomile (divorced); children (first marriage): Rebecca, Suzanne. *Education:* Attended Orange Coast College; attended Earnest Holmes School of Ministry, 1975.

ADDRESSES: Home—Lives in Malibu, CA. *Agent*—c/o Author Mail, Penguin Putnam, 375 Hudson St., New York, NY 10014.

CAREER: La Jolla Church of Religious Science, La Jolla, CA, minister, 1975-82; Terry Cole-Whittaker Ministries, San Diego, CA, founder and minister; Innerfaith Ministries, Palm Springs, CA, founder; former TV evangelist; Adventures in Enlightenment, founder and chairman; Foundation for Spiritual Study, founder.

WRITINGS:

What You Think of Me Is None of My Business, Oak Tree (La Jolla, CA), 1979.
How to Have More in a Have-Not World, Rawson (New York, NY), 1983.
The Inner Path from Where You Are to Where You Want to Be, Rawson (New York, NY), 1986.
Love and Power in a World without Limits: A Woman's Guide to the Goddess Within, Harper & Row (San Francisco, CA), 1989.
Having Beautiful Relationships (cassette), Hay House (Carson, CA), 1991.
Money Is God in Action (cassette), Hay House (Carson, CA), 1992.
Every Saint Has a Past, Every Sinner a Future: Seven Steps to the Spiritual and Material Riches of Life, Putnam (New York, NY), 2001.

SIDELIGHTS: In *How to Have More in a Have-Not World,* Terry Cole-Whittaker gives advice on how to become happy, healthy, rich, and a participant in God's plan. *Booklist* reviewer John Brosnahan claimed, "The volume's dynamic message is certain to find a receptive audience."

In *The Inner Path from Where You Are to Where You Want to Be,* Cole-Whittaker discusses how she became disappointed and overwhelmed with big business religion and her public ministry and decided to leave it all to search for personal growth and enlightenment.

Cole-Whittaker has also published self-help cassettes. In *Having Beautiful Relationships* she talks about her past unhappy relationships and how she changed herself and how others can change themselves. It also includes meditations for relaxation. In her cassette *Money Is God in Action,* Cole-Whittaker ties money to God's will. She discusses how money is a medium of exchange and asserts that if God is energy, then money is God in action. A reviewer for *Publishers Weekly* commented, "While the tape may stretch the bounds of self-help fare, its fundamental message holds universal appeal."

BIOGRAPHICAL AND CRITICAL SOURCES:

PERIODICALS

Booklist, January 1, 1984, John Brosnahan, review of *How to Have More in a Have-Not World,* p. 652.
Kirkus Reviews, October 1, 1983, review of *How to Have More in a Have-Not World,* p. 1074.
Library Journal, April 1, 1986, Elise Chase, review of *The Inner Path from Where You Are to Where You Want to Be,* p. 155; May 1, 1992, review of *Having Beautiful Relationships,* p. 135.
People Weekly, November 26, 1984, D. Keith Mano, "Terry Cole-Whitakker; Power, Money, Sex—America's Hottest Go-Go Evangelist Says You Can Have It All with No Guilt," p. 99.
Publishers Weekly, February 21, 1986, review of *The Inner Path from Where You Are to Where You Want to Be,* p. 158; May 4, 1992, review of *Money Is God in Action,* p. 27; April 23, 2001, review of *Every Saint Has a Past, Every Sinner a Future: Seven Steps to the Spiritual and Material Riches of Life,* p. 70.
Time, April 22, 1985, "Abrupt Exit; Woman Evangelist's Goodbye," p. 60.

OTHER

Terry Cole-Whittaker Web site, http://www.terrycolewhittaker.com/ (February 6, 2002), "About Dr. Terry Cole-Whittaker."*

*   *   *

CORRY, John A. 1931-

PERSONAL: Born November 17, 1931, in OH; son of Homer (a lawyer) and Cornelia (Adams) Corry; married Emily McKnight, 1963; children: Anne McKnight Corry. *Education:* Princeton University, B.A. (magna cum laude), 1953; Harvard Law School, J.D., 1956. *Religion:* "Protestant Christian."

ADDRESSES: Office—Davis Polk & Wardwell, 450 Lexington Ave., New York, NY 10017.

CAREER: Lawyer and writer. Davis, Polk & Wardwell, tax attorney, 1956-67, partner, 1967-97, senior counsel, 1997—.

MEMBER: New York State Bar Association (chair of tax section, 1992), Association of the Bar of the City of New York, American Bar Association, Tax Advisory Group of the American Law Institute Federal Income Tax Project.

WRITINGS:

1898: Prelude to a Century, self-published, distributed by Fordham University Press (Bronx, NY), 1998.
A Rough Ride to Albany: Teddy Runs for Governor, self-published, distributed by Fordham University Press (Bronx, NY), 2000.

WORK IN PROGRESS: A history of Lincoln's Cooper Union speech.

SIDELIGHTS: John A. Corry is a Harvard-educated tax lawyer who spent his career practicing in New York City. He has combined his love of writing with his love of history and self-published two books since his retirement as a partner in the law firm of Davis Polk and Wardwell. Fordham University Press distributes both books, *1898: Prelude to a Century* and *A Rough Ride to Albany: Teddy Runs for Governor.*

As a Princeton student, Corry was a reporter for, then editor-in-chief of, the *Daily Princetonian.* He continued writing all during his legal career, and as he approached retirement in the mid-1990s, he decided to combine his love of writing with a "long-standing interest in American and European history." "I picked the subject of my book on the year 1898 after determining that that year was much more important in United States and world affairs than 2000, which initially seemed an obvious choice because of its position as the first year of the century that was shortly to close," Corry told *CA.*

In researching his first book, Corry discovered an episode of Teddy Roosevelt's life that he came to believe had not been adequately covered elsewhere. He decided to write about the episode himself, and the result was the book *A Rough Ride to Albany.* In a review for *History: Review of New Books,* Larry Madaras noted that the book is a "good read because Corry captures the feel of the 1898 New York gubernatorial campaign." Included are portraits of other compelling characters in addition to Roosevelt himself, including the New York State Republican "Easy Boss" Thomas Collier Platt- an influential figure of the era who was often at odds with Roosevelt.

Corry told *CA:* "My goal is to write for the general reader, to whom history is most interesting when it is related in narrative form. As I did in my legal practice, my practice is to start writing before completing my research, since the discipline of putting words to paper often leads to further research which adds important details and insights to the final product."

BIOGRAPHICAL AND CRITICAL SOURCES:

PERIODICALS

Choice, June, 2001, S. L. Piott, review of *A Rough Ride to Albany: Teddy Runs for Governor,* p. 1852.
History: Review of New Books, winter, 2001, Larry Madaras, review of *A Rough Ride to Albany,* p. 57.
Library Journal, May 1, 1998, Brooks D. Simpson, review of *1898: Prelude to a Century,* p. 114.
New York Law Journal, January 2, 2001, Theodore R. Kupferman, review of *A Rough Ride to Albany,* p. 2.

*　　*　　*

CRAIG, Charmaine 1971(?)-

PERSONAL: Born c. 1971. *Education:* Harvard University, B.A. (magna cum laude); University of California at Irvine, M.F.A. (writing).

ADDRESSES: Home—Lives in Laguna Beach, CA. *Agent*—c/o Author Mail, Penguin Putnam Inc., 375 Hudson Street, New York, NY 10014.

CAREER: Novelist and actress. Film credits include *White Fang 2: Myth of the White Wolf,* Disney, 1994; television credits include *Northern Exposure.*

AWARDS, HONORS: Glimmer Train Press finalist, 1998, for *In a Whisper.*

WRITINGS:

The Good Men: A Novel of Heresy, Riverhead Books (New York, NY), 2002.

WORK IN PROGRESS: A novel inspired by her mother's family story and the struggle of the ethnic minority groups against the Burmese military junta.

SIDELIGHTS: Before Charmaine Craig embarked upon a literary career, she was actively engaged in the world of dramatic arts. In her earlier years, she appeared in community theater and student productions. During her studies at Harvard University, Craig was chosen for a role in *White Fang II,* and after graduation she appeared in the television series *Northern Exposure.* Despite her dramatic interests and experiences, however, an incident occurred during her student years that provided the impulse for laying aside her theatrical career.

While at Harvard Craig majored in medieval studies, a field in which she graduated with honors. As part of her historical research, she discovered the testimony of Grazida Lizier, a young woman who appeared before the judges of the Inquisition in 1320. Craig became "intrigued by Grazida's frank and plainspoken description of an affair she had with the village priest," explained *Orange County Register* contributor Valerie Takahama. Grazida was only fourteen years old when the affair began. "One thing that drew me to [Grazida]," Craig told Takahama, "is her relationship to her sexuality and her body and issues of pleasure seemed so contemporary."

Craig found it impossible to forget Grazida's story, and when she entered the writing program at the University of California at Irvine, she determined to write a novel based upon it. As she began the work, Craig imagined that she would write "a slim, lyrical volume of ecstasies," she told Takahama. What

emerged, however, was a 400-page novel accompanied by a timeline, definitions of heretical terms, and an impressive list of reference books.

The Good Men: A Novel of Heresy was based on testimony of the Cathars, a religious heretical group that flourished during the twelfth and thirteenth centuries in southern France. The Cathars followed a dualistic philosophy: they believed that God and Satan were co-creators of the world. The Cathars also believed that Christ had remained a pure spirit, never actually incarnating in human form, and therefore they rejected the Catholic Eucharist. As a result Pope Innocent III began a persecution of the sect, whose popularity he deemed dangerous to the Church. The last Cathar was executed in 1321. Craig used this historical background to examine the lives of the people of Montaillou, a medieval village located in the Pyrenees mountains. The novel, spanning three generations, describes what happens when neighbors turn against each other in a religious war.

Michelle Latiolais, quoted by Takahama, praised Craig's ability to inform modern readers about the Cathars, heresy, and the medieval Catholic Church. Latiolais remarked: "She dramatized it beautifully. I think the work that she did in educating a contemporary audience is masterful." A contributor to *Kirkus Reviews* considered *The Good Men* to be "a somewhat creaky debut true-life historical: part romance, part legal thriller, and a tour of some of the darkest corners of early Christianity." Kathryn Harrison of the *New York Times Book Review,* called Craig's work "an ambitious first novel." The critic stated: "There is much to admire in *The Good Men,* especially its deft juggling of complex intersecting story lines."

BIOGRAPHICAL AND CRITICAL SOURCES:

PERIODICALS

Kirkus Reviews, October 15, 2001, review of *The Good Men: A Novel of Heresy,* p. 1443.
New York Times Book Review, January 20, 2002, Kathryn Harrison, "*The Good Men:* A Sexually Obsessed Priest and the Inquisition."
Publishers Weekly, December 13, 2001, review of *The Good Men.*

OTHER

Glimmer Train Press, Inc., http://www.glimmertrain. com/ (March 7, 2002), "Very Short Fiction Award: Top 25 Winners and Finalists, Winter 1998."

MPR Books Web site, http://www.mpr.org/books/titles/ craig_thegoodmen.shtml (March 7, 2002), review of *The Good Men.*

Orange County Register, http://www.ocregister.com (January 21, 2002), Valerie Takahama, "Renaissance Woman."

Penguin Putnam Inc. Home Page, http://www. penguinputnam.com/ (March 12, 2002).*

*   *   *

CREMINS, Robert 1968-

PERSONAL: Born 1968, in Dublin, Ireland; married Melanie Danburg, 1993; children: David. *Education:* Trinity College, Dublin, B.A., 1990; University of East Anglia, England, M.A. *Religion:* Catholic.

ADDRESSES: Office—Strake Jesuit College Preparatory, 8900 Bellaire Blvd., Houston, TX 77036. *E-mail*—cremins_r@strakejesuit.org.

CAREER: American School, Paris, France, teacher; Strake Jesuit High School, Houston, TX, English teacher, 1993—.

WRITINGS:

A Sort of Homecoming: A Novel, Sceptre Books (London, England), 1998, W. W. Norton (New York, NY), 2000.

Send in the Devils, Sceptre Books (London, England), 2001.

Contributor of short stories to magazines; contributor of reviews to *Houston Chronicle.*

SIDELIGHTS: As a native of Ireland and part of the Irish diaspora himself, Robert Cremins is familiar with the topics explored in his first novel, *A Sort of Homecoming.* The tale is told through the eyes of the young, egotistical Tom Iremonger, who has just returned from a post-college fling around Europe funded by an inheritance from his grandfather. Tom plans to spend a year on the road, but after six months decides to make the obligatory trip home for Christmas. Expecting to dazzle his friends with his worldliness, he is surprised to find that home has changed as much as he has. His ex-girlfriend is dating someone new and has no interest in reuniting; his college pals have turned gangster; and all of his self-made "Rules of Cool" seem not to apply any longer. Tom compounds his self-absorption with alcohol and drugs, but the changes in his home turf finally start to effect a change in Tom, forcing him to take a closer look at who he has become.

Despite the seemingly serious plot, *A Sort of Homecoming* is quite funny. "Cremins sets [Iremonger] up to be not quite as well aware as he thinks," wrote Peter O' Malley in an online review for *Literal Mind.* "This makes for some seriously funny self-deception on Iremonger's part." The story is told in the first-person and primarily in the present tense, only moving to past tense when Iremonger reminisces. In this way, the reader gets the full effect of Iremonger's inflated ego and his eventual move toward maturity.

On another plane, Tom's story illustrates the tension between the old and the new Ireland. "Cremins uses his protagonist's delusion as a kind of warped prism through which to view larger issues facing contemporary Ireland: the constant exodus of its youth, troubled Catholic/Protestant relations and the erosion of Irish culture by the 'nouveau-riches' fad-conscious consumerism," wrote a *Publishers Weekly* reviewer.

Cremins garnered praise for his debut novel, and has been compared to Martin Amis by some British critics. The *Los Angeles Times* included *A Sort of Homecoming* in its "Best Books of 2000" list, observing that "Cremin's authorial control—his jazzy, sharp word riffs, his precise observation and his dark humor—mirror Amis', but he leaves out the ice kernel of misanthropy that lies at the heart of Amis' art; there is a soft center under the satisfyingly hard candy crunch of this book." George Needham noted in *Booklist:* "Admittedly, the coming-of-age premise is overworked, but Cremins manages to bring a fresh sensibility, an uncommon texture, and a unique environment to his tale. The characters are sharply etched, and the dialogue soars with a mixture of Irish, American, and Eurotrash slang."

Iremonger "is, in an exaggerated comic way—with a serious undertone—a distorted reflection of what happens when you withdraw one set of values but (another) set of values isn't there to take its place," Cremins explained to Fritz Lanham of the *Houston Chronicle.* Lanham concluded, "*A Sort of Homecoming* is a wise and funny novel. And for American readers, it opens a window on a relatively affluent, cosmopolitan Ireland that contradicts the stereotypes."

In 2002 Cremins followed up his literary debut with *Send in the Devils,* a humorous portrait of a young Irishman of wealthy lineage who moves to Maverick, Texas to escape a befuddled attempt at becoming a self-sufficient adult. When a friend who hopes to marry into the family is sent to the New World to bring home the errant John Paul Mountain, the cultures of upper-crust Ireland and Texas collide with typically surprising results.

BIOGRAPHICAL AND CRITICAL SOURCES:

PERIODICALS

Booklist, April 1, 2000, George Needham, review of *A Sort of Homecoming: A Novel,* p. 1432.
Houston Chronicle, August 23, 1998, Fritz Lanham, "Robert Cremins: Voice of the Irish Diaspora," p. 9.
Houston Chronicle (Houston, TX), October 7, 1998, Fritz Lanham, "Signature Authors," p. 7.
New York Times, April 16, 2000, Daniel Handler, "The Anti-Odyssey," p. 25.
Publishers Weekly, April 10, 2000, review of *A Sort of Homecoming,* p. 76.

OTHER

Company Magazine, http://www.companysj.com/ (April 3, 2000), "Someone You Should Know: Mr. Robert Cremins."
Literal Mind, http://www.literalmind.com/ (August 25, 2001), Peter J. O' Malley, review of *A Sort of Homecoming.*

*   *   *

CRUSE, Mary Anne 1825-1910

PERSONAL: Born 1825, in Huntsville, AL; died 1910; daughter of Samuel and Harriet Maria (Coleman) Cruse. *Religion:* Episcopalian.

CAREER: Writer, 1854-88.

WRITINGS:

The Little Episcopalian; or, The Child Taught by the Prayerbook, General Protestant Episcopal S. S. Union and Church Book Society (New York, NY), 1854.
Bessie Melville; or, Prayer Book Instructions Carried Out into Life: Sequel to the "Little Episcopalian," Daniel Dana (New York, NY), 1858.
Cameron Hall: A Story of the Civil War (novel), Lippincott (Philadelphia, PA), 1867.
Auntie's Christmas Trees: The Child's Gift-Book for the Christmas Holidays, General Protestant Episcopal S. S. Union and Church Book Society (New York, NY), 1875.
The Tiny Lawn Tennis Club, Dutton (New York, NY), 1880.
The Children's Kettledrum, Dean (London, England), 1881.
Little Grandpa, Whittaker (New York, NY), 1888.

SIDELIGHTS: Mary Anne Cruse was a southern writer who is probably best known as the author of *Cameron Hall: A Story of the Civil War,* which reflected her wartime experiences in a southern city occupied by Union forces. Cruse was born in Huntsville, Alabama in 1825. Growing up, she lived what Amy E. Hudock, writing in the *Dictionary of Literary Biography,* described as "an aristocratic lifestyle," and she enjoyed what Hudock called "leisure time for developing the mind and spirit." Cruse indulged a particular interest in theology, and in the 1850s she produced two books, *The Little Episcopalian; or, The Child Taught by the Prayerbook* and *Bessie Melville; or, Prayer Book Instructions Carried Out into Life: Sequel to the "Little Episcopalian,"* that Hudock summarized as "moral tales for children."

When the U.S. Civil War erupted in 1861, Alabama numbered among the Confederate states, but many citizens in Huntsville expressed sympathy for the Union cause. Despite their support, Huntsville residents saw their town regularly ravaged by Union troops which occupied the region for all but a brief period during the war. As Hudock noted, "Many Huntsville civilians suffered the loss of property, possessions, and dignity as the occupying Union forces attempted to paralyze the Confederate forces in the area by damaging the infrastructure of the society."

In 1867, two years after the war ended with the defeat of the Confederacy, Cruse—who had supported the losing side—published *Cameron Hall,* in which she re-creates life under Union occupation. The novel recounts the wartime experiences of the Cameron family, notably George Cameron and his sisters, Eva and Julia. While George defies family allegiances and joins the Union troops, Eva and Julia attempt to maintain domestic stability. Union soldiers, however, cruelly impose themselves, destroying homes and humiliating the citizenry. In one episode, an officer embarrasses Eva by reading aloud from her private love letters. "In this depiction of the indignities of war," wrote Hudock, "Cruse condemned not only the Union troops but also the capacity of war to turn men into monsters and make women the 'spoils of war.'" Eva eventually succumbs to insanity while futilely awaiting the return of her husband. But Julia, who had fled with her father—but failed to save his life—survives and returns to the family estate, as does her brother. Hudock contended, though, that "the ending is ultimately bleak," and she acknowledged Cruse's belief that "the only true hope in life was for Christian salvation, not military or political intervention."

In the years after its initial publication, *Cameron Hall* won recognition as a compelling depiction of Southern life during the Civil War. Hudock, for example, described the novel as "a fascinating firsthand examination of the life of an upper-class, white Southern woman," and she observed that the book "reveals the emotions of an occupied people." Hudock concluded her *Dictionary of Literary Biography* piece by stating, "Civil War fiction by women is part of the record of those tumultuous times, and *Cameron Hall* is a significant contribution to that genre."

In 1875 Cruse published another children's book, *Auntie's Christmas Trees: The Child's Gift-Book for the Christmas Holidays,* and in the ensuing decade she produced more juvenilia, including *Little Grandpa,* which appeared in 1888. Cruse then ceased writing books, although she lived another twenty-two years.

BIOGRAPHICAL AND CRITICAL SOURCES:

BOOKS

Dictionary of Literary Biography, Volume 239: *American Women Prose Writers, 1820-1870,* Gale (Detroit, MI), 2001, pp. 50-54.
Moss, Elizabeth, *Domestic Novelists of the Old South: Defenders of Southern Culture,* Louisiana State University Press (Baton Rouge, LA), 1992.

PERIODICALS

Southern Quarterly, summer, 1996, Robert Hunt, "Domesticity, Paternalism, and Isolation: Mary Anne Cruse and the Search for Moral Asylum," pp. 15-24.*

*   *   *

CZECH, Brian 1960-

PERSONAL: Born 1960. *Education:* University of Wisconsin, B.S. (wildlife ecology); University of Washington, M.S. (wildlife science); University of Arizona, Ph.D. (renewable natural resources); certified wildlife biologist. *Politics:* Independent/Green. *Hobbies and other interests:* Hiking, hunting, history.

ADDRESSES: Office—U.S. Fish and Wildlife Service, 4401 North Fairfax Dr., Arlington, VA 22203.

CAREER: San Carlos Apache Tribe Recreation and Wildlife Department, director; U.S. Fish and Wildlife Service, Arlington, VA, conservation biologist.

MEMBER: International Society for Ecological Economics, Wildlife Society, American Society for Ecological Economics (charter member), Society for Conservation Biology, Association for Politics and the Life Sciences, Society for Ecosystem Health, Ecological Information Network, Evans Scholars Foundation.

AWARDS, HONORS: National Leadership Award, Elks Club, 1978; Charles Lathrop Pack Essay Award, 1987; Hugo Winkenwerder Fellowship, 1987; U.S. Fish and Wildlife Service Star Award, 1999.

WRITINGS:

Shoveling Fuel for a Runaway Train: Errant and Shameful Spenders, and a Plan to Stop Them All, University of California Press (Berkeley, CA), 2000.
(With Paul R. Krausman) *The Endangered Species Act: History, Conservation Biology, and Public Policy,* Johns Hopkins University Press (Baltimore, MD), 2001.

Contributor to books, including *Rangeland Wildlife,* edited by P. R. Krausman, Society for Range Management (Denver, CO), 1996; and *Ecology and Management of Large Mammals in North America,* edited by S. Demarais and P. R. Krausman, Prentice Hall (Saddle River, NJ), 1999. Contributor of numerous articles to periodicals, including *Conservation Biology, Ecological Economics, Wildlife Society Bulletin, Endangered Species Update, Renewable Resources Journal, Environmental Conservation,* and *Journal of Range Management.* Guest editor, *Wildlife Society Bulletin,* 2000.

SIDELIGHTS: Brian Czech is a conservation biologist with the U.S. Fish and Wildlife Service. His *Shoveling Fuel for a Runaway Train: Errant and Shameful Spenders, and a Plan to Stop Them All* begins as an academic exercise and ends as a public tract designed to trigger a "steady state revolution" in the United States. *Shoveling Fuel* applies principles of wildlife science and evolutionary ecology to the workings of the human economy. It finds mainstream or "neoclassical" economic growth theory to be fallacious, dangerous, and most likely corrupted at the nexus of academia, corporatism, and government. Following a thorough debunking of Julian Simon's *Ultimate Resource 2, Shoveling Fuel* includes an overview of ecological economics and some of its leading theorists. Part two provides a blueprint for the steady state revolution, which is part academic, part social.

Theories of Darwin, Veblen, and Maslow are synthesized to reveal the "liquidator syndrome" afflicting many Americans. Three classes are identified: the wantonly wasteful liquidating class, the socially redeeming steady state class, and the watchful amorphic class.

Czech proposes that, once the motives of the liquidators and the effects of their behavior are revealed to a majority of Americans, the steady state class will begin to castigate the liquidating class, unleashing powerful motivational forces and a positive feedback process of "trickle-down consumption." This social movement, increasingly informed by the ecological economics movement in academia, will lead to the establishment of a steady state, sustainable economy. *Shoveling Fuel* concludes with a highly unconventional exhortation to the steady state class. A reviewer for *Publishers Weekly* claimed that "Czech is always clear but never condescending, serious but not without humor."

BIOGRAPHICAL AND CRITICAL SOURCES:

PERIODICALS

Kirkus Reviews, July 1, 2000, review of *Shoveling Fuel for a Runaway Train: Errant and Shameful Spenders, and a Plan to Stop Them All,* p. 930.
Publishers Weekly, August 14, 2000, review of *Shoveling Fuel for a Runaway Train,* p. 340.

D

DAMERON, Chip 1947-

PERSONAL: Born October 8, 1947, in Dallas, TX; son of Charles (a newspaper editor) and Madelyn (a homemaker; maiden name, Burgesser) Dameron; married Joan Farnham (a realtor), October 4, 1980; children: Michael. *Education:* Duke University, B.A., 1970; University of Texas at Austin, M.A., 1973, Ph.D. (English), 1985.

ADDRESSES: Office—University of Texas at Brownsville, 80 Fort Brown, Brownsville, TX 78520. *E-mail*—dameron@utb.edu.

CAREER: Poet and educator, University of Texas at Brownsville, professor of English, 1985—.

WRITINGS:

From Ben Bulben to the Rhine (travel), Gato Negro Press, 1981.
In the Magnetic Arena (poetry), Latitudes Press, 1987.
(With John Garmon and Marty Lewis) *Night Spiders, Morning Milk, Definition of Hours* (poetry), Hawk Press, 1990.
Hook & Bloodline (poetry), Wings Press, 2000.

Contributor of more than one hundred poems to literary magazines.

*   *   *

DeMARCO, Michael

PERSONAL: Married; wife's name Jennifer; children: Benjamin. *Education:* Williams College, B.A. (cum laude).

ADDRESSES: Home—Vienna, VA. *Agent*—c/o AMACON, 1601 Broadway, New York, NY 10019.

CAREER: Writer, management consultant with PricewaterhouseCoopers, and investment adviser.

WRITINGS:

Dugout Days: Untold Tales and Leadership Lessons from the Extraordinary Career of Billy Martin, AMACON (New York, NY), 2001.

Former editor of mutual fund newsletter.

SIDELIGHTS: Michael DeMarco is the author of *Dugout Days,* the first in-depth analysis of the managerial and leadership career of legendary baseball manager Billy Martin. Although *Dugout Days,* is a baseball book and a biography, it is primarily a management-through-leadership text. DeMarco shows how to apply Martin's strategies for success to today's winner-take-all corporate environment. How can a manager who was fired nine times and never stayed with a team for more than three consecutive seasons be a leadership model? As DeMarco makes clear, Martin earns the distinction because of his exceptional leadership style—at once tough, demanding, empowering, and protective—and his astounding turnaround record. In all of baseball history, Martin is the only manager to take two teams that had lost more than 100 games in a season—the Texas Rangers and the Oakland A's—and bring them into winning seasons the very next year.

At the core of the author's premise is that on today's cutthroat global playing field, the corporations that win are those that are driven by passionate, focused leaders. DeMarco asks readers to put aside any biases against Martin and to focus instead on the qualities that made him a winning manager and baseball icon. In each chapter, following the course of Martin's career, DeMarco summarizes key leadership skills (e. g., building a team of talented and dedicated players, putting yourself in your followers' shoes, getting the public on your side—reinforced by recollections from the many baseball legends, including Rod Carew, Ray Negron, Willie Horton, Phil Pepe and Mickey Rivers, whom he interviewed.

In an interview posted on *American Management Association Web site,* DeMarco related how Martin's style on the field teaches success in the business world. "Billy wanted his players to be aware at all times, regardless of whether they were in the game or on the bench. He wanted them to give their total focus to the game and to look for little opportunities to exploit. . . . The translation to business for any manager is simple: execution can outdo talent more than is commonly thought. Teach your employees the right way to do the job, talk to them constantly about why it is the right way, and then demand that the job get done correctly every day, not just sometimes. And when they do it, take notice!"

BIOGRAPHICAL AND CRITICAL SOURCES:

BOOKS

DeMarco, Michael, *Dugout Days: Untold Tales and Leadership Lessons from the Extraordinary Career of Billy Martin,* AMACON (New York, NY), 2001.

PERIODICALS

Booklist, May 15, 2001, Wes Lukowsky, review of *Dugout Days,* p. 1722.
Fortune, May 28, 2001, Jerry Useem, review of *Dugout Days,* p. 36.
Library Journal, May 1, 2001, Paul Kaplan, review of *Dugout Days,* p. 100.
Publishers Weekly, April 16, 2001, review of *Dugout Days,* p. 55.

OTHER

American Management Association Web site, http://www.amanet.org/ (February 2, 2002), interview with Michael DeMarco.*

* * *

DENKER, Alfred 1960-

PERSONAL: Born August 3, 1960, in Amsterdam, Netherlands; son of Alfred and Jeannette (Bakker) Denker. *Ethnicity:* "White." *Education:* University of Gröningen, M.A., 1982; University of Amsterdam, degree, 1985, Ph.D., 1997. *Politics:* "Liberal democrat."

ADDRESSES: Home—Pont de Cirou, 12800 Crespin, France; fax: 00-33-563-769418. *E-mail*—aldredden@aol.com.

CAREER: University of Amsterdam, Amsterdam, Netherlands, lecturer, 1986-87; Centre Philosophique, Les Trois Hiboux, France, managing director, 1988—. *Military service:* Worked at a military hospital, 1985-86.

MEMBER: Internationale Fichte Gesellschaft, Hegel Society of Great Britain, Martin Heidegger Gesellschaft.

WRITINGS:

Historical Dictionary of Heidegger's Philosophy, Scarecrow Press (Metuchen, NJ), 2000.
(Editor, with Marion Heinz) Theodore Kisiel, *Heidegger's Way of Thought: Critical and Interpretative Signposts,* Athlone Press London, England), 2001.
(Editor) Martin Heidegger and Heinrich Rickert, *Briefe, 1912-1933, und andere Dokumente,* Vittorio Klostermann, 2001.
(Editor, with Michael Vater) *Hegel's Phenomenology of Spirit: New Critical Essays,* Humanity Books (Amherst, MA), 2003.

WORK IN PROGRESS: A biography of Martin Heidegger, completion expected in 2015.

*   *   *

DePALMA, Anthony

PERSONAL: Born in Hoboken, NJ.

ADDRESSES: Home—Montclair, NJ. *Office*—New York Times, 29 West 43rd St., New York, NY 10036-3959.

CAREER: New York Times, New York, NY, began as reporter, became bureau chief in Mexico, bureau chief in Canada, 1993-99, became international business correspondent; writer.

WRITINGS:

Here: A Biography of the New American Continent, PublicAffairs (New York, NY), 2001.

Contributor to periodicals, including *Columbia Journalism Review, Harper's, New York Times Magazine,* and *Woman's Day.*

SIDELIGHTS: Anthony DePalma is a *New York Times* journalist who has worked as the newspaper's bureau chief in both Mexico and Canada. He is also the author of *Here: A Biography of the New American Continent. Here* "is a fine biography of the relationship between Canada, Mexico and the United States. It should be required reading for every American who wants to understand the forces that are causing North America to loom ever larger in our consciousness, slowly eroding the borders between its nations," Andrew Reding wrote in the *New York Times Book Review.* Although DePalma does examine the current trends towards integration, as Reding noted, he also discusses these three countries' diverse cultural histories, which often serve to push them apart. "There's no biography written without looking back into the history of where that person came from," DePalma told *NewsHour* interviewer Ray Saurez. "That really helps you understand, whether it be a person or a place." DePalma added that "although all three nations began at the same time and in the same place and were founded by people from roughly the same part of the world, being Europe, they developed in very different ways." He also observed, however, that "we have to acknowledge that we have a lot in common."

Upon its publication in 2001, *Here* won praise as an important contribution to the understanding of relations between the North American nations in the era of the North American Free Trade Agreement (NAFTA), which went into effect on January 1, 1994. *Maclean's* reviewer Brian Bethune called attention to *Here*'s "intricate account of converging economies and societies," which are both a cause and an effect of NAFTA. DePalma himself is often praised for his extensive knowledge of Mexico and Canada. "It would be hard to find a surer guide to the new American continent than Mr. DePalma," David M. Oshinsky wrote in the *New York Times.* He has "a sharp eye for cultural observation." Robert A. Pastor, meanwhile, noted in the *Atlanta Journal-Constitution* that *Here* "is a wonderful read that brims with poetry, anecdotes and blistering insights into the human and continental condition."

BIOGRAPHICAL AND CRITICAL SOURCES:

PERIODICALS

American Prospect, October 22, 2001, Jeff Faux, review of *Here: A Biography of the New American Continent,* p. 44.
American Studies International, June, 2002, Joel Hodson, review of *Here,* pp. 104-106.
Atlanta Journal-Constitution, September 9, 2001, Robert A. Pastor, "Post-Nafta: How North America Has Changed," p. D5.
Business Week, July 30, 2001, "Yankees, Meet Your Neighbors," p. 18.
Canadian Journal of History, April, 2002, Reginald C. Stuart, review of *Here,* pp. 95-101.
Choice, January, 2002, C. K. Piehl, review of *Here,* p. 937.
Economist, August 22, 2001, "And Gone Tomorrow?."
Library Journal, August, 2001, John E. Hodgkins, review of *Here,* p. 137.
Maclean's, August 13, 2001, Brian Bethune, "True North Strong," p. 50.
National Journal, October 13, 2001, Louis Jacobson, review of *Here,* p. 3195.

New York Times, July 18, 2001, David M. Oshinsky, "Blurring Borders in the New World," p. E10.

New York Times Book Review, July 8, 2001, Andrew Reding, "The Merger."

Time International, July 16, 2001, Stephen Handelman, "Meeting the Neighbors," p. 54.

OTHER

NewsHour, http://pbs.org/ (December 2, 2001), Ray Saurez, interview with Anthony DePalma.*

*   *   *

DEVLIN, Judith 1952-

PERSONAL: Born 1952. *Education:* Université Paris-Sorbonne (Paris IV), M.A., Més.L.; University of Oxford, D.Phil.

ADDRESSES: Office—University College Dublin, Belfield, Dublin 4, Ireland.

CAREER: Historian and educator. University College Dublin, Dublin, Ireland, lecturer and Newman Scholar in modern history.

MEMBER: Irish Association for Russian and East European Studies (president, board of directors).

WRITINGS:

The Superstitious Mind: French Peasants and the Supernatural in the Nineteenth Century, Yale University Press (New Haven, CT), 1987.

The Rise of the Russian Democrats: The Causes and Consequences of the Elite Revolution, Edward Elgar (Aldershot, England), 1995.

(Editor, with Ronan Fanning) *Religion and Rebellion: Historical Studies XX,* University College Dublin Press (Dublin, Ireland), 1997.

Slavophiles and Commissars: Enemies of Democracy in Modern Russia, St. Martin's Press (New York, NY), 1999.

Contributor of reviews to periodicals, including the *Times Higher Education Supplement.*

SIDELIGHTS: As a university lecturer, Judith Devlin specializes in the cultural and intellectual history of France and Russia in the nineteenth and twentieth centuries. She has used this expertise, combined with abundant research, to compile a number of scholarly works focusing on her area of academic interest, among them *The Superstitious Mind: French Peasants and the Supernatural in the Nineteenth Century* and *Slavophiles and Commissars: Enemies of Democracy in Modern Russia.*

Devlin's first book, *The Superstitious Mind,* is an exploration of the role of superstitions in the belief system held by the lower classes in nineteenth-century France. "Devlin's study draws on extensive readings of nineteenth-century accounts of belief and practice: folklorists' transcriptions of colorful tales, Catholic clerics' reports on the state of Christianity in French villages, physicians' descriptions of medical practice, and protopsychiatrists' observations on unusual states of mind," explained reviewer John Markoff in the *American Journal of Sociology.* Devlin proposes that the superstitions held by the peasants were devised in a rational manner, as a means of dealing with the trials and sufferings of their everyday lives; modern men and women, though not believing the same myths, are still in some ways equally superstitious.

R. D. Anderson praised *The Superstitious Mind* in *English Historical Review,* writing, "Devlin presents a mass of material in an elegant form and with a penetrating and sophisticated commentary." Eugen Weber, writing for the *Times Literary Supplement,* also praised aspects of the work: "Devlin's material is fascinating, and one's interest seldom flags. . . . The book is welcome because it breaks new ground." On the other hand, several reviewers found fault with the methods and sources the author used to support her theories. Markoff cautioned that Devlin's sources may not present the average mentality of the peasant population, but present instead the mentality of those on the periphery of society, because they are the ones who usually attract more attention. He also pointed out that at that time there were great variations in culture between different geographical areas in France, and one would expect variations in superstitions as well. Tom Shippey, writing in the *London Review of*

Books, remarked that the author works "from anecdote and supposition" and that *The Superstitious Mind* "gives those who are interested an introduction to a very considerable corpus of material on flying dragons, werewolves, sorcerers, grimoires, the patenôtre blanche and much else. It does not tell us how peasants thought, even in the nineteenth century, nor lead us into that strange world of instinctive reaction, half-conscious calculation, short-sighted meanness, and urgent necessity." Anderson concluded that while the book may have several downfalls, it "may well attract a large readership, and deservedly"; "it will perhaps prove more illuminating to students of popular culture in general than to historians of nineteenth-century France."

Devlin's 1995 work, *The Rise of the Russian Democrats: The Causes and Consequences of the Elite Revolution,* examines the democratic movement in post-*glasnost* Russia from 1987 to 1991, once again offering readers copious amounts of information. In her research Devlin reviewed Russian newspapers, magazines, published interviews, and documents from the archives of the Moscow Bureau for Information Exchange and concluded that while the Russian intelligentsia was responsible for much of the democratic movement, for a variety of reasons it failed to bring that democratic spirit to the larger public. "With respect to overcoming past prejudices and face-value characterizations, this study largely succeeds in attaining its stated objective: to revisit the eventful years from 1987 to 1991 and to offer a more sober account of Russia's anticommunist revolution than that found in many of the earlier works on this period. It is refreshing to read a book on contemporary Russia that neither pays particular homage to political actors simply because they are called 'democrats' nor consecrates their project because they have called it a 'democracy,'" noted Michael Urban in *Slavic Review.* Some reviewers had reservations about Devlin's study; as Ellen Carnaghan wrote in *Russian Review,* "at crucial points Devlin does not offer enough evidence to support [her argument]. . . . She has an annoying habit of making overly broad assertions—for instance, concerning the motivations behind the intellectuals' disinclination to reach out to ordinary people—without having any evidence to back them up." But Peter Lentini concluded in *Europe-Asia Studies,* "Devlin's book is a significant contribution to existing literature on the development of informal groups and movements and political party formation in the late Soviet and early post-Soviet period. . . . Her book is relevant for students and researchers in a number of areas and is very suitable as a supplementary text for courses on Soviet history, contemporary Russian politics, comparative post-communist politics and democratic transitions."

In *Slavophiles and Commissars* Devlin analyzes how Russian nationalism has filled the void of communism since 1989. The first part of the book examines the major ideologies at play, while the second part deals with the major events and political activities that followed the fall of the USSR in 1989. The author's assertion is that, since the fall of communism, leaders have exploited nationalism as a replacement for communism, with no real movement toward democracy. While Andreas Umland, writing in *Europe-Asia Studies,* commented that *Slavophiles and Commissars* might have been more comprehensive, he added that "Devlin's book is to be welcomed in that it contributes to filling a still glaring gap in the study of international right-wing extremism and post-Soviet affairs."

BIOGRAPHICAL AND CRITICAL SOURCES:

PERIODICALS

American Journal of Sociology, March, 1988, John Markoff, review of *The Superstitious Mind: French Peasants and the Supernatural in the Nineteenth Century,* pp. 1253-1254.

Choice, March, 1996, J. S. Zacek, review of *The Rise of the Russian Democrats: The Causes and Consequences of the Elite Revolution,* p. 1213; January, 2000, C. A. Linden, review of *Slavophiles and Commissars: Enemies of Democracy in Modern Russia,* p. 1006.

English Historical Review, January, 1990, R. D. Anderson, review of *The Superstitious Mind,* pp. 226-227.

Europe-Asia Studies, September, 1996, review of *The Rise of the Russian Democrats,* p. 1035; May, 2000, Andreas Umland, review of *Slavophiles and Commissars,* p. 574.

History: Reviews of New Books, summer, 1998, William B. Robison, review of *Religion and Rebellion,* pp. 208-209.

Journal of Modern History, September, 1990, Caroline Ford, review of *The Superstitious Mind,* p. 620.

London Review of Books, April 2, 1987, Tom Shippey, "Winners and Wasters," pp. 10-11.

Reference & Research Book News, November, 1999, review of *Slavophiles and Commissars,* p. 33.

Russian Review, October, 1997, Ellen Carnaghan, review of *The Rise of the Russian Democrats,* pp. 616-617; July, 2000, Eric Shiraev, review of *Slavophiles and Commissars,* p. 480.

Slavic Review, winter, 1994, Michael Urban, review of *The Rise of the Russian Democrats,* pp. 795-796.

Smithsonian, October, 1987, Charles Fenyvesi, review of *The Superstitious Mind,* p. 227.

Times Literary Supplement, April 24, 1987, Eugen Weber, "Magical Mud-slinging," p. 430.*

*　　*　　*

DIJKSTRA, Edsger W(ybe) 1930-2002

OBITUARY NOTICE—See index for *CA* sketch: Born May 11, 1930, in Rotterdam, Netherlands; died of cancer August 5, 2002, in Nuenen, Netherlands. Computer programmer, mathematician, educator, and author. Dijkstra's belief that things should be made as simple and direct as possible led to a number of innovations in computer programming. His work had an impact on everything from programming syntax to operating systems to global positioning systems (GPS). Originally intending to go into law, Dijkstra's natural talents in the sciences led him to study mathematics and physics instead. He graduated from the University of Leyden with a doctorate in 1956 and received another Ph.D. from the University of Amsterdam in 1959. Beginning his career on the staff of the Amsterdam Mathematics Center, where he worked on computer algorithms during the 1950s, he developed his Shortest Path algorithm, which determines the shortest route between two cities and is currently used in GPS technology. Dijkstra next became a professor of mathematics at Technical University in the Netherlands in 1962, and it was while there that he developed the multiprogramming system which greatly influenced the design of all subsequent operating systems. During his time at Technical University, he also advocated structured programming to simplify the way programmers wrote instructions, making it easier to read others' programs and trace any errors. This was followed by a position as a research fellow at the Burroughs Corporation in Neunen from 1973 to 1984, and another professorship at the University of Texas at

Austin from 1984 until his retirement in 1999. As an academic, Dijkstra turned more and more to mathematical methodology as his main field of interest. Despite this, he is best remembered for his programming work, including his solution to what became known as "the dining philosopher's problem," which solution later proved useful in designing computer networks and operating systems. Dijkstra was the author of several books, including *A Discipline of Programming* (1976), *Selected Writings on Computing: A Personal Perspective* (1982), and *Formal Development of Programs and Proofs* (1990). For his groundbreaking work he received numerous honors, including the prestigious 1972 Turing Award from the Association for Computing Machinery, the 1982 Computer Pioneer Award from the Institute of Electrical and Electronics Engineers, the 1989 Award for Outstanding Contributions to Computer Science Education from the Special Interest Group on Computer Science Education, and the 2002 Influential Paper Award at the Principles of Distributed Computing Conference. He was also the recipient of honorary doctorates from Queen's University in Belfast and the Athens University of Economics.

OBITUARIES AND OTHER SOURCES:

BOOKS

Who's Who in America, 55th edition, Marquis, 2001.

PERIODICALS

New York Times, August 10, 2002, p. A24.
Times (London, England), August 9, 2002.

OTHER

University of Texas at Austin Web site, http://www. utexas.edu/ (August 15, 2002).

*　　*　　*

DJIAN, Philippe 1949-

PERSONAL: Born May 3, 1949 in Paris, France; married Annèe (a painter); children: Loiec, Clara.

ADDRESSES: Agent—c/o Author Mail, Flohic Editions, 11 rue Rottembourg, 75012, Paris, France.

CAREER: Author.

WRITINGS:

50 contre 1, Editions BFB (Paris, France), 1981.
Bleu comme l'enfer, Editions BFD (Paris, France), 1982.
Zone érogène, Editions Barrault (Paris, France), 1984.
37.2° le matin, Editions Barrault (Paris, France), 1985, translation by Howard Buten published as *Betty Blue: The Story of a Passion,* Weidenfield & Nicolson (New York, NY), 1988.
Maudit mangége, Editions Barrault (Paris, France), 1986.
Echine, Editions Barrault (Paris, France), 1988.
Crocodiles, Editions Barrault (Paris, France), 1989.
Entre nous soit dit: conversations ave Jean-Louis Ezine / Philippe Djian, Editions Plon (Paris, France), 1989.
Lent Dehors, Editions Barrault (Paris, France), 1991.
Lorsque Lou, illustrated by Miles Hyman, Editions Gallimard (Paris, France), 1992.
Sotos, Editions Gallimard (Paris, France), 1993.
Assassins, Editions Gallimard (Paris, France), 1994.
Criminels, Editions Gallimard (Paris, France), 1997.
Sainte-Bob, Editions Gallimard (Paris, France), 1998.
Au plus près: entretiens avec Catherine Moreau / Philippe Djian, Editions Passe du vent (Paris, France), 1999.
Philippe Djian Revisité: Philippe Djian, rencontre avec Catherine Flohic, Les Flohic editeurs, (Paris, France), 2000.

Contributor to *Repenser les processus créateurs/Rethinking the Creative Processes,* edited by Françoise Grauby and Michelle Royer, P. Lang (Berne, Switzerland; New York, NY), 2001.

ADAPTATIONS: 37.2° le matin, was made into a movie of the same name by Jean-Jacques Beineix, France, 1986.

SIDELIGHTS: Although Philippe Djian has inspired an enthusiastic following in France for almost twenty years, he is relatively unknown in America. The irony of this is that Djian's work is informed almost exclusively by American writers. From his first book, the short story collection *50 contre 1,* critics have likened him to Henry Miller. Djian refers to American authors Jack Kerouac, Carlos Williams Whitman, J. D. Salinger, and Walt Whitman throughout his books, and

he also wrote a short story as homage to the American poet and novelist, Richard Brautigan, after Brautigan's suicide in 1989.

37.2° le matin, translated as *Betty Blue: The Story of a Passion* is the only book by Djian that has been translated into English. It was not translated until after a 1986 film adaptation by Jean-Jacques Beineix, which was a huge success for the director and for the film's stars, Beatrice Dalle and Jean-Hughes Anglade. Djian was not a fan of the adaptation, and he complained that the film had a completely different aesthetic from his book. He has commented that it is very frustrating to be known in the English-speaking world primarily by this film and by only one of his many works of fiction. "I think that there's no special interest from Americans in French work today," he said to Mireille Vignol on *Radio National.* "If you have the chance to have one of your books translated, most of the time it is only for one book. There is no special interest in your whole work."

The story of *Betty Blue* is told "with a conviction and sense of erotic finality," wrote an *Antioch Review* contributor, through the eyes of Zorg, a handyman and unpublished writer who works as a caretaker for a row of shacks on the west coast of France. Betty simply walks into his life, and the two have a passionate, obsessive love affair. They live life as a magical fantasy until their dreams collide with reality. Betty's increasingly manic behavior lands her in a mental hospital, where her passions are destroyed by electroshock treatments and tranquilizers. As Joseph Cotes commented in *Chicago Tribune Books,* "There is more than a hint here of Jack Kerouac and the Beat Generation—a parallel rejection of middle class values in an aimless search for meaning."

BIOGRAPHICAL AND CRITICAL SOURCES:

PERIODICALS

Antioch Review, fall, 1988, review of *Betty Blue: Story of a Passion,* p. 531.
Booklist, February 1, 1988, John Broshnan, review of *Betty Blue,* p. 903.
French Review, March, 1999, Kenneth J. Fleurant, review of *Criminels,* p. 775; May, 1993, Kenneth J. Fleurant, review of *Lent Dehors,* p. 1039.

L'Express, April 29, 1993, Angelo Rinaldi, review of *Sotos,* p. 5.

Library Journal, March 1, 1998, Marilyn Gaddis, review of *Betty Blue,* p. 76.

Publishers Weekly, February 26, 1988, Sybil Steinberg, review of *Betty Blue,* p. 76.

Times Literary Supplement, December 16, 1988, Andrew Hislop, review of *Betty Blue,* p. 1404.

Tribune Books (Chicago, IL), May 15, 1988, Joseph Coates, review of *Betty Blue,* p. 7.

OTHER

Online Philippe Djian, http://perso.infonie.fr (December 2, 2001), reviews and interviews with Philippe Djian.

Radio National (Australia), "Headspace #9," interview with Mireille Vignol, December 2, 2001.*

*   *   *

DODD, Quentin 1972-

PERSONAL: Born June 7, 1972, in Durham, NC; son of Robert (a wildlife biologist) and Suzanne (a teacher; maiden name, Hevron) Dodd; married Paula Myers (a physical therapist), May 28, 1994. *Education:* Wabash College, A.B., 1994. *Hobbies and other interests:* Ice hockey, antiques, B-movies, bonsai trees.

ADDRESSES: Home—1101 Danville Ave., Crawfordsville, IN 47933. *Office*—Wabash College, P.O. Box 352, Crawfordsville, IN 47933. *E-mail*—doddq@ quentindodd.com.

CAREER: Management Consulting and Research, Inc., Dayton, OH, programmer, 1994-99; Wabash College, Crawfordsville, IN, network administrator, 1999—. Writer, 1998—.

AWARDS, HONORS: Eleanor Cameron Award for best middle grades book, Golden Duck Awards, 2002, and Books for the Teen Age selection, New York Public Library, 2002, both for *Beatnik Rutabagas from beyond the Stars.*

WRITINGS:

Beatnik Rutabagas from beyond the Stars, Farrar, Straus & Giroux (New York, NY), 2001.

WORK IN PROGRESS: The Princes of Neptune, Farrar, Straus & Giroux (New York, NY), due 2004.

SIDELIGHTS: Quentin Dodd combines a day job as a computer network administrator with a night career of creating seriously funny and outlandish books for young readers. His 2001 title, *Beatnik Rutabagas from beyond the Stars,* is the tale of two teens who are spirited away in alien spaceships to lead competing intergalactic armies. Walter Nutria, a freshman in high school, is something of a video junkie, as is his sometimes girlfriend, Yselle Meridian. Together, they spend hours watching old science-fiction movies. One day, when he is busy skipping school, Walter is recruited by aliens to head the one-spaceship-strong Lirgonian fleet in its efforts to best their space enemies, the Wotwots. He jumps at the chance, but one thing Walter does not know is that Yselle has meanwhile been recruited to lead the Wotwots. Ultimately these two unlikely generals convince the warring sides that their real enemies are the Space Mice and the wicked Doctoral Candidate X.

Dodd's first novel earned mostly positive reviews. While Saleena L. Davidson, writing in *School Library Journal,* felt that the author "tries too hard to be funny and neglects character and plot development," other reviewers were more praiseworthy. A critic for *Publishers Weekly* noted similarities in Dodd's work to Douglas Adams's "Hitchhiker's Guide" series, dubbing the novel a "spunky debut," and further noting that Dodd's "agenda is laughs, and his extravagant imagination matches well with his flippant writing style." Similarly, a contributor for *Kirkus Reviews* applauded this "freewheeling debut," and commented that it "will draw chortles from readers who prefer their SF well-larded with surreal silliness." Greg Hurrell added to the praise in *Journal of Adolescent and Adult Literacy,* calling the book a "laugh-a-minute romp across the universe," and an "excellent first novel."

Dodd, who began his writing career with two novels that were not published, hopes to continue writing humorous stories for readers of all ages. For now he is riding the positive feedback from his first novel and is hard at work on a second that will combine, as he told Steve Penhollow in the Fort Wayne, Indiana, *Journal-Gazette,* "the 'my Dad owns a scientific island' genre of adventure fiction (i.e. Jonny Quest) with an intergalactic beauty pageant."

"I'm not much for trying to deliver a message," Dodd told *CA*. "A lot of books for kids, in my opinion, have a tendency to moralize excessively, and I think this can give the impression that reading is Serious Business, something that can't be done lightly or for enjoyment. My goal is to be the chocolate sundae of kids' literature: nutty, messy, and fun."

Dodd further commented to *CA:* "In writing, what I find most exciting is taking unrelated ideas and combining them in surprising ways. When I'm working on something, I rarely use traditional outlines, but instead cover my desk and my computer monitor with sticky notes that I can move and arrange into different patterns as the story takes shape. This means that I tend to research a lot of things that seem like good ideas at the time, but never end up on the page. I never throw anything away, though, and what doesn't fit in one story is sometimes the perfect ingredient for another."

BIOGRAPHICAL AND CRITICAL SOURCES:

PERIODICALS

Journal Gazette (Fort Wayne, IN), January 27, 2002, Steven Penhollow, "Writer Creates Far-out Aliens Kids Have Never Eyed Before," pp. E1, E6.
Journal of Adolescent and Adult Literacy, March, 2002, Greg Hurrell, review of *Beatnik Rutabagas from beyond the Stars,* p. 550.
Kirkus Reviews, August 1, 2001, review of *Beatnik Rutabagas from beyond the Stars,* p. 1120.
Publishers Weekly, August 20, 2001, review of *Beatnik Rutabagas from beyond the Stars,* p. 81.
School Library Journal, October, 2001, Saleena L. Davidson, review of *Beatnik Rutabagas from beyond the Stars,* p. 152.

OTHER

Quentin Dodd Web site, http://www.quentindodd.com/ (October 5, 2002).

*   *   *

DOLETZKI, Leo
See RÜHMKORF, Peter

DOMINO, Edward F(elix) 1924-

PERSONAL: Born November 20, 1924, in Chicago, IL; married Antoinetta F. Kaczorowski, November 20, 1948 (deceased); children: Karen, Laurence, Debra, Kenneth, Steven. *Ethnicity:* "Polish." *Education:* Attended University of Illinois—Urbana/Champaign, 1942-43, 1946-48; University of Illinois—Chicago Circle, B.S., 1949, M.S. and M.D. (with honors), both 1951. *Politics:* "Active." *Religion:* Episcopal. *Hobbies and other interests:* Arts, ecology, music.

ADDRESSES: Home—3071 Exmoor, Ann Arbor, MI 48104. *Office*—Department of Pharmacology, University of Michigan, Ann Arbor, MI 48109-0632; fax: 734-763-4450.

CAREER: University of Illinois—Chicago Circle, instructor in pharmacology, 1951-53; University of Michigan, Ann Arbor, instructor, 1953-54, assistant professor, 1954-58, associate professor, 1958-62, professor of pharmacology, 1962-99, professor emeritus, 1999—. Presbyterian Hospital, Chicago, IL, rotating intern, 1951-53; Lafayette Clinic, Detroit, MI, psychopharmacologist, 1958-83, director of Laboratory of Pharmacology, 1967-81, director of clinical psychopharmacology, 1981-83, director of Laboratory of Pharmacology and Neuropsychopharmacology Research, 1998-99. Wayne State University, visiting professor, 1965-84, clinical professor, 1984-86; Israel Institute of Biology, visiting pharmacologist, 1980; University of Colorado—Denver, Brady Visiting Professor, 1986; State University of New York—Buffalo, Pfizer Lecturer, 1986; University of Mississippi, William N. Creasy Visiting Professor in Clinical Pharmacology and Geriatric Psychopharmacology, 1987; University of Occupational and Environmental Health, Kitakyushu, Japan, visiting professor, annually 1988-94; Japan Marine Science and Technology Center, visiting scientist, 1988; University of Hiroshima, visiting professor, 1992; visiting pharmacologist in the USSR, 1971; visiting lecturer at other institutions, particularly in Japan; invited speaker at international conferences; also public speaker. U.S. Pharmacopeial Convention, delegate from University of Michigan, 1996—; consultant to federal government agencies and to the pharmaceutical industry; expert witness at hearings of the U.S. Food and Drug Administration. *Military service:* U.S. Naval Reserve, 1943-46.

MEMBER: Collegium Internationale Neuropsychopharmacologicum, International Society of Neurochemistry (emeritus member), American College of Neuropsychopharmacology (life fellow; member of council, 1969-70, 1983-85; vice president, 1976), American Clinical Neurophysiology Society (fellow; emeritus member), American Society for Pharmacology and Experimental Therapeutics (member emeritus; chair of symposium on mechanisms of drug sensitization, 1994), Society for Experimental Biology and Medicine (emeritus member), Society of Toxicology (emeritus member), Society of Medical Consultants to the Armed Services of the United States (emeritus member), American Association for the Advancement of Science (fellow; emeritus member), Central EEG Society (member emeritus), New York Academy of Sciences (emeritus member), University of Michigan Research Club (life member), Sigma Xi (emeritus member; member of council, 1961-63).

AWARDS, HONORS: Sigma Xi Prize in Medicine, University of Illinois—Chicago Circle, 1951; research award, Michigan Society for Neurology and Psychiatry, 1955; first prize, American Society of Anesthesiologists, 1963; American Medical Association, Certificate of Merit, anesthesiology section, 1964, and Physician's Recognition award, 1982, 1985; Nickolai Pavlovich Kravkov Memorial Medal, Academic Board, Institute of Pharmacology and Chemotherapy, Academy of Medical Sciences of the USSR, 1968; Certificate of Merit, Michigan Psychiatric Society, 1970; Distinguished Graduate Award for service to research and education, University of Illinois Alumni Association, 1981; Certificate for Service with High Distinction, Medical Research and Service Command, U.S. Army, 1982; grant from National Institute on Drug Abuse.

WRITINGS:

(Editor) O. S. Adrianov and T. A. Mering, *Atlas of the Canine Brain,* translated from the original Russian by E. Ignatieff, NPP Books (Ann Arbor, MI), 1964.

(Editor, with P. G. S. Beckett and T. H. Bleakley) *A Teaching Program in Psychiatry,* Volume 2: *Psychoneurosis, Organic Brain Disease, Psychopharmacology,* Wayne State University Press (Detroit, MI), 1968.

(Editor, with J. M. Davis) *Neurotransmitter Balances Regulating Behaviors,* NPP Books (Ann Arbor, MI), 1975.

(Editor, with W. E. Fann, R. C. Smith, and J. Davis) *Tardive Dyskinesia: Research and Treatments,* Spectrum Publications (New York, NY), 1980.

(Editor) *PCP (Phencyclidine): Historical and Current Perspectives,* NPP Books (Ann Arbor, MI), 1981.

(Editor, with J. M. Kamenka and P. Geneste) *Phencyclidine and Related Arylcyclohexylamines: Present and Future Applications,* NPP Books (Ann Arbor, MI), 1983.

(Editor, with J. M. Kamenka) *Sigma and Phencyclidine-like Compounds as Molecular Probes in Biology,* NPP Books (Ann Arbor, MI), 1988.

(Editor) *The Status of Ketamine in Anesthesiology,* NPP Books (Ann Arbor, MI), 1990.

(Editor, with T. Kameyama and T. Nabeshima) *NMDA Receptor-related Agents: Biochemistry, Pharmacology, and Behavior,* NPP Books (Ann Arbor, MI), 1991.

(Editor, with J. Kamenka) *Multiple Sigma and PCP Receptor Ligands: Mechanisms for Neuromodulation and Neuroprotection,* NPP Books (Ann Arbor, MI), 1992.

(Editor) *Brain Imaging of Nicotine and Tobacco Smoking,* NPP Books (Ann Arbor, MI), 1995.

(Editor, with T. Yanagita) *Japanese Michigan Fellows in Pharmacology,* NPP Books (Ann Arbor, MI), 1999.

Contributor to many medical and scientific books. Contributor of more than 700 articles to professional journals. Supporting editor, *Psychopharmacologia,* 1973-78; associate editor, *Experimental Neurology,* 1977-80; member of editorial board, *Journal of Pharmacology and Experimental Therapeutics,* 1958-65, *University of Michigan Medical Center Journal,* 1964-80, *Clinical Pharmacology and Therapeutics,* 1973-98, *Archives Internationale de Pharmacodynamie et Therapie,* 1975-90, *Progress in Neuro-Psychopharmacology,* 1976-79, *Reviews in Pure and Applied Pharmacologic Sciences,* 1980-83, *Research Communications in Drugs and Substances of Abuse,,* 1980—, and *Reviews in Clinical and Basic Pharmacology,,* 1984-90; member of editorial advisory board, *Neuropharmacology,* 1962-87, *Pharmacology, Biochemistry, and Behavior,* 1973-88, *Neurobiology and Aging,* 1980-82, *Primary Care Medicine Drug Alerts,* 1982—, *Drug Metabolism and Disposition: Biological Fate of Chemicals,* 1991-94, *Progress in Neuro-Psychopharmacology and Biological Psychiatry,* 1993—, and *Current Topics in Pharmacology* (India), 1994-97.

WORK IN PROGRESS: Sixty Years of University of Michigan Pharmacology; *Forty Years of Ketamine: Taming a Tiger.*

* * *

DONOHUE, Lynn 1957(?)-

PERSONAL: Born c. 1957; daughter of a policeman and tavern owner and a town clerk; married; children: two. *Education:* Trained as a bricklayer.

ADDRESSES: Office—P.O. Box 638, Marion, MA 02738. *E-mail*—brickbybrick@neaccess.net.

CAREER: Bricklayer and small business owner. Worked as a bartender in New Bedford, MA; became a bricklayer; Argus Construction, owner, 1982-97; Consolidated Brick of Rhode Island, top sales representative; Brick by Brick Foundation, founder, 1999.

MEMBER: New Bedford Bricklayers Union, Local 39.

WRITINGS:

(With Pamela Hunt) *Brick by Brick: A Woman's Journey,* Spinner Publications (New Bedford, MA), 2000.

SIDELIGHTS: Lynn Donohue's *Brick by Brick: A Woman's Journey* is the story of her life as the first female bricklayer in southeastern Massachusetts. Donohue dropped out of school at age fifteen and worked at the Belmont Club, a tavern that her father owned, as a bartender. She was making $3.10 an hour at age nineteen when she saw an advertisement offering vocational training in bricklaying. Donohue had seen other ads that said that bricklayers made $17 an hour, which sounded good to her. She took the three-month masonry course and embarked on a career as a bricklayer.

It took pressure from Donohue's mother, who was the town clerk of New Bedford, and the local Office of Equal Opportunity to convince the Bricklayers Union to give Donohue any work, and after she had gained employment her male coworkers still harassed her incessantly. She became one of the best bricklayers in the area, but she could never be foreman of her own crew because the other workers would not accept her. Finally, out of frustration Donahue started her own masonry company, which soon grew into a multi-million-dollar business. Then, after running the business for sixteen years, Donohue stopped taking on new projects and turned to writing *Brick by Brick* and becoming a motivational speaker. As a *Publishers Weekly* reviewer wrote "Donohue honors the will to survive and thrive" in her telling of her tale.

BIOGRAPHICAL AND CRITICAL SOURCES:

PERIODICALS

Boston Herald, July 26, 2001, Azell Murphy Cavan, "Building New Lives: Lynn Donohue Uses Her Rags-to-Riches Experience to Mentor Local Teens," p. 55.
Publishers Weekly, August 7, 2000, review of *Brick by Brick: A Woman's Journey,* p. 89.
Women's Review of Books, May, 2001, Susan Eisenberg, review of *Brick by Brick,* p. 8.

OTHER

Business Journal, http://www.thebizjournal.com/ (February 2, 2002), Karen White, "Laying the Foundation for Success."
Cape Cod Times, http://www.capecodonline.com/ (April 1, 2001), K. C. Myers, "Building Walls and Breaking Them."
SpeakersHome, http://www.speakershome.com/ (December 31, 2001), "Lynn Donohue."
Spinner Publications, http://www.spinnerpub.com/ (December 31, 2001).
Yuba-Sutter Economic Development Corporation, http://www.ysedc.org/ (December 31, 2001), "Keynote Speaker: Lynn Donohue."*

* * *

DRINKWATER, Carol 1948-

PERSONAL: Born April 22, 1948, in London, England; married; husband's name Michel.

ADDRESSES: Agent—c/o Author Mail, Overlook Press, One Overlook Drive, Woodstock, NY 12498.

CAREER: Stage, screen, and television actress; author. Actress in films, including *A Clockwork Orange,* 1971; *The Dawn Breakers; Queen Kong,* 1976; *Mondo Candido; The Shout,* 1978; *Joseph Andrews,* 1977; *Father,* 1989; *Magneto,* 1993; and *An Awfully Big Adventure.* Actress in television shows, including *All Creatures Great and Small, Chocky,* and *Golden Pennies.* Actress in made-for-television movies, including *Master of the Marionettes,* 1989, and *Coming Home,* 1998. Actress in television miniseries, including *Bouquet of Barbed Wire,* 1976; *The Haunted School,* 1986; and *Captain James Cook,* 1987.

AWARDS, HONORS: Edinburgh Festival First Fringe Award; TV Personality of the Year award, for portrayal of Helen Herriot in *All Creatures Great and Small; All Creatures Great and Small* was voted Britain's best drama series of all time; Chicago Film Festival award for a children's film, for *The Haunted School.*

WRITINGS:

Akin to Love, Hodder & Stoughton (London, England), 1991.
Mapping the Heart, Coronet (London, England), 1994.
An Abundance of Rain, Penguin Books (London, England), 1994.
Crossing the Line: Young Women and the Law, Livewire Books (London, England), 2000.
The Olive Farm: A Memoir of Life, Love, and Olive Oil in the South of France, Overlook Press (Woodstock, NY), 2001.
Because You're Mine, House of Stratus (London, England), 2001.

FOR CHILDREN

The Haunted School, Puffin Books (New York, NY), 1987.
Molly on the Run, Macdonald Young Books (London, England), 1996.
Twentieth-Century Girl: The Diary of Flora Bonnington, London, 1899-1900, Scholastic (London, England), 2000.
The Hunger: The Diary of Phyllis McCormack, Ireland 1845-1847, Scholastic (London, England), 2000.

SCREENPLAYS

The Haunted School (television miniseries), 1986.
Molly (made-for-television movie), 1995.

ADAPTATIONS: An Abundance of Rain is being developed as a film.

SIDELIGHTS: Carol Drinkwater is best known for her role in the British television series *All Creatures Great and Small,* based on the books of country veterinarian James Herriot, but she has been involved in theatre in many other roles as well. She was a member of the National Theatre under the direction of Sir Laurence Olivier, was awarded the Edinburgh Festival First Fringe Award for her work with a young experimental group, and has starred in theatrical performances in London's West End theater district on many occasions. From the theater Drinkwater moved into films and television. For her portrayal of Helen Herriott in *All Creatures Great and Small,* she was awarded the TV Personality of the Year Award. *All Creatures Great and Small* was voted Britain's top drama series of all time and has made Drinkwater quite a recognizable face in Britain.

Drinkwater has enjoyed a successful career as a writer as well. Her first adult novel, *Akin to Love,* benefits from a romantic island setting and characters drawn from a world that the author know well. Penny Morrison is a glamorous international star. She has written a film script that is a guaranteed success. The story is a thinly disguised retelling of her youthful relationship with the painter Harry Knowle, a man she met when she was a struggling actress visiting Crete as a backpacker. There she fell in love with Harry and discovered romantic Greece as well as the dark side of the dictatorship. Penny, now a star in London, returns to Crete to location filming and once again finds herself under the spell of the mysterious island.

Another of Drinkwater's novels, *Abundance of Rain,* is the story of Kate De Marly, who leaves a well-ordered life in England to travel to the Fijian island of Lesa. She is excited about her reunion with Sam McGuire, her father, who abandoned her as a child. On board ship she learns the meeting will never happen—her father has died. His sugar plantation is now hers. But as she settles into the rhythm of island life, she begins to suspect that her father's death was not an accident.

Drinkwater's young adult literature has also been well received. Her first book, *The Haunted School,* is set in a small mountain village in Australia during the late

1800s. The locals of Moogalloo believe that the abandoned old hotel is haunted by the ghost of a gold miner killed years before by a huge rock that rolled down from the mountain. People around town hold the ghost responsible for the death of the wife of a wealthy villager. Meanwhile, Fanny Crowe, a well-bred English governess, moves into the hotel and plans to turn it into a school, but first she has to convince the townspeople that the hotel is really ghost free. The story works out well for everyone when the ghost turns out to be only the dead miner's brother playing a trick on the town.

Twentieth-Century Girl: The Diary of Flora Bonnington, London, 1899-1900, is a coming-of-age book for girls set at the beginning of the twentieth century. Flora is a girl who is full of enthusiasm for the possibilities of the new century as well, even as she is becoming aware of the social injustices going on around her. In the same vein, *The Hunger: The Diary of Phyllis McCormack, Ireland 1845-1847* introduces young reader to the suffering of the Irish people during the potato famine years through the diary of protagonist Phllis McCormack.

In *Crossing the Line: Young Women and the Law,* young women describe what it's really like to end up in trouble with the police. They talk about what led them to "cross the line" and how that experience has changed their lives. The author has long been an advocate of programs for girls in trouble and is a frequent prison visitor. Her book offers an inside view of life on the other side of the European legal system.

In the late 1980s, Drinkwater moved to the south of France and bought a farm there. *The Olive Farm: A Memoir of Life, Love, and Olive Oil in the South of France* tells the story of how Drinkwater acquired this farm and how living there has changed her. The adventure begins with a cash deposit of her life savings to secure the ten-acre olive farm. In a interview with Tony Almond for the online magazine *Sameday Books,* Drinkwater recalled, "How we bought the property is nothing short of a miracle. We genuinely didn't have any money. . . . It would have remained a crazy dream except for the fact that Michel [Drinkwater's husband] came up with the idea of suggesting to the owners that we purchase the house and half the land first, then buy the other half at some later date."

Although the book is inevitably compared to Peter Mayles's *A Year in Provence* and Frances Mayes's *Under the Tuscan Sun,* reviewers found that the book has a unique niche of its own. "The views are breathtaking," Janet Ross wrote in *Library Journal,* and Drinkwater's success in realizing her dream is "a joyous relief." *Booklist* reviewer Margaret Flanagan called the book "warmly evocative," and a *Publishers Weekly* contributor similarly noted, "the book describes life in the South of France with lush, voluptuous appreciation."

Drinkwater says that her olive farm, Appassionata, has changed her life. She told Almond, "I have learnt commitment, faith, a deeper sense of responsibility, respect for the earth and its gifts to us. Even before I lived here I worked a bit for Greenpeace and the WWF but in those days my choices were born of ideas rather than practical experience. Appassionata has given me an inner joy. I am happy here; I love this little corner of the world. I love the colours of the Mediterranean, the warmth, the vegetation."

BIOGRAPHICAL AND CRITICAL SOURCES:

PERIODICALS

Booklist, July, 2001, Margaret Flanagan, review of *The Olive Farm: A Memoir of Life, Love, and Olive Oil in the South of France,* p. 1973.

Books for Keeps, September, 1996, Val Rendall, review of *Molly,* p. 16; July 2000, Colin Chapman, review of *Crossing the Line: Young Women and the Law,* p. 27.

Guardian (London, England), June 6, 2001, p. 13.

Journal of Reading, October, 1989, Susan Murphy and Robert Small, review of *The Haunted School,* p. 70.

Library Journal, April 15, 2001, Janet Ross, review of *The Olive Farm,* p. 123; October 15, 2002, Joseph L. Carlson, review of audio *The Olive Farm,* p. 112.

Publishers Weekly, April 23, 2001, review of *The Olive Farm,* p. 56.

Sunday Telegraph (London, England), September 24, 2000, Jane Slade, article on Carol Drinkwater.

Times Educational Supplement, August 25, 2000, Reva Klein, review of *Crossing the Line,* p. 24.

Washington Post Book World, May 27, 2001, Juliet Wittman, review of *The Olive Farm,* p. 123.

OTHER

Sameday Books, http://samedaybooks.co.uk/ (February 2, 2002), Tony Almond, interview with Carol Drinkwater.*

DUDMAN, Martha Tod 1952-

PERSONAL: Born January 4, 1952, in St. Louis, MO; daughter of Richard Beebe (a journalist) and Helen (a public relations director; maiden name, Sloane) Dudman; children: Georgia Manning, Richard Francis. *Education:* Antioch College, graduated, 1974.

ADDRESSES: Home—Northeast Bay, ME. *Office*—Dudman Communications Corp., 68 State St., #1129, Ellsworth, ME 04605-1924.

CAREER: Dudman Communications Corp., president and general manager, ended 1998; writer.

MEMBER: National Association of Broadcasters (member of board of directors), Bangor Rotary Club (vice president).

WRITINGS:

Dawn (novella and short stories), Puckerbrush Press (Orono, Maine), 1989.
Augusta, Gone: A True Story (memoir), Simon & Schuster (New York, NY), 2001.

Contributor to periodicals, including *Puckerbrush Review* and *New York Times.*

SIDELIGHTS: Martha Tod Dudman is a writer whose publications include *Augusta, Gone: A True Story,* a memoir that recounts her traumatic relationship with her teenage daughter. Dudman began writing in the mid-1970s after graduating from Antioch College, but after failing to interest publishers in a pair of manuscripts, she turned to working as a teacher. After becoming a wife and mother, Dudman befriended Constance Hunting, a University of Maine professor who published *Puckerbrush Review* and operated Puckerbrush Press. Dudman supplied various stories to *Puckerbrush Review,* and, in 1989, she issued her first book, *Dawn,* with Puckerbrush Press.

After her marriage ended in divorce, Dudman halted her literary career and assumed the presidency of Dudman Communications Corporation, which had been directed by her mother. "It was a tough decision,"

Dudman said in *Writers Write.* During the ensuing few years, Dudman wrote another book, but she otherwise devoted herself to parenting and to running the broadcasting business. "I felt like I didn't have any room in my head, just to wander around and think about writing," she told Cheryl Dellasega of *Writers Write.* "I learned how to run a business, and enjoyed it, but there was still something missing."

After leaving broadcasting in 1998, Dudman returned to writing, and, in 2001, she published *Augusta, Gone: A True Story,* "an unflinching description of an adolescent rebellion that nearly destroyed a family," as Martha Beck described it in the *New York Times Book Review.* The book is about Dudman's relationship with her teenage daughter as the child struggled with drugs, crime, and depression. Dudman's "searing honesty," Amy Waldman wrote in *People,* affected many reviewers. Ann Collette of *Book* wrote that *Augusta, Gone* is "compelling," and Daniel Paul Simmons III, in a *Publishers Weekly* piece, called it "visceral."

Dudman told Simmons that she kept *Augusta, Gone* from her daughter until the book reached the galley stage. "She kept bugging me to read it," Dudman told *Publishers Weekly,* "but I didn't want her to try to change it." When Dudman finally did let her daughter read an advance copy, her daughter was proud of the result. "She was living in San Diego at the time," Dudman told Cheryl Dellasega of *Writers Write,* "so I called and warned her that it might be tough to read, but that everything turned out okay. She must have sat down and read right through it, because she called back a few hours later and said she kept waiting to read that I didn't love her, and when that didn't happen, she realized how much I loved her."

BIOGRAPHICAL AND CRITICAL SOURCES:

PERIODICALS

Book, March, 2001, Ann Collette, review of *Augusta, Gone: A True Story,* p. 79.
Booklist, March 1, 2001, Vanessa Bush, review of *Augusta, Gone,* p. 1211.
Library Journal, February 15, 2001, Linda Beck, review of *August, Gone,* p. 192.
People, April 30, 2001, Amy Waldman, review of *Augusta, Gone,* p. 43.

Publishers Weekly, January 8, 2001, review of *Augusta, Gone,* p. 56; February 26, 2001, Daniel Paul Simmons III, "Like Mother, Like Mother," p. 26.

OTHER

Deer Leap, http://deerleap.com/ (December 2, 2001), review of *Augusta Gone.*

Writers Write, http://www.writerswrite.com/ (May, 2001), Cheryl Dellasega, interview with Dudman.*

*   *   *

DUHAMEL, Denise 1961-

PERSONAL: Born June 13, 1961, in Providence, RI; daughter of Normand (a baker) and Janet (a nurse) Duhamel; married Nick Carbo (a poet), August 22, 1992. *Education:* Emerson College, B.F.A. (creative writing), 1984; Sarah Lawrence College, M.F.A. (creative writing), 1987.

ADDRESSES: Office—Florida International University, 3000 Northeast 151st St., North Miami, FL 33181. *E-mail*—sedna61@aol.com.

CAREER: Poet and teacher. Has taught at Bucknell University, Lewisburg, PA, Lycomimg College, Williamsport, PA, and Bennington College, Bennington, VT; Florida International University, Miami, FL, assistant professor, 1999.

MEMBER: Academy of American Poets, PEN, Poetry Society of America, Poets House.

AWARDS, HONORS: Poetry fellowship, New York Foundation for the Arts, 1989; Crab Orchard Prize, 1998, for *The Star-spangled Banner*; poetry fellowship, National Endowment for the Arts, 2000.

WRITINGS:

Smile!, Warm Spring Press, 1993.
Girl Soldier, Garden Street Press, 1996.
How the Sky Fell, Pearl Editions (Long Beach, CA), 1996.

Kinky, Orchard Press (Alexandria, VA), 1997.
(With Maureen Seaton) *Exquisite Politics,* Tia Chucha Press (Chicago, IL), 1997.
The Star-spangled Banner, Southern Illinois University Press (Carbondale, IL), 1999.
(With Maureen Seaton) *Oyl,* Pearl Editions (Long Beach, CA), 2000.
Queen for a Day: Selected and New Poems, University of Pittsburgh Press (Pittsburgh, PA), 2000.
(With Maureen Seaton) *Little Novels,* Pearl Editions (Long Beach, CA), 2002.

Work represented in *The Best American Poetry,* 1993, 1994, 1998, 2000.

SIDELIGHTS: "Somewhere between [television series] *Sex and the City,* [poet] Sharon Olds and [monologist] Spalding Gray lies the poetry of Denise Duhamel," declared a *Publishers Weekly* reviewer in regard to *Queen for a Day: Selected and New Poems.* This volume joins such other works as *The Star-spangled Banner* in exploring some of the topics that Duhamel finds inspiring: sexuality, gender politics, and body image. She also investigates her husband's Filipino heritage and her place in the poetry community.

Unlike some of her poetic peers who would find anger in such subjects, Duhamel is an entertainer, in the view of *Booklist*'s Ray Olson. In *Queen for a Day,* the earlier poems are more serious, he said, while "her versions of sexually charged Inuit myths and famous fairy tales are lighter, though thoughtfully bemused rather than comic. Humor really enters her work in a series about the Barbie doll."

Some publishers, uncomfortable with Duhamel's sexual imagery, have chosen not to distribute her work. The banning of one of her books in Canada led the author to become an anticensorship advocate. Speaking to Nancy Lewis in a *Virginian Pilot* interview, Duhamel recounted the delay in the printing process for one of her books: "The printer came up with one excuse after another for not starting the press run. . . . After dragging its corporate feet for months, the company finally refused to print the book." As Duhamel added, "They said they never intended to print it, that it was pornographic." The book was eventually published, but the repercussions continued. According to Duhamel, even people from her Rhode Island hometown treat her differently upon learning that she is the author of a banned book.

Duhamel told *CA:* "When I was in high school, I believed that there were no living poets since the only poets I was exposed to in school were dead. It was not until I went to college that I was exposed to writers such as Kathleen Spivak, Bill Knott, and Sharon Olds—poets who really inspired me to try to be a poet myself."

BIOGRAPHICAL AND CRITICAL SOURCES:

PERIODICALS

Booklist, March 15, 1999, Ray Olson, review of *The Star-spangled Banner,* p. 1274; March 15, 2001, Ray Olson, review of *Queen for a Day: Selected and New Poems,* p. 1345.
Commercial Appeal (Memphis, TN), April 27, 1999, Fredric Koeppel, "Award-winning Poet to Read Here," p. C2.
Publishers Weekly, March 26, 2001, review of *Queen for a Day,* p. 86.
Virginian Pilot, October 12, 1996, Nancy Lewis, "Poet Tells of Combating Censorship," p. E5.

*   *   *

DYSON, A(nthony) E(dward) 1928-2002

OBITUARY NOTICE—See index for *CA* sketch: Born November 28, 1928, in Paddington, London, England; died c. July 30, 2002, in London, England. Educator, critic, social activist, editor, and author. Dyson held strong views on education, literature, and the laws that govern private life; his writings on these topics generated both respect and controversy. One of Dyson's early public campaigns involved his support for the decriminalization of homosexual behavior in private settings among consenting adults. He began with a 1958 letter to the London *Times* for which he secured the signatures of no fewer than thirty celebrated Britons. He then cofounded the Homosexual Law Reform Society and became active in a related support group, the Albany Trust. At about the same time, Dyson and his colleague Brian Cox established the *Critical Quarterly,* which attracted many well-known contributors and also became a vehicle for Dyson's wide-ranging opinions. In the late 1960s he challenged the British education system in a series of controversial "Black Papers" in which he criticized what he believed were the excesses of "progressive education" popular at the time, the dangers of the newly established, middle-level "comprehensive schools," and various other concerns. Dyson's third focus was literature. He taught English for many years, first at the University College of North Wales in Bangor, then at the new University of East Anglia in Norwich. He also edited a series of literature casebooks for the publisher Macmillan and Company, and wrote several books of his own. Dyson's writings include *The Crazy Fabric: Essays in Irony, The Inimitable Dickens,* and *Masterful Images: Metaphysicals to Romantics.* He edited several books as well, including *Twentieth-Century Mind* and *Education and Democracy.*

OBITUARIES AND OTHER SOURCES:

PERIODICALS

Independent (London, England), August 1, 2001, obituary by Brian Cox, p. 16.
Times (London, England), August 13, 2002.

E-F

EDWARDS, Thomas S. 1959-

PERSONAL: Born June 29, 1959, in Council Bluffs, IA; son of Charles (a physician) and Cecelia (a publications assistant; maiden name, Burger) Edwards; married Barbara Bywaters (a professor), July 28, 1990; children: Emily Lynell, Liam Thomas. *Ethnicity:* "White." *Education:* University of Nebraska—Omaha, B.A., 1981; Bowling Green State University, M.A., 1983, Ph.D., 1989.

ADDRESSES: Home—33 Highland Ave., Waterville, ME 04901. *Office*—Thomas College, 180 West River Rd., Waterville, ME 04901. *E-mail*—edwardst@ thomas.edu.

CAREER: University of New England, Westbrook College, Portland, ME, assistant professor of English and American studies, 1992-97; Castleton State College, Castleton, VT, associate academic dean, 1997-2000; Thomas College, Waterville, ME, vice president for academic affairs, 2000—. New England Faculty Development Consortium, member of board of directors, 1998—.

WRITINGS:

(Editor, with Karen L. Kilcup) *Jewett and Her Contemporaries: Reshaping the Canon,* University Press of Florida (Gainesville, FL), 1999.
(Editor, with Elizabeth A. De Wolfe) *Such News of the Land: U.S. Women Nature Writers,* University Press of New England (Hanover, NH), 2001.

(Editor, with Lorraine Anderson) *At Home on This Earth: Two Centuries of U.S. Women's Nature Writing,* University Press of New England (Hanover, NH), 2002.

Contributor of articles, translations, and reviews to periodicals. Translation editor, *Mid-American Review,* 1987-91.

SIDELIGHTS: Thomas S. Edwards told *CA:* "The collections I have been fortunate enough to work on have all grown out of teaching opportunities, and the collaborative nature of each publication has underscored all that I enjoy about the field of education. In each instance, a course or a question prompted the research that led to, in one case, a reevaluation of author Sarah Orne Jewett, and then, in a much broader context, a new focus on the role of women writers and their contributions to American literature. Ties between authors such as Willa Cather and Jewett were the first clue for me that regionalist writing, once dismissed as a relatively insignificant sideline of mainstream American literature, held the key to a wide range of perspectives on our evolving relationship with our landscape and our culture. *Such News of the Land: U.S. Women Nature Writers* outlines the critical foundation of the field that so many had noticed in different ways. *At Home on This Earth: Two Centuries of U.S. Women's Nature Writing* put together in chronological fashion an overview of the wealth and the beauty of nature writing."

BIOGRAPHICAL AND CRITICAL SOURCES:

PERIODICALS

Choice, June, 2000, J. W. Hall, review of *Jewett and Her Contemporaries: Reshaping the Canon,* p. 1816.

Legacy, June, 2001, Sarah Ann Wider, review of *Jewett and Her Contemporaries,* p. 242.

Library Journal, April 1, 2002, Maureen J. Delaney-Lehman, review of *At Home on This Earth: Two Centuries of U.S. Women's Nature Writing,* p. 104.

* * *

ELDER, Leon
    See YOUNG, Noel (B.)

* * *

ENGEL, Michael 1944-

PERSONAL: Born April 19, 1944, in New York, NY; married Jacqueline Haskins; children: Sara, Emily. *Education:* City College of the City University of New York, B.A., 1965, Ph.D., 1977; University of Wisconsin, M.A., 1972.

ADDRESSES: Home—43 Bryan Ave., Easthampton, MA 01027. *Office*—Department of Political Science, Westfield State College, Westfield, MA 01086.

CAREER: Westfield State College, Westfield, MA, professor of political science, 1976—.

WRITINGS:

State and Local Government: Fundamentals and Perspectives, Peter Lang (New York, NY), 1999.
The Struggle for Control of Public Education: Market Ideology versus Democratic Values, Temple University Press (Philadelphia, PA), 2000.

* * *

EVANS, A(lfred) Alexander 1905-2002

OBITUARY NOTICE—See index for *CA* sketch: Born August 22, 1905, in Bristol, England; died May 10, 2002. Evans, known to some as Alex, devoted his life to the education of young people. He began as a teacher of English, poetry, and drama at British

secondary schools. Later, under the auspices of the British Council, he filled posts in Germany, Hungary, and Turkey. In 1948 Evans was appointed deputy director of the Institute of Education at the University of Leeds. By this time he had moved from teaching children to training future teachers. In 1955 Evans became the headmaster of a school in London. For a brief period in the early 1970s he directed the London Centre for English Studies of Antioch College. Evans also served as the general secretary of the Association of Teachers in Colleges of Education. In addition to his contributions to books and periodicals, Evans produced editions of Shakespeare's plays and the verse collections *Poet's Tale, Victorian Poetry,* and *Contemporary: An Anthology of the Contemporary Poetry of Our Time, 1940-1964.*

OBITUARIES AND OTHER SOURCES:

PERIODICALS

Times (London, England), July 9, 2002, p. 30.

* * *

FABIAN, Ann 1949-

PERSONAL: Born August 18, 1949, in Pasadena, CA; daughter of Robert (a lawyer) and Virginia (a lawyer; maiden name, Ritt) Fabian; married Christopher Smeall (a lawyer), August 2, 1980; children: Andrew, Isabelle. *Education:* University of California—Santa Cruz, B.A. (with highest honors), 1971; Yale University, M.A., 1976, Ph.D., 1982.

ADDRESSES: Home—1165 Fifth Ave., New York, NY 10029. *Office*—Rutgers University, 131 George St., New Brunswick, NJ 08901-1414. *E-mail*—afabian@rci.rutgers.edu.

CAREER: Yale University, New Haven, CT, lecturer, 1982-84, assistant professor, 1984-91, associate professor of American studies and history, 1991-95, senior faculty fellow, 1991-92; University of California—Santa Cruz, associate professor of history, 1996; Rutgers University, New Brunswick, NJ, associate professor of American studies and history, 2000—, faculty fellow at Center for the Critical Analysis of Contemporary Culture, 2000-01. Columbia University, adjunct associate professor, 1996; Graduate Center of the City University of New York, adjunct associate professor, 1998; seminar leader. French-American School of New York, trustee, 1996-2000.

MEMBER: American Antiquarian Society (member of council, 2001), American Studies Association (member of council, 1999-2002; chair of Constance Rourke Prize committee, 2002), Western History Association, Columbia University Seminar on Early American History.

AWARDS, HONORS: Sidonie Miskimmon Claus Award for Excellence in Teaching the Humanities, Yale University, 1991; Stephen A. Botein fellow, American Antiquarian Society, 1994; fellow of Shelby Cullom Davis Center for Studies in History, Princeton University, 1996; William Y. and Nettie K. Adams fellow, School of American Research, Santa Fe, NM, 2002; Guggenheim fellow, 2002-03.

WRITINGS:

Card Sharps and Bucket Shops: Gambling in Nineteenth-Century America, Cornell University Press (Ithaca, NY), 1990, with a new introduction, Routledge (New York, NY), 1999.
The Unvarnished Truth: Personal Narratives in Nineteenth-Century America, University of California Press (Berkeley, CA), 2000.

Contributor to books, including *Under an Open Sky: Rethinking America's Western Past,* edited by William Cronon, Jay Gitlin, and George Miles, W. W. Norton (New York, NY), 1992; *Trading Cultures: The Worlds of Western Merchants; Essays on Authority, Objectivity, and Evidence,* edited by Jeremy Adelman and Stephen Aron, Berpols (Turnhout, Belgium), 2001; *Perspectives on American Book History: Artifacts and Commentary,* edited by Scott Casper, Joanne D. Chaison, and Jeffrey D. Groves, University of Massachusetts Press (Amherst, MA), 2002; *The Bondswoman's Narrative,* edited by Henry Louis Gates, Jr., Xanedu (Ann Arbor, MI), 2002; and *The Cultures of Collecting,* edited by Leah Dilworth, Rutgers University Press (New Brunswick, NJ), 2003. Contributor of articles and reviews to periodicals,

including *Yale Review, American Literary History,* and *South Atlantic Quarterly. Yale Journal of Criticism,* member of editorial collective, 1989-93, and editorial board; member of board of editors, *Western Historical Quarterly,* 1995-98; member of editorial board, *Reviews in American History.*

BIOGRAPHICAL AND CRITICAL SOURCES:

PERIODICALS

Biography, fall, 2000, James A. Good, review of *The Unvarnished Truth: Personal Narratives in Nineteenth-Century America,* p. 781.
Canadian Journal of History, August, 2001, Brian W. Dippie, review of *Card Sharps and Bucket Shops: Gambling in Nineteenth-Century America,* p. 388.

*   *   *

FARMBOROUGH, Florence 1887-1978

PERSONAL: Born April 15, 1887, in Steeple Claydon, Buckinghamshire, England; died August 18, 1974, in Heswall, England.

CAREER: Educator, nurse, and author. Taught English at University of Luis Vives, Valencia, Spain, c. 1930s, and in Kiev, Ukraine, and Moscow, Russia.

MEMBER: Red Cross, Royal Geographical Society.

WRITINGS:

Life and People in National Spain, Sheed & Ward (London, England), 1938.
Nurse at the Russian Front: A Diary, 1914-18, Constable (London, England), 1974, published as *With the Armies of the Tsar: A Nurse at the Russian Front, 1914-18,* Stein & Day (New York, NY), 1975; new edition, Cooper Square Press (New York, NY), 2000, abridged as *Russian Album 1908-1918,* edited by John Jolliffe, Michael Russell (Salisbury, England), 1979.

Contributor of articles to London *Times.*

SIDELIGHTS: English writer Florence Farmborough is most remembered for her volume of memoirs documenting her experiences as a volunteer nurse during World War I and the Russian Revolution. The book, titled *Nurse at the Russian Front: A Diary, 1914-18,* was a best seller in England when it was first published in 1974. The book contains Farmborough's first-hand observations of the miseries suffered by Russian soldiers and civilians during the revolution that created the communist state, as well as many of the hundreds of photographs she took with a plate camera and tripod during the era. The well-traveled Farmborough was also in Spain during its civil war in the 1930s, and she subsequently published a volume titled *Life and People in National Spain* about her experiences as the English language newsreader for broadcasts about the war that aired in England.

Farmborough was born April 15, 1887, in the English town of Steeple Claydon, in Buckinghamshire. After completing her education, she moved to the Ukrainian city of Kiev when she was just twenty-one years old, taking a job as an English teacher. Two years later, she moved to Moscow and served as a teacher for the two daughters of a Russian doctor. When World War I erupted in 1914, she volunteered her services with the Red Cross and then enrolled as a nurse at a hospital in Moscow before accompanying Russian troops on the battlefields of Poland, Austria, and Rumania. In 1917, the Russian troops she was with retreated back to Russia with the outbreak of the revolution. During the entire time, Farmborough made regular entries into a diary she was keeping and took hundreds of photographs, which many years later would become the basis for *Nurse at the Russian Front.*

Many critics felt that Farmborough's works provide a unique look at war. Critic Cecile M. Jagodzinski explained in an essay in *Dictionary of Literary Biography:* "Her memoirs . . . report on war from the viewpoint of an idealistic, sometimes naïve, and politically conservative young Englishwoman of the first decades of the twentieth century." The critic added, "Farmborough's writings demonstrate how wars and revolutions affect the personal histories of individuals and how the great events of history can transform or destroy the lives of ordinary people."

The diary entries in *Nurse at the Russian Front* also provide vivid descriptions of the inhumanity of war. For example, in one episode, Farmborough is traveling with Russian troops as they head for Poland: "As we continued our journey, we passed more than one battlefield. The dead were still lying around, in strange, unnatural postures—remaining where they had fallen: crouching, doubled up, stretched out, prostrate, prone, Austrians and Russians lying side by side." In the book Farmborough also describes the days leading up to the Russian Czar's abdication and his ousting by communist forces, an event she viewed with a good deal of skepticism.

Nurse at the Russian Front became a best seller and was also hailed by literary critics. A contributor to *Times Literary Supplement* felt the work offers "compelling reading" and constitutes "a remarkable and probably unique record of the desolation and horror of the Russian front." The same critic went on to call the book "not only a remarkable personal story, but also a striking historical document, adding to some important English testimony on the Russian army of those years." Likewise, a contributor for *Economist* believed Farmborough "produced a cool and yet moving record."

When the book was published in the United States as *With the Armies of the Tsar: A Nurse at the Russian Front, 1914-18,* it caught the notice of American critics as well. Rena Fowler of *Library Journal* praised Farmborough's efforts, noting that the "force of her sympathies creates an exciting and moving memoir." A contributor for *Saturday Review* called the work "fascinating," and went on to label the book "a work grounded in an irrepressible high spirit that is altogether rare in the bereft and convoluted literature of our times."

In 1979, Farmborough's book was abridged with the help of editor John Jolliffe and published as *Russian Album 1908-1918.* Divided into four parts, the work contains 170 illustrations, including photographs and maps. In addition to editing the work, Jolliffe also wrote an introduction in which he explains Farmborough's infatuation with Russia. "She loved Russia the most" because it taught her "the meaning of the word 'suffering.' It was a lesson, of course, learned principally in the days of war and revolution," Jolliffe wrote. Literary critic D. N. Collins of *British Book News* was particularly impressed with the photographs that accompany the text, which he felt form "an extremely valuable record of life in the Russian Empire at a crucial period in its history."

Despite her travels to and involvement with so many foreign lands, Farmborough always considered herself an Englishwoman. As she wrote in the introduction of *Life and People in National Spain:* "I am an Englishwoman. I introduce myself to you in this way so that you will readily understand that a person born and bred in the quietness and beauty of the English countryside, and whose father and forefathers have been true to their country and country's soil for so many centuries, must remain, despite much travel and despite life's vicissitudes, wholly English." Farmborough continued to travel the world for the remainder of her life, visiting Russia, which had left such an imprint on her soul, for the last time in 1962. She died in the English town of Heswall on August 18, 1974.

BIOGRAPHICAL AND CRITICAL SOURCES:

BOOKS

Dictionary of Literary Biography, Volume 204: *British Travel Writers, 1940-1997,* Gale (Detroit, MI), 1999.

PERIODICALS

British Book News, May, 1980, D. N. Collins, review of *Russian Album 1908-1918,* p. 318.
Economist, November 16, 1974, review of *Nurse at the Russian Front, 1914-1918,* p. 14.
Library Journal, May 1, 1975, Rena Fowler, review of *With the Armies of the Tsar: A Nurse at the Russian Front, 1914-1918,* p. 842.
Saturday Review, March 22, 1975, review of *With the Armies of the Tsar,* pp. 26-27.
Times Literary Supplement, October 4, 1974, review of *Nurse at the Russian Front,* p. 1080; January 4, 1980, review of *Russian Album 1908-1918,* p. 23.

OTHER

Spartacus, http://www.spartacus.schoolnet.co.uk/ (April 4, 2001).*

*   *   *

FARR, Moira 1958-

PERSONAL: Born September 2, 1958, in Barrie, Ontario, Canada; daughter of Ralph Vincent (a newspaper reporter and photographer) and Patricia (a nurse) Farr. *Education:* University of Toronto, B.A. (English and history; with honors), 1982; Ryerson School of Journalism, B.A. (journalism), 1985. *Hobbies and other interests:* Natural history, travel, bird watching.

ADDRESSES: Agent—Anne McDermid Agency, 12 Willcocks St., Toronto, Ontario, Canada M5S 1C8. *E-mail*—anne@mcdermidagency.com.

CAREER: Freelance writer and editor. Banff School of Fine Arts, Maclean-Hunter Creative Nonfiction program faculty editor, 2001; Carleton University School of Journalism, currently instructor in freelance writing for magazines; Ryerson Polytechnical University, currently teaching assistant and contributing editor.

MEMBER: Writers' Union of Canada, PEN Canada (member, board of directors).

AWARDS, HONORS: Norma Epstein Award for Creative Writing, University of Toronto, 1981, 1982; Maurice A. Code scholarship, University of Toronto, 1981; Kenneth R. Wilson Award for best feature article, 1986, for "Trouble at the University of Toronto School of Architecture"; National Magazine Award honorable mention, 1990, for "The Last Dinner," 1995, for "Women Beware Critics," 1997, for "Science Fair"; project grants for arts writers, Ontario Arts Council, 1991, 1995; writer's grant, Toronto Arts Council, 1992; Maclean Hunter Arts Journalism fellowship, Banff School of Fine Arts, 1992; "B" grant for fiction, Canada Council, 1997, 2000; Edmonton Journal's Top Pick for Nonfiction, 1999, for *After Daniel: A Suicide Survivor's Tale;* Pearson Prize for Nonfiction shortlist, Ottawa-Carleton Book Award, 1999, for *After Daniel;* silver medal, Canadian Council for the Advancement of Education, 2000, for article "The Thousand-Year Itch"; Canadian National Institute for the Blind TORGI Award shortlist, 2000, for *A Survivor's Tale;* Ottawa Arts Council fiction grant, 2001.

WRITINGS:

After Daniel: A Suicide Survivor's Tale, HarperCollins (Toronto, Canada), 1999.

Assistant editor, *Canadian Architect,* 1985-87; held various editorial jobs for *Financial Post Magazine,* 1987-90; editor, *This Magazine,* 1993, and *Equinox,* 1994-96.

ADAPTATIONS: After Daniel: A Suicide Survivor's Tale was the subject of a segment in a thirteen-part documentary series *Lives Interrupted* produced by Sleeping Giant Productions, which aired on Visio TV in the fall of 2001.

WORK IN PROGRESS: A novel.

SIDELIGHTS: Moira Farr's *After Daniel: A Suicide Survivor's Tale* tells the story of her relationship with Daniel Jones, a young writer who committed suicide in 1994, his death, and her responses to the loss. In *The Eye,* Kathy Shaidle commented that the book is "a searing, poignant memoir" and noted that "This is emphatically *not* a creepy, gossipy, self-pitying tell-all."

In the book, Farr notes that she did not want to glorify Jones's death by making it seem romantic, and she wanted to avoid being self-indulgent. Thus, she writes about wider issues as well as her own feelings, examining the broader social context of suicide and mental illness. She surveys current scientific knowledge of suicide, as well as current society's fascination with the act and the exploitation of suicide on the Internet. She notes how movies often use suicide as a plot device, "much as they would a car chase or an exploding building," remarked Paul S. Links in online *The Left Atrium,* and concludes that although the media can often educate the public about suicide, it can also "insensitive, torturing." Links noted that *After Daniel: A Suicide Survivor's Story* is "an offer of hope, a beautifully written journey of reclamation, and simply a very personal account of the author's own grief." Shaidle noted that although the book is not easy to read, it "is brimming with bittersweet beauty and a strange sort of hope, which might be the only kind there is."

BIOGRAPHICAL AND CRITICAL SOURCES:

PERIODICALS

Canadian Forum, September, 1999, Ginny Freeman MacOwan, "A Painful Subject Viewed through Impassioned Eyes," p. 36.
Edmonton Journal, July, 2001.

OTHER

Eye, http://www.eye.net/ (October 11, 2001).
Left Atrium, http://www.cma.ca/ (October 11, 2001).

FERGUSON, Craig 1962-

PERSONAL: Born May 17, 1962, in Glasgow, Scotland; married; wife's name Sascha.

ADDRESSES: Agent—William Morris Agency, Inc., 151 South El Camino Dr., Beverly Hills, CA 90212-2775.

CAREER: Actor, producer, writer. Television series appearances include *The Ferguson Theory,* 1994; *Freakazoid!,* 1995; *Maybe This Time,* ABC, 1995; *The Drew Carey Show,* ABC, 1996-2000; *Hercules,* syndicated, 1998. Appearances on episodic television include "Confidence and Paranoia," *Red Dwarf,* 1988; "Peeled Grapes and Pedicures," *Chelmsford 1 2 3,* 1988; *Have I Got News for You,* 1991; *The Brain Drain,* 1993; "Suites for the Sweet," *Almost Perfect,* CBS, 1996. Other television appearances include *Dream Baby,* PBS, 1992; *Drew's Dance Party Special,* ABC, 1998. Film appearances include *Modern Vampires,* Sterling Home Entertainment, 1998; *The Big Tease,* Warner Bros., 1999; *Saving Grace,* Fine Line Features, 2000; *Chain of Fools,* Warner Bros., 2000; *Born Romantic,* 2000. Film work includes (executive producer) *The Big Tease,* Warner Bros., 1999; (coproducer) *Saving Grace,* Fine Line Features, 2000. Stage appearances include *Bad Boy Johnny and the Prophets of Doom,* produced at the Theatre at Union Chapel, Islington, London, England, 1994.

WRITINGS:

The Big Tease (screenplay), Warner Bros., 1999.
(With Mark Crowdy) *Saving Grace,* Fine Line Features, 2000.

SIDELIGHTS: Known to American television audiences for his portrayal of the obnoxious boss Nigel Wick on *The Drew Carey Show,* Scottish actor Craig Ferguson is also a screen writer and producer. Among his film works is *The Big Tease,* in which Ferguson plays hairdresser Crawford MacKenzie. Under the impression that he has been invited to compete for the Platinum Scissors Award at the World Freestyle Championship in Los Angeles, MacKenzie flies out of Glasgow with a British documentary crew to follow his every move. As with another mock documentary about hapless Britons arriving on American shores, *This Is Spinal Tap,* things are not quite as MacKenzie expected: he has only been invited to the competition as a spectator. With the help of a Hollywood publicist played by Frances Fisher, however, "MacKenzie gets his chance to tease, comb, and mousse his way to the top," in the words of the *Los Angeles Times*'s Susan King. Bob Campbell in the New Orleans *Times-Picayune* called *The Big Tease* "the snappiest comedy sleeper since 'South Park,'" and described Ferguson's portrayal of MacKenzie as "the most endearingly outrageous U.K. export since Austin Powers."

Equally outrageous is the plot of *Saving Grace,* the title of which refers to the name of Brenda Blethyn's character. Suddenly widowed when her husband falls out of an airplane, and faced with heavy bills created by her husband's failed investments, Grace joins forces with her soon-to-be unemployed gardener (Ferguson) to start a profitable home-based business—growing marijuana. As the plot unfolds, it becomes apparent that more than a few upstanding citizens of the sleepy Cornish coastal town like to light up now and then. But the story consists of more than just a few giggles over dope, according to Joe Leydon in *Variety,* who described it as "more character-driven than plot-propelled."

"Although unlikely to prove this year's *Full Monty,*" wrote Graham Fuller in *Interview,* the film "should bring a little high to the late summer box office." Striking a similar note, Richard Schickel in *Time,* while noting that it is "not as tightly wound as the best of its breed," called *Saving Grace* "a genial way to pass the time." Lisa Schwarzbaum of *Entertainment Weekly* also expressed reservations about the film, but conceded that it has "dopey good vibes." Leydon in *Variety* was more outspoken in his praise, comparing the movie to *Local Hero* and pronouncing it a "spiritedly daft and droll gem of straight-faced lunacy."

BIOGRAPHICAL AND CRITICAL SOURCES:

BOOKS

Contemporary Theatre, Film, and Television, Volume 33, Gale (Detroit, MI), 2001.

PERIODICALS

Atlanta Journal-Constitution, February 25, 2000, Eleanor Ringel Gillespie, review of *The Big Tease,* p. P11.

Boston Globe, February 11, 2000, Jay Carr, review of *The Big Tease,* p. C6.
Entertainment Weekly, February 4, 2000, Lisa Schwarzbaum, review of *The Big Tease,* p. 48; August 11, 2000, review of *Saving Grace,* p. 52.
Interview, August, 2000, Graham Fuller, review of *Saving Grace,* p. 39.
Pittsburgh Post-Gazette, March 16, 2000, Susan King and Mitchell Hill, "A Quest for Stardom: Craig Ferguson, Who Left Scotland for Filmdom, Writes Screenplays between 'Drew Carey' Jokes," p. B5.
Time, August 14, 2000, Richard Schickel, review of *Saving Grace,* p. 78.
Times-Picayune (New Orleans, LA), April 14, 2000, Bob Campbell, review of *The Big Tease,* p. L32.
Variety, January 31, 2000, Joe Leydon, review of *Saving Grace,* p. 33.

OTHER

Craig Ferguson Online, http://www.angelfire.com/film/craigferguson/ (October 23, 2002).*

*   *   *

FERNAN GOMEZ, Fernando 1921-

PERSONAL: Born August 28, 1921, in Buenos Aires, Argentina (some sources say Lima, Peru); son of Carola Fernan Gomez (an actress); married Maria Dolores Pradera (an actress), 1945 (divorced, 1947); married Emma Cohen, 2000.

ADDRESSES: Agent—c/o Lolafilms, S.A, Velazquez 12, Madrid 28001, Spain.

CAREER: Actor, director, writer.

Film appearances include *Noche fantastica,* Cifesa, 1943; *La chica del gato,* Cifesa, 1943; *Viviendo al reves,* 1943; *Turbante blanco,* 1943; *Se vende un palacio,* 1943; *Rosas de otono,* 1943; *Mi enemigo y yo,* Cifesa, 1943; *Fin de curso,* Latina Films, 1943; *Cristina Guzman,* 1943; *Una chica de opereta,* Cifesa, 1944; *Empezo en boda,* 1944; *El destino se disculpa,* Cibeles Film, 1945; *El camino de babel,* Chamartin, 1945; *Bambu,* Ballesteros, 1945; *Domingo de car-*

naval, Aparicio, 1945; *Se le fue el novio,* Radio Films, 1945; *Espronceda,* 1945; *Es peligroso asomarse al exterior,* 1945; *Eres un caso,* 1945; *La proxima vez que vivamos,* 1946; *Los habitantes de la casa deshabitada,* 1946; *Embrujo,* Ernesto Gonzales, 1947; *La sirena negra,* 1947; *Noche sin cielo,* 1947; *La muralla feliz,* Boga, 1947; *Boton de ancla,* 1948; *Boliche y compania,* Latina Films, 1948; *La mies es mucha,* 1948; *Hoy no pasamos lista,* CEA Distribucion, 1948; *Carlos,* Vida en sombras, 1949; *Alas de juventud,* Delta, 1949; *Noventa minutos,* 1949; *La noche del sabado,* Suevia Films Excisa, 1950; *El ultimo caballo,* Procines Los Films del Buho, 1950; *Tiempos felices,* Universal, 1950; *Facultad de letras,* Francechs, 1950; *Balarrasa,* Cifesa, 1951; *La trinca del aire,* Suevia Films Excisa, 1951; *El capitan Veneno,* Samsa Films, 1951; *El sistema Pelegrin,* Warner Bros., 1952; *Me quiero casar contigo,* Hispano Foxfilm, 1952; *Los ojos dejan huellas,* Cifesa, 1952; *Rebeldia,* Cifesa, 1952; *La conciencia acusa,* RKO Radio Pictures, 1952; *Cincuenta años del real Madrid,* 1952; *Esa pareja feliz,* Iris Films, 1953; *Luis, aeropuerto,* Vifesa, 1953; *Nadie lo sabra,* Suevia Films Excisa, 1953; *Manicomio,* Selecciones Aparicio, 1954; *Morena Clara,* Cifesa, 1954; *La ironia del dinero,* Floralva Exclusivas, 1954; *La otra vida del Capitan Contreras,* Suevia Films Excisa, 1955; *Manuel,* El guardian del paraiso, 1955; *Congreso en Sevilla,* Cifesa, 1955; *El mansaje,* Procines, 1955; *Lo scapolo,* Cifesa, 1955; *La gran mentira,* As Films, 1956; *El fenomeno,* Goya Films, 1956; *El Malvado Carabel,* Floralva Exclusivas, 1956; *Viaje de novios,* C.B. Films, 1956; *Faustina,* Suevia Films Excisa, 1957; *Un marido de ida y vuelta,* Suevia Films Excisa, 1957; *Los Angeles del volante,* Ignacio Ferres Iquino Socieded Anonima, 1957; *Muchachas de azul,* Radio Films, 1957; *El inquilino,* Delta, 1957; *La vida por delante,* Mercurio Films, 1958; *Ana dice si,* Radio Films, 1958; *Soledad,* Emery, 1959; *Crimen para recien casados,* As Films, 1960; *La vida privada de Fulano de Tal,* Mundial Films, 1960; *Salo para hombres,* Radio Films, 1960; *Mimi Pompon,* C.E.A. Distribucion, 1961; *Fantasmas en la casa,* Floralva Exclusivas, 1961; *La venganza de Don Mendo,* C.B. Films, 1961; *Donde pongo este muerto?,* Hispano Foxfilm, 1962; *La mujer de tu projimo,* Cepicsa, 1962; *La Becerrada,* Dipenfa Filmayer Video, 1963; *Chasse a la mafia,* Cepicsa, 1963; *Benigno, hermano mio,* Tandem Films, 1963; *Visitando a las estrellas,* 1964; *El mundo sigue,* Nueva Films, 1965; *Ninette y un señor de Murcia,* Nueva Films, 1965; *Un vampiro para dos,* Rosa Films, 1965; *Mayores con reparos,* As Films, 1966; *La vil seduccion,* Academy Pictures, 1968; *Carola de dia, Carola de noche,* Incine, 1969;

Un adulterio decente, Paramount Films de España, 1969; *Estudio amueblado 2.P.,* Metro-Goldwyn-Mayer Iberica, 1969; *Por que pecamos a los cuarenta?,* C.B. Films, 1969; *Las panteras se comen a los ricos,* Atlantida Films, 1969; *De profesion, sus labores,* C.B. Films, 1970; *Crimen imperfecto,* Filmayer, 1970; *Vau seis,* 1970; *El triangulito,* Metro-Goldwyn-Mayer Iberica, 1970; *Pierna creciente, falda menguante,* Regia-Arturo Gonzalez Rodriguez, 1970; *Como casarse en siete dias,* Regia-Arturo Gonzalez Rodriguez, 1971; *Las ibericas F.C.,* C.B. Films, 1971; *Los gallos de la madrugada,* Regia-Arturo Gonzalez Rodriguez, 1971; *Don Quijote cabalga de nuevo,* Filmayer, 1972; *La leyenda del alcalde de Zalamea,* Suevia Films Excisa, 1973; *Ana y los lobos,* WorldWide Pictures, 1973; *El espiritu de la colmena,* Janus Films, 1973; *Vera, un cuento cruel,* 1973; *El amor del Capitan Brando,* Incine Distribuciones Cinematograficas, 1974; *El humo que mantiene las casas,* Hispamex, 1974; *Papa,* Incine Distribuciones Cinematograficas, 1975; *Yo soy fulana de tal,* Arturo Gonzalez Rodriguez, 1975; *Yo la vi primero,* Warner Espanola, 1975; *Sensualidad,* Jose Miguel Baixauli Alfonso, 1975; *Pim, pam, pum . . . fuego!,* J.F. Films de Distribucion, 1975; *Imposible para una solterona,* Lotus Films Internacional, 1976; *Eduardo,* La querida, 1976; *Parranda,* 1976; *Mas fina que las gallinas,* 1976; *Gulliver,* 1976; *Las cuatro novias de Augusto Perez,* Ismael Gonzalez Diaz, 1976; *Chely,* 1976; *Bruja, mas que bruja,* 1976; *El anacoreta,* Hispano Foxfilm, 1976; *Reina Zanahoria,* 1977; *La ragazza dal pigiama giallo,* 1977; *Los restos del naufragio,* 1978; *Milagro en el circo,* 1978; *Madrid al desnudo,* 1978; *Arriba hazana,* 1978; *Mama cumple cien años,* Universal Film Manufacturing, 1979; *Maravillas,* 1980; *127 millones libres de impuestos,* 1980; *Copia cero,* 1981; *Interior rojo,* 1982; *Besame, tonta,* 1982; *Apaga . . . y vamonos,* 1982; *Soldados de plomo,* 1983; *Juana la loca . . . de vez en cuando,* 1983; *Feroz,* C.B. Films, 1983; *La noche mas hermosa,* C.B. Films, 1984; *Los zancos,* 1984; *Leopoldo Contreras,* Stico, 1984; *El viaje a ninguna parte,* 1985; *Requiem por un campesino español,* 1985; *Marbella, un golpe de cinco estrellas,* Calepas International, 1985; *Mambru se fue a la guerra,* 1985; *Luces de bohemia,* 1985; *De hombre a hombre,* 1985; *La corte de Faraon,* 1985; *Pobre mariposa,* 1986; *La mitad del cielo,* 1986; *Delirios de amor,* 1986; *Cara de acelga,* 1986; *Mi general,* 1987; *Moros y cristianos,* United International Pictures y Cia, 1987; *El gran serafin,* 1987; *El rio que nos lleva,* 1989; *El mar y el tiempo,* 1989; *Marquis d'esquilache,* 1989; *Fuera de juego,* Columbia TriStar Films de Espana, 1991; *Marcellino,* 1991; *El rey pasmado,* 1991;

Belle epoque, Sony Pictures Classics, 1992; *Chechu y familia,* 1992; *The Absence,* 1993; *Cartas desde Huesca,* 1993; *Asi en el cielo como en la tierra,* 1995; *Pesadilla para un rico,* United International Pictures y Cia, 1996; *Tranvia a la Malvarrosa,* Columbia TriStar Films de España, 1996; *El abuelo,* Miramax, 1998; *Todo sobre mi madre,* Sony Pictures Classics, 1999; *Pepe Guindo,* Alta Films, 1999; *La lengua de las mariposas,* Miramax, 1999.

Film work as director includes *Manicomio,* Selecciones Aparicio, 1954; *El mansaje,* Procines, 1955; *El Malvado Carabel,* Floralva Exclusivas, 1956; *La vida por delante,* Mercurio Films, 1958; *La vida alrededor,* Mercurio Films, 1959; *Solo para hombres,* Radio Films, 1960; *La venganza de Don Mendo,* C.B. Films, 1961; *Los palomos,* Izaro Films, 1964; *El mundo sigue,* Nueva Films, 1965; *Ninette y un señor de Murcia,* Nueva Films, 1965; *Mayores con reparos,* As Films, 1966; *El extrano viaje,* Izaro Films, 1967; *Crimen imperfecto,* Filmayer, 1970; *Como casarse en siete dias,* Regia-Arturo Gonzalez Rodriguez, 1971; *Yo la vi primero,* Warner Española, 1975; *La querida,* 1976; *Bruja, mas que bruja,* 1976; *Mi hija Hildegart,* 1977; *Cinco tenedores,* 1979; *El viaje a ninguna parte,* 1985; *Mambru se fue a la guerra,* 1985; *El mar y el tiempo,* 1989; *Fuera de juego,* Columbia TriStar Films de España, 1991; *Siete mil dias juntos,* UPI y Cia, 1994; *Pesadilla para un rico,* United International Pictures y Cia, 1996; *A porta do sol,* 1998; *El Lazarillo de Tormes,* Lola Films Distribucion, 2000.

Television appearances include *Juan soldado,* 1973; *Fortunata y jacinta,* 1979; *La mujer de tu vida: La mujer perdida,* 1988; *La mujer de tu vida 2: Las mujeres de mi vida,* 1992. Work as television director includes *Juan soldado,* 1973; *La mujer de tu vida 2: Las mujeres de mi vida,* 1992.

AWARDS, HONORS: National Cinema Award, 1980.

WRITINGS:

La mujer de tu vida 2: Las mujeres de mi vida (Television script), produced 1992.

Wrote Television series *Los ladrones van a la oficina,* 1993.

Also author of the book *El mar y el tiempo,* (see below), 1989.

SCREENPLAYS

Manicomio, Selecciones Aparicio, 1954.
(And story creator) *El mansaje,* Procines, 1955.
El Malvado Carabel, Floralva Exclusivas, 1956.
(And story creator) *La vida por delante* (also known as *Life Ahead*), Mercurio Films, 1958.
(And story creator) *La vida alrededor* (also known as *Life around Us*), Mercurio Films, 1959.
Sólo para hombres, Radio Films, 1960.
La venganza de Don Mendo, C.B. Films, 1961.
Los palomos, Izaro Films, 1964.
El mundo sigue, Nueva Films, 1965.
Ninette y un señor de Murcia, Nueva Films, 1965.
Mayores con reparos, As Films, 1966.
Como casarse en siete dias, Regia-Arturo Gonzalez Rodriguez, 1971.
(And story creator) *Yo la vi primero* (also known as *I Saw Her First*), Warner Espanola, 1975.
(Additional dialogue) *Fuera de juego,* Columbia TriStar Films de España, 1991.
Pesadilla para un rico, United International Pictures y Cia, 1996.

Other screenplays include *La querida,* 1976; *Mi hija hildegart,* 1977; *Los zancos* (also known as *The Stilts*), 1984; *Stico,* 1984;
El viaje a ninguna parte (also known as *Voyage to Nowhere*), 1985; (and story creator) *Mi general* (also known as *My General*), 1987; (and story creator) *El mar y el tiempo* (also known as *The Sea and the Weather*), 1989; "La otra historia Rosendo Juarez," *Cuentos de Borges I,* 1991; *Lázaro de tormes,* 2001.

ADAPTATIONS: The 1983 film *Las bicicletas son para el verano October 1, 1980,* was based on a book by Fernan Gomez.

SIDELIGHTS: Son of the actress Carola Fernan Gomez, Spanish actor, director, and writer Fernando Fernan Gomez was born while his mother was on tour in South America in 1921. He moved to Spain in 1924, and many of the films in which he has appeared—written either by others or by Fernan Gomez himself—concern the Spain of the 1930s, either just before or during that country's bitter civil war.

According to Jonathan Holland of *Variety,* as an actor Fernan Gomez is a "gravel-voiced, irascible thesp" who "will be best remembered for a series of devastating social comedies in the 1950s." Among the dozens of screenplays he has written is *Los zancos* (*The Stilts*, 1984), in which a lonely professor named Angel is rescued from suicide by his lovely neighbor Terese, with whom he falls in love. There is only one problem: Terese has a lover and child, and though Angel and Terese embark on an erotic relationship, it is clear that their affair will come to an end.

The title of *Los zancos* refers to the name of a theatrical troupe to which Terese belongs, and travelling theatre shows are also central to the plot of *El viaje a ninguna parte* (*Voyage to Nowhere*, 1985). The latter is the story of a family of comedians who tour rural Spain during the 1940s and 1950s. Not only are these the dreary early years of Francisco Franco's dictatorship, but the family finds its entire means of livelihood threatened by the rise of television. Stepping far back in time for his material, Fernan Gomez adapted an anonymous sixteenth-century novel in *Lazarillo de Tormes* (2001). He also directed the movie, but José Luis Garcia Sanchez had to complete the project, after Fernan Gomez fell ill during the shooting.

BIOGRAPHICAL AND CRITICAL SOURCES:

BOOKS

Contemporary Theatre, Film, and Television, Volume 33, Gale (Detroit, MI), 2001.

PERIODICALS

Variety, October 1, 1980, "Principal Film Directors: Survival against the Odds and Flashes of Brilliance," pp. 44-45; August 15, 1984, review of *Los zancos,* p. 15; December 26, 1984, review of *Stico,* p. 16; October 11, 1989, review of *El mar y el tiempo,* p. 36; September 20, 1999, Jonathan Holland, "Fest Beholds Career of Fernan Gomez," p. 76; July 23, 2001, Jonathan Holland, review of *Lazaro de tormes,* p. 18.
World Literature Today, summer, 1989, David Ross Gerling, review of *El mar y el tiempo,* p. 458.*

*   *   *

FERRIS, David 1960-

PERSONAL: Born 1960. *Education:* New England Conservatory, B. Mus. (early music performance), 1982; Brandeis University, Ph.D. (music), 1993.

ADDRESSES: Office—Shepherd School of Music, Rice University, P.O. Box 1892, Houston, TX 77251-1892. *E-mail*—Ferris@rice.edu.

CAREER: Shepherd School of Music, Rice University, Houston, TX, assistant professor of musicology, 1998—. Previously taught at Amherst College, University of Houston, and Massachusetts Institute of Technology.

MEMBER: American Musicological Society, Society for Music Theory, American Bach Society.

WRITINGS:

Schumann's Eichendorff "Liederkreis" and the Genre of the Romantic Cycle, Oxford University Press (New York, NY), 2001.

WORK IN PROGRESS: C. P. E. Bach and the Forging of an Historical Identity.

SIDELIGHTS: David Ferris, a musicologist who specializes in the music of the late eighteenth and early nineteenth centuries, particularly German Romanticism, is the author of *Schumann's Eichendorff "Liederkreis" and the Genre of the Romantic Cycle.* Nineteenth century German composer Robert Schumann created the music of the *Liederkreis* during the year 1840 to accompany texts written by German Romantic poet Joseph von Eichendorff. "Ferris concentrates on the sources and content of the songs of 1840," reported Michael Musgrave, reviewing the book in the *Times Literary Supplement.* Musgrave also noted that these Romantic song cycles "vary from the highly organized . . . to much looser collections of poems and musical relationships," and added: "Ferris argues that much is lost in forcing such works into traditional 'organic' analytical moulds." C. Cai in *Choice* commended *Schumann's Eichendorff "Liederkreis" and the Genre of the Romantic Cycle* as "rewarding reading," and Musgrave concluded that "there is a good deal of information [in the volume] that usefully revises traditional assumptions about the way in which Schumann composed."

BIOGRAPHICAL AND CRITICAL SOURCES:

PERIODICALS

Choice, October, 2001, C. Cai, review of *Schumann's Eichendorff "Liederkreis" and the Genre of the Romantic Cycle,* p. 319.

Times Literary Supplement, October 12, 2001, Michael Musgrave, "Fragments of a Secret Life," pp. 18-19.*

*   *   *

FILENE, Benjamin 1965-

PERSONAL: Born June 1, 1965. *Education:* Brown University, A.B. (history; with honors), 1987; Yale University, Ph.D. (American studies), 1994.

ADDRESSES: Office—Minnesota Historical Society, 345 Kellogg Blvd. W., St. Paul, MN 55102-1906.

CAREER: Minnesota Historical Society, St. Paul, MN, exhibit developer.

AWARDS, HONORS: ASCAP-Deems Taylor award, Association for Recorded Sound Collection award, and Herbert Feis Award from the American Historical Association, all for *Romancing the Folk: Public Memory and American Roots Music.*

WRITINGS:

Romancing the Folk: Public Memory and American Roots Music, University of North Carolina Press (Chapel Hill, NC), 2000.

Contributor to periodicals, including *Minnesota History.*

SIDELIGHTS: Benjamin Filene's *Romancing the Folk: Public Memory and American Roots Music* grew out of the author's Yale University Ph.D. dissertation to become "an engaging analysis of the various interpretations of roots or vernacular music in the 20th century," according to *Choice* critic R. D. Cohen. The book begins with a look at Francis James Child, the Harvard-trained Shakespearean scholar who chronicled "pure" English and Scottish folk songs; and Cecil Sharp, who in 1916 established a link between Child's ballads and the songs of Appalachia. Other influences, from black spirituals to cowboy songs, helped shape the image of roots music. The author argues that the

popularity of folk songs in the early part of the twentieth century created a market for the kind of musician who would fit the "authentic" folksy image.

Song promoters of the twentieth century's early decades traveled far and wide in search of authentic music—in 1933 the father-and-son team of John and Alan Lomax visited the South, hauling a 350-pound recording machine, and came upon Huddie Ledbetter, who as Leadbelly "became the first folk 'primitive' sold as such," as *New York Times* reviewer Robert Christgau noted. The book recounts how Leadbelly's raw sound was tamped down to cater to the conservative tastes of mainstream listeners.

For Filene, Christgau continued, "no career epitomizes the professional quandary of the putative folk musician better than that of another Lomax discovery, Muddy Waters." The blues musician "never stopped adjusting to fashion," said the critic. But at his best, Waters "bent his overwhelming physical presence to recombinant interpretive genius, adapting usages he had absorbed in one place and time to the social and aural realities of another."

Waters, Leadbelly, Woody Guthrie, Pete Seeger, and Bob Dylan are all part of *Romancing the Folk,* as "Filene presents a case that perhaps these men were chosen and promoted to shape the public's perception of 'authentic,'" stated David Kidney in an online *Green Man Review* article. "It is an interesting argument. Is [Leadbelly] 'authentic' because he was the first? Or was he marketable and representative? Was he chosen by corporate America to represent 'roots' music because he had a good story, and a catchy tune?"

Library Journal reviewer Dan Bogey found *Romancing the Folk* "a learned and lively look at the development of our national music," adding that Filene covers territory that "is overlooked in [other] books on folk music." Christgau, however, had some criticism for the way Filene assesses the folk background of Bob Dylan, who "is so protean and prolix that you can use him to explore any number of things, and parsing his songs is a favorite ploy of intellectuals set on demonstrating their intimacy with popular culture. So given Filene's interest in the remade past, he should have gone easier on Dylan's [1960s] output, concentrating instead on the records of the ['90s], which he stuffs in at the very end." But the critic also acknowledged the author's contribution to musical history, saying that "the folklorists, academics, bureaucrats and entrepreneurs who dominate his story are colorful characters, and they are joined by artists who inspire Filene to critical heights few historians approach."

BIOGRAPHICAL AND CRITICAL SOURCES:

PERIODICALS

Choice, November, 2000, R. D. Cohen, review of *Romancing the Folk: Public Memory and American Roots Music,* pp. 554-555.
Library Journal, July, 2000, Dan Bogey, review of *Romancing the Folk,* p. 95.
New York Times, December 10, 2000, Robert Christgau, "Folk Lore."

OTHER

Green Man Review, http://www.greenmanreview.com/ (September 12, 2001), David Kidney, review of *Romancing the Folk.*
Minnesota Historical Society Web site, http://www.mnhs.org/ (September 12, 2001).

*   *   *

FITZPATRICK, Christina 1973-

PERSONAL: Born October 14, 1973, in Springfield, MA; daughter of Francis (a salesman) and Jennifer (a telecommunication specialist; maiden name, Chestnut) Fitzpatrick; married; children: three. *Ethnicity:* "Irish." *Education:* Emerson College, B.A., 1995; Sarah Lawrence College, M.F.A., 1999. *Religion:* Roman Catholic. *Hobbies and other interests:* Travel.

ADDRESSES: Agent—Wendy Weil Literary Agency, 232 Madison Ave., Suite 1300, New York, NY 10016.

CAREER: Midnight Oil Co., New York, NY, bartender, 1998—; Teachers and Writer's Collaborative, New York, NY, instructor, 2001—; Gotham Writer's Workshop, New York, NY, instructor, 2000; Iona College, New Rochelle, NY, freshman English teacher,

1999. Creative writing teacher at Valhalla Women's Prison and the Westside YMCA, 1997-98. Visiting artist at the American Academy in Rome, 2002.

MEMBER: Authors Guild.

WRITINGS:

Where We Lived, (short stories) HarperCollins (New York, NY), 2001.
What's the Girl Worth? (novel), HarperCollins (New York, NY), 2002.
The Nightstalker vs. Romance (novel), HarperCollins (New York, NY), 2003.

WORK IN PROGRESS: Research on the Italian language and the city of Rome.

SIDELIGHTS: In the opening pages of her debut book *Where We Lived,* Christina Fitzpatrick describes the lives of girls from the same New England town that embody the unhappiness, fear, ugliness and even horror many girls face while growing up. The girls in the book are portrayed as reckless, wild, and self-destructive while all the men and boys of the book are uniformly unsavory. A reviewer for *Publishers Weekly* wrote that the collection of slightly interconnected short stories merit but does not hold together as a novel. "There is a large talent at work here, but on this evidence it is better suited to unashamed short stories than to creating a bigger picture." Gillian Engberg, writing in *Booklist,* felt that "Fitzpatrick's dialogue is real, direct, and searing, and she evokes with remarkable honesty the complicated emotions—the shame, thrill, anger, and fear—of unhappy first sexual encounters and of leaving home."

Fitzpatrick told *CA:* "It was not entirely my choice to link the short stories in *Where We Lived.* My publishers felt that the stories would not sell enough as a collection, and consequently they specified in my contract that I *had* to connect the stories. I, of course, thought this stipulation was idiotic and aggravating, but at the same time I desperately, desperately wanted my work published—to the point that I thought I might explode. So I did the deed: I signed the contract, I linked the stories. And now . . . I have a writing career."

BIOGRAPHICAL AND CRITICAL SOURCES:

PERIODICALS

Booklist, June 1, 2001, Gillian Engberg, review of *Where We Lived,* p. 1840.

Publishers Weekly, June 11, 2001, review of *Where We Lived,* p. 57.

Los Angeles Times, July 15, 2001, Mark Rozzo, "Head First Fiction," p. 10.

*　　*　　*

FONTARA, Johannes
See RÜHMKORF, Peter

*　　*　　*

FORSYTH, Moira

PERSONAL: Born in Kilmarnock, Scotland; children: two. *Education:* Oxford University, Ph.D.

ADDRESSES: Home—Scotland. *Agent*—c/o Author Mail, St. Martin's Press, 175 Fifth Ave., New York, NY 10010.

CAREER: Poet and short story writer; leader of creative writing classes and workshops.

MEMBER: Words Inc, Highland Poets, Dingwall Writers' Group (chair), East Ross Writers.

AWARDS, HONORS: Writer's bursary, Scottish Arts Council, 1996.

WRITINGS:

What the Negative Reveals, ArtTM (Inverness, Scotland), 1999.

Waiting for Lindsay, Sceptre (London, England), 1999, St. Martin's Press (New York, NY), 2001.

David's Sisters, Sceptre (London, England), 2000.

Also contributor of poetry and short stories to anthologies.

SIDELIGHTS: Moira Forsyth was an accomplished writer of poems and short stories even before she released her first novel, *Waiting for Lindsay.* Set in her homeland of Scotland, the book tells the story of a family who lives under the shadow of thirteen-year-old Lindsay's disappearance during a family beach holiday. Thirty-four years later, Lindsay's cousins and brothers gather at that same beach facing new family struggles as well as the unspoken memories of their childhood tragedy.

The family is drawn together when Rob, the son of Lindsay's cousin Alistair, runs away to his aunt Annie, a childless woman of forty eager to have a son. Lindsay's brothers Jaime and Tom also pitch in to take care of Rob, but soon face their own domestic troubles. Annie, Alistair, Jaime, and Tom meet again at High House—the site of Lindsay's disappearance—with their private lives on the edge of disaster, seeking comfort and some form of closure in the mystery that has shaped their lives. A reviewer for *Publishers Weekly* suggested that *Waiting for Lindsay* would find its audience in "Anglophiles and *Masterpiece Theatre* devotees," but others found a broader appeal. Beth Warrell, writing for *Booklist,* called Forsyth's book "a quietly satisfying novel," and Susan Clifford Braun in *Library Journal* said that the author's "deft characterization and strong sense of place" made *Waiting for Lindsay* "well worth the read."

BIOGRAPHICAL AND CRITICAL SOURCES:

PERIODICALS

Booklist, July, 2001, Beth Warrell, review of *Waiting for Lindsay,* p. 1979.

Library Journal, July, 2001, Susan Clifford Braun, review of *Waiting for Lindsay,* p. 122.

Publishers Weekly, July 20, 2001, review of *Waiting for Lindsay,* p. 64.

Sunday Times (London, England), October 1, 2000, Moira Forsyth, "Escape: Time Off," p. 8.

Times (London, England), August 7, 1999, Christina Koning, review of *Waiting for Lindsay,* p. 22.

OTHER

BookBrowser, http://www.bookbrowser.com/ (June 16, 2001), Harriet Klausner, review of *Waiting for Lindsay.*

Words Inc., http://www.wordsinc.co.uk/ (February 20, 2002), "Writers from the Highlands and Islands."*

FOWLER, Brenda 1963-

PERSONAL: Born 1963, in IA.

ADDRESSES: Agent—c/o Author Mail, Random House, 201 East 50th St., 22nd Floor, New York, NY 10022.

CAREER: New York Times, New York, NY, correspondent in Vienna, Austria; writer.

WRITINGS:

Iceman: Uncovering the Life and Times of a Prehistoric Man Found in an Alpine Glacier, Random House (New York, NY), 2000.

Contributor to periodicals, including *New York Times.*

SIDELIGHTS: Brenda Fowler is the author of *Iceman: Uncovering the Life and Times of a Prehistoric Man Found in an Alpine Glacier,* which recounts the discovery of a frozen corpse, dubbed Ötzi, by two hikers crossing the Alps in 1991. In this "well-crafted and articulate book," as Joyce L. Ogburn described it in *Library Journal,* Fowler, who was stationed in Vienna as a correspondent for the *New York Times,* chronicles the events that follow the frozen figure's discovery.

Ötzi died during the Copper Age, four to five thousand years ago, but his corpse was in almost perfect condition. He was found with his tools, including a bow and arrows, a knife, and an axe, and he even had mushrooms with him. This well-preserved corpse proved to be a treasure trove for archeologists, and Fowler explains the scientific knowledge gleaned from Ötzi's body "in a way which is accessible to non-specialists," Tom Phillips wrote in *Contemporary Review.* Which archaeologists would have access to his corpse, however, as well as which country would benefit from the tourist dollars that such a popular exhibit could provide, were hotly contested by Italy, Austria, and the Italian province of South Tyrol. Fowler "offers a brisk and easy-to-follow narrative" both of the discovery and of these diplomatic wranglings, thought a *Publishers Weekly* critic.

BIOGRAPHICAL AND CRITICAL SOURCES:

PERIODICALS

Booklist, March 15, 2000, Gilbert Taylor, review of *Iceman: Uncovering the Life and Times of a Prehistoric Man Found in an Alpine Glacier,* p. 1323.
Chicago, May, 2000, Penelope Mesic, "Ice Escapades," p. 20.
Contemporary Review, February, 2002, Tom Phillips, review of *Iceman,* pp. 115-116.
Library Journal, March 1, 2000, Joyce L. Ogburn, review of *Iceman,* p. 122.
Publishers Weekly, February 14, 2000, review of *Iceman,* p. 180.
Scientific American, July, 2000, review of *Iceman.*
Seattle Times, May 1, 2000, David Williams, review of *Iceman.*

OTHER

Mummy Tombs.com, http://www.mummytombs.com/ (June 4, 2001), James M. Deem, review of *Iceman.**

*   *   *

FRAKES, Jonathan 1952-
(Jonathan Scott Frakes)

PERSONAL: Born August 19, 1952, in Bethlehem, PA; father, a professor of English literature; married Genie Francis (an actress), May 28, 1988; children: Jameson Ivor, Elizabeth Francis. *Education:* Attended Penn State University and Harvard University.

ADDRESSES: Office—Goepp Circle Productions, Paramount Pictures, 5555 Melrose Ave., Cooper #116, Los Angeles, CA 90038. *E-mail*—jonathanfrakes@ jonathanfrakes.net.

CAREER: Actor, director, and producer. Stage appearances include *Shenandoah,* New York City. Appeared in *The Common Glory, Every Good Boy Deserves Favor, Henry VIII,* and *Li'l Abner.* Appeared in productions at the Loeb Drama Center, Cambridge, MA.

Film appearances include *Camp Nowhere,* Buena Vista, 1994; *Star Trek: Generations,* Paramount, 1994; *Gargoyles: The Heroes Awaken,* Buena Vista, 1994; *Star Trek: First Contact,* Paramount, 1996; *Trekkies,* Paramount, 1997; *Star Trek: The Experience,* Paramount, 1998; *Star Trek: Insurrection,* Paramount, 1998; *Gargoyles: Brothers Betrayed,* 1998; *Gargoyles: The Force of Goliath,* 1998; *Gargoyles: The Hunted,* 1998. Film work as director includes *Star Trek: First Contact,* Paramount, 1996; *Star Trek: Insurrection,* Paramount, 1998; *Clockstoppers,* Paramount, 2001; *Total Recall 2,* Dimension Films, 2001.

Appearances on television pilots include *Beach Patrol,* ABC, 1979; *Roswell,* The WB, 1999. Appearances on TV series include *The Doctors,* NBC, 1977-78; *Bare Essence,* NBC, 1983; *Paper Dolls,* ABC, 1984; *Star Trek: The Next Generation,* syndicated, 1987-94; *Gargoyles,* syndicated, 1994-96; *The Paranormal Borderline,* UPN, 1996; *Gargoyles: The Goliath Chronicles,* ABC, 1996-97; *Beyond Belief: Fact or Fiction,* Fox, 1998; *The Lot,* AMC, 1999. Appearances on TV miniseries include *Beulah Land,* NBC, 1980; *Bare Essence,* CBS, 1982; *North and South,* ABC, 1985; *Dream West,* 1986; *North and South,* Book II, ABC, 1986; *Nutcracker: Money, Madness and Murder,* NBC, 1987; *John Jakes's Heaven and Hell: North and South,* Book III, ABC, 1994. Appearances in TV movies include *The Night the City Screamed,* 1980; *Star Trek: The Next Generation—Encounter at Farpoint,* syndicated, 1987; *The Cover Girl and the Cop,* NBC, 1989; *Star Trek: The Next Generation—All Good Things . . .,* syndicated, 1994; *Dying to Live,* UPN, 1999. Appearances on TV specials include *Gene Roddenberry: Star Trek and Beyond,* 1994; *Alien Autopsy: Fact or Fiction,* Fox, 1995; *Psychic Detectives: Search for Justice,* UPN, 1996; *Star Trek: 30 Years and Beyond,* UPN, 1996.

Appearances on episodic TV include "Angel on My Mind," *Charlie's Angels,* ABC, 1978; "Stages of Fear," *Barnaby Jones,* CBS, 1978; "The Legacy" and "The Lost Sheep," both *The Waltons,* CBS, 1979; "Separate Ways," *Eight Is Enough,* ABC, 1979; "Mrs. Daisy Hogg," *The Dukes of Hazzard,* CBS, 1981; "Harts and Palms," *Hart to Hart,* ABC, 1982; "An Arrow Pointing East," *Voyagers!,* NBC, 1982; "A Ghost of a Chance" and "The Face of Fear," both *Quincy, M.E.,* NBC, 1982; "Of Mouse and Man," *Hill Street Blues,* NBC, 1982; "A Divine Madness, a.k.a. Family Dispute," *Highway to Heaven,* NBC, 1984; "Always

Say Always," *The Fall Guy,* ABC, 1984; "Woman of Steele," *Remington Steele,* NBC, 1984; "But Can She Type?" *The Twilight Zone,* CBS, 1985; "The Angel," *Matlock,* NBC, 1986; "All's Fare," *Wings,* NBC, 1994; "Defiant," *Star Trek: Deep Space Nine,* syndicated, 1994; "Starting on the Wrong Foot," *Cybill,* CBS, 1995; "Don't Tug on Superman's Cape," *Lois and Clark: The New Adventures of Superman,* ABC, 1995; "Grief," *Gargoyles,* "Leader of the Pack," and "Upgrade," *Gargoyles,* syndicated, 1995; "Death Wish," *Star Trek: Voyager,* UPN, 1996; "Future Tense" and "Cloud Fathers," *Gargoyles,* syndicated, 1996; "Image," *Oh Baby,* Lifetime, 2000; "The Convention," *Roswell,* The WB, 2000; "Gwen, Larry, Dick, and Mary," *3rd Rock from the Sun,* NBC, 2000; Also appeared in episodes of *Falcon Crest,* CBS; *Fantasy Island,* ABC; *It's a Living,* ABC and syndicated; and *Married . . . with Children,* Fox. Other television appearances include *Brothers of the Frontier,* 1996; *The Alien Autopsy,* 1997.

Television work includes (executive producer, series) *Roswell,* The WB, 1999-2001 then UPN, 2001-02; (executive producer, movies) *Dying to Live,* UPN, 1999. Episodic television work as director includes *Star Trek: The Next Generation,* syndicated, episodes between 1987 and 1994; *University Hospital,* syndicated, 1995; "Meridian," *Star Trek: Deep Space Nine,* syndicated, 1994; "The Search, Part II," *Star Trek: Deep Space Nine,* syndicated, 1994; "Past Tense, Part II," *Star Trek: Deep Space Nine,* syndicated, 1995; "Parturition," *Star Trek: Voyager,* UPN, 1995; "Projections," *Star Trek: Voyager,* UPN, 1995; "Prototype," *Star Trek: Voyager,* UPN, 1996; Also directed episodes of *Diagnosis Murder,* CBS; and *Roswell,* The WB.

Voice recordings include the following video games: *Star Trek: The Next Generation Interactive Technical Manual,* Simon & Schuster Interactive, 1994; *Star Trek: The Next Generation—A Final Unity,* Microprose/Spectrum Holobyte, 1995; *Multimedia Celebrity Poker,* New World Computing/Dreamers Guild, 1995; *Star Trek: Generations,* Microprose/Spectrum Holobyte, 1997. Also appears in *Star Trek: The Next Generation Interactive VCR Board Game.* Director for the production of the video game *Star Trek: Klingon,* Simon & Schuster Interactive, 1996.

WRITINGS:

(With Dean Wesley Smith) *The Abductors: Conspiracy* (science fiction), Tor Books (New York City), 1996.

SIDELIGHTS: Like many former cast members of the various *Star Trek* television series, Jonathan Frakes is best known for his service aboard a spacecraft—in this case, his role as Commander William Thomas Riker on *Star Trek: The Next Generation* from 1987 to 1994. Much of his work since that time has likewise played on themes of space and extraterrestrial visitors to Earth. For example, Frakes served as executive producer for, and appeared in two episodes of, the series *Roswell,* which concerned a group of youthful aliens in the New Mexico town where a UFO supposedly crashed in 1947.

In addition to his work as an actor and director (which includes two *Star Trek* feature films), Frakes is the coauthor of a science-fiction novel, *The Abductors: Conspiracy.* Written with veteran sci-fi author Dean Wesley Smith, *The Abductors* begins with the search for a missing teen. Placed on the case, ex-cop Richard McCallum soon discovers evidence leading to a conclusion he initially cannot bring himself to believe: that what seems like a mere instance of a missing person could instead be a case of alien abduction. The unfolding events become much more personal for McCallum when he, too, is abducted.

BIOGRAPHICAL AND CRITICAL SOURCES:

BOOKS

Contemporary Theatre, Film, and Television, Volume 38 Gale (Detroit, MI), 2002.

PERIODICALS

Library Journal, July 1, 1996, review of *The Abductors: Conspiracy.*

OTHER

Jonathan Frakes Home Page, http://www.jonathan frakes.net/ (December 30, 2002).*

*   *   *

FRAKES, Jonathan Scott
 See FRAKES, Jonathan

FRATTAROLI, Elio

PERSONAL: Male. *Education:* Harvard University, B.A., 1969; attended the University of Chicago.

ADDRESSES: Home—Bala Cynwyd, PA. *Agent*—c/o Author Mail, Penguin Putnam, 375 Hudson St., New York, NY 10014. *E-mail*—elio@eliofrattaroli.com.

CAREER: Psychiatrist and psychoanalyst in private practice; University of Pennsylvania, Philadelphia, assistant professor; Psychoanalytic Center of Philadelphia, Philadelphia, PA, faculty member; Psychodynamic Psychotherapy Training Program, associate director.

MEMBER: American Psychoanalytic Association, American Psychiatric Association.

WRITINGS:

Healing the Soul in the Age of the Brain: Becoming Conscious in an Unconscious World, Viking (New York, NY), 2001.

Also author of numerous scholarly articles for peer-reviewed journals.

SIDELIGHTS: Psychiatrist Elio Frattaroli drew on his studies of English literature, the psychology of Bruno Bettelheim, and the psychiatry of Sigmund Freud in his first book, *Healing the Soul in the Age of the Brain: Becoming Conscious in an Unconscious World.* In it, Frattaroli presents a challenge to the "medical model" that dominates current psychiatric practice. He calls instead for a mode of psychotherapy that takes into account both human brain chemistry and the human soul. Frattaroli addresses not only the mistakes of the medical profession but also the ills of modern society, including the insistence on a "quick fix" for problems and the rise of managed care. Reviewing the book for the *Washington Post,* David Guy summarized Frattaroli's study: "Ultimately Frattaroli is criticizing our whole way of life. The question is whether we will get off our cell phones long enough to hear him."

To support his argument, Frattaroli uses insights from Shakespeare, Plato, and Descartes as well as major figures in psychology such as Erik Erikson and his former teacher Bruno Bettelheim. Most important to his argument, however, is the work of Sigmund Freud; E. James Lieberman, writing for *Library Journal,* suggested that the overall thrust of *Healing the Soul* "defends and improves upon Freudian psychology." In the end, Frattaroli does not propose an end to Prozac and other prescriptions for treating mental illness; rather, he calls for the use of long-term psychotherapy based on Freudian understandings of the unconscious.

Frattaroli's book was generally well received, though critics noted that the dense, lengthy tome is not an easy read. However, several reviewers suggested that *Healing the Soul* will nevertheless become a classic in the field. In *Library Journal,* Lieberman called the book "a major achievement," while a reviewer for *Publishers Weekly* predicted that "this thoughtful defense of the talking cure could be important and influential for many years to come."

BIOGRAPHICAL AND CRITICAL SOURCES:

PERIODICALS

Booklist, September 1, 2001, Gilbert Taylor, review of *Healing the Soul in the Age of the Brain: Becoming Conscious in an Unconscious World,* p. 30.
Library Journal, August, 2001, E. James Lieberman, review of *Healing the Soul in the Age of the Brain,* p. 139.
Philadelphia Inquirer, June 3, 2002, Stacey Burling, review of *Healing the Soul in the Age of the Brain.*
Psychiatric Times, September 1, 2002, David W. Krueger and Moshe S. Torem, review of *Healing the Soul in the Age of the Brain,* p. 58.
Publishers Weekly, July 30, 2001, review of *Healing the Soul in the Age of the Brain,* p. 68
Washington Post Book World, September 16, 2001, David Guy, "Popping the Pill Myth," p. T6.

OTHER

Elio Frattaroli Home Page, http://www.eliofrattaroli.com (February 13, 2002).
New Therapist, http://www.newtherapist.com/ (February 8, 2003), John Soderland, "Quiet Revolutionary" (interview with Frattaroli).*

FRAUENGLASS, Harvey 1929-

PERSONAL: Born August 1, 1929, in Hartford, CT; son of Jack (a pharmacist) and Lillian (Marcus) Frauenglass; married Dita Adam (divorced); married Gayle Fulwyler Smith (an artist), October 22, 1982; children: Mark, Andrew, Marni Frauenglass Keegan (deceased), Susan. *Education:* University of Chicago, A.B., 1949; attended University of Edinburgh, 1950-51; University of Iowa, M.F.A., 1959. *Politics:* "Progressive." *Hobbies and other interests:* Environmental protection activities.

ADDRESSES: Home—P.O. Box 56, Embudo, NM 87531. *Office*—Big Willow Farm, 50 County Dr. 1105, Embudo, NM 87531-0056. *E-mail*—gayle@cybermesa.com.

CAREER: Worked as writer, director, producer, and publicity manager in publishing and film industries, 1961-82; Big Willow Farm, Embudo, NM, apple grower and cider maker, 1983—. Los Alamos National Laboratory, Los Alamos, NM, worked as research editor for fourteen years. Acequia Junta y Cienega, commissioner, 1994-2000. *Military service:* U.S. Army, 1951-53; served in Germany.

WRITINGS:

Cidermaster of Rio Oscuro (nonfiction), University of Utah Press, 2000.

Author and producer of educational tape-slide presentations on environmental satellites, for National Aeronautics and Space Administration. Author of environmental essays.

BIOGRAPHICAL AND CRITICAL SOURCES:

PERIODICALS

Publishers Weekly, July 3, 2000, review of *Cidermaster of Rio Oscuro,* p. 61.

*   *   *

FREDSTON, Jill A. 1958(?)-

PERSONAL: Born c. 1958; married Doug Fesler (an avalanche expert). *Education:* Dartmouth College, bachelor's degree (environmental studies and physical geography); Cambridge University, graduate work (glaciology); has master's degree (polar studies/snow and ice).

ADDRESSES: Office—Alaska Mountain Safety Center, 9140 Brewsters Drive, Anchorage, AK 99156.

CAREER: Avalanche expert. Alaska Mountain Safety Center, Anchorage, AK, codirector; Alaska Avalanche School, codirector. Formerly a naturalist at Grand Canyon National Park.

WRITINGS:

(With Lynn D. Leslie and James L. Wise) *Snow Loads in Alaska,* Arctic Environmental Information and Data Center (Anchorage, AK), 1987.

(With Doug Fesler) *Snow Sense: A Guide to Evaluating Snow Avalanche Hazard,* fifth edition, Alaska Mountain Safety Center (Anchorage, AK), 2001.

Rowing to Latitude: Journeys along the Arctic's Edge, North Point Press (New York, NY), 2001.

SIDELIGHTS: Jill A. Fredston and her husband Doug Fesler are avalanche experts and codirectors of the Alaska Mountain Safety Center, a nonprofit organization that specializes in avalanche hazard evaluation, forecasting, mitigation, and education. They are also directors of the Alaska Avalanche School, which provides mountain safety training.

Fredston grew up in Larchmont, Connecticut. Her family's house was located on a small island in Long Island Sound, and Fredston was fascinated with the water. When she was ten, her parents gave her a small rowboat, which she rowed everywhere, even to school—even when, as she wrote in her book *Rowing to Latitude: Journeys along the Arctic's Edge,* "if it was low tide when school let out, I had to walk home and return later when there was enough water in the channel to float the boat." When she was eleven she rowed across the seven-mile-wide expanse of Long Island Sound to Long Island, accompanied by a friend in a tiny sailboat. They made landfall on Long Island, swam in a stranger's swimming pool, then headed back to Connecticut. A mile from shore, they were stopped by the Coast Guard. She wrote, "It hadn't occurred to us to think about the distance or the danger. We were simply heading for another shore."

Fredston's experiences in the boat solidified her love of the outdoors, ultimately leading her to settle in Alaska. Accompanied by her husband, she has trav-

eled more than 20,000 miles through the Arctic and subarctic in an oceangoing rowing shell, and she describes many of these trips in *Rowing to Latitude.* She and her husband have explored the rocky and frigid coasts of Alaska, Canada, Greenland, Spitsbergen, and Norway, and have encountered whales, grizzly bears, polar bears, and other northern wildlife, as well as twenty-foot-high waves. "It is hard to believe that two five-by-eight pages sprawled across your lap can evoke the same gut-wrenching fear as a Hollywood special-effects epic," Dana De Zoysa wrote in *January Magazine,* "but about a quarter of this book does just that." When Fredston started her book, she intended to focus almost entirely on these natural wonders, but her editor insisted that she also write about herself and her husband. As Fredston told interviewer Susan Elia in *Publishers Weekly,* she eventually agreed, since "it makes sense, really, as you're seeing everything from our point of view." This approach worked; as John Kenny noted in *Library Journal,* the book is "enjoyable and well-written."

BIOGRAPHICAL AND CRITICAL SOURCES:

BOOKS

Fredston, Jill, *Rowing to Latitude: Journeys along the Arctic's Edge,* North Point Press (New York, NY), 2001.

PERIODICALS

Alaska, August, 1990, Nan Elliot, "Jill Fredston: Long Distance Rower," p. 76.

Booklist, September 15, 2001, Allen Weakland, review of *Rowing to Latitude,* p. 188.

Christian Century, September 25, 2002, Patrick Henry, review of *Rowing to Latitude,* pp. 39-41.

Library Journal, October 15, 2001, John Kenny, review of *Rowing to Latitude,* p. 98.

Natural History, October, 2001, review of *Rowing to Latitude,* p. 78.

Publishers Weekly, August 6, 2001, Susan Elia, "PW talks with Jill Fredston," and review of *Rowing to Latitude,* p. 79.

Sports Illustrated Women, March 1, 2002, Karen Karbo, "So You Want to Escape to the Mountains: The Adventurer Jill Fredston," p. 102.

Women's Review of Books, January, 2002, Judith Niemi, review of *Rowing to Latitude,* p. 14.

OTHER

Booksense.com, http://www.booksense.com/ (February 8, 2003), Gavin J. Grant, "Very Interesting People: Jill Fredston" (interview).

FSB Associates, http://www.fsbassociates.com/ (January 15, 2002), review of *Rowing to Latitude.*

January Magazine, http://www.januarymagazine.com/ (February 8, 2003), Dana De Zoysa, review of *Rowing to Latitude.*

National Geographic News, http://www.nationalgeographic.com/ (February 8, 2003), Brian Handwerk, review of *Rowing to Latitude.*

Nova, http://www.pbs.org/ (February 8, 2003), "Avalanche!: Snow Sense."*

* * *

FUSILLO, Archimede 1962-

PERSONAL: Born February 19, 1962, in Melbourne, Australia; son of Ruggiero and Iolanda Fusillo; married, 1984; wife's name, Pina; children: Alyssa, Laurence. *Education:*Melbourne University, B.A. (psychology; with honors), 1983. *Politics:* "Personal." *Religion:* Roman Catholic. *Hobbies and other interests:* Flying, sports-car racing, and reading.

ADDRESSES: Agent—Jenny Darling & Associates, P.O. Box 413, Toorak, Victoria 3142, Australia.

CAREER: Author and teacher. Worked as a secondary school teacher in the late 1980s and early 1990s, teaching English and literature. Lecturer on literacy and reading throughout Australia.

MEMBER: Australian Society of Authors, Fellowship of Australian Writers, Victorian Writers Centre.

AWARDS, HONORS: Mary Grant Bruce Story Award for Children's Literature, 1989, for "The Farmhouse"; FAW Playwrights Award, 1994, for *A Christmas Dinner;* finalist, Australian BIA Master of Ceremonies Award, 1999; Australian Therapists Book of the Year, 2002, for *The Dons;* finalist, Mary Gran Bruce Award for Children's Literature, 2002, for *Uncorked;* finalist, "Italy in the World" Literature Awards; Alan Marshall Short Story Award; Lyndall Hardaw Short Story Award; Henry Savery Short Story Award; finalist, Teacher of the Year Awards.

WRITINGS:

Talking to the Moon (picture book), illustrated by Philippa Rickard, Macmillan Australia (South Melbourne, Australia), 1987.

Memories of Sunday Cricket in the Street (picture book), illustrated by Sally Mitrevska, Macmillan Australia (South Melbourne, Australia), 1987.

Short Stories: Reading to Write (young adult textbook), Oxford University Press (Melbourne, Australia), 1996.

Damien Parer: Putting the War on Film (young adult biography), Cardigan Street Publishers (Carlton, Australia), 1996.

Sparring with Shadows (young adult fiction), Penguin Books (Melbourne, Australia), 1997.

Imaginative Writer (textbook), Wizard Books (Ballarat, Australia), 2000.

The Dons (young adult fiction), Penguin Books (Melbourne, Australia), 2002.

Let It Rip ("Aussie Bites" series; picture book), Penguin Books (Melbourne, Australia), 2002.

Game or Not ("Aussie Bites" series; picture book), Penguin Books (Melbourne, Australia), 2003.

An Earful of Static (young adult fiction), Lothian Books (Melbourne, Australia), 2003.

Uncorked (novel), Word Weavers Press (Minneapolis, MN), 2003.

Feature writer for *Vive la Vie* and *Vive la Cuisine* magazines; freelance writer for other magazines.

WORK IN PROGRESS: Short story for new anthology in 2003; "Aussie Bites" titles for publication in 2004.

SIDELIGHTS: Archimede Fusillo told *CA:* "I have always loved the power of stories. As a child I listened to the stories my grandmother (Nonna) and my parents told me—of the war—of the trials of migration—of deprived childhoods—and of the comic side of life. Stories transported me to other times and places—and in them I saw a way to share with others my own 'take' on the world. Oral stories gave way to reading, and through reading I discovered how lasting a good story could be, and so I tried my hand at writing the sorts of stories that would make me laugh or cry or cringe. I found I loved communicating with an audience and enjoyed their responses."

"With all my writings my aim is to entertain, to take the reader on a journey. If the reader finds some solace, some insight in what they read, that's wonderful; but I write because I have stories I want to tell. I write with my audience in mind—and I write for all sorts of audiences; from young children (as in the 'Aussie Bites' books), to teenagers (*The Dons*), to adults (many of my short stories and text books). I read widely and always, from the classics to contemporary works—comic books to novels. My passion is the short story. A good short story requires precision of language, a keen sense of detail, and a ready sense of knowing what to leave out as much as what to include. My earliest success came with my short stories, which dealt with the characters and events of the area where I grew up, short stories set in places I knew intimately and could write about authentically."

"Writers are dreamers. We have to be if we are to see beyond the obvious and create stories which will grab and hold our readers. Writing is a craft which is never fully mastered, but honed through the act of doing, of polishing and refining. My advice to all who want to write is that there is no end point, just new tangents, with every new idea. Writing is as much breathing as it is commitment. I write because I cannot not write."

BIOGRAPHICAL AND CRITICAL SOURCES:

PERIODICALS

Magpies, November, 2001, Jo Goodman, review of *The Dons,* p. 39.

OTHER

Writers on the Road, http://www.statelibrary.vic.gov.au/ (January 7, 2003).

G

GARREN, Christine (Elizabeth) 1957-

PERSONAL: Born December 15, 1957, in Philadelphia, PA; daughter of William McElreath and Marjorie Faye (Sanders) Branham; married Samuel Baity Garren, May 24, 1980. *Education:* University of North Carolina-Greensboro, B.A., 1987, M.F.A., 1990. *Religion:* Society of Friends (Quaker).

ADDRESSES: Home—1608 North College Park Dr., Greensboro, NC 27403.

CAREER: Writer. Visiting writer-in-residence, Guilford College, Greensboro, NC, 1987.

AWARDS, HONORS: Poetry fellowship, National Endowment for the Arts, 1999.

WRITINGS:

Afterworld, University of Chicago Press (Chicago, IL), 1993.
Among the Monarchs, University of Chicago Press (Chicago, IL), 2000.

SIDELIGHTS: Christine Garren is a North Carolina-based poet whose work has won wide praise from critics. Her first book, *Afterworld,* was declared the best collection of contemporary American love poetry by *Georgia Review* contributor Fred Chappell. "The truth contained in Christine Garren's poems is immanent: there is no seam between thought and feeling, act and word," Bruce Murphy wrote in a review of the same collection in *Poetry.* He also praised Garren's poems for being "complex without being difficult; they don't have any of the 'figure it out for yourself' vulgarity, the up-turned nose of some 'avant-garde' poetics."

A *Kirkus Reviews* contributor noted the same quality in Garren's second collection, *Among the Monarchs.* "Garren's is a clear and unique voice, a rarity among university-sanctioned poets today," said that reviewer, who concluded, "the only wasted space [in this collection] is in the margins." Bradin Cormack in the *Chicago Review* also noted the poet's clarity and efficiency, writing that the poems "patiently and expertly explore the time and place of loss, the moods of grief" and praising Garren's economy of writing, attention to detail, and variety of tone and mood. "Confessionalism meets the enigmatic juxtapositions of the prose poem" in this collection, which deals in the first person with topics including abuse, abortion, and dysfunctional families, wrote a *Publishers Weekly* contributor, who noted that "the pieces are well-structured, and produce their effects with a sometimes grim efficiency."

BIOGRAPHICAL AND CRITICAL SOURCES:

PERIODICALS

Chicago Review, spring, 2001, Bradin Cormack, review of *Among the Monarchs,* p. 139.
Choice, December, 1993, review of *Afterworld,* p. 603.
Georgia Review, winter, 1993, Fred Chappell, review of *Afterworld,* p. 775.

Kirkus Review, October 1, 2000, review of *Among the Monarchs,* p. 1396.

Los Angeles Times Book Review, September 5, 1993, review of *Afterworld,* p. 6.

Poetry, December, 1995, Bruce Murphy, review of *Among the Monarchs,* p. 163; November, 2001, Christian Wiman, review of *Among the Monarchs,* pp. 93-95.

Publishers Weekly, July 31, 2000, review of *Among the Monarchs,* p. 90.

OTHER

National Endowment for the Arts, http://arts.endow.gov/ (February 19, 2003), "Writer's Corner: Christine Garren."

Poetry Daily, http://www.poems.com/ (September 15, 2001), "Poetry Daily Feature: Christine Garren."*

* * *

GERTLER, Stephanie (Jocelyn)

PERSONAL: Born in New York, NY; daughter of Menard M. and Anna (Paull) Gertler; married Mark B. Schiffer, September 19, 1981; children: David, Elyena, Benjamin. *Education:* New York University, B.A., 1974. *Hobbies and other interests:* Dance, exercise.

ADDRESSES: Office—23 Grand Park Ave., Scarsdale, NY 10583-7611. *E-mail*—SGert1211@aol.com.

CAREER: Journalist. *Newsweek,* Miami, FL, office manager, 1975-77; Grune & Strathon, New York, NY, senior production editor, 1978-81; *Greenwich News,* art/lifestyles editor, 1995-97; *Greenwich Post,* art/lifestyles editor, 1997; *Greenwich Magazine,* senior writer, 1997; *Westport,* senior writer, 1998.

AWARDS, HONORS: Award for general column, Society of Professional Journalists, 1997.

WRITINGS:

Ballet, Tap, and All That Jazz, 1997.
Jimmy's Girl, Dutton (New York, NY), 2001.
The Puzzle Bark Tree, Dutton (New York, NY), 2002.
Drifting, Dutton (New York, NY), 2003.

Contributor of articles to periodicals, including *Hour* (Norwalk, CT), *Wilton Villager,* and *Spotlight Magazine.* Columnist, *Advocate* (Stamford, CT).

SIDELIGHTS: Stephanie Gertler worked as a freelance writer for years before producing her first novel, *Jimmy's Girl.* She began writing even earlier, creating short stories and poetry and winning her school's annual literary award in the sixth grade. In her career, however, she focused on nonfiction, in essays, columns, and magazine articles, until she began work on *Jimmy's Girl.*

The book's heroine, Emily Hudson, is a married mother of four who grows dissatisfied with her seemingly ideal life. Her relationship with her husband, a workaholic attorney, has become passionless. She is inspired to find her first love, Jimmy, from whom she had separated when he went off to Vietnam and she became peace activist. Though he is also married with a child, they meet at the Vietnam War Memorial and spend a nostalgic, romantic weekend together in Washington, D.C. Together they discuss the past and the ways they have changed since then, and try to decide whether they should abandon their current lives to renew their relationship. The story is told from the perspective of both Emily and Jimmy, in alternating chapters, so that Gertler slowly reveals the differences between what each character says and what the other hears. On her Web site, Gertler explained that Emily's memories and emotions were linked to her own memories of first love. She wrote, "When I was writing *Jimmy's Girl,* I remembered what it felt like when 'he' would call, when I would mention 'his' name, when 'he' would ring the doorbell, put 'his' arm around me. When your heart is opened for the first time, even the agony is sweet."

Readers found that Gertler's story of young love touched a nerve. A reviewer for *Publishers Weekly* said that Gertler has produced an "assured debut," calling *Jimmy's Girl* "a winsome morality tale." Critics remarked on the universality of Gertler's main theme of "the road not taken," what Ellie Barta-Moran, in *Booklist,* described as "one of life's constant what-if questions." Joanna Burkhardt, writing for *Library Journal,* similarly commented that Gertler has created characters and problems with which her audience can identify, suggesting that "readers will react viscerally to the pain and pathos of their dilemma." In an interview on her Web site, Gertler herself imagined that "ninety-nine percent of people" wonder what happened to their first love. A critic for *Kirkus Reviews* called *Jimmy's Girl* "predictable fare," but nonetheless concluded that Gertler's novel "offers a tender evocation of lost love, and what it means to find it again."

Her second novel, *The Puzzle Bark Tree,* was published in 2002. In it, Gertler tells the story of Grace Hammond Barnett, whose emotionally distant parents commit suicide and leave behind a house Grace never knew of in the upstate New York village of Sabbath Landing. Her husband, Adam, refuses to go with her when she goes to check out the house, so she goes by herself. In Sabbath Landing she meets Luke Keegan, who knew Grace's family when she was a child and remembers things about them that Grace has long since forgotten or repressed. As Grace learns more secrets about her family's past, she also comes to understand the problems in her failing marriage. "Emotional without ever being overwrought or sappy, *The Puzzle Bark Tree* is a series of powerful and evocative revelations and repercussions," Roberta O'Hara wrote in a review for *BookReporter.com.*

BIOGRAPHICAL AND CRITICAL SOURCES:

PERIODICALS

Booklist, November 15, 2000, Ellie Barta-Moran, review of *Jimmy's Girl,* p. 618; May 15, 2002, Carolyn Kubisz, review of *The Puzzle Bark Tree,* p. 1574.

Kirkus Reviews, November 1, 2000, review of *Jimmy's Girl,* p. 68; April 1, 2002, review of *The Puzzle Bark Tree.*

Library Journal, October 15, 2000, Joanna Burkhardt, review of *Jimmy's Girl,* p. 101.

Publishers Weekly, October 16, 2000, review of *Jimmy's Girl,* p. 46; May 20, 2002, review of *The Puzzle Bark Tree.*

OTHER

Best Reviews, http://thebestreviews.com/ (January 6, 2002), Harriet Klausner, review of *Jimmy's Girl;* (March 2, 2002) Marilyn Heyman, review of *Jimmy's Girl.*

Bookreporter.com, http://www.bookreporter.com/ (February 19, 2003), "Author Profile: Stephanie Gertler"; interview with Gertler; Roberta O'Hara, review of *The Puzzle Bark Tree.*

GirlPosse, http://www.girlposse.com/ (February 19, 2003), "The Fifteen-Question E-Mail Interview with Stephanie Gertler."

Heartstrings, http://romanticfiction.tripod.com/ (February 19, 2003), interview with Gertler, C. L. Jeffries, review of *The Puzzle Bark Tree.*

Penguin Putnam Web site, http://www.pengiunputnam.com/ (October 7, 2001).

Romance Reader's Connection, http://www.theromancereadersconnection.com/ (February 19, 2003) Tracy Farnsworth, reviews of *The Puzzle Bark Tree* and *Jimmy's Girl.*

Romantic Times, http://www.romantictimes.com/ (February 19, 2003), Sheri Melnick review of *The Puzzle Bark Tree.*

Stephanie Gertler Web site, http://www.stephaniegertler.com/ (February 15, 2002).

Women Writers, http://www.womenwriters.net/ (May 1, 2002), Elizabeth Blakesley Lindsay, review of *Jimmy's Girl.*

Word Weaving, http://www.wordweaving.com/ (February 19, 2003), Cindy Penn, review of *The Puzzle Bark Tree.*

Written Voices, http://www.writtenvoices.com/ (February 19, 2003), "Featured Author: Stephanie Gertler."*

*   *   *

GIBSON, Henry 1935-

PERSONAL: Born Henry Gibson Bateman, September 21, 1935, in Germantown, PA; son of Edmund Albert and Dorothy (Cassidy) Bateman; married Lois Joan Geiger, April 6, 1966; children: Jonathan David, Charles Alexander, James Bateman. *Education:* Catholic University, B.A., drama, 1957; observer at the Royal Academy of Dramatic Arts, 1960.

ADDRESSES: Agent—Gold/Marshak/Liedtke Talent and Literary Agency, 3500 West Olive Ave., Suite 1400, Burbank, CA 91505.

CAREER: Actor, comedian, and writer. Made professional debut with the Mae Desmond Theatre Company, Philadelphia, PA, 1943; child actor and performer in

East Coast stock companies, 1943-57. Participant in National Teach-in, 1970; participant in Citizen's Committee on Population Growth and the American Future, 1972-75. *Military service:* U.S. Air Force, 1957-60, served in France in the 66th Tactical Reconnaissance Wing; becoming target intelligence officer.

Film appearances include *The Nutty Professor,* Paramount, 1963; *Kiss Me, Stupid,* Lopert, 1964; *The Outlaws Is Coming,* Columbia, 1965; *Charlotte's Web,* Paramount, 1973; *The Long Goodbye,* United Artists, 1973; *Nashville,* Paramount, 1975; *The Last Remake of Beau Geste,* Universal, 1977; *The Kentucky Fried Movie,* United Film, 1977; *A Perfect Couple,* Twentieth Century-Fox, 1979; *H.E.A.L.T.H.,* Twentieth Century-Fox, 1979; *The Blues Brothers,* Universal, 1980; *The Incredible Shrinking Woman,* Universal, 1981; *Tulips,* Avco-Embassy, 1981; *Monster in the Closet,* Troma, 1986; *Innerspace,* Warner Bros., 1987; *Switching Channels,* TriStar, 1988; *The 'Burbs,* Universal, 1989; *Night Visitor,* Metro-Goldwyn-Mayer/United Artists, 1989; *The Magic Balloon,* Showscan Film Corporation, 1990; *Gremlins 2: The New Batch,* Warner Bros., 1990; *Tune in Tomorrow,* Cinecom, 1990; *Brenda Starr,* Triumph Releasing, 1992; *Tom and Jerry: The Movie,* Miramax, 1993; *Cyber Bandits,* Columbia TriStar Home Video, 1995; *Bio-Dome,* Metro-Goldwyn-Mayer/United Artists, 1996; *Mother Night,* Fine Line Features, 1996; *Color of a Brisk and Leaping Day,* Artistic License Films, 1996; *Asylum,* Norstar Entertainment, 1996; *Stranger in the Kingdom,* 1997; and *Magnolia,* New Line Cinema, 1999.

Television series appearances include *The Tonight Show,* NBC, 1961-62; *Mike Wallace's P.M. East,* syndicated, 1962; *Rowan and Martin's Laugh-In,* NBC, 1968-71; *The Biskitts,* CBS, 1983; *The Wuzzles,* CBS and ABC, 1985; *Galaxy High School,* CBS, 1987; *The Adventures of Don Coyote and Sancho Panda,* syndicated, 1990; *Santo Bugito,* CBS, 1996; and *Sunset Beach,* 1999.

Appearances in TV movies include *Evil Roy Slade,* NBC, 1972; *Every Man Needs One,* ABC, 1972; *Escape from Bogen County,* CBS, 1977; *The Night They Took Miss Beautiful,* NBC, 1977; *Amateur Night at the Dixie Bar and Grill,* NBC, 1979; *For the Love of It,* ABC, 1980; *Nashville Grab,* NBC, 1981; *Slow Burn,* Showtime, 1986; *Long Gone,* HBO, 1987; *Return to Green Acres,* CBS, 1990; and *Escape to Witch Mountain (ABC Family Movie),* ABC, 1995. Appearances in

TV miniseries include *Around the World in Eighty Days,* NBC, 1989.

Appearances on episodic television include "We're Going to Have a Baby" and "The Baby Formula," *The Joey Bishop Show,* NBC, 1963; "A Man for Elly," *The Beverly Hillbillies,* CBS, 1964; "Grindl, Girl Wac," *Grindl,* NBC, 1964; "Ellie the Talent Show," *The Joey Bishop Show,* NBC, 1964; "The Great Manhunt," *The Littlest Hobo,* syndicated, 1964; "Danger, High Voltage," *My Favorite Martian,* CBS, 1964; "Liberty," "Physician, Heal Thyself" and "Carry Me Back to Cocoon Island," *Mr. Roberts,* NBC, 1965; "Pride of the Rangers," *Laredo,* NBC, 1965; "Pvt. Wrongo Starr," "Wrongo Starr and the Woman in Black," and "The Return of Wrongo Starr," *F Troop,* ABC, 1966; "Talk to the Snail," *The Dick Van Dyke Show,* CBS, 1966; "Aunt Harriet Wants You," *Hey Landlord,* NBC, 1967; "Samantha's French Pastry," *Bewitched,* ABC, 1968; "Love and the Shower," *Love, American Style,* ABC, 1969; "If the Shoe Pinches," *Bewitched,* ABC, 1970; "Love and the Note" and "Love and the Sweet 16," *Love, American Style,* ABC, 1971; "Love and the Christmas Punch," *Love, American Style,* ABC, 1972; "Love and the Spendthrift," *Love, American Style,* ABC, 1973; "Violence in Blue," *The Wide World of Mystery,* ABC, 1975; "Murder on High C," *Get Christie Love,* ABC, 1975; "Showdown at Times Square," *McCloud,* NBC, 1975; "Sharks Eat Sharks," *Barbary Coast,* ABC, 1975; "Don't Feed the Pigeons," *Police Woman,* NBC, 1975; "Screaming Javelins," *The New Adventures of Wonder Woman,* CBS, 1978; *W.E.B.,* NBC, 1978; "Anniversary and Mr. Hotel," *Fantasy Island,* ABC, 1978; "Father Goose," *The Bob Newhart Show,* CBS, 1978; "Victor, Bill, and Bobby, Sometimes," *Sweepstakes,* NBC, 1979; "Find Loretta Lynn," *The Dukes of Hazzard,* CBS, 1980; "Ghost Rig," *The Littlest Hobo,* 1980; "The Meek Shall Inherit Rhonda," *The Fall Guy,* ABC, 1981; "Candy Doctor," *Trapper John, M.D.,* CBS, 1982; "Mixed Doubles," *Magnum, P.I.,* CBS, 1982; "Fowl Play," *Simon and Simon,* CBS, 1982; "The Christmas Presence," *The Love Boat,* ABC, 1982; "Murder on Ice," *Quincy, M.E.,* NBC, 1983; "Endangered Detectives," *Small and Frye,* CBS, 1983; "Spanish Gambit," *Masquerade,* ABC, 1984; "The Million-Dollar Face," *Cover Up,* CBS, 1984; "Terror U.," *The Fall Guy,* ABC, 1984; "Murder in Mink," *Mike Hammer,* CBS, 1984; "Diplomatic Immunity," *Half Nelson,* NBC, 1985; "Welcome to Winfield," *The Twilight Zone,* CBS, 1986; "Voodoo Knight," *Knight Rider,* NBC, 1986; "Annabell Goes Punk," *Poofur,* 1987; "Who Threw the Barbitals in Mrs. Fletcher's

Chowder?," *Murder, She Wrote,* CBS, 1987; "Nobody Smurf," *The Smurfs,* NBC, 1987; "Father Goose," *Newhart,* 1989; "Harry's Will," *MacGyver,* ABC, 1990; "Deadly Silents," *MacGyver,* ABC, 1991; "Incident in Lot 7," *Murder, She Wrote,* CBS, 1991; "The Losers," *Eerie, Indiana,* NBC, 1991; "On the Air," *What a Dummy,* syndicated, 1991; "Chip off the Old Brick," *Evening Shade,* CBS, 1991; "Where's Harry," *Cutters,* CBS, 1992; "None but the Lonely Heart," *Tales from the Crypt,* HBO, 1992; "Out of the Ashes" and "The Cold Light of Day," *Sisters,* NBC, 1992; "Several Unusual Love Stories," *The John Larroquette Show,* NBC, 1994; "Turtle Word," *Coach,* ABC, 1995; "Dream Weaver," *Mad about You,* NBC, 1995; "A Room with a Bellevue," *Duckman,* 1996; "Trial by Fury," *Sabrina, the Teenage Witch,* ABC, 1997; "When Teens Collide," *Sabrina, the Teenage Witch,* ABC, 1998; "Profit and Lace," *Star Trek: Deep Space Nine,* UPN, 1998; *Buddy Faro,* CBS, 1998; "Angstgiving Day," *Maggie Winters,* CBS, 1998; "You Bet Your Life," *Providence,* NBC, 1998; *Rocket Power,* Nickelodeon, 1999; *Total Recall 2070,* Showtime, 1999.

Appearances on TV pilots include *Sheriff Who?,* NBC, 1966; *Honeymoon Suite,* ABC, 1972; *The Karen Valentine Show,* ABC, 1973; "The New Original Wonder Woman," *Wonder Woman,* ABC, 1975; *The Bureau,* NBC, 1976; *High School, U.S.A.,* NBC, 1984; and *Home Again,* ABC, 1988. Appearances on TV specials include *The Halloween That Almost Wasn't,* ABC, 1979; *Dorothy Hamill's Corner of the Sky,* ABC, 1979; *Robbut: A Tale of Tails,* 1985; *The Blinkins,* syndicated, 1986; *Opryland Celebrates 200 Years of American Music,* syndicated, 1988; *Rowan and Martin's Laugh-in Twenty-fifth Anniversary,* NBC, 1993; *Rowan and Martin's Laugh-In: A Valentine's Day Special,* NBC, 1994; and *Daisy-Head Mayzie,* TNT, 1995.

Stage appearances include *My Mother, My Father, and Me,* produced on Broadway, 1963. Recordings include *The Alligator and Other Poems,* Liberty Records, 1962, and *The Grass Menagerie,* Epic Records, 1971, and the singles "Artificial Flowers," Epic, 1971; "The Population Song," A&M, 1972; and "200 Years," ABC Records, 1975.

MEMBER: Academy of Motion Picture Arts and Sciences, National Academy of Television Arts and Sciences, Actors' Fund of America (West Coast advisory board, 1967-85), Keep America Beautiful (advisor, 1967-69); Environmental Defense Fund, Izaak Walton League (honorary president, 1975-76), United Nations Association.

AWARDS, HONORS: National Society of Film Critics Award, best supporting actor, 1976, for *Nashville.*

WRITINGS:

A Flower Child's Garden of Verses, New American Library (New York, NY), 1970.
Carnival of the Animals (poetry), Hollywood Bowl (Los Angeles, CA), 1971.
The Gift: The Illustrated History of the Statue of Liberty, Blackthorne, 1986.

Wrote lyrics to songs in *Nashville,* Paramount, 1975.

Contributor to periodicals, including *Audubon, National Wildlife, Environmental Quality, Progressive, Reader's Digest, Classic TV, Philadelphia Magazine, Los Angeles Times, Washington Post, Manchester Guardian,* and *California Living.*

SIDELIGHTS: In the film *Magnolia* (1999), actor and author Henry Gibson plays opposite William H. Macy's characterization of an aging former whiz kid. Gibson himself is a former child star, having had considerable success on the stage in the 1940s. Following a stint in the U.S. Air Force, he entered the world of film, debuting in Jerry Lewis's *The Nutty Professor* (1963). Since then, he has often—but certainly not always—portrayed sad, beleaguered figures that seemingly live in a dream world. Certainly that describes his best-known character from *Rowan and Martin's Laugh-In,* a gentle poet type who holds a daisy and appears befuddled by an insensitive world. During his stint on *Laugh-In,* which proved to be a career breakthrough for Gibson, he also published two books of poetry: *A Flower Child's Garden of Verses* (1970), and *Carnival of the Animals* (1971).

With *Nashville* (1975), one of his most acclaimed roles, Gibson portrays an entirely different persona in the character of Haven Hamilton, a dictatorial country and western singer. He also wrote songs for the movie. In *The Blues Brothers* (1980), he appears as the leader of the Illinois Nazi Party—a character clearly modeled on real-life American Nazi leader George Lincoln Rockwell, and a role that seems the polar opposite of Gibson's earlier turn as the meek poet. Outside of the film world, Gibson has maintained a career as a writer, publishing articles in magazines, as well as authoring *The Gift: The Illustrated History of the Statue of Liberty* (1986), which celebrates the great statue's centennial.

BIOGRAPHICAL AND CRITICAL SOURCES:

BOOKS

Contemporary Theatre, Film, and Television, Volume 32, Gale (Detroit, MI), 2000.*

*   *   *

GILL, Bartholomew
    See McGARRITY, Mark

*   *   *

GILLILAND, C. Herbert 1942-

PERSONAL: Born December 4, 1942, in Alton, IL; son of C. H., Sr. (a physician) and Marion Spjut (an anthropologist) Gilliland; married Carol Anne Gagnon (a college teacher), May 26, 1979; children: Anne-Marie, Alexandra, Elizabeth, Alice. *Education:* University of Florida, B.A., 1964, M.A., 1965, Ph.D., 1976. *Religion:* Protestant.

ADDRESSES: Home—607 Dunberry Dr., Arnold, MD 21012. *Office*—English Department, U.S. Naval Academy, 107 Maryland Ave., Annapolis, MD 21402. *E-mail*—gillilan@nadn.navy.mil.

CAREER: U.S. Naval Academy, Annapolis, MD, professor of English, 1986—. *Military service:* U.S. Naval Reserve, active duty 1965-69, 1982-85, and 1991; attained rank of captain.

AWARDS, HONORS: U.S. Navy Civilian Meritorious Service Medal, 1997.

WRITINGS:

(With Robert Shenk) *Admiral Dan Gallery: The Life and Wit of a Navy Original,* Naval Institute Press, 1999.

Translator from Catalan of a play by Manuel de Pedrolo; author of articles on Milton, Shakespeare, Andrew Marvell, writers of sea literature, and numismatics.

WORK IN PROGRESS: An edition of the journal of John C. Lawrence written aboard the U.S.S. *Yorktown* while interdicting slave trade from 1844-46 off the coast of Liberia with the African Squadron; research on naval literature and history; a biography.

SIDELIGHTS: C. Herbert Gilliland told *CA:* "As I write this I have one book [*Admiral Dan Gallery: The Life and Wit of a Navy Original*] in print and another nearly ready, and perhaps some others shaping up for later. For me, since I have a regular job, the hardest part of writing is finding the clear blocks of time to do it, especially the first draft, which seems to require the kind of thinking that cannot be done in half-hour segments.

"After training and working for years as a teacher and scholar of literature, I have become in recent years quite interested in biographical and historical works. My own background with the Navy, plus the holdings of the library of the Naval Academy, where I work, have led me to develop an interest in naval material. Though professional advantages accrue, my main motive now in writing is that I enjoy it. I learn a lot, I meet interesting people in the process and afterwards, and I hope to be giving readers pleasure and knowledge. I wish I'd started writing books sooner, and I thank my co-author Bob Shenk for getting me into it."

*   *   *

GOODMAN, Walter 1927-2002

OBITUARY NOTICE—See index for *CA* sketch: Born August 22, 1927, in New York, NY; died of kidney failure March 6, 2002, in Valhalla, NY. Journalist and author. Goodman was a reporter and editor for various newspapers and magazines and was well known for his 1968 book *The Committee: The Extraordinary Career of the House Committee on Un-American Activities.* Graduating from Syracuse University in 1949, he went on to complete his master's degree at the University of Reading in 1953. After college, he got a job in London with the Foreign Broadcast Information Service, but he returned to the United States to work as a writer for *New Republic.* This was followed by editorial stints at *Redbook* and *Playboy* from 1957 until 1974. In 1974 Goodman joined the *New York Times,* where he was deputy editor of the arts and leisure section until 1979. At this juncture he became executive editor and director of humanities programming for WNET in New York City until 1981. He next worked briefly for *Newsweek* as a senior writer before returning to the *New York Times.* Goodman's articles ranged from literary pieces to editorials, criticism, and television reviews; while at WNET he also worked on film documentaries. Besides *The Committee,* he wrote or cowrote eight other books, including *All Honorable Men: Corruption and Compromise in American Life, A Percentage of the Take,* and *The Family: Yesterday, Today, Tomorrow,* the last which he wrote with his wife, Elaine Goodman. Goodman also wrote another book with his wife, the nonfiction juvenile title *The Rights of the People: The Major Decisions of the Warren Court,* which won the Christopher Award in 1972. He was also the author of the children's book *Black Bondage: The Life of Slaves in the South.*

OBITUARIES AND OTHER SOURCES:

BOOKS

Who's Who in America, 55th edition, Marquis (New Providence, NJ), 2001.

PERIODICALS

Los Angeles Times, March 8, 2002, p. B15.
New York Times, March 7, 2002, p. C15.

*   *   *

GOUDZWAARD, Bob 1934-

PERSONAL: Born April 3, 1934, in Delft, Netherlands; son of Maurite Pieter (a printer) and Maria A. (van Tertoolen) Goudzwaard; married Riny van Helden, 1960; children: four. *Education:* Erasmus University, Ph.D., 1971. *Religion:* "Reformed."

ADDRESSES: Home—Oosterdwarslaan 3, 3971 AM Driebergen, Netherlands. *E-mail*—bob.goudzwaard@ext.vu.nl.

CAREER: Free University of Amsterdam, Amsterdam, Netherlands, professor of economics, 1972-99, professor of cultural philosophy, 1989-99, professor emeritus, 1999—. Center for Public Justice, Washington, DC, Kuyper lecturer, 1999. Dutch Parliament, member of house for Anti-Revolutionary Party, 1967-71. Advisor to World Council of Churches and World Alliance of Reformed Churches.

MEMBER: Institute for Christian Studies (Toronto, Ontario, Canada; fellow).

WRITINGS:

Ongeprijsde schaarste. Expretiale of ongecompensoerde effecten als economisch-politiek probleem, Van Stockum (The Hague, Netherlands), 1970.

Schaduwen van het groei-geloof, Kok (Kampen, Netherlands), 1974.

Kapitalisme en vooruitgang, 1978, 2nd revised edition translated and edited by Josina van Nuis Zylstra as *Capitalism and Progress: A Diagnosis of Western Society,* Eerdmans (Grand Rapids, MI), 1979.

Genoodzaakt goed te wezen: Christelijke hoop in een bezeten wereold, Kok (Kampen, Netherlands), 1981, translated by Mark Vander Vennen as *Idols of Our Time,* Inter-Varsity Press (Downers Grove, IL), 1984.

(With others) *Actie en bezinning,* (The Hague, Netherlands), 1983.

Economie, bewapening en ontwikkeling, Samson (Alps on the Rhine, Netherlands), 1985

Gonoeg van te veel, genoeg van te weinig, translated by Mark R. Vander Vennen as *Beyond Poverty and Affluence: Toward an Economy of Care with a Twelve-Step Program for Economic Recovery,* Eerdmans (Grand Rapids, MI), 1995.

(Author of foreword) *Bewogen realisma: economie, cultuur, oecumene,* Kok (Kampen, Netherlands), 1999.

Globalization and the Kingdom of God (Kuyper lecture), Baker Book House (Grand Rapids, MI), 2001.

BIOGRAPHICAL AND CRITICAL SOURCES:

PERIODICALS

Christian Century, May 28, 1980, Theodore R. Malloch, review of *Capitalism and Progress: A Diagnosis of Western Society,* p. 617.

Ethics, October, 1982, Arthur L. Stinchcombe, "On Softheadedness on the Future," pp. 114-128.

Maclean's, February 25, 1980, Robert Green, "Reluctant Rider on NATO's Wagon," p. 10.

Publishers Weekly, March 12, 2001, review of *Globalization and the Kingdom of God,* p. 79.

*   *   *

GRAAS, Ulrik
   See GRÄS, Ulrik

*   *   *

GRÄS, Ulrik 1940-

PERSONAL: Born October 15, 1940; son of Holger and Gerda Gräs; married Karen Skovbjerg (a journalist). *Education:* Graduated from secondary school, 1958 (apprenticed as a journalist); attended City of London College, 1960.

ADDRESSES: Agent—Tiderne skifter, Frederiksberg Alle 8, 1820 Copenhagen 5, Denmark.

CAREER: Sailor, novelist, journalist, and novelist. Radio host and journalist for Danish radio, beginning 1978. Cofounder of alternative press Attika, 1971; cofounder of a newspaper, 1973; correspondent for Dutch newspapers; freelance broadcast journalist, 1999—.

AWARDS, HONORS: Kaptajn H. C. Lundgreens legat, 1973; Cavlingprisen, 1978; Statens Kunstfond, 1973, 1974, 1977, 1978, 1979, 1980, 1981, 1982, 1983, 1984, 1985, 1986, 1988, 1990, 1991, 1992; Jul. Bomholts legatbolig, 1979; Martin Andersen Nexø legatet, 1984; Kulturministeriets nordiske rejsestipendium,

1984; Poeten Poul Sørensen og fru Susanne Sørensens legat, 1992; Danske journalister, 1995; Forfatterne Harald Kiddes og Astrid Ehrencron-Kiddes Legat, 2000.

WRITINGS:

Mandskabet (novellas), Borgen (Copenhagen, Denmark), 1965.

Kajplads, Borgen (Copenhagen, Denmark), 1967.

Fatimas hånd (novel), Attika (Copenhagen, Denmark), 1971.

Klapjagt, Attika (Copenhagen, Denmark), 1972.

Nabrzete, 1973.

Boulevardparken, Attika (Copenhagen, Denmark), 1973.

101 kilometerstenen, Attika (Copenhagen, Denmark), 1974.

Allah og den hellige jomfru, Attika (Denmark), 1975.

Noveller, Gyldendal, 1975.

Elskere elsk (novel), Attika (Nykøbing Mors, Denmark), 1976.

Mellemtime. Tre fortællinger fra vestbyen, Attika (Nykøbing Mors, Denmark), 1976.

Stammerne (novel), Attika (Nykøbing Mors, Denmark), 1978.

Historiens gang, Modtryk (Århus, Denmark), 1980.

Ny dansk prosa, 1978.

Mandeliv, 1980.

Hans Verden, Tiderme Shifter, 1980.

Ægteskabet er min rede, 1981.

Digterhjemmet Bomholts hus, 1981.

Gadekær og grillbar, Gyldendal, 1981.

Købmandsaften, 1982.

Hjerteslag (novel), Tiderne Skifter (Copenhagen, Denmark), 1983.

19 noveller, 1983.

Krigens Reporter, Tiderme Shifter, 1984.

Jern og krystaller, 1985.

Her og altid (novel), Tiderne Skifter (Copenhagen, Denmark), 1987.

(With Robert Jacobsen) *R. J.,* 1987.

Fredsdrømme, 1989.

(With Frede Troelsen) *Frede Troelsen,* Brandts klædefabrik (Odense, Denmark), 1992.

(With Robert Jacobsen) *Bernard—mesterens sparringspartner,* 1993.

Kærlighedens fortalelse, 1994.

Matige danshere, Minksgaard, 1995.

Berusede by (novel), Tiderne Skifter (Copenhagen, Denmark), 2000.

Also author of *Noveller fra '70'erne,* Gyldendal, and *Litteratur,* Gyldendal. Contributor of poems to anthology *Det lyse rum,* edited by Hans Hertel.

WORK IN PROGRESS: A novel about "a journalist caught at the crossing point between the revolutionary dreams of the past and present reality now twenty years on."

SIDELIGHTS: Danish author Ulrik Gräs has named William Faulkner, James Joyce, Joseph Conrad, Aksel Sandemose, and the beatnik generation as some of his most important literary inspirations. Through his work as a radio journalist and author, he has been an active participant on the cultural scene since the late 1960s. In addition to his radio work, in 1971 Gräs started an alternative press with fellow writers Johannes L. Madsen and Finn Krageskov called Attika, and he co-founded a newspaper in 1973 that was awarded the Cavlingprisen.

Gräs started Attika after other publishers rejected his novel *Fatimas hånd.* Attika is different from other publishing companies in that it is primarily concerned with its authors. Whereas a writer might normally receive a fifteen-percent book commission, Attika grants a fifty-percent commission on sales. The company has found great success, having published four hundred books by two hundred authors since its founding.

Some of Gräs's best-known novels include *Elskere elsk, Stammerne,* and *Hjerteslag.* These are both social realist novels dealing with the sexual and socioeconomic oppression of men. May Schack, writing in *Hug!,* pointed out that the men whom Gräs chose to write about in these works are not the privileged and the powerful few, but those at the bottom of the social-economic hierarchy. According to Schack, by writing about frustration, misery, and hopelessness from a male perspective Gräs's writing is similar to that of Danish author Vita Andersen, who is the author of books concerned with gender issues from a female perspective. Gräs analyzes the relationship between the sexes and how these conflicts are played out from a male perspective. He also looks at them from a class perspective.

In *Elskere elsk* Gräs shows how the male's situation is all the more painful because values, norms, and social patterns have changed so fundamentally that men are at a complete loss as to where they stand in society. They therefore react to their position in asocial, destructive, and self-destructive ways. The main protagonist in *Elskere elsk,* Karl Johan, and his friend Leif are both unemployed and have only minimal educations. Unable to deal with the problems of the times they are living in, they cling to the past in the unrealistic hope that society can return to the way it once was. With no personal resources and no ability to see themselves in a larger context, they neither understand nor identify with workers' and women's emancipation. Consequently, they aim their aggressions towards the liberals in the apartment below and also towards the women's movement. As the story progresses, Leif erupts in fits of increasingly violent intensity. Through a dialogue between Leif and the main female character in the story, Åse, the chauvinistic and oppressive ways of the man and the powerlessness experienced by both men and women is expressed in powerful ways. Åse clings to her own traditional sex role and is unwilling to take responsibility for her own life; the author lets the characters play their roles without intervening, commenting, or moralizing. By the end of the story, Åse has paid with her life for Leif's inability to deal with society.

Men's isolation from each other is one of the main themes of Gräs's novels. Men cannot express themselves openly, the author feels, and their last vestiges of pride lie in not showing signs of weakness or speaking about their feelings. Although Karl Johan sometimes feels vaguely interested in contacting the liberals in the apartment below him, he does not take this first step because of his feelings of inferiority. It would take away his dignity just to talk to them, so he avoids it altogether. Karl also feels uncomfortable when confronted with other men's feeling of insecurity.

In *Stammerne* the theme of male insecurity is further explored. The protagonist, Dino, is a communist who begins to doubt his political party as well as the stability of his relationship with his girlfriend, Jette. Traditional sex roles here have been reversed: Jette is the strong and active partner with a sense of purpose and self-confidence, and Dino is the weaker partner, feeling dependent and eager to please. He feels unhappy with the role of being the sweet attentive listener to women's problems and concerns. At the same time as Jette wants him to play this part, she is also attracted to a totally opposite kind of person: a strong and unyielding trade union leader. This concern about changing gender roles is also a theme addressed by other Danish writers such as Hans Jørgen Nielsen in *Fodboldenglen* and Kristen Bjørnkjær in *Krage søger måge.*

In the 1990s Gräs began working on portrait stories, such as *Kærlighedens fortalelse.* This genre involves soliloquies which explore the borderline between fiction and documentary. The dominant theme is how traumatic experiences from childhood can become determining factors in a person's adult life.

More recently, Gräs completed *Berusede by,* the story of Denmark during and after the German occupation. It is an attempt to view the events of World War II from a new and broader perspective. Many books have focused on the heroes of the war, such as those in the Resistance and those who helped Jews escape to Sweden. But these freedom fighters were in fact a small minority. The vast majority of Danes were passive and in some cases even cooperated with the Nazis. Gräs's book examines the social and psychological factors involved in this massive passivity. The narrator of *Berusede by* is a seventeen-year-old boy who lives in a typical Danish provincial town, where his grandfather is mayor. The boy is caught between loyalty towards his grandfather, who cooperates with the Germans, and a great pressure, as the Germans begin to lose, to be on the side of the Resistance, which his father has joined. The social-democratic mayor cooperates with the Germans, as do all of his colleagues in the nation, because he believes that this is the best choice for the city and the nation. In the frenzied days around Liberation Day, May 4, 1945, the city's inhabitants oust the mayor. *Politiken* reviewer Marie Tetzlaff criticized *Berusede by* for using too many clichés to describe the aristocrat "komtesse" of the town and the German commander, but she gave Gräs credit for writing an otherwise well-crafted and sensitive novel that brings to mind the present-day fears of foreigners "invading" from the south.

Gräs told *CA:* "I much preferred not to write at all; yet in order to survive and live in time and to react upon time, gaining an insight in our common history and sense of my own story, to me writing is as essential as breathing air."

"In fact every new novel is the same. Every novel is an extension of the previous novel, however, woven in an increasingly complex way—to harden the tissue."

"Like William Faulkner has a fictive town in Mississippi, 'Jefferson,' I have a fictive part of town in Denmark, 'Vestbyen;' it is both a state of mind and soul and a fictive image of actual places. In 'Vestbyen' I penetrate a district and the souls of its people, always digging—trying to reveal—new layers in history."

"Or: what I do is to *register* a spirit of a time in order to stage its expression backwards. Thus in old pictures (from the past) which are being developed in this new age, the story of our time becomes the story of our mind, right now, here, illumination in the present."

"In *101 kilometerstenen,* Arno, in *Stammerne,* Dino, in *Hjerteslag,* Reno, and in *Her og altid,* Kuno are all people who speak up against the world, people who do not want to be suppressed, who defy their environments and the communities they are given."

"Whether it is about journalism (Arno is a reporter from wars in the Middle East) or politics (Dino and Reno are socialists, however, critics of the socialist systems) or kinships as the masonic lodge which separates Kuno from his father, the central figures in my novels are in opposition."

"The energies I find at crossing points, in the collision, in the energy fields between parting and meeting, between what you are and what you could be."

"Artistically it is about achieving the most effective result. And if you want to hit you are to aim a bit above the target; because it is the spaces and the movements which contain opportunities—both ethically and aesthetically."

BIOGRAPHICAL AND CRITICAL SOURCES:

PERIODICALS

Andet, April, 2001.
Berlingske Tidende, September 26, 2000, Af Klaus Rothstein, "Ansvar eller svigt."

Hug!, August 27, 1980, May Schack, "Et køn med hemmeligheder. Tendenser i de sidste års mandelitteratur," pp. 61-72.

Litteratur/84, August 26, 1983, Erik Skyum-Nielsen, "Rejsen til hjerterødderme," pp. 58-59.

OTHER

Politiken, http://politiken.dk/ (August 5, 2001), Marie Tetzlaff, review of *Berusede by.*

*   *   *

GREGORY, Andre 1934-

PERSONAL: Born 1934; children: Nick.

ADDRESSES: Agent—The Gersh Agency, 130 West 42nd St., New York, NY 10036-7800.

CAREER: Producer, director, actor, and writer.

Stage appearances include *The Middle Ages,* Theatre at St. Peter's Church, New York, NY, 1983. Stage work includes (coproducer) *Deidre of the Sorrows,* Gate Theatre, New York, NY, 1959; (producer) *The Blacks,* St. Mark's Playhouse, New York, NY, 1961; (director) *P.S. 193,* Writers Stage, New York, NY, 1962; (director) *The Firebugs,* Seattle Repertory Theatre, Seattle, WA, 1963; (director) *Galileo,* Theatre of the Living Arts, Philadelphia, PA, 1965; (director) *Endgame,* Theatre of the Living Arts, 1965; (director) *Uncle Vanya,* Theatre of the Living Arts, 1966; (director) *Beclech,* Theatre of the Living Arts, 1966; (director) *Poor Bitos,* Theatre of the Living Arts, 1966; (director) *Leda Had a Little Swan,* Cort Theatre, New York, NY, 1968; (director) *Alice in Wonderland,* The Extension, New York, NY, 1970; (director) *Endgame,* New York University, New York, NY, 1973; (director) *Our Late Night,* The Manhattan Project Theatre, New York, NY, 1974; (director) *The Seagull,* Public Theatre, New York, NY, 1975; (advisor) *War on the Third Floor,* New Directors Project, Perry Street Theatre, New York, NY, 1984; (director) *All Night Long,* McGinn/Cazale Theatre, New York, NY, 1984; (director) *The Designated Mourner,* New York, NY, 2000; directed *Tartuffe,* 1967; *The Bacchae,* 1969; *Jinx's Bridge,* 1976; and *Alice in Wonderland,* Edinburgh Festival, Edinburgh, Scotland.

Film appearances include *My Dinner with Andre,* Pacific Arts, 1981; *Author! Author!,* Twentieth Century-Fox, 1982; *Protocol,* Warner Bros., 1984; *The Mosquito Coast,* Warner Bros., 1986; *Always,* International Rainbow Pictures, 1986; *My Favorite Fairy Tales Volume 4: The Wizard of Oz; The Magic Carpet; Alibaba and Forty Thieves,* 1986; *Street Smart,* Cannon, 1987; *The Last Temptation of Christ,* 1988; *Some Girls,* 1989; *The Bonfire of the Vanities,* 1990; *The Linguini Incident,* 1991; *Demolition Man,* 1993; *The Shadow,* 1994; *Vanya on 42nd Street,* 1994; *Last Summer in the Hamptons,* 1995; *Hudson River Blues,* Romance Classics, 1997; *Celebrity,* Miramax, 1998; and *Goodbye Lover,* Warner Bros., 1999.

Television movie appearances include *Alice in Wonderland,* 1983, and *Follies in Concert,* 1986.

WRITINGS:

(With Wallace Shawn) *My Dinner with Andre* (screenplay), Pacific Arts Video Records, 1981, published as *My Dinner with André: A Screenplay,* Grove Press (New York, NY), 1981.

(Author of story) *Vanya on 42nd Street,* Sony Pictures Classics, 1994.

SIDELIGHTS: Andre Gregory is probably the only writer in history to share a triple billing with Anton Chekhov and David Mamet, as he did in *Vanya on 42nd Street.* Gregory was behind the larger "frame story," if it can be called that, for the film, which focuses on the rehearsal of Chekhov's play *Uncle Vanya* (adapted by Mamet) on an unadorned stage in a Gothic building—"it looks like a fabulous ruin out of *Blade Runner,*" wrote Owen Gleiberman in *Entertainment Weekly*—just off Times Square. The 1994 film featured Julianne Moore, just then emerging into her own, with Wallace Shawn in the title role.

The pairing of Shawn and Gregory attracted particular critical interest because the two (along with director Louis Malle), had won a cult following more than a decade earlier in *My Dinner with Andre* (1981). Though the title indicates that the story (once again, if it can be called that) is presented from Shawn's point of view, in fact the screenplay was their joint creation. If *Uncle Vanya* seemed completely uncontrived—or, as some critics might have had it, completely contrived in its very lack of contrivance—then its predecessor was doubly so. The entire film consists of Shawn and Gregory sharing a dinner at a New York restaurant, and the "plot" (which is merely their conversation) takes place in real time.

"Considering the triumph of their first effort," wrote Gleiberman, ". . . it's amazing it has taken [Shawn, Gregory, and Malle] more than ten years to collaborate again. It was worth the wait, though." Stanley Kauffmann in the *New Republic* called *Vanya on 42nd Street* "A generally wonderful two hours," and praised its lack of artifice: "Nothing has been done to modernize the play. There are no costumes, no scenery, not even a samovar . . . but in every remotest cranny of spirit, this is Chekhov. It is not a flawless production, but it glows with affinity."

BIOGRAPHICAL AND CRITICAL SOURCES:

BOOKS

Contemporary Theatre, Film, and Television, Volume 33, Gale (Detroit, MI), 2001.

PERIODICALS

Christian Science Monitor, February 7, 1983, "Questioning, Searching" (interview with Gregory), p. 20; December 9, 1994, David Sterritt, review of *Vanya on 42nd Street,* p. 13.
Entertainment Weekly, November 25, 1994, Owen Gleiberman, review of *Vanya on 42nd Street,* p. 47.
Maclean's, May 15, 1995, Brian D. Johnson, review of *Vanya on 42nd Street,* pp. 73-74.
New Republic, November 7, 1994, Stanley Kauffmann, review of *Vanya on 42nd Street,* pp. 34-36.
New York Times, January 17, 1982, Vincent Canby, review of *My Dinner with Andre,* p. D1; October 16, 1994, Patricia Bosworth, "Why 'Vanya,' and Why Now," p. H13; July 21, 1995, review of *Vanya on 42nd Street,* p. B16; May 16, 1999, Mel Gussow, "My Lunch with Andre (and Wally)," p. 1.
Wall Street Journal, December 13, 1994, Julie Salamon, review of *Vanya on 42nd Street,* p. A16.*

GRIFFIN, Kitty 1951-

PERSONAL: Born July 26, 1951, in Aschafenberg, Germany; adopted daughter of Terence (a naval officer) and Rosemary (a homemaker; maiden name, O'Neill) Griffin; married Gerard Lagorio (a partner in a computer consulting firm); children: Ian Gerard (deceased), Danika, Beatrice. *Education:* Virginia Commonwealth University, B.S. (criminal justice), 1975; Carlow College, teacher certification (secondary social studies), 1989; studied screenwriting at Pittsburgh Filmmakers, 1999-2001. *Religion:* Catholic. *Hobbies and other interests:* Pottery, painting, biking, hiking, gardening, "caring for a Newfoundland dog, a ferret, cats, a canary, and a big, fat angel fish."

ADDRESSES: Home—241 Church Hill Rd., Venetia, PA 15367. *Agent*—Tracey Adams, McIntosh & Otis, 353 Lexington Ave., New York, NY 10016. *E-mail*—klagorio@cobweb.net.

CAREER: Author. Freelance journalist, 1998—; Community College of Allegheny County, Pittsburgh, PA, instructor, 2000—; Laroche College, Pittsburgh, PA, assistant professor, 2002.

MEMBER: Society of Children's Book Writers and Illustrators, Author's Guild, Carnegie Screenwriters.

AWARDS, HONORS: Honorable mention, best feature (weeklies) and second place, best design (weeklies), Spotlight Award-Keystone State Professional Chapter Society of Professional Journalists, 1999; honorable mention, children's fiction, *Writer's Digest* 2001 Writing Competition.

WRITINGS:

(With Kathy Combs) *Cowboy Sam and Those Confounded Secrets,* illustrated by Mike Wohnoutka, Clarion (New York, NY), 2001.
(With Kathy Combs) *The Foot-stomping Adventures of Clementine Sweet,* Clarion (New York, NY), in press.

WORK IN PROGRESS: Gretel, a novel; several picture books with Kathy Combs, including *Stinker and the Onion Princess; When the World Broke—Johnstown, May 31, 1889,* a novel; *Fisheye,* a screenplay.

SIDELIGHTS: Kitty Griffin commented to *CA:* "As a child I often felt out of place, out of time. It was a sense that I was someplace I didn't belong." Later, at age sixteen, she discovered that when she was three she had been adopted from an orphanage in Germany. Indeed, at one time she had another name, another language, another culture. Griffin feels this need to seek out the place she thought she should be set her on the path of writing. "I have always loved to read, and I read everything—fairy tales, mysteries, suspense, history, science fiction, I'm really not fussy. Here are books that I remember impacting me—*The King's Stilts* (Seuss), *The Roman, The Egyptian, The Etruscan* (all by Mika Walteri), *Foundation* (Asimov), and *Dune* (Herbert)."

In high school Griffin's teachers told her that she was a good writer and that she should be a lawyer. In college she majored in criminal justice, thinking she would be the next Perry Mason. Only when she had an opportunity to start interviewing convicts did she realize they were not all oppressed victims of an unjust society: these were real criminals. Griffin ended up working with juveniles and pre-delinquents and found it rewarding and challenging. For the next twenty years, much of her employment involved working with troubled and disadvantaged kids. For a couple of years, when she needed a break, she also worked as a postal carrier.

"My daughters were very demanding at bedtime and after reading three stories I'd turn out the light," Griffin recalled. "Then I would make a story up for them. Year after year of doing this released something inside my mind and characters began to take on shape and substance. Finally, these characters begged for more and I had to find out about writing. I was awarded a scholarship to attend a writing for children workshop at Rice University in Houston and that opened the portal. That was in 1991 and I haven't looked back." Even though it took a long time to get her first book published, Griffin felt good about saying she was a writer when people asked what she did.

Her Rice university scholarship let to Griffin's friendship with cowriter Kathy Combs, who lives in Houston, Texas. They attended other workshops together in different regions, from Indiana to Kentucky, from New York to New Jersey. Both *Cowboy Sam* and their second book, *The Foot-stomping Adventures of Clementine Sweet,* are Texas stories full of lyrical language. Their third collaboration, *Stinker and the Onion Princess,* is a lighthearted "Texas-sized" retelling of the Grimm tale "King Thrushbeard." Instead of a haughty princess, there is a stuck-up son of an oil baron (Big Daddy) and his wife, (Big Mama). "Oh whee, does that boy have an adventure as the Onion Princess helps him find his manners," remarked Griffin.

Griffin spent almost two years researching the story of the Johnstown Flood. This horrific event occurred on May 31, 1889, in the Conemaugh Valley just east of Pittsburgh, Pennsylvania. In less than an hour, over 2,000 people were brutally killed by a wave of rainwater that swept down the mountain into the valley below after a dam constructed to create a recreational lake broke. A visit to the flood museum in Johnstown left Griffin stunned, overwhelmed, and wanting to understand how such a tragedy could happen. Her background as a history teacher turned out to be a valuable asset as she began searching. With the help of several historians at local museums and libraries, her manuscript took shape. She often thinks of a quote from one of the survivors, Reverend David Beale (especially after the events of September 11, 2001) "it were vain to undertake to tell the world how or what we felt, when shoeless, hatless, and many of us almost naked, some bruised and broken, we stood there and we looked upon that scene of death and desolation." What Griffin learned from her study was the remarkable power people have to care for one another, to risk their lives for each other, and to pick up and carry on.

At the suggestion of friend Combs, Griffin took a screenwriting workshop and discovered a new and exciting way of looking at story. "Think of a screenplay as sending a series of electric postcards. Each scene has to push the main character further along." She feels that screenwriting has taught her a great deal about character development. That in turn has helped her become a better writer.

"I think of writing like white-water rafting," Griffin stated. "There are days when I am splashing and dashing madly along, and there are days when I'm caught in a whirlpool. Every story is a different adventure. Every story leads into new waters. My advice to those who want to write: Know when to hold on and when to paddle. It's one riot of a ride. The most exciting part is discovering where the story takes you. Of course it's rough, rejection hurts, but you know what? I've finally found where I want to be."

BIOGRAPHICAL AND CRITICAL SOURCES:

PERIODICALS

Kirkus Reviews, July 15, 2001, review of *Cowboy Sam and Those Confounded Secrets,* p. 1026.
Publishers Weekly, July 16, 2001, review of *Cowboy Sam and Those Confounded Secrets,* p. 180.
School Library Journal, December, 2001, Shara Alpern, review of *Cowboy Sam and Those Confounded Secrets,* p. 103.

*   *   *

GRIFFITH, Michael

PERSONAL: Born in Orangeburg, SC. *Education:* Princeton University, B.A. (Germanic languages and literature; summa cum laude), Louisiana State University M.F.A. (creative writing).

ADDRESSES: Agent—c/o Author Mail, Arcade Publishing, 151 Fifth Ave., New York, NY 10010. *E-mail*—mgriffi@lsu.edu.

CAREER: Associate editor, *Southern Review,* 1992—.

WRITINGS:

Spikes, Arcade (New York, NY), 2001.

WORK IN PROGRESS: The Blue Pencil of the Apocalypse, a novel of "grammar terrorists."

SIDELIGHTS: Michael Griffith is an editor of the *Southern Review.* His first novel, *Spikes,* is about golf and is unique in a genre that usually tends either to low comedy or mystical explorations of the game. As a sports novel, *Spikes* is overtly "literary," and as a literary novel it is unusual in being about golf. However it succeeds on both counts, because Griffith knows golf. His brother played professionally for a

while, and Griffith caddied for him. He became fascinated with the sub-culture of the mini-tours and the golfers that live in it.

The theme of Griffith's novel lies in the milieu of failure in success-driven America. As the novelist told Robert L. Hall for the online *Southern Scribe,* "There were guys like my main character, Brian—players who had expected to make a brief stop in the minors, but now who've been floundering for several years, failing players near the end of the string. I began to wonder what it must be like for someone to be a prodigy at something—whether violin or algebra or golf—and, after investing your entire youth in that skill, that bailiwick, that one happy preserve where you're THE BEST, to reach a point where you realize you can't hack it anymore. You are an also-ran, a mediocrity."

The hero of the novel, Brian Schwan, is over the hill at age twenty-six. He has been struggling along on the mini-tours—the lowest rung on the professional golf ladder—and isn't up to another day of it. His wife, Rosa, feels he has "thrown good money after bad golf" and wants him to quit and start a family. Even his father, who pushed Brian into golf, has lost faith. He has earned 19,000 dollars in four years and has never won a tournament. He's just shot a 77 to his partner Bird Soulsby's 59—the course record—and he's at the nadir of his career.

Just as Brian is throwing his golf bag in the trunk of his car and contemplating giving up golf for good, a beautiful television reporter mistakes him for Soulsby; he jumps at the chance to feel like a winner and takes on Soulsby's identity. Once he has decided to make the switch, he plays it to the hilt, even setting up a tryst with the lovely reporter Ellen. But Brian doesn't know who he is really trying to imitate or how strange things will get. As a reviewer for *Publishers Weekly* commented, "Griffith concocts a truly Nabokovian entertainment, which probes the natures of winners and losers, the love of the game and the eccentric subculture it spawns—though one needn't have the slightest interest in golf to be won over." Bradley S. Klein, in the *New York Times,* similarly wrote that Griffin's "writing is so vivid that even a nongolfer will be swept up for this breathless ride through the strip malls, night life and sleazy resorts of American schlock culture run amok." Reviewing the book for the *Online Houston Chronicle,* Eric Miles Williamson concluded that "There's golfing in *Spikes,* but it's not a novel about golf. *Spikes* is a comic novel at our follies and foibles, a brilliantly written examination of how we generate and cope with our personal miseries. With a prose style that is uniquely his own, Griffith's writing is as lush as Nabokov's, as intelligent as Saul Bellow's and as vivid as the best work of E. L. Doctorow."

BIOGRAPHICAL AND CRITICAL SOURCES:

PERIODICALS

Booklist, September 1, 2001, Bonnie Johnson, review of *Spikes,* p. 65.
Library Journal, December, 2000, Marylaine Block, review of *Spikes,* p. 272.
London Review of Books, October 4, 2001, James Francken, review of *Spikes,* p. 37.
New York Times, March 25, 2001, Bradley S. Klein, review of *Spikes,* p. 15.
Publishers Weekly, December 4, 2001, review of *Spikes,* p. 52.
Washington Post Book World, April 1, 2001, John Greenya, review of *Spikes,* p. T09.

OTHER

Hole by Hole, http://www.holebyhole.com/ (December 2, 2001), review of *Spikes.*
Houston Chronicle Online, http://www.chron.com/ (August 22, 2001), Eric Miles Williamson, review of *Spikes.*
Southern Scribe, http://www.southernscribe.com/ (December 2, 2001), Robert L. Hall, interview with Michael Griffith.

*   *   *

GRIMES, Paul 1924-2002

OBITUARY NOTICE—See index for *CA* sketch: Born May 8, 1924, in New York, NY; died from complications after hip surgery May 23, 2002, in Abington, PA.

Journalist, editor, and author. Grimes was best known as a travel writer who helped establish the magazine *Condé Nast Traveler.* After serving as a sergeant in the U.S. Army during World War II, he graduated from Cornell with a B.A. in 1948. He then embarked on a journalism career as a reporter and copy editor for the Kansas City *Star* and then as editor of *Women's Wear Daily* in New York City from 1949 to 1950. His time in Asia began when he took a job as an information officer for the U.S. Information Agency in Bombay during the early 1950s. From 1954 to 1955 he worked as editor of the *Bangkok Post* before returning to New York to join the *Daily News* staff as a copy editor. Grimes found himself working abroad in Pakistan, India, Afghanistan, and Bhutan as a foreign correspondent for the *New York Times* from 1957 to 1966. Returning to the United States, he joined the *Philadelphia Bulletin* for eight years before returning to the *New York Times* as a copy editor and travel columnist. He remained at the *New York Times* until 1987, when he became a founding editor and then editor-at-large for *Condé Nast Traveler* until his retirement in 2000. In addition to his numerous columns and articles, Grimes was the author of *The New York Times Practical Traveler* (1985).

OBITUARIES AND OTHER SOURCES:

BOOKS

Who's Who in the Media and Communications, first edition, Marquis (New Providence, NJ), 1997.

PERIODICALS

Los Angeles Times, April 25, 2002, p. B13.
New York Times, April 24, 2002, p. A26.

H

HALL, James W(ilson) 1947-

PERSONAL: Born 1947, in Hopkinsville, KY; married Evelyn (a schoolteacher), 1990. *Education:* Florida Presbyterian College (became Eckerd College); Johns Hopkins University, M.F.A., 1969; University of Utah, Ph.D., 1973.

ADDRESSES: Home—Miami, FL. *Office*—Florida International University, Miami, FL. *Agent*—Esther Newberg, International Creative Management, Los Angeles, CA. *E-mail*—James.Hall@jameswhall.com.

CAREER: Florida International University, Miami, teacher of literature and creative writing, 1974—; writer.

AWARDS, HONORS: John D. MacDonald Award; Critic's Choice Award, *San Francisco Review of Books,* for *Gone Wild;* nomination for Dashiell Hammett Prize, for *Buzz Cut.*

WRITINGS:

"THORN" CRIME NOVEL SERIES

Under Cover of Daylight, Norton (New York, NY), 1987.
Tropical Freeze, Norton (New York, NY), 1989.
Mean High Tide, Delacorte Press (New York, NY), 1994.

Buzz Cut, Delacorte Press (New York, NY), 1996.
Red Sky at Night, Delacorte Press (New York, NY), 1997.

CRIME NOVELS

Bones of Coral, Knopf (New York, NY), 1991.
Hard Aground, Delacorte Press (New York, NY), 1993.
Gone Wild, Delacorte Press (New York, NY), 1995.
Body Language, St. Martin's Press (New York, NY), 1998.
Rough Draft, St. Martin's Press (New York, NY), 2000.

OTHER

The Lady from the Dark Green Hills: Poems, Three Rivers Press (Pittsburgh, PA), 1976.
The Mating Reflex (poetry), Carnegie-Mellon University Press (Pittsburgh, PA), 1980.
Ham Operator: Poetry and Fiction, Ampersand Press (Bristol, RI), 1980.
False Statements (poetry), Carnegie-Mellon University Press (Pittsburgh, PA), 1986.
Paper Products: Short Stories, Norton (New York, NY), 1990.

Also author of poetry collections.

Columnist, *Sunshine,* 1998—. Contributor to periodicals, including *American Scholar, Antioch Review, Georgia Review, Kenyon Press, North American Review, Poetry,* and *Southern Poetry Review.*

SIDELIGHTS: James W. Hall is a versatile writer whose publications include poems, short stories, and novels. He is probably best known for his crime novels, including a series featuring Thorn, an unlikely protagonist who supports himself by making fishing lures in Key Largo. "I never intended Thorn to be a series character," Hall told an interviewer in *Mystery Pages.* He added, "I simply wanted to try to get a single novel published." On his own Web site, Hall describes Thorn as "a simple guy, a little grumpy sometimes, who mainly wants to be left alone." But Brewster Milton Robertson, writing in *Publishers Weekly,* acknowledged Thorn as a "rugged man of action [who] is also a poet and philosopher."

Hall introduced Thorn to readers in 1986 with *Under Cover of Day,* then allowed three years to pass before producing a second "Thorn" novel, *Tropical Freeze,* wherein the adventurous fisherman foils a cocaine-smuggling plot. An ensuing tale, *Mean High Tide,* finds Thorn averting ecological disaster while tracking his lover's killer, and a fourth story, *Buzz Cut,* relates Thorn's attempt to thwart a terrorist operation aboard a cruise ship. Mark Donovan, writing in *People Weekly,* concluded that *Buzz Cut* "packs a pretty good jolt," and a *Publishers Weekly* reviewer, assessing a sound recording of the novel, declared that the story serves as "a wickedly nasty slice-em-up thriller." Bill Ott in *Booklist* wrote that *Buzz Cut* possessed "the gut-level narrative drive of a disaster novel," and another *Publishers Weekly* critic affirmed that "this thriller will slice readers' sleep into slivers."

In *Red Sky at Night,* the next "Thorn" thriller, the resourceful sleuth discovers that a childhood friend is using maimed war veterans as unwitting subjects in bizarre scientific experiments. A *Publishers Weekly* critic claimed that *Red Sky at Night* amounted to an "awkward outing," but *Booklist* reviewer Bill Ott called it "popular fiction at its absolute best," and *People Weekly* reviewer Mark Donovan hailed it as a "readers' delight."

Hall's other crime thrillers include *Body Language,* in which Alexandra Rafferty, a forensic photographer with the Miami police, contends with horrific childhood memories and deranged acquaintances, including her senile father, while embroiled in a case involving a serial killer. In *Library Journal,* Francine Fialkoff deemed *Body Language* a "high-priority purchase for thriller fans," while Michael Adams, reviewing a sound recording of the novel, compared Hall unfavorably to Elmore Leonard and Carl Hiaasen but acknowledged the tale's "colorful dialogue." Another reviewer, writing in *Publishers Weekly,* alleged that the novel contains "distracting, superfluous plot threads." Even that reviewer, however, noted Hall's "poetic imagery in the landscapes and love scenes." *Booklist* reviewer Bill Ott wrote, "Only a too-pat romantic subplot and a slightly too happy ending keep this thriller from perfection."

Another crime novel, *Rough Draft,* concerns Miami police officer Hannah Keller, who becomes the bait in a government scheme to nab a homicidal banker responsible for the murder of Keller's parents. A *Publishers Weekly* reviewer, hailing Hall as an "expert creator of grotesque villains and fast action," declared that he "raises the crossbar with his sensitive insights into the human condition." Another enthusiast, Bill Ott, wrote in *Booklist* that Hall succeeds in "ratcheting tension while also dispensing fascinating information."

Hall's other writings include three poetry collections, *The Lady from the Dark Green Hills, The Mating Reflex,* and *False Statements,* and a short-story collection, *Paper Products.*

BIOGRAPHICAL AND CRITICAL SOURCES:

PERIODICALS

Booklist, April 15, 1996, Bill Ott, review of *Buzz Cut,* p. 1394; May 15, 1997, Bill Ott, review of *Red Sky at Night,* p. 1540; July, 1998, Bill Ott, review of *Body Language,* p. 1829; November 15, 1999, Bill Ott, review of *Rough Draft,* p. 579.

Library Journal, July, 1998, Francine Fialkoff, review of *Body Language,* p. 136; January, 1999, Michael Adams, review of *Body Language,* p. 184.

People Weekly, September 2, 1996, Mark Donavan, review of *Buzz Cut,* pp. 32-33; July 28, 1997, Mark Donavan, review of *Red Sky at Night,* p. 33.

Publishers Weekly, May 13, 1996, review of *Buzz Cut,* p. 53; July 1, 1996, review of *Buzzcut,* pp. 30-31; July 8, 1996, Brewster Milton Robertson, "James W. Hall: Serious South Florida Thrillers," pp. 62-63; May 26, 1997, review of *Red Sky at Night,* p. 63; July 13, 1998, review of *Body Language,* p. 62; November 22, 1999, review of *Rough Draft,* p. 43.

OTHER

James W. Hall Web site, http://www.jameswhall.com (April 6, 2001).
Mystery Pages, http://www.mysterypages.com (April 6, 2001), Paul A. Bergin, "Hard Boiled."*

*   *   *

HAMILTON, Masha

PERSONAL: Female; married David Orr; children: three.

ADDRESSES: Home—3961 North Jimsonweed Drive, Tucson, AZ 85749. *E-mail*—mashahamil@aol.com.

CAREER: Worked for ten years for Associated Press as a foreign correspondent in the Middle East. Later worked as a Moscow correspondent for the *Los Angeles Times.* Also reported for *NBC/Mutual Radio.*

WRITINGS:

Staircase of a Thousand Steps: A Novel, BlueHen Books (New York, NY), 2001.

Also contributing writer for the *Seattle Times.* Author of syndicated column, "Postcards from Moscow."

WORK IN PROGRESS: Working on a novel set in the Middle East with a journalist as the protagonist. *Lust of the Eye* is the working title.

SIDELIGHTS: Masha Hamilton started her writing career as a foreign correspondent for the Associated Press. When asked, in an interview posted on the Web site of Penguin Putnam, Inc., what attracted her to becoming a foreign correspondent, Hamilton replied that she wanted to "scrub my eyes clean." She believed she could do that by living in a foreign, or "exotic," environment, where she could experience a totally different lifestyle from her own. "I wanted to inhale unfamiliar scents," she stated. "I wanted new languages to sink into my head and roll off my tongue." She also revealed that both the Middle East and Russia represented, to her, places of "passion and energy," places in the midst of powerful transitions and "times of crisis."

A sampling of Hamilton's articles can be found in past issues of the *Seattle Times.* In the late 1980s, Hamilton wrote about the struggle in the Middle East, the *intefadeh,* or peace process, there, and the partial withdrawal of Israeli troops from Lebanon. She often reported from the Gaza Strip, noting the mounting tensions within the Muslim population and the general surrender to death accepted as the only means of freedom. Such sentiments can be read in her article for the *Times,* "Islam Seen as Key Factor in Gaza." "A sharp rise of Islamic fervor," Hamilton wrote in 1987, "has fueled clashes this month in the overcrowded seaside strip that Israel captured from Egypt in the 1967 Six Day War." What she found most threatening was the "mushrooming fundamentalism" that made Arab youths "fearless in the face of Israeli gunfire."

In 1988 Hamilton sent home another article for the *Times,* "Tactics in Arab-Israeli Unrest—Arabs Say Soldiers Have Hurt Those Not Protesting," in which she reported that "about 600 Palestinians" in Gaza City alone had been beaten by Israeli soldiers. Twenty percent of those beaten had been women. All of the victims claimed that they had not been actively protesting against the Israelis.

The following year, Hamilton moved to Moscow. From there, she sent home reports that covered such diverse topics as women's rights in Russia and political fears of the then-newly Westernized form of presidency. However, it was while in Moscow that Hamilton decided to give up her career as a journalist to write fiction. She reveals in the interview at Penguin Putnam that she was afraid that if she did not soon write about the characters filling her head, she would lose their stories. Her husband encouraged her to quit her job and focus on writing fiction, which she did.

Hamilton published her first novel, *Staircase of a Thousand Steps,* in 2001. The setting of the novel is a remote Jordanian desert village in the Middle East, which Hamilton has named Ein Fadr (a fictional place). The story is peopled with many interesting characters, including a young girl, Jammana, who learns of old family secrets through her clairvoyant abilities and who must unravel her past and weave the details back together in their proper places. There is also the midwife, Faridah, who has the healing gift of touch, but who finds the traditions that confine her to prescribed concepts of a woman's role in life distasteful. Harif, an older man who raises sheep, is a storyteller, who lives somewhat outside the customs of his village. Harif also has the gift of vision, but unlike his granddaughter, Jammana, Harif sees into the future. Jammana struggles to find her way between the world of her grandfather and the encroachment of modern customs, finding herself equally attracted to both.

The timeframe of the novel is the 1960s, before the Six-Day War with Israel. It is a time of mystery and change, a pivotal moment where past and future are about to clash. This tension "Hamilton movingly and beautifully expresses throughout this superior debut," wrote Faye A. Chadwell in a review for *Library Journal.* Bonnie Johnston, writing for *Booklist,* also found the prose in Hamilton's book "elegant." Johnston added that Hamilton's "subtle interweaving of the mystical and the mundane makes the novel delightfully compelling." Closely reflecting Johnston's words, a review for *Publishers Weekly* called Hamilton "a natural storyteller: she weaves past and present artfully together."

BIOGRAPHICAL AND CRITICAL SOURCES:

PERIODICALS

Booklist, April 15, 2001, Bonnie Johnston, review of *Staircase of a Thousand Steps,* p. 1534.
Library Journal, April 15, 2001, Faye A. Chadwell, review of *Staircase of a Thousand Steps,* p. 132.
Publishers Weekly, April 2, 2001, review of *Staircase of a Thousand Steps,* p. 37.
Seattle Times, December 20, 1987, "Islam Seen as Key Factor in Gaza," p. A20; January 27, 1988, "Tactics in Arab-Israeli Unrest—Arabs Say Soldiers Have Hurt Those Not Protesting," p. A3; March 12, 1989, "Overworked Soviet Women Seeing Red over Unequal Roles," p. A12; March 12, 1990, "Change in USSR.—Some Soviets Fear U.S.-Style Leader without the Checks," p. A3.

OTHER

Boulder Weekly, http://www.boulderweekly.com/ Lynn T. Theodose, review of *Staircase of a Thousand Steps,* (October 7, 2001).

Newsletter of Society of Southwestern Authors, http://www.azstarnet.com/ (June/July 2001).
Penguin Putnam, Inc., Web site, http://www.penguinputnam.com (October 7, 2001), "Reading Group Guides: *Staircase of a Thousand Steps.*"*

*   *   *

HANCOCKS, David 1941-

PERSONAL: Born May 5, 1941, Kinver, Worcestershire, England; son of Cecil, and Eva (Morgan) Hancocks; married Anthea Page Cook, February 16, 1982; children: Samuel Morgan, Thomas David, Morgan Page. *Education:* University of Bath, B.S. (with honors), 1966, B.S (architecture; with honors), 1968. *Hobbies and other interests:* Photography, gardening, music.

ADDRESSES: Home—1 Queensberry St., Carlton, Victoria 3052, Australia. *Office*—P.O. Box 460, Werribee, Victoria 3030, Australia. *Agent*—Spieler Agency, New York, NY. *E-mail*—dhancocks@zoo.org.au.

CAREER: Architect, Zoological Society of London, 1968-69; West of England Zoological Society, Bristol, 1970-72; Design coordinator, Woodland Park Zoological Gardens, Seattle, WA, 1973-74, director, 1975-84; private practice design, Melbourne, Australia, 1985-89; executive director, Arizona Sonora Desert Museum, 1989-97; consultant, Singapore Zoological Gardens, 1979-89, and Zoological Society, Victoria, Australia, 1986-89; director, Victoria's Open Range Zoo, Werribee, Australia, 1998—. Member of School of Renewable Natural Resources, University of Arizona, 1975; member of board of directors, Allied Arts of Seattle, 1976-85.

MEMBER: Royal Institute of British Architects (associate).

AWARDS, HONORS: Writing Award from the State of Washington Governor, 1974, for *Master Builder of the Animal World*; Distinguished Service Award, American Society of Landscape Architects, 1975; Outstanding Public Employee of the Year Award, Seattle Municipal League, 1983; WPZS Medal, Woodland Park Zoological Society, 1991; Book of the Year Award finalist, *Los Angeles Times,* 2001.

WRITINGS:

Animals and Architecture, H. Evelyn (London, England), 1971.
Master Builders of the Animal World, Harper and Row (New York, NY), 1973.
A Different Nature: The Paradoxical World of Zoos and Their Uncertain Future, University of California Press (Berkeley, CA), 2001.

WORK IN PROGRESS: In and out of the Zoo: Stories from My Career as a Zoo Architect and Zoo Director.

SIDELIGHTS: "To help save all wildlife, to work toward a healthier planet, to encourage a more sensitive populace: these are the goals of new zoos." This is David Hancocks's credo. Hancocks, for more than thirty years a zoo architect and director, has written extensively on the history of zoos and how we have related throughout history to captive animals. His concern with the plight of zoo animals began when he was a university student. Visiting the London Zoo, he remembers looking into the intelligent eyes of a captive gorilla. "I walked away feeling confused and depressed."

In his second book, *Master Builders of the Animal World,* Hancocks shows how animals build for themselves. The book provides a history of a wide spectrum of architecture. Dens of mammals, nests of various insects and birds, and even constructed shelter made by reptiles and fish are described, showing the architectural features involved. In *Animals and Architecture* Hancocks shows how the domestication of animals and their uses by man have led to specialized architectural types. In his discussion of the architecture of farm buildings, such as stables and menageries, Hancocks segues into the principal message of the book. It is Hancocks's fervent hope that zoo directors and architects can learn from animals themselves how to best duplicate, or simulate, the animals' natural habitats, life styles, and feeding and reproductive habits.

Published in 2001, *A Different Nature: The Paradoxical World of Zoos and Their Uncertain Future* continues Hancocks's sociological retracing back to Paleolithic times when "wild animal ownership bestowed prestige and power." Hancocks speculates that the first zoo was in Sumeria 4,300 years ago. Although some zoos, such as the Bronx Zoo, the Emmen Zoo in Holland, Arizona-Sonora Desert Museum, and Seattle's Woodland Park Zoo receive his praise, he stridently criticizes many zoo practices such as "disjointed exhibits" and cramped conditions. "My proposal is to uninvent zoos as we know them and to create a new type of institution, one that . . . engenders respect for all animals and that interprets a holistic view of Nature." Hancocks believes that the primary purpose of zoos is not to provide entertainment, but to educate visitors about animals and encourage preservation of their natural habitats. He argues that a zoo's focus should be upon whole ecosystems, particularly local systems.

"Visitors to the San Diego Zoo can hear messages about the threat of tiger extinction and nod their head in concern, then drive north to the San Diego Wild Animal park and hear messages about the depredation of elephants by poaching," he writes. Between the two institutions, the visitors will have traveled "through a region in which virtually every square inch of native chaparral has been destroyed." Although California has some of the most endangered ecosystems on Earth, no one mentions it. "It is just too uncomfortably close to home, an emphasis on exotic species and faraway habitats, such as the Amazon rain forest, serve to distract us from the problems of our own ecosystems, which are just as fragile. How many U.S. citizens know that North American hardwood forests are in danger of disappearing?" he asks. "We live today in a paradox: many children know more about exotic species like dolphins and pandas than their grandparents could have imagined, but next to nothing about their local flora and fauna." Hancocks believes important roles for today's zoos should be to fight for conservation and to provide education about local ecosystems.

William Conway, director of the Wildlife Conservation Society and the Bronx Zoo, writing about *A Different Nature* in *Wildlife Conservations* comments that "Giraffes, elephants, gorillas, snakes, and toucans respond poorly to the usual conventions of human architecture. Zoo architects usually respond no less poorly to the needs of animals. David Hancocks draws on a lifetime of experience working as a zoo director and zoo architect to explore the dilemma and offers a compelling vision for the future. This is an important book for those interested in conservation as well as for zoo and museum buffs." Reviewing the same book for

LA Weekly, Margaret Werthheim agreed that "[Hancocks] makes his case with convincing passion and unusually elegant prose. Given that declining biodiversity is probably the greatest of all the environmental problems we face, Hancocks's book has a special urgency. This is not a cry for the wild, but a call to arms."

BIOGRAPHICAL AND CRITICAL SOURCES:

BOOKS

Hancocks, David, *A Different Nature: The Paradoxical World of Zoos and Their Uncertain Future,* University of California Press (Berkeley, CA), 2001.
Hancocks, David, *Animals and Architecture,* H. Evelyn (London, England), 1971.
Hancocks, David, *Master Builders of the Animal World,* Harper and Row (New York, NY), 1973.

PERIODICALS

Booklist, May 15, 2001, review of *A Different Nature: The Paradoxical World of Zoos and Their Uncertain Future,* p. 1716.
Choice, April, 1974, review of *Master Builders of the Animal World,* p. 281.
Library Journal, November, 1973, Anne Luxner, review of *Master Builders of the Animal World,* p. 3275; September, 1971, David Gebhard, review of *Animals and Architecture,* p. 2626.
London Review of Books, June 21, 2001, Colin Tudge, review of *A Different Nature,* p. 38.
Publishers Weekly, May 7, 2001, review of *A Different Nature,* p. 233.
Science Books and Films, September, 1971, Clarence A. Porter, review of *Animals and Architecture,* p. 169.
Scientific American, Phillip and Phyllis Morrow, review of *Animals and Architecture,* p. 169.
Times Literary Supplement, August 27, 1971, review of *Animals and Architecture,* p. 1938.
Washington Post Book World, September 23, 1973, S.K. Oberbeck, review of *Master Builders of the Animal World,* p. 5.
Wildlife Conservation, August, 2001, William Conway, review of *A Different Nature,* p. 68.

OTHER

LA Weekly, http://laweekly.com/ (December 2, 2001), "How the Leopard Got Its Bars."
University of California Press Online, http://www.ucpress.org/ (December 12, 2001), review of *A Different Nature.*

*   *   *

HANSON, Curtis (Lee) 1945-

PERSONAL: Born March 24, 1945, in Los Angeles, CA (some sources cite Reno, NV).

ADDRESSES: Agent—United Talent Agency, 9560 Wilshire Blvd., Suite 500, Beverly Hills, CA 90212.

CAREER: Screenwriter, director, and producer. Editor and photographer for *Cinema* magazine. University of California, Los Angeles, chairperson of Film and Television Archive, 1999—.

Film work includes (producer and director) *Sweet Kill,* New World Pictures, 1973; (executive producer and director) *The Little Dragons,* Aurora, 1977; (associate producer) *The Silent Partner,* EMC, 1978; (director) *Losin' It,* Embassy, 1983; (director) *The Bedroom Window,* DEG, 1987; (director) *Bad Influence,* Triumph Releasing, 1990; (director) *The Hand That Rocks the Cradle,* Buena Vista, 1992; (director) *The River Wild,* Universal, 1994; (producer and director) *L.A. Confidential,* Warner Bros., 1997; (producer and director) *Wonder Boys,* Paramount, 2000; and (producer and director) *8 Mile,* 2002. Film appearances include *The Goonies,* Warner Bros., 1985, and *Adaptation,* 2002.

Television work includes (director) *The Children of Times Square,* ABC, 1986, and *Greg the Bunny,* 2002. Television appearances include *Killing at Hell's Gate,* 1981; *The Last Innocent Man,* 1987; *The Director's Vision: Hollywood's Best Discuss Their Craft,* Sundance Channel, 1998; *Hitchcock: Shadow of a Genius,* Turner Classic, 1999; and *Clint Eastwood: Out of the Shadows,* 2000.

AWARDS, HONORS: Audience Award and Grand Prix, Cognac Festival du Film Policier, 1992, for *The Hand That Rocks the Cradle;* shared (with Brian Helgeland)

Academy Award, Society of Texas Film Critics Award, Writers Guild of America Award, Broadcast Film Critics Association Award, and Southeastern Film Critics Association Award, all for best adapted screenplay, all 1997, all for *L.A. Confidential;* shared (with Helgeland) Bodil Award, Boston Society of Film Critics Award, Florida Film Critics Circle Award, Golden Satellite Award, Los Angeles Film Critics Association Award, National Society of Film Critics Award, New York Film Critics Circle Award, Chicago Film Critics Association Award, Online Film Critics Society Award, and USC Scripter Award, all for best screenplay, all 1997, all for *L.A. Confidential;* shared (with Arnon Milchan and Michael G. Nathanson) Edgar Allan Poe Award and Metro Media Award, Toronto International Film Festival, all for best motion picture, all 1997, all for *L.A. Confidential;* Boston Society of Film Critics Award, Florida Film Critics Circle Award, Los Angeles Film Critics Association Award, National Board of Review Award, National Society of Film Critics Award, New York Film Critics Circle Award, David Lean Award for Direction, British Academy of Film and Television Arts, Chicago Film Critics Association Award, ALFS Award, London Critics Circle, and Southeastern Film Critics Association Award, all for best director, all 1997, all for *L.A. Confidential;* Australian Film Institute Award for best foreign film, and ALFS Award, screenwriter of the year, both for *L.A. Confidential.*

WRITINGS:

The Children of Times Square (television movie script), ABC, 1986.

Former editor of *Cinema.*

SCREENPLAYS

(As Curtis Lee Hanson, with Henry Rosenbaum and Ronald Silkosky) *The Dunwich Horror,* AIP, 1970.
Sweet Kill (also known as *The Arousers* and *A Kiss from Eddie*), New World Pictures, 1973.
The Silent Partner, EMC, 1978.
(With Sam Fuller) *White Dog* (also known as *Trained to Kill*), Paramount, 1982.
(With Sam Hamm and Richard Cletter) *Never Cry Wolf,* Buena Vista, 1983.
The Bedroom Window, DEG, 1987.

(With Brian Helgeland) *L.A. Confidential* (based on the novel by James Ellroy), Warner Bros., published as *L.A. Confidential: The Screenplay,* Warner Books (New York, NY), 1997.

SIDELIGHTS: Curtis Hanson had written half a dozen movies, and directed several more, before he approached *L.A. Confidential* (1997), but though his directorial work in films such as *The River Wild* had been impressive, critics were unprepared for the cinematic tour-de-force that would sweep awards ceremonies throughout the world of film. Perhaps part of the secret to his success with *L.A. Confidential,* which he not only directed but cowrote with Brian Helgeland, is that Hanson had a solid background as a writer, first with *Cinema* magazine, and then, beginning in the early 1970s, for film.

Still, his achievement—and that of his extraordinary cast and crew—in *L.A. Confidential* was so impressive that numerous critics professed to be dumbfounded. Richard Schickel wrote in *Time,* "Try to imagine this: a mainstream American movie, rife with violent and often murderous behavior, yet so densely plotted, so richly peopled, that you can't summarize it in a sentence." The achievement was all the more remarkable because the work from which it was adapted—what Schickel described as "James Ellroy's brutal, bustling novel" by the same name—is not a book that readily invites adaptation. No wonder, then, that Schickel praised Hanson as an "alchemist-director."

The story, as Hanson renders it, is a tale of three very different men, placed together in the gaudy, sinister criminal underworld of Hollywood in the 1950s. All three are policemen, yet their relationship to law, truth, and honor is anything but uncomplicated. At opposite poles are Edmund Exley (Guy Pearce), the bespectacled, do-good cop determined to win promotion and abide by the letter of the law at all times, and Bud White (Russell Crowe), a tough guy who is most articulate with his fists. Between these two extremes is Jack Vincennes (Kevin Spacey), a hail-fellow-well-met who is instantly likeable despite, or rather because of his moral flabbiness. Together with the good-hearted prostitute Lynn Bracken (Kim Basinger), the sleazy gossip columnist Sid Hudgens (Danny DeVito), and the tough Irish police captain Dudley Smith (James Cromwell), the cast of characters could easily have degenerated into cliché. Critics considered it a tribute to numerous talents—not least that of the writer-director Hanson—that it did not.

"It is to the movie's credit," wrote John Simon in *National Review,* "that it works mostly by suggestion." Furthermore, "Everything has a fresh feel to it," including "the seamy operations of the forces of law in all their meanderings; the suddenness with which unconscionable violence strikes; the horrendous shoot-outs that register as more real than standard movie shootouts. The dead here look genuinely dead; more important, the living are genuinely alive in their imperfect, begrimed, vulnerable existences."

Many other reviewers likewise praised *L.A. Confidential* in unqualified terms. For example, Todd McCarthy in *Variety* described it thus: "Drenched in the tawdry glamour of Hollywood in the early 1950s and up to its ears in the delirious corruption of police and city politics, *L.A. Confidential* is an irresistible treat with enough narrative twists and memorable characters for a half-dozen films." Unlike most films, maintained David Ansen in *Newsweek,* with this one "you actually have to pay attention to follow the double-crossing intricacies of the plot. The reward for your work is dark and dirty fun."

BIOGRAPHICAL AND CRITICAL SOURCES:

BOOKS

Contemporary Theatre, Film, and Television, Volume 32, Gale (Detroit, MI), 2000.

PERIODICALS

America, October 18, 1997, Richard A. Blake, review of *L.A. Confidential,* pp. 22-23.
Entertainment Weekly, September 19, 1997, Owen Gleiberman, review of *L.A. Confidential,* p. 54; October 17, 1997, Lisa Schwarzbaum, review of *L.A. Confidential,* p. A65; January 16, 1998, Mark Harris, review of *L.A. Confidential: The Screenplay,* pp. 62-63.
Maclean's, September 22, 1997, Brian D. Johnson, review of *L.A. Confidential,* p. 76.
National Review, October 27, 1997, John Simon, review of *L.A. Confidential,* pp. 56-57.
New Leader, October 6, 1997, Raphael Shargel, review of *L.A. Confidential,* pp. 18-19.

New Statesman, October 31, 1997, John Diamond, review of *L.A. Confidential,* p. 37.
Newsweek, September 22, 1997, David Ansen, review of *L.A. Confidential,* p. 83.
People Weekly, September 29, 1997, Leah Rozen, review of *L.A. Confidential,* p. 19.
Time, September 15, 1997, Richard Schickel, review of *L.A. Confidential,* p. 100.
Variety, May 19, 1997, Todd McCarthy, review of *L.A. Confidential,* pp. 48-49.*

*   *   *

HARDY, Robert (Charles) 1925-

PERSONAL: Born October 29, 1925, in Cheltenham, England; son of Henry Harrison and Jocelyn (maiden name, Dugdale) Hardy; married Elizabeth Fox (marriage ended); married Sally Pearson. *Education:* Attended Magdalen College, Oxford.

ADDRESSES: Agent—Chatto & Linnit, Globe Theatre, Shaftesbury Ave., London W1, England.

CAREER: Actor. Shakespeare Memorial Theatre Company, England, member, 1949. *Mary Rose* Trust, longbow and weapons consultant.

Stage appearances include *Much Ado about Nothing,* Phoenix Theatre, London, 1952; *The River Line,* Lyric Theatre, then Strand Theatre, both London, 1952; *Henry VIII,* Old Vic Theatre, London, 1953; *Hamlet,* Old Vic Theatre, 1954; *Twelfth Night,* Old Vic Theatre, 1954; *Coriolanus,* Old Vic Theatre, 1954; *The Tempest,* Old Vic Theatre, 1954; *Macbeth,* Old Vic Theatre, 1954; *Love's Labour's Lost,* Old Vic Theatre, 1954; *The Taming of the Shrew,* Old Vic Theatre, 1954; *Richard II,* Old Vic Theatre, 1955; *Henry IV, Parts I and II,* Old Vic Theatre, 1955; *A Life in the Sun,* Edinburgh Festival, Edinburgh, Scotland, 1955; *Someone Waiting,* John Golden Theatre, New York City, 1956; *The Caine Mutiny Court Martial,* Hippodrome, London, 1956; *Camino Real,* Phoenix Theatre, 1957; *Four Winds,* Cort Theater, New York City, 1957; *All's Well That Ends Well,* Shakespeare Memorial Theatre Company, Stratford-upon-Avon, England, 1959; *A Midsummer Night's Dream,* Shakespeare Memorial Theatre Company, 1959; *Coriolanus,* Shakespeare Memorial Theatre Company, 1959; *King Lear,* Shakespeare Memorial Theatre Company, 1959; *Rosmerholm,* Comedy Theatre, London, 1960; *The Rehearsal,* Bristol Old Vic Theatre, then Globe Theatre, both London, 1961; *A Severed Head,* Bristol Old Vic Theatre, then Criterion Theatre, London, 1963; *Henry V,* Ravinia Theatre, Illinois, 1964; *Hamlet,* Ravinia Theatre, 1964; *The Constant Couple,* Prospect Productions, New Theatre, 1967; *I've See You Cut Lemons,* Fortune Theatre, London, 1969; and *Habeas Corpus,* Lyric Theatre, 1974. Major tours include *The Captain's Lamp,* 1955.

Film appearances include *Torpedo Run,* Metro-Goldwyn-Mayer, 1958; *The Spy Who Came in from the Cold,* Paramount, 1965; *Berserk,* Columbia, 1967; *How I Won the War,* United Artists, 1967; *Psychomania,* Scotia, 1971; *Demons of the Mind,* Cinemation, 1971; *10 Rillington Place,* Columbia, 1971; *Young Winston,* Columbia, 1972; *Le Silencieux,* 1972; *Night of the Lepus,* Metro-Goldwyn-Mayer, 1972; *Gawain and the Green Knight,* United Artists, 1973; *Yellow Dog,* Akari, 1973; *Dark Places,* Cinerama, 1974; *La Gifle,* Gaumont, 1974; *The Shooting Party,* European Classics, 1984; *Paris by Night,* Cineplex Odeon Films, 1988; *Year of the Comet,* Columbia, 1992; *A Feast at Midnight,* LIVE Entertainment, 1994; *Frankenstein,* TriStar, 1994; *Sense and Sensibility,* Columbia, 1995; *The Tichborne Claimant,* Redbus Film Distribution, 1997; *Mrs. Dalloway,* First Look Pictures Releasing, 1997; *The Barber of Siberia,* Intermedia Film Distribution/Worldwide Distribution, 1998; *An Ideal Husband,* 1998; *Thunderpants,* 2002; *Harry Potter and the Chamber of Secrets,* Warner Bros., 2002; and *The Gathering,* Fine Line/Granada, 2002.

Television movie appearances include *Twelfth Night,* 1957; *The Lady Is a Liar,* 1968; *Son of Man,* 1969; *Getting In,* 1971; *The Gathering Storm,* 1974; *The Secret Agent,* 1975; *Caesar and Claretta,* 1975; *Fothergill,* 1981; *The Zany Adventures of Robin Hood,* CBS, 1984; *Jenny's War,* syndicated, 1985; *The Woman He Loved,* CBS, 1988; *Marcus Welby, M.D.: A Holiday Affair,* NBC, 1988; *All Creatures Great and Small: Brotherly Love,* 1990; *The Master Blackmailer,* 1991; *Nancherrow,* 1999; *Lucky Jim,* 2002; and *The Falklands Play,* 2002. Appearances on TV miniseries include *An Age of Kings,* 1960; *The Spread of the Eagle,* 1963; *Elizabeth R,* 1971; *Shoulder to Shoulder,* 1974; *Edward the King,* 1975; *Winston Churchill: The Wilderness Years,* 1981; *The Far Pavilions,* HBO, 1984; *War and Remembrance,* ABC, 1989; *Gulliver's*

Travels, NBC, 1996; and *The Tenth Kingdom,* NBC, 2000. Appearances on TV series include *The Troubleshooters,* 1966-67 and 1969; *Manhunt,* 1969; *S. to S.,* 1974; *All Creatures Great and Small,* 1977-79; *Hot Metal,* 1986; *The Tenth Kingdom,* 2000; and *Foyle's War,* 2002.

Appearances on episodic television include "The Knight Who Owned Buckskin," *Buckskin,* 1959; "A Memory of Evil," *The Baron,* 1966; "The Desperate Diplomat," *The Saint,* 1968; *The Morecambe and Wise Show,* 1969; "Heart: No Choice for the Donor," *Strange Report,* 1971; "A Lady of Virtue," *The Duchess of Duke Street,* 1976; "To Catch a Thief," *Raffles,* 1977; "The Death of a Heart," *Masterpiece Theatre,* PBS, 1985; "Northanger Abbey," *Masterpiece Theatre,* PBS, 1987; "Death by Misadventure," *Bulman,* 1987; "The Pied Piper of Hamelin," *Long Ago and Far Away,* PBS, 1989; "Richard Burton: In from the Cold," *Masterpiece Theatre,* PBS, 1989; "Sherlock Holmes: The Master Blackmailer," *Mystery! PBS,* 1993; "Dead Man's 11," *Midsomer Murders,* 1993; "Middlemarch," *Masterpiece Theatre,* PBS, 1994; "Legal Systems," *Look at the State We're In!,* 1995; "Bramwell," *Mobil Masterpiece Theatre,* PBS, 1996; *Bramwell II,* 1996; "Twilight of the Gods," *Mystery! PBS,* 1996; and "Abraham," *Testament: The Bible in Animation,* HBO, 1997. Also appeared in "Vision of Crime," *The Veil.* Appearances on TV specials include *Twelfth Night,* BBC, 1980; *Winston Churchill,* PBS, 1986; *The Churchills,* PBS, 1996; *Castle Ghosts of England,* The Learning Channel, 1996; *Castle Ghosts of Wales,* The Learning Channel, 1997; *Castle Ghosts of Scotland,* The Learning Channel, 1997; and *Castle Ghosts of Ireland,* The Learning Channel, 1997.

AWARDS, HONORS: Commander of the Order of the British Empire, for services to acting.

WRITINGS:

Longbow: A Social and Military History, Stephens (Cambridge, England), 1976, reprinted, Bois d'Arc (Goldthwaite, TX), 1993.

Author of the documentary screenplays *Horses in Our Blood, The Longbow,* and *The Picardy Affair.*

SIDELIGHTS: Despite his dozens of movies and TV appearances, veteran English character actor Robert Hardy has remained largely a fixture of British rather than American cinema. Therefore, his most notable film work has been in such British movies as *The Spy Who Came in from the Cold* (1965), *Frankenstein* (1994), and *Sense and Sensibility* (1995). Hardy has also been a significant presence on the small screen, though again primarily in British productions. He appeared in *All Creatures Great and Small* series during the 1970s, and in 1981 earned enormous critical acclaim for his portrayal of the title character in *Winston Churchill: The Wilderness Years.* Thereafter he played Britain's great wartime prime minister in numerous other television miniseries, including *War and Remembrance* (1989). More recently, he has appeared on American television as Professor Illingworth in *The Lost World.*

While playing the lead in a stage production of Shakespeare's *Henry V,* Hardy became intrigued with the longbow. The longbow, though it existed in primitive forms much earlier, proved critical to the victories at Crecy and Agincourt during England's Hundred Years' War with France, a conflict in which Henry—and, on the opposite side and in another century, Joan of Arc—earned distinction. Hardy became such an expert on the longbow that when the sixteenth-century warship *Mary Rose* was recovered near Portsmouth, England, he became a longbow and weapons consultant for the *Mary Rose* trust. This interest also led to his writing *Longbow: A Social and Military History,* of which a reviewer in *Publishers Weekly* wrote, "Hardy's enthusiasm for the longbow, its technology and capability, and his appreciation of fine craftsmanship, are infectious."

BIOGRAPHICAL AND CRITICAL SOURCES:

BOOKS

Contemporary Theatre, Film, and Television, Volume 32, Gale (Detroit, MI), 2000.

PERIODICALS

Publishers Weekly, May 10, 1993, review of *Longbow: A Social and Military History,* pp. 64-65.*

* * *

HARRIS, Sheldon H(oward) 1928-2002

OBITUARY NOTICE—See index for CA sketch: Born August 22, 1928, in Brooklyn, NY; died of a blood infection August 31, 2002, in Los Angeles, CA. Historian, educator, and author. Although his original area of specialization was U.S. labor history, late in his career Harris became a hero in China for work that revealed how during World War II the Japanese conducted biological tests that killed thousands of Chinese civilians. An academic throughout his career, Harris earned his B.A. from Brooklyn College in 1949, his M.A. from Harvard University in 1950, and his Ph.D. from Columbia University in 1958. Teaching briefly at Brooklyn from 1957 to 1958, Harris was an associate professor of social sciences at Southeastern Massachusetts University until 1963. He spent the remainder of his academic career as a history professor at California State University, Northridge, retiring in 1991. Harris did not become involved in his research into wartime China until the early 1980s when, while on a trip to that country, he learned what the Japanese had done there from a Chinese colleague. Investigating the events of the war years, he discovered that over a quarter million people died in China after being deliberately infected with diseases ranging from cholera and typhoid to anthrax and bubonic plague. He also learned that the U.S. government knew about the research and had covered it up in order to protect the Japanese scientists who were providing Americans with their scientific data on the project. Harris published his findings in his 1994 book *Factories of Death: Japanese Biological Warfare, 1932-1945.* Gratifyingly, four days before his death Japanese officials admitted to their wartime crimes. In addition to *Factories of Death,* Harris was also the author of *Paul Cuffe and the African Return* (1972), *President Johnson's Decision to Intervene in Vietnam* (1972), and *Prohibition* (1973).

OBITUARIES AND OTHER SOURCES:

BOOKS

Writers Directory, 12th edition, St. James Press (Detroit, MI), 1996.

PERIODICALS

Chicago Tribune, September 5, 2002, section 2, p. 9.
Los Angeles Times, September 6, 2002, p. B13.
New York Times, September 4, 2002, p. A20.
Washington Post, September 7, 2002, p. B7.

HARTLEY, Mariette 1940-

PERSONAL: Born Mary Loretta Hartley, June 21, 1940, in New York, NY (some sources cite Weston, CT); daughter of Paul Hembree (an account executive) and Mary Ickes (a saleswoman and manager; maiden name, Watson) Hartley; married John Seventa, 1960 (divorced, 1962); married Patrick Francois Boyriven (a producer), August 13, 1978 (some sources cite 1974; divorced, 1996); children: (second marriage) Sean Paul, Julienne.

ADDRESSES: Agent—Don Buchwald and Associates, 6500 Wilshire Blvd., Suite 2200, Los Angeles, CA 90048.

CAREER: Actress, television journalist.

Television series appearances include *Peyton Place,* ABC, 1965-66; *The Hero,* NBC, 1966-67; *Goodnight, Beantown,* CBS, 1983-84; *The Morning Program,* CBS, 1986-87; *Wild about Animals,* syndicated, 1998; *To Have and to Hold,* CBS, 1998. Also guest host of *Good Morning, America,* ABC. Appearances on TV miniseries include *Passion and Paradise,* ABC, 1989, and *Heaven and Hell: North and South, Book III,* ABC, 1994. Appearances on TV movies include *Sandcastles,* 1972; *The Mystery in Dracula's Castle,* 1973; *Genesis II,* 1973; *The Killer Who Wouldn't Die,* 1976; *The Last Hurrah,* 1977; *Stone,* 1979; *The Love Tapes,* 1980; *The Secret War of Jackie's Girls,* 1980; *No Place to Hide,* 1981; *M.A.D.D.: Mothers against Drunk Drivers,* 1982; *Drop-out Father,* 1982; *Silence of the Heart,* CBS, 1984; *To Love, Honor, and Arrest,* ABC, 1986; *One Terrific Guy,* 1986; *My Two Loves,* 1986; *Murder C.O.D.,* NBC, 1990; *Diagnosis of Murder,* CBS, 1992; *The House on Sycamore Street,* CBS, 1992; *Child of Rage,* CBS, 1992; *Perry Mason: The Case of the Telltale Talk Show Host,* NBC, 1993; *Falling from the Sky: Flight 174,* ABC, 1995.

Appearances on episodic television include *Today,* 1952; *Gunsmoke,* CBS, 1962; "A Burying for Rosey," *The Legend of Jesse James,* 1962; "For I Will Plait Thy Hair with Gold," *Ben Casey,* 1963; "Cotter's Girl," *Gunsmoke,* CBS, 1963; "The Long Morrow," *The Twilight Zone,* 1964; "The Drifter," *The Virginian,* 1964; "Felicity's Springs," *The Virginian,* 1964; "Big Man, Big Target," *Gunsmoke,* CBS, 1964; "Right Is the Fourth R," *Bonanza,* 1965; "The Survivors," *Bonanza,* 1968; "Big Jessie," *Cimarron Strip,* 1968; "Is There Any Man Here?," *Bonanza,* 1969; "All Our Yesterdays," *Star Trek,* 1969; "The Impersonator," *The F.B.I.,* 1970; "Phoenix," *Gunsmoke,* CBS, 1971; "The Armageddon Contract," *Cade's County,* 1971; "The Iron Butterfly," *Bonanza,* 1971; *Ghost Story,* 1972; "The Judgement," *Gunsmoke,* CBS, 1972; "Shield of Honor," *The Streets of San Francisco,* 1973; "Have You Met Miss Dietz?," *The Bob Newhart Show,* 1973; "The Double Play," *The F.B.I.,* 1973; "Zero," *Emergency!,* 1973; "Snatches of a Crazy Song," *Owen Marshall: Counselor at Law,* 1973; "Cry Help!," *The Streets of San Francisco,* 1974; "The Iron Blood of Courage," *Gunsmoke,* CBS, 1974; "For My Lady," *Little House on the Prairie,* 1976; "Shanklin," *The Quest,* 1976; *The Oregon Trail,* 1977; "Futurepast," *Logan's Run,* 1978; "Married," *The Incredible Hulk,* CBS, 1978; "Paradise Cove," *The Rockford Files,* 1979; "Inga," *M*A*S*H,* CBS, 1979; *The Big Show,* 1980; *The Comedy Zone,* 1984; *WIOU,* CBS, 1990; "Night of the Coyote," *Murder, She Wrote,* CBS, 1992; "Caroline and the Twenty-Eight-Pound Walleye," *Caroline in the City,* NBC, 1996; *Animal Planet,* 1997; "O'er the Ramparts We Watched," *Twice in a Lifetime,* PAX, 1999.

Appearances on TV specials include *The African Queen,* 1977; *The Halloween That Almost Wasn't,* 1979; *The Second Time Around,* 1979; *Circus of the Stars IV,* 1979; *A Rainy Day,* 1981; *Blockheads,* 1982; *Small World,* 1982; *Television's Greatest Commercials,* 1982-1983; "Funny Girl," *Broadway Sings: The Music of Jule Styne,* PBS, 1987; *The CBS All-American Thanksgiving Parade,* CBS, 1990; *Guiding Light: The Primetime Special,* CBS, 1992; *Untold Stories: The Search for Amelia Earhart,* syndicated, 1992; *What about Me? I'm Only Three!,* CBS, 1992; *The Wild West,* syndicated, 1993; *The Seventh Annual Genesis Awards,* 1993; *The Ninth Annual Genesis Awards,* 1995; *Bill Bixby: The E! True Hollywood Story,* E! Entertainment Television, 1999; *James Garner: A Maverick Spirit,* Arts and Entertainment, 2000. Other television appearances include *Earth II,* 1971; *Columbo: Publish or Perish,* 1974; *Columbo: Try and Catch Me,* 1977; *Bride of the Incredible Hulk,* 1979. Also appeared in *Calloway's Climb.*

Film appearances include *Ride the High Country,* 1962; *Drums of Africa,* 1963; *Marnie,* 1964; *Ma-*

rooned, Columbia, 1969; *Barquero,* 1970; *The Return of Count Yorga,* 1971; *Skyjacked,* Metro-Goldwyn-Mayer, 1972; *The Magnificent Seven Ride!,* 1972; *Mystery in Dracula's Castle,* 1972; *Nightmare at 43 Hillcrest,* 1974; *Improper Channels,* 1979; *O'Hara's Wife,* 1982; *1969,* 1988; *Encino Man,* 1992; *Snitch,* Cargo Films, 1996; *Kismet,* 1998; *Baggage,* 1999.

Stage appearances include *A Winter's Tale,* American Shakespeare Festival, Stratford, CT, 1956-57; *Measure for Measure,* New York Shakespeare Festival in the Park, 1958-59; *The Merchant of Venice,* Goodman Theatre, Chicago, IL, 1959; *Antigone,* Theatre Group, University of California, Los Angeles, 1961-62; *The Miser,* Mark Taper Forum, Los Angeles, 1968; *Put Them All Together,* McCarter Theatre, Princeton, NJ, 1978, then Coronet Theatre, Los Angeles, 1982; *Detective Story,* Ahmanson Theatre, Los Angeles, 1984; *Delacorte Theatre,* New York City, 1988; *The Sisters Rosensweig,* Schubert Performing Arts Center, New Haven, CT, then James A. Doolittle Theatre, Hollywood, CA, both 1994; *The Trojan Woman,* CBS Studio Center, Los Angeles, 1995; *Sylvia,* Manhattan Theatre Club, New York City, 1995; *Deathtrap,* Palace Theatre, Columbus, OH, 1996. Major tours include *A Midsummer Night's Dream,* American Shakespeare Festival tour, 1959-60, and *A Winter's Tale,* American Shakespeare Festival tour, 1959-60.

Recordings include the videos *Women: Coming out of the Shadows,* 1993 and *Mine Eyes Have Seen the Glory,* 1996; and the album *Breaking the Silence,* 1990.

WRITINGS:

(With Anne Commire) *Breaking the Silence,* G. P. Putnam's Sons (New York, NY), 1990.

SIDELIGHTS: To Americans who are old enough to remember television from the late 1970s, the name "Mariette Hartley" probably conjures one image more than any other: the redheaded woman who paired with James Garner—many people mistakenly believed the two were married—in a witty series of Polaroid commercials. Yet Hartley has also appeared in numerous films and television shows, and the fact that those commercials remain so memorable is a tribute to her ability as an actress, and to the lively persona she projects.

According to Janine Gressel of the *Seattle Times,* Hartleey's "'sassy'" persona also characterizes the autobiography she wrote in 1990. Yet Gressel noted, "The book has the forbidding title *Breaking the Silence* . . . which [Hartley] and her coauthor, Anne Commire, hate," and "is marketed as the story of her life with alcoholic, suicidal parents, and her own similar battles." It was an unfortunate mistake, Gressel maintained, that *Breaking the Silence* would have been presented to the public in such a forbidding light, because "Actually, Hartley's memoirs are funny, bright, lively, a delight to read." Hartley herself was reportedly incensed over the portrayal of the book on *Entertainment Tonight* as "Mariette Hartley's bitter story." Rather than *Breaking the Silence,* she and Commire had used the working title "Breaking the Legacy," because, as Charles Champlin explained in the *Los Angeles Times,* "part of the emotional turmoil for Hartley in her earlier days was the terrible suspicion that suicide was a kind of toxin that she had inherited like the color of her hair."

Her father had killed himself in 1963, while Hartley was in the next room, and her mother had tried unsuccessfully to commit suicide as well. Both were, as Hartley wrote, "blackout, killer drinkers. Dad came to school football games drunk. I'd find Mom passed out in the bushes, scared and hiding." Hartley's mother was the product of an emotionally abusive home of a unique kind: her father was behavioral psychologist John B. Watson, who initiated the now almost universally rejected doctrine that children should not be held or shown physical affection. Not surprisingly, Watson's daughter grew up to be an emotionally aloof mother, and this had its effects on Hartley.

Though she would one day grow up to be a beautiful actress, at fourteen Hartley was gawky, and since she saw that her parents managed to suppress their problems with alcohol, she began drinking herself. She soon became sexually active, and, thinking she was pregnant, attempted suicide. In her late teens, she married a man who beat her, and over the years that followed, her life degenerated into a mire of alcoholism and depression before she joined Alcoholics Anonymous and began her slow but steady recovery from the pain that had characterized her background. Eventually she even reconciled with her mother, who died in 1990.

Despite all these painful notes, *Breaking the Silence* is full of humor, as befits its author, and is studded with anecdotes from Hartley's career as an actress. Genevieve Stuttaford in *Publishers Weekly* described the book as "Sometimes hilarious, sometimes horrifying, always on target."

BIOGRAPHICAL AND CRITICAL SOURCES:

BOOKS

Contemporary Theatre, Film, and Television, Volume 33, Gale (Detroit, MI), 2001.

Hartley, Mariette, with Anne Commire, *Breaking the Silence,* G. P. Putnam's Sons (New York, NY), 1990.

O'Donnell, Gail, and Michele Travolta, *Making It in Hollywood: Behind the Success of Fifty of Today's Favorite Actors, Screenwriters, Producers, and Directors,* Sourcebooks (Napierville, IL), 1995.

PERIODICALS

Ladies' Home Journal, October, 1990, Michael Bandler, "Mariette's Memories" (interview), p. 94.

Library Journal, October 1, 1990, Marcia L. Perry, review of *Breaking the Silence,* p. 96.

Los Angeles Times, October 30, 1990, Charles Champlin, "Mariette Hartley Breaks the Silence on Her Legacy," p. 3.

Publishers Weekly, September 7, 1990, Genevieve Stuttaford, review of *Breaking the Silence,* p. 72; November 2, 1990, review of *Breaking the Silence* (audio version), p. 52.

San Francisco Chronicle, November 8, 1990, Glenn Plaskin, "Hartley Confronted Her Terrors," p. B4.

Seattle Times, October 16, 1990, Janine Gressel, "'Sassy-as-Hell' Hartley Finds Humor in Painful Childhood," p. F3.*

*   *   *

HARTLEY, Mary Loretta
    See HARTLEY, Mariette

*   *   *

HARVEY, Matthea 1973-

PERSONAL: Born September 3, 1973, in Bad Homburg, Germany. *Education:* Harvard University, B.A., 1995; University of Iowa Writers' Workshop, M.F.A.

ADDRESSES: Home—Brooklyn, NY. *Office*—Bomb Magazine, 594 Broadway, Suite 905, New York, NY 10012. *E-mail*—matthea@bombsite.com.

CAREER: Poet. Columbia University Press, New York, NY, assistant editor, 1995-96; *American Letters and Commentary,* poetry editor; *Boston Review,* poetry review editor, 1998-2001; *Bomb* magazine, currently director of marketing and development.

AWARDS, HONORS: New England/New York Award, 1999; co-recipient of Publishing Online poetry competition prize.

WRITINGS:

Pity the Bathtub Its Forced Embrace of the Human Form (poetry), Alice James Books (Farmington, ME), 2000.

Contributor of poetry to periodicals, including *Denver Quarterly, Fence, Grand Street, Prairie Schooner, Paris Review, New Yorker,* and *New Republic.*

WORK IN PROGRESS: A collection of poems titled *Sad Little Breathing Machine.*

SIDELIGHTS: Pity the Bathtub Its Forced Embrace of the Human Form may have a "fussy title," according to a *Publishers Weekly* reviewer, but Matthea Harvey's poetry collection is nevertheless a "distinctive, substantial debut." Her form, said Catherine Daly in *Moria,* tends toward devices such as "syntactic doubling and ampersands" in place of traditional punctuation. *Pity the Bathtub* "provides prose poems which could be lineated, and lineated poems which could be prose," Daly summarized, adding that Harvey "doesn't break rules of punctuation; she doesn't use it in certain poems."

While *Big City Lit* reviewer Diana Manister deemed the collection "unrewarding" in its "pseudo stream-of-consciousness style," Matthew Thornburn of *Working Poet* hailed the book as one that "repeatedly raised my eyebrows and left me grinning, that had me racing ahead to see what's next and, just as often, doubling back to reread what I'd just read."

In an interview with Ruth E. C. Prince for the *Radcliffe Quarterly,* Harvey said that her decision to populate *Pity the Bathtub* with purely fictional characters was deliberate: "I've led a pretty normal life and didn't think it was such a fascinating subject for poems, but I did feel that my way of thinking about the world translated into another character's voice could be interesting." Her advice for aspiring poets: "Read a lot and write a lot, look at the world as if you were an alien or a detective, and use your imagination and let yourself invent what you think is a poem."

BIOGRAPHICAL AND CRITICAL SOURCES:

PERIODICALS

American Poet, spring, 2001, Dean Young, review of *Pity the Bathtub Its Forced Embrace of the Human Form,* p. 55.
Library Journal, February 1, 2001, Ann K. van Buren, review of *Pity the Bathtub Its Forced Embrace of the Human Form,* p. 100.
Publishers Weekly, November 6, 2000, review of *Pity the Bathtub Its Forced Embrace of the Human Form,* p. 85.
Radcliffe Quarterly, spring, 2001, Ruth E. C. Prince, "Imaginary Worlds."
Village Voice Literary Supplement, May, 2001, Karen Volkman, "Dangerous Muse."
Women's Review of Books, May, 2001, Cynthia Hogue, "Poets without Borders," p. 15.

OTHER

Big City Lit, http://www.nycbigcitylit.com/ (March, 2001), Diana Manister, "Trailing Clouds and Flashing Daffodils."
Moria, http://www.moriapoetry.com/ (autumn, 2001), Catherine Daly, review of *Pity the Bathtub Its Forced Embrace of the Human Form.*
Working Poet, http://www.workingpoet.com/ (August, 2001), Matthew Thornburn, review of *Pity the Bathtub Its Forced Embrace of the Human Form.*

*   *   *

HAY, Ashley 1971-

PERSONAL: Born 1971, in Bulli, Australia; daughter of Les (an engineer) and Marilyn (an artist) Hay. *Education:* Charles Stuart University, Australia, B.A. (communications), 1991; University of Technology, Sydney, Australia, B.A. (communications; with honors), 1995. *Politics:* "Left."

ADDRESSES: Home—3/16 Vicar St., Coogee, New South Wales 2034, Australia. *Office*—P.O. Box 177, Potts Point, New South Wales 2011, Australia. *E-mail*—ash_hay@bigpond.com.

CAREER: Independent Monthly, Sydney, Australia, staff writer and chief of staff, 1991-96; University of London, editorial assistant, 1997-98; *Bulletin,* Sydney, Australia, assistant editor, 1999—.

MEMBER: Australian Society of Authors.

AWARDS, HONORS: Open Fiction Award, *Sydney Morning Herald,* 1993; Banjo Paterson National Short Fiction Award, 1994.

WRITINGS:

The Secret: The Strange Marriage of Annabella Milbanke and Lord Byron, Duffy & Snellgrove (Sydney, Australia), 2000.
Gum: The Story of Eucalypts and Their Champions, Duffy & Snellgrove (Sydney, Australia), 2002.

SIDELIGHTS: Ashley Hay, in her debut biography, *The Secret: The Strange Marriage of Annabella Milbanke and Lord Byron,* has added another perspective to the already hundreds of books about Lord Byron's private and literary lives. Having had access to over four hundred boxes of Lady Byron's original correspondence and documents, Hay's biography focuses on the fifty-four-week marriage of Byron and Annabella Milbanke.

From the outset, it seemed a strange match: Byron, the archetypal Romantic, whom Lady Caroline Lamb famously described as "mad, bad and dangerous," marrying Annabella Milbanke, unanimously described as young, conservative and straight-laced, according to Hay, "a sensible, cautious prig of a girl."

Hay's biography explores many of the possible reasons for the marriage and subsequent separation, including allegations of incest between Byron and his half-sister, Augusta Leigh. Hay, however, remains unconvinced of this bit of period gossip and declines to give any pat answers.

Certainly, to the disappointment of many readers, the "secret," is never explained or revealed. Hay, however, brings to life the Regency milieu in which they lived and the complex social class system to which they belonged. As Sally Blakeney commented in *Biography,* "If Jane Austen were alive and working as an investigative reporter, she would write a book like *The Secret.* It is so full of probing, keen observations of human nature and slyly humorous turns of phrase that it makes previous assaults on the Gothic details of Lord Byron's weathered life look like battering rams."

BIOGRAPHICAL AND CRITICAL SOURCES:

BOOKS

Hay, Ashley, *The Secret: The Strange Marriage of Annabella Milbanke and Lord Byron,* Duffy & Snellgrove (Sydney, Australia), 2000.

PERIODICALS

Australian Book Review, August, 2000, Melissa Hart, review of *The Secret: The Strange Marriage of Annabella Milbanke and Lord Byron,* p. 60.
Biography, winter, 2001, Sally Blakeney, review of *The Secret,* p. 318.
Daily Mail (London, England), April 6, 2001, Val Hennessy, review of *The Secret.*
Law Society Journal, February, 2001, Rhonda Payget, review of *The Secret,* p. 93.
Times Literary Supplement (London, England), June, 22, 2001, Catherine Peters, review of *The Secret,* p. 26.

OTHER

Duffy & Snellgrove Web site, http://www.duffyandsnellgrove.com/ (April 12, 2002) biography of Ashley Hay.
Monster.com, http://www.monster.com/ (December 2, 2001), Jade Richardson, interview with Ashley Hay.

*   *   *

HERRERA, Robert A. 1930-

PERSONAL: Born October 31, 1930, in Spring Lake, NJ; son of S. J. (in import and export business) and Olga (a homemaker; maiden name, Coll) Herrera; married Deborah Donnelly (a professor of law), July 10, 1976. *Ethnicity:* "Spanish/Caucasian." *Education:* Attended Universidad Catolica (Havana, Cuba), and University of Madrid, 1976-78; New School for Social Research, M.A., Ph.D.; Seton Hall University, graduate study. *Politics:* "Conservative." *Religion:* Roman Catholic. *Hobbies and other interests:* Politics, literature, history, travel, languages.

ADDRESSES: Home—102 Central Ave. E., Morris Plains, NJ 07950, fax: 973-642-8748. *E-mail*—herrde@shu.edu.

CAREER: Educator and author. Seton Hall University, South Orange, NJ, instructor, 1968-70, assistant professor, 1972, professor of philosophy, 1979-98, professor emeritus, 1998—, consultant to Judeo-Christian Institute, 1981-98; Rutgers University, New Brunswick, NJ, assistant professor of philosophy, 1971-72. Real Colegio Maria Cristina (Spain), professor at summer institute, 1970-75, chancellor, 1974-75; Bernard Baruch College of the City University of New York, lecturer, 1971-72; New School for Social Research (now New School University), lecturer, 1977-79; Consejo Superior de Investigaciones Cientificas (Spain), visiting scholar, 1989-90; lecturer in the United States and abroad. North American Anselm committee, member.

AWARDS, HONORS: Grants from Carnegie Foundation, 1970, Christian Commonwealth Institute, 1974, National Center for Scientific Research (France), 1982, 1989, New Jersey Humanities Council, 1987, Marguerite Ayer Wilbur Foundation, 1993, and Earhart Foundation, 1997.

WRITINGS:

John of the Cross: Introductory Studies, Editorial de Espiritualidad (Madrid, Spain), 1968.
Anselm's Proslogion: An Introduction, University Press of America (Washington, DC), 1979.
Lamps of Fire: Studies in Christian Mysticism, St. Bede's Publications (Petersham, MA), 1986.
(Associate editor and contributor) *Scholars, Savants, and Their Texts: Essays in Honor of Arthur Hyman,* Peter Lang Publishing (New York, NY), 1989.
(Editor and contributor) *Saints, Sovereigns, and Scholars: Essays in Honor of F. D. Wilhelmsen,* Peter Lang Publishing (New York, NY), 1993.

(Editor and contributor) *Mystics of the Book: Themes, Topics, and Typologies,* Peter Lang Publishing (New York, NY), 1993.

Donoso Cortes: Cassandra of the Age, William B. Eerdmans Publishing (Grand Rapids, MI), 1995.

Orestes Brownson: Sign of Contradiction, ISI Press (Wilmington, DE), 1999.

Reasons for Our Rhymes: An Inquiry into the Philosophy of History, Eerdmans (Grand Rapids, MI), 2001.

Contributor to books, including *God in Contemporary Philosophy,* Nauwelaerts (Louvain, Belgium), 1977; *Augustine: Mystic and Mystagogue,* 1994; and *Augustine: Biblical Exegete,* 2000. Contributor of articles and reviews to periodicals, including *Augustiniana, Sophia, Modern Age, Anselm Studies, Continuity, Philosophy Today, Modern Schoolman,* and *World and I.* Contributing editor, *Abraxas,* 1971-72, and *Triumph,* 1973-75; member of editorial board, *Faith and Reason,* 1980—.

WORK IN PROGRESS: Silent Music: The Life and Work of St. John of the Cross, for Eerdmans (Grand Rapids, MI), completion expected 2003.

SIDELIGHTS: Robert A. Herrera told *CA:* "There was a popular song, in the sixties I believe, titled 'Stop the World, I Want to Get Off.' Writing does that. You create a private enclave, a little world of your own, immune to the vicissitudes of real existence. It is a nice escape, as is my interest in philosophy and religion, especially when a third of one's life has been spent in explosive situations—in countries such as Spain, France, and Cuba.

"My style is a pastiche, perhaps a blend of Cardinal Newman, G. K. Chesterton, and the very worst of Ortega. Thought-wise, my first influence was St. Thomas Aquinas, followed by Duns Scotus, then the modern thinkers, with Franz Leibniz in the lead. As far as contemporaries are concerned, I was influenced by Boris Goldenberg, who I met in Havana, and Hans Jonas, my mentor for both graduate degrees. A further influence is the literature of fantasy (Jorge Borges) and religious authors such as the Pseudo-Denis and St. Theresa.

"My writing process is disorderly. After collecting the relevant notes, I sit down at the typewriter and pound out ten or so pages of unadulterated garbage—free

association. Then I proceed to structure, change, and polish until the finished product comes to light. Insofar as my choice of topics is concerned, I believe the only topics worthy of consideration are God, my soul, and human destiny, with a nod to St. Augustine."

BIOGRAPHICAL AND CRITICAL SOURCES:

PERIODICALS

Booklist, June 1, 2001, Steven Schroeder, review of *Reasons for Our Rhymes: An Inquiry into the Philosophy of History,* p. 1830.

*　　*　　*

HEYERDAHL, Thor 1914-2002

OBITUARY NOTICE—See index for *CA* sketch: Born October 6, 1914, in Larvik, Norway; died of brain cancer April 18, 2002, in Colla Michari, Italy. Anthropologist, explorer, and author. Heyerdahl, a zoologist, had many adventures, including at least one that captured the imagination of the world. Heyerdahl attended the University of Øslo as a zoology student, but left for the Polynesian island Fatu Hiva, where he and his wife conducted plant and animal research while living primitively. On Fatu Hiva Heyerdahl began to theorize that there had been contact between South America and Polynesia. He believed that the first settlers of Polynesia could have been South American, not Asian as believed, and they could have traveled there via some type of ocean vessel. The idea was generally scoffed at, with most scholars believing no type of boat could have been created that would have survived the ocean voyage. To prove his point, in 1947 Heyerdahl built a balsa-log raft similar to that which South American people might have designed and used, assembled a crew of five men, and set sail from Peru to an island near Tahiti. It took 101 days to cover the 4,300 miles, but Heyerdahl was successful and the story of his adventure on the "Kon-Tiki" was a hit. The book *Kon-Tiki: Across the Pacific by Raft* sold more than 30 million copies and has been published in 67 languages. A documentary of the trip won an Academy Award in 1951. Heyerdahl agreed that his journey did not necessarily prove his theory, but he considered it a success because it proved the trip could be done. Heyerdahl built other boats out of reeds and other ancient materials and sailed between Morocco and Barbados. He took a trip down the Tigris River to the Persian Gulf to show that Sumerians might have moved between Asia and Arabia. Credited with leading the first real archeological expedition to Easter Island, Heyerdahl received awards from countries around the globe and wrote numerous books, including *Aku-Aku: The Secret of Easter Island, Sea Routes to Polynesia, The Maldive Mystery,* and *Easter Island: The Mystery Solved.* His autobiography, *Green Was the Earth on the Seventh Day,* was published in 1996.

OBITUARIES AND OTHER SOURCES:

PERIODICALS

Los Angeles Times, April 19, 2002, p. A1.
New York Times, April 19, 2002, p. A25.
Times (London, England), April 19, 2002.
Washington Post, April 19, 2002, p. B9.

*   *   *

HILTON, R. H.
    See HILTON, Rodney (Howard)

*   *   *

HILTON, Rodney (Howard) 1916-2002
    (R. H. Hilton)

OBITUARY NOTICE—See index for *CA* sketch: Born November 17, 1916, in Middleton, Lancashire, England; died June 7, 2002, in Birmingham, England. Historian, educator, and author. Hilton taught medieval history at the University Birmingham from a distinctly Marxist perspective. His primary interest was the peasantry and peasant revolts during the Medieval period. His comprehensive survey *Bond Men Made Free: Medieval Peasant Movements and the English Rising of 1381* spans several centuries and supports his argument that class conflict and rebellion against poverty and inequality preceded the modern age and the birth of capitalism by many hundreds of years. Hilton bolstered his thesis by studying the history of

British and European economies through the ledgers and account books of many medieval estates. Another of his books is *Class Conflict and the Crisis of Feudalism: Essays in Medieval Social History.* Hilton wrote extensively on the development of agrarian capitalism, sometimes under the name R. H. Hilton, but he was also interested in the importance of towns and townspeople in the medieval world, where he believed they were an integral and longstanding part of medieval society rather than a herald of the modern age to come. In the 1950s Hilton allied himself with a group of Marxist historians who later established the journal *Past and Present;* he remained a steady contributor to that influential journal from its inception in 1952. At Birmingham, as the head of the university's school of history in the 1960s, Hilton encouraged the scholarly but reportedly boisterous informal seminars from which emerged the graduates sometimes described collectively as "the Birmingham school." In the 1970s Hilton expanded his range of interest to include historical research on such diverse topics as women and ballads and embraced emerging technologies like medieval archaeology that could shed new light on the way medieval people thought and lived. He was elected a fellow of the British Academy in 1977.

OBITUARIES AND OTHER SOURCES:

PERIODICALS

Guardian (London, England), June 10, 2002, obituary by Christopher Dyer, p. 20.
Los Angeles Times, June 20, 2002, p. 13.
New York Times, June 14, 2002, p. C11.
Times (London, England), June 21, 2002.

*   *   *

HOLDEN, Wendy 1965-

PERSONAL: Born 1965, in Yorkshire, England; daughter of a printer and a secretary; married Jon (a political consultant) in 1993. *Education:* Cambridge University, degree in English literature.

ADDRESSES: Agent—c/o Author Mail, Hodder Headline, 338 Euston Rd., London NW13BH, England.

CAREER: Tatler, former deputy editor; has worked for magazines and newspapers including *Harpers & Queen* and *Sunday Times,* London, England; full-time writer and novelist, 1999—.

WRITINGS:

Simply Divine, Plume (New York, NY), 2000.
Bad Heir Day, Plume (New York, NY), 2001.
Farm Fatale, Headline (London, England), 2001.
(With Susan Travers) *Tomorrow to Be Brave,* Free Press (New York, NY), 2001.
Pastures Nouveaux, Plume (New York, NY), 2002.

Contributor to numerous magazines and newspapers, including the London-based *Independent* and *Daily Mail.*

SIDELIGHTS: Journalist Wendy Holden has taken a career turn as a novelist, spinning out outrageous and pun-filled stories about young Brits in search of romantic and professional happiness. Her debut novel *Simply Divine* has been favorably compared to Helen Fielding's best-selling novel *Bridget Jones's Diary* and was itself a best-selling book in England. A second outing, *Bad Heir Day,* follows in the same vein, earning milder reviews. Both works showcase Holden's passion for puns, her interest in the publishing world, and her joy in poking fun at rich, silly, husband-chasing twenty-somethings.

The young protagonist of *Simply Divine,* works for a British magazine. Employed by the women's glossy *Gorgeous,* Jane Bentley is already tired of writing about celebrities when she gets the assignment of serving as ghost writer for the ditzy socialite Champagne D'Vyne. Her life seems to be falling apart at home as well, where her live-in boyfriend is growing distant. Jane is surprised when she finds herself drawn into Champagne's world, where she finds a new love interest. Another plot element involves Jane's friend Tally, who is desperate to save the family mansion from being destroyed.

Reviews of *Simply Divine* stressed its currency and humor. *Booklist*'s Michele Leber called the novel "A delicious romp with a nice satirical edge." A reviewer for *Publishers Weekly* felt that the descriptions of

Champagne's excesses grow tiresome, but nevertheless recommended the book for its "Witty puns, glittery silliness and a down-to-earth heroine [that] provide both style and substance." In an *Entertainment Weekly* review, the critic recommended the "a pun-a-minute read" for a refreshing, vacation diversion.

Reviewers often make note of similarities between *Simply Divine* and *Bridget Jones's Diary. Library Journal*'s Francine Fialkoff deemed *Simply Divine* was "as clever as Bridget . . . [and] a cut above intellectually, though the puns may wear thin and the British allusions may draw blanks." Fialkoff also compared the work to Mary Sheepshanks's *A Price for Everything.* According to a *Kirkus Reviews* writer, Holden probably "benefited and suffered from the [Helen] Fielding influence." This critic admired the novelist's "smart, clear eye" but was annoyed by her penchant for puns and sometimes raw humor. Conversely, Lisa Allardice commented in the *Spectator* that "The gags come thick and fast, mostly hitting the mark." But she also warned that jokes about current events and the Bridget Jones resemblance threaten to make the book "a little last-season."

With *Bad Heir Day* Holden invents a comic drama about a young woman who also hopes to succeed in the publishing world and is looking to trade in her boyfriend for a more rewarding mate. Anna Farrier has a handsome but promiscuous lover named Sebastian, who apparently has been intimate with most of the female guests at a wedding he and Anna attend. Hoping to escape Sebastian while also learning the trade from a best-selling writer, Anna takes a job as a live-in assistant to novelist Cassandra Knight. Her primary responsibility, however, proves to be serving as nanny to Knight's young son. But Anna's fortunes improve when she meets and marries Jamie, a waiter who also happens to be a castle-owning Scottish lord.

Not all reviewers were pleased with *Bad Heir Day*'s puns and dramatic twists. A reviewer for *Publishers Weekly* bemoaned its "awkward puns, shallow characters and predictable plot lines." However, a *Books Magazine* writer called the novel "deliciously witty." And *Booklist*'s Diana Tixier Herald, who was eager to read a follow up to *Simply Divine,* dubbed the story a "deliciously wicked and hugely entertaining romp."

BIOGRAPHICAL AND CRITICAL SOURCES:

PERIODICALS

Booklist, April, 1, 2000, Michele Leber, review of *Simply Divine,* p. 1435; December 1, 2000, Diana Tixier Herald, review of *Bad Heir Day,* p. 698.
Books, summer, 2000, review of *Bad Heir Day,* p. 23.
Entertainment Weekly, June 16, 2000, review of *Simply Divine,* p. 85.
Kirkus Reviews, February 15, 2000, review of *Simply Divine,* p. 194.
Library Journal, February 1, 2000, Francine Fialkoff, review of *Simply Divine,* p. 117.
Publishers Weekly, February 14, 2000, review of *Simply Divine,* p. 173; January 22, 2001, review of *Bad Heir Day,* p. 301.
Spectator, March 20, 1999, Lisa Allardice, review of *Simply Divine,* pp. 70-71.

*   *   *

HOPKINS, (Paul) Jeffrey 1940-

PERSONAL: Born September 30, 1940, in Providence, RI. *Education:* Harvard University, B.A. (English literature; magna cum laude), 1963; University of Wisconsin, Ph.D. (Buddhist studies), 1973.

ADDRESSES: Office—Department of Religious Studies, Box 400126, University of Virginia, Charlottesville, VA 22904-4126. *E-mail*—jhopkins@virginia.edu.

CAREER: Scholar, translator, and writer. University of Virginia, Charlottesville, assistant professor of Tibetan and Buddhist studies, 1973-77, associate professor of Tibetan and Buddhist studies, 1977-89, professor of Tibetan and Buddhist studies, 1989—, director of Center for South Asian Studies, 1979-82, 1985-94. University of British Columbia, distinguished visiting professor of religious studies, 1983-84. University of Hawaii, School of Hawaiian, Asian, and Pacific Studies, Yehan Numata Distinguished Visiting Professor of Buddhist Studies, 1995. Founded programs in Buddhist studies and Tibetan studies and language at the University of Virginia. Institute for Asian Democracy, Washington, DC, and University of Virginia, organizer

and director of Nobel Peace Laureates Conference on Human Rights, Conflict, and Reconciliation, 1998; Institute for Asian Democracy, president, 1994-2000; International Campaign for Tibet, moderator for "Symposium on China's Policies toward Religion in Tibet," 1996; Institute of International Education, served on national screening committee for South Asia for Fulbright and foreign-sponsored awards, 1994; Official interpreter on lecture tours for His Holiness the Dalai Lama in the United States in 1979, 1981, 1984, 1987, 1989, and 1996; in Canada in 1980; in Southeast Asia and Australia in 1982; in Great Britain in 1984; and in Switzerland in 1985.

MEMBER: International Association of Buddhist Studies, Society for Buddhist/Christian Studies, Tibet Society, American Academy of Religion, Ellen Bayard Weedon Foundation (member of board of trustees).

AWARDS, HONORS: Leverett Poetry Prize, Harvard University, 1963; University of Virginia research grant, 1974, 1975; University of Virginia Sesquicentennial Associateship research grant, 1978, 1985, 1992, 1999; American Institute of India Studies research grant, 1975-76, 1979; Fulbright senior fellowship, 1982; Ellen Bayard Weedon travel grant, University of Virginia, 1987, 1988, 1999, 2000; Project for the Development of Proficiency-based Tibetan Language Instructional Materials, grant from Department of Education for International Research and Studies Program, University of Virginia, 1990-92; recognized by the Order of the Rook for contribution to the University of Virginia, 1997; Philip E. Lilienthal Asian Studies Endowment Award, University of California Press, 1997; Fulbright-Hays Faculty Research Abroad fellowship, 2002-03.

WRITINGS:

Meditation on Emptiness, Wisdom Publications (London, England), 1983, second edition, 1999.
The Tantric Distinction, Wisdom Publications (London, England), 1984, second edition, 1999.
Emptiness Yoga, Snow Lion Publications (Ithaca, NY), 1987, second edition, 1996.
(General editor and coauthor, with William Magee and Elizabeth Napper,) *Fluent Tibetan: A proficiency-oriented Learning System, Novice and Intermediate Levels* (textbook and CD-ROM), four volumes, Snow Lion Publications (Ithaca, NY), 1993.

Sex, Orgasm, and the Mind of Clear Light, North Atlantic Books (Berkeley, CA), 1998.

Dynamic Responses to Dzong-ka-ba's "The Essence of Eloquence," University of California Press (Berkeley, CA), Volume 1: *Emptiness in the Mind-only School of Buddhism,* 1999, Volume 2: *Reflections on Reality,* 2001, Volume 3: *Absorption in No External World,* in press.

(General editor and coauthor, with William Magee, Elizabeth Napper, and Alex Chapin) *Fluent Tibetan: The Vocabulary and Dialogues: A Multimedia Supplement with Additional Dialogues* (textbooks and CD-ROM), Snow Lion Publications (Ithaca, NY), 1999.

(Editor) *The Art of Peace: Nobel Peace Laureates Discuss Human Rights, Conflict, and Reconciliation,* Snow Lion Publications (Ithaca, NY), 2000.

Cultivating Compassion: A Buddhist Perspective, Broadway Books (New York, NY), 2001.

Also author of numerous articles, booklets, and professional papers. Serves on editorial board of *Contemporary Buddhism: An Interdisciplinary Journal.*

EDITOR

Tantra in Tibet, edited and annotated by the Dalai Lama and Tsong-ka-pa, Allen & Unwin (London, England), 1978, Snow Lion Publications (Ithaca, NY), 1987.

(With Lati Rimboche) *Death, Intermediate State, and Rebirth in Tibetan Buddhism,* translated by Yang-jen-ga-way-lo-drö, Gabriel Press (Ithaca, NY), 1980.

Kensur Ngawang Lekden, *Compassion in Tibetan Buddhism* (lectures; part of Tsong-ka-pa's commentary on Chandraksrti's *Supplement to the Middle Way*), Snow Lion Publications (Ithaca, NY), 1980.

Yoga of Tibet, translated and annotated from the Tibetan by the Dalai Lama and Tsong-ka-pa with a supplementary analysis, Allen & Unwin (London, England), 1981, published as *Deity Yoga,* Snow Lion Publications (Ithaca, NY), 1987.

Khetsun Sangpo, *Tantric Practice in Nyingma* (lectures), Rider/Hutchinson (London, England), 1982, Snow Lion Publications (Ithaca, NY), 1983.

(With Lati Rinbochay, Locho Rinbochay, and Leah Zahler) Pan-chen So-nam-drak-ba, *Meditative States in Tibetan Buddhism* (lectures), Wisdom Publications (London, England), 1983, second edition, 1997.

Dalai Lama, *Kindness, Clarity, and Insight* (lectures), Snow Lion Publications (Ithaca, NY), 1984.

Kalachakra Tantra: Rite of Initiation for the Stage of Generation, translated by Kay-drup and the Dalai Lama, Wisdom Publications (London, England), 1985, 2nd edition, 1999.

Yeshi Donden, *Health through Balance: An Introduction to Tibetan Medicine* (lectures), Snow Lion Publications (Ithaca, NY), 1986.

The Dalai Lama at Harvard (seminar on Buddhist philosophy), Snow Lion Publications (Ithaca, NY), 1989.

(With Geshe Lhundup Sopa) *Cutting through Appearances: The Practice and Theory of Tibetan Buddhism,* translated and annotated by the Fourth Panchen Lama and Gön-chok-jik-may-wang-bo, Snow Lion Publications (Ithaca, NY), 1990.

Dalai Lama, *The Meaning of Life from a Buddhist Perspective* (lectures), Wisdom Publications (Boston, MA), 1992.

Tibetan Arts of Love, translated by Gedün Chöpel, Snow Lion Publications (Ithaca, NY), 1992.

Geshe Gedun Lodro, *Walking through Walls: A Presentation of Tibetan Meditation* (lectures), Snow Lion Publications (Ithaca, NY), 1992, revised edition published as *Calm Abiding and Special Insight,* 1998.

(With Lati Rimpoche) *Buddhist Advice for Living and Liberation: Nagarjuna's Precious Garland,* translated from the Tibetan and Sanskrit by Nagarjuna and the Tibetan by the Seventh Dalai Lama, Snow Lion Publications (Ithaca, NY), 1998.

Dalai Lama, *How to Practice: The Way to a Meaningful Life,* Simon & Schuster (New York, NY), 2002.

ADAPTATIONS: How to Practice: The Way to a Meaningful Life has been recorded as an audio book, Audio Book Club.

WORK IN PROGRESS: Tantric Techniques, historical and doctrinal analysis delineating the difference between the two main forms of Buddhist practice, sutra and tantra, according to three of the four major orders of Tibetan Buddhism; *Primordial Enlightenment: The Nying-ma View of Luminosity and Emptiness,* presentation of the Nying-ma view of basic reality and primordial enlightenment based on the writings of Ju Mi-pam-gya-tso; *Magical Feats in Yoga Tantra,* the third volume of the *Great Exposition of Secret Mantra; Tibetan-Sanskrit-English Dictionary; Overview of Mantra,* translation, oral commentary, and analysis of Nga-wang-bel-den's *Grounds and Paths of Secret Mantra; Basic Tibetan Grammar: Si-tu's Commentary on "The Thirty,"* the foremost indigenous work on Tibetan grammar.

SIDELIGHTS: Jeffrey Hopkins told *CA:* "Until the early years of the twentieth century, the region of Tibetan Buddhist influence stretched from Kalmuck Mongolian areas near the Volga River (in Europe) through Outer and Inner Mongolia, the Buriat Republic of Siberia, Ladakh, Bhutan, Sikkim, much of Nepal, and areas that earlier in that century were part of Tibet proper but are included in present-day China—all of Ch'ing-hai Province as well as parts of Gansu, Yunnan, and Sichuan Provinces. This Tibetan Buddhist cultural area, now controlled to a great extent by Russia and China, was long a cradle of the dynamic development of Buddhist philosophy and practice. Its language of religious and philosophical discourse was Tibetan, and the large monastic universities of Tibet at its center drew students from the entire region, in some ways like Rome for Catholics.

"Isolated from extensive contact with the rest of the world, Tibetan traditions developed a complex and intellectually rigorous system of philosophical inquiry centered in monastic universities. My specialty, the Ge-luk-ba order of Tibetan Buddhism, became the dominant (but certainly not the only) cultural influence within Tibetan Buddhism in the seventeenth century. With a curriculum based on five great books of the Indian Buddhist tradition, separate colleges within the order—each with its own textbook literature—competed with each other in debate. This rivalry spawned a large body of scholastic commentary, characterized by a vast, synthetic worldview that attempts to form a seamless whole of the many strands of Buddhist philosophy and systems of practice through rigorous analysis seeking to penetrate (or inventively re-create) the intention of the Indian texts that are the roots of the tradition. It continues to this day as a living tradition.

"My ongoing work—which includes research in the Nying-ma-ba, the oldest tradition of Tibetan Buddhism, and the Jo-nang-ba order, the primary philosophical opponents of the founder of Ge-luk-ba—falls into four areas: analytical expositions, annotated translations of central Tibetan texts written by Tibetan and Mongolian scholars, edited translations of oral presentations by Tibetan scholars, and creation of a Tibetan-Sanskrit-English word-list."

Hopkins, who founded the University of Virginia's Tibetan and Buddhist studies program, has written several books on Tibetan and Buddhist themes, including *Cultivating Compassion: A Buddhist Perspective.* In this book the author, stated James R. Kuhlman in *Library Journal,* "clearly details meditative exercises designed to build one upon the other" to develop a sense of compassion, which is a major theme in Buddhist tradition. Crediting Hopkins's use of jargon-free, everyday language, a *Publishers Weekly* reviewer said the book could be of use to both newcomers and seasoned followers of Buddhism.

In 2000 Hopkins's book *The Art of Peace: Nobel Peace Laureates Discuss Human Rights, Conflict, and Reconciliation* was published. This book is the result of a 1998 conference, directed by Hopkins, that brought together eight Nobel laureates, including Archbishop Desmond Tutu, Betty Williams, and Oscar Arias Sanchez, to share their views. Hopkins's question-and-answer format, noted *Booklist*'s Mary Carroll, "may be this volume's unique contribution, clarifying each laureate's approach to the personal change and activism that peace demands."

BIOGRAPHICAL AND CRITICAL SOURCES:

PERIODICALS

Booklist, June 1, 2000, Mary Carroll, review of *The Art of Peace: Nobel Laureates Discuss Human Rights, Conflict, and Reconciliation,* p. 1809.
Houston Chronicle, May 5, 2001, review of *Cultivating Compassion: A Buddhist Perspective,* p. 1.
Library Journal, May 1, 2000, Graham Christian, review of *The Art of Peace,* p. 121; February 1, 2001, James R. Kuhlman, review of *Cultivating Compassion,* p. 101.
Publishers Weekly, June 20, 1986, John Mutter, review of *Health through Balance: An Introduction to Tibetan Medicine,* p. 94; January 29, 2001, review of *Cultivating Compassion,* p. 83.

*   *   *

HOROWITZ, Anthony 1955-

PERSONAL: Born April 5, 1955, in London, England; son of Mark (a lawyer) and Joyce Horowitz; married Jill Green (a television producer), April 15, 1988; children: Nicholas, Cassian. *Education:* Attended Rugby school; University of York, B.A.

ADDRESSES: Office—c/o Greenlit Productions, 13 D'Arblay St., London W1, England. *Agent*—Peters, Fraser & Dunlop, 34-43 Russell St., London WC2B 5HP, England. *E-mail*—ajhorowitz@aol.com.

CAREER: Writer.

WRITINGS:

Enter Frederick K. Bower, Arlington (London, England), 1979.
The Sinister Secret of Frederick K. Bower, illustrated by John Woodgate, Arlington (London, England), 1979.
Misha, the Magician and the Mysterious Amulet, illustrated by John Woodgate, Arlington (London, England), 1981.
The Kingfisher Book of Myths and Legend, illustrated by Frances Mosley, Kingfisher (London, England), 1985, published as *Myths and Mythology,* Little Simon (New York, NY), 1985.
(Adaptor) *Adventurer* (based on a television script by Richard Carpenter), Corgi (London, England), 1986.
(Adaptor with Robin May) Richard Carpenter, *Robin of Sherwood: The Hooded Man* (based on a television play), Puffin (Harmondsworth, England), 1986, published as *The Complete Adventures of Robin of Sherwood,* Puffin (Harmondsworth, England), 1990.
Groosham Grange (also see below), illustrated by Cathy Simpson, Methuen (London, England), 1988.
Starting Out (play), Oberon (London, England), 1990.
Groosham Grange II: The Unholy Grail, Methuen (London, England), 1991, published as *The Unholy Grail: A Tale of Groosham Grange* (also see below), Walker (London, England), 1999.
The Puffin Book of Horror Stories, illustrated by Daniel Payne, Viking (London, England), 1994.
Granny, Walker (London, England), 1994.
(Editor, and contributor) *Death Walks Tonight: Horrifying Stories,* Puffin (New York, NY), 1996.
The Switch, Walker (London, England), 1996.
The Devil and His Boy, Walker (London, England), 1998, Puffin (New York, NY), 2001.
Horowitz Horror: Nine Nasty Stories to Chill You to the Bone, Orchard (London, England), 1999.
Groosham Grange; and, The Unholy Grail: Two Stories in One, Walker (London, England), 2000.

Mindgame (play), Oberon (London, England), 2000.
More Horowitz Horror: Eight Sinister Stories You'll Wish You Never Read, Orchard (London, England), 2000.
The Phone Goes Dead, Orchard (London, England), 2002.
The Night Bus, Orchard (London, England), 2002.
Twist Cottage, Orchard (London, England), 2002.
Burnt, Orchard (London, England), 2002.
Scared, Orchard (London, England), 2002.
Killer Camera, Orchard (London, England), 2002.

Creator of the television series *Midsomer Murders,* writing the episodes "The Killings at Badgers Drift," "Strangler's Wood," "Dead Man's Eleven," and "Judgement Day"; *Murder in Mind,* writing "Teacher," "Echoes," "Mercy," "Torch Song," and other episodes; and *Foyle's War,* writing "The German Woman," "The White Feather," "A Lesson in Murder," and "Eagle Day." Author of "The Last Englishman" and "Menace," for the television series *Heroes & Villains,* British Broadcasting System (BBC) 1; Has also written television screenplays for *Agatha Christie's Poirot, Crime Traveller,* and *The Saint.* Also author of a screenplay based on his novel *Stormbreaker.*

Books by Horowitz have been translated into Spanish, French, German, Danish, Swedish, Hebrew, Japanese, Flemish, Italian, and other languages, and published in Braille editions.

"DIAMOND BROTHERS" SERIES

The Falcon's Malteser (also see below), Grafton (London, England), 1986, published as *Just Ask for Diamond,* Lions (London, England), 1998.
Public Enemy Number Two, Dragon (London, England), 1987.
South by South East, Walker (London, England), 1991.
I Know What You Did Last Wednesday, Walker (London, England), 2002.
The Blurred Man (published with *The Falcon's Malteser*), Walker (London, England), 2002.

"POWER OF FIVE" SERIES

The Devil's Door-Bell, Holt (New York, NY), 1983.
The Night of the Scorpion, Pacer (New York, NY), 1984.
The Silver Citadel, Berkley (New York, NY), 1986.
Day of the Dragon, Methuen (London, England), 1989.

"ALEX RIDER" SERIES; JUVENILE NOVELS

Stormbreaker, Walker (London, England), 2000, Puffin (New York, NY), 2001.
Point Blanc, Walker (London, England), 2001, Philomel (New York, NY), 2002.
Skeleton Key, Walker (London, England), 2002, Philomel (New York, NY), 2003.
Eagle Strike, Walker (London, England), 2003, Philomel (New York, NY), 2004.

ADAPTATIONS: Stormbreaker was adapted for audiocassette, Listening Library, 2001; *Point Break* is also available on audiocassette. *The Gathering* was released as a motion picture by Dimension Films, 2003.

WORK IN PROGRESS: A new "Alex Rider" book, forthcoming in 2004.

SIDELIGHTS: The name Anthony Horowitz is well known to young British fans of horror stories. The editor of *The Puffin Book of Horror Stories,* Horowitz has also chilled youngsters' blood for over a decade with such heart-stopping books as *Death Walks Tonight: Killer Stories* and the novels *Scared* and *Twisted.* More recently, American readers have been introduced to Horowitz through his popular series of books featuring protagonist Alex Rider, the teenage nephew of a former British secret agent who find himself thrust into a series of daring adventures. "There are times when a grade-B adventure is just the ticket for a bored teenager," maintained *Booklist* reviewer Jean Franklin, "especially if it offers plenty of slam-bang action, spying, and high-tech gadgets." According to Franklin, the "Alex Rider" novels *Stormbreaker, Point Blanc,* and *Skeleton Key* provide just that.

Fourteen-year-old Alex Rider makes his fiction debut in *Stormbreaker.* When his guardian, Uncle Ian, is killed in a car wreck, Alex questions whether the police have correctly classified the death as accidental after he finds a number of bullet holes in his uncle's car. After his curiosity over his uncle's death almost gets him killed as well, Alex discovers Ian was an agent for British Intelligence and decides that joining the agency himself might be the best way to stay alive. Leaving prep school for two weeks of intensive training as an MI6 agent, Alex is given a collection of spy gadgets and sent on his first assignment: to infiltrate a training group run by demented inventor Herod Sayles, who is trying to wipe out Great Britain's children by using biological weapons introduced through an in-school computer system known as "Stormbreaker." Noting that "satirical names abound . . . and the hard-boiled language is equally outrageous," a *Publishers Weekly* reviewer nonetheless wrote that "these exaggerations only add to the fun" for readers. *Stormbreaker* was deemed "an excellent choice for reluctant readers" by *School Library Journal* contributor Lynn Bryant due to its "short cliff-hanger chapters and its breathless pace."

In *Point Blanc,* the second installment in the "Alex Rider" series, the teen operative finds himself back in prep school, only this time it is an exclusive prep school called Point Blanc that is located in the French Alps and designed to house the young black sheep in Britain's wealthiest families. Run by a South African named Dr. Grief, the school has surprisingly good luck in making these rich teen troublemakers tow the line. But why? After Alex, now trapped at the school, discovers that brainwashing by Grief is only one of the ways these young men are controlled, he begins to worry about his own safety. Fortunately, as a *Kirkus Reviews* critic assured readers, "Horowitz devises a string of miraculous circumstances that keeps Alex alive and spying throughout." Propelled by hidden passages, frightening medical experiments, and a protagonist who barely stays one step away from death, *Point Blanc* was described by Franklin as a "non-stop thriller" in her *Booklist* review.

Many of Horowitz's books feature young teens who find their mundane lives suddenly turned upside down by an evil force. Such is the case in *The Devil's Door-Bell,* one of Horowitz's first novels for young readers. Published in 1983 as the first segment in the "Power of Five" series, it tells the story of thirteen-year-old Martin Hopkins, whose parents' tragic death forces him into the care of a foster mother named Elvira who takes him to live on her country farm in Yorkshire, England. Upset at being newly orphaned and nervous over Elvira's strange demeanor and intimations that Martin's time will also soon be up, the teen realizes that his suspicions are not just due to stress: Elvira is actually a witch, and her coven is planning something that will cause him harm. A clue left by a murdered friend leads Martin and journalist friend Richard Cole to an ancient circle of stones known as the "Devil's Door-Bell" where Elvira's plans to unleash a malevolent supernatural horror energized by a nearby nuclear power station are revealed. Calling *The Devil's Door-Bell* "a satisfyingly scary book," *School Library Journal* contributor Anne Connor added that Horowitz creates a "chilling atmosphere of horror" despite the novel's "sketchy characterization . . . and . . . unbelievable plot." As the author revealed to *CA,* Horowitz is rewriting *The Devil's Door-Bell* for a new edition.

The "Power of Five" series, which focuses on young people who are fated to do battle with the forces of an ancient evil, continues with *The Night of the Scorpion.* Here Martin and Richard once again find themselves forced to close a portal into hell after a mysterious explosion almost kills a group of Martin's classmates. This time the pair must travel to Peru, where their efforts to battle the demons known as the Old Ones are thwarted by human accomplices who arrest Richard as soon as he gets off the plane. Left alone in a strange country, Martin meets another boy named Pedro, a descendant of the Incas who, like Martin, is destined to do battle with the Old Ones. "Horowitz packs enough suspense and violence into the story to satisfy the most avid thriller fans," according to a *Publishers Weekly* contributor, while *English Journal* reviewer Regina Cowin noted that "the reader is drawn into this story of ancient mysticism just as inexorably as Martin and Pedro are drawn into" their battle against ancient evil. Other "Power of Five" novels include *Day of the Dragon,* published in 1989.

Horowitz's readers are in for even more travels through time in his novel *The Devil and His Boy.* Set in Elizabethan England, this 2000 novel finds a servant boy named Tom Falconer thrust into an alien world after he is ordered to accompany a friend of his master's to London, but his companion is murdered along the way. Befriended by a pickpocket named Moll, Tom joins a troupe of thespians and suddenly finds himself enmeshed in political intrigue and drawn into the illegal activities of some of his new friends. Cast in a play titled "The Devil and His Boy" which is being produced by the secretive Dr. Mobius, Tom winds up in the lap of the Queen of England herself. "Horowitz paints his characters . . . with broad strokes and keeps the melodramatic story moving at a rapid clip," wrote *School Library Journal* contributor Barbara Scotto, dubbing *The Devil and His Boy* a "rol-

licking good tale that is mostly based on historical fact." Ilene Cooper also cited the historical basis of the novel, adding that, "to his credit, [Horowitz] does not try to pretty up Elizabethan life for his audience. . . . dirty and disfigured characters are described in detail."

In addition to series and stand-alone novels, Horowitz has published a number of short-story collections, some as editor and some as sole author. In *Horowitz Horror: Nine Nasty Stories to Chill You to the Bone* and its sequel, *More Horowitz Horror: Eight Sinister Stories You'll Wish You'd Never Read,* readers can consider themselves forewarned. Noting that "none will disappoint readers with an appetite for ghoulish happenings," *School Librarian* reviewer Peter Hollindale praised several stories included in the second of the two books, commending Horowitz's creative use of irony, subtlety, and "creepy and surprising variants on familiar themes."

Writing children's books is only one of several areas where Horowitz has used his writing talents; the other is in authoring series and segments for British television, an activity that has helped Horowitz the novelist imbue his stories with a strong cinematic sense and draw even reluctant readers into his tales of horror and suspense. He also oftentimes includes film references in his books, particularly in his "Diamond Brothers" series about the P.I. brothers who star in such novels as *The Falcon's Malteser, Public Enemy Number Two,* and *South by South East.* Calling the books "rattling good yarns," Jo Goodman noted in a *Magpies* review that "*South by South East* contains, amongst others, the windmill scene from [Hitchcock's film] *Foreign Correspondent* and the crop duster from *North by Northwest.*" *The Falcon's Malteser* references the classic film *The Maltese Falcon* starring Humphrey Bogart, while *Public Enemy Number Two* is a take-off on the gangster film *Public Enemy Number One.*

Horowitz told *CA:* "It seems that kids who don't like to read love my books! They're written for anyone who loves adventure, excitement, humor, and non-stop action. *Stormbreaker* and *Point Blank,* which are about a fourteen-year-old spy, were both inspired by James Bond, and when you read my books I hope you'll be able to 'see' them—to imagine them as movies. I write a lot for television and the cinema too, particularly horror and murder mystery. There is a dark side to my writing, but mainly I believe in having fun."

BIOGRAPHICAL AND CRITICAL SOURCES:

PERIODICALS

Booklist, January 1, 2000, Ilene Cooper, review of *The Devil and His Boy,* p. 922; September 1, 2001, Kelly Milner Halls, review of *Stormbreaker,* p. 97; April 1, 2002, Jean Franklin, review of *Point Blank,* p. 1319.

English Journal, October, 1985, review of *The Night of the Scorpion,* p. 82.

Kirkus Reviews, March 15, 2001, review of *Stormbreaker,* p. 410; February 15, 2002, review of *Point Blank,* p. 258.

Magpies, March, 2001, Jo Goodman, "So You Want to Be a Private Investigator?," pp. 14-15.

New Statesman, April 30, 2001, Andrew Billen, "A Few Twists Too Far," p. 49.

Publishers Weekly, March 1, 1985, review of *The Night of the Scorpion,* p. 81; May 21, 2001, review of *Stormbreaker,* p. 109; May 13, 2002, review of *Point Blank,* p. 72.

School Librarian, summer, 2001, Peter Hollindale, review of *More Horowitz Horror,* p. 102.

School Library Journal, April, 1984, Anne Connor, review of *The Devil's Door-Bell,* p. 124; July, 1994, Mary Jo Drungil, review of *Myths and Legends,* p. 124; April, 2000, Barbara Scotto, review of *The Devil and His Boy,* p. 136; June, 2001, Lynn Bryant, review of *Stormbreaker,* p. 150; March, 2002, review of *Point Plank,* p. 232.

Spectator, February 11, 1995, Ian Hislop, "Last of a Kind," p. 47.

Voice of Youth Advocates, April, 2000, review of *The Devil and His Boy,* p. 35.

*   *   *

HOWD MACHAN, Katharyn 1952-
(Katharyn Machan Aal)

PERSONAL: Born 1952; married Eric Machan Howd (a poet); children: CoraRose, Benjamin. *Education:* College of St. Rose, B.A. (English and speech), 1974; University of Iowa, M.A. (English), 1975; Northwestern University, Ph.D. (performance studies), 1984.

ADDRESSES: Office—254 Park Hall, Ithaca College, Ithaca, NY 14850. *E-mail*—Machan@ithaca.edu.

CAREER: Poet, teacher. Ithaca College, Ithaca, NY, associate professor of writing and women's studies. Ithaca Community Poets, coordinator; director of Feminist Women's Writing Workshops and the annual daylong college-community conference, "Women Speak."

AWARDS, HONORS: Poetry in Public Places Award, New York City Subway Placard Series, 1978; Celia B. Wagner Award, Poetry Society of America, 1982; Cecil Hemley Award, Poetry Society of America, 1984; first place award, Signpost Press National Chapbook Competition, 1986; Best-of-Issue Award for Essay, *AID Review,* 1987; poetry fellowship, Virginia Center for the Creative Arts, 1987; Ravenswood Prize for poetry, 1987; Tompkins County Individual Artist Awards for poetry, 1987, 1988; first place award, CrazyQuilt Press National Chapbook Competition, 1988; first place award, *Lyra* essay competition, 1990; Carolyn Kizer Poetry Award, *Calapooya Collage,* 1991; Goodman Award for poetry, Thorntree Press, 1991; Tompkins County Individual Artist Award for playwriting, 1992; Womanspace Poetry Award, *Korone,* 1992; first place award, *In Praise of Poetry,* 1994; Ithaca College faculty grants for poetry, 1987, 1991, 1995, 1996; poetry award, Creative Artists Partnership of Tompkins County, 1998.

WRITINGS:

POETRY

(With Kenneth Winchester) *Bird on a Wire,* self-published, 1970.

The Wind in the Pear Tree, self-published, 1972.

The Book of the Raccoon, Gehry Press, 1977.

Looking for the Witches, Fine-Arts Bluesband and Poetry Press (Roslindale, MA), 1980.

Where the Foxes Say Goodnight, Scarlet Ibis Press, 1981.

Conversations, Liberty Press (Wichita, KS), 1982.

Seneca Street Poems, Coalition of Publishers for Employment (New York, NY), 1982.

Raccoon Book, McBooks Press (Ithaca, NY), 1982.

(With Barbara Crooker) *Writing Home,* Gehry Press, 1983.

Women: A Pocket Book, Grass Roots Press (Edmonton, Alberta, Canada), 1983.

Along the Rain Black Road, Camel Press, 1986.

When She Was the Good-time Girl, Signpost Press (Hudson, WI), 1987.

Redwing Voices, 1888, Dawn Valley Press, 1988.

From Redwing, Foothills Publishing (Kanona, NY), 1988.

Redwing Women, CrazyQuilt Press (San Diego, CA), 1989.

The Kitchen of Your Dreams, Thorntree Press (Winnetka, IL), 1992.

Belly Words, Sometimes Y Publications, 1994.

EDITOR

Rapunzel, Rapunzel: Poems, Prose, and Photographs by Women on the Subject of Hair, McBooks Press (Ithaca, NY), 1980.

(And contributing as Katharyn Machan Aal) *The Wings, the Vines: Poems by Katharyn Machan Aal, Alice Fulton, Karen Marie Christa Minns, and Sybil Smith,* McBooks Press (Ithaca, NY), 1983.

Contributor of poetry to numerous magazines, including *Yankee, Nimrod, South Coast Poetry Journal, Hollins Critic, Seneca Review,* and *Louisiana Literature.*

SIDELIGHTS: Katharyn Howd Machan is a teacher of creative writing and women's studies at Ithaca College, where she is an assistant professor. She has coordinated feminist writing workshops and programs and published essays on feminist themes ("In Their Own Voice") as well as the creative process ("On Writing Poetry") and performance ("Breath into Fire: Feminism and Poetry Readings").

Howd Machan is also a prolific poet whose work has appeared in numerous literary publications and more than fifty anthologies and textbooks. She lives in Ithaca, New York, with her husband, the poet Eric Machan Howd, and their two children.

BIOGRAPHICAL AND CRITICAL SOURCES:

OTHER

Bedford-St. Martin's Press Web site, http://www.bed fordstmartins.com/litlinks/poetry/ (September 15, 2001).

Ithaca College Web site, http://www.ithaca.edu/ (February 14, 2001).*

HUEBNER, Timothy S. 1966-

PERSONAL: Born October 13, 1966, in Orlando, FL; son of John L. (in sales) and Sylvia S. (a teacher) Huebner; married Kristin M. Lensch (a musician), May 29, 1999. *Ethnicity:* "White." *Education:* University of Miami, B.A., 1988; University of Florida, M.A., 1990, Ph.D. (U.S. history), 1993. *Politics:* Democrat. *Religion:* Protestant. *Hobbies and other interests:* Hiking, cycling.

ADDRESSES: Office—Department of History, Rhodes College, 2000 North Parkway, Memphis, TN 38112. *E-mail*—Huebner@Rhodes.edu.

CAREER: University of Miami, Coral Gables, FL, visiting assistant professor of history, 1993-94; Florida International University, Miami, visiting assistant professor of history, 1994-95; Rhodes College, Memphis, TN, assistant professor of history, 1995—. Tennessee Cultural Heritage Preservation Society, advisory board member, 1999—.

MEMBER: Organization of American Historians (Southern Chapter), Association for Tennessee History, Phi Beta Kappa (secretary, gamma of Tennessee chapter).

AWARDS, HONORS: Samuel Proctor Award for Outstanding History Teaching Assistant, University of Florida, 1991-92.

WRITINGS:

The Southern Judicial Tradition: State Judges and Sectional Distinctiveness, 1790-1890, University of Georgia Press (Athens, GA), 1999.

Contributor to *Local Matters: Race, Crime, and Justice in the Nineteenth-Century South,* edited by Christopher Waldrep and Don Nieman, University of Georgia Press, 2001; and to various periodicals, including *Georgia Historical Quarterly, Journal of Southern Legal History, Virginia Magazine of History and Biography, Journal of Supreme Court History,* and *Tennessee Historical Quarterly.* Book review editor, *American Journal of Legal History.*

WORK IN PROGRESS: The U.S. Supreme Court under Roger B. Taney, for ABC-Clio, 2004.

SIDELIGHTS: Timothy S. Huebner told *CA*: "Having studied with the renowned historian of the South, Bertram Wyatt-Brown, and with leading legal historian Kermit L. Hall, my work has focused on the legal history of the nineteenth-century American South, a field long neglected by historians and legal scholars alike. Much of my scholarship reflects my interest in the 'legal culture' of the South: the cultural and political assumptions held by southern jurists and how those values influenced the interpretation of the law. Although nearly all of my work has dealt with judges and courts, I am becoming more interested in southern constitutional values and hope to pursue research in this area in the future."

I-J

IGLÌCKA, Krystyna 1964-

PERSONAL: Born June 13, 1964, in Warsaw, Poland; daughter of Janusz (a sociologist) and Zofia (a psychologist) Iglìcki; married; children: Narek. *Ethnicity:* "Polish." *Education:* University of Warsaw, M.Sc., 1988; Warsaw School of Economics, Ph.D., 1993.

ADDRESSES: Office—Institute for Social Studies, University of Warsaw, Ul. Stawki 5/7, 00-183 Warsaw, Poland; fax: 831-49-33.

CAREER: Warsaw School of Economics, Warsaw, Poland, researcher, 1988-99, assistant professor at Institute for Statistics and Demography, 1993-99; University of Warsaw, member of Center for Migration Studies, 1994-96, assistant professor at Institute for Social Studies, 1999—, institute deputy director, 2000—, director of Migration and Eastern Policy Program at Institute of Public Affairs, 2002—. University of London, London, England, School of Slavonic and East European Studies, coordinator of Polish migration project, 1996-98; University of Pennsylvania, coordinator of research project, 1999-2000.

MEMBER: International Sociological Association, European Association for Population Studies.

AWARDS, HONORS: Grants from Centre d'Etudes et de Recherches Internationales, Paris, France, 1993, Soros Foundation, 1994-96, United Nations Economic Commission for Europe, 1994-96, Weltschaftswissenschaftszentrum, Berlin, Germany, 1995, and Polish Scientific Committee, 1995-96; senior Fulbright fellow, 1999-2000.

WRITINGS:

Regionalne zroznicowanie plodnosci w Polsce, 1931-1988 (title means "Regional Differentiation of Fertility in Poland, 1931-1988"), Warsaw School of Economics Press (Warsaw, Poland), 1994.

Analiza zachowan migracyjnych w wybranych regionach Polski, 1975-1994 (title means "An Analysis of the Migratory Behaviors in Selected Regions of Poland, 1975-1994"), Warsaw School of Economics Press (Warsaw, Poland), 1998.

(Editor, with Keith Sword, and contributor) *The Challenge of East-West Migration for Poland,* Macmillan (London, England), 1999.

(Editor, with F. E. I. Hamilton, and contributor) *From Homogeneity to Multiculturalism: Minorities Old and New in Poland,* School of Slavonic and East European Studies, University of London (London, England), 2000.

Poland's Post-War Dynamic of Migration, Ashgate Publishing (Burlington, VT), 2001.

Contributor to books, including *Usefulness of Demographic Modeling,* edited by J. Jozwiak and I. E. Kotowska, Warsaw School of Economics Press (Warsaw, Poland), 1991; *Causes and Consequences of Migration in Central and Eastern Europe: Podlasie and Slask Opolski; Basic Trends in 1975-1994,* University of Warsaw Press (Warsaw, Poland), 1996; and *Causes and Consequences of Migration from Central and Eastern Europe: The Case of Poland,* edited by T. Frejka, M. Okolski, and Keith Sword, United Nations Economic Commission for Europe (Geneva, NY), 1998. Contributor to professional journals in Poland and around the world, including *Europe-Asia Studies, Journal of Population Geography, Journal of Ethnic and Migration Studies,* and *International Migration.*

BIOGRAPHICAL AND CRITICAL SOURCES:

PERIODICALS

Europe-Asia Studies, September, 1999, Joanne Van Selm-Thorburn, review of *The Challenge of East-West Migration for Poland,* p. 1121.

*   *   *

IVES, David 1951-

PERSONAL: Born 1951. *Education:* Attended Northwestern University and Yale University School of Drama.

ADDRESSES: Agent—c/o Publicity Director, Harper-Collins, 10 East 53rd St., New York, NY 10022.

CAREER: Playwright and writer.

AWARDS, HONORS: Guggenheim Fellowship in playwriting.

WRITINGS:

PLAYS

Ancient History, Dramatists Play Service (New York, NY), 1990.
Long Ago and Far Away, Dramatists Play Service (New York, NY), 1994.
Don Juan in Chicago (produced in New York, NY, 1995), Dramatists Play Service (New York, NY), 1995.

All in the Timing: Fourteen Plays, Vintage Books (New York, NY), 1995.
Mere Mortals: Six One-Act Comedies, Dramatists Play Service (New York, NY), 1998.
The Land of Cockaigne and English Made Simple, Dramatists Play Service (New York, NY), 1998.
The Red Address, Dramatists Play Service (New York, NY), 1998.
Lives of the Saints: Seven One-Act Plays, Dramatists Play Service (New York, NY), 2000.
Time Flies and Other Short Plays, Grove Press (New York, NY), 2001.

OTHER

Monsieur Eek (juvenile), HarperCollins (New York, NY), 2001.

Also author of *Five Very Alive,* a collection of five one-act plays produced at Atlantic Theater Company, New York, NY, in the early 1990s.

SIDELIGHTS: David Ives was once described as a playwright with a "dandy, dark wit" by interviewer Randall Short in *New York* magazine. A native of Chicago, Ives grew up in the same neighborhood as film director David Mamet and came to New York after college. While paying the rent as an assistant editor of *Foreign Affairs,* he wrote plays. He attended Yale University School of Drama and according to Short, "forc[ed] the English language through an increasingly giddy series of hoops."

Many of Ives's plays are one-acts. In the early 1990s he offered *Five Very Alive,* a bill of five one-act plays. Sy Syna, reviewing the Atlantic Theater Company production in *Back Stage,* described them as "all funny, all current, a few aimed at easy satiric targets, and, at least one, trenchant." *Don Juan in Chicago,* according to Amy Rieter, reviewing the Primary Stages production for *Back Stage,* is "fantastically quirky and clever. The characters speak most of the play in verse, and the rhymes are so silly and fun that you find yourself hanging on every delicious word."

However, the Ives play that has attracted the most notice is *All in the Timing.* James S. Torrens, reviewing this work in *America,* noted, "Ives does not work so much with clever patter or droll character as with comic ideas and situations." *All in the Timing* consists of six "surreal miniplays, united only in their treatment of time as a substance that can be sliced, poured or frozen," stated Stefan Kanfer, writing in *New Leader.* Richard Corliss began his *Time* review: "A scantily dressed stage. A few dexterous actors. And, offstage, a hotel-desk bell. In David Ives' fertile world, these are the only requirements for theater that aerobicizes the brain and tickles the heart." Larry S. Ledford, reviewing the Primary Stages production of *All in the Timing* in *Back Stage,* concluded, "If, as one of the characters says, 'Language is the opposite of loneliness,' Ives et al. have the tools to keep a theatre full of company for many months to come." In an interview with Randall Short in *New York* magazine, Ives said, "If I have a style, I don't plan it. It's not something like Mamet, instantly recognizable by the number of profanities in it, or like the Jamesian locutions of Edward Albee. I hate writing the same play twice, and so I don't feel I use a single style for everything. I think it would be hard for me to recognize my style, and even harder for somebody to parody it. When I reach the point where I'm recognizable, I think I'll retire."

Ives has also penned a children's novel, *Monsieur Eek.* Set in a tiny fictional town with a population of twenty-one, the story revolves around a shipwreck. Susan Dove Lempke, writing in *Booklist,* commented that Ives "mixes historical fiction, fantasy, and mystery into an entertaining story." A reviewer in *Publishers Weekly* commented that the book is a "fairy tale-like story full of absurd characters who make bizarre interpretations" and that the result is "a fun read with a thoughtful message." Ellen Fader, reviewing the book in *School Library Journal,* recommended it for those "who like nonstop action, a bit of shivery mystery leavened by humor, and a happily ever after ending."

BIOGRAPHICAL AND CRITICAL SOURCES:

PERIODICALS

America, August 27, 1994, James S. Torrens, review of *All in the Timing,* p. 25.

American Theatre, July-August, 1994, Stephanie Coen, review of *All in the Timing,* p. 25; April, 1999, Celia Wren, "Irrational Exuberance," p. 37.

Back Stage, November 22, 1991, David Lefkowitz, review of *Off the Beat and Path,* p. 40; January 17, 1992, Sy Syna, review of *Five Very Alive,* p. 52; January 21, 1994, Larry S. Ledford, review of *All in the Timing,* p. 40; March 31, 1995, Amy Reiter, review of *Don Juan in Chicago,* p. 42; May 31, 1996, David A. Rosenberg, review of *Ancient History/English Made Simple,* p. 48; May 9, 1997, Irene Backalenick, review of *Mere Mortals and Others,* p. 42.

Bloomsbury Review, November, 1995, Dallas Crow, review of *All in the Timing,* p. 33.

Booklist, June 1, 2001, Susan Dove Lempke, review of *Monsieur Eek,* p. 1883.

New Leader, February 14, 1994, Stefan Kanfer, review of *All in The Timing,* p. 22; September 22, 1997, Stefan Kanfer, review of *Mere Mortals and Others,* p. 22.

New York, April 3, 1995, Randall Short, "Sharp as Ives," p. 50; April 10, 1995, John Simon, review of *Don Juan in Chicago,* p. 75; June 3, 1996, John Simon, review of *Ancient History,* p. 96.

Publishers Weekly, May 28, 2001, review of *Monsieur Eek,* p. 89.

School Library Journal, June, 2001, Ellen Fader, review of *Monsieur Eek,* p. 150.

Time, January 31, 1994, Richard Corliss, review of *All in The Timing,* p. 106.*

*   *   *

JACQUETTE, Dale 1953-

PERSONAL: Born April 19, 1953, in WI; married Tina Traas, August 14, 1976; children: Scott K. Templeton. *Ethnicity:* "White." *Education:* Oberlin College, B.A. (with high honors), 1975; Brown University, M.A., 1981, Ph.D., 1983. *Hobbies and other interests:* Photography.

ADDRESSES: Home—311 South Sparks St., State College, PA 16801. *Office*—Department of Philosophy, 246 Sparks Bldg., Pennsylvania State University, University Park, PA 16802; fax: 814-865-0119. *E-mail*—dlj4@psu.edu.

CAREER: Pennsylvania State University, University Park, professor of philosophy and director of philosophy graduate logic program, both 1986—. University of Venice, Fulbright lecturer, 1996; University of Pittsburgh Center for Philosophy of Science, associate, 1999—; speaker at numerous universities in the United States and abroad, including University of Windsor, University of Lethbridge, University of Memphis, Free University of Amsterdam, University of Toronto, Universidad del Pais Vasco, and State University of New York—Buffalo.

MEMBER: International Society for the Study of Argumentation, Internationale Franz Brentano Gesellschaft, North American Schopenhauer Society, American Philosophical Association, Society for Exact Philosophy, Hume Society, American Society for Aesthetics, Association for Informal Logic and Critical Thinking, Österreichische Ludwig Wittgenstein Gesellschaft, Eastern Pennsylvania Philosophical Association, Phi Beta Kappa.

AWARDS, HONORS: Grant from National Endowment for the Humanities, 1984; fellow of Alexander von Humboldt-Stiftung at University of Mannheim, 1989-90, and University of Würzburg, 2000-01.

WRITINGS:

Philosophy of Mind, Prentice-Hall (Englewood Cliffs, NJ), 1994.
Meinongian Logic: The Semantics of Existence and Nonexistence, Walter de Gruyter and Co. (Berlin, Germany), 1996.
Wittgenstein's Thought in Transition, Purdue University Press (West Lafayette, IN), 1998.
Six Philosophical Appetizers, McGraw-Hill (New York, NY), 2001.
Philosophical Entrées: Classic and Contemporary Readings in Philosophy, McGraw-Hill (New York, NY), 2001.
David Hume's Critique of Infinity, Brill Academic Publishers, 2001.
Ontology, Acumen Books, 2002.
On Boole, Wadsworth Publishing (Belmont, CA), 2002.

Contributor to books, including *Argumentation Illuminated,* edited by Frans H. van Eemeren and others, International Society for the Study of Argumentation (Amsterdam, Netherlands), 1992; *The School of Franz Brentano,* edited by Liliana Albertazzi, Massimo Libardi, and Roberto Poli, Kluwer Academic Publishers , 1996; *Austrian Philosophy Past and Present: Essays in Honor of Rudolf Haller,* edited by Keith Lehrer and Johannes Christian Marek, Kluwer Academic Publishers (Dordrecht, Netherlands), 1997; *Interpretation, Relativism, and the Metaphysics of Culture: Themes in the Philosophy of Joseph Margolis,* edited by Michael Karusz and Richard Shusterman, Humanity Books (Amherst, NY), 1999; and *The Cambridge Companion to Schopenhauer,* edited by Christopher Janeway, Cambridge University Press (New York, NY), 1999. Contributor of more than 150 articles and reviews to periodicals, including *Social Epistemology, Philosophical Explorations, Continental Philosophy Review, British Journal of Aesthetics, History of European Ideas, Journal of Applied Philosophy, Metaphilosophy, History of Philosophy Quarterly, Logical Analysis and History of Philosophy,* and *Facta Philosophica.*

EDITOR

(And author of introduction) J. N. Findlay, *Meinong's Theory of Objects and Values,* Ashgate Publishing (Burlington, VT), 1995.
(And contributor) *Schopenhauer, Philosophy, and the Arts,* Cambridge University Press (New York, NY), 1996.
(With Andrew R. Martinez) *Symbolic Logic,* includes interactive logic exercises on accompanying CD-ROM by Nelson Pole, Wadsworth Publishing (Belmont, CA), 2001.
(With Liliana Albertazzi and Roberto Poli; and contributor) *The School of Alexius Meinong,* Ashgate Publishing (Burlington, VT), 2001.
(And contributor) *A Companion to Philosophical Logic,* Blackwell Publishers, 2002.
(And contributor) *Philosophy of Logic: An Anthology,* Blackwell Publishers, 2002.
(And contributor) *Philosophy of Mathematics: An Anthology,* Blackwell Publishers, 2002.
Philosophy, Psychology, and Psychologism: Critical and Historical Essays on the Psychological Turn in Philosophy, Kluwer Academic Publishers (Dordrecht, Netherlands), in press.

Editor, *American Philosophical Quarterly,* 2002—; editor of special issues of *Philosophy and Rhetoric,* 1997, and *Journal of Value Inquiry,* 2001; member of editorial board, *Brentano Studien* and *Journal of Speculative Philosophy.*

WORK IN PROGRESS: Pathways in Philosophy: An Introductory Guide, for Oxford University Press (New York, NY); *The Philosophy of Schopenhauer,* for McGill-Queen's University Press; *Journalistic Ethics: Moral Responsibility in the Media,* for Prentice-Hall (Tappan, NJ); editing *The Cambridge Companion to Brentano,* Cambridge University Press (New York, NY); research on "mathematical entity."

BIOGRAPHICAL AND CRITICAL SOURCES:

PERIODICALS

Mind, October, 1998, Graham Oppy, review of *Meinongian Logic: The Semantics of Existence and Nonexistence,* p. 894.
Review of Metaphysics, March, 2000, Stephen R. Grimm, review of *Wittgenstein's Thought in Transition,* p. 708.

OTHER

Dale Jacquette Web site, http://www.personal.psu.edu/dlj4/ (January 11, 2003).

*   *   *

JAGENDORF, Zvi 1936-

PERSONAL: Born 1936, in Vienna, Austria. *Education:* Hebrew University, Jerusalem, Ph.D., 1978. *Religion:* Jewish.

ADDRESSES: Home—Jerusalem, Israel. *Office*—c/o Dewi Lewis Publishing, 8 Broomfield Road, Heaton Moor, Stockport SK4 4ND, England.

CAREER: Hebrew University, Jerusalem, Israel, senior lecturer, 1983-95, associate professor, 1995-2001, professor emeritus, 2001—.

AWARDS, HONORS: Longlist nomination for Booker Prize, 2001, for *Wolfy and the Strudelbakers.*

WRITINGS:

The Happy End of Comedy: Johnson, Molière, and Shakespeare, University of Delaware Press (Newark, DE), 1984.
Wolfy and the Strudelbakers, Dewi Lewis Publishing (Stockport, England), 2001.

Also author of articles on Shakespeare, Primo Levi, and Jewish literature, published in journals, including *Modern Language Review, Modern Hebrew Literature, Raritan,* and *Shakespeare Quarterly.* Author of *Freud's Last Case,* a play in Hebrew, produced in 1993.

SIDELIGHTS: Zvi Jagendorf had a long and distinguished career as a professor of English and theatre before writing his first book of fiction. With *Wolfy and the Strudelbakers,* Jagendorf changed his focus, shifting from serious studies of Shakespeare and the dynamics of theatrical performance to a comedic portrayal of a young Jewish boy from Vienna living in exile with his family in London. Jagendorf's first novel was a tremendous success, earning both a nomination for the very prestigious Booker Prize and comparisons to such authors as Gustave Flaubert, James Joyce, and Bruno Schulz (sometimes called the Polish Kafka).

Wolfy and the Strudelbakers opens in 1939 Vienna, where the Helfgott family is planning to flee the country to escape persecution by the Nazis. In a series of thirteen vignettes, Jagendorf portrays Wolfy, his brother Bernie, his parents, and his Onkle Mendl and Tantie Rosa struggling both to assimilate and to preserve their faith and their culture in wartime London. Jagendorf's observations on the clash of cultures provides much of the humor, as when Wolfy wins a prize from the Bishop of Lichfield, a holy card with a picture of the Virgin Mary and Jesus, which his parents later throw in the fireplace. In another chapter, the boys' Hebrew classes, intended to help them retain their Jewish identity, meet in an area notorious for prostitutes. Yet the book is also full of sadness: Wolfy's mother dies unexpectedly, and the brothers gradually learn stories about their uncles and their father that reveal the kind of hardships they have escaped.

Readers were enthusiastic about *Wolfy and the Strudelbakers.* Writing for the London *Guardian,* James Hopin remarked on Jagendorf's flair for characterization, noting, "Every character leaps into life with a telling detail or phrase. . . . these are personalities of vitality and charm." Toby Clements, reviewing *Wolfy and the Strudelbakers* in the London *Daily Telegraph,* wrote that Jagendorf succeeds in distinguishing his work from the formulaic novel of Jewish coming of age, a model created by Philip Roth's *Portnoy's Complaint* in 1969. Clements cited Jagendorf's "quiet good humor and the high quality of his writing" as elements that set his work apart, in addition to his "gentle refusal to accept that all the Sturm und Drang of the past is a thing of the past, or that the narrator's life is necessarily less interesting just because nothing much happens in it." In a review for the online *Guardian Unlimited Books,* Tim Adams also commented on the quality of the writing in *Wolfy and the Strudelbakers,* saying, "I am not sure whether [Jagendorf] has lived in England, but the novel reads like the best kind of personal memoir, full of the little intimacies of family life, and written with a sustained and generous vision of the particular joys and disappointments of finding your way in a foreign land."

BIOGRAPHICAL AND CRITICAL SOURCES:

PERIODICALS

Choice, April, 1985, H. L. Ford, review of *The Happy End of Comedy,* p. 1155.
Daily Telegraph (London, England), July 21, 2001, Toby Clements, "Mad about the Goy."
Guardian (London, England), September 15, 2001, James Hopkin, review of *Wolfy and the Strudelbakers,* p. 10.
Shakespeare Quarterly, summer, 1986, Maurice Charney, review of *The Happy End of Comedy,* pp. 264-65.

OTHER

Dewi Lewis Publishing Web site, http://www.dewilewis publishing.com/ (October 7, 2001), reviews of *Wolfy and the Strudelbakers.*
Guardian Unlimited Books, http://books.guardian.co.uk/ (August 26, 2001), Tim Adams, "Hormones, Scars, and a Promised Land."
Hebrew University Web site, http://www.huji.ac.il/ (March 19, 2002), home page of Zvi Jagendorf.*

*   *   *

JENKINS, Lee Margaret

PERSONAL: Female. *Education:* Cambridge University, B.A., M.A., and Ph.D.

ADDRESSES: Office—University College, Cork, Faculty of Arts, O'Rahilly Building, Western Road, Cork, Ireland. *E-mail*—l.jenkins@ucc.ie.

CAREER: University College, Cork, Ireland, lecturer in Modern English, 1994—.

MEMBER: Irish Association for American Studies, British Association of American Studies, Modernist Studies Association, Wallace Stevens Society, William Faulkner Society.

AWARDS, HONORS: British Academy postdoctoral research fellowship, 1992-94; research fellow at Darwin College, Cambridge, 1992-94; Government of Ireland research fellowship, 2002-03.

WRITINGS:

Wallace Stevens: Rage for Order, Sussex Academic Press (Brighton, England), 1999.
(Co-editor with Alex Davis) *The Locations of Modernism: Region and Nation in British and American Modernist Poetry,* Cambridge University Press (New York, NY), 2000.

Contributor to academic journals, including *The Irish Review, Ariel, Contemporary Literature,* and *Nineteenth-Century Studies.*

SIDELIGHTS: In her work as a lecturer in English literature, Lee Margaret Jenkins has focused on modern American and Irish poetry, and in 2000 she co-edited *The Locations of Literary Modernism: Region and Nation in British and American Modernist Poetry.* In this collection, contributors explore the regional and national influences on modernist poets, who are often seen as beyond a particular time and space. Different essays focus on the local contexts of such poets as Ezra Pound, Langston Hughes, and Elizabeth Bishop, with a chapter by Jenkins herself on Wallace Stevens (1879-1955). Jenkins's fuller views on this major American poet are set forth in *Wallace Stevens: Rage for Order.* In this revisionist study, she contrasts the early promise of his first book, *Harmonium,* with what she sees as a more disappointing middle phase focused on a will-bound poetic of "major men" and a return to doubt in his later writings. While commenting in the *Times Literary Supplement* that "few among Stevens's admirers will be convinced" by Jenkins's thesis, Stephen Burt nevertheless saluted her "impressive research." Edward Ragg, furthermore, argued in the *Journal of the Irish Association for American Studies* that Jenkins's book is "the most significant study of Wallace Stevens to have appeared on either side of the Atlantic for several years."

BIOGRAPHICAL AND CRITICAL SOURCES:

PERIODICALS

Journal of the Irish Association for American Studies, Volume 9, 2000, Edward Ragg, "The Violence Within and the Violence Without," pp. 247-252.
Times Literary Supplement, December 31, 1999, Stephen Burt, "The Heavy Nights," p. 27.

*   *   *

JONES, Allen Morris 1970-

PERSONAL: Born March 16, 1970, in Charleston, WV; son of Burl and Eunice (Holmes) Jones. *Ethnicity:* "Caucasian." *Hobbies and other interests:* Fishing, hunting, piano, tennis.

ADDRESSES: Home—2101 South Fourth W., Missoula, MT 59801. *E-mail*—amjones@mcn.net.

CAREER: Freelance writer. Former editor of *Big Sky Journal*; Bangtail Press, Bozeman, MT, editor and co-publisher.

WRITINGS:

A Quiet Place of Violence: Hunting and Ethics in the Missouri River Breaks, Bangtail Press (Bozeman, MT), 1997.
(Editor, with Jeff Wetmore) *The Big Sky Reader,* St. Martin's (New York, NY), 1998.
Last Year's River, Houghton Mifflin (Boston, MA), 2001.

WORK IN PROGRESS: A novel about an escaped slave, set in Appalachia.

SIDELIGHTS: Allen Morris Jones is the former editor of *Big Sky Journal,* a literary periodical focusing on the work of writers of the American West. After five years in this position, Jones resigned to write his novel, *Last Year's River.* Described as a "luminous" first novel by a *Publishers Weekly* reviewer, the story, which begins in 1919, explores the passionate relationship between two very different, but equally lonely people. Seventeen-year-old New York debutante Virginia Price is already feeling lost and alienated as a result of her father's death, feelings that only become worse when she is raped by her boyfriend, Charlie Stroud. When her mother finds out that she has become pregnant as a result of the rape, Virginia is sent with her aunt to the Wyoming ranch of Frank Mohr, where they will stay until the baby is born.

Virginia is unsettled by ranch life, so different from her Manhattan upbringing, and by the people she meets: Frank Mohr's abused Native American wife, Rose, and cowboys Dewey and Adze, who work on the ranch. She is also unused to her new situation as a "fallen woman" and is upset by the locals' curiosity about her past. However, she manages to make friends with Mohr's twenty-four-year-old son, Henry, who is just back from fighting in World War I, and they begin a secret relationship.

Things become complicated when Charlie Stroud shows up, wanting to marry Virginia and take her to Boston, where they can renew their life together. However, Virginia has nothing but contempt for him. Tensions rise through a series of ensuing dramatic events. A *Publishers Weekly* reviewer commented that the book is "impressive" and noted, "the novel should make the reader impatient for Jones's next effort." In *People Weekly,* Lori Gottlieb wrote that the novel was "keenly felt and powerfully told." David Abrams wrote in *January Magazine* that the book "haunts and sustains like a piano chord resonating long after the fingers have lifted from the keyboard. The music of Jones's words will also linger long after the eye has lifted from the page."

The Big Sky Reader, which Jones edited with *Big Sky Journal* founder Jeff Wetmore, is an anthology of nearly forty articles that appeared in *Big Sky Journal* between 1992 and 1997. Although some are fiction, most of the pieces are nonfiction about the West, featuring ranching, rodeos, hunting, fishing, and saloons, with an emphasis on Montana. A *Booklist* reviewer called the anthology "a satisfying collection for those who love the area and enjoy reading of its mystique."

In *A Quiet Place of Violence: Hunting and Ethics in the Missouri River Breaks,* Jones describes a year of hunting and fishing in Montana's Missouri River Breaks. Discussing the ethics of hunting, he explores why people hunt, as well as how hunting can be done in an ethical and respectful manner.

BIOGRAPHICAL AND CRITICAL SOURCES:

PERIODICALS

Booklist, December 1, 1998, Fred Egloff, review of *The Big Sky Reader,* p. 644; September 15, 2001, Bill Ott, review of *Last Year's River,* p. 192.

Kirkus Reviews, September 1, 2001, review of *Last Year's River,* p. 1236.

Library Journal, November 15, 1998, Cynde Bloom Lahey, review of *The Big Sky Reader,* p. 67: October 1, 2001, Karen Anderson, review of *Last Year's River,* p. 140.

People Weekly, November 12, 2001, p. 47.

Publishers Weekly, September 10, 2001, review of *Last Year's River,* p. 58.

OTHER

January Magazine, http://www.januarymagazine.com/ (December 2, 2001), David Abrams, "Big Sky, Noisy River."

*   *   *

JONES, Philippe
See ROBERTS-JONES, Philippe

K

K., Alice
See KNAPP, Caroline

*   *   *

KAMINSKY, Peter 1947(?)-

PERSONAL: Born c. 1947; married; two children. *Education:* Princeton University, BA.

ADDRESSES: Home—Brooklyn, NY. *Agent*—c/o Hyperion Editorial Department, 77 West 66th St., 11th Floor, New York, NY 10023.

CAREER: Writer, television producer.

WRITINGS:

Fly Fishing for Dummies, IDG Books Worldwide (Foster City, CA), 1998.
(With Jim McCann) *Stop and Smell the Roses: Lessons from Business and Life,* Ballantine (New York, NY), 1998.
(With Peggy Fleming) *The Long Program: Skating toward Life's Victories,* Pocket (New York, NY), 1999.
(With John Madden) *John Madden's Ultimate Tailgating,* Gramercy (New York, NY), 2000.
(With Gray Kunz) *The Elements of Taste,* Little, Brown (Boston, MA), 2001.
The Moon Pulled upan Acre of Bass: A Flyrodder's Odyssey at Montauk Point, Hyperion/Theia (New York, NY), 2001.

Fishing for Dummies: An Illustrated Reference for the Rest of Us, Courage Books (Philadelphia, PA), 2002.

WORK IN PROGRESS: Contributor of articles, especially on food and the outdoors, to magazines and newspapers including the *New York Times'* "Outdoors" column, *New York, Food & Wine, Outdoor Life,* and *Sports Afield.*

SIDELIGHTS: In *The Moon Pulled up an Acre of Bass: A Flyrodder's Odyssey at Montauk Point,* Peter Kaminsky celebrates a yearly ritual: the running of vast schools of striped bass off Montauk Point, New York, and the fishermen and women who follow them. Kaminsky describes the hunt for the fish in what *People Weekly* writer Jack Friedman called "a joyous, beautifully written evocation of time and place." Combining observations of the fly-fishing guides, the fish, and those who seek to catch them, Kaminsky gives an insider's view of this fishing paradise. In *Publishers Weekly,* a reviewer wrote, "most Eastern fly rodders will revel in Kaminsky's walkabout."

Fly Fishing for Dummies is a distillation of fly-fishing's ins and outs for novices to the sport. Despite the sport's mystique, Kaminsky explains in the book that it actually does not require "the touch of a surgeon, the body mechanics of Tiger Woods, and the spirit of a Zen master." Providing tips on gear, flies, casting, techniques, and fishing strategies, the book also gives the location of the best trout rivers in North America.

In *Fishing for Dummies,* Kaminsky helps readers become acquainted with a variety of fishing techniques, such as flyfishing, spinning, or baitcasting, and methods to improve them. The book includes information on how to identify the most common freshwater and saltwater fish, tie knots, secure lures, and choose the right bait. Optimistically, it also tells how to clean and cook the catch of the day. *Fishing for Dummies* also describes how disabled people can become involved in the sport and gives Internet resources for fishers.

John Madden's Ultimate Tailgating, written with sportscaster John Madden, is a compendium of over eighty recipes for tailgate parties. Divided into regional cuisines, the book features sidebars with tidbits of local history. Kaminsky's collaboration with four-star chef John Gray, *The Elements of Taste,* contains over 130 contemporary recipes with discussions of how and why their ingredients work well together. Kaminsky also colloborated with Olympic gold medal-winning figure skater Peggy Fleming on her autobiography, *The Long Program: Skating toward Life's Victories.*

BIOGRAPHICAL AND CRITICAL SOURCES:

PERIODICALS

Booklist, October 15, 1999, Wes Lukowsky, review of *The Long Program,* p. 409.
Library Journal, October 15, 1999, Bonnie Collier, review of *The Long Program,* p. 76.
People Weekly, November 1, 1999, p. 409; September 10, 2001, p. 51.
Publishers Weekly, March 23, 1998, review of *Stop and Sell the Roses,* p. 86; September 27, 1999, review of *The Long Program,* p. 89; July 23, 2001, review of *The Moon Pulled up an Acre of Bass,* p. 61.

OTHER

Time-Warner Web site, http://www.twbookmark.com/ (October 7, 2001), review of *The Elements of Taste.*
ESPN Outdoors, http://espn.go.com/outdoors/ (January 26, 2003), Joe Healy, interview with Peter Kaminsky.*

*   *   *

KANE, Paul 1950-

PERSONAL: Born March 23, 1950, in Cobleskill, NY; son of T. Paul (a judge) and Jeanne (maiden name, Meagher) Kane; married Christine Reynolds (a textile conservator), June 21, 1980. *Education:* Yale University, B.A. (English), 1973; Melbourne University, M.A. (English), 1985, Ph.D. (English), 1990. *Politics:* "Independent."

ADDRESSES: Home—8 Big Island, Warwick, NY 10990. *Office*—Vassar College, 124 Raymond Ave., Poughkeepsie, NY 12604. *Agent*—Kyung Cho, Henry Dunow Agency, 22 West 23rd St., New York, NY 10010. *E-mail*—kane@warwick.net.

CAREER: Vassar College, Poughkeepsie, NY, professor of English, 1990—.

MEMBER: PEN American Center, American Association of Australian Literary Studies.

AWARDS, HONORS: National Endowment for the Humanities fellowship, 1998; Guggenheim fellowship, 1999.

WRITINGS:

The Farther Shore (poetry), George Braziller (New York, NY), 1989.
(With William Clift) *A Hudson Landscape* (photographs and prose), William Clift Editions, 1993.
(Editor, with Harold Bloom) *Ralph Waldo Emerson: Collected Poems and Translations* (poetry), Library of America (New York, NY), 1994.
(Editor) *Poetry of the American Renaissance* (poetry), George Braziller (New York, NY), 1995.
Australian Poetry: Romanticism and Negativity (criticism), Cambridge University Press (Melbourne, Australia), 1996.
Drowned Lands (poetry), University of South Carolina Press (Columbia, SC), 2000.

Contributor of poems, articles, and reviews to periodicals, including *New Republic, Paris Review, Poetry, Raritan, New Criterion, Antipodes,* and *Australian Book Review.*

WORK IN PROGRESS: Work on Emerson's poetry; Mont St.-Michel and Shiprock; a book of poems.

SIDELIGHTS: Paul Kane both writes his own poetry and edits the works of other poets. In the latter role, he produced *Ralph Waldo Emerson: Collected Poems and Translations,* a volume that was praised by a *Publishers Weekly* contributor as an "exhaustive, sensitive compilation" that "offers up poetic reiterations of Emerson's more popular essays . . . and serves to re-open the case for Emerson as a poet."

In *Australian Poetry: Romanticism and Negativity,* Kane begins his investigation of Australia's romantic tradition by examining works "from the likes of De Man, Bloom and Harmann," according to *Australian Literary Studies* critic Martin Duwell. "He also faces the objections of new historicists who wish to see the matter returned to an historically specific event in the face of the suspicion that romanticism is in danger of becoming a vague coverall term." In addition, Kane "covers the philosophical history of 'negativity' in a useful summary, comparing Hegelian and Freudian uses of it, so that the absence of romanticism can be treated as something more than a lack."

BIOGRAPHICAL AND CRITICAL SOURCES:

PERIODICALS

Australian Literary Studies, May, 1997, Martin Duwell, review of *Australian Poetry: Romanticism and Negativity,* p. 107.
Hudson Review, autumn, 1990, Dick Allen, review of *The Farther Shore,* p. 509.
Library Journal, November 1, 1995, Frank Allen, review of *Poetry of the American Renaissance,* p. 69.
Nation, October 3, 1994, Thomas M. Disch, review of *Ralph Waldo Emerson: Collected Poems and Translations,* p. 350.
Overland, autumn, 1997, Jeffrey Poacher, review of *Australian Poetry,* p. 88.
Publishers Weekly, June 27, 1994, review of *Ralph Waldo Emerson,* p. 66.
Times Literary Supplement, May 31, 1991, Glyn Maxwell, review of *The Farther Shore,* p. 12.

*   *   *

KARSH, Yosuf
  See KARSH, Yousuf

*   *   *

KARSH, Yousef
  See KARSH, Yousuf

KARSH, Yousuf 1908-2002

OBITUARY NOTICE—See index for *CA* sketch: Born December 23, 1908, in Mardin, Armenia (now Turkey); died after surgery, July 13, 2002, in Boston, MA. Photographer and writer. Karsh is remembered all over the world as photographer to the rich and famous. Considered a master of light and darkness, his work represents the epitome of formal studio portraiture. Karsh of Ottawa, as he was known, took thousands of pictures in his career, which began in the early 1930s. It was a 1941 photograph of British Prime Minister Winston Churchill—capturing the statesman's dogged, determined, and pugnacious attitude in the face of war—that launched the photographer's dazzling international career. Though sometimes criticized as formulaic, it is generally agreed that Karsh's portraits of royalty, military leaders and politicians, literary figures, and scions of business, science, industry, the church, and the arts have shaped the visual images by which the world at large identifies these figures today. Critics have written that Karsh excelled in distilling the very essence of his subjects as he believed—or they believed—the world perceived them. He was sent on assignment by the Canadian magazine *Saturday Night* and America's *Life* magazine. His photographs have appeared on postage stamps and in permanent museum collections, official biographies and history textbooks, and numerous exhibitions; he was also the official photographer for the annual posters of the Muscular Dystrophy Association. Karsh published his work in more than a dozen books, accompanying them with captions and anecdotes he wrote himself. One of the first was *Faces of Destiny,* published in 1946. His 1983 retrospective was expanded in 1999 as *Karsh: A Sixty-Year Retrospective.* Karsh was awarded a U.S. Presidential citation for service on behalf of the handicapped and decorated a Companion of the Order of Canada. His given name was sometimes spelled "Yosuf" or "Yousef."

OBITUARIES AND OTHER SOURCES:

BOOKS

Karsh, Yousuf, *In Search of Greatness: Reflections,* Knopf (New York, NY), 1962.

PERIODICALS

Los Angeles Times, July 14, 2002, obituary by Jon Thurber, p. B16.

New York Times, July 15, 2002, p. A19.
Times (London, England), July 15, 2002.
Washington Post, July 14, 2002, obituary by Richard
    Pearson, p. C6.

OTHER

Diary of a Portraitist (television special), Canadian
    Broadcasting Corp., 1967.
Profile of Karsh (television special), Canadian
    Broadcasting Corp., 1970.

*   *   *

KAUFFMAN, Stanley L.
    See KAUFMAN, Lloyd

*   *   *

KAUFMAN, Lloyd 1945-
    (Louis Su, Samuel Weil, Stanley L. Kauffman,
    Samuel L. Weil)

PERSONAL: Born December 30, 1945 in New York,
NY; son of Stanley Lloyd (a lawyer) and Ruth (maiden
name, Fried) Kaufman; married Patricia Swinney (a
state film commissioner), July 13, 1974; children: Lily-
Hayes, Lisbeth, Charlotte.

ADDRESSES: Office—Troma Entertainment, Inc., 733
Ninth Ave., Second Floor, New York, NY 10019-7297.

CAREER: Director, producer, cinematographer, writer.

Film work includes (production manager) *Joe,* 1970;
(production manager) *Sweet Savior,* 1971; (producer,
director, and editor) *The Battle of Love's Return,*
Standard Films, 1971; (producer) *The Newcomers,*
1973; (executive producer) *Sugar Cookies,* General,
1973; (producer) *Big Guss What's the Fuss,* 1973;
(producer, director, and editor) *The Divine Obsession,*
Oppidan, 1975; (location executive) *Saturday Night
Fever,* Paramount, 1977; (producer and
cinematographer) *The Secret Dreams of Mona Q.,*
Troma, 1977; (cinematographer) *My Sex-Rated Wife,*
Melody, 1977; (cinematographer) *Lustful Desires,*

Tigon, 1978; (production supervisor) *Slow Dancing in
the Big City,* United Artists, 1978; (associate producer)
Mother's Day, United Film Distribution, 1980;
(associate producer and unit production manager) *The
Final Countdown,* United Artists, 1980; (producer,
director, and cinematographer) *Squeeze Play,* Troma,
1980; (production manager) *My Dinner with Andre,*
New Yorker, 1981; (executive producer) *Adventure of
the Action Hunters,* Troma, 1982; (producer, director,
and cinematographer) *Waitress,* Troma, 1982;
(producer, director, and cinematographer) *Stuck on
You!,* Troma, 1983; (producer, director, and
cinematographer) *The First Turn-on!!,* Troma, 1984;
(executive producer) *When Nature Calls,* Troma, 1984;
(executive producer) *Screamplay,* Troma, 1984;
(producer and creative consultant) *Splatter University,*
Troma, 1984; (executive producer) *Girls School
Screamer,* Troma, 1984; (executive producer) *The Dark
Side of Midnight,* Troma, 1984; (executive producer,
director, and cinematographer) *The Toxic Avenger,*
Troma, 1985; (executive producer) *The G.I. Execu-
tioner,* Troma, 1985; (producer, director, and camera
operator) *Class of Nuke 'em High,* Troma, 1986;
(executive producer) *Combat Shock,* Troma, 1986;
(executive producer) *Lust for Freedom,* Troma, 1987;
(producer) *Surf Nazis Must Die,* Troma, 1987;
(executive producer) *Monster in the Closet,* Troma,
1987; (executive producer) *Blood Hook,* Troma, 1987;
(producer and director) *War,* Troma, 1988; (executive
producer) *Redneck Zombies,* Trans World Entertainment, 1988; (executive producer) *War Cat,* Trans
World Entertainment, 1988; (producer and director)
The Toxic Avenger, Part II, Troma, 1989; (producer
and director) *The Toxic Avenger Part III: The Last
Temptation of Toxie,* 1989; (producer) *Fortress of
Amerikkka,* 1989; (executive producer) *Jakarta,* 1989;
(producer, director, and camera operator) *Sergeant Kabukiman N.Y.P.D.,* 1990; (producer) *A Nymphoid
Barbarian in Dinosaur Hell,* 1990; (producer) *Class of
Nuke 'em High Part II: Subhumanoid Meltdown,* 1991;
(producer) *Class of Nuke 'em High 3: The Good, the
Bad, and the Subhumanoid,* 1994; (producer) *Blondes
Have More Guns,* 1995; (producer, director, and
camera operator) *Tromeo and Juliet,* Troma, 1996;
(coproducer) *Hellinger,* Rounds Entertainment, 1997;
(producer) *The Legend of the Raven: Chosen One,*
1998; (producer) *The Rowdy Girls,* Troma, 1999;
(director) *Terror Firmer,* Troma Team Video, 1999;
(director) *Citizen Toxie: The Toxic Avenger Part 4,*
Troma, 1999; (producer) *Class of Nuke 'em High IV,*
Troma, 2000; (producer) *Sidney Pink on "Pyro",* 2001;
(executive producer) *Parts of the Family,* 2001;
(producer) *All the Love You Cannes!,* 2002; (director)
Apocalypse Soon, 2002.

Film appearances include *The Battle of Love's Return,* Standard Films, 1971; *Sweet Savior,* 1971; *Cry Uncle!,* 1971; *Sugar Cookies,* General, 1973; *Rocky,* United Artists, 1976; *Slow Dancing in the Big City,* United Artists, 1978; *The Final Countdown,* United Artists, 1980; *Rocky V,* 1990; *Troma,* 1996; *Cannes Man,* Rocket Pictures Home Video, 1996; *Orgazmo,* October Films, 1997; *Terror Firmer,* Troma Team Video, 1999; *Tomorrow by Midnight,* Capitol Films, 1999; *Evocandus,* 2000; *Nikos,* 2002; *The Book of Orgazmo,* 2002; *All the Love You Cannes!,* 2002; *Quest for the Egg Salad: Fellowship of the Egg Salad,* 2002.

Television appearances include (specials) *Canned Ham: Bowfinger,* Comedy Central, 1999. Television work includes (series creator) *Toxic Crusaders,* 1991.

WRITINGS:

(With James Gunn) *All I Need to Know about Film-making I Learned from the Toxic Avenger* (autobiography), Berkley Boulevard (New York, NY), 1998.

(With Trent Haaga and Adam Jahnke) *Make Your Own Damn Movie!: Secrets of a Renegade Film Director,* St. Martin's Griffin (New York, NY), 2002.

SCREENPLAYS

(And composer with Andre Golino) *The Battle of Love's Return,* Standard Films, 1971.

(With Theodore Gershuny) *Sugar Cookies,* General, 1973.

(As Louis Su; with David Wynn and Robert Kalen) *The Divine Obsession,* Oppidan, 1975.

(As Samuel Weil; with others) *Stuck on You!,* Troma, 1983.

(As Samuel Weil; author of additional material) *The First Turn-on!!,* Troma, 1984.

(With Joe Ritter, Gay Terry, and Stuart Strutin) *The Toxic Avenger* (based on a story by Kaufman), Troma, 1985.

(As Samuel Weil; with Haines, Stuart Strutin, and Mark Rudnitsky) *Class of Nuke 'em High* (also known as *Nuke 'em High*), Troma, 1986.

(With Michael Dana, Eric Hattler, and Thomas Martinek) *War* (also known as *Troma's War;* based on a story by Kaufman), Troma, 1988.

(As Samuel Weil; with Gay Terry) *The Toxic Avenger, Part II* (based on a story by Kaufman), Troma, 1989.

The Toxic Avenger Part III: The Last Temptation of Toxie (based on a story by Kaufman), Troma, 1989.

Sergeant Kabukiman N.Y.P.D., 1990.

(And lyricist, theme song) *Class of Nuke 'em High Part II: Subhumanoid Meltdown,* 1991.

Class of Nuke 'em High 3: The Good, the Bad, and the Subhumanoid, Troma, 1994.

(And composer of theme song) *Tromeo and Juliet,* Troma, 1996.

Terror Firmer (based on his book *All I Need to Know about Filmmaking I Learned from the Toxic Avenger*), Troma Team Video, 1999.

Citizen Toxie: The Toxic Avenger Part 4, Troma, 1999.

All the Love You Cannes!, Troma, 2002.

Also author of *Big Guss What's the Fuss* (also known as *Ha-Balash Ha'Amitz Shvartz*), 1973.

SIDELIGHTS: One of the remarkable figures to appear at the fringes of late twentieth-century American cinema has been Lloyd Kaufman, who has written, directed, and produced numerous films released by Troma Studios. Troma, which Kaufman founded in 1974 with friend Michael Herz, has brought the world such cinematic milestones as *The Toxic Avenger* (1985), *The Class of Nuke 'em High* (1986), and numerous sequels to each.

The premise of *The Toxic Avenger* is vintage Kaufman, filled as it is with grotesquerie, humor, and the dark underside of a post-industrial society gone awry. These films are set in Tromaville, "toxic capital of the world," where a tutu-clad, mop-wielding youth falls into a vat of radioactive waste to become the Toxic Avenger, or "Toxie." Reviewing *Citizen Toxie: The Toxic Avenger Part 4* (2001), Lisa Nesselson of *Variety* described the protagonist as a "polite, muscular, carbuncle-covered superhero with one eye sliding down his corrugated cheek and mellifluous vocal intonations modeled on Tony Randall." The film, as she went on to indicate, leaves nothing sacred, portraying "the Almighty as a trash-talking dwarf." She summed up the fourth installment in the "Toxic Avenger" series as "Ebulliently irreverent from first frame to last."

Reviewing *Terror Firmer* (1999), Kevin Thomas in the *Los Angeles Times* maintained that "the gross and the savage and the imbecilic aren't as funny as they used to be in Troma productions." In contrast, Nesselson called it "a lock, schlock, and barrel-of-laughs pic that fearlessly—nay, proudly—scrapes the bottom of said barrel."

Kaufman's over-the-top style has won him a considerable fan base, as demonstrated in his 2002 documentary *All the Love You Cannes!*, which depicts three years' worth of visits to the Cannes Film Festivals by the Troma entourage. Nesselson called the film "frequently funny and borderline unwatchable," yet Kaufman's work and reputation are no joke. Not only have his films helped launch the careers of Kevin Costner, Marisa Tomei, and Billy Bob Thornton, but they have influenced directors Quentin Tarantino, Kevin Smith (*Clerks*), and even Peter Jackson (*The Lord of the Rings: The Fellowship of the Ring*).

The director shared his ideas and experiences in *All I Need to Know about Filmmaking I Learned from the Toxic Avenger* (1998), of which a reviewer in *Publishers Weekly* wrote, "Kaufman's gross-out humor and rambling style will wear thin for all but the most devoted Troma fans, but his perspective on independent film production stands to benefit low-budget auteurs everywhere." Mike Tribby of *Booklist* summed up the work with greater enthusiasm, noting that with "Troma's patented assortment of nymphomaniacs, surf Nazis, and sleazy monsters, this is not-to-be-missed pop culture stuff."

BIOGRAPHICAL AND CRITICAL SOURCES:

BOOKS

Contemporary Theatre, Film, and Television, Volume 35, Gale (Detroit, MI), 2001.
Kaufman, Lloyd, with James Gunn, *All I Need to Know about Filmmaking I Learned from the Toxic Avenger* (autobiography), Berkley Boulevard (New York, NY), 1998.
Kaufman, Lloyd, with Trent Haaga and Adam Jahnke, *Make Your Own Damn Movie!: Secrets of a Renegade Film Director,* St. Martin's Griffin (New York, NY), 2002.

PERIODICALS

Atlanta Journal-Constitution, June 18, 2002, Bob Longino, "Toxic Avenger's Crusade: Make Your Own Movie: Cult Favorite Pushes Guide to Producing Independent Films," p. E1.

Booklist, August, 1998, Mike Tribby, review of *All I Need to Know about Filmmaking I Learned from the Toxic Avenger,* pp. 1949-1950.
Los Angeles Times, October 29, 1999, Kevin Thomas, review of *Terror Firmer,* p. 12.
Publishers Weekly, June 29, 1998, review of *All I Need to Know about Filmmaking,* p. 43.
Variety, September 29, 1997, Monica Roman, "N.Y.'s Strange Bedfellows: B-Movie Kingpin, Film Commish Husband-and-Wife Boosters for City," pp. S51-52; June 7, 1999, Lisa Nesselson, review of *Terror Firmer,* p. 48; June 25, 2001, Lisa Nesselson, review of *Citizen Toxie: The Toxic Avenger Part 4,* p. 25; June 10, 2002, review of *All the Love You Cannes!,* p. 36.
Village Voice, December 5, 2000, Nick Rutigliano, "Toxic Avengers," p. 138.*

*   *   *

KAVIEFF, Paul R. 1947-

PERSONAL: Born August 29, 1947, in Detroit, MI; son of Melvin C. Kavieff (a public school system director of vocational education); married Deborah A. Carson, February, 1990 (marriage ended December, 1999). *Ethnicity:* "Russian/Jewish." *Education:* Oakland University, B.A. (magna cum laude), 1975, and graduate study. *Politics:* Liberal. *Hobbies and other interests:* Classic cars, performance engineering.

ADDRESSES: Home—2630 Trafford Rd., Royal Oak, MI 48073.

CAREER: Detroit Public Schools, Detroit, MI, stationary/operating engineer, 1966-93; writer. Wayne State University, stationary/operating engineer, 1979—; licensed mechanical contractor; consultant on organized crime. *Military service:* U.S. Navy, 1965-68.

AWARDS, HONORS: Stuart and Venice Gross Award for Literature, Saginaw Valley State University, c. 2001, for *The Violent Years.*

WRITINGS:

The Purple Gang, Barricade Books (Fort Lee, NJ), 2000.
The Violent Years, Barricade Books (Fort Lee, NJ), 2001.

WORK IN PROGRESS: A biography of a New York gangster; a history of Murder Inc.; ongoing research on the history of organized crime in the United States.

SIDELIGHTS: Paul R. Kavieff told *CA:* "The primary motivation for my writing is a lifelong fascination with how the underworld and the upperworld mesh. My first two books, *The Purple Gang* and *The Violent Years,* are the first history/reference works ever written about the Detroit underworld. I am particularly interested in how the social order in the U.S. Prohibition Era underworld worked.

"As a U.S. organized crime historian, my writing process begins with a careful and usually exhaustive search for historical materials related to my subject. After digesting what sometimes is many thousands of pages of material, I begin writing. I find that, if I waited to get inspired, I would accomplish very little. Therefore my writing process often consists of forcing myself to write something every day. The hardest thing for any writer is to get something on paper. Once my thoughts are written and I can look at the product objectively, I can then begin to shape the book."

*   *   *

KELLY, Nora 1945-

PERSONAL: Born 1945, in Paterson, NJ; son of John Stephenson and Nancy (Elliott) Kelly; children: Julian Clarke. *Education:* University of British Columbia, B.A. (with honors); Simon Fraser University, Ph.D., 1979. *Hobbies and other interests:* Travel, food, wine, art, tending long-lived friendships.

ADDRESSES: Home—Vancouver, British Columbia, Canada. *Office*—c/o Poisoned Pen Press, 6962 East First Ave., Suite 103, Scottsdale, AZ 85251. *Agent*—c/o Author Mail, A. P. Watt Ltd., 20 John St., London WC1N 2DR, England.

CAREER: Writer.

MEMBER: Writers' Union of Canada, Crime Writers of Canada, Sisters in Crime.

AWARDS, HONORS: Arthur Ellis Award, Crime Writers of Canada, 1998, for best Canadian mystery.

WRITINGS:

In the Shadow of King's (novel), St. Martin's (New York, NY), 1984.
Blue's Folly (screenplay), Canadian Broadcasting Corp., 1986.
My Sister's Keeper (novel), St. Martin's (New York, NY), 1992.
Bad Chemistry (novel), St. Martin's (New York, NY), 1994.
Old Wounds (novel), Poisoned Pen Press (Scottsdale, AZ), 1999.
Hot Pursuit (novel), Poisoned Pen Press (Scottsdale, AZ), 2002.

Also contributor of short story "Quebec Street" to *Capilano Review,* 1998.

SIDELIGHTS: Nora Kelly has written a number of well-received mysteries. Many critics believe that she has a flair for creating intelligent, well fleshed-out characters. Her first book, *In the Shadow of King's,* introduces readers to super sleuth Gillian Adams, a history professor who travels back and forth between the Pacific Northwest and the United Kingdom, much like Kelly herself.

Gillian Adams, besides being intelligent, insightful, and quite clever, is in love with Scotland Yard's Edward Gisborne, who helps Gillian solve murders when she is in England. This is true in *In the Shadow of King's,* in which Gillian is back at her alma mater, King's College. She has been invited to Sunday lunch, during which she witnesses the attempted murder of her host, Alistair Greenwood. Pompous and cruel, Professor Greenwood is not a well-liked man. He bitterly insults a woman sitting at the table, and she in turn pulls out a gun and attempts to kill him. Although the bullet misses its aim, Greenwood does not avoid death much longer. Shortly after the first attempt on his life, he is shot dead in a lecture room at King's College at the conclusion of a lecture that Gillian is giving. With Gisborne's assistance, Gillian gathers all the clues and eventually finds the murderer.

Kelly's excellent literary skills were praised in a *Library Journal* review of *In the Shadow of King's.* The reviewer wrote: "She displays both literary skills and a talent for adroit plotting." Lynette Friesen, also writing for *Library Journal,* complimented Kelly's "flowing prose style," although she was less convinced about Kelly's ability to build meaningful suspense. Nonetheless, Friesen concluded that "overall this [book] is excellent."

In Kelly's second book, *My Sister's Keeper,* Gillian has to deal with the politics of sexism on the campus of a university in the Pacific Northwest. The novel takes place in the 1990s, shortly after the murder of fourteen female students by a crazed man who believed that feminists had ruined his life. The plot is based on the Montreal Massacre, an actual event in Canada in which fourteen women engineering students were murdered by a crazed man who believed that feminists had ruined his life. The plot of the novel grew out of the tense and hostile atmosphere that pervaded many campuses in the wake of the massacre, when more women began challenging male traditions that they believed fostered sexist attitudes.

Kelly sets up an angry tone that centers on a rally organized by her female characters against the misogyny that exists at the university. In this agitated environment, the Feminist Union comes under attack. While most of the college administrators view the student harassment of the Union as mere pranks, Gillian is a little more wary. When one of the more radical feminist students loses her fellowship and then is found murdered, Gillian is hot on the trail. A critic for *Publishers Weekly* referred to Kelly's second book as a "thought-provoking, smoothly written mystery" and "an often riveting novel."

Bad Chemistry once again demonstrates Gillian's intelligence in solving crimes. Gillian has returned to the United Kingdom and finds herself in the city of Cambridge, where almost everyone knows everyone else. Wendy Fowler, a fellow in the chemistry department of the university, is found murdered. She had been a volunteer at the local Pregnancy Information Service in town, and following her murder it is discovered that she was pregnant, the result of a clandestine affair with a married man.

Wendy was also a very ambitious young chemist. She did not try to conceal her drive to succeed, and this irked many of her male colleagues. Although the murder shocks the townsfolk, who find it hard to believe that such hatred could exist in their midst, Gil-

lian uncovers evidence of venomous rivalries that exist among Wendy's peers. Then there is a second murder, and although the local police do not link the two murders, Gillian is not so naive. She and her lover, Gisborne, work through the clues until the crime is solved.

A *Publishers Weekly* reviewer found that Kelly "effectively integrates her feminist ideas with the story line" in *Bad Chemistry;* and Gail Pool, writing for the *Wilson Library Bulletin,* observed, "Kelly uses the complexities of the case to probe the complexities of women's lives as they struggle with feminism and ambition, misogyny and love."

In *Old Wounds* the locale changes again, as Gillian visits her ailing mother in the Hudson River Valley of New York State. To keep herself financially afloat, Gillian accepts a position as guest lecturer at a small rural school. The setting is quiet, but this changes when a young student, Nicole Bishop, is murdered and left on one of the country back roads. At first it is believed that Nicole was shot in a hunting accident. Later it is discovered that the young woman was stabbed. Upon further investigation, authorities learn that Nicole had been leading a double life.

Gillian is familiar with many of the local inhabitants, having known them since childhood. As she investigates the crime, she runs into old acquaintances, not all of them remembered fondly. In confronting them, Gillian must revisit her past and in the process stir up memories that she would rather have forgotten. Also, in dealing with her mother's impending death, Gillian must learn to change roles, becoming the caretaker of the person who once nurtured her. She must come to terms with a future she had not previously spent much time contemplating: a world without the presence of her mother.

Carolyn A. Van Der Meer, in a review of *Old Wounds* for *Mystery Review,* stated that Kelly's "real coup . . . is her ability to capture the psychological elements present in a crime of passion"; while *BookBrowser's* Harriet Klausner concluded: "The story line allows the delightful characters to show their true disposition and motives that dictate much of their behavior." A critic for *Publishers Weekly* praised Kelly's fourth book as "a richly rewarding story of old wounds opened, probed and ultimately healed." *Old Wounds* won the 1998 Arthur Ellis Award for best Canadian mystery.

BIOGRAPHICAL AND CRITICAL SOURCES:

PERIODICALS

Library Journal, January 1985, Lynette Friesen, review of *In the Shadow of King's,* p. 103.

Mystery Review, fall, 1999, Carolyn A. Van Der Meer, review of *Old Wounds.*

Publishers Weekly, November 9, 1984, review of *In the Shadow of King's,* p. 61; October 19, 1992, review of *My Sister's Keeper,* p. 58; April 25, 1999, review of *Bad Chemistry,* pp. 60-61; November 22, 1999, review of *Old Wounds,* p. 45.

Wilson Library Bulletin, February 1993, review of *My Sister's Keeper,* pp. 92-93; May 1994, Gail Pool, review of *Bad Chemistry,* p. 87.

OTHER

BookBrowser, http://www.bookbrowser.com/ (September 22, 1999), Harriet Klausner, review of *Old Wounds.*

*   *   *

KING, Laurie R. 1952-

PERSONAL: Born September 19, 1952, in Oakland, CA; daughter of Roger R. (a furniture restorer) and Mary (a retired librarian and curator; maiden name, Dickson) Richardson; married Noel Q. King (a professor emeritus), 1977; children: Nathanael, Zoe. *Education:* University of California, Santa Cruz, B.A., 1977; Graduate Theological Union, M.A., 1984. *Religion:* Episcopal. *Hobbies and other interests:* Swimming, gardening, travel.

ADDRESSES: Home—P.O. Box 1152, Freedom, CA 95019. *Agent*—Linda Allen, 1949 Green St., No. 5, San Francisco, CA 94123.

CAREER: Writer. Worked as a manager of Kaldi's (Now Los Gatos Coffee Roasters), at various volunteer posts in the Pajaro United School District, and as a counselor for La Leche League International.

Laurie R. King

MEMBER: International Association of Crime Writers, Crime Writers Association U.K., Mystery Writers of America, Sisters in Crime.

AWARDS, HONORS: Edgar Allan Poe Award, Mystery Writers of America, 1994 and John Creasey Dagger, 1995, both for *A Grave Talent;* Agatha Award nomination, 1994, and American Library Association best book citation, 1996, for *The Beekeeper's Apprentice;* Nero Wolfe Award, 1995, for *A Monstrous Regiment of Women;* Edgar Allan Poe Award nomination, 1996, for *With Child* and for "Paleta Man"; Gail Rich Award, 1998; honorary doctorate from Church Divinity School of the Pacific.

WRITINGS:

"KATE MARTINELLI" SERIES

A Grave Talent, St. Martin's Press (New York, NY), 1993.

To Play the Fool, St. Martin's Press (New York, NY), 1995.

With Child, St. Martin's Press (New York, NY), 1996.

Night Work, Bantam (New York, NY), 2000.

"MARY RUSSELL" SERIES

The Beekeeper's Apprentice; or, On the Segregation of the Queen, St. Martin's Press (New York, NY), 1994.
A Monstrous Regiment of Women, St. Martin's Press (New York, NY), 1995.
A Letter of Mary, St. Martin's Press (New York, NY), 1997.
The Moor, St. Martin's Press (New York, NY), 1998.
O Jerusalem, Bantam (New York, NY), 1999.
Justice Hall, Bantam (New York, NY), 2002.

OTHER

A Darker Place, Bantam (New York, NY), 1999, published as *Birth of a New Moon* (London, England), 1999.
Folly, Bantam (New York, NY), 2001.
Keeping Watch, Bantam (New York, NY), 2003.

SIDELIGHTS: Laurie R. King's unconventional take on the mystery genre has led to the development of two popular series characters: Mary Russell, the detective wife of Sherlock Holmes, and Kate Martinelli, a San Francisco policewoman. Through a number of books featuring each protagonist, King has formed their characters—and those of their cohorts—while consistently crafting tense thrillers, many with religious themes. The author began her career auspiciously, when her first published book, *A Grave Talent,* won both the Edgar Allan Poe Award and Britain's John Creasey Dagger. Since then she has produced a significant body of "thoughtful, intelligent, innovative, imaginative mysteries," stated reviewer Emily Melton in *Booklist.*

"I began writing in 1987 at the age of thirty-five when my younger child started preschool, freeing up three entire mornings every week," King told the *St. James Guide to Crime and Mystery Writers.* King earned an advanced degree in religious studies, but when she began to write she concentrated on fiction, drawing on her specialized knowledge and her experience as a world traveler. Her first completed novel was *The Beekeeper's Apprentice; or, On the Segregation of the Queen,* but due to its use of Sherlock Holmes as a character, certain copyright issues had to be resolved

before it could be published. In the meantime, her first "Martinelli" book, *A Grave Talent,* was released, earning warm reviews and major awards.

King's two protagonists, Russell and Martinelli, could not be more different in time or place. Kate Martinelli is a modern-day inspector with the San Francisco Police Department, while Mary Russell is a teenage girl coming of age in England during World War I. But both characters are keen detectives, relying on intellect and courage to solve crimes. With the creation of Mary Russell, King is "confronted with furious resistance from Sherlockian purists," noted interviewer Mia Stampe. However, in the opinion of *MysteryGuide. com* reviewer JP, this first book in the "Mary Russell" series "captures the spirit of the Holmes adventures with a great deal of love, while allowing room for female fans to more easily project themselves into the story." In her first outing, Russell meets Sir Arthur Conan Doyle's legendary sleuth, Sherlock Holmes, whom she matches "wit for wit and soon becomes his willing and eager apprentice," according to *St. James Guide to Crime and Mystery Writers* writer Susan Oleksiw in an essay on King's work. *The Beekeeper's Apprentice* finds Sherlock coming out of retirement to help Russell solve the case of the kidnapped daughter of a U.S. senator. *Booklist* critic Emily Melton found the novel "funny, heartwarming and full of intrigue." Purist resistance notwithstanding, Pat Dowell stated in the *Washington Post Book World* that King "has relieved Holmes of the worst effects of his misogyny and, by so doing, salved the old hurt that comes to every female reader of literature, usually at a very young age, when she realizes with great disappointment that she is excluded from the circle of presumed readers and fellow adventurers: that sinking feeling that 'They didn't mean me.'"

The second "Mary Russell" mystery, *A Monstrous Regiment of Women,* takes the Holmes-Russell relationship a step forward, with the aging master sleuth "indeed [losing] his heart" to the plucky young woman, as Marilyn Stasio commented in a *New York Times review.* "He also flings aside his idiosyncratic genius and his proud, disdainful ways to mince along in the shadow of his protege—even to the point of drawing her bath and preparing her meals. It is not a pretty sight." Dick Adler in the Chicago *Tribune Books* deemed the second installment "as audacious as it is entertaining and moving," adding that King's research, "here and elsewhere is both prodigious and seamless:

Fact and fiction blend smoothly." After establishing the character of a retired Holmes, King sets her third Holmes-Russell novel, *A Letter of Mary,* in 1923. By now Russell is a full-fledged detective, investigating the suspicious death of an archaeologist in possession of a history-making discovery. What caught the attention of a *Publishers Weekly* reviewer was the interplay between the two main characters who, though generations apart, "share intellectual camaraderie, companionable humor and sexual attraction."

King's other series detective, Kate Martinelli, stars in several mysteries that Melton noted are "not as popular as her 'Mary Russell' novels, but . . . a solid choice for those who like tough female cops." As she did with Russell, the author develops Martinelli emotionally and professionally throughout the series, paying special attention to Martinelli's sexual orientation and the challenges it presents in her career. The reader gets to know Martinelli, from her beginnings as the wary partner to a male detective, to her emergence as a "confident, dynamic gay woman," according to Oleksiw. Adler, reviewing *With Child* in the Chicago *Tribune Books,* described the character as "the kind of person you'd like to know and talk with over many lunches, a smart and tough woman confident in her lesbian sexuality."

In *With Child,* King has the Bay Area officer traveling to the Pacific Northwest to track a killer. While readers may beat Martinelli to the conclusion, noted a *Publishers Weekly* critic, "the pleasure of her company and the accelerating suspense preceding the climax make for a compelling read." As for how a married, straight woman came to write about a lesbian police officer, King says with a laugh that "'the effrontery of it sometimes takes me aback!'" as she was quoted in a *Publishers Weekly* review.

Night Work is the series' fourth novel in which Martinelli investigates the vigilante murders of abusive men. Two topics close to King's heart, feminism and religion, figure prominently, and a reviewer for *Publishers Weekly* noted that King's use of the esoteric to form her narrative makes *Night Watch* "a highly unusual—and memorable—novel . . . compelling, effective." As the plot unfolds, the author also focuses on Martinelli's efforts to rebuild her severely damaged relationship with life-partner Lee while remaining committed to her work. This tension between her personal and work lives increases dramatically when

evidence suggests that a friend of hers may be responsible for the vigilante murders. In her *Library Journal* review of the book, Nancy McNicol asserted, "King once again gives the reader a superbly structured plot played off a set of intellectually stimulating characters. . . . Fans of the three previous Martinelli books will be gratified."

Comparing the characters of Russell and Martinelli, Oleksiw remarked that while the historical figure "represents a struggle women believe they have long since won—the right of women to exert influence and act—Kate Martinelli embodies the restrictions that remain, the more subtle ones that prevent women from claiming an authentic identity within the supposedly broader bounds of contemporary society and living according to that identity." Both series offer King opportunities to explore feminist issues in subtle and broader ways. Whether it is a discovery of the role Mary Magdalen played in Jesus Christ's ministry in *A Letter of Mary* or the murderous impulses of extremist feminists in *Night Work,* King remains engaged with the place of women in society both past and present.

The use of series characters also enables the author to explore how character shapes destiny over time. "As a writer I like the structure of a mystery," King told *Authors and Artists for Young Adults.* "It enables me the skeletal structure upon which to hang story or plot, something to keep me going forward in narrative, to allow the people in the book to move around and develop while the plot unfolds. Mysteries also are often series, and you have the opportunity to get to know characters over a length of time. You can develop them and really get to know them in a series."

King's stand-alone mysteries include *A Darker Place* and *Folly.* In *A Darker Place,* FBI agent Anne Waverley infiltrates a mysterious cult, placing herself and other members in jeopardy as she seeks to discover the group's deadly aims. A *Publishers Weekly* reviewer described King's character Anne Waverley as "a complicated and enigmatic heroine who perfectly fits the task of illuminating . . . religious cults." In the *New York Times Book Review,* Marilyn Stasio likewise praised Waverley as "just the kind of person to rescue the psychological suspense genre from its surfeit of perfect heroines." In *Folly,* Rae Newborn seeks a cure for her depression by working on a dilapidated and isolated house willed to her by an uncle she never knew. One *Publishers Weekly* reviewer stated that in

Folly King "skillfully portrays psychological illness." Still, this novel seems to have met with less enthusiasm from King's readers. Another *Publishers Weekly* reviewer complained, "Beautiful prose and intriguing characters can't quite save the confusing, and at times needlessly complicated plot of this challenging psychological thriller"; the reviewer goes on to cite the overwhelming "complexity of detail" and the "hokey" denouement as further evidence of the book's weaknesses. Whitney Scott of *Booklist* mocked what she called King's "formulaic interludes" in her review: Rae "takes her tenuously healed body and raw wound of a mind to a deserted island. . . . Rae performs the obligatory scene of casting her antidepressants and tranquilizers into the sea, followed by the equally requisite discovery of—gasp!—a Friday-esque footprint." Although in reviewers' minds King may have missed the mark with this novel, she is certain to have taken note of their responses. In her interview with Mia Stampe for the *Kriminal Litteraere Nyheder* Web site, King revealed her outlook. "A good reviewer . . . can point out things that the lowly writer had not realized: that parts of the plot the writer thought so very clever are actually terribly cliched, that plots creak if not well oiled. . . . I pay attention to reviews, and bleed when they are bad. But I learn."

King once commented in *Authors and Artists for Young Adults:* "Any good novel tells the truth in some way. It's the responsibility of an author to entertain, but it's also the job of any good novel to allow us all to learn something about what it means to be a thinking human being, to see how we work and function in the world. . . . I am never happier than when someone writes to say they have re-read my books. This indicates that there is a depth to them that you don't get with just one reading."

AUTOBIOGRAPHICAL ESSAY:

Laurie R. King contributed the following autobiographical essay to *CA:*

Is a writer—is any artist, for that matter—born, or made? Or is it some near-random combination of chance and drive that shapes the person?

Well, yes.

My mother married my father in part because she was drawn to his family's stability, that his still-married parents had lived in the same house they'd bought upon moving from Minnesota to the San Francisco Bay area when he was three years old. She, daughter of a much-broken home, envisioned a secure life, in a house bought and paid for, with decades of raising children and getting to know the neighbors. Instead she got a string of rentals and a man with itchy feet—or, as family rumor had it, one who read his way through a library and then moved on.

We moved so often when I was young, it wasn't until high school that I entered the same school in September that I'd been in the previous June. By then, I'd more or less given up on the tedious process of making friends, since libraries were always nearby, and books were much better companions anyway. So for most of my childhood, in Santa Cruz and San Jose, California, then the suburbs of Tacoma, Washington, I lived in a community of fictional individuals—those of Walter Farley and Marguerite Henry and Albert Payson Terhune; Ray Bradbury and Robert Heinlein and Isaac Asimov; Rosemary Sutcliff and Madeleine L'Engle—plus biographies of pretty much everyone, travel books, teach-yourself Esperanto, you name it. I even read Dickens, whom nobody had yet told me was boring. So as we migrated up and down the West Coast, I was at home, because there were always libraries.

I am a writer, because I love and have been nurtured by books.

Ancestor Worship:

My mother was born in San Francisco, as was her mother before her. My grandmother remembered camping in a tent in Golden Gate Park after the 1906 quake, waiting for the flames to subside. My grandfather, who had been in his twenties, always told us that had he been a good, law-abiding Christian, he would have been killed in his bed. But because he was out at an all-night poker game when the quake struck, he came home to find a brick chimney dropped neatly across where his sober, more virtuous self might have laid down.

My grandfather's name was Robert J. Dickson, known inevitably to all as Dick. He came out from Chicago after a year of university, when his eyesight began to fail and his doctor suggested a more active style of life. (This seems to have been a common prescription in the ill-lit nineteenth century: Richard Henry Dana's experience on a sailing ship, written up as *Two Years Before the Mast*, also began with a spell of blindness caused by study.) Dick's modicum of higher education qualified him for the nickname "Doc," particularly during the needy years of the world-wide flu epidemic following the First World War. Dick raised peaches and white asparagus in the Sacramento River delta, and married a woman seventeen years his junior, Florence Adderley, in 1920. Their two children were Mary Jane, born in 1922, and Robert J., Jr., in 1925.

The Adderleys were minor English gentry who had migrated to the Bahamas in the seventeenth century. Over the next three centuries, the family gave rise to planters (read: slave owners), a sponge diver, a privateer, an unlicensed whaler, and eventually a Commander of the Order of the British Empire, King's Counsel, and speaker of the House of Assembly in Nassau. One branch ended up in San Francisco. When her parents separated, my mother was more or less raised by two English aunts, maiden ladies who took their toast with marmalade, drank tea shipped in wooden chests from England, and never, ever contemplated applying for American citizenship. Mother graduated from San Mateo High, and started at University of California Berkeley before finances demanded that she take a job at Macy's in San Francisco. When the war came, she took work making delicate and essential vacuum tubes—Rosie the Riveter in miniature.

My father's people, the Richardsons, were more of a hodge-podge, so that he claimed to be a little of everything including Czechoslovakian, which last delighted me as a child although I suspect it was coined for that very purpose. As Disbrows, the family was in the New World by 1719, so that I could claim to be a Daughter of the American Revolution, were I so inclined. His family came from Minneapolis to the Bay Area when he was young. He interrupted his college career at Redlands in Southern California to enlist in the Army, fought his war in the South Pacific, and married my mother upon his return. His list of employment reads a bit like that of a stereotypical mystery writer, from nurseryman to real estate agent to gas station attendant to itinerant furniture repairman, but he never wrote anything more involved than letters, and sadly died before he could hold his daughter's first book in his hands.

Early Life:

I was born in Oakland, California, across the bay from San Francisco—we lived in Walnut Creek, where my

The author with her mother, 1952

father worked for a nursery, but Oakland held the nearest Kaiser hospital. My sister was seven years older; my brother, three years younger than I, was born in Walnut Creek; when he was small we moved to the beach community of Santa Cruz, the first house and town I can remember. In the summers we would stand alongside busy Mission Street and shout, "Tourist go home!" at the passing cars. On warm afternoons, which near the ocean would more likely be in May or September than in the actual summer months, we would walk down the hills to the beach. Fifteen years later, when I moved to the Santa Cruz area as a college student, I would be constantly taken aback by coming around some corner or driving up some street and finding myself on familiar ground. My daughter, in 2002, lived across the street from a hillside where my tricycling brother nearly shot under a car in 1958.

The beach claimed by us locals was on the other side of the wharf from the glitzy Boardwalk, or, if the tide allowed, along the bank of the San Lorenzo River south of the bright lights, where the water was calm but the scum and scraps from the upstream tannery a seagull-attracting annoyance. We did venture onto the

Boardwalk sometimes—for the Fourth of July fireworks, certainly. I was a whiz at the game of skeeball, but the only Boardwalk ride I really enjoyed was the ever-magical merry-go-round, its steam calliope, all parts visible, blasting out music as the shiny horses went up and down and the bigger kids stretched out to catch the brass rings. The town itself was away from the beach: Woolworth's with its cheap temptations and its soda fountain with my mother, the darkly fragrant United Cigar shop with my father (who confused me by calling it the "hot stove league," although there was no stove I could see, just magazine racks where he bought *Astounding* and *Argosy*, John D. MacDonald and the Doc Savage stories, along with those paperback novellas printed in a delightful, back-to-back format which meant that both covers made for a new beginning). And always, the library.

The Santa Cruz Public Library was a tall, dark-shingled Aladdin's cave of riches, which I remember draped with vines although I suspect that later imagination provided that decoration. I still have a small pin, brass and blue enamel, given me by the summer reading club when I was six. And in first or second grade, *The Hobbit* must have swum into the edges of my ken (although I cannot have been old enough to read it, and don't recall my parents reading it to me) because I can remember as if it were yesterday sitting in the sunny classroom and composing a story about a small creature that lived under a hill, illustrating each extra-wide line of the pulp paper with small, precise drawings of mysterious figures and round red doors set into grassy hillsides—and remember too the hot humiliation of failing the assignment because the illustrations had taken me so long, I ran out of time to do the text.

Thus the writer's first lesson: Finish the story.

Forty years later, it is a lesson I am still learning. The temptations to decorate, to revise and tinker with a horribly bald and incomplete manuscript instead of bashing through to The End are perpetual, but the mantra that runs through my mind every day of writing a first draft is: Finish the thing, then see what's there.

*

One of the great pleasures in being the sort of writer I am, in having published *The Beekeeper's Apprentice*, is looking up during a signing and seeing myself in the back row. The book, which begins with the heroine fifteen years old yet easily capable of meeting the great Sherlock Holmes as an equal, is the story I wish I had when I was twelve or fourteen. Fantasy, affirmation, a hint of romance, a dash of adventure: along with those shy girls in the back row, I *am* Mary Russell. Or I was at that age, in my mind.

In truth, I was socially inept, physically awkward, excruciatingly shy, and always an outsider. We moved north to Washington state in 1961, and although we did our share of camping in state parks and going clamming on the wide ocean beaches, and I spent two summers in the camp on what used to be Spirit Lake before Mount St. Helens erupted, mostly I sat with my nose in a book. My after-school hours in fifth and sixth grades were spent (when not reading) either in the company of a girl who alternated between using me as an audience for her renditions of *West Side Story* ballads ("I'm So Pretty" warbled while primping at the mirror) and creating devious ways to torment me, or else in the privacy of my room, where I had constructed an entire universe out of plasticine clay, horses and people, dogs and houses.

Picture, if you will, a small, neat house in the early 1960s, overlooking Puget Sound, that inland sea on top of which giant rafts of logs head down to Tacoma's foul-smelling paper mills and Japanese freighters come to load up, while below the surface nuclear submarines and pods of Orca play. Dash Point is a small community astride the road between Tacoma and Seattle (little changed thirty-five years later, although the Richardson family probably couldn't afford to live there now) with Janet's general store, a Presbyterian church, and an elementary school of six classes and a hundred students. When it snows, the steep road looping down to the water is closed to all but sledders, and in alternate summers the town hosts a fund-raising Dock Dinner barbecue. The town's public hall is perched halfway up the hillside, a place where the PTA and volunteer fire department hold their meetings, one room of which has walls covered with padlocked cabinet doors. Behind those doors, revealed at odd hours during the week, is the Dash Point Public Library, its limitations overcome by regular transfusions and exchanges with the main branch in town. A regular visitor—in fact the daughter of the part-time librarian—is a tall, gawky ten year old with cropped hair and a squint (for she will not get her first glasses until the following year). She surveys the new books, hoping for something as compelling as *The Black Stal-*

In seventh grade, 1964

lion or *The Diamond in the Window,* or that biography of Thoreau she read recently in which the young Henry speculated about the oddity of his sister "making" a bed, as if with hammer and saw. Today she finds nothing so appealing, but takes down a book she has enjoyed before, about some teenagers who have marvelous adventures in the sea, including having a foot trapped by a giant clam. She makes out the card with her name, Laurie Richardson, in round, upright script, and heads up the hill and through the blackberry-lined shortcuts to her house. Past the garden with the hateful bee-swarming hydrangea that makes lawn-mowing such a hazard, over the front lawn, in the door past the eight-foot grand piano (taken long ago by her father as commission in a real estate deal, its size for years determining which houses they could rent and which would be too small). Up the stairs, past her high-school-aged sister's cubby, into the room she shares with her younger brother, the nicest room in the house with a panoramic view of the Sound and Whidbey Island. But the view is not of interest to young Laurie. Instead, she settles down on a high stool near the tall, deep plywood shelving unit her father has built, reaches for the crudely modeled figures of grey-blue clay, and enters into the world of her imagination.

I thought of it as an extension of the Walter Farley stories, the "Black Stallion" and "Island Stallion" series brought to three-inch, sticky life, every figure the dreary color of the much-reworked clay. It was, without a doubt, a strange preoccupation for a child— had it been the 1990s instead of the 1960s, I would surely have been in therapy and subjected to a regimen of mood-relieving drugs. As it was, those long hours of fitting the figures onto the horses' backs and imagining the sensations of riding free were my first excursion into telling myself stories.

I occasionally wonder, particularly when I've been talking to a group of kids, if I would have become a writer earlier had I actually met such an alien creature. But these were the days before book tours and author interviews, before schools brought in artists of various flavors to demonstrate the attainability of such ways of life, and the only person I knew associated with the world of books was a neighbor girl whose photograph appeared in a children's book on Hawaii. As far as I was concerned, it was God who put the books on library shelves, not mere mortals. Slow learner that I am, it didn't occur to me to write my own stories until I was in my thirties.

Education

Moving more or less yearly is not conducive to an even education. The differences in curricula meant that I repeated several subjects (I can still diagram a mean sentence) while others (states' capitals, for example) eluded me entirely. My parents separated for two years, during which time my mother and I lived in Saratoga, California, a wealthy community (except for us) on the outskirts of San Jose, nestling into the Santa Cruz mountains in which I would live as an adult. The Beatles roared into the scene while I lived in Saratoga, and the Vietnam war got into gear.

In the summer of 1967, while the hippies were flocking into San Francisco with flowers in their hair, I was headed in the opposite direction. My mother and I rejoined my father and brother in a house at the southern end of Tacoma, where I attended a high school fed by nearby Fort Lewis (this at the height of the Vietnam war) where I was the weird kid with long hair and gold-rimmed glasses, Army jacket with green-for-ecology peace patch on the shoulder, the school's only hippie. High school found me more interested in science fiction than science, reading novels than writing papers, and my lackluster grades hardly encouraged counselors to seek me out with the stimulation of college dreams.

I seem to have had a certain grasp of language even in my teens. During my first year at Franklin Pierce High, I wrote the following paragraph, a homesick fifteen year-old putting her longing into words:

> San Francisco, as I last saw it, was enough to stir the heart of any native Californian. The scene was movingly beautiful. I can remember it as if I saw it just yesterday. It was from the freeway leaving the city, looking down through the tall, intricately woven expansion of the Golden Gate Bridge. The angular outlines of the downtown buildings were softened by a light gray fog. The mist cleared over the water, letting the morning sun shine down onto the bay. Alcatraz, foreboding yet lonely, protruded from the clear surface of the blue-gray water. An ocean liner slowly made its way past the tiny sailboats on its journey to the ocean. The scene slowly disappeared behind the hills surrounding the bay. The last things to be hidden from sight were the tall, proud pillars of that beautiful bridge.

This sentimental paragraph garnered an A, with the teacher's comment that the word selection showed it to be "quality communication." Still, an ability with language hardly amounts to a full-time university scholarship, and there was no way the family could manage to put both my brother and me through college. In the end, I more or less backed into university, when the aunt with whom I lived after finishing high school insisted I keep myself busy by enrolling at the local junior college.

It is extraordinary, how often in life ideas and teachers reach out and grab a person. A teacher by the name of Norman Miller—overworked, under-challenged, perpetually rumpled, the very essence of curmudgeonly—was my own encounter on the road to Damascus. This gruff individual taught logic, philosophy, and religious studies, and was the first to suggest that religion was a passion that could permeate all life, a drive like any other, not some ethereal wimpiness. Typical of Miller was the debate staged between him and a philosopher whose difficult belief it was that all matter was illusion. Miller's response was to pick up the nearest chair and heave it at the man, which rather ended the debate.

Unfortunately, the provisions for the study of religion at a junior college in the 1970s were limited. However, just down the road was the shiny-new University of California campus at Santa Cruz, which had a program in religious studies. I applied in 1973, was accepted as a junior transfer, and spent the next two and a half years in ecstasy.

On the surface, it was a ridiculous choice, leaving me unprepared for any real employment. But I loved the study of religion, in which I perceived the blend of human yearnings and passions intertwining with rationality and observation. Religion was the way the human being sang with his or her entire being, the way we confronted the universe and tried to find out place in it. The subject chose me, and I could only go with it.

Anaïs Nin came to speak at Santa Cruz, and Houston Smith and Henry Chadwick. I studied Chinese language and Russian spirituality, Jungian archetypal psychology and Alchemical symbolism. I labored in the campus organic garden, planting red cabbages under the guidance of a garrulous and nearly incomprehensible Sikh, and wrote bad poetry about the experience. I read Lao Tse and Jacob Neusner and Carl Jung and Frank Waters, all of whom had something to say about the human religious experience. I wrote a thesis project on the role of the fool in Western culture, drawing on the New Testament and on American Indian Trickster mythology. I read and listened and talked, and I was at home.

In other words, a typical liberal arts education from what was already known as the University of California's "touchy-feely" campus. A B.A. that took me seven years (since I was working my way through) and left me with the first university degree in my family. One that was completely worthless in terms of employment, yet which has, oddly enough, proven to be the basis for everything I now do.

I never took a course in creative writing, never signed up for any English class other than the basic requirement. If I had, no doubt what I write now would be very different. Instead, I followed my interests, and when I had fulfilled my Bachelor's requirements, I turned to graduate school, again staying close to home and applying to the Graduate Theological Union in Berkeley.

The GTU is, as the name indicates, a union of the various graduate schools—seminaries—that have taken root on "holy hill" to the north of the UC Berkeley campus. It is a tree-shaded residential area with one incursion of student life, a short block of shops, cafés, and bookstores surrounded by shingled houses and god-talk. The GTU is an independent organization that utilizes the staff and facilities of the individual church schools to put together its academic degrees. In other words, if you wish to enter the ministry, you go into a seminary; if you want an academic degree, you go into the GTU. I affiliated myself with the Episcopalians, the Church Divinity School of the Pacific, but headed more deeply into academia, with the idea that my B.A. had given me a sense of the world's religion, but now it was time to look at my own heritage.

I spent seven more years doing a three-year Master of Arts degree, somewhat slowed by work, marriage, the raising of children, the renovation of houses, and round-the-world travel, about all of which I will say more later. Gradually, I found myself drawn to Old Testament instead of New, although I took Koiné Greek and attended classes in New Testament, church history, and Patristics. What really interested me was the tracing of roots and themes: how a phrase or image can be traced through the millennia.

There is a phrase from the Sufi mystic Rumi, referring to God as the thread that runs through the pearls of the world's religions. That thread is what drew me, tracing that quivering high-tension line of energy that begins in one place and comes out in another, thousands of miles away, millennia removed, changed but recognizable.

For example, in the Old Testament, the personal, or covenantal, name for the God of Israel was Yahweh, but there are other names as well, prominent among them forms of "El." For a long time it was assumed that El simply meant "god," which indeed it does. However, with the 1928 discovery of Ugarit in northern Syria, it became clear that El was also *a* god, king of the pantheon, a bearded and remote male who

hands down decrees from his tented throne. This figure contributes his own vocabulary to the poems and descriptions of the Hebrew Yahweh, winding through the Hebrew Bible's concept of God as El Shaddai and Elohim, before ending up on the ceiling of the Sistine Chapel with Michelangelo's visualization of God as all-powerful and bearded.

Similarly, one finds a thread of God as female. Yahweh is male, invariably referred to with the masculine pronoun, yet images of the feminine persist, so that the Hebrew God is described as crying out in birth, or acting the midwife for "his" people, or comforting the people "as a mother comforts her child." But the thing that interested this M.A. student most was the other side of the feminine, that which at ancient Ugarit was personified in the goddess Anat, close sister to India's Kali. Anat loves warfare, lives for slaughter, exists for the joy of meeting soldiers in battle, and her attributes, phrases from her hymns, became linked with Yahweh; when the people Israel needed a vocabulary to describe the wrath of God, one of the sources they drew from was that of the violent goddess.

During my time at the GTU I also co-taught a course on "Women and Leadership in the Early Church," which looked at the roles of women in the first centuries of the Christian movement. But in the end, I chose as my thesis topic "Feminine Aspects of Yahweh," digging into the textual roots of the question. Had I not had other obligations, I would no doubt have persisted, going on to a Ph.D. involving six languages and countless trips to hot and fly-blown archaeological sites, and my published works would have borne titles such as "Problems in Ugaritic Phraseology" and "Elephantine: God's Wife or Wishful Translation?" instead of *A Grave Talent* and *The Beekeeper's Apprentice*.

But our choices are molded around our circumstances, and by the time the M.A. hood was lowered around my neck, I also had two small children and a husband nearing retirement age. Entering a lengthy Ph.D. program would have been irresponsible.

Life:

For some fortunate individuals, higher education is a period unto itself, a time when close concentration on the joys of the ivory tower is uncluttered by such concerns as bills and diapers. For many of us, particularly women, this is not the case. We put ourselves through, or do it in the corners of our lives free of other responsibilities, occasionally brushed by the wistful speculation of what it would be like to attend school full time, or to live in a dorm, or to hang around after class and drink a beer instead of returning to care for an infant or cook a meal.

Still, it is not granted to many young women to interrupt their graduate studies for a honeymoon in Papua New Guinea followed by a six-month tour across the southern Pacific Ocean, from Ayer's Rock to Machu Piccu. I had not intended to marry, and neither I think had he, but we are, as I said, shaped by our circumstances, and when, some months after graduation, I took a day off my job as manager of Kaldi's Fine Coffees and Teas in Los Gatos to visit a professor whom I hadn't seen for some time, and found our conversation entering interesting avenues, well, marriage seemed a good idea. Twenty-five years later, it still does.

Noel King was born in what was then India, is now Pakistan, in 1922. His family was Anglo-Indian, his father employed by the railroad to lay telegraph line across the northern face of the country, as far as Lhasa in 1924. After the war, Noel entered Oxford, then did a higher degree at Nottingham, and was ordained in the Anglican Church. He spent the next fourteen years in Africa, setting up programs in religious studies first in Accra, Ghana, then in Makerere, Uganda. He and his family came to the newest campus of the University of California in 1967, hired again to begin a program in comparative religion. That is where I met him.

We married in 1977. Our daughter was born three years later, a son three years after that, and I found, somewhat to my surprise, that I liked being a mother. Aside from the sheer physical fascination of infants, I never cared much for the babies of other people, and often thought their children more irritating than compelling; fortunately, however, I found my own two a source of endless fascination and intense amusement, particularly when they became old enough to communicate verbally. They are young adults today, and still make me laugh like no other people can.

My son turned one as I was writing my M.A. thesis, "Feminine Aspects of Yahweh" (an academic exercise considerably enriched by the recent personal experi-

The author and her husband, Noel King, Easter Island, 1978

ences of childbirth, nursing, and the nurturing of small children). While the children were small, my work was within the bounds of the farm—raising food and children is a full time job, and I was well and truly entered into the householder life. I volunteered at school, sat on various committees, became a leader of La Leche League, helping new mothers figure out how to juggle all the elements of their lives. And, because my husband was raised in colonial India when servants were a way of life, and is far better with a concordance than he is with a circular saw, for me the householder life involved not only shovels, kitchen stove, washing machine, and canning jars, but also Skil saws, framing hammers, paintbrushes, and electrical drills. How To books sprang up like mushrooms beside my volumes of textual criticism and feminist theology. I became, quite literally, a home-maker.

Building was an unanticipated satisfaction, the creation of shelter and comfort, the externalization of an idea, a joining of muscle and mind. I will admit that I never grew entirely comfortable with either plumbing or electricity, both of which can leak with disastrous results, but I did everything else, from putting up track shelves to installing a pantry in the kitchen and finally designing and building a two-story addition on the old farmhouse. This last involved everything from the ground up: foundations and framing, windows and insulation, sheetrock and siding. We built it so the kids could have separate rooms—and so I could have, in Virginia Woolf's words, a room of my own (although the attendant five hundred pounds a year Woolf includes in her essay would have to wait a bit).

Ironically, in marrying a peripatetic man, I found what my mother did not: stability. We have owned three houses in all these years, plus a house in England to which we go occasionally. Each has had its own strong personality, each was suited to our time of life then.

Our first house was on the side of a redwood-lined creek in Santa Cruz, small and quirky, a typical cabin with rooms added on over the years, with a deck perched over the water and a dirt road above. We heated with a wood stove, brought our daughter home to the house, and soon realized it would never do for an active child, much less two.

So we moved, to an eighty-year-old farmhouse on two acres of rich Pajaro Valley soil, with an orchard, a field, and a separate house for the grandparents who had semi-retired from the Pacific Northwest. For fifteen years the kids ran wild there, gobbling raspberries off the bushes, racing after our Irish Wolfhound, collecting brown, white, and pastel blue eggs from beneath the chickens, picking green beans and apricots, whacking down the nuts from the old walnut tree every October. All summer the kitchen was fragrant with jams, catsup, chutneys, applesauce; at holidays the walls bulged with relations.

Now we live on the top of a hill overlooking that same Pajaro Valley, above the Monterey Bay summer fogs, a mile from the epicenter of the big 1989 earthquake. The house is quieter, surrounded by live oaks and a few redwoods, visited by coyotes, hummingbirds, and red-tail hawks. We go regularly to England, where we have family, and maintain the yellow-brick terrace house in Oxford, one street in from the River Isis, within sound of the bells at Christ Church.

Travel:

Settled as a home-maker I might have been, but travels have always been a part of my married life. I married at twenty-five and set off almost immediately for an England so freezing the gas in the wall-heaters refused to glow anything but a sullen red, so jammed with pre-Christmas traffic the imperturbable London cabbies threw up their hands and made for the pubs, so near mid-winter the sun barely rose above the horizon before it was setting again. London in December opens one's eyes to the bleaker aspects of Dickens.

After three weeks, my new husband and I parted company, him to Africa and Pakistan, me to close up my rented apartment in Santa Cruz and await visas. Ten weeks later, having heard not one word from him since we had parted at Heathrow, not knowing if his plans had changed, if his mind had changed, or if he'd even made it out of the subcontinent in one piece, I set off across the Pacific, washing up a day or twenty later, hugely jet-lagged and queasy from an airline breakfast of near-raw Australian steak, in Port Moresby, Papua New Guinea. In that state, nothing much would have surprised me, including to find myself at the hot end of the world without a clue of what to do next, or where to go. It was rather like a dream, in which getting off the plane to find my husband waiting at the terminal was less a relief than a part of a natural, if confusing, sequence of events. But then, much of my life has felt like that.

Moresby itself was unrelenting, hot and crass and plagued by crime. It was a joy to head for the highlands, up into the misty reaches of a land where one could still meet individuals who recalled the arrival of the first white face, a land where the Bird of Paradise flitted, where men donned formal leaf aprons, elaborate head-gear, and face paint to embark on the repair of a bridge, where pigs were used as currency, where a third of the world languages—*languages*, not dialects—were born.

We stayed at missions, mostly Catholic and Lutheran. As an introduction to a foreign culture, it was a dramatic as a person could ask for, a constant surprise, from the gas-run washing machine to the smoke-scented string bags used to carry everything from yams to babies. I studied Pidgin English with a woman named Yasiame, who lived near the mission with her

Traveling in Australia, 1978

two children, although I never met her husband. She wove me a string bag from bright wool I sent her from Australia, with some old kina coins woven into it; when I put it to my face, I can still smell the highlands in its fibers.

We stayed in the highlands for a month, flying in and out of tiny air strips, hitching rides with locals to pig kills and the colorful ceremonies called sing-sings, seeing how the Christian church interacted and intertwined with local belief and custom, learning how utterly foreign yet similar people can be. When we left, we spent another week in the Sepik River area, exploring grass-swamps in a boat carved from a tree and powered by outboard motor, gaping at *Haus Tamborans* (spirit houses), and twitching from chloroquin. Then back to Moresby, and on to Australia.

The next months saw us island-hopping across the Pacific, spending a month in Australia, then to New Zealand, followed by Tonga, the two Samoas, Tahiti,

and Easter Island. Because we were going to spend some time in South America, I had been working my way through a Spanish grammar I picked up in Melbourne, which made for tremendous confusion in French-speaking Tahiti, but helped somewhat after that. Easter Island was incredible, unreal, provocative—and cursed with the worst airport I have ever seen, a swirl of heat and shoving and bureaucrats with guns, run by the Chilean military with more concern for homeland security than the sensibilities of tourists. Still, the great stone heads stand looking out across the now-barren landscape, with the half-cut statues lying still in their quarry.

Santiago, La Paz, and Lake Titicaca; the Spanish colonial Cuzco and the Inca capital of Machu Pichu; Lima's desert archaeology and the tensions in a country on the edge of a revolt; the foul air and tumult of Mexico City.

Santa Cruz seemed bizarrely calm, on our return.

I returned to the GTU, my husband to his responsibilities at the university. And eighteen months after our daughter was born, we packed up and moved to northern India for a six month stint at the Punjabi University.

Travel with a small child is an experience. Worries and labors are increased a hundredfold, of course, from figuring out how to dry cloth diapers in the frigid climate of the lower Himalayas to keeping the shopkeeper's affectionate hand (which you have just seen being used to blow his nose into a gutter) away from your small blond daughter's rosy cheek. However, joys are magnified as well—doors are opened, hearts poured out, the traveler becomes something far more than just another tourist. Cooks and tailors allowed her (and us in her wake) to wander freely through their jealously guarded realms. Airline clerks miraculously conjured up adjoining seats in sold-out flights. Hardened civil servants melted. The Dalai Lama dandled her on his knee and made her chortle. I recommend taking a child along, if your nerves are strong enough.

Two years later, my M.A. granted and my career as a writer but a shape on the distant horizon, we took both children to Israel. There, too, hearts opened. An Italian woman atop Masada took one look at the blue-eyed boy riding on my back and the curly-headed girl clutching my hand and exclaimed, "You are so brave!" A stern Palestinian gardener allowed the kids to pluck his roses. The eyes following us were gentler, and certainly more interested, than they would have been, had we been intruding as two mere adults.

Writing:

But what do a much-uprooted childhood, a love of theology, travel to distant places, and the establishment of three homes have to do with the Laurie R. King entry in *Contemporary Authors*? If my husband had not been so near to retirement age, I might well have gone on into doctoral studies, become a Biblical scholar, and had a far different entry. Or if back in high school my math teachers had been more encouraging, my other secret passion might have taken root, leading me into architecture, in which case a Laurie King biography would have been found in another series entirely. Or if life had tugged just slightly harder in another direction, I might have pursued the mysteries of birth, and plunged into the joyous obscurity of a midwife, known only to those whose babies she had caught.

The author with her daughter, Zoe, India, 1981

Instead, in September of 1987, when my daughter was in her second grade classroom and my son off to his preschool three mornings a week, I sat down with the Waterman fountain pen I had bought on the Oxford high street the summer before and wrote on a canary pad the words, "I was fifteen when I met Sherlock Holmes, fifteen years old with my nose in a book as I walked the Sussex Downs, and nearly stepped on him."

And like that, I was a writer.

Where does this drive for fiction come from? How does a person who had expressed no recognizable urge toward storytelling since her sixth-grade immersion in the plasticine land of make-believe sit down and write an entire novel in a month? And then have the good sense to rewrite it so it was better, then continue on and write another, and a third—before any publisher expressed the faintest interest? And how long would I have gone on, I often wonder, how many unsold manuscripts would I have produced before giving up on the idea of writing and getting a real job?

Many writers in my own genre come into print by a similar path, finding in writing a second career after a decade or two practicing law or journalism or raising children. Some writers, of course, begin in college, with a degree in creative writing, learning the skills and never looking back. For others of us, writing is a little like going to a foreign country to learn a language. At first, one listens, gradually absorbing nouns and verbs, taking on the patterns of grammar (or storytelling) and thinking about the means of expression. Eventually, however, the urge to say something grows too strong to deny. And on that day one speaks out, or takes pen in hand.

I had, of course, been producing words in considerable volume all during the years of college and graduate school. Even though the sort of writing produced for a class in, say, Church Fathers has a different aim from the sort which builds a novel, the ultimate aim is that of communication. And there is no doubt that, as with the journalist who turns novelist, being accustomed to produce words regularly makes a person less intimidated by a blank page than most. Too, the study of Bible as a text emphasizes the importance of words, each word, as well as the rhythm of language and the subtle purposes behind the story one is telling.

Perhaps if I had undergone formal training in the writing of fiction, I would write in a very different way. Like taking a language in school, learning to write in a program naturally stresses the structural aspects of creating fiction, whereas learning by absorbing, imitating, and transforming comes more slowly. I, on the other hand, am one of those who write without an outline, with only the vaguest idea of what the story is about or where it is going. This is not a system for everyone—many writers need a visible outline of where the novel is going before they feel comfortable with sitting down to page one. Others of us merely shove ideas and images around in the back of our heads until either looming bills or internal pressures conspire to drive us to pen or keyboard.

In any case, whether through ignorance or inclination, when I sat down to write about my new imaginary friends in what became *The Beekeeper's Apprentice*, I felt as if I were setting out in an uncharted system of caves with a questionable flashlight in hand. (Truth to tell, I feel the same every time I begin a book, although after fourteen times, it is a sensation I have come to anticipate.) This is the story of a young woman, just fifteen when the book opens, who meets the retired Sherlock Holmes on the Sussex Downs in southern England, impresses him with the sharpness of her eyes, wits, and tongue, and becomes first his apprentice, then his partner. She is, one might say, a young, female, twentieth-century version of the Great Detective; the two mix like oil and vinegar.

I wrote the book in September and October of 1987, penning (literally, with that Waterman fountain pen) the core 280 pages in 28 days, a pace I have rarely matched since then. At the beginning of 1988 I began sending it out to publishers, collecting a fair number of rejection slips over the next two years before it occurred to me that I could either write or send, but not both. In 1989 I found an agent, Linda Allen in San Francisco, the first professional to look at my work and see it as—well, my work.

But before I got in contact with Linda, I wrote another Russell and Holmes book, called *A Letter of Mary*, which eventually became the third in the series. And when that was finished and the publishing world was not beating down my door, I changed times and locations to write *A Grave Talent*, a contemporary novel about a world-rank woman artist—a "female Rembrandt"—who is being investigated for the murder of three young girls. As luck would have it, this third book was the first to sell, in December 1991, to be published by St. Martin's Press in January, 1993.

A Grave Talent was the first in a series of (at present) four books concerning Kate Martinelli, a homicide inspector with the San Francisco Police Department. A year later, *The Beekeeper's Apprentice* came out; two weeks after its publication, my editor called to announce that *A Grave Talent* had been nominated for the Edgar award for best first novel by the Mystery Writers of America. My then fourteen-year-old daughter and I went to the awards banquet in New York in May, where I was completely stunned to hear my name announced as the winner. The only thing I'd ever won in my life was a box of brandied cherries at a community bingo game in the Dash Point town hall, a prize quickly confiscated by my parents as I was only ten at the time. As I write these words, Edgar sits brooding from the corner of my bookshelf, at his side the later prizes I have won, including the beautifully carved Creasey dagger, a stolid bust of a scowling Nero Wolfe, and the certificate noting that in October 1997 Laurie Richardson King was granted the honor-

The King family, 1987: (clockwise, from left) husband Noel, Laurie, daughter Zoe, son Nathan

ary degree of Doctor of Humane Letters from the Church Divinity School of the Pacific, my old seminary.

One of the purposes of this essay is to attempt an illustration of how one person became a writer, and how her life had formed her work. In that vein, I would like to take a closer look at the writing itself.

The Martinelli Books:

Following the publication of *A Grave Talent* and *The Beekeeper's Apprentice*, I continued to alternate the exploits of Russell and Holmes with the somewhat less frivolous stories concerning Kate Martinelli. The Martinelli books, which are written in fairly straightfor-

ward American English and in the third person, are often classified as police procedurals, for the simple reason that the main characters are cops. In truth, I was one of the many writers surprised to be told that her novel is actually a mystery. Genre classifications ("He is a mystery writer; she writes horror") are more for the convenience of booksellers and the publishers' sales reps than any true description of what is inside the covers of a particular book. Jane Smiley, Ron Hansen, Michael Chabon, and other "literary" writers have all produced crime fiction, whereas some of my books lodged in that category are only suspense by the most generous description. The hat of "mystery writer" does chafe occasionally, but for the most part I am comfortable with it.

In any case, *A Grave Talent*, featuring as it does a homicide detective and some dead bodies, was called a mystery. And although I had not thought of it as the first in a series—indeed, by the time I finished the book I was more than ready to heave Kate and the rest of them off the Golden Gate Bridge—my editor was interested enough in the cast of players to ask for another. So a topic I had been pushing around in the back of my mind for some time came into play: What would a holy fool look like in twentieth century America?

The holy fool is by his (or occasionally her) nature the product of a rigid society. His function is to embody chaos, to throw the concrete structures of feudalism into question, to let in the creative forces of disorder. It can be a dangerous game—fools were regularly locked up or beheaded for their chronic impertinence—but a necessary one. Who but a fool would speak the truth to a king? The religious elements of foolishness are myriad, from the antics of Zen masters to the declaration by St. Paul that he is a fool for Christ's sake, chiding the church in Corinth for their self-aggrandizement (I Corinthians 4). And since the fool is by nature the product of a tightly controlled social order—Lear's fool only exists because of the nature of royal power—I asked myself, could such a creature function in a society such as that of contemporary California, where chaos rules and the means of tweaking the powerful are many and varied?

I thought it possible, and wanted to write a novel about what such a person would look like. Thus it is, in *To Play the Fool,* that Kate Martinelli meets a homeless holy fool named Brother Erasmus, an escapee from the author's undergraduate thesis. Erasmus lives in three worlds: among San Francisco's poor and homeless, to whom he ministers; inside the ivory-tinged walls of Berkeley's Graduate Theological Union, where he embodies the rich contradictions of the Christian message; and among the tourists of Fisherman's Wharf, showing them the neediness beneath their wealth.

As I began to write Erasmus, I found an unexpected side of the man: He speaks only in the words of others. He preaches, orders breakfast, and answers the questions of his interrogators entirely in quotations, a challenge to a writer I do not think I would care to attempt again. It was a book I thought would be too quirky for the taste of most readers, but I have been pleased to find that its popularity remains steady, and for some readers, Erasmus's story is their favorite.

Kate's next outing, *With Child,* involves her in the lives of two teenagers, one a homeless boy, the other the daughter of her partner Al Hawkin's new bride. The book received several nominations, either despite or because of its being less a mystery than the story of Kate's personal involvement in the lives of the two young people. Written at a time my own children were entering the dark undergrowth of adolescence, it is also a mother's reflection on the vulnerability of the young—a recurring theme in the novels.

Kate's latest story, the fourth, is *Night Work,* which immerses her in the worlds of women's shelters, leather bars, Kali worship, and bride burning. (Just a typical outing for a San Francisco cop . . .) It plays with the idea of how far a woman can go to defend herself and her own, and uses as its theme the figure of Kali, the Indian goddess who glories in bloodshed, whose wholesale slaughter of men and monsters lays the groundwork for rebirth and healing. Kate the cop has to believe that it is wrong for a woman to lay violent hands on an abusive man; Kate the woman isn't so sure.

The Russell Books:

In the meantime, the Russell stories were also making their appearance. This is a very different kind of a series, not only because they are written in a formal, even ornate British English, and in the first person, but because of their style and humor. Early King reviewers, in fact, found it difficult to be sure that the Laurie R. King of *A Grave Talent* was the same one credited with *The Beekeeper's Apprentice,* an ongoing problem of categorization which eventually gave rise to the sales flyer produced by Bantam proclaiming, "What Laurie King writes next is always a mystery!"

But indeed, the two authors are the same, although readers continue to believe in the opening sequence wherein my intrepid UPS delivery woman deposits the Russell manuscripts on my doorstep, leaving me to decipher and transcribe them. It is, I generally assure such innocents, but a literary device, done to explain how one Laurie King comes to speak in the voice of Mary Russell—and to collect her royalties.

The series opens when our heroine is fifteen, which may explain in part the popularity of the books with bright adolescent girls. Mary is mature beyond her years, brilliant enough to get the better of The Great Detective, and if the attentive reader begins to suspect a certain degree of electricity between the girl and the considerably older man, well, only the most devout Sherlockians have been offended with how it all turns out. The book was chosen by the American Library Association as one of their notable books for young adults, which honor I cherish.

As mentioned already, the book I wrote after *Beekeeper* was actually the third in the series, *A Letter of Mary*. As I was writing *Beekeeper*, it became increasingly clear that the relationship between my two detectives was not going to be that of mere intellectual and professional partners, but rather a partnership in every aspect of their lives. However, because I had no idea how I was going to get them to that point, I put aside the next to write the third instead. Then, once I had seen what their marriage looked like and the balances and compromises it entailed, I could go back and write the story of how they reached that point. It is, incidentally, a method I occasionally resort to within an individual book: If I am not sure where the story is going, I skip forward a chapter or five and write a scene I am certain about, after which I have a clearer picture of what I need to do to get there.

A Monstrous Regiment of Women opens in the waning days of 1920. Mary is on the eve of her coming of age when she meets an old friend and is introduced to a woman religious leader in London. Mary is already feeling torn between her desire for a feminist independence as an Oxford intellectual on the one hand and a greater commitment to the always-difficult Sherlock Holmes on the other; meeting Margery Childe only brings the conflict into greater contrast. In the course of the book, Russell spends considerable effort in tutoring the woman on the feminine aspects of God to be found in the Bible, overlooked because of translations and expectations.

A Letter of Mary finds Mary's decision made, and the duo married for nearly three years. (And no, I do *not* intend to write about the Russell-Holmes honeymoon. When it comes to those two, dignity is paramount.) She is working on an academic paper, Holmes is (as often the case) bored with inactivity, when to their Sussex house comes an archaeologist friend from their time in Palestine. She brings Mary a papyrus document, apparently written by Mary Magdalene, who refers to herself as a disciple of Jesus. When the

archaeologist is killed, the duo is launched on an investigation that may or may not hinge on the potentially transformative, even revolutionary effects the Magdalene's letter would have on Christendom.

The fourth Russell (*The Moor*) takes Mary and Holmes to Dartmoor where, with *The Hound of the Baskervilles* echoing in the background, they investigate a suspicious death and a smattering of supernatural sightings. Holmes describes to Russell the discovery of a body, a discovery suspiciously akin to a former Holmes adventure on Dartmoor. Mary responds:

"No! Oh no, Holmes, please." I put up my hand to stop his words, unable to bear what I could hear coming, a thundering evocation of one of the most extravagant phrases Conan Doyle ever employed. "Please, please don't tell me that 'on the ground beside the body, Mr Holmes, there were the footprints of a gigantic hound.'"

He removed his pipe from his mouth and stared at me. "What on earth are you talking about, Russell? I admit that I occasionally indulge in a touch of the dramatic, but surely you can't believe me as melodramatic as that."

I drew a relieved breath and settled back in my chair. "No, I suppose not. Forgive me, Holmes. Do continue."

"No," he continued, putting the stem of his pipe back into place. "I do not believe it would be possible to distinguish a hound's spoor from that of an ordinary dog—not without a stretch of ground showing the animal's loping stride. These were simply a confusion of prints."

"Do you mean to tell me . . . "I began slowly.

"Yes, Russell. There on the ground beside the body of Josiah Gorton were found"—he paused to hold out his pipe and gaze at the bowl, which seemed to me to be drawing just fine, before finishing the phrase "—the footprints of a very large dog."

I dropped my head into my hands and left it there for a long time while my husband sucked in quiet satisfaction at his pipe.

Holmes, it will be noted, does from time to time get the better of Russell.

One of the pleasures of *The Moor* for its author was encountering the eminent Victorian Sabine Baring-Gould, real-life squire of Lew Trenchard manor in Devon, author of hundreds of books from pot-boiler novels to lives of the saints and natural histories of werewolves, composer of hymns such as "Onward Christian Soldier" and "Now the Day Has Ended," and collector of folklore and traditional songs. When I came across the man, first through his books and later in an article in *Smithsonian* magazine, I knew I just had to have him. I was immensely pleased to find that, if I hurried, I wouldn't even have to interfere with the date of his death.

The next book in the series, *O Jerusalem*, takes place out of sequence, going back five years to the time of *The Beekeeper's Apprentice*, to present in greater detail an episode referred to only in passing. Here, Russell and Holmes travel to what was then called Palestine, during the early days of the British mandate over the country, to investigate a problem for Holmes' mysterious brother Mycroft, who is something to do with British Intelligence. This is 1919, when General Allenby governed the country, T. E. Lawrence was struggling for Arab rights at the Paris peace talks, and decisions were being made that continue to reverberate to this day. One of the more interesting challenges in writing the book was precisely that sense of reverberations: A 1919 conversation about the hopes for peaceful cooperation among Christian, Muslim, and Jew rings loud to a reader in the year 2000 who knows that those hopes would be continually dashed. On another level, because the book is set when Russell and Holmes are still master and apprentice, her internal speculations concerning the nature of their relationship allows the reader a small and superior smile—at least, the reader who has met the series already.

The most recent volume in the Russell saga is *Justice Hall*, with links to the characters of *O Jerusalem* that serve to explain the latter's out-of-sequence

publication. When the two Bedouin "brothers" who guided Russell and Holmes through Palestine appear in England in 1923, they are under decidedly different guise. *Justice Hall* concerns the British aristocracy, and the dreadful injustices that occurred during the Great War. It also permitted the author to create a pair of glorious houses, giving full rein to her architectural fantasies. (A typical letter to one of my antiquarian bookseller friends began, *If you could have any half dozen books in your library, what would they be?*) But the book goes on to examine the burdens that go with such riches, the responsibilities to family and king that cost a young man everything.

The seventh Russell will appear in spring of 2004, and will be set in India.

Stand-alone Novels:

In 1998, after publication of *The Moor*, I reluctantly said good-bye to my beloved St. Martin's Press editor, Ruth Cavin, and moved to Kate Miciak at Bantam Books, which had been doing my paperbacks all along. My first book there was also my first stand-alone novel. *A Darker Place* (published in England as *The Birth of a New Moon*) is the story of Anne Waverley, an expert on modern religious movements who occasionally consults for the FBI by going undercover into religious communities—groups the media invariably condemns as "cults"—to help judge their stability and internal security. Here, she encounters the movement "Change," a movement using the language and symbolic activities of the medieval alchemist to speak its spiritual truths. I wrote the book to explore the question of how a religious movement becomes mainstream—Christianity, after all, began as a lunatic offshoot of Judaism, which itself was at least in part a radical reworking of Canaanite beliefs.

A second stand-alone, *Folly*, came out in 2001. In it Rae Newborn, a woodworker with a long history of severe depression, goes to a deserted island in the northern reaches of Puget Sound to rebuild a house, and ends up rebuilding her life. The physical process of building, from clearing ground and laying the building's foundations to raising the walls and roof, is mirrored by the story of Rae's building recovery. It also allows the author to flaunt her familiarity with the minutiae of load-bearing two-by-fours and eight-penny nails.

Being punted by Nathan on the River Cherwell, Oxford, England, 1999

Toward the end of *Folly* a character is introduced named Allen Carmichael. He is a minor player in the book, but is central to *Keeping Watch* (2003), which marks the first time I've written a novel with a male protagonist. Allen is a Vietnam vet who finds his purpose in the rescue of abused children and their mothers: He gets them away, he hides them, he finds them new lives. In the course of his work he rescues a young boy who turns out to be more than he appears, and we enter into the question of how a killer is made, what forces have to conspire to make a child pick up a gun.

Endpiece:

In this account of the novels, I have attempted to show the number of places at which the author's former lives have surfaced in her fiction: an undergraduate study in alchemy here, a B.A. thesis on the fool or a Master's thesis on the feminine aspects of God there, a trip to India, the hands-on experience of housebuild-

ing and a childhood spent in the Pacific Northwest and a close familiarity with Oxford and an intimate grasp of a parent's nightmares—why, there are even brief mentions of breastfeeding babies and canning fruit (in *A Grave Talent* and *Keeping Watch*). It is truly extraordinary how often the interests of an author and her characters coincide. . . .

This is less a case of the old rule for beginning writers, "Write what you know," than it is a matter of building on, and with, what fascinates the author. In fact, the primary thrust of a book may well be something about which I know little or nothing at all—the art world, modern religious movements ("cults"), and Vietnam are just a few. I tend to use the things I have done or studied as background, to lend dimension to the story or to characters.

One of the unanticipated side-benefits of writing about religious matters has been that my novels are taken seriously in some interesting quarters. Several of the books are required reading in English courses scattered across the country, *Folly* is being used in a psychology class to illustrate depression, and in the spring of 2002 I spent a week as writer-in-residence at Hanover College in southern Indiana, a small school with a strong interest in matters theological.

But, as I asked at the beginning: Is a writer born, or made?

And as I answered at the beginning, yes. An innate love of language and storytelling may lay a foundation, but opportunity, a breadth of experience, and above all a stiff-necked refusal to bend to the voice of harsh reality, are essential.

I love my job. Never would I have believed, when I was a dreamy child, that one day I would be paid to tell myself stories.

BIOGRAPHICAL AND CRITICAL SOURCES:

BOOKS

Authors and Artists for Young Adults, Volume 29, Gale (Detroit, MI), 1999.

Heising, Wiletta L., *Detecting Women 2,* Purple Moon Press, 1996-1997.

St. James Guide to Crime and Mystery Writers, 4th edition, St. James Press (Detroit, MI), 1996.

PERIODICALS

Armchair Detective, fall, 1996, p. 402.

Booklist, February 1, 1993, Marie Kuda, review of *A Grave Talent,* p. 972, Mary Romano Marks, review of *A Grave Talent,* p. 975; February 1, 1994, Emily Melton, review of *The Beekeeper's Apprentice; or, On the Segregation of the Queen,* p. 997; February 15, 1995, Emily Melton, review of *To Play the Fool,* p. 1062; September 1, 1995, p. 45; February 1, 1996, Emily Melton, review of *With Child,* p. 919; November 1, 1996, p. 522; January 1, 1998, Emily Melton, review of *The Moor,* p. 784; April 15, 1998, review of *The Moor,* p. 1360; December 15, 1998, review of *The Moor* (audio version), p. 761; January 1, 1999, Emily Melton, review of *A Darker Place,* p. 837; April 15, 1999, Stephanie Zvirin, review of *O Jerusalem,* p. 1480; December 1, 1999, Emily Melton, review of *Night Work,* p. 687; May 1, 2000, Shelle Rosenfeld, review of *The Beekeeper's Apprentice,* p. 1609; February 15, 2001, Whitney Scott, review of *Folly,* p. 1116; February 1, 2002, GraceAnne A. DeCandido, review of *Justice Hall,* p. 907.

Drood Review of Mystery, January, 2001, review of *Folly,* p. 20.

Globe and Mail, February 13, 1999, review of *A Darker Place,* p. D13; June 12, 1999, review of *O Jerusalem,* p. D19.

Kirkus Reviews, December 1, 1993, review of *The Beekeeper's Apprentice,* p. 1491; August 1, 1995, p. 1063; December 15, 1995, p. 1735; January 1, 1999, review of *A Darker Place,* p. 10; April 1, 1999, review of *O Jerusalem,* p. 489; December 15, 1999, review of *Night Work,* p. 1920.

Kliatt, September, 1996, p. 11; March, 1998, review of *A Letter of Mary,* p. 12; January, 1999, review of *The Moor* (audio version), p. 46; March, 1999, review of *The Moor,* p. 12; July, 1999, review of *The Beekeeper's Apprentice,* p. 2.

Lambda Book Report, March, 2000, Lynne Maxwell, "Serial Detectives at Work," p. 26.

Library Journal, January, 1993, Rex E. Klett, review of *A Grave Talent,* p. 169; September 1, 1995, p. 212; October 1, 1998, review of *The Moor* (audio version), p. 150; January, 1999, Nancy McNicol, review of *A Darker Place,* p. 152; May 1, 1999, Laurel Bliss, review of *O Jerusalem,* p. 117; January, 2000, Nancy McNicol, review of *Night Work,* p. 160; July, 2000, Patsy E. Gray, review of *O Jerusalem,* p. 162.

New York Times Book Review, February 19, 1995, p. 25; September 17, 1995, Marilyn Stasio, review of *A Monstrous Regiment for Women,* p. 41; February 18, 1996, p. 20; January 5, 1997, Marilyn Stasio, review of *A Letter of Mary,* p. 20; January 11, 1998, review of *The Moor,* p. 19; May 31, 1998, review of *The Moor,* p. 30; March 7, 1999, Marilyn Stasio, review of *A Darker Place,* p. 20; February 20, 2000, Marilyn Stasio, review of *Night Work.*

People Weekly, March 19, 2001, review of *Folly,* p. 48.

Publishers Weekly, January 3, 1994, review of *The Beekeeper's Apprentice,* p. 73; December 12, 1994, review of *To Play the Fool,* p. 52; July 10, 1995, review of *A Monstrous Regiment for Women,* p. 46; December 4, 1995, p. 55; October 21, 1996, p. 48; November 18, 1996, p. 64; December 21, 1998, review of *A Darker Place,* p. 54; May 3, 1999, review of *O Jerusalem,* p. 69; January 17, 2000, review of *Night Work,* p. 46; January 15, 2001, review of *Folly,* p. 55; February 18, 2002, Robert C. Hahn, "*PW Talks with . . . ,*" and review of *Justice Hall,* pp. 78-79.

School Library Journal, July, 1994, Susan H. Woodcock, review of *The Beekeeper's Apprentice,* pp. 128-129; June, 1997, Susan H. Woodcock, review of *A Letter of Mary,* p. 151; April, 1998, review of *The Moor,* p. 158; December, 1998, review of *The Moor,* p. 29; July, 1999, review of *A Darker Place,* p. 115.

Tribune Books (Chicago, IL), September 3, 1995, Dick Adler, review of *A Monstrous Regiment of Women,* p. 4; January 7, 1996, Dick Adler, review of *With Child,* p. 6; January 5, 1997, p. 4.

Voice of Youth Advocates, April, 1998, reviews of *A Grave Talent* and *The Beekeeper's Apprentice,* p. 41; October, 1998, John Charles, review of *The Moor,* p. 274; December, 1998, review of *The Moor,* p. 333.

Wall Street Journal, February 5, 1997, p. A16.

Washington Post Book World, February 20, 1994, Pat Dowell, "Sherlock Rusticates," p. 8; February 19, 1995, p. 6; October 15, 1995, p. 6; December 15, 1996, Maureen Corrigan, review of *A Letter of Mary,* p. 10; July 18, 1999, review of *O Jerusalem,* p. 5.

Wilson Library Bulletin, February, 1995, Gail Pool, "Murder in Print," p. 72.

OTHER

Capitola Book Café, http://www.capitolabookcafe.com/ (March 6, 2001), "Andrea's Page: Interview with Author Laurie King."

Kriminal Litteraere Nyheder, http://www.webfic.com/
kriminyt/art/ (March 6, 2001), Mia Stampe,
"Interview with Laurie R. King."

MysteryGuide.com, http://www.mysteryguide.com/
(March 26, 2002), review of *The Beekeeper's
Apprentice.**

* * *

KNAPP, Caroline 1959-2002
   (Alice K.)

OBITUARY NOTICE—See index for *CA* sketch: Born
1959, in Cambridge, MA; died of complications from
lung cancer June 4, 2002, in Cambridge, MA. Journalist, editor, columnist, and author. Knapp worked as a
journalist, editor, and columnist for the *Boston Business Journal* and the *Boston Phoenix,* the latter an
alternative weekly, beginning in 1988. Under the
sobriquet Alice K., she also wrote "Out There," a
humorous column for single cosmopolitan women
which later culminated in the book *Alice K.'s Guide to
Life: One Woman's Quest for Survival, Sanity, and the
Perfect New Shoes.* Knapp became an instant celebrity
with the publication of her memoir, *Drinking: A Love
Affair.* The revelation that she had been a secret
alcoholic since her teen years surprised the people
who had observed her as an excellent student and a
hard-working, award-winning journalist. Knapp's
autobiography became a bestseller and won the author
several glowing reviews for the talent of her writing
and the honesty of her confession. Knapp's successful
fight against alcohol was promoted by the media,
including an *Oprah* broadcast, as a positive model for
other women and young people to follow. Two years
later Knapp wrote another love story, *Pack of Two:
The Intricate Bond between People and Dogs,* about
the pet she had rescued from an animal shelter. This
volume also achieved bestseller status and was generally popular with critics. Knapp was reportedly writing another book on addictions at the time of her death.

OBITUARIES AND OTHER SOURCES:

BOOKS

Contemporary Literary Criticism, Volume 99: *Year-
book 1996,* Gale (Detroit, MI), 1997, pp. 47-53.
Knapp, Caroline, *Drinking: A Love Story,* Dial Press
(New York, NY), 1996.

Knapp, Caroline, *Pack of Two: The Intricate Bond
between People and Dogs,* Dial Press (New York,
NY), 1998.

PERIODICALS

Boston Globe, June 5, 2002.
Boston Herald, June 5, 2002, obituary by Tom Mash-
berg, p. 40; June 6, 2002.
Globe and Mail (Toronto, Ontario, Canada), June 19,
2002.
Los Angeles Times, June 22, 2002, obituary by Jon
Thurber, p. B18.
New York Times, June 5, 2002, p. A23.
Washington Post, June 8, 2002, p. B7.

* * *

KOCH, Kenneth (Jay) 1925-2002

OBITUARY NOTICE—See index for *CA* sketch: Born
February 27, 1925, in Cincinnati, OH; died of
leukemia July 6, 2002, in New York, NY. Educator,
poet, playwright, fiction writer, and librettist. As a
founding member of the avant-garde movement called
the New York school which emerged in Manhattan in
the 1950s, Koch created a vernacular poetry of urban
life that dazzled the critics who understood his
intentions. He was praised for the humor and wit that
infused even his most serious work, for the infinite
range of subject matter that fueled his imagination,
and for the excitement, spontaneity, and pure joy that
burst without restraint from whatever poetic form he
chose to frame his thoughts. Koch published many
poetry collections over a fifty-year period, including
*One Train: Poems; On the Great Atlantic Rainway:
Selected Poems, 1950-1988,* for which he was awarded
a Bollingen Prize from Yale University in 1995; and
New Addresses: Poems, a somewhat autobiographical
collection published near the end of his life that earned
him a National Book Award in 2000. Described as a
dedicated and enthusiastic teacher, Koch was a professor of English and comparative literature at Columbia
University for many years, but he taught poetry writing to people of all ages, resulting in the books *Wishes,
Lies, and Dreams: Teaching Children to Write Poetry*
and *I Never Told Anybody: Teaching Poetry Writing in
a Nursing Home.* Koch was awarded the Rebekah
Johnson Bobbitt National Prize for Poetry in 1996. He
also wrote short stories, short plays, and librettos.

OBITUARIES AND OTHER SOURCES:

BOOKS

Contemporary Dramatists, 6th edition, St. James Press (Detroit, MI), 1999.
Contemporary Poets, 7th edition, St. James Press (Detroit, MI), 2001.

PERIODICALS

Los Angeles Times, July 9, 2002, obituary by Reed Johnson, p. B10.
New York Times, July 8, 2002, obituary by Alan Feuer, p. A16.
Times (London, England), July 29, 2002.

*   *   *

KRAFT, Kenneth 1949-

PERSONAL: Born July 16, 1949, in Cincinnati, OH; son of Lewis and Eve Kraft; married; wife's name, Trudy; children: Eva, Louise. *Education:* Harvard University, B.A. (cum laude), 1971; University of Michigan, M.A., 1978; Princeton University, Ph.D., 1984.

ADDRESSES: Home—780 Millbrook Lane, Haverford, PA 19041 1229. *Office*—Maginnes Hall, Lehigh University, Bethlehem, PA 18015. *E-mail*—klk2@lehigh.edu.

CAREER: Lehigh University, Bethlehem, PA, professor of religion studies, 1990—, college seminar program director, 1992-95, chair of religion studies department, 1997-2000. Taught at University of Pennsylvania, Swarthmore College, and Stanford University Japan Center in Kyoto. Spoke at the Parliament of the World's Religions, Cape Town, South Africa, 1999, and at Communitarian Network Summit, Washington, DC, 1999. Service on advisory boards, editorial boards, and steering committees has included Buddhist Peace Fellowship (Berkeley, CA); The Buddhism Project: Art, Buddhism, and Contemporary Culture (New York, NY); Forum on Religion and Ecology, Harvard University Center for the Study of World Religions; *Journal of Buddhist Ethics;* Religion Working Group on Genetically Modified Organisms, University of Pennsylvania Center for Bioethics; Rochester Zen Center (Rochester, NY); World Bank World Faiths Development Dialogue.

AWARDS, HONORS: Postdoctoral fellowship, Harvard University, 1984-85; Outstanding Academic Book, *Choice,* 1992, for *Eloquent Zen: Daito and Early Japanese Zen.*

WRITINGS:

(Editor and contributor) *Zen: Tradition and Transition,* Grove Press (New York, NY), 1988.
(Author of preface) Philip Kapleau, *The Three Pillars of Zen,* Doubleday (New York, NY), 1989.
(Editor and contributor) *Inner Peace, World Peace: Essays on Buddhism and Nonviolence,* State University of New York Press (Albany, NY), 1992.
Eloquent Zen: Daito and Early Japanese Zen, University of Hawaii Press (Honolulu, HI), 1992.
The Wheel of Engaged Buddhism: A New Map of the Path, Weatherhill (New York, NY), 1999.
(Editor) *Zen Teaching, Zen Practice: Philip Kapleau and the Three Pillars of Zen,* Weatherhill (New York, NY), 2000.
(Editor, with Stephanie Kaza) *Dharma Rain: Sources of Buddhist Environmentalism,* Shambhala Publications (Boston, MA), 2000.

Contributor to anthologies, including *The Path of Compassion: Writings on Socially Engaged Buddhism,* edited by Fred Eppsteiner, Parallax Press (Berkeley, CA), 1988; *This Sacred Earth: Religion, Nature, Environment,* edited by Roger S. Gottlieb, Routledge (New York, NY), 1996; *Buddhism and Ecology: The Interconnection of Dharma and Deeds,* edited by Mary Evelyn Tucker and Duncan Williams, Harvard University Press (Cambridge, MA), 1997; *Engaged Buddhism in the West,* edited by Christopher Queen, Wisdom Publications (Boston, MA), 2000. Contributor to journals, including *Tricycle, Journal of Buddhist Ethics,* and *Zen Bow.*

SIDELIGHTS: Professor and author Kenneth Kraft is considered to be at the forefront of contemporary Buddhist thought. He has written extensively on engaged Buddhism, including the "greening" of Buddhism—

the use of Buddhist doctrines and practices to foster ecological awareness and integrity. He has also written authoritatively on Zen's relationship to language.

The first book Kraft edited, *Zen: Tradition and Transition,* collects original essays by eleven contemporary Zen scholars and masters. The book traces the history of Zen as well as its expression in contemporary life. The book also addresses the challenges faced by Zen in the West. *Booklist* reviewer Sheila E. McGuinn-Morrer called the book "accessible and interesting." Kraft's second book, *Inner Peace, World Peace: Essays on Buddhism and Nonviolence,* explores Buddhist teachings on nonviolence and their relevance in the modern world. Called a "valuable source book" by critic Ruben Habito in *Religious Studies Review,* this book is one of the first assessments by Western scholars of Buddhist peacemaking.

Eloquent Zen: Daito and Early Japanese Zen was chosen by *Choice* as an Outstanding Academic Book in 1992. This book is a pioneering study of the medieval Japanese Rinzai Zen master Daito Kokushi (also known as Myocho). In the *Journal of Asian Studies,* reviewer Steven Heine stated that Kraft "makes an important contribution to studies of Zen and Japanese Buddhist history and thought." Daito helped to bring Zen from China to Japan. Kraft highlights Daito's use of capping phrases, which are, as he writes, "supposed to be able to make a comment, resolve a specific conundrum, convey a Zen insight, transform another's awareness, resonate like a line of poetry, or perform several of these functions simultaneously." Reviewer Robert H. Scharf wrote in the *Journal of Religion* that "Kraft has performed a worthy service in presenting the Daito of tradition," and called the book "sensitive" and "a welcome addition to Zen scholarship."

Kraft's other projects include *The Wheel of Engaged Buddhism: A New Map of the Path* and *Zen Teaching, Zen Practice: Philip Kapleau and the Three Pillars of Zen.* The former extends Kraft's exploration of engaged Buddhism, with emphasis on the ways that individuals can integrate spiritual awareness and action in the world. The latter tells the story of Roshi Philip Kapleau, one of the first Westerners to train in Zen in Japan. Several of Kapleau's leading disciples show how American Zen has matured since the mid-1960s.

Between the publication of *Eloquent Zen* and *The Wheel of Engaged Buddhism,* Kraft gave an address, "The Greening of Buddhist Practice," to the Kyoto Seminar for Religious Philosophy that was reprinted in *Cross Currents.* Here Kraft stated that "Buddhists around the world have begun to immerse themselves in environmental issues, attempting to approach urgent problems from the inside as well as the outside. An increasing number of practitioner-activists believe that the only way to stop the boat of ecological disaster is to deepen our relationship to the planet and all life within it."

Kraft shows how the practices of Buddhism can help anyone to become more aware of the environmental implications of activities we do every day. For example, washing one's hands can become a mini-meditation on the preciousness of water, and an occasion for renewing one's dedication to the environment. This theme is explored further in *Dharma Rain: Sources of Buddhist Environmentalism.* Forty contributors of diverse backgrounds cover issues such as reverence for life, ecological precepts, and universal responsibility. According to reviewer James R. DeRoche in *Library Journal,* the book "explicates the Buddhist notion that at root, everything is one. Trees, animals, rocks, air and water are all, simply, us." Contributors include the Dalai Lama, composer Philip Glass, and Vietnamese Zen master Thich Nhat Hanh.

Kraft maintains that the deepest teachings of the great religions are especially relevant in troubled times. "That's really the spirit of engaged Buddhism," he said in an interview with Sandhya Jha in *Interfaith Alliance,* "not to shrink from the work that needs to be done." Kraft seems to be living up to this aspiration through his teaching and writing.

BIOGRAPHICAL AND CRITICAL SOURCES:

BOOKS

Kapleau, Philip, *Awakening to Zen,* Scribner (New York, NY), 1997.

Kraft, Kenneth, *Eloquent Zen: Daito and Early Japanese Zen,* University of Hawaii Press (Honolulu, HI), 1992.

This Sacred Earth: Religion, Nature, Environment, edited by Roger S. Gottlieb, Routledge (New York, NY), 1996.

PERIODICALS

Booklist, April 15, 1988, Sheila E. McGinn Moorer, review of *Zen: Tradition and Transition,* pp. 1372-1373.

Choice, March, 1989, D. R. Eastwood, review of *Zen: Tradition and Transition,* p. 1186; December, 1992, M. F. Nefsky, review of *Eloquent Zen,* p. 634.

Commonweal, December, 1992, Frederick Franck, review of *Inner Peace, World Peace,* p. 30.

Japanese Journal of Religious Studies, December, 1993, Michel Mohr, review of *Eloquent Zen,* pp. 331-344.

Journal of Asian Studies, February, 1992, review of *Eloquent Zen,* pp. 213-214.

Journal of Religion, July, 1994, Robert H. Scharf, review of *Eloquent Zen,* pp. 432-433.

Kirkus Reviews, April 1, 1988, review of *Zen: Tradition and Transition,* p. 517.

Library Journal, December, 1999, James F. DeRoche, review of *Dharma Rain,* p. 142.

Publishers Weekly, December 13, 1999, review of *Dharma Rain,* p. 97.

Religious Studies Review, October, 1994, Ruben L. F. Habito, review of *Inner Peace, World Peace,* p. 355.

OTHER

Interfaith Insights, http://www.interfaithinsights.org/ (September 1, 2000), interview with Sandhya Jha.

KRAUS, Richard G(ordon) 1923-2002

OBITUARY NOTICE—See index for *CA* sketch: Born October 21, 1923, in New York, NY; died of colon cancer March 28, 2002, in Lower Gwynedd Township, PA. Recreation expert, educator, and author. Kraus was well known as a professional square-dance caller and helped promote recreation as an important part of education. He earned a B.A. from the City College of the City University of New York in 1942 and his M.A. and Ed.D. from Columbia University. During his early career he was active in the "cooperative movement" that promoted cooperative housing initiatives. As part of this work, he became involved in organizing recreational activities for children and was a part-time recreation leader and dance teacher for the YWCA during the early 1940s. Kraus was assigned to government intelligence work in Texas during World War II, and at this time he also became more interested in square dancing. After the war he called dances in New York, recorded square dance albums, and made appearances on television shows. He also taught students about recreation at several institutions, including Columbia University's Teachers College, Lehman College of the City University of New York, and Temple University. At Lehman and Temple he served as chairman of the schools' recreation departments. Kraus authored over two dozen books on recreation and dance, including *Recreation and the Schools, Social Recreation: A Group Dynamics Approach,* and *Recreation Programming: A Benefits-driven Approach.*

OBITUARIES AND OTHER SOURCES:

PERIODICALS

New York Times, April 20, 2002, p. A15.

L

LABOVITZ, Trudy A. 1954-

PERSONAL: Born April 11, 1954, in Pittsburgh, PA; daughter of Carl and Pearl Tulip Labovitz. *Education:* University of Pittsburgh, B.A. (Chinese), 1975, M.B.A. (human resources), 1982. *Politics:* "You betcha." *Hobbies and other interests:* Reading, feral cats, cats.

ADDRESSES: Agent—c/o Publicity Director, Spinsters Ink, P.O. Box 22005, Denver, CO 80022. *E-mail*— Labovitz@concentric.net.

CAREER: Writer.

WRITINGS:

Ordinary Justice (mystery), Spinsters Ink (Denver, CO), 1999.
Deadly Embrace (mystery), Spinsters Ink (Denver, CO), 2000.

Also the author, with Kathy Emery, of two cryptic crosswords published in *Games.*

SIDELIGHTS: In her debut mystery novel *Ordinary Justice,* Trudy Labovitz introduces Zoe Kergulin, an ex-Department of Justice employee turned private investigator. Described by *Booklist*'s Whitney Scott as "A promising newcomer to the growing ranks of feminist detectives," Zoe has moved from Washington, D.C., to her West Virginia hometown to start a new life after witnessing her best friend's murder by an abusive husband. But her rural environment is not immune to violence either, and soon Zoe is involved in the disappearance of a neighbor who is another victim of domestic violence. While the author "doesn't delve deeply enough into Zoe's background," according to a *Publishers Weekly* reviewer, *Ordinary Justice* nonetheless "has a good momentum" and "packs an unexpected punch." Rex E. Klett of *Library Journal* deemed Labovitz's debut novel "a real gem," citing her "eye for detail."

Deadly Embrace, the second Zoe Kergulin adventure, finds the detective involved in a murder in her hometown and wondering whether her past as a government agent is behind the crime. Reviewing the book in *Library Journal,* Rex Klett praised its "enticing and complex plot" and "focused clarity." Neda Ulaby of the *Lambda Book Report* praised the book as "an intelligent, tersely told tale that relies upon masterful suggestion and confident internal logic."

Labovitz told *CA* that her primary motivation for writing is "the writing itself. It makes me feel fulfilled. When I write, I can get out of myself, and yet, get into myself. The focus is the important part. Plus, I believe I have something to say that no one else seems to be saying." She discussed the influences on her writing: "I know I am inspired to write more when I'm reading something that's particularly well-written. The other influences are the deep opinions I hold. Also, I know that in everyday life I don't hold much hope for the world, but I seem to find some kind of optimism when I write."

For Labovitz, the hardest part of the writing process "is sitting down and doing it. I don't outline. When writing a mystery, I know who did the deed, and I know my protagonist will figure out who the murderer is. I don't always know what lies in between until a few drafts later."

Labovitz's choice of subject is determined in part by her view of the world, whose condition she describes as "bleak." "Writing fiction allows me to remake the world in a more pleasing image. Yes, there's murder in my fictional world, but it always has a motive, and the murderer is always caught. Like Zoe, I still believe in the concepts of justice and truth."

BIOGRAPHICAL AND CRITICAL SOURCES:

PERIODICALS

Booklist, April 15, 1999, Whitney Scott, review of *Ordinary Justice,* p. 1480.
Lambda Book Report, November, 2000, Neda Ulaby, "Less Is More," p. 22.
Library Journal, April 1, 1999, Rex E. Klett, review of *Ordinary Justice,* p. 133; October 1, 2000, Rex E. Klett, review of *Deadly Embrace,* p. 150.
Publishers Weekly, April 19, 1999, review of *Ordinary Justice,* p. 65.
Record (Bergen County, NJ), June 18, 1999, review of *Ordinary Justice,* p. 44.

*   *   *

La BREE, Clifton 1933-

PERSONAL: Born June 25, 1933, in Monson, ME; son of Raymond (a painter) and Evelyn (Heaney) La Bree; married Yolande Coache, December 26, 1954 (marriage ended, December 22, 1977); married Pauline Pare, September 1, 1984; children: Evelyn, Vivian, Gerald, Sharon, Michael, Kevin. *Ethnicity:* "White American." *Education:* Attended Boston University, 1951-52; University of New Hampshire, B.S., 1955. *Politics:* Republican. *Religion:* Protestant. *Hobbies and other interests:* Antique automobiles, hiking, camping.

ADDRESSES: Home—102 Wilson Hill Rd., New Boston, NH 03070. *E-mail*—cplabree@groien.com.

CAREER: U.S. Forest Service, Bangor, ME, research aide, 1955; New Hampshire Cooperative Extension Service, Durham, county forester, 1955-57; New York State College of Forestry, Syracuse, supervisor, 1957-59; self-employed consulting forester, 1958—. Town of New Boston, NH, member of Forestry Commission, 1975-88.

MEMBER: Society of American Foresters.

WRITINGS:

The Gentle Warrior: General Oliver Prince Smith, USMC, Kent State University Press (Kent, OH), 2001.

Author of five novels, not yet published.

WORK IN PROGRESS: Research on several World War II commanders.

SIDELIGHTS: Clifton La Bree told *CA:* "I have been a student of military history for most of my adult life. I wrote *The Gentle Warrior: General Oliver Prince Smith, USMC* because of my respect and admiration for his military career. To me he represented the ultimate soldier.

"I was a young boy during World War II, and it has left a lasting impression on the way I view the world around me. It was a period of monumental sacrifice and suffering of the American family. A community spirit permeated every home. Those who received tragic news of lost sons, brothers, or fathers bore their pain with dignity and grace, and it was shared by the nation as a whole. It was a serious and sober period of great anxiety. The Depression years had conditioned the nation to hardships, but little did people know how severely they would be tested on the field of battle.

"I admire the courage and values that sustained the everyday working family through the most horrendous conditions imaginable. It was a time when American citizen-soldiers collectively rolled up their shirt sleeves and began the serious task of defeating two of the most militaristic nations on earth, Japan and Germany.

"When the war was over, people removed their uniforms and got on with their lives with the same determination they displayed on the battlefield. Their embrace of the future was complete. Perhaps the most defining characteristic of the World War II generation was the ability to accept the responsibilities and consequences of choices made. I admire those people for that noble trait and shall continue to write about the way it was."

BIOGRAPHICAL AND CRITICAL SOURCES:

PERIODICALS

Naval War College Review, winter, 2002, Donald Chisholm, review of *The Gentle Warrior: General Oliver Prince Smith, USMC,* p. 160.

*   *   *

LaPALMA, Marina deBellagente 1949-

PERSONAL: Born January 10, 1949, in Milan, Italy; daughter of Edoardo and Theresa (Luigia) deBellagente; married Richard J. Goldstein, December 29, 1979; children: Henry Chase. *Education:* Mills College, B.A., 1979; University of California—San Diego, M.F.A. (1984); City University of New York, Ph.D., 1990. *Politics:* Independent. *Religion:* Buddhist. *Hobbies and other interests:* Yoga, gardening, music, travel.

ADDRESSES: Home—526 Hopkins Street, Menlo Park, CA 94025. *E-mail*—lapalma@well.com.

CAREER: University of California—San Diego, writing instructor, 1981-84; Otis Parsons College of Art, Los Angeles, CA, professor of literature and composition, 1984-99, professor of art history, 1985-87, 1990; Hunter College, New York, NY, teaching assistant, 1987-89; San Francisco Art Institute, San Francisco, CA, 1995-96. Chair, board of directors, children's book project, 1995—; member of arts commissioner, City of Menlo Park, 1997—.

MEMBER: Association International des Critiques d'Art, American Association of Italian Studies, Modern Language Association, American Italian Historical Association, National Writers Union (treasurer, Local 3).

WRITINGS:

Neurosuite, Kelsey Street Press, (Berkeley, CA), 1975.
Casablanca Carousel, HCB Productions, 1976.
Grammars for Jess, Kelsey Street Press (Berkeley, CA), 1980.
Facial Index, State One Press (Oakland, CA), 1983.
Murmurs, Present Press, (Los Angeles, CA), 1984.
Able Was I, Present Press (Los Angeles, CA), 1986.
Persistence (prose poetry), Diderot Press, 1996.
Poessagi (essays), 1998.

Academic papers published in *Romance Languages Annual, Italian Studies,* and other scholarly journals.

WORK IN PROGRESS: From Rooms (poetry); *Guilia Niccolai* (poetry); resarch on women in contemporary Islamic culture and on *La Chene*—a study of the 1991 French-Romanian film by Lucien Pintilie.

SIDELIGHTS: Marina deBellagente LaPalma told *CA:* "My work in a variety of media over the years—literary, visual, musical, sculptural, performance—has always had at its core the tactile and sensual properties of language. The form I have most intimately lived with is the once and future pamphlet, the chapbook. Portable and concise, it more than sufficed (was no doubt even glamorous) for Eighteenth-century Europe. But in these global, electronic, and bio-engineered times, the form of address must be fluid, hybrid, labyrinthine, multiple—like the addressee. Composed of both rupture and continuity, my life traces a path (like DNA) in the form of a spiral, rambling through seemingly discordant terrains, only to return again and again to the same set of themes, concerns at different phases. My aesthetic practices have always teetered (or even cavorted) somewhere on margins or thresholds between legibility and illegibility; language and decorative pattern (a version of form and content); transparency versus opacity; ambiguity and structure; fluidity and rigidity; singing and speech, and so on. The beautiful word 'liminality' offers the implication that these are not oppositions but rather the ends of a spectrum: Transformation, recombination, and the rhythmic interweaving of motifs in works built up through experimentation. These ideas had a heyday as theater, performance, collage, text-sound, poetry, new music, painting, photography, installation, and sculpture all contaminated, overlapped, and mimicked one another. I was there.

"Two intellectual landmarks of the twentieth century: One: the work begun by early avant garde artists (how truly shocking collage and randomness were when introduced into artistic practices around the turn of the last century). Two: the structuralist enterprise, which made us aware of our obsession with and dependence upon categories that are more or less invented, more or less arbitrary, more or less alienated from their basis in the phenomenal and the molecular—categories to keep track of the plenitude of the world and its manifestations. These paradigmatic leaps have allowed certain leeways: the text or artwork may be viewed not just as an unchanging artifact but also as a field for play or struggle (or one masquerading as the other); a shift of emphasis in the role of the audience—reader, viewer, whatever—as enabled arbiter of what a text means and to what uses it shall be put. Information woven with invention, redundant and reflexive on hard drives, extending itself into laptops, Palm Pilots, and Newtons, Phenoms, Softbooks, Rocketbooks—a proliferation of devices for transferring, storing, capturing, displaying, transforming, manipulating (a word rooted in the manual, the hand). Throughout this complex field of becoming, ideas, migratory and potentially contagious, adapt and attach to other ideas, propagating themselves through human vectors with the thriving fragility of thought.

"Though despots and demagogues seize it as weakness, our incompleteness is our strength. Language can sometimes seem like a strange and alien mutation we haven't quite mastered. Depending on how you look at it, this can be either a whimsical sophistry or an ominous sign of how tenuous and incidental civilization really is. Whether comforting or alarming, this notion of language as a virus from outer space has its own quirky appeal. But it hinges on the rusty assumption of a hard and fast division between mind and body.

"I view poetry as a crux where mind and body, heaven and earth, intersect (It can also, therefore, be a crucifixion), and feel the pull between the tendency toward expansion, connection, and linking of various themes, ideas, obsessions, and interests and the feeling one must try to curtail the overlaps, to contain, at least a little, the proliferation.

"What I seek, gentle reader, is a discursive strategy that illustrates via the bleeding that goes on among my texts the inherent ambiguity of various types of boundaries. A protocol that lets me retain some control over them, though each is a kind of hybrid, a monstrous (maybe sacred) semantic offspring, made up of parts from several others. Always, some part of me leans in the other direction. Toward vagrancy or migration, nomads and exile, diffusion, dispersal, subtlety that folds around itself in a gossamer stillness. The intersection of personal narratives with public history, the layering of information, a quest for the hidden, sometimes contradictory meanings embedded in human artifacts: Discovering one's writing voice entails realizing how internal and potentially unique that voice is and—at the same time—how multiple. Not only in the sense of having different modes, but of how much of others is in our deepest subjective feelings and ideas, how hybrid we are as human, how we are formed and defined as much by our culture as by our biology, shaped by memes as much as genes. For language, as Mikhail Bakhtin tells us, 'is not a neutral medium that passes freely and easily into the private property of the speaker's intentions; it is populated, overpopulated, with the intentions of others.' My writing, then, consists of migratory dispatches from the frontier. Like a garden (that mediating space between inside and outside, private and public, open and closed) they can never really be finished."

*   *   *

LASCH-QUINN, Elisabeth 1959-

PERSONAL: Born September 8, 1959, in Washington, DC; daughter of Christopher (a historian and educator) and Nell (Commager) Lasch; married Raymond Quinn (a song writer and sculptor), June 8, 1991; children: Isabel, Honoré. *Education:* University of Virginia, Charlottesville, B.A., 1981; University of Vermont, M.A., 1984; University of Massachusetts, Amherst, Ph.D., 1990.

ADDRESSES: Office—Department of History, 145 Eggers Hall, Syracuse University, Syracuse, NY 13244.

CAREER: Syracuse University, Syracuse, NY, assistant professor, 1990-95, associate professor, 1996-2002, professor of history, 2002—. Visiting research fellow, Whitney Humanities Center, Yale University, 1993-94; visiting assistant professor, Yale University, 1994; fellow, Woodrow Wilson International Center for Scholars, Washington, DC, 1998-99.

WRITINGS:

Black Neighbors: Race and the Limits of Reform in the American Settlement House Movement, 1890-1945, University of North Carolina Press (Chapel Hill, NC), 1993
(Editor) Christopher Lasch, *Women and the Common Life: Love, Marriage, and Feminism,* W. W. Norton (New York, NY), 1997.
(Editor with Elizabeth Fox-Genovese) *Reconstructing History: The Emergence of a New Historical Society,* Routledge (New York, NY), 1999.
Race Experts: How Racial Etiquette, Sensitivity Training, and New Age Therapy Hijacked the Civil Rights Revolution, W. W. Norton (New York, NY), 2001.

Also contributor of numerous articles and essays to *Washington Times* and *New Republic,* and to anthologies, including *American Reform and Reformers,* edited by Paul Cimbala and Randall Miller, Greenwood Press, 1996.

WORK IN PROGRESS: A book on the family; a book on the history of moral conscience; numerous articles, essays, and songs.

SIDELIGHTS: Elisabeth Lasch-Quinn has had a formidable family legacy to maintain as the daughter of historian Christopher Lasch. Lasch-Quinn later embarked on her own successful career in history, focusing primarily on race and culture, and in some of her works she continued in her father's ideological tradition. Her assessments of both race relations and the "culture wars" of the twentieth century, and many other aspects of recent social and cultural history, are controversial but widely read by scholars and general readers of many political persuasions.

Lasch-Quinn's first book is *Black Neighbors: Race and the Limits of Reform in the American Settlement House Movement, 1890-1945.* Settlement houses were a nineteenth-century phenomenon, persisting until World War I, where white, middle-class Americans did the cultural work of assimilating immigrants. When the waves of immigrants ended, African-Americans from the south moved into the areas served by the settlement houses. Lasch-Quinn observes that, while the settlement houses did not similarly work with African-American migrants, agencies including the YWCA, Urban League, church groups, and industrial schools took over settlement work. Lasch-Quinn argues that while racism was one reason the original settlement movement did not assist African-Americans, secularism was another cause, because settlement workers rejected the religion that infused many African-American communities.

Black Neighbors is generally acknowledged by reviewers as a useful contribution to the history of the settlement house movement as well as African-American history in general. Margaret Spratt, writing in the *Journal of Urban History,* wrote that Lasch-Quinn's interpretation of the movement has "important consequences when analyzing social reform in the twentieth century," adding that her study "changes the direction of our inquiry and opens up new areas of research." Similarly, a critic for the *Antioch Review* maintained that "Lasch-Quinn refigures the whole field" by broadening the boundaries of the settlement house movement. Arnold R. Hirsch, reviewing the book in *Reviews in American History,* commented on the nuance and insight of Lasch-Quinn's study, and called *Black Neighbors* "a balanced and judicious commentary that sheds some new light on this much studied phenomenon."

Lasch-Quinn's next major project was to edit a collection of her father's last essays on gender and culture, entitled *Women and the Common Life: Love, Marriage, and Feminism.* Lasch was a critic of the idea of progress, which he maintained had been transformed into an entirely materialist, consumerist concept. Lasch charged that feminism had been subsumed by this idea of progress, defining success in the marketplace as the highest goal. Lasch-Quinn's contribution to the collection is a memoir of her father's life and work, including an account of his last weeks and her sense of his influence on her own work.

Lasch-Quinn has also edited, with historian Elizabeth Fox-Genovese, a collection of essays by scholars of the Historical Society: *Reconstructing History: The*

Emergence of New Historical Society. The Historical Society convened in 1998 to provide an alternative to what members saw as the dogmatic leftist ideology of historical scholarship. Members of the society are not necessarily conservative, however; of those represented in *Reconstructing History,* many are simply skeptical of postmodernism and its dismissive attitude toward historical traditions. Reviewer Eugen Weber called *Reconstructing History* "eloquent, thoughtful, and sometimes virulent," adding that the essays by a collection of authors from across the academic and political spectrum were united in that they "either assume or set out to demonstrate the incompatibility of post-modernism and historical study." Charles K. Piehl, in *Library Journal,* similarly suggested that although some essays were genuine contribution to the discipline of history, "others reveal emotions that may prove as counterproductive as the trends they condemn." Penelope J. Cornfield, however, writing in the *Journal of Contemporary History,* concluded, "the collective effect of so much anxious argument from such an array of serious and thoughtful historians, from both right and left on the political spectrum in the USA, should not be ignored." Lasch-Quinn's own concerns involve the rise of academic over-specialization, the loss of intellectual community, and the waning of the intellectual's public presence.

Among the intellectuals follies attributed to postmodernism by the Historical Society are relativism and political correctness. Lasch-Quinn addresses both of these in her second book on racial issues, *Race Experts: How Racial Etiquette, Sensitivity Training, and New Age Therapy Hijacked the Civil Rights Revolution.* Lasch-Quinn maintains that racial issues have been mired in the language of psychology, feeling, and self-esteem, preventing the possibility of resolving problems of social injustice through political action. Lasch-Quinn criticizes workplace diversity training and well-intentioned children's literature for keeping alive racial stereotypes and equating bad manners with racism. Lasch-Quinn's book won numerous endorsements, including from Michael Meyers, executive director of the New York Civil Rights Coalition, and Eugene Genovese, founder of the Historical Society, and the eminent sociologists Peter Berger and William Julius Wilson.

BIOGRAPHICAL AND CRITICAL SOURCES:

PERIODICALS

Academic Questions, spring, 2000, Thomas C. Reeves, review of *Reconstructing History,* p. 92.

Antioch Review, spring, 1994, review of *Black Neighbors,* p. 373.
Choice, March, 1994, D. R. Jamieson, review of *Black Neighbors,* p. 1208.
First Things, March, 2000, review of *Reconstructing History,* p. 95.
Journal of Contemporary History, July, 2000, Eugen Weber, "From the Culture Wars Front," pp. 467-478; January, 2001, Penelope J. Corfield, "The State of History," pp. 153-161.
Journal of Urban History, September, 1997, Margaret Spratt, review of *Black Neighbors,* pp. 770-776.
Library Journal, January, 1997, Janet Clapp, *Women and the Common Life,* p. 127; September, 1999, Charles K. Piehl, review of *Reconstructing History,* p. 212.
New Statesman, March 21, 1997, Melissa Benn, review of *Women and the Common Life,* pp. 53-54.
New York Times, December 9, 2001, Alan Wolfe, "I'm O.K.—You're a Racist," p. 27L.
New York Times Book Review, January 19, 1997, Andrew Delbanco, "Consuming Passions," p. 8.
Publishers Weekly, July 23, 2001, review of *Race Experts,* p. 58.
Reviews in American History, September, 1994, Arnold R. Hirsch, review of *Black Neighbors,* pp. 480-486.
Wilson Quarterly, winter, 1997, Robyn Geary, review of *Women and the Common Life,* pp. 96-97.

OTHER

Syracuse University Web site, http://www.maxwell.syr.edu/ (October 7, 2001), "Elisabeth Lasch-Quinn."

*   *   *

LAURENS, Camille
  See RUEL-MéZIÈRES, Laurence

*   *   *

LAWLOR, Laurie 1953-

PERSONAL: Born April 4, 1953, in Oak Park, IL; daughter of David (a teacher) and Audrey (a teacher; maiden name, Trautman) Thompson; married John Lawlor (an attorney), June 8, 1974; children: Megan,

John. *Education:* Northwestern University, B.S.J., 1975; National-Louis University, M.A.T., 1992. *Hobbies and other interests:* Traveling, reading, camping.

ADDRESSES: *Home*—2103 Noyes, Evanston, IL 60201. *Agent*—Jane Jordan Browne, Multimedia Product Development, 410 South Michigan, Ste. 724, Chicago, IL 60605. *E-mail*—Laurie@laurielawlor.com.

CAREER: Freelance writer and editor, 1977-89; teacher of college-level writing courses and coordinating elementary and junior-high school writing workshops throughout the Midwest.

MEMBER: Authors Guild, Authors League of America, Society of Children's Book Writers and Illustrators, Society of Midland Authors, Children's Reading Round Table (Chicago, IL).

AWARDS, HONORS: Children's Literature Award (Utah), 1989, Nebraska Golden Sower Award, 1989, Rebecca Caudill Young Reader's Book Award nomination, 1990, and Iowa Children's Choice Award, 1990, all for *Addie across the Prairie;* KC Three Award, 1990-91, for *How to Survive Third Grade;* Nebraska Golden Sower Award nomination, Iowa Children's Choice Award, and North Dakota Flicker Tale Award, all 1992, all for *Addie's Dakota Winter;* Society of Children's Book Writers and Illustrators/Anna Cross Giblin Nonfiction Grant.

WRITINGS:

How to Survive Third Grade, illustrated by Joyce Audy Zarins, A. Whitman (Morton Grove, IL), 1989.
Daniel Boone, illustrated by Burt Dodson, A. Whitman (Morton Grove, IL), 1989.
Second-Grade Dog, illustrated by Gioia Fiammenghi, A. Whitman (Morton Grove, IL), 1990.
The Worm Club, Simon & Schuster (New York, NY), 1994.
Shadow-Catcher: The Life and Work of Edward S. Curtis, Walker Publishing (Morton Grove, IL), 1994.
Little Women (novelization of the movie based on the novel by Louisa May Alcott), Minstrel Books (New York, NY), 1994.
Gold in the Hills, Walker (New York, NY), 1995.

The Real Johnny Appleseed, A. Whitman (Morton Grove, IL), 1995.
Come Away with Me ("Heartland" series), Pocket Books (New York, NY), 1996.
Take to the Sky ("Heartland" series), Pocket Books (New York, NY), 1996.
The Biggest Pest on Eighth Avenue, illustrated by Cynthia Fisher, Holiday House (New York, NY), 1997.
Where Will This Shoe Take You?: A Walk through the History of Footwear, Walker (New York, NY), 1998.
The Worst Kid Who Ever Lived on Eighth Avenue, illustrated by Cynthia Fisher, Holiday House (New York, NY), 1998.
Window on the West: The Frontier Photography of William Henry Jackson, Holiday House (New York, NY), 1999.
Wind on the River, Jamestown Publishers (Lincolnwood, IL), 2000.
Helen Keller: Rebellious Spirit, Holiday House (New York, NY), 2001.
Old Crump: The True Story of a Trip West, illustrated by John Winch, Holiday House (New York, NY), 2002.
Magnificent Voyager: The Story of Captain Cook's Last Expedition, Holiday House (New York, NY), 2002.

"AMERICAN SISTERS" SERIES

West along the Wagon Road, 1852, Pocket Books (New York, NY), 1998.
A Titanic Journey across the Sea, 1912, Pocket Books (New York, NY), 1998.
Adventure on the Wilderness Road, 1775, Pocket Books (New York, NY), 1999.
Crossing the Colorado Rockies, 1864, Pocket Books (New York, NY), 1999.
Voyage to a Free Land, 1630, Pocket Books (New York, NY), 1999.
Down the Rio Grande, 1829, Pocket Books (New York, NY), 2000.
Horseback on the Boston Post Road, 1704, Aladdin (New York, NY), 2000.
Exploring the Chicago World's Fair, 1893, Pocket Books (New York, NY), 2001.
Pacific Odyssey to California, 1905, Aladdin (New York, NY), 2001.

"ADDY ACROSS THE PRAIRIE" SERIES

Addie across the Prairie, illustrated by Gail Owens, A. Whitman (Morton Grove, IL), 1986.

Addie's Dakota Winter, illustrated by Toby Gowing, A. Whitman (Morton Grove, IL), 1989.

Addie's Long Summer, illustrated by Toby Gowing, A. Whitman (Morton Grove, IL), 1992.

George on His Own, illustrated by Toby Gowing, A. Whitman (Morton Grove, IL), 1993.

Luck Follows Me, A. Whitman (Morton Grove, IL), 1996.

Addie's Forever Friend, illustrated by Helen Cogancherry, A. Whitman (Morton Grove, IL), 1997.

SIDELIGHTS: Laurie Lawlor told *CA:* "When I was growing up, we had strange and powerful creatures living in our house. Jack Frost and the Fat Lady were my first attempts at fiction. I'm proud to say that they successfully terrorized my five younger brothers and sisters for years. To this day, no one willingly goes into the attic alone. Why would anyone wish to create such characters? The answer, quite simply, is adventure. It's much more exciting living in a house with witches in the clothes chute than living in a normal house in a normal Chicago suburb. Creating adventure really is at the heart of what I enjoy about writing. I also believe it is at the heart of what children enjoy reading.

"*Addie across the Prairie* began as a personal adventure. For years I had heard stories passed down to my mother by my grandmother about how my Great Aunt Laura and her brothers and sisters traveled from Iowa to Dakota Territory to homestead. This family folklore intrigued but did not satisfy me. Perhaps it was my training as a journalist that made me want to know *exactly* what happened. What was it like to be nine years old, my Great Aunt Laura's age, and leave everything familiar behind? How did her family adjust? How did they survive? Ten lined, yellowed notebook pages launched my search. I discovered an account written by my Aunt Laura when she was married, fifty years old, and struggling to make a go of a homestead west of the Missouri river. On these pages, titled 'Pioneering,' she told in simple, unassuming language the story of her childhood in Dakota. On the last page, her last sentence drifts toward a blot in the bottom corner. 'As I grow older it seems that every year is more like pioneering.' And that was all she wrote.

"The events described in *Addie across the Prairie* occurred more than one hundred years ago. What I particularly enjoy about historical fiction is the way it can explode time barriers. When a period of history is described as realistically and truthfully as a writer knows how, historical fiction allows readers a unique opportunity. They become time travelers, comparing and contrasting their own modern lives with that of a book's characters.

"What struck me again and again as I worked on *Addie* was the marvelous way humans can adapt. When our environment forces us, we can re-learn just about anything; how to find water, how to farm, how to build our houses, how to find fuel. We adjust, we adapt. Think about it. How different is the settlement of remote, hostile parts of the American West from the settlement of remote, hostile parts of our galaxy? The same child reading about Addie's adventures and comparing them with his or her own might one day really experience 'homesteading' in a space colony somewhere. It is this sense of possibility, of adventure, that I hope to convey to readers. What happens to Addie could have—or might one day—happen to them."

Lawlor's books have received high praise for making history, particularly the history of settling of the American West in the nineteenth century, come alive for young readers more than a hundred years later. In biographies of real-life legends such as Daniel Boone and Johnny Appleseed, as well as in novels such as the "Addie across the Prairie" and "American Sisters" series, Lawlor teaches children about the social, political, and cultural milieu that makes sense of her characters' lives, and allows her readers to more accurately gauge their struggles as well as their triumphs. While Lawlor is occasionally faulted for paying less attention to character development than to historical context, she has also been praised for composing well-written, exciting historical narratives for children.

Lawlor first became known for her "Addie across the Prairie" series. This series showcases the author's strengths as a writer of historical fiction for children, including a child-centered narrative that is grounded in both a child's reality and in the history of pioneering the West in the 1880s. Other fictional attempts to bring to life this era include *Gold in the Hills* and *Old Crump: The True Story of a Trip West.* In *Gold in the Hills,* a man who has recently lost his wife becomes convinced he can make a fortune panning for gold in the Colorado mountains and leaves his children, Hattie and Pheme, with his cousin Tirzah while he gives it a try. The children's abandonment leaves them vulnerable to the meanness of Tirzah, and Hattie and Pheme are in danger of losing heart until they are befriended by an elderly woodsman. "Readers will be drawn into the mental anguish of these people as they evolve and show some emotional growth," predicted Rita Soltan in *School Library Journal.* Elizabeth Bush, writing in the *Bulletin of the Center for Children's Books,* praised Lawlor's effective characterization as well as her exciting plot, concluding that *Gold in the Hills* should be "as appealing to outdoorsy adventure buffs as it will be to orphan-story fans." *Old Crump: The True Story of a Trip West* is set earlier in the same century, during the long, perilous journey over the mountains and across Death Valley to reach California in 1849. The title character, Old Crump, is the family's faithful ox who tirelessly carries them across the rough terrain and is put out to pasture in gratitude once they arrive. Although a contributor to *Kirkus Reviews* found some factual inaccuracies in the text, a reviewer in *Publishers Weekly* noted that the story is based on period diaries, "making this a solid introduction to the historical journey to the West."

Young readers with a fascination for the world of Laura Ingalls Wilder will likely be attracted to Lawlor's "American Sisters" series, some critics noted. These are novels for middle-grade readers that inspired by the author's research into pioneer history. Each narrative is interspersed with excerpts from the diaries of the actual people on whom Lawlor based her stories. In *Adventure on the Wilderness Road, 1775,* an eleven-year-old girl narrates her large family's arduous and dangerous journey on Daniel Boone's Wilderness Road to settle in Kentucky. Hazel Rochman, who reviewed the book for *Booklist,* remarked that a greater insight into the barely-glimpsed lives of the Native Americans would have been a welcome addition; yet "Lawlor's research is meticulous, and her narrative is true to the white child's viewpoint of the family adventure." In *West along the Wagon Road, 1852,* the first novel in the series, another eleven-year-old girl, one of seven girls and three boys in the family, narrates her family's

journey in a covered-wagon caravan into Oregon Territory. "Lawlor's well-researched text and readable writing style make this book an excellent choice" for young fans of historical fiction, remarked Robin L. Gibson in *School Library Journal.* Two stepsisters appear in *Down the Rio Grande, 1829,* the sixth volume in the series. Although *School Library Journal* critic Betsy Barnett faulted Lawlor's use of magic to rescue her characters from the worst of their predicaments, she also praised the author's depiction of the boat trip, the topography, and the era, as well as "excellent descriptions of Mexican culture, traditions, language, and people."

Lawlor is also known for her biographies for middle-grade readers. Among these is *Shadow-Catcher: The Life and Work of Edward S. Curtis.* Curtis spent the major part of his life tirelessly photographing the Native Americans of the American West, and while his work—including thirty volumes of haunting photographs and a film—did not garner success during his lifetime, it is now considered a priceless contribution to American history as it provides in many cases the only record of a people, a culture, and a way of life that have since disappeared. "Kids reading the book will get a real sense of the steady erosion of the once all-encompassing civilizations," remarked Deborah Stevenson in *Bulletin of the Center for Children's Books.* Other critics noted that Lawlor refuses to gloss over the less-appealing aspects of Curtis's personal life, sacrificing his relationship with his family in pursuit of his ambition, for example. Through this biography, "the reader will get a feel for the life and dedication of this artist as well as the sacrifices that he made," observed Susan DeRonne in *Booklist.*

A biography of another noted photographer of the nineteenth-century frontier, William Henry Jackson, also garnered critical praise. In *Window on the West: The Frontier Photography of William Henry Jackson,* Lawlor brings to light the last quarter of the nineteenth century, a time of cowboys, Indians, and the ever-expanding railroad. As in her other works, the strength of this book is considered to be its portrait of the America through which her subject walked. As a contributor to the *Horn Book* put it: "The reader gets only quick glimpses of [Jackson], yet the changing world in which he operated is abundantly explored." "This is much more than a look at early photography," proclaimed Randy Meyer in *Booklist,* "it's a memorable, bittersweet valentine to the Old West."

Lawlor investigates a legendary figure in another biography, *The Real Johnny Appleseed.* Here, relying extensively on her knowledge of the history of the era to fill in the gaps in the historical record, the author paints a portrait of John Chapman, who spent much of his life planting apple orchards in pursuit of the Swedenborgian ideal of helping others. "Lawlor's clear narrative style and impeccable scholarship combine to make this . . . an outstanding choice," wrote Susan Scheps in *School Library Journal.* A more recent notable American hero is the subject of another well regarded biography in *Helen Keller: Rebellious Spirit.* As in Lawlor's earlier biographies, her subject's life is well-grounded in its historical context, "making [Keller's] achievements seem all the more astounding given the era's prevailing discrimination against women and the disabled," remarked a contributor to *Horn Book.* And, as in her biography of Edward S. Curtis, reviewers favorably noted Lawlor's willingness to note her subject's flaws along with her virtues.

Lawlor moves out of the nineteenth century and into the twentieth with her "Heartland" series, beginning with *Come Away with Me* and *Take to the Sky,* both set in the early 1900s. Here the stage is set for stories that focus on the conflict between the demands of tradition and the lure of modern innovation, as Emily Kutler noted in *School Library Journal.* In *Come Away with Me,* twelve-year-old Moe gets into some scrapes when two older, more ladylike, cousins come for a visit, and in *Take to the Sky,* Moe and her best friend, Otto, build an airplane. "The books are humorous and well-paced," wrote Kutler.

Lawlor has also written several light-hearted contemporary mysteries, including *The Worst Kid Who Ever Lived on Eighth Avenue* and *The Biggest Pest on Eighth Avenue.* In the *Worst Kid,* the kids on Eighth Avenue become suspicious when they see a man burying something in his parents' backyard. In *The Biggest Pest,* these same kids are constantly annoyed in their preparations for a scary play by the interruptions of pesky little brother Tommy.

Reviewers delighted in Lawlor's history *Where Will This Shoe Take You?,* which a contributor to *Child Life* dubbed "a unique and cool way to look at history, one foot at a time." In this book, Lawlor states that throughout history, footwear has been an indicator of social and economic status, political tendencies, and level of power; she also surveys superstitions and

traditions related to shoes. "Read this and you'll never look at your old sneakers the same way again," stated Elizabeth Bush in the *Bulletin of the Center for Children's Books.*

BIOGRAPHICAL AND CRITICAL SOURCES:

PERIODICALS

Booklist, August, 1992, Deborah Abbot, review of *Addie's Long Summer,* p. 2011; September 1, 1993, Kay Weisman, review of *George on His Own,* p. 61; December 1, 1994, Susan DeRonne, review of *Shadow-Catcher: The Life and Work of Edward S. Curtis,* p. 661; June 1, 1995, Frances Bradburn, review of *Gold in the Hills,* p. 1771; September 1, 1995, April Judge, review of *The Real Johnny Appleseed,* p. 71; November 15, 1996, Susan DeRonne, review of *Where Will This Shoe Take You?: A Walk through the History of Footwear,* p. 583; November 15, 1997, Susan Dove Lempke, review of *Addie's Forever Friend,* p. 560; May 1, 1998, Ilene Cooper, review of *The Worst Kid Who Ever Lived on Eighth Avenue,* p. 1524; December 1, 1998, John Peters, review of *West along the Wagon Road, 1852,* p. 667; April 1, 1999, Hazel Rochman, review of *Adventure on the Wilderness Road, 1775,* p. 1426; February 15, 2000, Randy Meyer, review of *Window on the West: The Frontier Photography of William Henry Jackson,* p. 1098; June 1, 2000, Helen Rosenberg, review of *Wind on the River,* p. 1882; April 1, 2001, Ilene Cooper, review of *Exploring the Chicago World's Fair, 1893,* p. 1483; September 1, 2001, Susan Dove Lempke, review of *Helen Keller: Rebellious Spirit,* p. 99.
Book Report, May-June, 1995, Tena Natale Litherland, review of *Shadow-Catcher,* p. 54; March-April, 1996, Pam Whitehead, review of *Gold in the Hills,* p. 36; March-April, 1997, Joan Chezem, review of *Where Will This Shoe Take You?,* p. 58.
Bulletin of the Center for Children's Books, November, 1988, p. 77; December, 1989, p. 87; March, 1990, p. 168; November, 1992, p. 78; February, 1995, Deborah Stevenson, review of *Shadow-Catcher,* p. 205; July-August, 1995, Elizabeth Bush, review of *Gold in the Hills,* p. 388; November, 1995, Elizabeth Bush, review of *The Real Johnny Appleseed,* p. 97; January, 1997, Elizabeth Bush, review of *Where Will This Shoe Take You?,* p. 178.

Child Life, April-May, 1998, review of *Where Will This Shoe Take You?,* p. 20.

Entertainment Weekly, January 27, 1995, A. J. Jacobs, review of *Little Women,* p. 8.

Horn Book, January-February, 1995, Peter D. Sieruta, review of *Shadow-Catcher,* p. 75; March-April, 1997, Elizabeth S. Watson, review of *Where Will This Shoe Take You?,* p. 212; March, 2000, review of *Window on the West,* p. 214; September, 2001, review of *Helen Keller: Rebellious Spirit,* p. 611.

Horn Book Guide, fall, 1995, Martha V. Parravano, review of *Gold in the Hills,* p. 300; spring, 1998, Maeve Visser Knoth, review of *The Biggest Pest on Eighth Avenue,* p. 56; fall, 1998, Maeve Visser Knoth, review of *The Worst Kid Who Ever Lived on Eighth Street,* p. 313; fall, 1999, Bridget Mc-Caffrey, review of *West along the Wagon Road, 1852* and *A Titanic Journey across the Sea,* p. 295.

Kirkus Reviews, February 15, 1998, review of *The Worst Kid Who Ever Lived on Eighth Street,* p. 270; March 1, 2002, review of *Old Crump: The True Story of a Trip West,* p. 337.

New York Review of Books, Alison Lurie, review of *Little Women,* p. 3.

Publishers Weekly, June 10, 1988, review of *How to Survive Third Grade,* p. 80; December 5, 1994, review of *Shadow-Catcher,* p. 78; May 29, 1995, review of *Gold in the Hills,* p. 86; June 24, 1996, review of *Come Away with Me,* p. 61; September 28, 1998, review of *West along the Wagon Road, 1852,* p. 102; January 17, 2000, review of *Window on the West,* p. 58; July 2, 2001, review of *Helen Keller,* p. 77; February 11, 2002, review of *Old Crump,* p. 185.

School Arts, May, 2000, Kent Marantz, review of *Window on the West,* p. 62.

School Library Journal, October, 1986, Elaine Lesh Morgan, review of *Addie across the Prairie,* p. 178; September, 1988, Annette Curtis Klause, review of *How to Survive Third Grade,* p. 184; December, 1988, Katharine Bruner, review of *Daniel Boone,* p. 128; January, 1990, Sylvia S. Marantz, review of *Addie's Dakota Winter,* p. 104; June, 1990, Leslie Barban, review of *Second-Grade Dog,* p. 103; November, 1992, Elizabeth Hamilton, review of *Addie's Long Summer,* p. 95; July, 1993, JoAnn Rees, review of *George on His Own,* p. 86; February, 1995, Nancy E. Curran, review of *Shadow-Catcher,* p. 121; August, 1995, Rita Soltan, review of *Gold in the Hills,* p. 142; January, 1996, Susan Scheps, review of *The Real Johnny Appleseed,* p. 120; November, 1996, Emily Kutler, review of *Come Away with Me* and *Take to the Sky,* p. 108; May, 1997, Wendy D. Caldiero, review of *Where Will This Shoe Take You?,* p. 148; February, 1998, Rosalyn Pierini, review of *Addie's Forever Friend,* p. 86; March, 1998, Sharon R. Pearce, review of *The Biggest Pest on Eight Avenue,* p. 182; April, 1998, Maura Bresnahan, *The Worst Kid Who Ever Lived on Eighth Avenue,* p. 102; December, 1998, Robin L. Gibson, review of *West along the Wagon Road, 1852,* p. 128; November, 1999, Betsy Barnett, review of *Adventure on Wilderness Road, 1775,* p. 160; March, 2000, Steven Engelfried, review of *Window on the West,* p. 256; January, 2001, Betsy Barnett, review of *Down the Rio Grande, 1829,* p. 132; August, 2001, Janie Schomberg, review of *Exploring the Chicago World's Fair, 1893,* p. 185; December, 2001, Kathleen Baxter, "We Could Be Heroes: From an Outspoken Boxer to a Teenage Saint, Four Amazing Lives," p. 39; June, 2002, Ruth Semrau, review of *Old Crump,* p. 98.

Washington Post Book World, May 7, 1995, Ilan Stavans, review of *Shadow-Catcher,* pp. 13, 18.

Wilson Library Bulletin, April, 1995, Linda Perkins, review of *Shadow-Catcher,* p. 116.

OTHER

Laurie Lawlor Web site, http://www.laurielawlor.com (January 18, 2003).*

*   *   *

LEAHEY, Michael I. 1956-

PERSONAL: Born September 24, 1956, in Nyack, NY; son of Edward Berry and Mary Catherine (Carlin) Leahey; married Lynn K. Davey (an editor), January 19, 1991; children: two. *Ethnicity:* "Irish-American." *Education:* Fordham University, B.A., 1978; Babson College, M.B.A., 1981. *Politics:* Independent. *Religion:* Catholic. *Hobbies and other interests:* History, philosophy, music, golf, baseball.

ADDRESSES: Home—Westchester, NY. *Office*—c/o Office of Clinical Trials, Columbia Presbyterian Medical Center, PH 15 Center, Suite 1540, 622 West 168th St., New York, NY 10032.

CAREER: Columbia University and New York Presbyterian Hospital, administrator and business manager, 1982-87, director of the Office of Clinical Trials, 1992—; Jackson Steel Products, president, 1987-90; management consultant and writer, 1990-91.

MEMBER: Mystery Writers of America, Historical Mystery Writers, New York Academy of Sciences.

AWARDS, HONORS: Washington Irving Award, Westchester Library Association, 2000.

WRITINGS:

Broken Machines, St. Martin's Press (New York, NY), 2000.
The Pale Green Horse, St. Martin's Press (New York, NY), 2002.

SIDELIGHTS: Author Michael I. Leahey had a distinguished career in management and finance before beginning his career as a mystery writer. As the director of the Office of Clinical Trials at the prestigious Columbia Presbyterian Medical Center in New York City, Leahey successfully promoted the Center as a site for clinic trials and overseen its multimillion dollar clinical trials fund. The New York world of his detective series, however, is dark, gritty, and full of sleazy characters, inspired by such authors as Dashiel Hammett, Raymond Chandler, and Rex Stout.

Leahey began his crime novelist career with the book *Broken Machines.* In it, he introduces the investigative team of James Joseph Donovan and Dr. Boris Mikail Koulomzin, neighbors in an apartment watched over by a wacky doorman and an elderly Russian widow. Donovan's friend Janet Fein, a social worker, brings the pair the case of Ruby Brice, a murdered prostitute, and her orphaned son Clifford, a precocious ten year old. The detectives follow a trail to the National Manufacturing Corporation in Brooklyn, where Donovan begins working undercover. Embezzlement, gunrunning, and sweatshop conditions for exploited immigrant laborers are only the beginning of the evils Donovan and his partner discover in the course of solving a growing list of murders.

With its strong language, dark atmosphere, and complex protagonist, *Broken Machines* earned Leahey comparisons to popular writers of detective fiction including Rex Stout, Elmore Leonard, and Robert Parker. Writing for *Booklist,* reviewer Gary Niebuhr called *Broken Machines* "a promising debut featuring an appealing team of sleuths." Harriet Klauser, for the online review *BookBrowser,* also commented on Leahey's skill with characterization, noting that "although the plot is tense and loaded, the cast makes this tale work." Klausner concluded that Leahey's characters "provide the right amount of intelligence, chutzpah, and reality to transform [his] novel into a triumphant urban noir." A critic for *Kirkus Reviews* suggested that Leahey's quirky characters make the novel somewhat inconsistent, writing that the author "needs to decide whether he wants to be hard-boiled or terminally cute." A reviewer for *Publishers Weekly,* however, predicted that "readers will be eager for more adventures of this engaging PI and his compatriots."

Donovan's next adventure unfolds in *The Pale Green Horse* wherein his ex-wife Kate, editor of a fashion magazine, plays a larger role. His partner the doctor gets mixed up in an apparent case of mistaken identity that puts them on a trail of a killer named Johnny St. John. In an interview with *Authors on the Web,* Leahey noted that "the pale green horse was the fourth rider of the apocalypse and his companion was death." Leahey told *Authors on the Web* that although he enjoys writing, he must give much of his time to other commitments: "I have a day job running a research program for Columbia University and New York Presbyterian Hospital. At any given time we have about 400 active research studies. I also have two small children, ages 5 and 2, who are my greatest gifts and with whom I spend virtually all my spare time when they aren't sleeping. Writing must fit around these activities, which is hard, but not impossible."

Leahey told *CA:* "I want to make it clear that my writing does fit in around my other commitments. What suffers is my personal down time. For me, writing is the one passion I have always had. I will continue to write and, hopefully, improve with each new book."

BIOGRAPHICAL AND CRITICAL SOURCES:

PERIODICALS

Booklist, November 15, 2000, Gary Niebuhr, review of *Broken Machines,* p. 623.
Kirkus Reviews, August 1, 2000, review of *Broken Machines,* p. 1078.

Library Journal, September 1, 2000, Rex Klett, review of *Broken Machines,* p. 255.

Publishers Weekly, August 28, 2000, review of *Broken Machines,* p. 58.

OTHER

BookBrowser, http://www.bookbrowser.com/ (September 1, 2000), Harriet Klausner, review of *Broken Machines.*

Book Reporter, http://www.bookreporter.com/ (December 2, 2002), review of *The Pale Green Horse.*

Michael I. Leahey Home Page, http://www. michaelileahey.com (October 7, 2001).

Mystery Reader, http://themysteryreader.com/ (October 7, 2001), Jennifer Monahan Winberry, review of *Broken Machines.*

Office of Clinical Trials, Columbia Presbyterian Medical Center Web site, http://cpmcnet.columbia.edu/ (March 25, 2002), biography of Michael I. Leahey.

*   *   *

LEBERT, Benjamin 1982-

PERSONAL: Born January 9, 1982, in Freiberg, Germany. *Nationality:* German. *Education:* Castle Nueseelen Boarding School.

ADDRESSES: Home—Munich, Germany.

CAREER: Writer for young-adult supplement of *Süddeutsche Zeitung,* Munich, Germany.

WRITINGS:

Crazy, translated by Carol Brown Janeway, Knopf (New York, NY), 1983.

ADAPTATIONS: Crazy was filmed by director Hans-Christian Schmid and won numerous awards in Germany, 2000.

SIDELIGHTS: Benjamin Lebert, sometimes called a *wunderkind* in the world of contemporary German literature, achieved immediate success with the publication of his coming-of-age novel, *Crazy.* Written when the author was only fifteen, the book was an overnight sensation among German youth. By the end of 2001 the book had sold over 300,000 copies in Germany alone, and its American publication marked another milestone for the then eighteen-year-old Lebert. The novel was translated into twenty-five languages.

The protagonist of this semi-autobiographical novel also bears the name Benjamin Lebert, and, like the author, he is partially crippled and a school dropout. *Crazy* tells the story of a boy who has failed at several boarding schools and has now entered a new one in a last-ditch attempt to graduate. He soon acquires several colorful friends, who join him in a mutual journey of self-discovery, experimenting with drugs, sex, smoking, and alcohol while reflecting often on the meaning of their lives.

Benni, as he is called, joins his friends on several escapades, including a raid on the girls' dorm and a forbidden trip to Munich. Despite his growing feeling of belonging, Benni in the end does not improve his grades and is forced to leave the school.

In an interview with Simon Hattenstone in the *Guardian,* Lebert said that he began writing monster stories around the age of nine, beginning *Crazy* during weekends at home from school. While writing, he told Hattenstone, "You can invent your own world. There's a kind of purity . . . you have to be very honest and very close to yourself." He indicated that he was angered to find that some reviewers thought the book was actually written by his father, a journalist. His former teachers, he said, had little confidence in his writing abilities: "They said I was a loser. . . . But I feel in some way everyone is not a loser. Everyone is brave in some way."

Lebert's rise to fame began when German author Maxim Biller read one of Lebert's pieces in a youth supplement to a German newspaper and faxed it to his own publishing house, which later decided to publish and promote *Crazy.* The book's often-mentioned similarities to J. D. Salinger's *Catcher in the Rye* prompted Lebert to remark to Allison Linn in an interview in *Book,* "Without *Catcher in the Rye,* this book never would have been written." Linn noted that "Lebert has clearly captured the hearts of so many

German teens in part because he so unabashedly revealed his insecure and sensitive side in the novel— the child still trapped in the teen-ager."

Most reviews of *Crazy* agreed that Lebert is a promising young writer. In the *New York Times Book Review,* Jeffrey Eugenides commented on the book's tendency to "blather on and on" as "Lebert's band of schoolboys wax philosophic," and criticized the "sketchy characterization" and "unjustified behavior" evident in the story. But Eugenides also found that "on a purely linguistic level [Lebert] writes clearly and adequately." Max Brzezinski in the *Antioch Review* called the book "cliché-ridden" and "superficial" but acknowledged that it "shows genuine promise." Hattenstone concluded that "*Crazy* is a beautiful book about someone grasping freedom for the first time."

Online critic Jane Downs appreciated the book for providing a glimpse into the secret world of youth _ not youth as it would like to be seen, but youth amongst itself, behind closed doors. "Lebert tells of that curious mix of anxiety, ambition, fear and optimism that characterizes adolescence."

Booklist reviewer Kristine Huntley felt that "Lebert's voice is enticing from the first page, and his witty but simple observations make this book an impressive first novel from a talented young writer." A reviewer for Time Europe described Lebert's style as "fresh, raw and even poetic writing" that hints of crazier things to come.

Crazy was adapted into a film by producers Jakob Claussen and Thomas Wobke, whose film *Beyond Silence* was nominated for the Best Foreign Film Oscar in 1997. With a screenplay by Michael Gutmann, the film raked up a multitude of German film awards and toured Australia. It was filmed on location at the actual prep school that Lebert attended.

BIOGRAPHICAL AND CRITICAL SOURCES:

PERIODICALS

Antioch Review, winter, 2001, Max Brzezinski, review of *Crazy,* p. 111.
Booklist, February 15, 2000, Kristine Huntley, review of *Crazy,* p. 1052.

Guardian (London, England), July 31, 2000, Simon Hattenstone, "Portrait: Flawed Genius," p. 8.
Library Journal, April 1, 2000, Judith Kicinski, review of *Crazy,* p. 130.
Los Angeles Times, April 28, 2000, Heller McAlpin, "Thoughtful Teens Populate Young Writer's Coming-of-Age Tale," p. E3.
New York Times Book Review, May 14, 2000, Jeffrey Eugenides, "Pup Fiction," p. 12.
Publishers Weekly, March 20, 2000, review of *Crazy,* p. 73.
School Library Journal, August, 2000, Sheryl Fowler, review of *Crazy,* p. 212.

OTHER

Book, http://www.bookmagazine.com/archive/issue10 (May-June, 2000), profile of Lebert and excerpt from *Crazy.**

*   *   *

LEE, Chana Kai 1962-

PERSONAL: Born 1962. *Education:* Holds degrees in history and African-American studies. University of California at Los Angeles, Ph.D., 1993.

ADDRESSES: Office—Department of History, University of Georgia, Athens, GA 30602.

CAREER: University of Georgia, Athens, associate professor of history.

MEMBER: Editorial consultant, Femenist Studies, University of Maryland, College Park.

AWARDS, HONORS: Letitia Woods Brown Prize, Willie Lee Rose Prize from Southern Association for Women Historians, and semi-finalist, Robert F. Kennedy Book Award, all for *For Freedom's Sake: The Life of Fannie Lou Hamer.*

WRITINGS:

For Freedom's Sake: The Life of Fannie Lou Hamer, University of Illinois Press (Urbana, IL), 1999.

(Contributor) *Gender and the Southern Body Politic,* Edited by Nancy Bercaw, University Press of Mississippi (Jackson, MS), 1997.

WORK IN PROGRESS: A collection of essays about historical memory, black feminism, and women's sexuality.

SIDELIGHTS: Chana Kai Lee is the author of *For Freedom's Sake, The Life of Fannie Lou Hamer,* a biography of the prominent black civil rights activist of the 1960s. Lee describes Hamer as one who was born among the "ruralest and the poorest of the poorest" in Jim Crow Mississipi. The book recounts Hamer's courageous crusade to empower the poor in the segregated South. Publisher University of Illinois Press noted on its Web site: "Lee renders Hamer's acute political instincts, her rhetorical prowess, and her skill in retooling her past to serve strategic political purposes, as well as her deep frustration with a society that was willing to hold her up as an example of individual heroism but resisted her efforts at complex understanding of how sexism and racism intersected both to spur the civil rights movement and to shape, and sometimes restrict, women's roles within it. Lee illuminates the abiding links between political activism and economic transformation within the civil rights movement."

In a review for *Boston Research Center Newsletter,* critic Judith Nies notes that the book captures Hamer's life of hard work and marginalization. "Hamer's struggles were not limited to race. Within the Civil Rights movement she found little support from an all-male black Baptist clergy, famously negligent in giving recognition or voice to women leaders. More background and context about white supremacist Mississippi and the male African-American leadership would add depth to this poignant life story, but Lee's work fills an important gap in the history of the two-pronged struggle of black women in the 1960s."

In *Gender and the Southern Body Politic,* Lee joins several scholars in attempting to broaden readers' understanding of politics and history.

BIOGRAPHICAL AND CRITICAL SOURCES:

PERIODICALS

Publishers Weekly, August 9, 1999, review of *For Freedom's Sake,* p. 331.

OTHER

Boston Research Center Newsletter, www.brc21.org/ newsletters/ (fall, 2001).*

*   *   *

LEINWAND, Theodore B.

PERSONAL: Male. *Education:* Johns Hopkins University, Ph.D., 1980.

ADDRESSES: Office—Department of English, The University of Maryland, College Park, MD 20742. *E-mail*—tl5@umail.umd.edu.

CAREER: University of Maryland, associate professor of English, Graduate Research Board, 1989-92, Arts and Humanities PCC, 1993-95; acting director of undergraduate studies, spring 1994.

MEMBER: Folger Library Colloquium and Seminar Screening Committees.

WRITINGS:

The City Staged: Jacobean Comedy 1603-1613, University of Wisconsin Press (Madison), 1986.
Theatre, Finance, and Society in Early Modern England, Cambridge University Press (Cambridge, England), 1999.

Contributor to academic journals, including *Kenyon Review, Shakespeare Quarterly, Shakespeare Studies, Journal of Medieval and Renaissance Studies,* and *Clio.* Serves on the editorial board for *Renaissance Drama.*

WORK IN PROGRESS: A work about Thomas Middleton's *Michaelmas Term,* for Oxford University Press.

SIDELIGHTS: Theodore B. Leinwand is an associate professor of English at the University of Maryland and the author of *The City Staged: Jacobean Comedy,*

1603-1613. Leinwand studies the plays of George Chapman, Thomas Middleton, John Webster, and others in comparing and defining the social relations between art and the stage and to explain how Londoners saw themselves, both in the city and on the stage. He examines various citizens, including the gentleman and his family, the merchant, the maid, the whore, and the independent woman. Leinwand looks at the degree of realism of characters portrayed on stage and how audiences reacted to them. C. C. Harbour noted in *Choice* that the definitions given to the stage versions are made clearer by comparing them to those found in poems, satires, sermons, pamphlets, and conduct books. Harbour wrote that Leinwand "clearly articulates his concept of the complex relationship between art and society."

Gail Kern Paster wrote in *Shakespeare Quarterly* that Leinwand "wants to examine how city comedy's major plot and characterization formulae represent the city to itself. He focuses particularly on how the overdetermined social roles into which three crucial status groups of merchants, gallants, and women cast each other are refracted onto the stage in exaggerated or distorted ways. And he concludes that these typifications caused members of the city-comedy audience to re-examine their own interpretations of themselves and of others." Paster called *The City Staged* "a major contribution to our understanding of Jacobean comedy."

Criticism reviewer Richard C. McCoy wrote that Leinwand feels the theatrical and social stereotypes "serve an ideological function, confirming the social order and its hierarchical structure. Leinwand regards drama as a collective enterprise, and, citing Jeffrey Sammons's *Literary Sociology and Practical Criticism,* he contends that all literature is, 'in some measure, the joint production of author and public.' At the same time, he sees a need to comprehend the historical circumstances of such collective productions." McCoy felt that there are "shortcomings" in Leinwand's analyses of plays but found them to be "generally intelligent and persuasive," and "nearly always provocative and illuminating."

In *Shakespeare Quarterly,* Shakespearean scholar Lars Engle reviewed *Theatre, Finance and Society in Modern England,* calling it "concise, well-focused and ineresting." Engle commends Leinwand for resisting the tendency of other authors to "read the present into the past" when examining the economics of Shakespeare's England. Engle notes: "Leinwand has read widely in economic history as well as literary criticism and theater history. One of the most important contributions his book makes is to undermine some of the oppositions that have been important to economic critics of drama: oppositions between landed gentry and merchants, aristocrats and new men, for instance." Engle dubbed the book so worthwhile that he planned to "send students to it."

BIOGRAPHICAL AND CRITICAL SOURCES:

PERIODICALS

Choice, December, 1986, p. 636.
Criticism, summer, 1987, pp. 403-405.
Kenyon Review, spring, 2002, "On Sitting down to Read Shakespeare Once Again."
Modern Philology, May, 1989, p. 423.
Renaissance Quarterly, autumn, 2000, review of *Theatre, Finance and Society in Early Modern England.*
Review of English Studies, August, 1988, p. 429.
Shakespeare Quarterly, summer, 1988, pp. 257-58; Volume 52, number 1, 2001, pp.157-159.

*   *   *

LEMAITRE, Corene 1967-

PERSONAL: Born 1967. *Education:* New York University; B.F.A. (with honors); studied acting with Stella Adler.

ADDRESSES: Home—London, England.

CAREER: Novelist. Circle Repertory Theater Company, New York, NY, worked in literary office; host of television talk show *Authors Etc.,* broadcast in Philadelphia, PA.

WRITINGS:

April Rising (novel), Carroll & Graf (New York, NY), 1999.

Past editor of *The Source.*

SIDELIGHTS: Corene Lemaitre grew up with two passions: writing and acting. She went to New York to study drama under Stella Adler. Her career path turned away from acting when she moved to Edinburgh, Scotland to edit a literary magazine. Her first novel, *April Rising,* was published while she was still editing the magazine.

April Rising is the story of a wayward young woman who travels abroad for two years and then returns home. When she comes back to her parents' suburban house, everything has changed, including a new inhabitant in her bedroom, a junk-food-addicted woman named April who is dating her brother.

In an interview with *fireandwater.com,* Lemaitre says the book should provoke readers to examine their own lives. "The two girls in *April Rising,* though initially hostile towards each other are nevertheless two halves of the same person. Ellen's parents are equally two halves of the same person, who learn that you have to work at the process of becoming one. This is the challenge of any relationship. It's not easy to bond with another human being, but it's a noble and worthwhile goal."

New York Times Book Review contributor Nell Casey gave *April Rising* a favorable critique. "The story is told with impressive eccentricity. Like April herself, the novel has an offbeat good spiritedness that eventually wins you over."

BIOGRAPHICAL AND CRITICAL SOURCES:

PERIODICALS

New York Times Book Review, January 23, 2000, Nell Casey, review of *April Rising,* p. 20.
Publishers Weekly, October 11, 1999, review of *April Rising,* pp. 51-52.

OTHER

Corene Lemaitre Home Page, http://www.icdc.com/~corene/ (April 3, 2003).
FireandWater.com, http://www.fireandwater.com/ (April 3, 2003).
HarperCollins Web Site, http://www.harpercollins.co.uk/ (February 3, 2003).*

LEO, John P. 1935-

PERSONAL: Born June 16, 1935, son of Maurice M. and Maria M. (Trincellita) Leo; married Stephanie Wolf, December 30, 1967 (divorced); children: Alexandra. *Education:* University of Toronto, B.A., 1957; Marietta College, Litt.D. (honors), 1996. Politics: "Social Conservative."

ADDRESSES: Office—*U.S. News & World Report,* 1290 6th Avenue, Suite 600, New York, NY 10104.

CAREER: Bergen Record, Hackensack, NJ, editor, 1957-60; *Catholic Messenger,* Davenport, IA, editor, 1960-63; *Commonweal,* New York, NY, associate editor, 1963-67; *New York Times,* New York, NY, reporter, 1967-69; New York City Department of Environment Protection, department administrator, 1970-73; *Village Voice,* New York, NY, press columnist, 1973-74; *Time,* New York, NY, associate editor and senior writer, 1974-88; *U.S. News & World Report,* New York, NY, columnist, 1988—.

AWARDS, HONORS: Excellence in the Advancement of Men's Issues Award, National Coalition of Free Men, 1996; Harry S. Murphy Award, Queens County Board of the Ancient Order of Hiberians, 1996, for outstanding contribution to support the teachings of the Catholic Church, 1996.

WRITINGS:

How the Russians Invented Baseball and Other Essays of Enlightenment, Delacorte Press (New York, NY), 1989.
Two Steps ahead of the Thought Police, Simon & Schuster (New York, NY), 1994.
Incorrect Thoughts: Notes on Our Wayward Culture, Transaction Publishers (New Brunswick, NJ), 2000.

SIDELIGHTS: John P. Leo, a senior writer and columnist for *U.S. News & World Report,* considers himself a social conservative, one who never shies away from controversial topics. His weekly column, which is distributed to publications nationwide by Universal Press Syndicate, reflects his outspoken views on topics such as the controversy regarding the memorial to fallen firefighters at the site of the World Trade Center disaster and his belief that the best college graduates in the United States should enter the fields of public service and national security rather than taking lucrative jobs in the corporate business world.

Leo has been a journalist since 1957 and a columnist or senior writer since 1973; this has allowed him plenty of time to reflect on the culture and politics of the United States. One of his favorite topics is morality and his objections to the lyrics of popular music, teenage sex, assisted suicide, media bias, and partial-birth abortions, to name a few. In an interview with Warren Bird of *Christianity Today,* Leo defined the "driving theme" in his weekly columns: "I think people are hungry for strong analysis to rub up against. They may not agree with me, but they believe I mean what I say. If I say it strongly, they'll say, 'Yeah, that's right' or 'I think he's full of beans and I'm going to explain why.' Either way it makes people think."

In the same interview, Leo gave his views on political correctness. "I think PC [political correctness] is a real threat. . . . It's an attempt to shake the whole foundation accusing it of being partial, bigoted, too white, too male, and needing to be replaced. . . . I hit PC hard because I think it's a very grave crisis." It is from these beliefs that Leo's words flow, into his columns and eventually into his books, which are collections of previously published columns. He writes with a sense of humor on issues many contemporary journalists shy away from.

In 1989 Leo put together his first collection, *How the Russians Invented Baseball and Other Essays of Enlightenment,* containing pieces written while Leo was working for *Time.* It was during this period that he created a fictional married couple, Wanda, a liberal feminist, and Ralph, a conservative masculinist (as Leo calls him). Through this imaginary couple Leo attempts to decimate some of the more left-wing cultural concepts, giving Wanda a voice but using her mostly as a foil for her husband's arguments. Leo still uses this couple in his columns for *U.S. News & World Report.*

A *Publishers Weekly* reviewer called Wanda and Ralph Leo's "would-be trendy couple." The same reviewer referred to Leo's writing, overall, as "zingers . . . aimed at whatever tempted the journalist's pitiless observations on society." The writer concluded that the book "calls for laughs, cheers and tears." *Booklist*'s Ray Olson called the book "Hilarious!"

Leo's second collection, *Two Steps ahead of the Thought Police,* was published five years later in 1994. Again, it is a collection of Leo's columns, having first been published in *U.S. New & World Report,* where Leo has worked since 1988. In *Two Steps ahead of the Thought Police,* Leo deals with the debate over politically correct language, systems, programs, and actions. *New Criterion*'s Terry Teachout noted a column Leo wrote concerning Brown University's Third-World Transition Program. Through this program, "all nonwhite freshmen are invited to school three days early to meet and interact under the helpful ministrations of nonwhite advisors and teachers." Leo points out that with this statement from Brown, the university implies that all Third-World students are nonwhite. Another assumption, according to Leo, is that the university believes that students from Hong Kong have much in common with students from Harlem, since both groups are lumped together as nonwhites.

Michael Wreszin, in his review of *Two Steps Ahead of the Thought Police* for the *Washington Post Book World,* described Leo's writing as containing "warmth and grace that belie his general tone of urgency." Wreszin saw as one of Leo's main focuses in this collection the ridicule of "the penchant for victimhood in America." Leo's favorite victim is what he refers to as the SWAM (straight white American male), who is suffering from racial quotas in colleges and in the business world.

In 2000 Leo published his third collection of columns, *Incorrect Thoughts: Notes on Our Wayward Culture.* It is divided into seven sections, with the subject headings media, education, family and gender, race and minorities, politics and law, culture and language, and, finally, society and social behavior. All of the topics are filtered through Leo's favorite lens, political correctness, which he sees not as anecdotal quirkiness but as a social movement that is sweeping through all the various aspects of American culture. These include U.S. schools, courts and media, as well as the feminist movement and the art world. Leo views this movement as coercive and censoring. Some of the individual column titles include: "The Selling of Rebellion," "Dumbing down Teachers," "Killing off the Liberals," "Let's Lower the Bar," "Promoting No-Dad Families,"

"Our Addiction to Bad News," and "Decadence the Corporate Way."

In an article posted on *Town Hall* online, Leo stands up for the right of a free press. In his article, "The Public's Right to Know Exists Even in Wartime," in which Leo reflects on National Security Advisor Condoleeza Rice's suggestions as to what television stations should and should not be presenting, Leo comments that although "respect for the grave responsibilities of the administration is admirable," especially during a time of crisis, the media should not be censored. Instead, the news business should find "a way to say clearly that it expresses its patriotism by aggressively defending the public's right to know what's going on. That's the job of a free press, even in wartime." Leo definitely believes in a free press as well as his right to express his views, which he often does, as Silver wrote in his review, with a "mordant wit."

A contributor to the online *Conservative Chronicle* described Leo as "insightful." "Leo is not afraid to jump off the bandwagon of popular opinion and ask pertinent (and impertinent) questions," noted the contributor.

BIOGRAPHICAL AND CRITICAL SOURCES:

PERIODICALS

Booklist, August, 1989, Ray Olson, review of *How the Russians Invented Baseball and Other Essays of Enlightenment,* p. 1926; July, 1994, Gilbert Taylor, review of *Two Steps ahead of the Thought Police,* p. 1895.
Christianity Today, October 7, 1996, Warren Bird, "Counterpunch Morality: How Columnist John Leo Challenges the Moral Assumptions of the Cultured Elite," pp. 62-63.
Commonweal, November 18, 1994, Robert G. Hoyt, review of *Two Steps ahead of the Thought Police,* pp. 38-39.
Kirkus Reviews, June 15, 1989, review of *How the Russians Invented Baseball and Other Essays of Enlightenment,* p. 896.
Library Journal, July, 1989, A. J. Anderson, review of *How the Russians Invented Baseball and Other*

Essays of Enlightenment, p. 80; June 15, 1994, A. J. Anderson, review of *Two Steps ahead of the Thought Police,* p. 85.
National Review, November 24, 1989, Priscilla L. Buckley, review of *How the Russians Invented Baseball and Other Essays of Enlightenment,* p. 58; August 29, 1994, Jack Fowler, review of *Two Steps ahead of the Thought Police,* p. 65.
New Criterion, September, 1994, Terry Teachout, "So Terribly Correct."
New York Times Book Review, December 31, 2000, Douglas A. Sylva, review of *Incorrect Thoughts: Notes on Our Wayward Culture,* p. 14.
Publishers Weekly, June 9, 1989, Genevieve Stuttaford, review of *How the Russians Invented Baseball and Other Essays of Enlightenment,* pp. 50-51; May 23, 1994, review of *Two Steps ahead of the Thought Police,* p. 70.
Time, April 9, 1984, John A. Meyers, "John Leo Tells Story of Ralph and Wanda," p. 3.
Vanity Fair, July, 1994, Elise O'Shaugnessy, review of *Two Steps ahead of the Thought Police,* pp. 32-35.
Wall Street Journal, February 6, 2001, Daniel J. Silver, review of *Incorrect Thoughts: Notes on Our Wayward Culture,* p. A16.
Washington Post Book World, September 4, 1994, Michael Wreszin, review of *Two Steps ahead of the Thought Police,* p. 6.

OTHER

Conservative Chronicle, http://www.conservative chronicle.com/ (January 14, 2003).
Town Hall, http://www.townhall.com/ (February 2, 2002), John Leo, "The Public's Right to Know Exists Even in Wartime."
Universal Press Syndicate Web site, http://www. uexpress.com/ (January 16, 2003).*

*   *   *

LICHTBLAU, Myron I(vor) 1925-2002

OBITUARY NOTICE—See index for *CA* sketch: Born October 10, 1925, in New York, NY; died March 17, 2002, in Syracuse, NY. Educator and author. Lichtblau was a professor of Spanish and Latin-American literature who wrote extensively on these subjects. He earned his B.A. from the City College of the City University of New York in 1947 after serving in the U.S. Army during World War II. His master's degree, received in 1948, was from National University of Mexico, and he received his Ph.D. from Columbia in 1957. After earning his master's degree, Lichtblau taught Spanish at secondary schools in New York City until 1957, when he joined the faculty at Indiana University, Bloomington. Most of his career was spent at Syracuse University, where he was a professor from 1959 to 1998, chairing the department of foreign languages from 1967 to 1974. Lichtblau published several books during his career, including *The Argentine Novel in the Nineteenth Century* (1959), *Manuel Galvez* (1972), and *An Annotated Bibliography of the Argentine Novel* (1997). He also edited such works as *Emigration and Exile in Twentieth-Century Hispanic Literature* (1988) and *Manuel Galvez: La maestra normal* (1991).

OBITUARIES AND OTHER SOURCES:

BOOKS

Writers Directory, 16th edition, St. James Press (Detroit, MI), 2001.

PERIODICALS

Post-Standard (Syracuse, NY), May 20, 2002, p. B4.

*   *   *

LIEBERMAN, Richard 1946-

PERSONAL: Born September 13, 1946, in Akron, OH; son of Harry (a physician) and Sarah (Tuchman) Lieberman; married Christine Scheve, June 19, 1971; children: Todd, Claire. *Education:* Miami University, B.A., 1968; University of Cincinnati Law School, J.D., 1971. *Hobbies and other interests:* Music, skiing.

ADDRESSES: Home—625 Oak St., Winnetka, IL 60093. *Office*—Ross & Hardies, 150 North Michigan Avenue, Suite 2500, Chicago, IL 60601. *E-mail*—Richard.Lieberman@RossHardies.com.

CAREER: Seyfarth & Shaw, attorney, 1974-83; Ross & Hardies, Chicago, IL, attorney and partner, 1983—. Attorney for National Labor Relations Board, 1971-73, and Equal Employment Opportunity Commission, 1973-74. Trustee for Goodman Theater, University of Cincinnati Board of Visitors.

MEMBER: American Bar Association

AWARDS, HONORS: Honorable mention for nonfiction, Midland Author Society, 2002.

WRITINGS:

Personal Foul: Coach Joe Moore vs. the University of Notre Dame, Academy Chicago Publishers, (Chicago, IL), 2001.

SIDELIGHTS: Richard Lieberman is a Chicago attorney who took on a high-profile age discrimination case against Notre Dame University and documents it in the courtroom drama *Personal Foul: Coach Joe Moore vs. the University of Notre Dame.* Popular offensive line coach Joe Moore sued the University of Notre Dame for age discrimination—but matters got much worse when the lawsuit uncovered disquieting evidence of unethical and inappropriate conduct in a football program widely regarded as a model of probity. The story began in November 1996, when Bob Davie was hired as head coach to replace the beloved Lou Holtz. In one of his first—and most fateful—executive decisions, Davie fired sixty-four-year-old Joe Moore in order to replace him with a younger person. Attorney Lieberman took on Moore's case. *Personal Foul* describes the trial and the tensions to which litigants like Moore are subject.

During litigation attorneys for Notre Dame tried to destroy Moore's reputation as both a coach and a man. In the process, Davie's own background came under close scrutiny because a reporter's investigation revealed embarrassing parts of his own past. As the trial proceeded, Notre Dame's football program was discovered to be rife with legal improprieties and inappropriate behavior involving both coaches and administrators. Patrick Mahoney wrote in *Library Journal* that "unfair hiring practices are only the tip of the iceberg as Lieberman reveals a storied football program rife with ethical problems in the hiring of its coaches and the treatment of some of the players themselves." A *Publishers Weekly* contributor called *Personal Foul* "intriguing for its close look at the suit and at Lieberman's own legal stratagems."

BIOGRAPHICAL AND CRITICAL SOURCES:

PERIODICALS

Booklist, June 1, 2001, Wes Lukowsky, review of *Personal Foul: Coach Joe Moore vs. the University of Notre Dame,* p. 1824.
Library Journal, June 1, 2001, Patrick Mahoney, review of *Personal Foul,* p. 190.
Publishers Weekly, June 4, 2001, review of *Personal Foul,* p. 65.
Washington Post, November 6, 2001, Allen St. John, "A Bunt, a Punt, and an Ace," p. C02.

*   *   *

LIPPMAN, Laura

PERSONAL: Born in Atlanta, GA; daughter of Theo Lippman, Jr. (a retired journalist) and a children's librarian; married John Roll. *Education:* Studied journalism at Northwestern University. *Hobbies and other interests:* Eating, drinking, socializing with family and friends, and exercise.

ADDRESSES: Office—c/o Baltimore Sun Company, 501 North Calvert Street, P.O. Box 1377, Baltimore, MD 21278. *E-mail*—jroll@erols.com.

CAREER: Mystery writer and newspaper reporter for *Baltimore Sun.* Former reporter for *Waco Herald-Tribune* and *San Antonio Light.*

AWARDS, HONORS: Nominated, Shamus Award for best new novel, 1996, for *Baltimore Blues;* Edgar Award and Shamus Award, both for best paperback original novel, both 1997, both for *Charm City;* Agatha Award and nominations for Shamus and Edgar awards, all 1998, all for *Butcher's Hill.*

WRITINGS:

MYSTERY NOVELS; "TESS MONAGHAN" SERIES

Baltimore Blues, Avon (New York, NY), 1997.
Charm City, Avon (New York, NY), 1997.
Butcher's Hill, Avon (New York, NY), 1998.
In Big Trouble, Avon (New York, NY), 1999.
The Sugar House, Morrow (New York, NY), 2000.

SIDELIGHTS: Feature journalist for the *Baltimore Sun* and mystery novelist Laura Lippman's "Tess Monaghan" series features reporter-turned-private-investigator Tess Monaghan. Her series has been critically well received: the first novel in the series, *Baltimore Blues,* was nominated for a Shamus Award for best first novel. Subsequent books in the series have garnered other prestigious awards and award nominations, including an Edgar Allan Poe Award, Shamus Award, and Agatha Award.

Asked by online *MysteryNet* about the similarities between Tess and herself, Lippman comments: "She's the person I might have been if I had lost my job in my 20s—a rougher exterior, but a much softer interior, full of self doubts. Like many fictional characters, she gets to say the rude/funny things I would never dare to say out loud. She is brave and principled, two things I like to think I am, but perhaps not to the extent Tess is." Asked about her favorite book and the authors who influenced her writing, she answered: "Favorite book? *Lolita,* which does have whodunit elements and quite a few clues sprinkled throughout. In the mystery field, I was heavily influenced by James Cain, Sara Paretsky, Carl Hiaasen, Walter Mosley and inevitably, I suppose Raymond Chandler. One of my alltime favorites is Phillip Roth. I also read a lot of what I call 'girl fiction,' a term I use with great affection and the highest respect for the work of Joanna Trollope, Alice Adams, Gail Godwin, Cathleen Schine and Laurie Colwin, among others."

Lippman's "Tess Monaghan" series has received largely positive reviews from critics as well as readers in the United Kingdom, Japan, France, Norway, and Portugal. Elizabeth Pincus in the *Voice Literary Supplement* called Monaghan "a dame with the old-fashioned hubris of Phillip Marlowe and a thoroughly modern, unruly mind." She added, "There's a pulpy little thrill in finding the best mystery writing around within the gaudy, palm-sized pages of a massmarket release." Lippman's latest work is *The Sugar House.*

Lippman said in an interview with *Books 'n Bytes* contributors Jon Jordan that she enjoys setting all of her books in Baltimore. "I know parts of Baltimore well, but it's an extremely complicated city. I'd be skeptical of anyone who claimed to master all its cultures and subcultures, not to mention its history. It's like a really good song, a standard that a lot of people have covered over the years . . . say, 'My Funny Valentine.' I have my version, and it's authentic, but not authentic."

BIOGRAPHICAL AND CRITICAL SOURCES:

PERIODICALS

Publishers Weekly, December 30, 1996, review of *Baltimore Blues,* p. 64; August 18, 1997, review of *Charm City,* p. 89; June 1, 1998, review of *Butcher's Hill,* p. 48B; July 26, 1999, review of *In Big Trouble,* p. 88; November 29, 1999, Judy Quinn, "No Mystery to Laura Lippman's Leap," p. 32.
Voice Literary Supplement, October-November, 1999, Elizabeth Pincus, "The Lonesome Star," p. 135.

OTHER

Books 'n Bytes, http://www.booksnbytes.com (April 4, 2003).
MysteryNet, http://www.mysterynet.com/. (February 3, 2000).
Charlotte Austin Review, http://www.charlotteaustin review.com.
Laura Lippman's Web site, http://www.lauralippman. com.*

*   *   *

LOMAX, Alan 1915-2002

OBITUARY NOTICE—See index for *CA* sketch: Born January 31, 1915, in Austin, TX; died July 19, 2002, in Sarasota (some sources cite Safety Harbor), FL. Musicologist, folksinger, photographer, filmmaker, record producer, television personality, and author. Lo-

max dedicated his entire life to collecting and recording the world's folk music. He began as a teenager, traveling with his folklorist father through the byways of the American South, hauling a primitive, five-hundred-pound recording machine. He continued his quest, by road, rail, and river, until he amassed thousands of songs and produced dozens of recordings. Lomax recorded Woody Guthrie for the Library of Congress and introduced into American culture the talents of such performers as Huddie "Leadbelly" Ledbetter, Muddy Waters, and Jelly Roll Morton. A self-described "obsessive" collector, Lomax traveled around the world, and he did not stop there, but disseminated the music and the stories behind the songs in many ways. He performed as a folksinger for record albums, and in the 1940s he hosted nationally broadcast radio programs. He wrote, directed, and produced documentary films, including *The Land Where the Blues Began* in 1985. He also wrote, directed, narrated, and produced a public television series, *American Patchwork,* for which he received the National Medal of the Arts. In the 1980s Lomax began working on a massive song and dance database called "Global Jukebox," and in the 1990s was working on the vast "Lomax Collection" with Rounder Records. His memoir, *The Land Where the Blues Began,* earned him a National Book Critics Circle Award for nonfiction in 1993. Lomax's groundbreaking work has allowed hundreds of performers to carry folk tradition into the twenty-first century, each in his or her own way, but it was Lomax himself who preserved the flavor and integrity of the original work.

OBITUARIES AND OTHER SOURCES:

BOOKS

Lomax, Alan, *The Land Where the Blues Began,* Pantheon Books (New York, NY), 1993.

PERIODICALS

Los Angeles Times, July 20, 2002, p. B15.
New York Times, July 20, 2002, obituary by Jon Pareles, pp. A1, A13.
Times (London, England), July 25, 2002.

LONG, Marie K.

PERSONAL: Married Elgen M. Long (a pilot).

CAREER: Author. Served as a public relations consultant with the Western Aerospace Museum in Oakland, CA.

WRITINGS:

(With Elgen M. Long) *Amelia Earhart: The Mystery Solved,* Simon & Schuster (New York, NY), 1999.

SIDELIGHTS: Marie K. Long and her husband, Elgen M. Long, spent more than twenty-five years researching their book, *Amelia Earhart: The Mystery Solved.* In the process, they traveled more than 100,000 miles to interview more than 100 sources. Andrea Higbie said in a *New York Times Book Review* article that the recitation of events is "dry," but felt that "for aviation buffs the book may be of some interest."

Earhart, the first woman to cross the Atlantic, in 1928, disappeared during an around-the-world flight in 1937 with her navigator, Fred Noonan. Many have speculated on their fate. Carolyn See wrote in *Washington Post Book World* that "according to the Longs, there weren't any skulking Japanese or hungry cannibals in the Earhart narrative." The authors note the travel route of Earhart and Noonan, the stops at small airports, their routine, and the plane parts that routinely failed. They write that in Lae, Noonan had too many drinks and became tangled in his mosquito netting. "But think of it," said See, "Lae, New Guinea, before World War II! Wouldn't you have a few Scotches? Earhart and Noonan were walking (flying) a tenuous line between the ancient 'unknown' and feckless Western attempts at 'civilization.' They'd touched down at El Fashar, Khartoum, Massawa, Bandoeng; they'd searched up and down the West African coast for Dakar the way we'd search for a hotel at the end of a fourteen-hour drive to an unfamiliar city."

The Longs detail the problems facing Earhart and Noonan, including faulty equipment, insufficient fuel, high winds, and their inability to communicate by Morse Code. They, three ships in the area, and Howland Island were in three different time zones. People on the ground listened for messages as they headed toward the island, a destination they would never reach. The book provides the details of Earhart's life, marriage to publisher G. P. Putnam, and her celebrity. A *Publishers Weekly* reviewer said that the Longs' examination of Earhart's career and a history of the early days of aviation "affords a host of other pleasures, chief among them a nearly moment-by-moment description of the fatal flight itself."

In a *Seattle Times* review, Adam Woog wrote: "The latest book is perhaps the most level-headed and persuasive of all. Elegen M. Long and Marie K. Long have been studying Earhart for decades and are widely recognized, decidely non-crackpot authorities." Woog, who also wrote a book on the missing pilot, quoted Earhart biographer Mary S. Lowell, saying that if anyone has solved the mystery of Earhart's disappearance, it is probably the Longs. "The conclusion they reach is almost diappointing in its reliance on common sense and hard evidence," Woog wrote. "After exhaustively studying everything from fuel consumption ratios to the (sometimes contradictory) logs kept by radiomen in contact with her, the Longs conclude that Earhart simply ran out of fuel near her destination of Howland Island, crashed and did not survive."

In a review for *Data Quality Journal,* James Hurysz argued that often Americans want to remember heroes and heroines, and will take their accomplishments out of context. While the Longs are able to provide a factual portrayal of the difficulties and pressures Earhart faced by flying in the middle of the Great Depression, Hurysz argued that too many unanswered questions remain regarding the navigation decisions Earhart was forced to make on her last flight. "The Longs raise as many questions about Earhart's . . . disappearance as they settle." Hurysz wrote. "It appears that we will have to wait until Earhart's *Electra* is discovered before the mystery of her disappearance begins to be solved."

BIOGRAPHICAL AND CRITICAL SOURCES:

PERIODICALS

Data Quality Journal, September, 1999.
New York Times Book Review, January 2, 2000, Andrea Higbie, review of *Amelia Earhart.*
People Weekly, November 15, 1999, review of *Amelia Earhart,* p. 49.

Publishers Weekly, October 4, 1999, review of *Amelia Earhart,* p. 53.

Washington Post Book World, December 17, 1999, Carolyn See, "Earhart, Lost in the Details," p. C02.

Seattle Times, January 2, 2000, review *Amelia Earhart,* by Adam Woog.*

*   *   *

LONGLEY, Lawrence D(ouglas) 1939-2002

OBITUARY NOTICE—See index for *CA* sketch: Born November 12, 1929, in Bronxville, NY; died of cancer March 20, 2002, in Appleton, WI. Educator and author. Longley was a political science professor and expert on U.S. presidential elections. He earned his Ph.D. from Vanderbilt University in 1969, after which time he enjoyed a long academic career at Lawrence University where he became a full professor of government in 1989. An active worker for the Democratic Party, he served on the Democratic National Committee (DNC) and was a consultant to the U.S. Senate Judiciary Committee. In 1996 and 1997 Longley was also a member of the DNC's executive committee. An authority on the electoral college, Longley contributed to a number of books on the subject and was the coeditor for such works as *The People's President: The Electoral College in American History and the Direct Vote Alternative* and *The Electoral College Primer 2000.*

OBITUARIES AND OTHER SOURCES:

BOOKS

Who's Who in American Politics, 17th edition, Marquis (New Providence, NJ), 1999.

PERIODICALS

Washington Post, March 24, 2002, p. C8.

*   *   *

LOVELACE, Linda
See MARCHIANO, Linda Boreman

LUKE, Pearl 1958-

PERSONAL: Born March 21, 1958, in Peace River, Alberta, Canada; daughter of Ronald and Florence (Chapman) Luke; life partner of Robert Hilles (a novelist and poet); children: Amanda; stepchildren: Breanne, Austin. *Education:* University of Calgary, Alberta, Canada, B.A., 1991, M.A., 1998. *Religion:* Agnostic. *Hobbies and other interests:* Travel, art, design.

ADDRESSES: Home—1208 14th Ave. S.W., #705, Calgary, Alberta, Canada T3C 0V9. *Agent*—Denise Bukowski, The Bukowski Agency, 14 Prince Arthur Ave., Suite 202, Toronto, Ontario, Canada M5R 1A9. *E-mail*—pluke@shaw.ca.

CAREER: Writer, 1988—. In sales, 1975-87; commercial real estate agent, 1987-89; high school teacher in Mexico, 1992; editorial assistant, Carswell Publishing, 1993-94; instructor, DeVry Institute of Technology, 1997-2001; full-time freelance writer, 2001. Writer-in-residence, Taipei, Taiwan.

MEMBER: Writers' Union of Canada.

AWARDS, HONORS: Globe and Mail notable book of the year, 2000, for *Burning Ground;* Commonwealth Prize for Best First Book in Canada and the Caribbean, 2001, for *Burning Ground.*

WRITINGS:

Burning Ground, HarperFlamingoCanada (Toronto, Ontario, Canada), 2000.

Also contributor of short fiction to various literary magazines and anthologies; regular contributor to *Calgary Herald.*

WORK IN PROGRESS: Madame Zee, for HarperCollins Canada, expected 2003.

SIDELIGHTS: Pearl Luke's *Burning Ground* stars Percy Turner, a young woman who spends five months alone in the wilderness, living in the Envy River fire tower and keeping watch over the forest. At the same time, she keeps watch on her own thoughts, exploring her memories and yearnings. After seven years working on a fire tower, she is finally relieved of some of her isolation by an Internet connection. Through her computer, she chats and flits with Gilmore, another fire tower operator who is hundreds of miles away but whose voice on the radio intrigues her. At the same time, though, she assesses her painful relationship with her childhood sweetheart, Marlea. Told partly in flashback and partly through Percy's intimate e-mail messages and letters, the story describes Percy's childhood in a trailer park in remote Oldrock, Alberta, bares family secrets, and depicts how Percy's love for Marlea began. The tale ends with unexpected danger and surprises for Percy. In *Quill and Quire,* Karen X. Tulchinsky praised Luke's "memorable and passionate" characters, as well as her "witty, engaging, and real" prose.

BIOGRAPHICAL AND CRITICAL SOURCES:

PERIODICALS

Canadian Geographic, July, 2001, p. 90.
Globe and Mail (Toronto, Ontario, Canada), August 12, 2000.
Quill and Quire, July, 2000, Karen X. Tulchinsky, review of *Burning Ground,* p. 34.
Toronto Star, August 27, 2001.

OTHER

Commonwealth Writers Web site, http://www.common wealthwriters.com/ (December 4, 2002).

M

MacLEOD, Catriona 1963-

PERSONAL: Born May 8, 1963, in Stornoway, Scotland; daughter of Angus and Karin (Kaeten) MacLeod; married Neil H. G. Garrioch (an architect), July 20, 1991; children: Isabella R. M. *Education:* University of Glasgow, M.A., 1986; Harvard University, Ph.D., 1992.

ADDRESSES: Office—Department of Germanic Languages and Literatures, University of Pennsylvania, 745 Williams Hall, Philadelphia, PA 19104-6305; fax: 215-573-7794. *E-mail*—cmacleod@mail.sas.upenn. edu.

CAREER: Oxford University, Oxford, England, Randall McIver junior research fellow at St. Hugh's College, 1992-93; Yale University, New Haven, CT, assistant professor, 1993-99; University of Pennsylvania, Philadelphia, visiting assistant professor, 1998-99, assistant professor, 1999-2001, associate professor of Germanic languages and literatures, 2001—, faculty research fellow of Pennsylvania Humanities Forum, 2000-01.

MEMBER: International Association of Word and Image Studies, Modern Language Association of America, Goethe Society of North America (member of editorial advisory board, 2001—), American Association of Teachers of German, American Society for Eighteenth Century Studies.

AWARDS, HONORS: Whiting fellow, 1991-92; Poorvu Family Prize for Teaching, Yale University, 1996.

WRITINGS:

Embodying Ambiguity: Androgyny and Aesthetics from Winckelmann to Keller, Wayne State University Press (Detroit, MI), 1998.

WORK IN PROGRESS: A book on sculpture and narrative.

BIOGRAPHICAL AND CRITICAL SOURCES:

PERIODICALS

Germanic Review, fall, 2000, Robert Tobin, review of *Embodying Ambiguity: Androgyny and Aesthetics from Winckelmann to Keller,* p. 317.
Modern Language Review, January, 2001, Jeff Morrison, review of *Embodying Ambiguity,* p. 256.

*   *   *

MacRAYE, Lucy Betty
See WEBLING, Lucy

*   *   *

MADDOX, Bruno 1969-

PERSONAL: Born 1969, in England; son of Sir John (former editor of *Nature* and a science writer) and Brenda (a biographer) Maddox. *Education:* Attended Harvard University.

CAREER: Novelist and book reviewer. *Washington Post,* book reviewer; *New York Times,* book reviewer; *Spy magazine,* reporter, 1996, editor, 1997-98.

WRITINGS:

My Little Blue Dress, Viking (New York, NY), 2001.

SIDELIGHTS: Born to a British literary family, Bruno Maddox has written a first novel which, according to Tom Dart in the London *Times,* "reads like the offspring of *Bridget Jones's Diary* and *Being John Malkovich.*" The book was begun hurriedly after Maddox's tenure at the failed *Spy* magazine ended and he submitted a five-page proposal to a publisher. His frantic efforts to finish the book are reflected in *My Little Blue Dress,* which purports to be a memoir of an old lady in New York who was born at the turn of the century. It is written by "Bruno Maddox," a twenty-something hack writer who takes care of the woman but spends as much time talking about the hip Manhattan scene and his own hangups as he does telling her story—most of which he invents himself.

Part of the irony of the story is the narrator's own ignorance of history, which he attempts to cover up by talking in generalities and relating bits and pieces of the garbled history he does know. "The result," wrote Mario Russo in *Salon.com,* is "an extravagantly silly, anachronism-filled parody of one of those precious 'rural childhood' memoirs." Bruno follows the woman's story from her idyllic childhood in an English village, to a post-World War I sojourn in decadent Paris, to a job as a tea-server in a military outpost during World War II. Then, in a hurry to finish his manuscript, Bruno flashes to the end of the woman's life in New York's Chinatown, where she spends her shabby existence reminiscing about the past. Finally he lapses into what Russo called a "satire of the media world's social scene," with descriptions of some of the New Yorkers who frequent Bruno's world: "There was some eighteen-year-old guy who just made a film about cripples. A guy who writes a column for *Rogue* magazine. Some actress. And that guy Gordon Gundersson . . . a book author who has his own television commercial."

Critics were generally favorable toward *My Little Blue Dress,* while expressing some reservations about the loosely structured narrative. Brian Kenney, writing in *Booklist,* found that "what begins as a wonderfully inventive mock memoir skillfully molts into a delightfully twisted non-coming-of-age story." A *Publishers Weekly* critic wrote, "Maddox's writing is purposely uppity, but the kitschy, honest overtones communicate a very witty take on love and life." Sarah Brennan on the *Bookreporter.com* Web site felt that at times the novel "smacks of desperate contrivance" but also called it an "hilarious satire of modern society's twin evils—memoir writing and pop culture trivia in lieu of textbook history." In a review in the *Washington Post Book World,* Keith Gessen called attention to Maddox's debt to a 1980 book titled *Amazons,* an earlier example of the fake memoir genre. Gessen felt that Maddox has "talent to waste; this does not mean that he should be wasting quite so much of it." In the *New York Times Book Review,* Emily Barton stated that some readers may be "put . . . off with the broadness of [Maddox's] humor and the boozy laxity of his prose" but nevertheless called the book a "winsome and vastly entertaining novel." A London *Times* review by Alex O'Connell said of *My Little Blue Dress,* "For a single-joke book it sustains itself very well. . . . This is a clever and stylish first novel."

Nina Blount, a critic for *iVenus.com,* was not sure if Maddox is trying to pre-empt criticism or invite it by working mistakes into his plot. "There is a sense, though, in which all that whimsy makes the critic feel a bit churlish about trying to pick apart the book. The incongruities and errors are meant to be there, the reason it reads like the rantings of a sleep-deprived neurotic is that that's exactly what it is." Maddox told Blount that he drew inspiration from the Bret Easton Ellis's 1991 novel *American Psycho.* "I'm a big *American Psycho* fan. That convinced me that maybe it was OK to make one's book deliberately annoying in parts."

BIOGRAPHICAL AND CRITICAL SOURCES:

PERIODICALS

Daily Telegraph (London, England), May 12, 2001, Andrew Biswell, "Brunamaddoxy: Andrew Biswell Hails a Ludic Debut.
New York Times Book Review, May 27, 2001, Emily Barton, "Enough about Me," p. 4L.
Times (London, England), May 16, 2001, Alex O'Connell, "Whose Life Is It Anyway?,"p. 15;

June 2, 2001, Tom Dart, "All about Me: Life Stories," p. 62.

Washington Post Book World, June 16, 2001, Keith Gessen, "New York Meta-Stories," p. C2.

OTHER

Bookreporter.com, http://www.bookreporter.com/ (December 2, 2001), Sarah Brennan, review of *My Little Blue Dress.*

Salon.com, http://www.salon.com/ (December 2, 2001), Maria Russo, review of *My Little Blue Dress.*

iVenus.com, http://www.iVenus.com/, Nina Blount, review of *My Little Blue Dress,* 2001.*

* * *

MAHONY, Phillip 1955-

PERSONAL: Born March 26, 1955, in New York, NY; children: four. *Education:* New York University, B.A., 1977, M.A., 1982.

ADDRESSES: Home—21-65 46th St., Astoria, NY 11105.

CAREER: Police officer in New York, NY, 1980—; writer. New York University, New York, NY, adjunct poetry instructor, 1996—.

WRITINGS:

POETRY

Catching Bodies, North Atlantic Books (Berkeley, CA), 1986.
Supreme, North Atlantic Books (Berkeley, CA), 1989.
(Editor) *From Both Sides Now: The Poetry of the Vietnam War and Its Aftermath,* Scribner (New York, NY), 1998.

WORK IN PROGRESS: Case Active, a novel.

SIDELIGHTS: Phillip Mahony is a New York City police officer who has also published several volumes of poetry. His first book, the 1986 collection *Catching Bodies,* features such poems as "Complaint #313485, 77 pct., 10/23/81," which was inspired by the gunshot death of a robbery victim whom Mahony had accompanied to the hospital. Mahony's second volume, *Supreme,* is an ambitious, twenty-three-part epic chronicling the violent endeavors of three youths. Andrew Rosenstein, writing in *New York,* affirmed that *Supreme* "springs from the everyday horror of life in Bushwick." Rosenstein added that Mahony considers himself to be a poet who works as a police officer. "Putting on the uniform doesn't mean you become a different person," Mahony observed.

Mahony is also the editor of *From Both Sides Now: The Poetry of the Vietnam War and Its Aftermath,* which *Progressive* reviewer John Nichols hailed as "the finest poetry anthology of 1998." The volume, arranged chronologically to reflect the war's development, includes works by such North American writers as Grace Paley, Allen Ginsberg, and Margaret Atwood, but it also features poems by both war veterans, including Air Force pilot Walter McDonald, and Vietnamese natives such as Nguyen Chi Thien. "In many senses," contended Nichols, "this book is more history than standard poetry anthology." Frank Allen, meanwhile, wrote in *Library Journal* that *From Both Sides Now* serves as a "useful anthology of multicultural, war-scarred poetry."

BIOGRAPHICAL AND CRITICAL SOURCES:

PERIODICALS

Library Journal, October 1, 1998, Frank Allen, review of *From Both Sides Now,* p. 94.
New York, August 28, 1989, Andrew Rosenstein, "Beat Poet," p. 24.
Progressive, December, 1998, John Nichols, review of *From Both Sides Now,* p. 43.

* * *

MALKIN, Irad

PERSONAL: Born in Israel; son of Yaakov Malkin and Felice Pazner; married, wife's name Jeanette. *Education:* Tel Aviv University B.A. (summa cum laude), 1972; University of Pennsylvania, Ph.D., 1981.

ADDRESSES: Office—Department of History, Tel Aviv University, Tel Aviv, 69978 Israel, fax: 972-3-640-9457 *E-mail*—malkin@taunivm.

CAREER: Tel Aviv University, Tel Aviv, Israel, professor of ancient Greek history, 1982—; writer. Visiting professor at University of Montreal, 1988; visiting scholar at University of California, Berkeley, 1994-95. Guest lecturer at various institutions, including Brown University, Harvard University, Columbia University, Stanford University, Cornell University and Swedish Institute at Athens.

AWARDS, HONORS: Fellowship, Center of Hellenic Studies, 1990-91; fellowship, National Endowment of the Humanities, 1994-95.

WRITINGS:

Religion and Colonization in Ancient Greece, E. J. Brill (New York, NY), 1987.

(Editor with R. L. Hohlfelder, and contributor) *Mediterranean Cities: Historical Perspectives,* F. Cass (Totowa, NJ), 1988.

(Contributor) S. Almog and M. Heyd, editors, *Chosen People, Elect Nation, and Universal Mission,* [Jerusalem], 1991.

(Editor with Zeev Tzahor) *Leaders and Leadership in Jewish and World History,* Historical Society of Israel (Jerusalem), 1992.

Myth and Territory in the Spartan Mediterranean, Cambridge University Press (New York, NY), 1994.

(Contributor) Y. Malkin, editor, *Lecture, Discussion, Persuasion: Proficiencies and Values in Verbal Communication,* [Tel Aviv, Israel], 1994.

(Editor with Z. W. Rubinsohn) *Leaders and Masses in the Roman World: Studies in Honor of Zvi Yavetz,* E. J. Brill (New York, NY), 1995.

(Contributor) R. Haegg, editor, *The Role of Religion in the Early Greek Polis,* Swedish Institute at Athens (Athens, Greece), 1996.

The Returns of Odysseus: Colonization and Ethnicity, University of California Press (Berkeley, CA), 1998.

Contributor to periodicals, including *Athenaeum, Classical Antiquity, Classical Quarterly, Classical Philology, Journal of Hellenic Studies, Kernos,* and *Mediterranean Historical Review.*

WORK IN PROGRESS: A History of Greek Colonization; editing and contributing to *Ancient Perceptions of Greek Ethnicity,* for Harvard University Press.

SIDELIGHTS: Irad Malkin is an historian specializing in ancient Greece. In his first book, *Religion and Colonization in Ancient Greece,* he examines the responsibilities of *oikists,* decision-makers with regard to religious matters in Greek colonies from the eighth to the fourth pre-Christian centuries. Oikists, who were appointed by the Delphic oracle, determined the designations of temples for specific gods, dictated the geographical placement of temples, and even authorized funding for worshipful cults. Jon D. Mikalson, writing in *American Historical Review,* affirmed that "little is known of historical *oikists*" and allowed that "Malkin's *oikist* model remains in the realm of theory." He also observed that oikist lore constitutes "a mishmash of myth, legend, and history." According to Mikalson, "Malkin picks his way through this heterogeneous evidence methodically . . . and he meticulously details modern interpretations." Mikalson concluded his review by declaring that "Malkin contributes much to understanding the [oikist] processes." Another reviewer, Robert E. Bennet, wrote in *Religious Studies Review* that *Religion and Colonization in Ancient Greece* serves as "a thorough treatment" of oikist lore, and he noted that the volume is "well researched."

Myth and Territory in the Spartan Mediterranean, another of Malkin's notable writings, explores the various mythological tales exploited by Spartans to justify their occupation of Greek lands in ancient times. In his *American Historical Review* assessment, Pericles Georges declared that the volume "provides a densely detailed and richly annotated gazetteer of every myth concerning Sparta," and he added that it "portrays a people whose self-identity included . . . a view of themselves as a pan-Mediterranean presence." Georges added that the work "resonates with implications that illuminate much of Sparta's *histoire evenementielle* before Alexander." J. Fischer, meanwhile, wrote in *Choice* that *Myth and Territory in the Spartan Mediterranean* is an "extraordinarily well researched and well written book," and Bradley P. Nystrom concluded in *Religious Studies Review* that the volume will prove "useful and interesting" to devotees of the subject. Malkin collaborated with Z. W. Rubinsohn in editing *Leaders and Masses in the Roman World: Studies in Honor of Zvi Yavetz,* which features eleven essays on class distinctions in ancient Greece and ancient Rome. W. Jeffrey Tatum, in a *Religious Studies Review* appraisal, remarked that the various essays are "worth reading."

Among Malkin's other publications is *The Returns of Odysseus: Colonization and Ethnicity,* which relates the hero of Homer's classic epic to Greek colonization campaigns and commercial endeavors. Robin Osborne contended in the *Times Literary Supplement* that Malkin regards the legends of Odysseus as "the very stuff of the history of Greek exploration of the western Mediterranean" and "the lasting textual trace of the Greek expansion of the eighth and seventh centuries." Osborne concluded his review by declaring that *The Returns of Odysseus* "should redirect historical endeavors." *New Republic* reviewer Peter Green, meanwhile, was especially impressed with Malkin's ability to expose the more questionable aspects of what are considered historical facts. "Malkin's book," Green related, "abounds in endless varieties of manipulated or revamped evidence to bring the past into line with current requirements: did these people consciously know what they were doing?" According to Green, "What grabs Malkin . . . are the varieties of colonial propaganda, which . . . depend on the creative re-shaping of myth." Green deemed *The Returns of Odysseus* "erudite, richly documented, and stringently argued."

BIOGRAPHICAL AND CRITICAL SOURCES:

PERIODICALS

American Historical Review, June, 1990, pp. 792-793; April, 1996, pp. 459-460.
Choice, May, 1995, p. 1506.
New Republic, July 12, 1999.
Religious Studies Review, January, 1989; July, 1995, p. 227; January, 1996, p. 65.
Times Literary Supplement, June 18, 1999, p. 45.*

*   *   *

MANASTER, Kenneth A. 1942-

PERSONAL: Born 1942, in Chicago, IL; married Ann Brandewie; children: Jenny, Cole. *Education:* Harvard College, A.B., 1963; Harvard Law School, LL.B., 1966. *Hobbies and other interests:* Violin.

ADDRESSES: Home—Los Altos, CA. *Office*—Santa Clara University, School of Law, 500 El Camino Real, Santa Clara, CA 95053. *E-mail*—kmanaster@scu.edu.

CAREER: Author and educator. Santa Clara University, Santa Clara, CA, law professor, 1972—; has also taught law at the University of Texas and the University of California's Hastings College of the Law; visiting scholar, Harvard Law School and Stanford Law School; U.S. District Court, Chicago, law clerk; State of Illinois, assistant attorney general, heading Chicago office of Environmental Control Division. Bay Area Air Quality Management District Hearing Board, member, 1973-90, chair, 1978-89.

AWARDS, HONORS: Fulbright fellowship for research in Peru.

WRITINGS:

(With Daniel P. Selmi) *State Environmental Law,* two volumes, Boardman (New York, NY), 1989.
(Editor, with Daniel P. Selmi) *California Environmental Law and Land-Use Practice,* six volumes, Bender (New York, NY), 1989.
Environmental Protection and Justice: Readings and Commentary on Environmental Law and Practice, Anderson (Cincinnati, OH), 1995, second edition, 2000.
Illinois Justice: The Scandal of 1969 and the Rise of John Paul Stevens, University of Chicago Press (Chicago, IL), 2001.

SIDELIGHTS: With more than thirty years of professional experience to draw upon, lawyer and law professor Kenneth A. Manaster has written or edited several books on various aspects of environmental law. Manaster's most recent work, *Illinois Justice: The Scandal of 1969 and the Rise of John Paul Stevens,* details a legal scandal that took place in Chicago in the late 1960s, resulting in the resignation of two Illinois State Supreme Court justices. The case also propelled the relatively unknown lawyer John Paul Stevens on a course that ended with a seat the U.S. Supreme Court.

Manaster, who lives with his wife and two children in Los Altos, California, earned his law degree from Harvard Law School in 1966 and then traveled to Peru to study on a Fulbright fellowship. Manaster's long professional career, which he began in Chicago as a federal court law clerk in the late 1960s, includes an appointment as an Illinois assistant attorney general heading Chicago's Environmental Control Division in the early 1970s. In addition, between 1973 and 1990 Manaster was a member of the Bay Area Air Quality Management District Hearing Board, serving as its chairman for more than ten years. Manaster also chaired the public advisory committee to the U.S. Environmental Protection Agency's study of toxic pollution in the Santa Clara Valley. In 1972, after teaching stints at both the University of Texas and the University of California's Hastings College of Law, Manaster joined the faculty of Santa Clara University, where he continues to teach environmental protection law and tort law. He has drawn on his knowledge of environmental law to publish numerous law review articles as well as his first three books. The first, which he cowrote with Daniel P. Selmi, is a two-volume work called *State Environmental Law.* Manaster teamed up again with Selmi to coedit a six-volume effort titled *California Environmental Law and Land-Use Practice,* which he followed up with *Environmental Protection and Justice: Reading and Commentary on Environmental Law and Practice.*

In *Illinois Justice* Manaster recalls the scandal that rocked Illinois political and legal circles in the summer of 1969. As Manaster explains, the scandal began when a political gadfly named Sherman H. Skolnick accused a State Supreme Court justice of having an improper relationship with a political operative. A special commission, led by John Paul Stevens, was formed to investigate the matter. At the time Stevens was just an obscure antitrust lawyer. Manaster, who worked with Stevens and the special commission, shows how the investigation and the political environment became extremely charged, largely fueled by a partisan press. As Manaster explains, under Stevens's leadership, the commission tracked down enough evidence in six weeks to prove that two Supreme Court justices had been corrupted in an earlier judicial case over which they were presiding. Manaster describes the courtroom drama in which Stevens displayed his brilliance. Ultimately the two justices resigned, and Stevens's career took off.

Manaster's book was published not long after a similar investigation was conducted by independent prosecutor Kenneth Starr into President Bill Clinton's affairs,

and the author comments on the similarities, or lack thereof. In the foreword, cowritten by Justice Stevens himself, the two allude to Starr's investigation. The highly charged political environment surrounding it was quite similar to the scandal of 1969. However, Manaster points out, Stevens was able to separate himself from the politics of the moment. Although a contributor for *Publishers Weekly* felt that Manaster's jargon and prose am "overly lawyerly," the reviewer did call *Illinois Justice* a "well-researched" effort with an "enlightening" foreword. More laudatory reviews were written by a number of other critics with legal experience. For example, Wayne W. Whalen wrote in *American Lawyer* that "if you enjoy reading about how law is practiced—by the very best when the stakes are high and the shot clock is about to run—this book has it." And *Judicature* contributor James J. Alfini said, "*Illinois Justice* is that rare book that accomplishes its intended purpose, and then some. . . . Professor Manaster's trenchant analysis and insights . . . make this book a must read for anyone interested in judicial system reform and improvement."

BIOGRAPHICAL AND CRITICAL SOURCES:

PERIODICALS

American Lawyer, April, 2002, Wayne W. Whalen, "Before the Robes," pp. 63-65.
Booklist, September 1, 2001, Vernon Ford, review of *Illinois Justice: The Scandal of 1969 and the Rise of John Paul Stevens,* p. 23.
Baltimore Sun, September 9, 2001, Michael Pakenham, "Judicial Corruption in Illinois: A Caveat for the Whole Nation," p. 10E.
Harvard Law Review, November, 2001, review of *Illinois Justice,* p. 551.
Judicature, January, 2002, James J. Alfini, "Judicial Scandal," pp. 202-203.
New York Law Journal, September 11, 2001, Robert W. Bennett, "The Lawyer's Bookshelf," p. 2.
Publishers Weekly, July 30, 2001, review of *Illinois Justice,* p. 69.
Wilson Quarterly, winter, 2002, Katy J. Harriger, review of *Illinois Justice,* p. 123.

OTHER

Santa Clara University Web site, http://www.scu.edu/ (March 12, 2002).

MARCHANT, Fred 1946-

PERSONAL: Born 1946. *Ethnicity:* "Caucasian" *Education:* Attended Providence College, Brown University, and the University of Chicago.

ADDRESSES: Office—Suffolk University, Department of English, 8 Ashburton Place, Boston, MA 02108. *E-mail*—fjmarchant@aol.com.

CAREER: Harvard University, Cambridge, MA, lecturer; Boston University, Boston, MA, assistant professor; Suffolk University, Boston, MA, professor of English, director of creative writing program. Resident at McDowell Colony, Yaddo, Ucross, and Heinrich Böll Cottage, Achill Island, Ireland. Affiliate member of William Joiner Center for the Study of War and Its Social Consequences. *Military service:* U.S. Marine Corps; became lieutenant.

MEMBER: Academy of American Poets, Poetry Society of America, PEN New England (member of executive board), New England Poetry Club.

AWARDS, HONORS: Washington Prize for poetry (1993) for *Tipping Point;* King's English Award.

WRITINGS:

Tipping Point, Word Books, 1994.
Full Moon Boat, Graywolf Press (Saint Paul, MN), 2000.
House on Water, House in Air, Dedalus Press (Dublin, Ireland), 2002.

WORK IN PROGRESS: With Nguyen Ba Chung, translating the poetry of Tran Dang Khoa.

SIDELIGHTS: Fred Marchant served in the U.S. Marine Corp as a lieutenant, an experience that appears to have marked him for life. During his tour of duty in Vietnam, he requested and received an honorable discharge on the basis of conscientious objection. He was one of the first officers ever to accomplish this. Since then, he has become involved with the William Joiner Center for the Study of War and Its Social

Consequences, located on the campus of the University of Massachusetts, Boston, where he teaches summer writers' conferences.

Marchant's title poem in his first collection, *Tipping Point* (1994), reflects the moment of decision when he applied for conscientious objector status. However, the war in Vietnam is not the only topic of this collection. Marchant also writes about other moral dilemmas, some very personal, such as poetic memories of his mother and father's sometimes abusive relationship. He also writes about his father's death, the poet's own aging body, and a loving tribute to his grandfather, who holds the poet in his arms during a baptismal ceremony.

In a review by Sam Cornish for *Ploughshares,* Marchant's "honest emotion" was noted with admiration. Cornish also mentioned that this collection of Marchant's "is about a whole life without self-pity." Marchant is able to talk about his memories intelligently, Cornish believed, without falling into clichés of "confessional poetry." His poems are "anything but self-serving," Cornish concluded.

It was Marchant's mastery of language that caught the attention of a reviewer for *Publishers Weekly.* "Its distinction lies in his chiseled control of language," the reviewer reported. This reviewer concurred with Cornish in stating that Marchant "never overdramatize[s]" any of the situations about which he writes. Rather, this reviewer continued, "Marchant is melodiously severe" in describing the people on whom he focuses in his poetry.

Marchant's second collection, *Full Moon Boat,* also focuses on aspects of war, but his voice and vision have matured. His poems read more like meditations on various aspects of war and its consequences. He looks at the world with a trained eye, pointing out details that others miss. The details are not the objects appearing in front of him, but, rather, the meaning behind all of those things. Often, he meditates on war veterans, like himself. His experiences enlighten the lives and hidden emotions of ex-soldiers. Such is his tribute to one man who travels to Ha Noi in Vietnam to retrieve the bones of his brother, dead for ten years. The man boards a train with a "rucksack bundled in his arms." In order not to draw attention to his bag, "he tries to be casual." It is, Marchant informs his reader, forbidden to ride on the train "with the remains of a body."

Marchant then lists the names of the bones in the bag and relates how they are mingled with the live brother's clothing and toiletries. Only with the last line does Marchant hint at the brother's emotions, which he describes as "dry-hardened" as the bones he carries.

A review of *Full Moon Boat* was published by *Ploughshares* and written by H. L. Hix, who explained that the title of Marchant's second collection, plus the title poem, names "an odyssey inverted, defining an alternative to the ideal of the heroic return from war." Rather than the hero, Hix stated, Marchant's poems establish the pacifist's return.

BIOGRAPHICAL AND CRITICAL SOURCES:

PERIODICALS

Ploughshares, fall, 1994, Sam Cornish, review of *Tipping Point,* p. 247; winter, 2001-02, H. L. Hix, review of *Full Moon Boat.*
Publishers Weekly, June 27, 1994, review of *Tipping Point,* p. 69; October 30, 2000, review of *Full Moon Boat,* p. 73.
River Poetry, spring, 2002, review of *Full Moon Boat.*
Ruminator Review, winter, 2000, review of *Full Moon Boat,* p. 32.

OTHER

Graywolf Press Web site, http://www.graywolfpress. org (March 2, 2002)."

*   *   *

MARCHIANO, Linda Boreman 1949-2002
(Linda Lovelace)

OBITUARY NOTICE—See index for *CA* sketch: Born January 10, 1949, in the Bronx, NY; died of injuries from a car crash April 22, 2002, in Denver, CO. Pornographic film star and author. Marchiano became nearly a household word under the stage name Linda Lovelace when she starred in the first feature-length pornographic movie, 1972's *Deep Throat.* Marchiano grew up in New York the daughter of a retired police officer and a domineering mother. To escape her mother's physical and emotional abuse, Marchiano moved in with an ex-Marine named Chuck Traynor. According to Marchiano's autobiography *Ordeal,* co-written with Mike McGrady, Traynor forced her into prostitution and sex with men he introduced her to. Eventually he began filming the encounters and that led to *Deep Throat,* made for an estimated $30,000 to $40,000 and earning more than $600 million worldwide. Marchiano claims she received no payment for the film and that she was forced into it by Traynor, who had also forced her to marry him so she could not testify against him. Marchiano escaped from Traynor in the mid-1970s and married Larry Marchiano, with whom she had two children. After her book was published Marchiano hit the lecture circuit and discussed the debilitating effects of pornography for those who are part of the scene, campaigning against the victimization of women and children. Marchiano followed with a second autobiography, also written with McGrady, in 1986: *Out of Bondage.* Other works, under the name Linda Lovelace, include *Inside Linda Lovelace,* a book of photographs, and *The Intimate Diary of Linda Lovelace,* written with Carl Wallin.

OBITUARIES AND OTHER SOURCES:

PERIODICALS

Chicago Tribune, April 23, 2002, section 2, p. 8.
Los Angeles Times, April 23, 2002, p. B11.
New York Times, April 24, 2002, p. A26.
Times (London, England), April 24, 2002.

*   *   *

MARILLIER, Juliet

PERSONAL: Born in Dunedin, New Zealand. *Education:* Otago University, B.A.

ADDRESSES: Home—Perth, Western Australia. *Agent*—c/o Author Mail, Tor Books, 175 Fifth Avenue, New York, NY 10010.

CAREER: Author; also worked as a teacher and lecturer of music history, and as a professional singer and choral conductor.

AWARDS, HONORS: Readers' Choice Award for Best Fantasy Novel, *Romantic Times,* 2000, and Alex Award, American Library Association, both for *Daughter of the Forest;* Aurealis Award for Fantasy Novel, 2000, for *Son of the Shadows.*

WRITINGS:

Daughter of the Forest, (first novel in "Sevenwaters" trilogy), Tor Books (New York, NY), 2000.
Son of the Shadows, (second novel in "Sevenwaters" trilogy), Tor Books (New York, NY), 2001.
Child of the Prophecy, (third novel in "Sevenwaters" trilogy), Tor Books (New York, NY), 2002.
Wolfskin, Tor Books (New York, NY), June, 2003.

SIDELIGHTS: On her Web site, Juliet Marillier says that while growing up in Dunedin, New Zealand, where "the influence of the Celtic immigrants who settled the area is still vibrantly evident in the local culture," she "was surrounded by the music and stories of Scotland and Ireland." This served as an inspiration for the setting in her "Sevenwaters" fantasy trilogy. "It's not surprising I ended up with a lifelong affinity for history and folklore," Marillier says. "The threads of traditional storytelling are woven very strongly into the fabric of my writing."

The first book in the trilogy is *Daughter of the Forest,* set in ancient Ireland. It is the story of Sorcha, only daughter and youngest of the seven children of Lord Colum of Sevenwaters. Their wicked stepmother transforms her brothers into swans. Only Sorcha can restore her brothers by weaving them each a shirt from a plant that tears her skin to shreds. *Library Journal*'s Jackie Cassada called *Daughter of the Forest* "a rich and vibrant novel that belongs in most fantasy collections." A *Publishers Weekly* reviewer wrote, "Marillier is a fine folklorist and a gifted narrator who has created a wholly appealing and powerful character in this daughter of the forest."

In *Son of the Shadows,* Sorcha's daughter Liadan has a gift of seeing and hearing what others cannot. She is also a healer of mind, body, and spirit. Her gift results in a meeting with a mercenary and enemy of her family. Liadan comes to love this man, but she realizes this love cannot be fulfilled. Reviewing the book for *Library Journal,* Jackie Cassada noted, "Marillier

blends old legends with original storytelling to produce an epic fantasy." *Booklist's* Patricia Monaghan commented, "Marillier's virtuosic pacing and vivid, filmic style make this an engaging continuation" of *Daughter of the Forest. Child of Prophecy* is the final book in the Sevenwaters Trilogy and concludes the story of Sorcha and her family.

BIOGRAPHICAL AND CRITICAL SOURCES:

PERIODICALS

Booklist, April 15, 2000, Patricia Monaghan, review of *Daughter of the Forest,* p. 1534; April 1, 2001, Stephanie Zvirin, review of *Daughter of the Forest,* p. 1461; May 15, 2001, Patricia Monaghan, review of *Son of the Shadows,* p. 1738.
Library Journal, May 15, 2000, Jackie Cassada, review of *Daughter of the Forest,* p. 129; May 15, 2001, Jackie Cassada, review of *Son of the Shadows,* p. 167.
Locus, April, 2000, Faren Miller, review of *Daughter of the Forest,* p. 23.
Publishers Weekly, April 17, 2000, review of *Daughter of the Forest,* p. 57; April 16, 2001, review of *Son of the Shadows,* p. 49.
Voice of Youth Advocates, December, 2000, Marsha Valance, review of *Daughter of the Forest,* p. 362.

OTHER

Fantastica Daily, http://www.mervius.com/ (December 31, 2001), Eva Wojcik-Obert, review of *Son of the Shadows.*
Slow Glass, http://www.slowglass.com.au/ (December 31, 2001), "Interview with Juliet Marillier."
Juliet Marillier's Web site, http://www.vianet.net.au/~marill/ (December 31, 2001).*

*   *   *

McCLAFFERTY, Carla Killough 1958-

PERSONAL: Born July 11, 1958, in Little Rock, AR; daughter of Raymond (a farmer) and Maxine (a homemaker; maiden name, Rucker) Killough; married Patrick Michael McClafferty (a vice president in electric sales), August 26, 1978; children: Ryan

Patrick, Brittney Leigh, Corey Andrew (deceased). *Education:* Graduate of Baptist Medical Center School of Radiologic Technology, 1978. *Religion:* Baptist.

ADDRESSES: Home—8013 Coleridge Dr., North Little Rock, AR 72116. *E-mail*—c.mcclafferty@comcast.net.

CAREER: Rebsamen Memorial Hospital, staff radiologic technologist, 1978-83; part-time work in orthopedic clinics, 1983—. Women's Sunday School Teacher, Victory Missionary Baptist Church, 1998—.

MEMBER: Society of Children's Book Writers and Illustrators, Authors Guild, American Society of Radiologic Technologists, American Registry of Radiologic Technicians.

AWARDS, HONORS: Work-in-progress grant, Society of Children's Book Writers and Illustrators, 1997; New York Public Library List, and Children's Book Council selection for Outstanding Science Trade Book, both 2002, both for *The Head Bone's Connected to the Neck Bone: The Weird, Wacky, and Wonderful X-Ray.*

WRITINGS:

Forgiving God: A Woman's Struggle to Understand When God Answers No, Discovery House (Grand Rapids, MI), 1995.
The Head Bone's Connected to the Neck Bone: The Weird, Wacky, and Wonderful X-Ray, Farrar, Straus & Giroux (New York, NY), 2001.

Contributor to periodicals, including *Cricket, German Life,* and *Radiologic Technologist.*

WORK IN PROGRESS: A children's book about Marie Curie and radium, working title, *Marie Curie and Her Liquid Sunshine.*

SIDELIGHTS: Carla Killough McClafferty first came to writing as a way to cope with her grief over the loss of her fourteen-month-old son. In *Forgiving God: A Woman's Struggle to Understand When God Answers No,* the author describes the spiritual journey that began when her son fell off a backyard swing and died from the injury to his head, which led McClafferty to question her belief in the goodness of God. Coming through on the other side with her faith renewed, McClafferty felt moved to tell her story in the hope of helping others. Along the way, she discovered a love of writing, and soon came *The Head Bone's Connected to the Neck Bone: The Weird, Wacky, and Wonderful X-Ray,* McClafferty's first children's book. A much different work from her first, this science book for young adults was inspired by McClafferty's first career as an x-ray technologist. It details "the fascinating and often strange history of the X-ray," according to Mary R. Hofmann in *School Library Journal,* running from its invention by a German scientist in the nineteenth century to its early medical and entertainment uses, to the important role it currently plays in the medical panoply. A *Book Report* reviewer called *The Head Bone's Connected to the Neck Bone* "a compelling and very readable narrative," while a critic for the *Voice of Youth Advocates* said, "McClafferty presents a clear and amusing discussion of the X-ray." Todd Morning contended in *Booklist,* the strength of the book is in McClafferty's emphasis on "human stories, which makes for fascinating reading."

McClafferty once explained: "Every book begins with a seed of an idea. The seed that grew to become *The Head Bone's Connected to the Neck Bone* was planted with one unanswered question. While working at an orthopedic clinic, I looked up Wilhelm Conrad Röntgen, the man who discovered X-rays, in a book of short medical biographies. The article said Röntgen was expelled from school when he was a boy, but it didn't say why. And I wanted to know why. So I began digging up information about Dr. Röntgen and the early days of X-rays and was fascinated by the funny, sad, and ridiculous stories I found. I just had to write a children's book to share this information. The challenge in writing it came from blending information that covers a wide variety of topics over a period of more than one hundred years, beginning with the discovery and ending with how X-rays are used in science and industry today."

BIOGRAPHICAL AND CRITICAL SOURCES:

PERIODICALS

Booklist, November 1, 2001, Todd Morning, review of *The Head Bone's Connected to the Neck Bone: The Weird, Wacky, and Wonderful X-Ray,* p. 465.

Book Report, March/April, 2002, review of *The Head Bone's Connected to the Neck Bone,* p. 75.

EPISD Reviews, April 23, 2002, review of *The Head Bone's Connected to the Neck Bone,*

Horn Book, July-December, 2001, review of *The Head Bone's Connected to the Neck Bone,* p. 151.

Louisville Eccentric Observer, June 5, 2002, review of *The Head Bone's Connected to the Neck Bone.*

Reading Teacher, April, 2002, review of *The Head Bone's Connected to the Neck Bone,* p. 700.

School Library Journal, December, 2001, Mary R. Hofmann, review of *The Head Bone's Connected to the Neck Bone,* p. 165.

Voice of Youth Advocates, July, 2002, Linda Perkins, review of *The Head Bone's Connected to the Neck Bone.*

*   *   *

McGARRITY, Mark 1943-2002
(Bartholomew Gill)

OBITUARY NOTICE—See index for CA sketch: Born July 22, 1943, in Holyoke, MA; died in an accidental fall July 3, 2002, in Morristown, NJ. Author. McGarrity gained acclaim as the author of the "McGarr" mystery series, which he wrote under the pseudonym Bartholomew Gill. He was a graduate of Brown University, where he received a B.A. in 1966, and Trinity College, where he earned a master's degree in 1971. McGarrity earned his living as a writer, beginning with novels published under his own name, including *Lucky Shuffles* (1973) and *White Rush/Green Fire* (1991). His first "McGarr" novel, *McGarr and the Politician's Wife,* was published in 1973. The author's interest in his Irish heritage is reflected in the "McGarr" books, which are notable for their realistic portrayals of life in modern Ireland. The hero of the series appeared in sixteen novels altogether, including the Edgar Award-nominated *The Death of a Joyce Scholar* (1989) and *Death in Dublin,* which was published posthumously in 2003. In addition to his novels, McGarrity was a regular contributor to the Newark, New Jersey *Star-Ledger,* for which he wrote a column covering such topics as environmental conservation and the outdoors.

OBITUARIES AND OTHER SOURCES:

BOOKS

Writers Directory, 16th edition, St. James Press (Detroit, MI), 2001.

PERIODICALS

Chicago Tribune, July 7, 2002, section 4, p. 7.
Los Angeles Times, July 6, 2002, p. B19.
New York Times, July 11, 2002, p. A25.

*   *   *

McLAUGHLIN, Michael 1949-2002

OBITUARY NOTICE—See index for *CA* sketch: Born June 14, 1949, in Wray, CO; died c. June 25, 2002, in Santa Fe, NM. Restaurateur, chef, and author. McLaughlin will be remembered for the hundreds of tasty and unusual recipes he developed and published in nearly two dozen cookbooks. He first gained recognition as a collaborator on *The Silver Palate Cookbook,* which was nominated for the Tastemaker Award of the R. T. French Company and included in the Cookbook Hall of Fame of the James Beard Foundation. McLaughlin developed his culinary expertise as the manager of the Silver Palate restaurant in New York City. He later became a partner and chef for the original Manhattan Chili Company, but he was best known for his cookbooks and numerous magazine articles. McLaughlin's other books include *The Manhattan Chili Company Southwest American Cookbook, The New American Kitchen, The Back of the Box Gourmet, The Jimtown Store Cookbook,* and (as coauthor) *Lusty California Cooking.* He also contributed to popular magazines such as *Bon Appetit, Food and Wine,* and *Spice.*

OBITUARIES AND OTHER SOURCES:

PERIODICALS

Los Angeles Times, July 13, 2002, p. B17.
New York Times, July 12, 2002, obituary by Regina Schrambling, p. A17.

*   *   *

McNALLY, Tom 1923-2002

OBITUARY NOTICE—See index for CA sketch: Born March 8, 1923, in Berlin, NH; died of a stroke July 29, 2002, in Ennis, MT. Journalist, photographer, sportsman, and author. McNally was an avid outdoorsman and hunter who was a respected newspaper columnist for the *Chicago Tribune.* Serving in the U.S. Army as a paratrooper during World War II, he received his B.S. from Loyola College in 1949. After working for a couple years as a manager for National Sporting Goods Co. and Montgomery Ward, he got a job as the outdoor editor for the *Baltimore Sun* in 1952. In 1956 he joined the *Chicago Tribune,* where he remained until his death. McNally wrote the regular columns "Woods and Waters" and "Mostly about Dogs," as well as the "Sportsman's Travel Guide," which appeared in the paper's travel section. Setting three world records for his fishing skills, McNally was also an accomplished nature photographer. He put his writing and photographer's skills to work in a series of outdoors books, many of which were for juveniles, including *Fishing for Boys* (1962), *Camping for Boys and Girls* (1966), and *Camping* (1972). Works for adults include *Tom McNally's Fishermen's Bible* (1970; third edition, 1976), *Tom McNally's Complete Book of Fisherman's Knots* (1975), and *The Complete Book of Fly Fishing* (1993).

OBITUARIES AND OTHER SOURCES:

PERIODICALS

Chicago Tribune, July 30, 2002, section 2, p. 9.

*   *   *

MEIER, Leslie
   See RÜHMKORF, Peter

*   *   *

MILLIGAN, Spike
   See MILLIGAN, Terence Alan

*   *   *

MILLIGAN, Terence Alan 1918-2002
   (Spike Milligan)

OBITUARY NOTICE—See index for *CA* sketch: Born April 16, 1918, in Ahmednagar, India; died of kidney failure February 27, 2002, in Rye, Sussex, England. Comedian, actor, and author. Milligan, always known

as Spike, rose to fame in the 1950s when he teamed with Peter Sellers, Harry Secombe, and Michael Bentine to star in the wildly popular British radio series *The Goon Show.* It has been said that, as the show's chief writer, Milligan reached heights of absurdity that approached genius. His comedy sketches featured ridiculous characters like Count Moriarty, Blubottle, and Eccles, whose quest to save the British Empire through their misadventures entertained listeners for nearly ten years. After *The Goon Show* went off the air, Milligan became a solo performer. He also wrote more than fifty books, ranging from children's books like *Sir Nobunk and the Terrible, Awful, Dreadful, Naughty, Nasty Dragon* to verse collections like *Fleas Knees and Hidden Elephants* and novels like the parody *Lady Chatterly according to Spike Milligan.* His more serious writings include *The Bedsitting Room,* a well-received play he wrote with John Antrobus. He was also the coauthor of *Depression and How to Survive It,* inspired by his own experiences with crippling depression throughout most of his adult life. Despite his ongoing criticism of "the establishment," which was not always masked by humor, Milligan was admired by the British people for the pleasure he brought into their lives. One of his biggest fans was Prince Charles, the patron of the Goon Show Preservation Society, who bestowed upon Milligan an honorary knighthood in 2000.

OBITUARIES AND OTHER SOURCES:

BOOKS

Farnes, Norma, editor, *The Spike Milligan Letters,* M. Joseph (London, England), 1977.
Milligan, Spike, *Adolf Hitler: My Part in His Downfall,* M. Joseph (London, England), 1971.
Scudamore, Pauline, editor, *Dear Robert, Dear Spike: The Graves-Milligan Correspondence,* A. Sutton (Gloucester, England), 1991.

PERIODICALS

Chicago Tribune, February 28, 2002, section 2, p. 9.
Los Angeles Times, February 28, 2002, p. B13.
New York Times, February 28, 2002, obituary by David Binder, p. A25.
Times (London, England), February 28, 2002, p. 39.
Washington Post, February 28, 2002, obituary by Adam Bernstein, p. B6.

MILLMAN, Marcia (Honey) 1946-

PERSONAL: Born 1946, in New York, NY; daughter of Harry and Esther Millman. *Education:* Brandeis University, B.A. (history), 1967, Ph.D. (sociology), 1972; Yale University, postgraduate studies, 1967-68.

ADDRESSES: Office—University of California, Santa Cruz, Department of Sociology, Santa Cruz, CA 95064.

CAREER: University of California, Santa Cruz, professor of sociology, 1971—, department chair, 1988-91.

AWARDS, HONORS: National Endowment for the Humanities fellowship, 1974.

WRITINGS:

(Editor with Rosabeth Moss Kanter) *Another Voice: Feminist Perspectives on Social Life and Social Science,* Anchor Press/Doubleday (Garden City, NY), 1975.

The Unkindest Cut: Life in the Backrooms of Medicine, William Morrow (New York, NY), 1977.

Such a Pretty Face: Being Fat in America, photographs by Naomi Bushman, W. W. Norton (New York, NY), 1980.

Warm Hearts and Cold Cash: The Intimate Dynamics of Families and Money, Free Press (New York, NY), 1991.

The Seven Stories of Love: And How to Choose Your Happy Ending, William Morrow (New York, NY), 2001.

SIDELIGHTS: As a professor of sociology, Marcia Millman specializes in family dynamics, social psychology, deviance and conformity, social interaction, occupations and professions, and the study of popular representations and narratives of social life. She has written a number of books in her field, and is coeditor, with Rosabeth Moss Kanter, of *Another Voice: Feminist Perspectives on Social Life and Social Science.* In this academic collection, twelve sociologists, all but one of them women, examine a range of sociological subfields, including the sociology of organizations, medical sociology, the sociology of education, urban sociology, race, social stratification,

deviance, and social change. Recommendations are made by the contributors, who examine the models that have traditionally been used, as to steps that must be taken to ensure that sociological research portrays both sexes fairly. They focus on less-studied aspects of female life, including working-class women, black female heads of families, work-related illness, and women's progress in the professions. To counter studies in areas dominated by men, they suggest that areas in which women are prominent should receive more attention, including playgrounds, beauty shops, and nurseries. *Booklist* reviewer Mary Jane McKinven noted that the contributors also fault "the tendency to focus on rationalism and logic at the expense of emotional factors." A *Publishers Weekly* contributor said that in those areas that were neglected before the feminist movement, "this book makes a significant contribution." *Library Journal* reviewer Sandy Whiteley called the volume "a state-of-the-art report."

"The combination of review, critique, and theoretical resynthesis is an exceedingly difficult but also exceptionally important accomplishment," wrote Myra Marx Ferree in *Contemporary Sociology.* "By and large, the articles succeed in providing a sufficient review of the field for the sociologist not specializing in the area to feel comfortable with the material as well as enough new theoretical insight into familiar material so as not to bore the specialist. The clear and unlabored quality of the prose in most of the articles and the generally high level of success achieved make this very tricky balancing act look almost easy."

The Unkindest Cut: Life in the Backrooms of Medicine was called "a behind-the-scenes syllabus of medical errors" by a *Booklist* reviewer. The volume is a result of Millman's two years of observations in the wards, operating rooms, emergency rooms, and staff meetings of three private metropolitan teaching hospitals affiliated with prestigious medical schools. The events are real, but the names have been changed, with Millman calling the composite hospital "Lakeside." She notes the factors that contribute to medical error, including conflict within different levels of staff and between medical staff and administration. She discusses regulation, or lack thereof, when it comes to new medical procedures and the promotion of high-priced procedures that are not universally accepted as necessary. *Library Journal* contributor Peggy Champlin wrote that *The Unkindest Cut* "understandably does not consider the *good* care many hospitals give. It is thus a frightening book."

Judith Lorber reviewed *The Unkindest Cut* in *Contemporary Sociology*. Lorber felt the long section titled "Overlooking Medical Mistakes" to be the "best part" in a book that she considered "uneven." Lorber wrote that "[Millman's] chapter on the ritualistic collusion and pretense at professional criticism produced at a typical Medical Mortality Conference, which is supposed to review medical mistakes, demonstrates clearly the myriad ways doctors redefine and neutralize their mistakes to protect their 'gentlemen's agreement' that they are competent, self-sufficient, and all-knowing practitioners."

Millman's *Such a Pretty Face: Being Fat in America* is the result of her study of the U.S. obsession with weight and our reaction to those who are overweight, based on interviews with Americans, mostly women, who fall into this category. An *Atlantic* reviewer said that what Millman "has turned up is largely predictable." Jane Howard said in the *New York Times Book Review* that "it is odd, as Miss Millman points out, that 'the women's movement has been remarkably silent on the issue of weight. . . . Indeed, it is puzzling that the pressure to be stylishly thin and the toll this takes on women has received practically no attention.'" Howard wrote that Millman "reports sympathetically on her visits to a camp for fat children and on several meetings for obese grown-ups. Horror stories abound (one woman had to be sewn by her mother into one and a half wedding dresses; a seven-year-old got so big she had to start wearing women's sizes), as do less dramatic insights: 'Later on in life, women often gain a few pounds to achieve a false sense of control over their husband's lack of sexual interest.'"

"Thankfully . . . there are no suggestions for an exercise and weight-reduction plan," wrote Melanie Pulik in *Saturday Review*. "American readers know how to get thin; some of them just aren't psychologically able to." Sylvia Rabiner wrote in the *New Republic* that Millman "wisely refrains from offering pat reasons for why people gain weight. She suggests a variety: economics, for one. There are many more poor overweight Americans than affluent ones. Ethnic background counts too. Psychological explanations aside, there is probably no neurotic component to a pasta addiction acquired childhood. Where psychological explanations apply, Millman offers some interesting ones: getting fat is not always a loss of control but a form of it; one may eat to defy a parent, to retreat

from the sexuality of a father, and avoid competition with a still-needed mother." Millman also points out how different fat men are treated compared to fat women. As Anatole Broyard explained in a *New York Times* review, "a woman who weights 20 or 30 pounds more than the norm is considered fat, [but] a man at 50 pounds more is not." Men can also be manipulative of overweight women. Women categorize such men as either nursers, dealers, or users. "A nurser needs no explanation," wrote Broyard. "A dealer is a man who enters into a mutual no-criticism pact with the fat woman because he, too, has something to be 'ashamed of.' The user is a man who simply exploits the fat woman's loneliness and low self-esteem."

Rabiner said that "though Millman makes a compassionate plea for a better understanding of the problems of extreme overweight, her real point is that a society whose highest standard of feminine beauty is an anorexic twenty-one-year-old makes victims of us all." Broyard concluded that *Such a Pretty Face* "raises interesting questions, for example, about the image of the self and its various distortions, about the role and the definition of beauty in our society, about control as an index of anxiety." Even for readers who do not consider themselves overweight, *Such a Pretty Face* was recommended by *Ms.* critic Judith Thurman for "the transcripted interviews, [which] seem to come straight from Gertrude Stein. Here are the rhythms of American speech and life behind its clichés, rendered passionate by their exactness."

A *Kirkus Reviews* contributor who reviewed *Warm Hearts and Cold Cash: The Intimate Dynamics of Families and Money* said that Millman's "unsentimental view—not that money buys love but that money *is* love-gives a valuable jolt to ways of assessing family relationships." Millman explores the expected situations, such as divorce, where money is often used to hurt and control, but she also shows how the power within a marriage is often determined by who earns, or has control over, the money, how parents' spending on children reveals how they are valued, and how, even after death, some use money to reward or punish relatives through their wills. Millman demonstrates how people use money to satisfy their personal agendas and emotional needs.

"She also deals with class differences in rules concerning the distribution and management of money in families," wrote Miriam M. Johnson in the *American*

Journal of Sociology, "noting that the middle class, being the most individualistic, has the fewest rules. But these few many be changing. In an earlier generation, middle-class parents expected to give only cultural capital and a college education to their children. . . . Now middle-class young (and not so young) adults are finding themselves unable to maintain a middle-class life-style without help from their parents. These changes are causing generational strain with children expecting more from their parents than their parents had expected to give."

"Ms Millman sees no value in holding on to sentimentality about family love," wrote Louis Auchincloss in the *New York Times Book Review.* "She favors prenuptial agreements. And she also believes that both spouses should be self-supporting, because being financially dependent sets up a person to become a child again." In a *Women's Review of Books* article, Patricia Aufderheide said that Millman "does make a case for treating financial affairs as legitimate symptoms of family attitudes and crises, rather than as aberrations in or betrayals of loving relationships. She takes us up to the point where we can acknowledge that we do use money to control and measure our love lives, and that it's virtually impossible in a commoditized universe of values to avoid doing so."

Millman's *The Seven Stories of Love: And How to Choose Your Happy Ending* is based on a class she developed and taught. Her seven stories are "First Love," "Pygmalion," "Obsessive Love," "The Downstairs Woman and the Upstairs Man," "Sacrifice," "Rescue," and "Postponement and Avoidance." Millman contends that all relationships fall into one, or a combination of, these categories. She draws on individual cases and uses books, including *Jane Eyre, The Girls' Guide to Hunting and Fishing, Rebecca,* and *Endless Love,* and scripts, including *Pretty Woman, Fatal Attraction, Casablanca,* and *Dirty Dancing,* to make her points. A *Publishers Weekly* reviewer said Millman "offers a clear-sighted and illuminating view of why romantic relationships play out as they do."

BIOGRAPHICAL AND CRITICAL SOURCES:

PERIODICALS

America, October 2, 1976, review of *The Unkindest Cut: Life in the Backrooms of Medicine,* p. 197.

American Journal of Sociology, March, 1992, Miriam M. Johnson, review of *Warm Hearts and Cold Cash: The Intimate Dynamics of Families and Money,* pp. 1511-1513.

Atlantic, March, 1980, review of *Such a Pretty Face: Being Fat in America,* p. 101.

Booklist, December 1, 1975, Mary Jane McKinven, review of *Another Voice: Feminist Perspectives on Social Life and Social Science,* p. 496; February 15, 1977, review of *The Unkindest Cut,* p. 864.

Contemporary Sociology, March, 1977, Myra Marx Ferree, review of *Another Voice,* pp. 256-257; January, 1978, Judith Lorber, review of *The Unkindest Cut,* p. 108; January, 1992, Linda M. Blum, review of *Warm Hearts and Cold Cash,* p. 70.

Family Health, May, 1980, Maryann Brinley, review of *Such a Pretty Face,* p. 45.

Journal of Comparative Family Studies, autumn, 1992, Sheldon Goldenberg, review of *Warm Hearts and Cold Cash,* p. 483.

Journal of Contemporary Ethnography, January, 1993, Jerome Rabow, review of *Warm Hearts and Cold Cash,* p. 501.

Kirkus Reviews, February 15, 1991, review of *Warm Hearts and Cold Cash,* p. 234.

Library Journal, September 15, 1975, Sandy Whiteley, review of *Another Voice,* pp. 1644-1645; December 15, 1976, Peggy Champlin, review of *The Unkindest Cut,* p. 2589; March 15, 1980, Virginia A. Doser, review of *Such a Pretty Face,* p. 735.

Ms., May, 1980, Judith Thurman, review of *Such a Pretty Face,* p. 30; May, 1985, review of *Such a Pretty Face,* p. 144.

New Republic, April 12, 1980, Sylvia Rabiner, review of *Such a Pretty Face,* pp. 34-36.

New York Times, February 15, 1980, Anatole Broyard, "Books: Not So Jolly," p. C24.

New York Times Book Review, March 16, 1980, Jane Howard, "Fat Women," p. 12; May 12, 1991, Louis Auchincloss, "Home Is Where the Checkbook Is," p. 10.

Psychology Today, May, 1980, Elsa Dixler, review of *Such a Pretty Face,* p. 112.

Publishers Weekly, July 21, 1975, review of *Another Voice,* p. 71; March 5, 2001, review of *The Seven Stories of Love: And How to Choose Your Happy Ending,* p. 77.

Saturday Review, February 16, 1980, Melanie Pulik, review of *Such a Pretty Face,* p. 50.

School Library Journal, August 1980, Cyrisse Jaffee, review of *Such a Pretty Face,* p. 84.

Social Science Quarterly, December, 1992, Craig J. Forsyth, review of *Warm Hearts and Cold Cash,* p. 969.

Weight Watcher's, August, 1980, Anita Haber, review of *Such a Pretty Face,* p. 8.

Women's Review of Books, June, 1991, Patricia Aufderheide, "Can't Buy Me Love?," pp. 7-8.

Yale Review, summer, 1980, review of *Such a Pretty Face,* p. 14.

*   *   *

MNOOKIN, Wendy M. 1946-

PERSONAL: Born November 1, 1946, in New York, NY; daughter of Seymour (a psychiatrist) and Marjorie (a social worker; maiden name, Strachstein) Miller; married Arthur Piccinati (divorced); married James Paul Mnookin (a financial manager), May 24, 1970; children: Seth Andrew, Abigail Sarah, Jacob Paul. *Education:* Radcliffe College, B.A. (English), 1968; Vermont College, M.F.A. (writing), 1991.

ADDRESSES: Home—40 Woodchester Drive, Chestnut Hill, MA 02467. *E-mail*—jwmnookin@mediaone.net.

CAREER: Poet.

AWARDS, HONORS: National Endowment for the Arts, fellowship in poetry, 1999.

WRITINGS:

POETRY

Guenever Speaks, Round Table Publications, 1991.
To Get Here, BOA Editions (Rochester, NY), 1999.
What He Took, BOA Editions (Rochester, NY), 2002.

*   *   *

MOE, Doug

PERSONAL: Married; wife's name, Bette; children: Quinn, Olivia. *Education:* University of Wisconsin—Madison, received degree, 1979.

ADDRESSES: Home—Madison, WI. *Office*—P.O. Box 8060, Madison, WI 53708. *E-mail*—dougmoe@madison.com.

CAREER: Journalist. *Capital Times,* Madison, WI, columnist, 1997—; WMMM-FM, Madison, WI, radio commentator. Has also worked as editor of *Madison Magazine.*

WRITINGS:

The World of Mike Royko, University of Wisconsin Press (Madison, WI), 1999.

WORK IN PROGRESS: Lords of the Ring: The Triumph and Tragedy of College Boxing's Greatest Team, a history of the University of Wisconsin's boxing team.

SIDELIGHTS: Once voted the best local columnist in Madison, Wisconsin, Doug Moe pays tribute to a renowned Chicago columnist in *The World of Mike Royko.* Royko set a high standard as the populist scourge of the powerful who really knew his city's neighborhoods and could bring them to life for his readers in short, sharp sentences. Shortly after his death in 1997, his columns were collected and published as *One More Time.* "A different but equally satisfying nosh awaits fans in this brief, lavishly illustrated biography," wrote a reviewer for *Booklist.* In *The World of Mike Royko,* Moe tells the story of Royko's childhood, living over a tavern in a Polish-American neighborhood, his years in the Air Force, where he edited the weekly newspaper, the 1963 launch of his daily column, and his emergence as "The Man Who Owned Chicago," covering politics, local celebrities, racial conflict, and the daily ordeal of the "little guy" against the system. While some reviewers faulted its uncritical approach, others appreciated this first biography of the man behind the columns. In his review for the *Chicago Tribune,* Roger Simon wrote, "I was prepared to dislike Doug Moe's book. . . . I was, I am happy to say, dead wrong. It is not only a fascinating and well-written book, but a visually attractive one."

BIOGRAPHICAL AND CRITICAL SOURCES:

PERIODICALS

Booklist, November 1, 1999, Mary Carroll, review of *The World of Mike Royko,* p. 484.

Chicago Tribune, January 23, 2000, Roger Simon, *The World of Mike Royko.*

New York Times Book Review, January 9, 2000, Laura Green, review of *The World of Mike Royko,* p. 21.

*   *   *

MOINOT, Pierre 1920-

PERSONAL: Born March 29, 1920, in Fressines, Deux-Sèvres, France; married Madeleine Sarrailh, 1947; children: one son, four daughters. *Education:* Attended University of Paris, University of Caen, and University of Grenoble. *Hobbies and other interests:* Hunting, carpentry.

ADDRESSES: Home—44 Rue du Cherche-Midi, 75006 Paris, France.

CAREER: Senior civil servant in France, 1946—; technical adviser for André Malraux, 1959-61; Theatres and Cultural Action, director, 1960-62; Union Général Cinématographique, administrator, 1960—; president of Commission on Advances in Long Films, France, 1964-72, and Commission on Audiovisual Problems, 1981—. UNESCO, French delegate, 1966, director general of Arts and Letters, 1966-69, chief advisor to Audit Office, 1967, president, 1978, attorney general, 1983-86. *Military service:* Served in the military; received Bronze Star.

MEMBER: Academy Francaise.

AWARDS, HONORS: Prix Femina, 1979, for *Le Guetteur d'ombre;* Prix du Roman de l'Academie Française; Prix des Libraires de France; Legion d'honneur (grand officer) Arts et des Lettres.

WRITINGS:

Armes et bagages (novel), Gallimard (Paris, France), 1951.

La chasse royale (novel), Gallimard (Paris, France), 1953, translated by Ralph Manheim as *The Royal Hunt,* Knopf (New York, NY), 1955.

La Blessure: Nouvelles, Gallimard (Paris, France), 1956.

Le sable vif (novel), Gallimard (Paris, France), 1963, translated by Francis Price as *An Ancient Enemy,* Macmillan (London, England), 1966.

Héliogabale, Gallimard (Paris, France), 1971.

La Griffe et la dent, Denoël (Paris, France), 1977.

Mazarin: Scénario et dialogues d'une série de quatre films télévisés, Gallimard (Paris, France), 1978.

Le Guetteur d'ombre, Gallimard (Paris, France), 1979.

Discours de réception de M. Pierre Moinot à l'Academie française et response du Révérend Père Carré, Gallimard (Paris, France), 1983.

Discours Prononcés dans la séance publique tenue par l'Académie française pour la reception de M. Pierre Moinot le Jeudi 20 Janvier 1983, Institut de France (Paris, France), 1983.

Jeanne d'Arc: Le pouvoir et l'Innocence, Flammarion (Paris, France), 1988.

La Descente du fleuve (novel), Gallimard (Paris, France), 1991.

Tous comptes faits: Entretiens avec Frederic Badre et Arnaud Guillon, Quai Voltaire (Paris, France), 1993.

Attention à la peinture (novel), Gallimard (Paris, France), 1997.

Le Matin vient et aussi la nuit (novel), Gallimard (Paris, France), 1999, translated by Jody Gladding as *As Night Follows Day,* Welcome Rain Publishers (New York, NY), 2001.

SIDELIGHTS: Pierre Moinot has held positions in the military and in the arts in France. He was elected in 1982 as an immortal of the Academie Française, a literary society made up of forty immortals devoted to maintaining the purity of the French language.

Moinot's novel *Le Guetteur d'ombre* won the Prix Femina in 1979. It is the story of a man who leaves his job as a newspaper editor, his family, and the comforts of home, to hunt a deer in the forest. He sees the deer once in the beginning of his pursuit, but is unable to shoot it. During the beginning of his hunt a man dying from cancer accompanies him. The hunter's real quest is to find a sense of self-identity and his ties to nature. In the end he finally gives up and returns to his wife and daughter and his demanding job. Reviewing the book for *French Review,* Paul A. Mankin called the book "a brilliant prose style, rich in nuances of inner moods and meticulous in the description of the forest." Reviewing the book for *World Literature Today,* Sergio Villani wrote, "*Le Guetteur d'ombre* is a powerful literary work, well deserving the Prix Femina, from a humanist of great depth and compassion."

Moinot's *As Night Follows Day* is a mystery about the consequences of murder in a French village after World War II. The murder is of two young men while they were out planting corn. The villagers become fearful and for the first time doors are locked, guns are prepared, and everyone is a suspect. *Booklist* critic Connie Fletcher called it "a masterful literary thriller."

BIOGRAPHICAL AND CRITICAL SOURCES:

PERIODICALS

Booklist, April 1, 2001, Connie Fletcher, review of *As Night Follows Day,* p. 1455.
French Review, April, 1981, Paul A. Mankin, review of *Le Guetteur d'ombre,* p. 767.
Publishers Weekly, May 28, 2001, "June Publications," p. 54.
World Literature Today, winter, 1981, Sergio Villani, review of *Le Guetteur d'ombre,* pp. 63-64.

*   *   *

MONELLE, Raymond 1937-

PERSONAL: Born August 19, 1937, in Bristol, England; son of Ray (a band leader) and Grace (Grindon) Monelle; children: Catherine, Julia. *Education:* Pembroke College, Oxford, M.A., 1960; Royal College of Music, London, B.Mus. (with first class honors), 1966. *Religion:* Christian.

ADDRESSES: Home—80 Marchmont Rd., Edinburgh EH9 1HR, Scotland. *Office*—Faculty of Music, Alison House, University of Edinburgh, 12 Nicolson Sq., Edinburgh EH8 9DF, Scotland. *E-mail*—r.monelle@ music.ed.ac.uk.

CAREER: University of Edinburgh, Edinburgh, Scotland, reader in music, 1969—. International Musical Signification Project, member.

MEMBER: Royal Musical Association, Society for Music Theory.

WRITINGS:

Linguistics and Semiotics in Music, Harwood Academic Publishers (Philadelphia, PA), 1992.
The Sense of Music: Semiotic Essays, Princeton University Press (Princeton, NJ), 2000.

WORK IN PROGRESS: The Musical Topic.

BIOGRAPHICAL AND CRITICAL SOURCES:

PERIODICALS

Choice, April, 2001, F. Goosen, review of *The Sense of Music: Semiotic Essays,* p. 1472.
Music and Letters, February, 1994, Kofi Agawu, review of *Linguistics and Semiotics in Music,* p. 120.
Notes, March, 1994, Robert S. Hatten, review of *Linguistics and Semiotics in Music,* p. 1002.

*   *   *

MONTI, Dean 1957-

PERSONAL: Born September 12, 1957, in Oak Park, IL; son of James (an insurance agent) and Doylene Monti; married Elizabeth, February 28, 1997 (divorced June 29, 2000). *Ethnicity:* "Caucasian." *Education:* DePaul University, B.A., 1995.

ADDRESSES: Home—10 Sterling Circle #202, Wheaton, IL 60187. *E-mail*—nadimneto@aol.com, dmonti@aad.org.

CAREER: Writer, editor, and novelist. American Veterinary Medical Association, Schuamburg, IL, writer/editor, 1998-2000; American Academy of Dermatology, Schaumburg, IL, writer/editor, 2000-01.

MEMBER: Writer's Guild.

WRITINGS:

The Sweep of the Second Hand, Academy Chicago Publishers (Chicago IL), 2001.

WORK IN PROGRESS: But We're Still Sinking, a short story collection; *Never Better,* a novel.

SIDELIGHTS: Although Dean Monti's first novel is not autobiographical, Monti and his protagonist, Malcolm, both had some trouble with getting started and keeping things going with their lives. In Monti's first novel, *The Sweep of the Second Hand,* Malcolm Cicchio inexplicably begins losing one minute of sleep with each passing night; at that rate he figures his heart will explode in sixteen months. He's sure that if he can just find his watch, the one his girlfriend gave him and then took back, his life just might get better. But his life is a disaster about to happen and the other characters in this debut novel are at about the same point as Malcolm. Whether Malcolm can get it together is played out in a string of days that might just let Malcolm come out on top. A *Publisher Weekly* reviewer called *The Sweep of the Second Hand* "sweet, slow and slightly bizarre, this is an intriguing debut." In a review for *Library Journal* Bob Lunn wrote that "a comic novel all too often can be little more than a string of gags, but Monti begs comparison with Woody Allen and Nick Hornby."

Monti told *CA:* "When I was sixteen I was dating a girl who was keeping me on just so she'd have a date for homecoming. The first time we made out, she complained I was a lousy kisser. I don't know what her model was—her method was one of odd twisting and contortion of the face while going at it, but at the same time I thought she knew something I didn't. As the years past, we put romance away for good and became close friends. By the time I was in my late twenties we were still friends and I had written many short stories and plays. She suggested I should write a novel. I had never considered it. I told her I couldn't— that the task was beyond my talents and capabilities. But I began to hammer away at a novel a little at a time and finished a 380-page draft some six months later. I believe the main reason I went about it so diligently is that I couldn't be known as a person who could not kiss and could not write novels. My writing improved as I wrote. My kissing, I'm told, got better, too."

Monti told *CA:* "I was certain that the first novel I wrote would be recognized as the next great thing in the literary world. A wise writing teacher suggested I get on 'eye level' with my characters. I took this advice and wrote my first published novel, *The Sweep of the Second Hand.* Writing the second novel was easier because I had already put in the physical hours demanded of novel writing. The same wise writing teacher told me, 'Maybe you wrote that first novel so that you could get to the second one.' Indeed."

BIOGRAPHICAL AND CRITICAL SOURCES:

PERIODICALS

Booklist, June 1, 2001, Marlene Chamberlain, review of *The Sweep of the Second Hand,* p. 1848.
Library Journal, May 15, 2001, Bob Lunn, review of *The Sweep of the Second Hand,* p. 164.
Publishers Weekly, May 28, 2001, review of *The Sweep of the Second Hand,* p. 1848.
Wall Street Journal, July 20, 2001, Merle Rubin, review of *The Sweep of the Second Hand,* p. W8.

*   *   *

MOORE, Timothy J. 1959-

PERSONAL: Born 1959. *Education:* Millersville University, B.A.; University of North Carolina, Ph.D.

ADDRESSES: Office—University of Texas, Department of Classics, 211 Waggener Hall, Austin, TX 78701. *E-mail*—timmoore@utxvms.cc.utexas.edu.

CAREER: University of Texas at Austin, assistant professor, 1992-98, associate professor of classics, 1998—, department chair, 2002—; Harvard University, Mellon faculty fellow, 1991-92; Texas A & M University, assistant professor, 1986-91; University of Colorado at Boulder, visiting assistant professor, summer, 1989; Texas A & M Study Center in Italy, assistant professor, summer, 1988; University of North Carolina at Chapel Hill, teaching assistant, 1983-86, L'Année Philogique, research assistant, 1981-84.

MEMBER: American Institute of Archaeology, American Philological Association, American Classical League, Classical Association of the Middle West and South, Texas Classical Association.

AWARDS, HONORS: Mellon faculty fellowship, Harvard University, 1991-92; American Academy in Rome fellowship, 1998-99; Alexander von Humboldt fellowship, 1999-2000; President's Associates Teaching Excellence Award, University of Texas, 2002.

WRITINGS:

Art[r]istry and Ideology: Livy's Vocabulary of Virtue, Athenäum (Frankfurt am Main, Germany), 1989.
The Theater of Plautus: Playing to the Audience, University of Texas Press (Austin, TX), 1998.

WORK IN PROGRESS: Researching music in Roman comedy.

SIDELIGHTS: Timothy J. Moore, an associate classics professor at the University of Texas at Austin, specializes in new and Roman comedy (especially Plautus), Roman historiography and modern views of the Romans. His first book, *Art[r]istry and Ideology: Livy's Vocabulary of Virtue,* is a revision of his doctoral dissertation at North Carolina. It is a study of fifty concepts found within Livy's treatment of the virtues of the Romans. Moore begins by asking readers to recall the virtues that made Rome great and the vices that led to its downfall, as most of the 142 books in Livy's *Vocabulary* deal with Rome's decline. *Art[r]istry and Ideology* consists of six chapters: "Bravery and Industry," "Justice and Loyalty," "Forbearance and Self-control," "Humanity and Kindness," "Wisdom and Knowledge," and "Innocence and Seriousness."

Moore concentrates on constant, not temporary virtues. He describes meaning and context for each concept, or word. For example, he notes that such words as *modestia* and *patientia* were used to describe a wide variety of peoples, while *moderatio, perseverantia,* and *constantia* applied mainly to Romans. He relates this information to Livy's own perception of the subjects of his study: from plebeians to patricians, Romans and non-Romans. Moore, also comparing Livy's text to the Polybian original and with Claudius Quadrigarius, concludes that Livy's vocabulary and moral ideas are original, and have an original slant. Moore adds six detailed appendices.

In *Classical Review,* John Briscoe said Moore makes little "attempt to examine the usage of the words under consideration in earlier Latin, or to relate the discus-

sion to the central questions of the stylist level of L[ivy]'s vocabulary and the innovation he makes." Other critics were more praiseworthy. Konrad Gries wrote in *Classical World:* "Thorough and meticulous (perhaps a bit too much so), this study is a useful compilation. Of particular value are the discussions of *fides, sapentia, gravitas, severitas,* and *magnus animus.*" T. J. Luce, writing in the *American Journal of Philology,* called Moore's interpretation of Livy's words "sensible," and Moore's exposition "crisp and clear," and following a "regular pattern." Luce concludes that "altogether, this is a useful and commendable monograph."

Moore also wrote *The Theater of Plautus: Playing to the Audience.* This work studies the comedies of Plautus, who was a very successful writer in Rome, and sets them within their historical and cultural context. Specifically, Moore "demonstrates with admirable thoroughness the extent to which Plautine comedies are theatrically self-conscious," according to Erich Segal in a *Times Literary Supplement* review. "His actors are not merely playing characters but rather actors *playing* actors who are playing characters." Moore goes on to study how Plautus used various techniques to hold his audience's interest in his plays, and he provides a background for understanding how the actors and audiences of the time would have likely viewed and reacted to these plays. For those interested in classical theater, *The Theater of Plautus* "should prove a very useful book," according to *Religious Studies Review* critic Richard Hunter.

BIOGRAPHICAL AND CRITICAL SOURCES:

PERIODICALS

American Journal of Philology, summer, 1991, T. J. Luce, review of *Art[r]istry and Ideology,* pp. 276-279.
Classical Review, Volume 40, number 1, 1990, John Briscoe, review of *Art[r]istry and Ideology,* pp. 40-42.
Classical World, March-April, 1991, Konrad Gries, review of *Art[r]istry and Ideology,* p. 316.
Religious Studies Review, October, 1999, Richard Hunter, review of *The Theater of Plautus: Playing to the Audience,* p. 41.
Times Literary Supplement, May 28, 1999, Erich Segal, "Pay Attention, Folks," p. 4.

OTHER

University of Texas Web site, *http://ccwf.cc.utexas.edu/* (March 25, 2003), "Timothy J. Moore."

*   *   *

MORLEY, Neville (G. D.)

PERSONAL: Married Clarne Atkinson; children: Ronald, Kenneth, Christine.

ADDRESSES: Office—Department of Classics and Ancient History, University of Bristol, 11 Woodland Rd., Bristol BS8 1TB, England. *E-mail*—n.g.d. morley@bris.ac.uk.

CAREER: Educator and historian. University of Bristol, Bristol, England, senior lecturer in ancient history and director of Centre for the Classical Tradition.

WRITINGS:

Metropolis and Hinterland: The City of Rome and the Italian Economy, 200 B.C.-A.D. 200, Cambridge University Press (New York, NY), 1996.
Writing Ancient History, Cornell University Press (Ithaca, NY), 1999.
Ancient History: Key Themes and Approaches, Routledge (New York, NY), 2000.

SIDELIGHTS: British author Neville Morley is a professor of ancient history at the University of Bristol. His primary interests are economic history, particularly the economic history of ancient Rome, and historiography and historical theory. Morley's *Metropolis and Hinterland: The City of Rome and the Italian Economy, 200 B.C.-A.D. 200* is the first comprehensive study of the economic relationship between Rome and the rest of the Italian peninsula during the peak of the Roman Empire. Morley uses twentieth-century economic theory to emphasize the view of the consuming city as an engine of economic growth rather than as a parasite on the productive forces of rural areas. *Metropolis and Hinterland* consists largely of summaries of other scholar's work rather than of original hypotheses by Morley himself, which might be attributable to the fact that the book began as Morley's Ph.D. dissertation. Despite this, critics largely commended the author for presenting a clear, logical, and well-written overview of the current state of scholarship on this subject.

After *Writing Ancient History,* Morley's book about the problems a scholar confronts when writing histories of ancient times, he published *Ancient History: Key Themes and Approaches.* Containing several hundred excerpts from secondary historical sources written by over two hundred scholars, the book is intended to provide an overview of the current scholarship on ancient Greece and Rome. The first part of *Ancient History,* "Key Themes and Debates," is arranged by topic. Over seventy subjects, ranging from agriculture, architecture, and art to technology, tyranny, and war, are each given their own section. The second part, titled "Key Writers," collects statements about the ancient world from a wide range of modern scholars, including Foucault, Marx, Nietzsche, and Weber, as well as other lesser-known historians.

While critics have generally recognized the usefulness of having a representative sample of opinions conveniently arranged by topic, several reviewers questioned the sound-bite-like style of many of the selections. Some of the excerpts are one-liners, including Professor J. R. Patterson's famous "Crisis: what crisis?" and Hammond's conclusion on Alexander: "In brief, he had many of the qualities of the noble savage." Without the whole of the discussion from which such quotations are excerpted, students unfamiliar with such scholars' arguments might fail to understand the significance of such statements, noted some critics. While *Times Literary Supplement* contributor Mary Beard dubbed Morley's approach "impossibly crude" and "an insult both to those who wrote them [the excerpted passages] and to the students who may use the book," Darryl A. Phillips was more approving in his appraisal of *Ancient History* in the online *Bryn Mawr Classical Review.* Phillips commended Morley's selection and arrangement of sources, especially the way Morley often provokes readers to draw their own conclusions by putting two contradictory sources back to back. He also noted that source books are not supposed to contain complete academic debates, but should instead provide an interesting overview of the topic and encourage students to pursue further reading.

BIOGRAPHICAL AND CRITICAL SOURCES:

PERIODICALS

American Journal of Archaeology, April, 1998, J. Theodore Peña, review of *Metropolis and Hinterland: The City of Rome and the Italian Economy, 200 B.C.-A.D. 200,* pp. 451-452.
Choice, June, 1997, R. I. Curtis, review of *Metropolis and Hinterland,* p. 1718.
Classical World, May, 1998, Allen M. Ward, review of *Metropolis and Hinterland,* p. 437.
Journal of Urban History, May, 2000, Peregrine Horden, "The Abrams Test: Ancient and Medieval Cities in Recent Historiography," pp. 479-492.
Times Literary Supplement, April 28, 2000, Mary Beard, review of *Ancient History: Key Themes and Approaches,* p. 33.

OTHER

Bryn Mawr Classical Review, http://ccat.sas.upenn.edu/ (April 18, 2001), Michael Meckler, review of *Metropolis and Hinterland,* Darryl A. Phillips, review of *Ancient History.*
University of Bristol Web site, http://www.bris.ac.uk/ (August 21, 2001).*

*   *   *

MORRICE, J(ames) K(enneth) W(att) 1924-2002
(Ken Morrice)

OBITUARY NOTICE—See index for *CA* sketch: Born July 14, 1924, in Aberdeen, Scotland; died March 28, 2002, in Aberdeen, Scotland. Psychiatrist and poet. Morrice was a poet who wrote in both English and Scots and drew on his experience in psychiatry to compose his verses. After serving from 1957 to 1949 in the Royal Naval Volunteer Reserve, where he became a surgeon lieutenant, he received his D.P.M. from the University of London in 1951, and his M.D. from the University of Aberdeen in 1954. From 1956 until 1985 Morrice was a consultant psychiatrist at hospitals in Scotland and also practiced for a year in Denver, Colorado. He was also a clinical senior lecturer at the University of Aberdeen from 1968 to

1985. Morrice turned to private practice in 1985, the same year he became an honorary fellow at the University of Aberdeen, but retired in 1989. As a writer, Morrice did not release his first book of verse, *Prototype,* until he was in his forties. These and later works were characterized by their exploration of the human condition and the author's dry wit. He followed this collection with half a dozen more books, including *Relations, Twal Mile Roon, The Scampering Marmoset,* and *Selected Poems.* He also wrote two collections under the name Ken Morrice: *For All I Know* and *When Truth Is Known.*

OBITUARIES AND OTHER SOURCES:

PERIODICALS

Scotsman (Edinburgh, Scotland), April 2, 2002, p. 14.
Times (London, England), April 19, 2002.

*   *   *

MORRICE, Ken
See MORRICE, J(ames) K(enneth) W(att)

*   *   *

MORRISSEY, Mary Manin

PERSONAL: Female; divorced; children: four. *Education:* M.A. (counseling psychology). *Religion:* "New Thought."

ADDRESSES: Office—c/o Living Enrichment Center, 29500 Southwest Grahams Ferry Rd., Wilsonville, OR 97070-9516. *E-mail*—mary@lecworld.org.

CAREER: Minister, 1975—.

MEMBER: Association for Global New Thought (president, 2001—).

AWARDS, HONORS: Doctorate of Humane Letters.

WRITINGS:

Alchemy of the Heart: The Transformative Power of Everyday Life, Peanut Butter Publications (Portland, OR), 1995.

Building Your Field of Dreams, Bantam Books (New York, NY), 1996.

No Less than Greatness: Finding Perfect Love in Imperfect Relationships, Bantam Books (New York, NY), 2001.

(Editor) *New Living Begins with New Thinking: Words of Wisdom from New-Thought Ministers and Teachers on Health, Prosperity, Creativity, Relationship, and Spirituality,* Jeremy P. Tarcher/ Putnam (New York, NY), 2002.

ADAPTATIONS: Building Your Field of Dreams, a one-hour PBS documentary.

SIDELIGHTS: Author and minister Mary Manin Morrissey began a church in her living room that eventually grew to a 3,000-member "megachurch" with a ninety-five-acre property in suburban Portland, Oregon. As a teenager, she was a homecoming queen who was forced to marry at the age of sixteen, when she became pregnant. She was expelled from high school and eventually endured the near death of one of her four children, life-threatening kidney disease, poverty, and divorce. Morrissey credits her determination and her reliance on God's direction for her ability to build her popular ministry and rebuild her life.

In an interview with Linda Ross Swanson for *New Times,* Morrissey described her approach to spirituality and the theology of her Living Enrichment Center (LEC). The center is part of a larger organization called the International New Thought Alliance, which Morrissey calls an "umbrella organization" connecting New Thought churches, which also include Religious Science and Unity churches. Morrissey teaches "life-centered spirituality," which she described to Swanson as "a practical and relevant spirituality applicable to today's living." Citing the influences of life-centered spirituality, Morrissey said, "life centered spirituality combines [Meister] Eckhart's teachings with the transcendentalist teachings of both Emerson and Thoreau," calling it a way of thinking that "enables us to become conscious co-creators with God."

Morrissey's 1996 book *Building Your Field of Dreams* offers a step-by-step guide to becoming a co-creator. In it, she tells the story of her development from a frightened pregnant teenager to the minister of a church of her own creation as an example of the power of her method. She commends spiritual disciplines including tithing, and challenges readers to reflect on whether their dreams actually represent their "true calling" from a higher power. Morrissey draws from traditional Christian thought and authors including Marianne Williamson, Norman Vincent Peale, and Deepak Chopra, a mix some reviewers found effective, others a bit trite. A reviewer for *Publishers Weekly* described *Building Your Field of Dreams* as "sincere," but suggested that Morrissey "often uses tired spirituality clichés." Ilene Cooper, writing for *Booklist,* found that while there is "nothing very new" in *Building Your Field of Dreams,* "the roadmap she offers readers for their own empowerment is eminently practical" and will "speak to many."

Morrissey's next book, *No Less than Greatness: Finding Perfect Love in Imperfect Relationships,* applies the principles of her ministry—and *Building Your Field of Dreams* specifically—to personal and intimate relationships. Morrissey discusses the importance of forgiveness and generosity, and recommends practices that include visualization, journaling, affirmations, and creating daily rituals. A reviewer for *Publishers Weekly* suggested that the book is a rehash of familiar ideas, and said that "Morrissey's approach demonstrates only a superficial awareness of both psychology and crucial relationship issues." The reviewer found that *No Less than Greatness* focuses on relationship problems that "often seem trite," ignoring serious issues like addiction, poverty, and abuse. However, readers in the spirituality community responded favorably to Morrissey's approach. Frederic and Mary Ann Brussat reviewed *No Less than Greatness* for the online *Spirituality and Health,* finding that "reading this inspiring work will lift your spirit and compel you to put more time and energy into being yourself—a child of God expressing love."

In addition to writing, Morrissey is very active in her own church and in international issues. She has participated in dialogues with the Dalai Lama and other spiritual leaders, scientists, philosophers, and ecologists. As a representative of New Thought churches, she attended the 1999 Parliament of World Religions in Cape Town, South Africa. She served as the U.S. cochair for the Season for Nonviolence, an annual campaign begun in 1997 in honor of Mahatma Gandhi and Martin Luther King, Jr., and addressed the

United Nations on the campaign's behalf. She broadcasts a weekly radio show through Radio for Peace International and hosts conferences and lectures with nationally known speakers at Living Enrichment Center's Namaste Retreat Center. Speaking to Swanson in *New Times* about her hopes for the future, Morrissey said, "I think that one hundred years from now New Thought's recognition will be lost. It will naturally dissolve into what is universal spirituality honoring all paths in the presence of one God. I'd like to be remembered as one of the midwives for the new emerging spirituality of the twenty-first century, someone who helped nurture it into being."

BIOGRAPHICAL AND CRITICAL SOURCES:

PERIODICALS

Booklist, August, 1996, Ilene Cooper, review of *Building Your Field of Dreams,* p. 1860.
Publishers Weekly, June 10, 1996, review of *Building Your Field of Dreams,* p. 92; July 23, 2002, review of *No Less than Greatness: Finding Perfect Love in Imperfect Relationships,* p. 73.

OTHER

Living Enrichment Center Web site, http://www.lecworld.org/ (October 7, 2001).
New Times, http://www.newtimes.org/ (June, 1997), Linda Ross Swanson, "Listening to God's Voice, with Rev. Mary Manin Morrissey."
Spirituality and Health, http://www.spiritualityhealth.com/ (October 7, 2001), Frederic and Mary Ann Brussat, review of *No Less than Greatness.**

*   *   *

MURPHY, Francis Xavier 1914-2002
(Xavier Rynne)

OBITUARY NOTICE—See index for *CA* sketch: Born June 26, 1914, in Bronx, NY; died while suffering from Parkinson's disease and after cancer surgery, April 11, 2002, in Annapolis, MD. Priest and author. Murphy wrote more than twenty books during his career, but it was a series of articles written under the pseudonym Xavier Rynne that caught the attention of

the Vatican and indeed, the world. Murphy grew up in New York and entered the seminary when he was fourteen. In 1937 he received his bachelor's degree from St. Alphonsus and was ordained in 1940. He followed with a master's degree and doctorate from Catholic University of America in 1942 and 1944, respectively. Shortly after he became a chaplain with the U.S. Naval Academy and served there until 1947. Murphy worked in several parishes around New York and became an army chaplain in Korea, receiving a Bronze Star for offering Mass on the front lines during combat. In 1959 he became a professor of moral theology at the Vatican-affiliated Lateran University. Murphy was in Rome during the historic Second Vatican Council and began writing a series of reports on Vatican II for the *New Yorker.* The first article, "Letter from Vatican City," was published in 1962 under the name Rynne, and caused a ruckus inside and outside the church for its insider's view of the meetings and the intrigue surrounding them. *Letters from Vatican City: Vatican Council II (First Session): Background and Debates* was published in 1963. All Murphy's articles from the *New Yorker* were published in 1968 as *Vatican Council II.* Murphy was asked repeatedly if he were Xavier Rynne, but would always answer that his name was Francis Murphy, thus avoiding the question. Other books by Murphy include *A Monument to St. Jerome; Essays on Some Aspects of His Life, Works, and Influence; Moral Doctrines of the Early Church Fathers;* and *Patristic Heritage in the Renaissance and Modern Age.* After leaving Rome, Murphy returned to the United States and lectured at numerous universities, including Johns Hopkins and Seton Hall. In 1985 he became a priest at St. Mary's Catholic Church in Annapolis and St. Christopher Catholic Church on Kent Island.

OBITUARIES AND OTHER SOURCES:

PERIODICALS

Los Angeles Times, April 13, 2002, p. B18.
New York Times, April 15, 2002, p. A25.
Washington Post, April 12, 2002, p. B6.

*   *   *

MYRSIADES, Linda (Suny) 1941-

PERSONAL: Surname is pronounced "Mer-sigh-addes"; born 1941, in Philadelphia, PA; daughter of George (a businessman and conductor of Armenian music) and Arax (a homemaker; maiden name,

Kesdekian); married Kostas Myrsiades (a professor of comparative literature), June 6, 1965; children: Yani, Leni. *Education:* Beaver College, B.A., 1963; Indiana University, M.A., 1965; Athens University, certificate in modern Greek, 1966; Indiana University, Ph.D., 1973; Temple University, postgraduate study, 1986-87; Temple University School of Law, postgraduate study and guided research, 1994-95; Communications Research Associates, certified in basic mediation, 1995. *Hobbies and other interests:* Exercise, travel.

ADDRESSES: Home—370 North Malin Rd., Newtown Square, PA 19073. *Office*—529 Main Hall, English Department, West Chester University, West Chester, PA 19383. *E-mail*—lmyrsiades@wcupa.edu.

CAREER: Delaware County Community College, Media, PA, adjunct professor, 1971-78; Pierce-Deree College, Athens, Greece, adjunct professor, 1973-74; Gwynned-Mercy College, Fitzgerald-Mercy Hospital, Lansdowne, PA, 1976-78; Pennsylvania State University, Lima, PA, adjunct professor, 1977; Widener University, Chester, PA, adjunct professor, 1976-85, assistant professor, 1985-89; West Chester University, West Chester, PA, adjunct professor, 1988-90, assistant professor, 1990-95, associate professor, 1995-2000, professor, 2000—. National Endowment for the Humanities, peer review evaluator, 1996.

MEMBER: Society for the Advancement of Management, Association for Business Communication, American Comparative Literature Association, Modern Greek Studies Association, Modern Language Association.

AWARDS, HONORS: Research grant, Hellenic-American League, 1972-73; research fellowship, National Endowment for Humanities, 1981-82; RAM Award, Association of Human Resource Management and Organizational Behavior, 1987; Organizational Development Award, Association of Human Resource Management and Organizational Behavior, 1987; SSHE Award, Temple University, 1994.

WRITINGS:

The Karagiozis Heroic Performance in Greek Shadow Theater, with translations by husband, Kostas Myrsiades, University Press of New England (Hanover, NH), 1988.

Culture and Comedy in the Greek Puppet Theater, with translations by Kostas Myrsiades, University of Kentucky Press (Lexington, KY), 1992.

(Editor, with Kostas Myrsiades) *Margins in the Classroom: Teaching Literature,* University of Minneapolis Press (Minneapolis, MN), 1994.

(Editor, with Kostas Myrsiades) *Race-ing Representation: Voice, History, and Sexuality,* Rowan and Littlefield (Lanham, MD), 1998.

(Author of introduction and contributor) *Karagiozis: Three Classic Plays,* translated by Kostas Myrsiades, Pella Publishing, 1999.

Cultural Representation in Historical Resistance: Complexity and Construction in Greek Guerrilla Theater, with translations by Kostas Myrsiades, Bucknell University Press (Lewisburg, PA), 1999.

(Editor, with Kostas Myrsiades) *Un-disciplining Literature: Literature, Law, and Culture,* Peter Lang (New York, NY), 1999.

Splitting the Baby: A Cultural Study of Abortion in Literature and Law, Rhetoric and Cartoon, Peter Lang (New York, NY), 2002.

Contributor to periodicals, including *Scholars, Cultural Studies, Journal of Management Development, Journal of Modern Greek Studies, Turcica, Southern Folklore, Ellinika, College Literature, Education and Society,* and *Journal of the Hellenic Diaspora.* Associate editor, *College Literature,* 1990—.

WORK IN PROGRESS: A book on cultural constructions of the yellow fever epidemic in Philadelphia in 1793.

SIDELIGHTS: West Chester University English professor Linda Myrsiades is an authority on aspects of the relationships between language and literature, law, and culture. Working in another very different academic field, she has also teamed up with her husband, West Chester teaching colleague Kostas Myrsiades, to chronicle the history and development of Karagiozis puppetry in Greek theater during the late nineteenth and early twentieth centuries.

Assessing their collaboration, *The Karagiozis Heroic Performance on Greek Shadow Theater, Choice* reviewer C. R. Hannum wrote, "This work illuminates a corner of theater history often shadowed by neglect, particularly by implying links between classic Greek Phlyakes (farce), Greek Old Comedy, and the Karagiozis performance." Assessing the same work for *World Literature Today,* reviewer John Rexine explained, "The authors hope that their work will reinforce the now readily accepted argument that the Karagiozis theater is an integral part of Greek folk tradition."

Reviewer B. Harlow, also writing in *Choice,* noted that the book *Cultural Representation in Historical Resistance: Complexity and Construction in Greek Guerrilla Theater* "focus[es] specifically on the example of Greek guerrilla theater in the period of Greece's resistance to the Nazis during WW II." Harlow advised that the book is of interest "both as an anthology and as a contribution to the archive of 'resistance literature' and its theoretical practice."

Splitting the Baby: A Cultural Study of Abortion in Literature and Law, Rhetoric and Cartoon is, as the title suggests, a scholarly investigation of abortion in American literature, law, rhetoric and cartoons.

BIOGRAPHICAL AND CRITICAL SOURCES:

PERIODICALS

Cardozo Studies in Law and Literature, fall/winter, 2000, Marinos Diamantides, "Review Essay: the Long Way to an Un-Disciplined Literature," pp. 293-316.

Choice, February, 1989, C. R. Hannum, review of *The Karagiozis Heroic Performance in Greek Shadow Theater,* p. 952; January, 2000, B. Harlow, review of *Cultural Representation in Historical Resistance: Complexity and Construction in Greek Guerrilla Theater,* p. 926.

Journal of Modern Greek Studies, 1993, Anna Stavrakopoulou, "Karagiozis"; Volume 14, number 1, 1996, p. 123; May, 2002, Eleni Tsalia, review of *Cultural Representation in Historical Resistance and Karagiozis: Three Classic Plays,* p. 157.

Journal of the Hellenic Diaspora, 1989, John Rexine, "The Karagiozis Heroic Performance."

Reference & Research Book News, June, 1993, review of *Karagiozis: Culture and Comedy in Greek Puppet Theater,* p. 36.

Translation Review Supplement, December, 1999, review of *Complexity and Construction in Greek Guerrilla Theater,* p. 42.

World Literature Today, winter, 1989, John E. Rexine, review of *The Karagiozis Heroic Performance in Greek Shadow Theater,* p. 144.

N

NÄGELE, Rainer 1943-

PERSONAL: Born August 2, 1943, in Triesen, Liechtenstein; son of Alwin and Irma (Sele) Nägele; married Beryl Schlossman. *Education:* University of California—Santa Barbara, Ph.D.

ADDRESSES: Home—69 Penny Lane, Baltimore, MD 21209. *Office*—Department of German, Johns Hopkins University, Baltimore, MD 21218; fax: 410-516-7212. *E-mail*—rainernagele@cs.com.

CAREER: Johns Hopkins University, Baltimore, MD, professor of German, 1979—.

WRITINGS:

Reading after Freud: Essays on Goethe, Höderlin, Habermas, Nietzsche, Brecht, Celan, and Freud, Columbia University Press (New York, NY), 1987.

Theater, Theory, Speculation: Walter Benjamin and the Scenes of Modernity, Johns Hopkins University Press (Baltimore, MD), 1991.

Echoes of Translation: Reading between Texts, Johns Hopkins University Press (Baltimore, MD), 1997.

Lesarten der Moderne: Essays, Edition Isele (Eggingen, Germany), 1998.

Literarische Vexierbilder: Drei Versuche zu einer Figur (essays), Edition Isele (Eggingen, Germany), 2001.

Echos: Übersetzen; Lesen zwischen Texten, Urs Engeler Editor (Basel, Switzerland), 2002.

BIOGRAPHICAL AND CRITICAL SOURCES:

PERIODICALS

Criticism, summer, 1999, Angelika Rauch-Rapaport, review of *Echoes of Translation: Reading between Texts,* p. 409.

NAGOURNEY, Adam 1954-

PERSONAL: Born October 10, 1954, in New York, NY. *Education:* State University of New York, B.A., 1977.

ADDRESSES: Office—*New York Times,* 229 West 43rd Street, New York, NY 10036.

CAREER: Gannett Westchester Newspaper, journalist, 1977-83; *New York Daily News,* Albany bureau chief, Albany, NY, 1988-90; *USA Today,* national political correspondent, 1990-92, White House correspondent, 1993; *New York Times,* New York, NY, political correspondent, 1996—.

WRITINGS:

(Coauthor with Dudley Clendinen) *Out for Good: The Struggle to Build a Gay Rights Movement in America,* Simon & Schuster (New York, NY), 1999.

SIDELIGHTS: Adam Nagourney has worked as a journalist since graduating from the State University of New York with a degree in political economics. He worked as a national political correspondent and then as White House correspondent for *USA Today.* He joined the *New York Times* in 1996 as a political correspondent. He spent his first year there covering Bob Dole in the 1996 presidential campaign, and then covering the state and city politics in New York.

From 1994 until he joined the *New York Times* in 1996, Nagourney was working on *Out for Good: The Struggle to Build a Gay Rights Movement in America*, with coauthor Dudley Clendinen, an editorial writer for the *New York Times*. *Out for Good* is an account of the gay rights movement in the United States, beginning with the riot at Stonewall Inn, a gay bar in New York City, in June 1969 and ending with the founding of ACT UP in 1987. The coauthors gathered their information from hundreds of personal interviews and press accounts. *Nation* reviewer Martin Duberman called the book a "vivid but determinedly untheoretical history of 'the struggle to build a gay rights movement in America.'" *Library Journal*'s E. James Van Buskirk claimed, "This journalistic account engagingly weaves intimate details into the broad canvas."

BIOGRAPHICAL AND CRITICAL SOURCES:

PERIODICALS

Atlanta Journal-Constitution, June 13, 1999, Shane Harrison, "*Out for Good* Ably Traces Gay Rights Drive," p. L13.

Booklist, June 1, 1999, Brad Hooper, review of *Out for Good: The Struggle to Build a Gay Rights Movement in America,* p. 1782.

Lambda Book Report, July-August, 1999, Bob Summer, review of *Out for Good,* p. 29.

Library Journal, June 15, 1999, E. James Van Buskirk, review of *Out for Good,* p. 94.

Nation, June 14, 1999, Martin Duberman, "Uncloseted History," p. 51.

Publishers Weekly, April 12, 1999, review of *Out for Good,* p. 60.

OTHER

BookPage, http://www.bookpage.com/ (December 31, 2001), Connie Miller, review of *Out for Good.*

365 Gay, http://www.365gay.com/ (December 31, 2001), Robb Michaels, review of *Out for Good.*

New York Times on the Web, http://www.nytimes.com/ (January 8, 2002), David J. Garrow, "Slamming the Closet Door," "Adam Nagourney, Political Correspondent."*

NAHAI, Gina Barkhordar 1961(?)-

PERSONAL: Born c. 1961, in Iran. *Education:* University of California—Los Angeles, M.A. (international relations); University of Southern California, M.F.A., 1988. *Religion:* Jewish.

ADDRESSES: Home—Beverly Hills, CA. *Agent*—Lowenstein Associates Inc., 121 West 27th St., Suite 601, New York, NY 10001.

CAREER: Novelist. Adjunct professor in master's writing programs, University of Southern California and University of California at Los Angeles; consultant in Iranian affairs for RAND Corporation.

WRITINGS:

Cry of the Peacock, Simon & Schuster (New York, NY), 1991.

Moonlight on the Avenue of Faith, Washington Square Press (New York, NY), 2000, Persian translation by the author published as *Mahtab dar kuchah-i Sidaqat,* Intisharat-i Dawr-i Dunya (Tehran, Iran), 2000.

Sunday's Silence, Harcourt (New York, NY), 2001.

SIDELIGHTS: Cry of the Peacock, Gina Nahai's first novel, tells the story of Iran over the last two hundred years. Most of the story focuses on the Iranian Jews, the oldest Jewish community still in existence. These Jews have been there, hardly noticed by the outside world, for over twenty-five hundred years. Nahai devoted eight years to the project. As the author commented in an interview posted on the *University of Southern California Professional Writers Degree Program Web site,* "Part of that was there was nothing written about Iranian Jews in any language, anywhere—nothing substantial. So it was hard to gather the needed information."

Cry of the Peacock begins with its protagonist, an Iranian-Jewish woman named Peacock, incarcerated in a women's prison in post-revolutionary Iran. The preceding two hundred years of history of Peacock's family and, by extension, of the Iranian-Jewish community, is then told through flashbacks interwoven with discussions of Iranian history. Nasrin Rahimieh, writing in *World Literature Today,* praised Nahai's technique, noting that "The novel not only brings to light the suppressed history of the Iranian Jews, but it does so by reclaiming a historical space they have traditionally been denied." Sharon Dirlam commented in the *Los Angeles Times Book Review* that the novel "rings with truth, but it's also a spellbinding story that's hard to put down."

Nahai's second novel, *Moonlight on the Avenue of Faith,* begins in the Jewish ghetto in Tehran during the reign of the Shah. In the tradition of magic realist fiction, extraordinary and unbelievable thing happen to ordinary people. When the oppressed Roxanna's mother finds feathers in her daughter's bed and tries to push her off a roof, Roxanna's invisible wings save her. After fleeing her home and taking up with an aging courtesan known as Alexandra the Cat, Roxanna inadvertently casts a spell on her future husband, Sohrab, who finds her wandering the streets and takes her back to his house on the Avenue of Faith. Treated cruelly by the women of her husband's family, Roxanna mysteriously disappears, leaving behind a daughter, Lili. The rest of the novel focuses on Lili, who with the rest of the family ends up in California after the Iranian revolution. Edward Hower, reviewing the book for the *New York Times,* characterized Nahai as "a skilled and inventive writer" and praised her characters, especially Lili's aunt, Miriam, "an endearingly earthy woman who often embarrasses her pretentious relatives—on a shopping trip in Los Angeles, for example, when she fingers expensive clothes 'as if she were buying live sheep.'"

After her two novels set in Iran, Nahai set *Sunday's Silence* in Appalachia, a place described by a *Publishers Weekly* contributor as "another region whose people seem to be united by a fundamentalist faith, their beliefs as exotic to, and misunderstood by most Western readers as those of the people of Iran." The story centers on Adam, the bastard son of a snake-handling preacher. Adam has become a foreign correspondent in Beirut and has spent twenty years trying to distance himself from his origins. When he returns to Tennessee following his father's death, he becomes passionately involved with a Kurdish immigrant woman who may have had a hand in his father's demise. "One of the things that strikes me when I talk about my first book," Nahai commented in an interview on the web site of the Professional Writers Program at USC, "[is that] everyone always says, oh, my God, all

this stuff happened in Iran or the Middle East, how outrageous, or how violent or backwards. But I always say if you just look around the corner, you see the same kinds of things happening right here in the most developed country in the world. . . . Human reactions are strange and unpredictable all over the world, not just in some Middle Eastern country."

BIOGRAPHICAL AND CRITICAL SOURCES:

PERIODICALS

Booklist, February 15, 1999, Bonnie Johnson, review of *Moonlight on the Avenue of Faith,* p. 69; November 1, 2001, Joanne Wilkinson, review of *Sunday's Silence,* p. 460.

Kirkus Reviews, September 15, 2001, review of *Sunday's Silence,* p. 1318.

Library Journal, April 15, 1991, Andrea Caron Kempf, review of *Cry of the Peacock,* p. 123; February 15, 1999, Janet Ingraham Dwyer, review of *Moonlight on the Avenue of Faith,* p. 184; October 15, 2001, Reba Leiding, review of *Sunday's Silence,* p. 109.

Los Angeles Magazine, November, 2001, Robert Ito, review of *Sunday's Silence,* p. 136.

Los Angeles Times Book Review, July 28, 1991, Sharon Dirlam, review of *Cry of the Peacock,* p. 6.

New York Times, May 30, 1999, Edward Hower, review of *Moonlight on the Avenue of Faith,* p. 19.

People Weekly, December 10, 2001, review of *Sunday's Silence,* p. 49.

Publishers Weekly, March 29, 1991, review of *Cry of the Peacock,* p. 79; January 4, 1999, review of *Moonlight on the Avenue of Faith,* p. 69.

School Library Journal, November, 1991, Diane Goheen, review of *Cry of the Peacock,* p. 159.

World Literature Today, spring, 1992, Nasrin Rahimieh, review of *Cry of the Peacock,* p. 396.

OTHER

Book Sense, http://www.booksense.com/ (January 13, 2003), Gavin J. Grant, interview with Gina Nahai.

Jewish Journal of Greater Los Angeles, http://www.jewishjournal.com/ (January 27, 2003), "Doctors, Lawyers, and Other Jewish Women."

University of Southern California Professional Writers Degree Program Web site, http://www.usc.edu/dept/LAS/mpw/ (January 13, 2003), interview with Gina Nahai.*

*   *   *

NICHOLS, Mike 1931-

PERSONAL: Original name, Michael Igor Peschkowsky; surname legally changed, 1939; born November 6, 1931, in Berlin, Germany; became naturalized U.S. citizen, 1944; son of Nicholaievitch (a physician) and Brigitte (Landauer) Peschkowsky; married Patricia Scott (a singer), 1957 (divorced 1960); married Margot Callas, 1963 (divorced 1974); married Annabel Davis-Goff (a screenwriter) (divorced); married Diane Sawyer (a television journalist), April 29, 1988; children: (first marriage) Daisy; (third marriage) Max, Jenny. *Education:* Attended University of Chicago, 1950-53; trained for the stage with Lee Strasberg, 1954. *Hobbies and other interests:* Breeding Arabian horses.

ADDRESSES: Office—Icarus Productions. *Agent*—Creative Artists Agency, 9830 Wilshire Blvd., Beverly Hills, CA 90212.

CAREER: Actor, stage and film director, producer, and writer. Playwrights Theatre Club (improvisational theatrical company, later became Compass Players and then Second City), Chicago, IL, founder and member, 1955-57; performer (with Elaine May) in an improvisational comedy act, appearing in nightclubs and cabarets throughout the United States, 1957-61. Producer and director of plays and films; producer and director of television series, specials, and movies, including *The "Annie" Christmas Show,* 1977, *Family,* 1976-80, *The Gin Game,* 1981, *The Thorns,* 1988, and *Working Girl,* 1990. Appearances on television programs include *Jack Paar Presents, The Nineteenth Annual Tony Awards, The Fourteenth Annual Kennedy Center Honors, American Masters, The American Film Institute Salute to Jack Nicholson,* and *Nichols and May—Take Two.*

Director of motion pictures, including *Who's Afraid of Virginia Woolf?,* Warner Brothers, 1966, *Catch-22,* Filmways, 1970, *The Day of the Dolphin,* Avco-Embassy, 1973, *Gilda Live,* Warner Brothers, 1980, *Biloxi Blues* (also known as *Neil Simon's Biloxi Blues*), Universal, 1988, *Working Girl,* Twentieth Century-Fox, 1988, and *Wolf,* Columbia, 1994. Director and producer of motion pictures, including *The Graduate,* Embassy, 1967, *Carnal Knowledge,* Avco-Embassy, 1971, *The Birdcage* (also known as *La Cage aux folles*), Metro-Goldwyn-Mayer/United Artists, 1996, *Primary Colors,* First Look Pictures, 1997, *The Designated Mourner,* First Look Pictures, 1997, *What Planet Are You From?,* Columbia/Tristar, 2000, *All the Pretty Horses,* Columbia/Tristar, 2000, and *Wit,* HBO Studios, 2001. Executive producer of *The Longshot,* Orion, 1986. Director and producer of films, including (with Don Devlin) *The Fortune* (also known as *Spite and Malice*), Columbia, 1975; (with Michael Hausman) *Silkwood,* Twentieth Century-Fox, 1983; (with Robert Greenhut) *Heartburn,* Paramount, 1986; (with John Calley) *Postcards from the Edge,* Columbia, 1990; and (with Scott Rudin) *Regarding Henry,* Paramount, 1991. Producer, with John Calley and Ismail Merchant, of *The Remains of the Day,* Columbia, 1993.

Director of plays, including *Barefoot in the Park,* produced at Biltmore Theatre, New York, NY, 1963, *The Knack,* produced at New Theatre, New York, NY, 1964; *Luv,* produced at Booth Theatre, New York, NY, 1964; *The Odd Couple,* produced at Plymouth Theatre, New York, NY, 1965; *The Apple Tree,* produced at Shubert Theatre, New York, NY, 1966; *The Little Foxes,* produced at Vivian Beaumont Theatre, New York, NY, 1967; *Plaza Suite,* produced at Plymouth Theatre, New York, NY, 1968; *The Prisoner of Second Avenue,* produced at Eugene O'Neill Theatre, New York, NY, 1971; *Uncle Vanya,* produced at Circle in the Square/Joseph E. Levine Theatre, New York, NY, 1973; *Comedians,* produced at Music Box Theatre, New York, NY, 1976; *Streamers,* produced at New York Shakespeare Festival, Mitzi E. Newhouse Theatre, New York, NY, 1976; (and producer, with Hume Cronym) *The Gin Game,* produced at Long Wharf Theatre, New Haven, CT, then John Golden Theatre, New York, NY, 1977; *Drinks before Dinner,* produced at New York Shakespeare Festival, Public Theatre, New York, NY, 1978; *Who's Afraid of Virginia Woolf?,* produced at Long Wharf Theatre, New Haven, CT, 1980, *Lunch Hour,* produced at Ethel Barrymore Theatre, New York, NY, 1980, *Fools,* produced at Eugene O'Neill Theatre, New York, NY, 1981; *The Real Thing,* produced at Plymouth Theatre, New York, NY, 1984, *Hurlyburly,* produced at Goodman Theatre,

Chicago, IL, then Promenade Theatre, New York, NY, 1984; *Social Security,* produced at Ethel Barrymore Theatre, New York, NY, 1986; *Standup Shakespeare,* produced at Theatre 890, New York, NY, 1987; *Waiting for Godot,* produced at Mitzi E. Newhouse Theatre, New York, NY, 1988; *Elliot Loves,* produced at Goodman Theatre, Chicago, IL, then Promenade Theatre, New York, NY, 1990, and *Death and the Maiden,* produced at Brooks Atkinson Theatre, New York, NY, 1992.

Also directed *The Importance of Being Earnest,* Vancouver, British Columbia, Canada. Directed and produced several play tours as well as stage and film productions. Acted in *An Evening with Mike Nichols and Elaine May,* 1960, *A Matter of Position,* 1962, *Who's Afraid of Virginia Woolf?,* 1980, and *The Designated Mourner,* 1996.

MEMBER: Actors' Equity Association, American Federation of Television and Radio Artists, Society of Stage Directors and Choreographers, Screen Actors Guild, American Guild of Variety Artists, Writers Guild of America.

AWARDS, HONORS: Grammy Award, best comedy recording, National Academy of Recording Arts and Sciences, 1961, for *An Evening with Mike Nichols and Elaine May*; Emmy Award, Academy of Television Arts and Sciences, c. 1962, for *Julie and Carol at Carnegie Hall*; Antoinette Perry ("Tony") Award, best director, 1964, for *Barefoot in the Park*; Tony Award and *Variety*-New York Critics' Poll Award, both for best director, both 1965, both for *The Odd Couple* and *Luv*; Outer Critics' Circle Award, 1965, for directing four current hits; Sam S. Shubert Foundation Award, 1965, for outstanding contributions to the New York legitimate theater for the 1964-65 season; *Cue* magazine award, 1965, entertainer of the year for directorial achievements; Famous Fives Poll, outstanding director, Academy Award nomination, best director, British Academy of Film and Television Arts Award, best film from any source, and Golden Globe Award nomination, best motion picture director, all 1966, all for *Who's Afraid of Virginia Woolf?*; Academy Award, best director, New York Film Critics' Award, best director, and Directors Guild of America Award, outstanding directorial achievement, all 1967, all for *The Graduate*; Golden Globe Award, best motion picture director, Hollywood Foreign Press Association,

and British Academy of Film and Television Arts award, best film director, all 1968, all for *The Graduate*; Tony Award, best director, 1968, for *Plaza Suite*; Tony Award, best director, 1972, for *The Prisoner of Second Avenue*; Tony Award nomination, best director of a drama, 1974, for *Uncle Vanya*; Tony Award nomination, best director of a play, 1977, for *Comedians and Streamers*; Tony Award (shared), best musical, 1977, for *Annie*; Tony Award nomination, best director of a play, 1978, for *The Gin Game*; Academy Award nomination, best director, and Golden Globe Award nomination, best director, both 1983, both for *Silkwood*; Tony Award, best director of a play, 1984, for *The Real Thing*; Ellis Island Medal of Honor, National Ethnic Coalition of Organizations, 1986; Academy Award nomination, best director, and Golden Globe Award nomination, best director, both 1988, both for *Working Girl*; Academy Award nomination, best picture, 1993, and British Academy of Film and Television Arts Award nomination, best film, 1994, both for *The Remains of the Day*; Film Society of Lincoln Center, Lifetime Achievement Award, 1999; Directors Guild of America, national honoree, 2000.

WRITINGS:

(With Ken Welch) *Julie and Carol at Carnegie Hall* (TV special), CBS, 1962.
(Author of special material for the stage production) *The Carol Burnett Show,* produced at Greek Theatre, Los Angeles, CA, 1966.
(Adapter for the stage production, with Albert Todd) *Uncle Vanya,* produced at Circle in the Square/ Joseph E. Levine Theatre, New York, NY, 1973.

SIDELIGHTS: Mike Nichols was born Michael Igor Peschkowsky in 1931. After immigrating to the United States from Germany, his father, Nicholaievitch Peschkowsky, legally changed the family name to Nichols, and his own first name to Paul. By 1939 Mike Nichols and his younger brother had joined their father in New York City. Paul Nichols, a physician, died a few years later, leaving his wife to raise their two sons alone. In 1944 Nichols became a naturalized U.S. citizen.

Nichols enrolled in a premedicine program at the University of Chicago but soon found himself interested in the theater. He moved back to New York, where he studied acting with Lee Strasberg for nearly two years. After returning to Chicago, he joined the Compass Players, later to be known as Second City, and began working with Elaine May.

Nichols and May developed and performed comedic routines that impressed audiences seeking satire. After performing to sell-out audiences in New York City, they reached Broadway. The award-winning *An Evening with Mike Nichols and Elaine May* ran from 1960 to 1961. Shortly thereafter, Nichols appeared in a play, and the comic duo split up. At a friend's suggestion, Nichols made a career change and directed his first play, Neil Simon's *Barefoot in the Park, The Odd Couple* and *Luv.* All three plays garnered directing awards for Nichols.

Nichols then turned his attention to filmmaking. He received critical acclaim for directing *Who's Afraid of Virginia Woolf?.* The award-winning film *The Graduate* quickly followed this success. Of his concept and creative process in *The Graduate,* Nichols once commented to interviewer Gavin Smith in *Film Comment,* "I can love a piece of material, but [not] know for some time whether I see it as a movie, whether I literally see things that'll be a movie. When I begin to see those things, it's always a moment or a scene that is the hook that pulls me into it. Sometimes it becomes so specific that the movie in the end is very much what I saw in the beginning. That's certainly true of *The Graduate, Virginia Woolf, Carnal Knowledge.*" After directing *Carnal Knowledge,* a film about men's views of women, Nichols directed two more films, *Day of the Dolphin* and *The Fortune.* Nichols then took a seven-year break from directing motion pictures.

Nichols was hardly idle during that hiatus. He returned to the theater to direct the plays *Plaza Suite* and *The Prisoner of Second Avenue,* both of which received Tony Awards. By the mid-1970s, however, even the theater work seemed to lessen in importance. He turned to television for a time and became the executive producer of *Family.* By the late 1970s Nichols had returned to Broadway to produce the musical *Annie,* a production that earned another Tony Award. In the 1980s Nichols was active in both theater and television but returned to filmmaking with *Silkwood,* a controversial, fact-based story about a plutonium plant employee, Karen Silkwood, who died under suspicious circumstances en route to speak to a union representative about dangerous conditions at the plant.

Nichols commented to Smith that *Silkwood* "was so much about people who don't spend a lot of time talking about relationships, talking about what's wrong, so that there was a constant obbligato, a kink of underside of what's really happening between the people. And that's what I liked about working on it, that what is going on between the people is still quite visible even when they don't talk about it. It's also what drew me to the theater to begin with. You find ways to express the underneath without words; sometimes it's the opposite of the words, or a tangent of the words. I think *Silkwood* has a lot of those things—unexpressed undercurrents that are palpable." Nichols went on to make two more movies during the 1980s, *Heartburn* and *Biloxi Blues.*

After coping with some health concerns and marriage problems, Nichols divorced, then married television journalist Diane Sawyer. Nichols was soon back at work. He directed a stage production of Beckett's *Waiting for Godot* as well as a string of successful films, including *Working Girl, Postcards from the Edge,* and *Regarding Henry.* By the mid-1980s Nichols was directing Jack Nicholson in another controversial movie, *Wolf.* Richard Schickel, writing in *Time,* called *Wolf* "a genre movie for grownups." Schickel commented, "There is a well-measured sense of pity for Will [the protagonist]. You could . . . find in him a symbol for all kinds of human bedevilment." Henry Sheehan, writing in *Knight-Ridder/Tribune News Service,* noted that, "while Nichols knew he was dealing in pure fantasy, he also wanted to treat that fantasy in a subtly realistic way."

Two years later *The Birdcage,* a remake of the French farce *La Cage aux folles,* was released. Elaine May wrote the script, and Nichols directed. David Ansen, writing in *Newsweek,* stated, "The movie's method and its message, are as old as comedy itself, as the lords of misrule rout the spoilsports who would try to legislate love." Owen Gleiberman, reviewing the film for *Entertainment Weekly,* noted, "*The Birdcage* is an enchantingly witty and humane entertainment . . . that actually improves upon its source." Tom Gliatto, reviewing *The Birdcage* in *People,* called the film "a dextrous remake." Guy Flatley, writing in *Cosmopolitan,* remarked, "In its farcically subversive way, this lark has more to say about true family values than a stadium-full of fiery born-again orators."

The next May and Nichols collaboration was *Primary Colors.* Stuart Klawans, writing in *Nation,* stated, "If you look at *Primary Colors* as allegory, you will find it corresponds all too closely with political life as we know it." A reviewer in *Maclean's* observed, "We end up caring about these political lives more than we care to admit. And in the final analysis, the movie embraces moral ambiguity with a poignantly tortured liberalism." Lisa Schwarzbaum, writing in *Entertainment Weekly,* called the movie a "witty diversion." David Ansen, reviewing it in *Newsweek,* said, "Mike Nichols's *Primary Colors* isn't a vulgar take on today's headlines— it's complex, funny and sad." Todd McCarthy, writing in *Variety,* described the film as a "modern immorality tale with a keen, observant edge."

Nichols has also directed *What Planet Are You From?* and produced the films *All the Pretty Horses,* and *Wit,* the latter based on Margaret Edson's 1997 Pulitzer Prize-winning play of the same name.

BIOGRAPHICAL AND CRITICAL SOURCES:

BOOKS

Contemporary Theatre, Film, and Television, Volume 28, Gale (Detroit, MI), 2002.
Encyclopedia of World Biography Supplement, Volume 20, Gale (Detroit, MI), 2001.

PERIODICALS

Back Stage, April 3, 1992, Martin Schaeffer, review of *Death and the Maiden,* p. 40; December 1, 2000, Mike Salinas, "DGA Announces Honorees for 2000," p. 6.
Cosmopolitan, May, 1996, Guy Flatley, review of *The Birdcage,* p. 28.
Entertainment Weekly, October 23, 1992, Ty Burr, review of *The Graduate,* p. 68; March 15, 1996; Owen Gleiberman, review of *The Birdcage,* p. 44; March 27, 1998; Lisa Schwarzbaum, review of *Primary Colors,* p. 44; March 10, 2000; Owen Gleiberman, "Cosmos Guy: As the Horny Alien of *What Planet Are You From?, Garry Shandling Really Has a Rocket in His Pocket,*" p. 46.
Film Comment, May, 1999, Gavin Smith, "Mike Nichols," p. 10.
Interview, April, 1998, Brendan Lemon, "Nichols and . . . Timing," p. 102; March, 2000, Elizabeth Richardson, review of *What Planet Are You From?,* p. 110.

Knight-Ridder/Tribune News Service, June 17, 1994, Henry Sheehan, "*Wolf* Director Brings Different Sensibility to the Horror-Movie Genre," p. 617; March 14, 1996, Mal Vincent, "Director and Stars Talk about Making Hit Comedy *The Birdcage,*" p. 314.
Los Angeles Magazine, July, 1994, Rod Lurie, review of *Wolf,* p. 143.
Maclean's, March 30, 1998, "The Presidential Hustle: *Primary Colors,*" p. 62.
Nation, April 27, 1998, Stuart Klawans, review of *Primary Colors,* p. 35.
National Catholic Reporter, April 26, 1996, Joseph Cunneen, review of *The Birdcage,* p. 10.
New Republic, March 24, 1997, Stanley Kauffmann, review of *The Designated Mourner,* p. 28.
Newsweek, March 18, 1996, David Ansen, review of *The Birdcage,* p. 71; May 6, 1996, Jack Knoll, "Why Mike Nichols Is Working without a Net: The Brilliant Director Is Taking a Risky Turn on the London Stage in a Dark Wallace Shaw Play," p. 84; March 23, 1998, David Ansen, review of *Primary Colors,* p. 63; March 6, 2000, David Ansen, "Lover from Another Planet: Shandling Is from Mars, Women Are from Venus," p. 68.
People, March 11, 1996, Tom Gliatto, review of *The Birdcage,* p. 19.
Time, July 15, 1991, Richard Corliss, review of *Regarding Henry,* p. 72;
June 20, 1994, Richard Schickel, review of *Wolf,* p. 62.
Variety, March 16, 1998, Todd McCarthy, review of *Primary Colors,* p. 63; May 10, 1999, Peter Bart, "Gotham's Guiding Light," p. 4; February 19, 2001, Eddie Cockrell, review of *Wit,* p. 39; June 18, 2001, Todd McCarthy, review of *Catch-22,* p. 18.*

*   *   *

NIVEN, Larry
   See NIVEN, Laurence Van Cott

*   *   *

NIVEN, Laurence Van Cott 1938-
  (Larry Niven)

PERSONAL: Born April 30, 1938, in Los Angeles, CA; son of Waldemar Van Cott (a lawyer) and Lucy Estelle (Doheny) Niven; married Marilyn Joyce Wiso-

Larry Niven

waty, September 6, 1969. *Education:* Attended California Institute of Technology, 1956-58; Washburn University of Topeka, A.B., 1962; attended graduate courses at University of California—Los Angeles, 1962-63. *Politics:* Libertarian. *Hobbies and other interests:* Science-fiction conventions, computer games, folk singing.

ADDRESSES: Home and office—11874 Macoda Lane, Chatsworth, CA 91311.

CAREER: Writer, 1964—. Co-founder, Citizen's Advisory Council for a National Space Policy.

MEMBER: Science Fiction Writers of America, Los Angeles Science Fantasy Society.

AWARDS, HONORS: Hugo Awards, World Science Fiction Convention, 1967, for story "Neutron Star," 1971, for *Ringworld,* 1972, for story "Inconstant Moon," 1975, for story "The Hole Man," and 1976, for novelette "The Borderland of Sol"; Nebula Award, Science Fiction Writers of America, 1970, and Ditmar Award, 1972, both for *Ringworld;* E. E. Smith Memo-

rial Award, 1978; Japanese fiction awards for *Ringworld* and "Inconstant Moon," both 1979; Inkpot Award, San Diego Comics Convention, 1979; L.L.D., Washburn University of Topeka, 1984.

WRITINGS:

"KNOWN SPACE" NOVELS; AS LARRY NIVEN

World of Ptavvs, Ballantine (New York, NY), 1966.
A Gift from Earth, Ballantine (New York, NY), 1968.
Protector, Ballantine (New York, NY), 1973.
A World out of Time, Holt (New York, NY), 1976.
Three Books of Known Space (includes *World of Ptavvs, A Gift from Earth,* and short stories), Ballantine (New York, NY), 1996.
Destiny's Road, TOR Books (New York, NY), 1997.

"MAN-KZIN WARS" SERIES; AND EDITOR, AS LARRY NIVEN

(With Poul Anderson and Dean Ing) *The Man-Kzin Wars,* Baen Books (New York, NY), 1988.
(With Dean Ing and S. M. Stirling) *Man-Kzin Wars II,* Baen Books (Riverdale, NY), 1989.
(With others) *Man-Kzin Wars III,* Baen Books (Riverdale, NY), 1990.
(With others) *Man-Kzin Wars IV,* Baen Books (Riverdale, NY), 1991.
(With others) *Man-Kzin Wars V,* Baen Books (Riverdale, NY), 1992.
(With others) *Man-Kzin Wars VI,* Baen Books (Riverdale, NY), 1994.
(With others) *Man-Kzin Wars VII,* Baen Books (Riverdale, NY), 1995.
(With others) *The Best of All Possible Wars: The Best of the Man-Kzin Wars,* Baen Books (Riverdale, NY), 1998.
(With others) *Man-Kzin Wars IX,* Baen Books (Riverdale, NY), 2002.

"RINGWORLD" SERIES; AS LARRY NIVEN

Ringworld, Ballantine (New York, NY), 1970.
The Ringworld Engineers, Holt (New York, NY), 1980.
The Ringworld Throne, Ballantine (New York, NY), 1996.
Ringworld's Children, Tor (New York, NY), 2004.

"INTEGRAL TREES" SERIES; AS LARRY NIVEN

The Integral Trees, Ballantine (New York, NY), 1984.
The Smoke Ring, Ballantine (New York, NY), 1987.
Ghost Ships, in press.

"GIL HAMILTON" SERIES; AS LARRY NIVEN

The Long ARM of Gil Hamilton, Ballantine (New York, NY), 1976.
The Patchwork Girl, Ace Books (New York, NY), 1979.
Flatlander, Del Rey (New York, NY), 1995.

COLLABORATIONS; AS LARRY NIVEN

(With David Gerrold) *The Flying Sorcerers* ("Svetz" series), Ballantine (New York, NY), 1971.
(With Jerry Pournelle) *The Mote in God's Eye,* Simon & Schuster (New York, NY), 1974.
(With Jerry Pournelle) *Inferno,* Pocket Books (New York, NY), 1976.
(With Jerry Pournelle) *Lucifer's Hammer,* Playboy Press (Chicago, IL), 1977, reprinted, Ballantine (New York, NY), 1998.
(With Steven Barnes) *Dream Park,* Ace Books (New York, NY), 1981.
(With Jerry Pournelle) *Oath of Fealty,* Simon & Schuster (New York, NY), 1981.
(With Steven Barnes) *The Descent of Anansi,* Pinnacle Books (New York, NY), 1982.
(With Jerry Pournelle) *Footfall,* Ballantine (New York, NY), 1985.
(With Steven Barnes and Jerry Pournelle) *The Legacy of Heorot,* Simon & Schuster (New York, NY), 1987.
(With Steven Barnes) *Dream Park II: The Barsoom Project,* Ace Books (New York, NY) , 1989.
(With Steven Barnes) *Achilles' Choice,* illustrated by Boris Vallejo, Tor Books (New York, NY), 1991.
(With Jerry Pournelle and Michael Flynn) *Fallen Angels,* Baen Books (Riverdale, NY), 1991.
(With Steven Barnes) *The California Voodoo Game,* Ballantine (New York, NY), 1992.
(With John Byrne) *Green Lantern: Ganthet's Tale,* DC Comics (New York, NY), 1992.
(With Jerry Pournelle) *The Gripping Hand* (sequel to *The Mote in God's Eye*), Pocket Books (New York, NY), 1993.

(With Jerry Pournelle and Steven Barnes) *Beowulf's Children,* Tor Books (New York, NY), 1995.
(With Jerry Pournelle) *The Burning City,* Pocket Books (New York, NY), 2000.
(With Steven Barnes) *Saturn's Race,* Tor Books (New York, NY), 2000.

STORY COLLECTIONS; AS LARRY NIVEN

Neutron Star, Ballantine (New York, NY), 1968.
The Shape of Space, Ballantine (New York, NY), 1969.
All the Myriad Ways, Ballantine (New York, NY), 1971.
The Flight of the Horse, Ballantine (New York, NY), 1973.
Inconstant Moon, Gollancz (London, England), 1973.
A Hole in Space, Ballantine (New York, NY), 1974.
Tales of Known Space, Ballantine (New York, NY), 1975.
The Magic Goes Away, Ace Books (New York, NY), 1978.
Convergent Series, Ballantine (New York, NY), 1979.
Niven's Laws, Owlswick Press (Philadelphia, PA), 1984.
The Time of the Warlock, SteelDragon (Minneapolis, MN), 1984.
Limits, Ballantine (New York, NY), 1985.
N-Space, Tor Books (New York, NY), 1990.
Playgrounds of the Mind, Tor Books (New York, NY), 1991.
Crashlander, Ballantine (New York, NY), 1994.

OTHER; AS LARRY NIVEN

(Editor) *The Magic May Return,* Ace Books (New York, NY), 1981.
(Editor) *More Magic,* Berkley Publishing (New York, NY), 1984.
(Editor) *Alien Sex: Nineteen Tales by the Masters of Science Fiction and Dark Fantasy,* Dutton (New York, NY), 1992.
Rainbow Mars ("Svetz" series), Tor Books (New York, NY), 1999.

Also contributor to books, including *Dangerous Visions: Thirty-three Original Stories,* edited by Harlan Ellison, Doubleday (New York, NY), 1967; *The Craft of Science Fiction,* edited by Reginald Bretnor, Harper (New York, NY), 1976; and other anthologies.

Contributor of short stories to periodicals, including *Magazine of Fantasy and Science Fiction, Galaxy, Playboy,* and others.

SIDELIGHTS: "There is a certain type of science fiction story that is completely incomprehensible to the non-SF reader," Gerald Jonas wrote in the *New York Times Book Review.* "Devotees know it as the 'hard science' story. . . . [They] recognize Larry Niven as one of the masters of this rather specialized subgenre." Niven's novels are speculations about the technologies of the future, but his speculations closely follow current trends in scientific research to their logical, if optimistic, conclusions. According to Raymond J. Wilson writing in the *Dictionary of Literary Biography,* "much of Larry Niven's fiction reveals a love affair with technology. Niven's pro-technology heroes take the positive position that the problems raised by technology can be solved and are, in any case, a small price to pay for the benefits of technological advance." Niven's heavy emphasis on science is acknowledged by the author himself. Speaking to Jeffrey Elliot in *Science Fiction Review,* Niven explained: "I wait for the scientists' [research] results and then write stories about them. . . . I try to make my stories as technically accurate as possible."

Born in Los Angeles, Niven was raised in Beverly Hills and attended school both there and at the Cate School in Carpinteria. He graduated in mathematics from Washburn University in Kansas and did a year of graduate work in math at the University of California at Los Angeles before he decided to devote all his time to writing. By 1964 he had sold his first story, "The Coldest Place," to *Worlds of If.* Two years later he turned another short story into his first published novel, *World of Ptavvs,* the book which initiated his "Known Space" series. In *World of Ptavvs,* the planet Thrintun wants to enslave all other races through their power of mind control. The "ptavv" in the title is their word for slave, and that is the plan for the planet Earth: to create a world of slaves. Kzanol is the alien representative marooned on Earth, and his human opposite is Larry Greenberg, who executes a memory transfer with the Thrintun alien. According to Wilson, "The novel's success lies in its differentiation of human and alien perspectives."

In his Hugo and Nebula award-winning book *Ringworld* and its sequel, *The Ringworld Engineers,* Niven creates an artificial planet shaped like a giant ring. It

has a diameter of 190 million miles, and is built in orbit around a sun. Along its outer edge is a range of thousand-mile-high mountains, which keeps the atmosphere from spinning off as the planet rotates. The top surface of Ringworld—an area three million times larger than the surface of the Earth—has been terraformed to sustain life, while the underside is made of an incredibly strong material. Between Ringworld and the sun are a series of orbiting screens which serve to block sunlight at regular intervals to simulate night and day. The planet is, Bud Foote wrote in the *Detroit News,* the "greatest of fictional artifacts."

Ringworld is based on speculations first made by prominent physicist Freeman Dyson that in time humanity will acquire the necessary technology to convert the gaseous planets of the solar system into heavier elements and use this material to construct a string of artificial planets in Earth's orbit. This project would provide mankind with more room for its expanding population. While strictly adhering to scientific possibility, Niven's *Ringworld* takes Dyson's idea a step further, envisioning a single huge planet rather than many smaller ones. As Niven states in *The Ringworld Engineers,* Dyson "has no trouble believing in Ringworld."

By the time *Ringworld* and *The Ringworld Engineers* take place, the builders of the planet are long dead, and Ringworld is populated by barbarian descendants of the builders who no longer understand the advanced technology which created their world. Because of the immense space available on the planet, an area impossible for any human to explore in a lifetime, a wide variety of races and cultures have evolved.

In both books, this immense diversity is lavishly presented. In *Ringworld* a human expedition crash-lands on the planet and is forced to journey across its width to safety, encountering many different peoples along the way. In *The Ringworld Engineers* some stabilizer rockets which keep the planet in proper orbit have been removed by a culture using them to power their spaceships. An Earthling and an alien set out to find the repair center of Ringworld so they can make the repairs needed to get the planet back in orbit again. Their search takes them through a host of cultures. Reviewing *The Ringworld Engineers,* Galen Strawson of the *Times Literary Supplement* stated that "the book is alive with detail. There is *rishathra,* sex between species; there are silver-haired vampires with supercharged pheromones; there are shadow farms and flying cities, quantities of different social forms and incompatible social *mores*. Faults of construction cease to matter in the steady stream of invention. This is in part a guidebook to (a minute fragment of) the Ringworld."

Niven did not originally intended to write a sequel to *Ringworld*, but the amount of interest science-fiction readers showed in his award-winning novel—and certain technical questions they raised—eventually convinced him to write *The Ringworld Engineers*. Besides explaining a few engineering details about the planet's construction, *The Ringworld Engineers* also includes new ideas suggested by Niven's readers. As Strawson explained, Niven wrote the book "partly to answer questions and partly to incorporate details not of his own imagining." Because of this, Strawson saw a problem in the novel's structure. "The incidents [in *The Ringworld Engineers*] often seem set up to provide frames for the imparting of information about Ringworld's construction; so that although they are individually well conceived and executed, and jointly testify to Niven's remarkable powers of imagination, they fail to develop smoothly into one another."

Despite some criticism, the "Ringworld" books have proven enormously popular, and Niven has written a third book in the series. In *The Ringworld Throne*, Louis Wu returns to the artificial planet as its Central Protector. Seeking to discover who is destroying incoming spacecraft, he soon finds himself joining with other humanoids to battle protectors who have transformed into vampires.

Niven is also the author of such popular sci-fi novels as *A World out of Time* and the fantasy *The Magic Goes Away*. The former, a story about cryogenics in which Jaybee Corbell awakens in the twenty-second century after being frozen for two hundred years, is a mixture of "hard science with mind-boggling concepts of time and space," according to a *Publishers Weekly* contributor. Niven departs from his usual hard-science format in *The Magic Goes Away*, in which four magicians team up to attempt to replenish the supply of mana, the source of magic in the world. Algis Budrys of *Booklist* noted that Niven, though prominent for his "excellent science fiction," is "equally deft with fantasy."

In *Integral Trees* and *The Smoke Ring*, Niven takes readers to a ring of breathable air surrounds a neutron star. It is here that a group of mutineering space adventurers have set up a new civilization. The humans have adapted to life in a low-gravity environment. Reviewing *The Integral Trees*, Roland Green of *Booklist* noted that the "world described here is almost too rich" for a book of this size and called the work "a major sf novel, likely to be in demand almost everywhere." A *Publishers Weekly* reviewer agreed, describing the novel as "marvelous, sense-of-wonder, hardcore SF." With the sequel, *The Smoke Ring*, Niven produced a more character-oriented book, relying less on raw adventure than usual. Reviewing that book, *Booklist*'s Green commented that "this solid, well-paced story, featuring a richness of scientific concepts" is bound to be welcome in all public libraries.

Niven has also written short-story collections with tales that introduced well-known Niven characters such as Gil Hamilton and Beowulf Shaeffer, as well as stories that deal with time travel, warlocks, and hard science. His award-winning stories appear both in individual volumes as well as in anthologies such as *N-Space* and *Playgrounds of the Mind*. Niven is also well known for his collaborations with other science-fiction writers. His "Man-Kzin Wars" series consists of shared-world anthologies in which noted science-fiction authors set original tales in a world of Niven's creation: namely, Known Space, which is constantly under attack by the aggressive and catlike Kzin. The novels *The Mote in God's Eye* and its sequel, *The Gripping Hand*, were both penned in collaboration with Jerry Pournelle. In *The Mote in God's Eye* humans have their first contact with another sentient species, the Moties, which are monkey-like creatures living in a highly developed social system. Fredric Jameson, writing in *New Republic*, described *The Mote in God's Eye* as "foreign policy Sci-fi, insofar as it raises the basic policy issue: is peaceful coexistence with the Mote desirable or even possible, and at what cost?" Echoing the conclusion that the United States reached about communism, *The Mote in God's Eye* "sets out to demonstrate that in spite of the possible good will of individual moties, the danger lies in their system itself," Jameson noted. In *The Gripping Hand* the Moties are reproducing rapidly and are on the verge of breaking free of their star system. Two humans who survived the original onslaught of the Moties, Horace Bury and Captain Renner, patrol the galaxy to make sure that does not happen. When two researchers discover a possible solution to the population boom, Bury and Renner are convinced to take a crew that includes the researchers' children and go to the Mote system. "The Niven-Pournelle touch is as sure and as golden as it has ever been," Tom Easton wrote in *Analog Science Fiction and Fact.* Niven has also collaborated with Pournelle on several other books, including *Inferno,* a take-off on the work by Dante Alighieri; *Lucifer's Hammer,* a best seller about a comet striking Earth; and the highly acclaimed *Footfall,* in which an alien invasion forces the United States and Russia to join forces to defeat them.

With Steven Barnes, Niven has written several books, including *Dream Park, Dream Park II: The Barsoom Project,* and the third book in the series, *The California Voodoo Game.* Set in California in the twenty-first century, *Dream Park* is the ultimate virtual reality: a computerized holographic theme park. It is a fantasy world into which murder as well as industrial espionage suddenly appear, "a good inventive SF with the makings of an excellent mystery," according to a *Publishers Weekly* critic. About its sequel, *The Barsoom Project,* a reviewer for *Kliatt* noted that YA readers would enjoy "the skillful and fast-paced blend of fantasy, SF, and mystery elements in this novel."

Niven, Pournelle, and Barnes joined forces on *The Legacy of Heorot* and its sequel, *Beowulf's Children.* Based loosely on the Beowulf legend, the books employ a monstrous Grendel for their action. Colonists from Earth are settling the planet Avalon, still in its prehistoric age. Things are idyllic on this untouched Eden until the entrance of the beast. A reviewer for *Kliatt* noted that characters and action in the first of the Beowulf books "involve the reader totally in this fast-moving, tension-filled story." The storyline progresses two decades for the second installment of the tale, *Beowulf's Children,* "an example of panoramic sf at its best," according to a *Library Journal* reviewer.

Niven has created worlds within worlds with his novels and short stories. His percolating imagination has lent reality to fantasy for legions of readers. Combining a quirky blend of action, punning humor, and hard science, he has carved out new ground in the science-fiction genre, a sort of Niven-land, instantly recognizable to readers.

AUTOBIOGRAPHICAL ESSAY:

Larry Niven contributed the following autobiographical essay to *CA:*

The Niven File

I'm a compulsive teacher, but I can't teach. I lack at least two of the essential qualifications.

I cannot "suffer fools gladly." The smartest of my pupils would get all my attention, and the rest would have to fend for themselves. And I can't handle being interrupted.

Writing is the answer. Whatever I have to teach, my students will select themselves by buying the book. And nobody interrupts a printed page.

I knew what I wanted when I started writing. I've daydreamed all my life, and told stories too. One day the daydreams began shaping themselves into stories. I wanted to share them.

Astrophysical discoveries made peculiar implications, worlds stranger than any found in fantasy. I longed to touch the minds of strangers and show them wonders.

I wanted to be a published science fiction writer, like Poul Anderson and Jack Vance.

I wanted a Hugo Award!

Getting rich formed no part of that. Science fiction writers didn't get rich. (Robert Heinlein excepted. Kurt Vonnegut, Junior, excluded.) I used money to keep score: how many people had I reached?

I had my Hugo Award three years after I sold my first story. Within science fiction fandom one becomes a Grand Old Man fast. Now what?

Now: become a better writer. I'll always have things to learn. I still have trouble writing about the things that hurt me most. In my earlier novels almost nobody got old or sick.

Today? Well, I get allergy attacks. Alcohol, dry air, lack of sleep, or any combination thereof can cause me to wake up blind and in pain, with deep red eyes and puffy eyelids. I have to use a humidifier, or go to sleep with a wet towel. Now you know . . . but you wouldn't have the right to know if I hadn't given the same allergy to Gavving in *The Integral Trees* and Rather in *The Smoke Ring.* I did that for story purposes, and I had to nerve myself up to it.

Parts of my life are private. My computer erases my early drafts, and that's fine. My mistakes are not for publication.

*

Born April 30, 1938, in Los Angeles, California, USA.

Father: Waldemar Van Cott Niven.

The author in his office with his wife, Marilyn, 1978

Mother: Lucy Estelle Doheny Niven Washington.

Raised in Beverly Hills, California. Hawthorne Public School (Beverly Hills); Cate School in Carpinteria.

Entered California Institute of Technology, September 1956. Flunked out February 1958, after discovering a bookstore jammed with used science-fiction magazines.

Gainful employment: gas station attendant, summer 1960.

Graduated Washburn University, Kansas, June 1962: B.A. in mathematics with minor in psychology. Half the university was scattered to the winds by a tornado a month after I left. One year graduate work in mathematics at UCLA before I dropped out to write.

First story publication: "The Coldest Place," *Worlds of If,* December 1964.

Married Marilyn Joyce Wisowaty, September 6, 1969. We met at the NYcon, 1967. No children. We reside in Tarzana, California.

I have written at every length. Most of my work is fiction, but there have been speculative articles, speeches for high schools and colleges, television scripts, political action in support of the space program, and seventeen weeks of a newspaper comic strip.

I've collaborated with a variety of writers.

Interests: Science fiction conventions. Computerized games. AAAS meetings and other gatherings of people at the cutting edge of the sciences. The L5 Society. Filksinging.

Saving civilization and making a little money. Moving humankind into space by any means, but particularly by making space endeavors attractive to commercial interests.

In 1982 Jerry Pournelle talked me and Marilyn into hosting a gathering of the top minds in the space industry in an attempt to write a space program, with goals, timetables, costs. The Citizens Advisory Council for a National Space Policy has met five times over five years, for harrowing three-day weekends. The attendees include spacecraft designers, businessmen, NASA personnel, astronauts, lawyers. Adding science fiction writers turns out to be stunningly effective. We can translate: we can force these guys to speak English. We've had some effect on the space program . . . not enough, but some.

I grew up with dogs: keeshonds, the show dogs my mother has raised for fifty years. I live with cats. I have passing acquaintance with raccoons and ferrets. Associating with nonhumans has surely given me some insight into alien intelligences.

I've written on computers for nearly ten years. I don't know anything else about computers. What I do is, I buy what Jerry Pournelle tells me to. He's the Users Column for *Byte* magazine. I buy two, to get a spare *and* spare parts, and because *Marilyn* understands and loves computers.

I remember typewriters. I remember typing whole pages to make two or three corrections; I remember Liquid Paper and scissors and Scotch tape. A word processing program is a magic typewriter. Writing the first draft is almost as much work as it used to be—the computers don't do *that* yet!—but subsequent drafts are so easy that every time I read a passage over, I find myself rewriting.

*

My life has changed over the years.

Most photographs show me with a pipe in my mouth. I quit smoking on August 11, 1987, about 6:30 p.m.

Joe Haldeman persuaded me and Jerry to quit drinking during February every year, just to prove we aren't alcoholics. Why February? Shortest month. We switched to January, though, because there's less social activity in January. At this point I'm a teetotaller; the reasons are medical, not philosophical.

Steven Barnes—another collaborator who teaches several varieties of martial arts—urges new exercise programs on us from time to time. There was a Marci Mark 2 weight-lifting system, a torture implement that occupied one wall of our bedroom. There's an hour of aerobics with weights, on a cassette: *The Firm Workout*. The latest is a Versa Climber: a device that allows us to climb mountains without leaving home.

We were looking good, until I injured a knee and Marilyn ruptured a spinal disk . . . and then my back went out too. . . . For most of a year it was as if our warranties had run out. We've been healing, though. At this point we're both in shape to hike.

*

Awards: Hugos (or Science Fiction Achievement Awards) for "Neutron Star," 1966; *Ringworld,* 1970; "Inconstant Moon," 1971; "The Hole Man," 1974; "The Borderland of Sol," 1975. Nebula, Best Novel 1970: *Ringworld.* Ditmars (Australian, Best International Science Fiction) for *Ringworld,* 1972, and *Protector,* 1974. Japanese awards for *Ringworld* and "Inconstant Moon," both awarded 1979. Inkpot, 1979, from San Diego Comic Convention. Various Guest-of-Honor plaques.

Doctor of Letters, honorary, from Washburn University, May 1984.

*

Other novels clamor to be written, if I had the time. I stopped signing contracts (almost) long ago. It doesn't help. A story ready to be written always feels like an obligation.

Thraxisp, A Memoir

John and Bjo Trimble were science-fiction fans long before I was. I met them the night I found the Los Angeles Science Fantasy Society.

They're organized.

They've led treks into the desert when it's blooming. On such a trek I discovered a plant called squaw cabbage: a green vase with a tiny scarlet flower at the tip. It looks like something seeded from Mars . . . and I examined it in awe and delight while the rest of the trekkers stared at me.

Fans remember Jack Harness discovering the blazing desert starscape on another trek. He stretched out on his sleeping bag and lay there, staring up . . . and they found him in the morning, *on* his sleeping bag, half frozen.

The Trimbles are compulsive organizers. They created Equicon, an annual science-fiction convention local to Los Angeles. Equicon merged with Filmcon, which is media-oriented: movies, TV, comic books, posters, role-playing games. Then—

*

The World Building Project was Joel Hagen's idea. He had made the suggestion to other convention committees. When he talked to John and Bjo Trimble, they said *Yes.*

Joel Hagen is a sculptor. The work he displays at conventions is generally bones: skeletons from other worlds. Sometimes they come with provenances, details on the worlds where they were exhumed, signed by UPXAS, the United Planets Xenoarcheological Society.

Joel chose and assembled the rest of us: Art Costa, Don Dixon, Patricia Ortega, Rick Sternbach (all artists), Paul Preuss and me (writers of fiction), and Dr. William K. Hartmann (astronomer, artist, writer of articles and fiction).

*

At Equicon/Filmcon, in April 1981, the Trimbles gave us eight hotel rooms plus a big lecture room on the mezzanine. The World Builders Room was to remain open twenty-four hours a day. We eight artists and writers would spend as much of the convention there as we could. Actually we were more than eight; Rick Sternbach's wife Asenath was present most of the time, Marilyn kept wandering in, and there were others.

Most of us arrived Thursday night. We gathered on Friday morning and set to work.

I feared that we would duplicate the results of another world-building consortium, Harlan Ellison's Medea-building group. The World Builders chose a tidally locked habitable moon of a superJovian world, like Ellison's Medea. (Nobody used the term "brown dwarf star" yet.) But we changed some parameters to get something different.

Due to orbital elements chosen by Dr. Hartmann, *Thrassus* (too Latin! I changed it), *Thraxisp* is heated by both its sun and the superJovian planet. It's too hot for life except at the poles and in the seas.

Life would crawl out onto the land at each pole. Life thenceforth would travel separate evolutionary paths.

So Saturday we split into two groups.

I got tired of saying *crawl.* "My creatures will fly onto the land!" I cried. Flight first, then lungs . . . our flying lungfish would eventually nest in trees, then evolve legs and design a civilization. The volleks would be natural pilots. Okay, Preuss, top that!

"Mine will *roll,*" Paul gloated. His team designed a sand dollar. It rolled onto the land mass at the south pole and became a miner. The tunneks became a race of sessile philosophers, sensing their world with taste and seismic effects, getting their nourishment by chemical mining, consuming nothing organic.

*

The room was open to all. Convention attendees could wander in at any time. At set times we would lecture on our progress. At all times the artwork would be on display, and somebody would always be there to talk.

There was a globe of Thraxisp. There were paintings as seen from the surface, with the brown dwarf hanging tremendous in the sky; Joel was making and refining sculptures of the volleks and tunneks and their more primitive ancestors.

Convention attendees did wander in, but not many. We could have used more action.

But *we* were having fun.

What we were evolving was two races of natural space travelers.

They would have everything going for them. The tunneks would work on understanding physics. The volleks were natural pilots and explorers. For mines and chemical sources we had tunneks and the Tea-kettle: an asteroid-impact crater on the equator, facing directly toward the primary: a confined region where the ocean boils gently at all times, precipitating interesting salts and chemicals into glittering hills. Thraxisp's gravity is low; it has to be, because otherwise the gas torus effect will give it too much atmosphere (see *The Integral Trees*). That makes escape velocity low. We gave them an endless variety of moons to explore, all easily accessible to the most primitive spacecraft. And first contact with alien intelligence would come for both of them before ever they left the atmosphere!

*

By mid-Sunday, the end of the convention, we had hoped to introduce human explorers. My memory says we didn't get that far.

We didn't get as much crowd as we earned. The movie fans weren't interested. The Trimbles were disappointed.

But we eight continued to work.

Bill Hartmann wrote up the convention and published in *Smithsonian* magazine, March 1982, with some of our illustrations. The money was shared. Our plan was to share every nickel of fallout, 12.5 percent each.

The thought of an eventual book must have been in the back of every mind. Now we dared speak of it, and now we dared make more elaborate plans. We sent human explorers to Thrax, aboard the Ring City taken from my "Bigger than Worlds" article. The artists modified it extensively. We set up a loose plot

With a Pierson's puppeteer (a Niven creation), Boston, 1989

Here we stalled.

*

What happened?

Too many artists, not enough writers. Five and a half artists, two and a half writers, counting Hartmann as split down the middle. That's good for building a convention display, but bad for a book. It turns out Paul doesn't like the short story form; *that* didn't help.

Too much ingenuity. Ideas scintillated back and forth, and each had to be considered . . . added to the canon . . . memorized by all . . . worked into the larger picture . . .

In a normal collaboration, each of two people has to be willing to do about 80 percent of the work. With eight of us, and with the enormous complexity the project attained, organization took far too much of the effort available. We'd each be doing 80 percent of the work . . . for 12.5 percent of the take.

Granted that the project was a true kick in the ass, a mind stretcher, the kind of awesome world building the mundanes can't even dream about, an experience to shape the rest of our lives. It's still true that each of us could earn more, faster, more surely, by working alone.

I've no reason to think that this ever crossed anyone's mind but mine. I've never asked.

And on the gripping hand . . . with eight successful writers/artists working on a long term project, isn't it obvious that one or another would get involved in something else? Other collaborations or other obligations, or personal problems, or something to bring in quicker money . . . It was my first thought when Joel conned me into this. We tried it anyway.

*

Somebody was lured away, and it was me.

The first major step on the road to success: learn how to turn down bad offers. The second major step: learn how to turn down good offers. This can be very

line, in blocks of short story embedded in artwork of intense variety. Volleks would meet the Ring City in orbit in primitive comic-book spacecraft. The payoff would be the discovery, by inference, of the tunneks, whose existence the volleks are hiding. We assigned each other blocks of text.

More material emerged. The tunneks became musicians: they built great wind-operated pipe systems from careful deposits of slag. We have the recordings. We argued back and forth about designs for Ring City. Elaborate maps emerged, and sociological studies too.

We gathered—never all eight of us together—at universities and conventions to display our work.

We gathered (only five of us) to correlate notes, and to try to sell a book on the basis of what we had. We didn't have enough, or else it wasn't organized enough. The publisher's representative was interested but not sufficiently.

difficult. I say this in my own defense: Jerry Pournelle and I worked these rules out as a basic truth; but I was better at using it, or else I needed the money less. Jerry is still trying to dig out from under too many obligations, all these years later.

But I was snowed under when it was Thraxisp time. I was working on a book with Steven Barnes and a book with Jerry and at least one of my own. That one could be slighted—none of my publishers have ever complained about lateness, Ghod bless them—but the rent is always presumed due for my collaborators. Fair's fair.

This was how it ended—

November 18, 1986

Generic Thraxisp Participant

Dear Generic,

Paul isn't interested in blitzing Thraxisp. I haven't been able to reach Dr. Hartmann by phone. Me, I would need to be re-inspired. We are the three writers in the Thraxisp Group, and it is we who would need to write text.

So. My position is this:

1) We've had a learning experience. It was pleasant and educational too.

2) The trick is to make money by having fun. But none of the writers is available to turn Thraxisp into a book. It follows that we can only make money by selling individual contributions.

3) The artists have busted their asses at this; and I include Dr. Hartmann as both writer and artist. The artists may sell their artwork and keep the money, no strings attached. (I don't know of any piece of artwork that was a collaboration. If such exists, work your own deals.)

4) The writers may sell whatever they write in future, no strings attached, using the Thraxisp system as a communal idea pool. This includes fiction and also articles. (Bill, you sold an article with illustrations and split the money with us all. Thank you. I hope that the ethics of changing the rules now don't bother you; but give us some input.)

I presently have no such stories in mind; but such might arise in future.

Artists may also make and sell new material, no strings attached.

5) I don't know what to do about existing text. Some of the text was done in solo flights, and those blocks should belong to the author; but I suggest that any of the eight of us may quote from any of the text, making it a communal pool.

6) Obviously, illustrations are available for fiction and articles. I suggest that the artists and writers can cut their deals in the usual fashion.

7) Whatever happens, I suggest we keep each other informed.

8) I don't plan any more eight-part collaborations. The only thing wrong with this bag of snakes is, it was too big!

I'm well aware that the one who ran out of time to work was me. It's embarrassing . . . and I don't want to go through that again either.
Best wishes,
Larry Niven

*

The true heir to all of this is an annual event called *Contact.*

At *Contact,* all of the invited guests are "soft" scientists—biologists, anthropologists, sociologists—or science-fiction writers with an emphasis in the "soft" sciences. There are lectures, there are displays—not like the usual convention Art Show, but more of an anthropological museum display. At night there are films suitable for a college class. The badges are neat. They feature Joel Hagen's alien skulls.

Contact was Jim Funaro's idea. Seven or eight of us carved out details while sitting around a big table in the bar at a Westercon. Joel Hagen and I were there. At the first *Contact* Paul Preuss was also among the guests: three out of eight veterans of the World Builders Project at Equicon/Filmcon.

Contact includes the Bateson Project: a world-building exercise. The paying guests get to watch ten to fifteen very good minds shaping worlds in the fashion of the World Builders: artwork, sociology charts, a globe or two, sculpture. At set times the participants lecture on what they've accomplished.

At the first *Contact* the guests had to produce their worlds from scratch. Didn't work. Anthrobiosociologists break laws of physics without noticing.

At the second Joel Hagen handed us a sculpture, a thing that was mostly legs . . . and no anus. We made Joel put one in. We called it a *squitch* and extrapolated a world.

Ideally the *Contact* guests need a world to start with. Jim invites a hard science-fiction writer or two (Poul Anderson, Jerry Pournelle, me) to make one. He arrives Thursday night with a stack of notes and maps, and lectures on the physics, orbits, climatology, etc. Then the life-sciences people take over.

It's always been two teams. One handles the aliens. One team designs a human culture; and that can be weirder yet. On Sunday they run 'em together, on stage.

*

Ending is much too strong a word.

Niven, c. 1978

Thraxisp hasn't disappeared. We have all the material for an elaborate franchise universe.

Each of us has learned. Cooperation is not easy for professional dreamers. Keeping a dream world consistent isn't easy for anyone. We gave our creatures biology, history, cultures, art forms, vehicles and habitats.

We learned how to play. It's damned few of our five billion who are really good at that.

Biographical Sketches

Milford Writers' Conferences: Tradition says that a novice writer learns nothing from a writers' conference.

I knew this. I attended the Milford Conferences hosted by Kate Wilhelm Knight and Damon Knight; but for fear of losing my ability to write, I skipped every other year. Presently I dropped out, or was dropped; my memory won't tell me which.

The Milford conferences were serious. Each attendee brought several copies of at least one manuscript. During the day the others would read it. The attendees would gather in a Vicious Circle to offer comments, criticism, suggestions.

Of three stories I took to Milford (and Madiera Beach, when the Knights moved there) only one was improved. That was "For a Foggy Night."

It's still true that the Milford Conferences were different. My urge to write did not die because I went to Milford. On the contrary, I always enjoyed myself; I always went home inspired, one way or another; and I met people I'd wanted to know since I was a little boy.

James Blish brought the first section of a novel, *A Torrent of Faces,* and described what he had planned for the rest. An asteroid is due for collision with Earth . . . an Earth inhabited by a trillion people, with no margin of error for any such catastrophe. Bombs are placed to blow away pieces of the rock; lasers fired from the Moon are to boil away some of the surface; but too much of it will touch down . . .

My turn. "Suppose you fire those lasers at just one side of the body? Boil one side. Vapor pressure, law of reaction. Couldn't you cause it to miss the Earth?"

Blish said, "I hope not."

It took me a moment to join the laughter . . . to realise that I'd suggested a way to shoot down the plot for his novel!

But Blish did what a professional would do (and I learned by seeing what he did). He made the laser just powerful enough to shift the impact point of the meteoroid from Chicago to a place not so heavily populated . . . and it still destroyed too much.

*

Arthur C. Clarke brought a Questar telescope and set it up on the Knights' porch. It was early afternoon and we all took turns looking at Venus.

Many years later, during a radio interview in Los Angeles, Arthur was asked, "Who's your favorite writer?" You know the answer to that, surely. You can't name one, or many; you'll offend all the rest.

He said, "Larry Niven." And apologized to Jerry Pournelle, that night at a Pournelle party.

Jerry tells a similar tale, and in fact lots of us can do so. Arthur Clarke is the kind of man you want to kill someone for, just so he knows.

*

I'd discovered **Lester Del Rey**'s juveniles at the same time as Robert Heinlein's. Here he was in the flesh, generating wicked arguments on every possible topic.

I met **Piers Anthony** at the Madiera Beach conference, but we never got to talking. We got a dialogue going many years later, when I sent him a fan letter after reading *Omnivore.*

Gordon Dickson and others talked about working for an agency for reading fees. There was mention of a novice writer whose wonderful characters never got involved in anything like a story, and another who mistook funny hats for characterization. They never got the point, and the readers never stopped caring . . . and could never tell anyone to quit.

Harlan Ellison wanted unqualified praise. Any suggestion that a story could be improved was met with verbal vitriol. The circle of critics saw a lot of that.

This grated. If a story didn't need fixing, why bring it? Then again, he brought very good stories, and his suggestions for improving others' stories were pointed and useful.

Years later, my whole attitude flipflopped.

I sent "Inconstant Moon" to Damon Knight for *Orbit.* He rejected it.

Damon Knight was then one of the foremost critics of speculative fiction. The other was James Blish. Algis Budrys was making a reputation; Spider Robinson didn't exist. And *Orbit* was definitive: it was the literary end of the spec fic spectrum throughout the New Wave period.

What I wrote was never New Wave; but there's never been a time when I didn't want to expand my skills. I thought I'd made it this time. A solid study of character; no visible hardware; a love story. New Wave for sure, even if I was writing in complete sentences.

I recently unearthed Damon's long rejection letter. He made a good deal of sense, more than I remembered. Even a Hugo Award winning story can be improved.

At the time I was furious. I questioned his critical skill. This story was perfect, and only an idiot would have questioned, etc.

Maybe a writer needs that much arrogance. Else he'll never send out his first story, never make his first sale.

*

The Famous Writers School taught me how to know when I was a writer. I knew it when I saw the check.

It was signed by **Frederik Pohl.**

Fred bought my first four stories, and many others, for the Galaxy chain. The third was a novella called "Relics of Empire." He retitled it "World of Ptavvs," got Jack Gaughan to do a stack of interior illos for it, and paid in peanuts. He also took it to Betty Ballantine (the science fiction arm of Ballantine Books) and suggested that it could become a novel.

Fred has figured large in my life.

He was an usher at my wedding.

At my first science-fiction convention I was a lost neofan; but a writer too, because Fred Pohl knew me.

Early on, he suggested that I write stories about odd astrophysical domains: very hot and cool stars, hypermasses, Hal Clement's kind of thing; we'd pair them with articles on the same, and paintings. . . . That notion fell through, but he set me to looking for the odd pockets in the universe.

When Fred left the Galaxy chain, someone should have warned me to go with him. His replacementment, Ejier Jakobssen, was a recycled editor from "pulps" days. Ejier rejected a story months aftet "buying" it (saying he'd take it, but not sending a check). He "bought" "The Flying Sorcerers" as four-part serial, demanded references for all of the Tuckerized friends in the book (which ruined all the jokes for me), then rejected the first section! *Then* rejected the rest. I'd heard horror tales about the days of the pulps. Now I got to live through them.

*

William Rotsler was part of the LASFS crowd when I joined. He's easygoing, curious about his fellow man, easy to get to know. His life follows his whims.

He collects epigrams for what will someday be an enormous volume; meanwhile he sometimes sends them to *Reader's Digest.* ("Everything starts as someone's daydream." Larry Niven, fifty bucks for five words.)

He's a photographer . . . of "fumetti," of bottom-budget movies, of naked ladies. (Models, that is. Naked ladies? "She gets the benefit of the doubt, just like you, dear.") At science-fiction conventions his tendency was to escort supernaturally beautiful women, "Rotsler women."

If things get dull at a science-fiction convention banquet, look for the cluster of interested, amused, excited people. Bill Rotsler has gotten bored. So he's started drawing . . . on his notepad, the tablecloth . . . When things were slow in starting at a banquet some years back, Bill began illustrating the butter dishes. The restaurant must have been dismayed at how many butter dishes went home with the guests. Mine was a dialogue:

"What does a collaborator do?"

"He adds his name to a work which would not otherwise have the luster."

But I didn't grab my favorite. It's "The Memorial Vincent Van Gogh Coffee Cup," with the handle for an ear and a bandage drawn on the other side!

Once upon a time his whim had him making badges. He made a great many of them. Some were for sale, for charities. Some, personalized, were for friends. So there were badges labeled *Not Larry Pournelle* and *Not Jerry Niven.* I wore *Jerry Pournelle's Voice Coach* for awhile, and when I'd got my fair share of fun out of that, I gave it to Jerry's wife. I wear *LARRY NIVEN, Friend of the Great and Near-Great* to conventions. (Which are you? Well, if you're standing close enough to read the badge . . .) I no longer wear *Have Sex Outside My Species* because it's been too long since *The Ringworld Engineers,* and because I once forgot to take it off when I left the hotel.

You can identify inner-circle fandom by the Rotsler badges.

*

I met **Tom Doherty** by walking into the Ace party at the World Science Fiction Convention in Florida. Tom had just taken over at Ace Books.

He met me at the door. He knew my name. He had a good smile and (I tend to notice) an impressively large head, roomy enough for the brain of a blue whale. He was talking to Adele Hull of Pocket Books, and he started to tell me how good she was . . . and caught himself. It occurred to him that he shouldn't be praising the opposition in front of a solid author.

I said, "I have to tell you, it probably will never cost you a nickel."

"Why not?"

Oh my God. He didn't know! And I realized that I was going to have to tell him. Who else would?

So I did. "Nobody deals with Ace Books unless all the other choices are used up. Nobody expects royalties; the advance is *it.* Overseas money is never reported. . . . "

Tom Doherty is a careful businessman. He didn't take over Ace without checking first. He checked back for two years and found no complaints lodged against

Ace . . . not because there weren't any, as he thought, but because the whole field had long since given up on ever getting money due from the old Ace Books.

The encounter with Larry Niven was his second awful shock of the day. He had already met Jerry Pournelle that afternoon.

"I'm Jerry Pournelle, president of SFWA, and we want to look at your books!"

Tom wound up paying several hundred thousand dollars in back fees to authors.

*

After he and James Baen parted company with Ace, Tom formed his own company, Tor Books. Then Jim dropped away and formed Baen Books. In this field we tend to train each other.

I see Tom fairly frequently. Once we met at a Boskone (annual Boston convention) and he took me and Marilyn off to Loch Ober, along with his editor, his wife, and his daughter. He talked four of us into ordering lobster Savannah.

The lobster is cut open along the back; the meat is cooked, chopped and mixed with herbs, then put back. Lobster Savannah looks like it could *heal.* These beasts ran three pounds each. I started talking to my dinner:

"Doctor McCoy will see you now."

"The Federation doesn't think you can defend yourselves without our aid."

"Now, wretched bottom-feeder, you will tell us of your troop movements!"

By dinner's end I had arranged a mutual defense treaty with the baked Alaska. And by the time we reached the hotel, I had been dubbed *Speaker-to-Seafood.*

*

The last time Marilyn and I were in New York, I came to realize that Tom had bought me five meals—though he was only present at two!

I was told early: when you eat with an editor or publisher, that's who pays the check. It's surprisingly easy to get used to such a tradition . . . but enough is enough. Hell, I'd never even sold him a book.

N-Space started with a phone call from Bob Gleason, one of my favorite editors. He and Tom had got to talking over a dinner . . . and it emerged that Larry Niven was going to have been a published author for twenty-five years, real soon now. Why not publish a retrospective volume? So Bob called.

It sounded good to me.

In May 1989, Tom Doherty and Bob Gleason stayed at my house for a few days before the SFWA Nebula Awards. We did a fair amount of work on the book. And I fed Tom Doherty by *cooking* several meals.

I even picked up a restaurant check once, by previous negotiation. He tried to back out afterward, but I wouldn't let him.

*

We called **Don Simpson** the Eldritch Doom because of the things he kept in his room. He's an artist and inventor, of that breed that never gets rich, because he invents new art forms. By the time anything could become successful, he'd be on to something else.

He had a wonderful time with some glass engraving equipment.

I'd been leaving Michelob beer bottles all over the clubhouse: the old lovely vase-shaped bottles too tall to quite fit in a refrigerator. At my fanquet (the banquet given for a LASFS member who has made a professional sale) Don presented me with a beer bottle engraved with Jack Gaughan's illustration of one of my aliens. I got him to do two more for me, then a Baccarat decanter and some Steuben crystal. . . .

He was in the LASFS then. Later he moved to San Francisco, but I don't think he gave up his habits.

*

Frank Gasperik was an oddity. When I met him he was a biker and a hippie and a science-fiction fan.

Niven at his home in Tarzana, California, 1978

Among bikers he carried a guitar and called himself The Minstrel. At science-fiction conventions he sang filk.

Jerry and I put him in *Lucifer's Hammer* as Mark Czescu. We put his song in too. He makes a good character . . . though he tends to take over a book, like kudzu.

We put him in *Footfall* too, as Harry Reddington, and commissioned a ballad from him. By then Frank had been through major changes. He'd been rear-ended twice within two weeks while driving two different cars, neither of which had headrests. His insurance company was giving him the runaround and his lawyer told him he'd look better on a witness stand if he didn't get well too quick. So he was avoiding major efforts to walk normally. It's all true . . . and Jerry and I screamed at him separately and together until we made him see that he wasn't being paid enough to stay sick!

We were working near the end of *Footfall* at my house when Frank phoned about another matter. I told him, "We're at the poker table deciding Hairy Red's fate."

"Give me a heroic death," he said. So we killed him.

*

Dan Alderson is classic. At Jet Propulsion Laboratories they called him their "sane genius." He designed a program used by most of the free world countries for deep space probes. Computer nerd, sedentary, white shirt with infinite pens and pencils in a plastic holder in the pocket. Diabetic.

Characteristic cry: "Weep! Wail!"

From Dan came the germ of a short story, "There Is a Tide." He worked out the exact instability of the Ringworld; it took seven years. I went to him for numbers for the Ringworld meteor defense.

He was Dan Forrester in *Lucifer's Hammer*. The list of what Forrester would need after Hammerfall is his, because Jerry asked him.

He's the hero of one of Jerry's tales of asteroid colonization.

He likes Known Space. He's published intricately plotted outlines for stories that would vastly extend Known Space if they were written.

*

Judy-Lynn Benjamin Del Rey entered the field as an editor under Fred Pohl at Galaxy Science Fiction. When Fred quit, she continued with Ejler Jakobssen for awhile. She wound up at Ballantine Books and became one of the most powerful editors in the field.

She was a dwarf. One got over noticing that. She was charming, intelligent, enthusiastic, competent. She was tactful within limits: she generally wouldn't lie to an author.

She liked stuffed animals. When I introduced her to the cat-tail (see *World out of Time*) which Takumi Shibano had brought me from Japan, she fell in love with it. Takumi got me another, and I passed it on.

She wanted to chop hell out of *A Mote in God's Eye*. Jerry and I wouldn't have that, so the book wound up with Simon and Schuster and Bob Gleason. In later years her comment on that decision was, "I don't want to talk about it."

She never bid on books at auction. Thus she lost *Footfall* to Fawcett . . . and got it back when Ballantine bought Fawcett!

Let me tell you about the last time I noticed her height.

We were walking along a Philadelphia sidewalk, talking: me and Marilyn and Judy-Lynn and Lester, who is kind of short himself. Suddenly I was sitting on the sidewalk, dazed, looking up, with blood dripping down my nose from a wedge-shaped notch in my forehead. I saw something massive and metallic hanging over the sidewalk at eyebrow height.

In Philadelphia they put construction equipment where it can bite pedestrians. If I hadn't been looking down I'd have seen it. As it was, I had to go into the construction site and borrow Kleenex and a Band-Aid.

*

David Gerrold came to the LASFS in peculiar fashion. He came as a big name pro, unknown to all, who had never published in any magazine nor sold any novel. But he had written the script for a *Star Trek* episode, "The Trouble with Tribbles."

This should be remembered: there had been no bad *Star Trek* shows. Nothing like the first season of *Star Trek* had ever been seen. Gene Roddenberry had lured real by-Ghod science-fiction writers to write scripts! One season was all it took to alienate them. They weren't used to seeing their precious prose rewritten by inept hacks or (in one case) Gene Roddenberry's secretary.

David was a novice. *Everybody* rewrote "Tribbles," and he took it for granted. From listening to David and others I have gathered that the best stories see the most rewriting. Everybody wants to have had something to do with building a good show.

Marilyn and I invited David and a date over for dinner one night. He turned up alone. In the course of conversation, we discussed writing a story together . . . and kept talking, and looked through a dictionary for definitions for "As A Mauve," and kept talking. . . .

David did more of the first-draft writing. He types like a jackrabbit: lots of speed, lots of typos. The story ("The Misspelled Magicians") grew to the size of a two-part serial. I chopped it back to size before we extended the story.

It was fun. We'd take turns at the typewriter. I remember him jumping up from the typewriter, startling me, shouting, "All right, I've got them into a riot! You stop it."

I read what he'd written. I said, "Stop it, hell—" and wrote the riot.

David wrote fast and wordy. I found I was expected to do the cutting. I should have cut deeper; but it felt *wrong* to be chopping at another writer's precious prose. I didn't develop the necessary savagery until the second rewrite of *A Mote in God's Eye.*

We've worked together since. David was story editor for the Saturday morning animated show *Land of the Lost.* The fun went out of it when invisible executives began to interfere with the first script. They chopped out our best character. They were about to take the river out of "Downstream"! I washed my hands of it . . . and then they put the river back. . . . And when David told me that he needed help with more scripts, I saw a neat convergence.

I could do the first drafts. David as story editor could decide what changes were needed, and as my collaborator he could then *make* them. I need never worry about the changes in my precious prose. So we did two more.

*

Steven Barnes stands about five eight or nine. He's black. He's in perfect physical condition. He's smiling. He's probably talking (though he listens good too) and as he talks, he bounces around like he really ought to be tied to a railing, just in case.

Steve isn't exactly your typical fan. Then again, he is. Kids picked on him in high school for an intellectual bookworm. They wouldn't let him be nice. He took up martial arts. He teaches several varieties. Now they let him be nice whenever he wants to.

But . . . he's a science-fiction fan. We're *different.* He didn't stop with learning how to survive Conan the Cimmerian.

He wants to know everything that the human body can be made to do. He wants his friends to be healthy and safe. He teaches self-defense classes at the LASFS. He tries out exercise modes, and when he *knows* something works, he passes it on to his friends.

Writing? Oh, *writing!* Jerry Pournelle and I think we're pretty good. We could have made *The Legacy of Heorot* a fine tale of interstellar colonization; but we don't have the right mind-set for a horror novel. What it took was the guy who wants me to see *The Texas Chain-Saw Massacre* for its artistic merit.

Steven's first solo novel *(Street Lethal)* was based on a working love potion, for God's sake! A monogamy treatment. I wouldn't have had the nerve.

The television industry loves him too. Remember a show called *The Wizard?* They were about to drop it. Then they saw Steven's script. It involved a robot suspected of murder.

Suddenly they were talking about this one saving the show! They swapped scripts around to put his in the right place; they found enough money somehow; and when the producer made script changes, the director changed it back and swore it was already perfect. They think he's pretty good.

There's money in scripts too.

You be nice to him, or he'll spend all his time writing scripts.

*

Jerry Pournelle raised the subject of collaboration, and it sounded like fun to me. Working with David Gerrold had been fun.

Jerry wouldn't work in Known Space, because he couldn't believe in the politics or the history. But he had a thousand years of a future history that uses the faster-than-light drive designed by our mutual friend Dan Alderson. I looked it over. Peculiar. A thousand inhabited planets and no intelligent beings save humans?

Then I realised that the laws of the Alderson Drive allowed me to insert an undiscovered alien civilization right in the middle.

That did it: there was going to be a novel. I had abandoned a novella two-thirds written; I dug it out and resurrected the alien. We spent a wild night extrapolating from the Motie Engineer form, to a dozen varieties of Motie, to a million years of history and three planet-busting wars. We swore we would write the novel we wanted to read when we were twelve.

Writing is the hard part. Every time we thought we were finished, we found we weren't.

Jerry sent our "finished" manuscript to a friend: Robert Heinlein. Robert told us that he could put one terrific blurb on the cover *if* we made some changes. The first hundred pages had to go. . . .

And we did that, and reintroduced characters and moved background data from the lost Prologue to a later scene set on New Scotland, and did more chopping throughout. "There's a scene I've *never* liked," I told Jerry, and our whole relationship changed. This was when we learned not to be too polite to a collaborator; it hurts the book.

And we sent it back to Robert, *who did a complete line editing job.*

I know of a man who once offered Robert Heinlein a reading fee! The results were quite horrid. But in the case of *Mote,* Robert hadn't expected us to take his advice. Nobody ever had before, he tells us. But if "Possibly the finest science-fiction novel I have ever read" were to appear on the cover, above Robert Heinlein's name, then the book had to *be* that.

It took us forever to write. We won the LASFS's "Sticky" Award for "Best Unpublished Novel" two years running. It was worth every minute.

*

Jerry and I had begun work on *Oath of Fealty* when I remembered Dante's *Inferno.* I'd read it in college,

With collaborator Jerry Pournelle

twice in quick succession, then daydreamed about a lost soul trying to escape that awful landscape.

The *Divine Comedy* is good fantasy, but only because of the passage of time. It was the first hard science-fiction novel. It has all the earmarks: not just because it's a trilogy, and not only for its tremendous scope. Dante used a wide spectrum of the knowledge of the time: theology, the classics, architecture, geography, even astrology. He designed a perfect Easter for his protagonist's trip through Hell and Purgatory and the Earthly Paradise and Heaven. He invented the Southern Cross, as Swift invented the moons of Mars, for story purposes.

I remembered the daydreams, and I remembered that I was a writer now. I remembered that Jerry Pournelle had a strong theological education, and that we'd already written a novel together. I put it to him that we should write a sequel.

Every other book has taken us two to three years to write. Once we got into text, we wrote *Inferno* in four months. Why so fast? Because the territory is terribly unpleasant. We wanted out!

Pocket Books put *Inferno* in a royalties pool with *Mote.* That is, royalties from *A Mote in God's Eye* would go to repay the advance on *Inferno,* because Pocket Books had little faith in *Inferno.* It is understood, in such cases, that second book will at least be published . . . but *Inferno* sat on some shelf for over a year. By the time we noticed and raised some hell, Pocket Books had paid not a penny for *Inferno.*

Inferno has had good critical acclaim. In college courses it has been taught as critical commentary on Dante, which of course it is.

I must add that we should have put it through another draft. We had the time, courtesy of Pocket Books' mistake, and *we didn't know it.*

*

Since Jerry and I first began writing together, our tendency has been to meet to plot out the book, assign each other scenes, then go off to write them. Near the end of *Footfall* we changed our habit. We wrote in my office, taking turns at the typewriter.

The mood became frenetic.

The more we wrote, the more we saw of scenes that needed to be written. Text in the beginning and middle needed rewriting. The end of the book receded before us like a ghost. Spring became summer . . . yet what we were writing was *superb,* it was *needed,* and the end *was* inching near.

Came the day we worked on the penultimate chapter. We planned a wrap-up-the-threads chapter to follow.

Jerry took his turn. *Will the aliens honor a conditional surrender? The Threat Team dithers. The President makes his choice. . . .*

My turn, with the aliens. *Surrender, or all will die! But the Herdmaster must have permission of the females . . .* I was typing fast enough to break

bones . . . *set their feet on the Herdmaster's chest.* I jumped up. "If I don't quit now I'll go into Chayne-Stokes breathing," I said.

Jerry read it through. "I can improve this," he said, and typed, "-30-" (The End).

Laws

From time to time I publish this list; from time to time I update it. I don't think it's possible to track its publishing history. The most recent appearance was in Niven's Laws *from Owlswick Press. In this version I've amplified a little.*

To the best I've been able to tell in fifty years of observation, this is how the universe works. I hope I didn't leave anything out.

NIVEN'S LAWS

1a) Never throw shit at an armed man.

1b) Never stand next to someone who is throwing shit at an armed man.

You wouldn't think anyone would need to be told this. Does anyone remember the Democratic National Convention of 1968?

2) Never fire a laser at a mirror.

3) Mother Nature doesn't care if you're having fun.

You will not be stopped! There are things you can't do because you burn sugar with oxygen, or your bones aren't strong enough, or you're a mammal, or human. Funny chemicals may kill you slow or quick, or ruin your brain . . . or prolong your life. You can't fly like an eagle, nor yet like Daedalus, but you can fly. You're the only Earthly life form that can even begin to deal with jet lag.

You can cheat. Nature doesn't care, but don't get caught.

4) FxS=k.

The product of Freedom and Security is a constant. To gain more freedom of thought and/or action, you must give up some security, and vice versa.

These remarks apply to individuals, nations, and civilizations. Notice that the constant k is different for every civilization and different for every individual.

5) Psi and/or magical powers, if real, are nearly useless.

Over the lifetime of the human species we would otherwise have done something with them.

6) It is easier to destroy than to create.

If human beings didn't have a strong preference for creation, nothing would get built.

7) Any damn fool can predict the past.

Military men are notorious for this, and certain writers too.

8) History never repeats itself.

9) Ethics changes with technology.

10) Anarchy is the least stable of social structures. It falls apart at a touch.

11) There is a time and a place for tact.

(And there are times when tact is entirely misplaced.)

12) The ways of being human are bounded but infinite.

13) The world's dullest subjects, in order: a) Somebody else's diet. b) How to make money for a worthy cause. c) Special Interest Liberation.

14) The only universal message in science fiction: There exist minds that think as well as you do, but differently.

Niven's corollary: The gene-tampered turkey you're talking to isn't necessarily one of them.

15) Fuzzy Pink Niven's Law: Never waste calories.

Potato chips, candy, whipped cream, or hot fudge sundae consumption may involve you, your dietician, your wardrobe, and other factors. But Fuzzy Pink's Law implies:

Don't eat soggy potato chips, or cheap candy, or fake whipped cream, or an inferior hot fudge sundae.

16) There is no cause so right that one cannot find a fool following it.

This one's worth noticing.

At the first High Frontier Convention the minds assembled were among the best in the world, and I couldn't find a conversation that didn't teach me something. But the only newspersons I ran across were interviewing the only handicapped person among us.

To prove a point one may seek out a foolish Communist, thirteenth-century Liberal, Scientologist, High Frontier advocate, Mensa member, science-fiction fan, Jim Bakker acolyte, Christian, or fanatical devotee of Special Interest Lib; but that doesn't really reflect on the cause itself. *Ad hominem* argument saves time, but it's still a fallacy.

17) No technique works if it isn't used.

If that sounds simplistic, look at some specifics:

Telling friends about your diet won't make you thin. Buying a diet cookbook won't either. Even reading the recipes doesn't help.

Knowing about Alcoholics Anonymous, looking up the phone number, even jotting it on real paper, won't make you sober.

Buying weights doesn't give you muscles. Signing a piece of paper won't make Soviet missiles disappear, even if you make lots of copies and tell every anchorperson on Earth. Endlessly studying designs for spacecraft won't put anything into orbit.

18) Not responsible for advice not taken.

19) Think before you make the coward's choice. Old age is not for sissies.

NIVEN'S LAWS FOR WRITERS

1) Writers who write for other writers should write letters.

2) Never be embarrassed or ashamed by anything you choose to write.

(Think of this before you send it to a market.)

3) Stories to end all stories on a given topic, don't.

4) It is a sin to waste the reader's time.

5) If you've nothing to say, say it any way you like.

Stylistic innovations, contorted story lines or none, exotic or genderless pronouns, internal inconsistencies, the recipe for preparing your lover as a cannibal banquet: feel free. *If what you have to say is important and / or difficult to follow, use the simplest language possible.* If the reader doesn't get it then, let it not be your fault.

6) Everybody talks first draft.

POSTSCRIPT

Larry Niven contributed the following update in 2002:

May 30, 2002:

Viewed from today, the year 2001 CE feels like a dividing line across my life.

It started with a stock market crash—sorry, recession. I never paid much attention—typical science-fiction fan—but Marilyn has taken up watching the stock market's vagaries on TV. I can't avoid it.

We'd bought a house that costs more to maintain than the Tarzana house did. I never thought we'd leave Tarzana and the house where about sixty of us evolved the plan that drove the Soviet Union bankrupt, but we'd run out of room for our stuff. The seller in Chatsworth left us with some nasty surprises. I was still adjusting.

I do sometimes have to remind myself that there are people who would kill to have my problems.

I was in depression. I needed a break, a change. In April I got it. I should be more careful of my wording when I make wishes.

What follows is electronic mail from 2001, rewritten a bit for the sake of lucidity.

*

This went out to friends, via e-mail, on April 16, 2001.

Hi, everybody! I've injured myself. I've torn a tendon my knee, the one that leads right up the front of the thigh.

According to the emergency room crew, it's "partly torn." As I begin this, I haven't seen my own doctor yet.

What happened:

I flew up to Seattle for Norwescon, the northwest regional science fiction convention, on Thursday. Steve Barnes, my longtime collaborator, picked me up a little after noon. We talked *Ringworld's Child,* and he led me through some valuable insights. We followed maps to Brenda Cooper's new apartment. She's a more recent collaborator: short stories and an unfinished novel. There, as planned, we three changed for a yoga class that is held at a temperature of 106 degrees.

However crazy that sounds—my wife Marilyn hated the idea—what could happen? It's classic yoga, and I'm bracketed by collaborators.

The yoga went okay. The heat got to me halfway through; not unusual; I lay down to get past that. Finished the class.

We were outside, still hot in Seattle's damp weather. Presently, ready to make for the car, I tried to stand up. My left slipper slid on the slippery pavement—slid back under me—and I felt and saw my kneecap slide out of place. Yoga had softened all those muscles.

One of us called 911. An ambulance and stretcher arrived. I was told my kneecap was in place, so I straightened my leg and found I could stand up. Steve was up quick, telling me to grab him for support, and I did. One step and I learned that my knee was buckling without resistance.

I got X-rays. Came home with them. They'll have to be returned.

The ER doctor said: "Partly torn tendon. Don't bend the leg for (usually) four to six weeks." And I was given a leg brace, a torture implement to hold my leg straight by force. Yes, I sleep with it.

The next couple of days were . . . interesting. It could have been a nightmare . . . but Brenda wheeled me around in a hotel wheelchair all Friday, brought me ice to ice the knee, etc. Without her it would have been a mess.

Toilets have to be negotiated carefully when you can't bend your knee, even toilets for handicapped.

You notice a lot of handicapped at conventions, when you're damaged yourself. Algis Budrys is in a wheelchair for a while. Charles Brown caught us on camera, and we'll appear in tandem in *Locus.*

People keep asking the same question. How'd I do it?

I barely slept Thursday. Friday I got over that: went to sleep in the filk concert room, entertained to sleep, stretched out on four chairs. Brenda thought I was applauding in my sleep, but I wasn't; I was aware of the music.

The handicapped elevator to half the meeting rooms goes up from the kitchen!

By Saturday I'd tired of the wheelchair. I could stand up, and I developed a halfarc footstep. Brenda stuck with me. I could fall over. I was trying not to bring her, and Steve, down.

What could have been a nightmare, wasn't. People are too solicitous for that: friends, strangers, and the ones whose names I should remember, were all kindly and sympathetic.

Marilyn had called my own doctor. Appointment Monday.

Saturday evening: the plan had been to fly home for a traditional Easter egg hunt. I called Alaska Friday and got upgraded to First Class with a bulkhead. Only, it didn't take. The seat was given me only through Portland. That had to be fixed.

It got fixed. I flew home Main Cabin, in a bulkhead seat with room to stick my leg past the bulkhead into First. At one point a delighted flight attendant announced she'd got me all three seats . . . then realized, as I had, that the arms don't come up; the trays are in them. From Portland I was riding with a woman and child, part of a group of nine skiing enthusiasts. The flight attendant didn't like me "blocking" them.

Hey, I can stand up and let them past. The only thing I can't do is bend my leg.

*

Easter Sunday was fun. I'm mobile enough if Marilyn drives and I stretch out in the back of the wagon. Lunch was good, and the conversations were a delight. Thank you all. Kim, thanks for the charity egg. I never found one. With Sandy's wit I would have found many: they were hidden all around the big chair in the living room.

*

So I'm home, and it's Monday, April 16, 2001, and I'm planning an altered life.

My quadriceps tendon is torn loose from my kneecap. The doctor told me that this is the major muscle in the leg, that if it isn't reattached I may never get function back. It must happen fast. On Wednesday they're going to reattach the tendon.

Then—maybe I'm in a cast; if not, it's something else that absolutely immobilizes the leg. I spend the first night in the hospital.

Marilyn is optimistic. We've had knee surgery before. (Torn meniscus.) This isn't as extreme as knee replacement, which we may face someday. I hope she's right, and I intend to emulate her attitude.

The restaurant forays we planned depend on my being able to straighten my leg. I hadn't planned any trips until July, so there's no need to dread an airplane seat.

I can't sit in a barber's chair. I feel shaggy already.

Jerry, I'll be mobile, even if on crutches, by the time you and Roberta come back from Paris. Come and visit me. No hike.

Brother Mike, the visits to Mom won't resume for—I can't guess. Mom should find it interesting when I do wobble in, and Marilyn will be there; she has to drive me.

Nephews: I'm open to visits until I can come to you.

Eleanor and all editors: my output may slow down. Again, maybe it won't. I'll be trapped at home, with nothing to do but dream and write.

*

I was afraid I'd go nuts without company. We missed the Nebula Awards dinner, but the Dohertys, the Pournelles, and my agent Eleanor came to visit. I got enough visitors to keep me sane. Thanks, all.

This went out six weeks later:

*

It strikes me that I owe all of you a progress report on my life. Trouble is, nothing much changes when you're laid up.

I'm still not allowed to bend my left leg.

For two and a half weeks I was in a cast. I've been in a leg brace for three. The brace is just like a cast except I can open it and wash my leg.

I can't go upstairs, so I'm camping out in the den downstairs in a rented hospital bed. Jerry Pournelle and Eric Pobirs have set up my computer equipment in the library.

I can write. I did 1,600 words yesterday on *Burning Tower*. Friday the Pournelles took me on a research mission to the Los Angeles County Museum of Art, claiming that museums are wheelchair-friendly. They were dead right, and the display of Olmec history was invaluable. Our characters—as of 14,000 years ago, when magic still worked—aren't going where we thought they were. The Aztecs' legendary origin, called Aztlan, may have been where Chaco Canyon is, right on the continental divide. We'll climax the story there.

My skills as an invalid grow. I hope my knee is growing back together too. So I wait.

What I want to tell you about is making breakfast.

Six-plus weeks after the accident, five-plus weeks after the operation, yesterday Marilyn asked, "Can I sleep late tomorrow morning?"

"Sure."

"Can you make your own breakfast?"

"Sure." I'd done it before, up to a point.

Morning. Marilyn bought a papaya; I saw it in the fridge. I want half the papaya, toast with peanut butter and jam, and a cappuccino.

Step one: use the walker. (Hopping on my right leg, with the left stuck out.) I can't carry anything with the walker, but I can turn around with something in one hand, the other on the walker. I go to the refrigerator and get the papaya, peanut butter, jam, putting them on the island. (It's an island kitchen.) I get a knife from the knife rack. (From the wheelchair it's too high.) Cut the papaya. Teaspoon: clean out the seeds. I bag half and put it back in the fridge. I put toast in the toaster oven.

Forget any of that and I lose two or three minutes.

Step two: hop back to the den, transfer to the wheelchair. Marilyn found me a box-shaped carry thing with a strap. The strap goes around my waist. I can carry solid things in my lap now. I can't carry fluids in it.

I put a plate in the carry thing. The toaster pops and I put that in the plate and move it to the island. I deal with the toast. I roll into the dining room where there's a new translation of the Odyssey sent to me by Owen Lock. Eat and read.

What's left? The cappuccino.

I've got an expensive cappuccino maker in the bar. It's two steps down. For weeks I thought that couldn't be done. Then a trip to visit Tim and Shannon Griffin, my nephew and his wife, hit me with a two-step, and I found out I could do it with the walker.

So: back to the walker. *Lunge* to place the walker, hop two steps down. Pour grounds, run the coffee, add milk, steam it all. Marilyn has to keep water and milk and ground coffee supplied; I can't carry anything with the walker. But I can turn around and put coffee on the bar proper.

What I can't do is take it anywhere.

I can carry a magazine in the wheelchair. I put a magazine where I'm going to sit. I try to use a chair there, but my straight leg defeats me. So I hop the walker to the wheelchair and sit in that while I drink my cappuccino.

Somewhere in there the cat nags me into feeding her. All that takes is the carry thing, if the cat will only get out of my way and let me wheel into the pantry. . .

Breakfast.

It's a lifestyle. I can hope it won't last more than six months.

*

I developed an appreciation for why married people live longer than singles. Sometimes you need the help.

We skipped the West Coast Science Fiction Convention. Those friends who also skipped came over for a party. They and Marilyn did all the work: barbecued my hamburger, and moved my wheelchair outside and back in. With all those friends around, I opted to use the swimming pool. My first swim: a rite of passage.

"You're crazy, Niven. How do you plan to get back out?"

"I plan to crawl out." Seemed obvious enough.

The doctor finally let me bend the knee a little, then a lot, and put me on physical therapy. Another rite of passage was letting my foot go all the way around on a stationary bike. Therapy lasted months.

We went to the World Science Fiction Convention over Labor Day in Chicago. By then I had my leg back. I packed a pull-apart walking stick.

*

Saturday, September 15, 2001:

I feel slow and stupid. It's taken four days to sink in. Persons unknown have perpetrated the most awesome act of terror since Genghis Khan's tower of heads.

Thursday at the Los Angeles Science Fantasy Society meeting, various people spoke on the destruction of the World Trade Center. They spoke of personal feelings and proposed courses of action. I found myself mute.

Long ago I did have something to say.

I was watching an early TV play on *Masterpiece Theater,* a fairy tale in which the king offered his daughter and other valuable considerations to the man whose achievement was judged most wonderful. Suitors presented wonders. One was a marvelous clock, with moving figures for the hours. Another contender hacked it to pieces.

The judges were ready to proclaim him the winner.

That, I said heatedly, was stupid. Fairy tales should teach better than that. Creation is vastly more difficult than destruction. It's only because we're natural creators that we ever get anything built at all.

*

The World Trade Center lived up to its billing. The two towers were supposed to stand up to an airplane impact. They did. Fire brought them down by melting the structural steel, but the towers stood long enough to allow most of the people to get out. The rubble collapsed inward rather than spilling across the city.

I was in the World Trade Center once, many years ago.

Jerry Pournelle and I had come to sell a book. Robert Gleason, the editor, took us up to the top of the World Trade Center for cocktails. A big elevator lofted us from that vast lobby, accelerating hard, and rattling because plenty of slack had been allowed for its high speed.

Typically—I'm too often a self-centered son of a bitch—I didn't remember that Jerry is an acrophobe. I've seen how he handles it: sliding along a ledge narrower than his feet, twelve feet up, wearing a backpack, leading a troop of Boy Scouts up IronCreek. You only need to give him time to screw up his courage. In the elevator he was a little quiet.

We reached the top. Conversation resumed as we walked toward a shallow flight of stairs and, beyond, a wraparound floor-to-ceiling picture window. I noticed Jerry wasn't with us.

He was still at the top of the stairs. "Get a table. I'll be with you in a minute," he said.

We did. Presently Jerry joined us. "That was weird," he said. "I didn't have any warning. I remember climbing to the top of the Statue of Liberty. It scared hell out of me. Now the Statue of Liberty is right out there, and I'm looking down on it like it's a toy!"

On the way down Bob and I were doing macho dominance games, trying to get Jerry involved, to distract him from the tremendous drop below that vibrating elevator.

*

I'm a bit of an acrophobe too. I don't think I can ever write of the events of September 11. It's too easy to imagine.

The World Trade Center was an amazing achievement. Bringing it down . . . well. It's amazing that men would train so hard and long to commit suicide; but our warriors do that too.

*

October 2001:

This is to be a trip report. I'm expanding it from handwritten notes as and when I can.

Many months ago I agreed to be Guest of Honor at Albacon, October 5 through 7, 2001. 1 figured I'd visit New York too. We keep the publishing industry there. I'd visit some old and new friends.

Then "they" destroyed the World Trade Center, using 767s as big bombs.

Jerry Pournelle and I have been making notes toward a sequel to our version of *Inferno,* which was a sequel to Dante's *Inferno.* It seems reasonable to work on *Purgatorio* this trip.

*

Sunday

All day I couldn't get my mind straight. I couldn't write. I'm good at daydreaming, good at building stories, but all my internal stories since September 11 involve terrorists on airplanes.

I settled for a 10 A.M. flight from LAX, to get a direct flight. We're being told to arrive two hours early because of enhanced security. Marilyn and I decided to spend the night next to LAX at the Marriott. $200+, but we can get up at 6:00 instead of 4:00 and take the Marriott shuttle. LAX won't let automobiles in the airport.

*

Monday

I'm still pretty jittery. I hit the Marriott's buffet rather than decide what to eat.

Rumor is you can't carry much aboard a plane now. Is my day pack too large?

"Did you take a fanny pack?"

"No." I'd thought of it, then not done it. So we stop in the hotel shop and get an over-the-shoulder thing little enough to go in my pack.

Marilyn leaves me at the shuttle.

I check in. Allow two hours, right. Smooth as silk. They let me keep my pack. Murphy magic works. (That is, you enlist the cussedness of the universe by preparing for the event you would prevent. If the spell doesn't work, hey, you're still prepared!)

I stop to buy notepads; I want to write this up. I'm an hour and a half early at the gate.

I'm the only suit and tie in sight. Bad idea, I think. At best I'm way out of style. I should take a zipper jacket so I know where everything is.

The waiting area isn't crowded. If we all came two hours early, it should be packed. Travelers must be sparse. Nobody seems nervous, though. There are lots of children.

Maybe I'm seeing remnants. There are folk who promised to travel before September 11. We are the ones who haven't backed out. When we run short, is it disaster for the airlines?

What the terrorists did to us is known. But what can we be made to do to ourselves as a result?

I saw lots of police on the streets, guiding traffic. All the rules around LAX have changed.

News yesterday: an attempted armed robbery at the Promenade, a shopping center we frequent. The perp is dead. Trigger fingers are quicker these days. Does that mean crime will go down? Or are we distracting our police, and will crime go up?

Consider: we could arm all passengers on commercial flights. Terrorists would be outnumbered.

Nah. A shootout would go to the faster draw. Holes in the hull would cause explosive decompression.

What if we required glaser bullets? (They shatter on impact.)

You'd still get a few shootouts with no terrorists involved. Some asshole smokes in a lavatory, boom!

Consensus among my friends says arm the pilots, at least.

I wonder how the LAX Theme Restaurant is doing? Closed, I bet, given that the new rules don't allow parking.

Belatedly, I'm in the Admiral's Club. I still don't see suits or ties. The coffee is welcome.

I'm still daydreaming fights on airplanes. Several friends sent me a speech by a pilot. *Mob them. Throw things at them. Blanket over his head.* Would his suggestion work? On one terrorist with a blade, yeah. Five?

Boarded.

I've heard "Mack the Knife" as background twice today. It's come to me: "Mack the Knife" is a filk! Mack Heath was the antihero in a play, maybe *Threepenny Opera.* Jerry would know.

Nothing about Hell in the way of insights—except that Niven & Pournelle's *Purgatorio* (sequel to our version of *Inferno*) will fill up with terrorists unless I'm careful.

September 11 was such a complex cluster of sins! Pride, murder of innocents, grand theft, perversion of scripture, violation of visa terms, defacing a national monument, probably coveting thy neighbor's property. Do sinners commute? Can a sinner be scattered through Hell, in several places at once?

Consecutively, I think. Where did Billy the Kid go after the demons got him (in our *Inferno*)? To some other sin to be expiated.

*

HELL: Never grow older. Heal from anything.

HEAVEN: Perfect in the flesh. No hurts to heal from, but you'd heal.

LATE KNOWN SPACE, my most extensive future history: Never grow old. Heal from anything. This is the ideal we've been pursuing all along, and Dante passed it out free in Hell. Life Extension Foundation, take note.

*

American Airlines' upgrade is wonderful. I'm riding a 767-300. First Class has full horizontal recline into a bucket-shaped shield. Business Class seats (mine, due to an upgrade) are so far apart that my extended legs don't reach by several inches. Nearly full recline, two switches to adjust the leg rest. It's wonderfully comfortable. I haven't seen Tourist Class.

Lunch was high end. Dessert: "You only get chocolate sauce on ice cream in First. Here it's just ice cream." Or tiramisu, which was delicious.

I stopped worrying as soon as the flight attendant served me a Mimosa before takeoff. Now, three and a half hours after takeoff, what would bandits be waiting for?

Airplanes in Hell? We built one already, a glider, and introduced a Shuttle pilot. Air Force? I don't think Dante's demons flew, except Geryon. Jerry? We'll HIJACK GERYON!

(Gun to the demon's head.) "Geryon, remember that I have an ethical right to lie to you. Make me an offer I can accept."

The setup: Carpenter runs across a soul, Winford, who has to reach Earth. Carpenter doesn't care where he is as long as there are souls to be helped and puzzles to be solved. So he helps.

Winford could avert a disaster if only he were alive, or could talk to someone alive on Earth.

The route lies uphill, against the flow of Hell, through the impassable wall and into Dante's Wood. Check location: southern hemisphere, just opposite Rome, by Dante's map. If we make it back to Earth, we get to play ghosts. Purgatory for Carpenter is both Hell and Earth

The guy next to me is a reader. Doesn't talk.

I'm down. Marilyn, there's seating in the baggage area! How polite!

Not a wasted day. Still, I may have learned as much as I ever will from looking down on clouds, and that was all fantasy, of course: *The Magic Goes Away.*

Incoming, we didn't pass over any scar in the skyline, nor any city at all. It looked like swamp and sea.

No baggage is moving.

AA must have upgraded just before the stock market went bad. Then, September 11. That will cost them.

Because the United States built so many planes, and sold them everywhere, it has come about that you must speak English to fly, or at least land. If we lose our command of commercial air, we lose a big piece of what makes us great.

*

Baggage moving. Here's mine.

My driver's a kick. He braced me as I was searching through a maze of fences for a taxi stand. He's got a limo. "$40." A sign had warned me that these guys are illegal, but I felt lucky so I took it.

"What was it like for you on the 11th?"

"It was great!" At Kennedy lots of people were canceling their flights. Then they all needed taxis. They were willing to ride four at a time, four different stops, sixty bucks each, no problem.

He wants to know what happens next. I couldn't tell him. Jeez, and me an SF writer. He thinks Bush will smell like a rose at the end of his term. Hey, he knows more than I do. Predicting the near future is the hardest.

He's from Trinidad. He used to own a shoe store. His English is good. He likes politics and he likes to lecture. I got an earful of how the USA is perceived by the underclasses in foreign climes.

Meddlesome. You just can't do business if the big foreign neighbor can step in and change the rules at any time.

Most of my rocket scientist friends feel exactly the same way about NASA. Libertarians feel that way about government agencies in general: arrogant, meddlesome, too powerful. But we can't let ourselves be hurt this badly. We're going to meddle hard.

Hating—and mocking—thy neighbor is an old tradition. Hating/mocking thy most conspicuous neighbor is easiest: it doesn't test your memory or your acting ability or make your head hurt. They want to tear us down because we block their view.

The New York streets are all screwed up. Thank God for Eleanor Wood's directions.

My first impression of the Gramercy Park Hotel: nice. Little. European. First suite we tried, the door lock wasn't working. Second suite, looked nice. Tiny bathroom.

The restaurant is wonderful.

I didn't try to use the toilet in 1405 until way late.

It's blocked by a radiator. No problem if your left leg has been amputated high enough up. I got my leg up on the radiator and made it work. Yes, my injured leg, still healing nicely, never gave me a bit of trouble on the plane. I notice there's a bar in the tub for handicapped. Does anyone really expect a handicapped person to use this toilet?

I'll have to change rooms again.

*

Tuesday

New room, looks good. A guy with long legs would still be blocked from the toilet. My telephone is clicking regularly: message from Eleanor Wood, after the phone rang with nobody on. It took me ten minutes, four phone calls, to get it to stop clicking.

Lunch date at Simon & Schuster, with John Ordover and Eleanor. I got there early. I finally met John. He seems fannish, and why not? In his youth (he says) I pulled him into the *Magic Goes Away* universe.

He immediately got me talking about *Ringworld's Child.* (Maybe make that "Children".) He loves it. Forget that I'm writing it for TOR, he's still into new stories.

Lunch was delightful. Afterward Eleanor took me to her new office. I never saw her old office. The new one, several rooms, has a cluttered look, but she loves it. Then she took me by subway (I wouldn't go in there without a guide) to the Rose Center for Earth and Space at the American Museum of Natural History.

Marilyn found this place for me in an *LA Times* article: "The Cosmic Cathedral." It's so new that some of the buttons in the downstairs exhibits aren't installed yet. But it's mostly complete, and it's wonderful. What it will teach best is a sense of proportion. Circling that great sphere in the center takes you from the size of the universe down to the size of a quark. Down the ramp covers the age of the universe . . . that still varies a little, twelve to fourteen billion years. (It was eighteen billion when I first memorized a number; fifteen when I was writing the DC Comics background.)

I went back to the hotel by cab and turbaned driver, along Fifth Avenue, a nostalgic trip.

Prix fixe menu, mussels, and a very good duck.

The park is only open 7 to 7. Yes, I thought of taking a cab to the disaster area, and didn't.

I no longer have access to the Internet when I'm away from home. I'll have to get Eric to set that up. Last time it was like pulling teeth.

I hate the touchpad feature of this keyboard. Every time my thumb brushes it, I lose the cursor. Then again, I hate not having backup when I realize that my

mouse has quit working. Oh, futz, it's probably safe to get it disabled.

*

Wednesday

Breakfast. This hotel is short on fruit, but they're solicitous. I got the doorman to let me into the park, and rapidly wished that I'd saved bread from breakfast. Squirrels and pigeons surrounded me.

Walked to the *Analog* offices, eleven blocks. Bought a camera. My leg is feeling the exercise, but holding up.

Lunch with Stan Schmidt and a young editor ran well. I got my fruit fix. Stan's eager for short fiction, no surprise. He thinks "Finding Myself" is absolutely wonderful.

I hope I printed the correspondence with Brenda Cooper when we were building "Finding Myself." I want it in *Scatterbrain,* my forthcoming retrospective collection from TOR. The letters have disappeared off the bottom of my file, but I may have copied them and sent the stack to Bob Gleason. Or Brenda might have them. I spent a lot of wordage telling Brenda how difficult a story she was telling, where every aspect of the environment is optional. Eventually the fixes became the story.

Bob Gleason's out of town. Too bad, I would have liked to talk to him.

I bought a second camera because I thought I'd messed up the first one. Now I think I didn't. I'll use up both. Ghu, these things are cheap. I found three produce markets on Park; bought cashews and a banana and fake maple fudge.

I got myself into the little locked park again. There's one wonderful two-faced sculpture (out of a selection). I took several pictures. I was afraid I'd missed the squirrels; not hardly! One accepted a cashew.

I don't want to see the scar of the World Trade Center! What would I see? Only rubble that hasn't been trucked away. I don't want to be a camera-laden tourist in sight of, or in the way of, people who are doing real work. I didn't want to last night—a dangerous notion anyway—and I don't want to this afternoon. The news is giving all the detail one could possibly want, and more. Somebody mentioned the stench; it must be awful, with 6,300 *(later reduced to 3,000)* dead and irretrievable inside all that concrete. I have enough data to describe a rubble pile in Hell well enough to raise echoes in a reader's mind.

I want to see the New York around me, and listen to the stories.

Stan Schmidt of *Analog* was in town September 11 (he only comes once a week). The trains were stopped for a while, and then ran limited, filling up, then stopping at every stop, and apparently not collecting tickets. He feared the tunnels collapsing but getting out was worth the risk.

I met Eleanor Wood and Tom and Tanya Doherty in the hotel bar. Off to a play, *Metamorphoses*. It's based on Ovid's legends, and worth seeing: it's played largely in a shallow pool of water.

Dinner at "11 Madison." Very nice, I'd like to go back. We talked politics in a high noise level that eased as diners became less of a mob. Tom agrees with the limo driver and me: our government has been characteristically meddlesome. He knows way more than I do about current events, and he dubs the government clumsy, too. "We should never have broken up the Ottoman Empire—"but they were supporting the Axis, so it must have looked good then. And how can we not meddle in Afghanistan after September 11?

We put Eleanor in a taxi, and then the Dohertys walked me back to the hotel.

*

Thursday

I walked to the Flatiron Building, to TOR's new offices. You can't lose it: it's angled on the sky. I hate getting lost.

Tom got me to sign some books, gave me a copy of *Ender's Game*—which I should have read years ago, it's wonderful—then introduced me to Jennifer Marcus. She's publicity director. We spent some time talking.

I saw two bookstalls on the sidewalk. Best-sellers generally; nothing by me. I wanted to photograph one, but a guy—maybe a clerk—stopped me with gestures. I think he was putting me on, but I let him.

The trip to Albany was hassle free, but loud: propeller engines. Joe Berlant picked me up. He played tour director going in. Schenectady is a wonderful town. I was told repeatedly about the weather forecast: two days hot, then cold.

Signed in. At six, went to join the Art Show crew for work and pizza. I helped set up, moving pipes and so forth, then assembling the maze. I've never done that before. I'm still unskilled labor, but . . . have to try this at LosCon.

*

Friday

Kurt Siegel picked me up for a tour, as promised. He's a fireman; he was active in the rescue operations at the World Trade Center. He grew up here and knows it all. We drove, then walked around the Stockade area, where all the houses are centuries old. He pointed out marks of age and damage and renovation. Brick that sags, bricks that were put in endwise in alternate rows. Steel rods that pull a brick house back together, their external endpoints marked with decorative stars. Back yards huge in extent. The river.

Asphalt siding that turns a building into a tinderbox, on newer buildings outside the Stockade.

Lunch at an ancient market: turkey sandwiches, from a whole turkey fresh out of the oven. We explored the college and the wonderful Nott Memorial. I forgot I had a camera on me, dammit. I'm not used to carrying one.

The convention started 4 P.M. My panel was at six. Afterward I got coat and tie and joined Dave Hartwell and his family, and Hal Clement. We couldn't get into our first restaurant so we followed Joe's directions to a steakhouse. Back too late for the Ice Cream Social, but the Regency Ball was in progress. I got my wonderful vest, bought with Marilyn's approval at a craft show in Santa Monica, and danced. Left to attend the Art Show Reception; dropped leftover grapes off at the Con Suite; danced some more; watched a horrible movie; returned to my room.

Half past midnight: found a message from Eleanor. Call her, at home if need be. Vince Gerardis needs a decision.

I called.

It was about movie rights. I wish Eleanor had said, "This is not for discussion." But I probably woke her up.

*

Saturday

As promised, it rained this morning and it's still gloomy. I brought sweaters. Walking past the video room, I caught *The Slaver Weapon* playing.

Breakfast in the Con Suite. Librarian with a puppet dragon. Falsetto: "Hi, kids, I'm the dragon who teaches you to read!"

I said, "Lends new meaning to the term 'bookwyrm'."

"Who said bookworm?"

"Me."

"Genius!"

I saw him later and he'd labeled the dragon, correctly spelled: *BOOKWYRM.*

Panels ran okay, maybe better than okay. I doze off only when I'm in the audience. What I caught of the New Planets panel sounded interesting. If a red or brown dwarf has a fat gas giant companion, it'll be tidally locked, but the moons won't be locked to the sun. You'll get day and night. That's half the stars in the sky. I'd better tell the chirpsithra: give them companion species.

Tony and Sue Lewis got in midnight Friday. Sue caught me in the hall Saturday. The plan: meet for dinner, then do a 9 P.M. interview. It all worked. We went with Joe and Edie Siclari. The restaurant was slow, the food good, and we were back in time to catch some anniversary cake.

The interview ran just fine. Having told Marilyn about the Mandell accord, I felt free to speak of it to the audience. It never occurred to me that I was speaking for the Internet, for someone who would garble the data.

Joe and Edie threw a sweet wines room party. Very nice. I went on to other room parties, watched a few minutes of *Flesh Gordon,* then bed. No surprises this time.

*

Sunday

Pills, breakfast, exercise, and swim. Autograph at eleven. Sunday's panels didn't look exciting.

I drafted David Stephenson for lunch; we'd been seeing each other on panels and everywhere. Hotel restaurant was vacant of staff. We rethought, then followed Joe and Edie Siclaris' directions to Mike's Diner. Good sausage sandwich. Conversation: getting into space, of course. David doesn't trust Zubrin's "Mars Direct": another ten-year plan, like Apollo.

Conversations in the reception area.

Joe Berlant took us back to the steak house: me, Hal Clement, and the bookseller Larry Smith.

Reception area, more conversations. Too much about Bin Laden. We're bombing Afghanistan. I wonder how that will affect airport security.

*

Monday

Breakfast with Hal Clement. Joe took me to the airport and Hal to his train.

I'm hoping for an uneventful flight. Memo: carry ear plugs when flying. Propeller planes are worse than the jets.

Again I arrived with two hours to spare and found no hassles. I wanted a picture of Security at Albany Airport. Asked. The woman got her supervisor. He gave permission. Then one of a line of armed soldiers took it back.

There's a Meditation Room at the airport, and I did snap a picture of that. There's no icon for any specific religion, just a nice, relaxing place.

The flight was pleasant, the seats not so far apart, but far enough. My seatmate and a woman ahead of her were interacting, trading information, hard at work. Dinner was earlyish: lunchtime by LA time. The movie: *Tomb Raider*. If I'd turned the volume up enough I'd be deaf now, so I didn't try to follow the plot.

Marilyn wasn't in Baggage Claim. LAX wasn't allowing cars inside the airport when I left eight days ago, so she was probably at Lot B. I tried to call her cellphone. Failed.

My luggage didn't arrive.

I put in a bid at the luggage office. The woman's guess proved correct: it didn't get loaded from the Albany flight. Airlines never have hired enough baggage handlers, and now they must have fired a few.

I pushed my way onto a Lot B bus. There wouldn't have been room for my suitcase, I think. Cheerful crowd: glad to land without a sniff of a terrorist, just like me. Marilyn was at Lot B. She'd pushed the wrong button on her phone.

I was ready for dinner again, and Marilyn had missed hers. We stopped at an IHOP, then home.

*

Tuesday

Call from Vince Gerardis, my TV/movie agent. I called back.

He's seen an announcement on a Hollywood Web page. It derives from what I said during Saturday evening's interview. Vince is sure it'll shoot down any movie deal that might have been made.

Damn! I wasn't told to keep my mouth shut, but I also didn't realize I was talking for the Internet.

My luggage arrived late afternoon.

*

Conclusion:

This trip, I never tried to make anything happen. I took whatever was thrown at me, and wrote it up. Mostly it went fine. New York is functioning after September 11. Schenectady is wonderful if you can sightsee with the eyes of a firefighting native. The airlines are working, hassle-free if you don't need your luggage right away. The airports are another matter; you have to plan around that.

Once we ruled the air: most passenger airplanes were built by the United States. Is that age over? It might not even be tragic. The age of flight may be given over to the age of communication. Modems, virtual reality, tourism without tears.

Computer gurus train themselves, by playing with computers until they learn how to program. Only in a free country can they do that. We will rule the worldwide net too.

*

Trip report: Salt Lake City

Life, the Universe, and Everything

At the outset this seemed a wonderful opportunity. I'd been laid up with a ruined knee, housebound except for Marilyn's good offices. Came an offer to see Salt Lake City again, I jumped at it. I could see what's happened to Hansen Planetarium in twenty years.

Later it seemed stupid. Utah, in February, with the city clogged by the Olympics?

Hannah Jensen suggested that I get here early, watch some Olympic competition. Sure, why not?

Then I got a message: they're short of hotel space, would I mind being put up at someone's house?

This sounded like disaster. I asked for hotel space. I suggested coming for just the symposium. Yeah, right. When it all fell out, I was coming Monday for a symposium that starts Thursday—Tickets for an Olympic event had been arranged Tuesday.

I went wary, carrying all manner of names and addresses.

It got better.

The flight: Marilyn expected a rush hour, so we got there two-and-a-half hours early. I brought a book. The flight went fine. Mason Emerson picked me up: I wore my CONTACT ID badge. He volunteered tourist duty before the run to the motel.

In an art gallery, one Michael Porrazzo (Porrazzo Strategic Technologies Inc.) spotted me by the badge. He told me about Discover Navajo, ongoing in the vicinity. He gave me some names and introductions. He may have generated something else too: an unusual market. We'll see.

Dinner: Rhodesio, one of those places where they carve samples of meat at your table. I tasted crocodile and snake sausages, and excellent chicken and beef.

Next day Mason took me back for Discover Navajo. He's been really helpful. We went through an educational tour that's going straight into *Burning Tower*. Between the proto-Aztecs at Aztlan and Condigeo, I'll embed Navajo physics.

Tuesday was my first experience at an Olympic event: James Clegg took me to Women's Hockey, Russia vs. Germany. My first hockey event too. My, that puck moves fast. I saw not much violence but a lot of falling. It was a shutout, 5-0, but it looked to me like both sides were very good, very fast.

At I-CON X conference, Long Island, NY, April 1991

Wednesday two ladies, Susan Kroven and Patricia Castelli, took me (by way of a dynamite southwestern restaurant) back to Hansen Planetarium at my request. It's changed some. They've got some wonderful displays, and a great show—music and astrophysics—and a new version of "the most wonderful object in the universe." The ladies toured me around the Temple area, and we happened to catch a concert in the Mormon Tabernacle.

Wednesday night we met at Aleta and James Clegg's house. (They've got *The Last Hero,* by Terry Pratchett, and showed it to me. I bought it later.) Purpose: symposium business, and a banquet, and something odder: a *Star Trek* role-playing game played at the local grade school. The computer equipment is wonderful. I played captain in a crew of fifteen. We got lectured on Star Fleet history, then ran a mission. We got about halfway through. I think I fluffed our hyperspace jump.

Thursday through Saturday: something like a convention, something like a symposium. It ran smoothly. At all times I had transportation, and food was available. It's still a university convention, and that means an out-of-town guest is pretty well stuck. You want a shower or sleep, you don't look for an elevator, you find someone with a car. I was lucky: I held up throughout the convention. The motel had a pool and spa, too. (So does my house, but they're outside, in the Chatsworth winds.)

There was a session that (again) fit right into *Burning Tower*. It was on using other cultural myths in stories, but mostly the panelists concentrated on the Americas, southwest USA and on south.

Thursday night, a Mormon bishop took me to dinner.

Friday night, a writer group did that, then brought me back for good filking. (Singing, that is: parody songs as written by fantasy and science fiction fans.)

Saturday, a medieval banquet at the U, then dancing I actually knew. Hole-in-the-wall, I think, with flute music to the same tune the Friends of the English Regency use. Then visits to emeritus teachers, and I was given a quilt. I was packing too much: I was ready to refuse when Lisa Done volunteered to carry it for me.

Sunday's flight home ran smooth by today's standards. I had to take off my shoes for Security. The airport offered no trace of breakfast. In flight, stay in seats for half an hour after takeoff and half an hour before landing, on penalties we didn't explore. Marilyn met me as planned.

A generally good trip. But I wouldn't have spent two extra days to get to a single Olympic event, and flying is getting to be a more serious hassle.

*

May 28, 2002:

After we left the emergency room, Brenda and Steve suggested that this would be seen as an incident, not a life change. Maybe they were right.

My leg has done everything I've asked of it.

I've joined a hiking group, I climb rocks at Stony Point, and I've started playing racquetball . . . where tennis elbow is a problem, but the knee is up to it.

Healing from this and other injuries has been like getting old in reverse. I could mark moments of improvement: the day I could make breakfast, bend my knee, attend physical therapy, ride in the front seat of a car, hike. The night I could drive, Marilyn was ecstatic.

The depression I felt at the beginning of the year disappeared as soon as I had something real to worry about.

I have worried about my writing.

The cure for that is to write. If a novel wasn't moving fast enough, I moved to another novel, or wrote a short story. I'm working on two collaborations, both nearly finished, I think. *Scatterbrain,* due next year, is finished. I've written many short stories lately.

*

The future isn't what I thought it would be. Some of us saw more clearly than others, and those, I guess, were the pessimists.

Foreigners of Eastern origin are being turned away from USA flight training schools. We're losing that aspect of our civilization: we'll no longer rule the skies. We were supposed to have cities on the Moon by now.

I predicted that Mecca wouldn't survive into the twenty-first century. My reasoning was that Muslims are just too good at pissing people off. I've missed the deadline, obviously, but . . . somebody with a nuke, somewhere, is going to decide he's had enough.

I never thought I was a prophet. I've looked for, and written about, basic truths. There aren't many. What I've seen has usually found its way into the "Draco Tavern" stories, where all sufficiently general questions have answers.

BIOGRAPHICAL AND CRITICAL SOURCES:

BOOKS

Authors and Artists for Young Adults, Volume 27, Gale (Detroit, MI), 1999.

Beacham's Encyclopedia of Popular Fiction, Beacham (Osprey, FL), 1996.

Contemporary Literary Criticism, Volume 8, Gale (Detroit, MI), 1978.

Contemporary Popular Writers, St. James Press (Detroit, MI), 1997.

Dictionary of Literary Biography, Volume 8: *Twentieth-Century American Science-Fiction Writers,* Gale (Detroit, MI), 1981.

Gunn, James, editor, *New Encyclopedia of Science Fiction,* Viking (New York, NY), 1988.

Legends in Their Own Time, Prentice Hall (New York, NY), 1994.

Platt, Charles, *Dream Makers,* Volume II: *The Uncommon Men and Women Who Write Science Fiction,* Berkley Publishing (New York, NY), 1983.

Reginald, Robert, *Science-Fiction and Fantasy Literature, 1975-1991,* Gale (Detroit, MI), 1992.

Science-Fiction Writers, 2nd edition, Scribner's (New York, NY), 1999.

St. James Guide to Science-Fiction Writers, 4th edition, St. James Press (Detroit, MI), 1995.

Stringer, Jenny, editor, *The Oxford Companion to Twentieth-Century Literature in English,* Oxford University Press (New York, NY), 1996.

Vrana, Stan A., *Interviews and Conversations with Twentieth-Century Authors Writing in English,* Scarecrow Press (Metuchen, NJ), 1986.

PERIODICALS

Analog Science Fiction & Fact, March, 1978; February, 1979; July, 1993, p. 250; January, 1996, p. 273; June, 1999, review of *Rainbow Mars,* p. 134.

Booklist, February 1, 1979, Algis Budrys, review of *The Magic Goes Away,* p. 856; February 1, 1984, Roland Green, review of *The Integral Trees,* p. 770; March 1, 1987, review of *The Smoke Ring,* p. 948; December 15, 1992, Carl Hays, review of *The Gripping Hand,* p. 699; March 1, 1999, review of *Rainbow Mars,* p. 1160.

Detroit News, April 20, 1980, Bud Foote, review of *Ringworld.*

Future, number 3, 1978.

Kirkus Reviews, December 1, 1992, review of *The Gripping Hand,* p. 1472; September 1, 1995, p. 1232; April 1, 1996, p. 495; January 15, 1999, review of *Rainbow Mars,* p. 111.

Kliatt, January, 1989, review of *The Legacy of the Heorot,* pp. 22-23; January, 1990, review of *Dream Park II,* pp. 20-21; May, 1994, p. 18; July, 1988, review of *Destiny's Road,* p. 20.

Library Journal, September 15, 1995, review of *Beowulf's Children,* p. 97; May 15, 1996, p. 86; February 15, 1999, review of *Rainbow Mars,* p. 188.

Locus, February, 1993, p. 30; September, 1994, p. 69; February, 1995, p. 38; April, 1999, review of *Rainbow Mars,* pp. 25, 29.

Los Angeles Times Book Review, April 19, 1981; November 8, 1981; November 21, 1982.

Magazine of Fantasy and Science Fiction, September, 1971.

New Republic, October 30, 1976, Fredric Jameson, "Science Fiction as Politics," pp. 34-38.

New York Times Book Review, January 12, 1975; October 26, 1975; October 17, 1976; November 13, 1977; January 31, 1993, p. 25.

Publishers Weekly, September 16, 1974, review of *The Mote in God's Eye,* p. 54; August 23, 1976, review of *A World out of Time,* p. 61; February 22, 1980, review of *The Patchwork Girl,* p. 107; March 13, 1981, review of *Dream Park,* pp. 86-87; January 4, 1985, review of *The Integral Trees,* p. 68; December 28, 1992, review of *The Gripping Hand,* p. 70; December 6, 1993, p. 70; October 16, 1995, p. 46; May 13, 1996, review of *The Ringworld Throne,* p. 60; January 25, 1999, review of *Rainbow Mars,* p. 77; December 3, 2001, review of *Man-Kzin Wars IX,* p. 44.

School Library Journal, March, 1975, Joni Bodari, review of *The Mote in God's Eye,* p. 112; March, 1980, K. Sue Hurwitz, review of *The Ringworld Engineers,* p. 147.

Science Books and Films, special edition, v. 32, 1998, review of *Ringworld,* p. 22; September, 1999, review of *Rainbow Mars,* p. 207.

Science-Fiction Review, July, 1978, Jeffrey Ellior, "An Interview with Larry Niven," pp. 24-27.

Times Literary Supplement, November 7, 1980, Galen Strawson, review of *The Ringworld Engineers,* p. 1265.

Voice of Youth Advocates, June, 1981, review of *The Ringworld Engineers,* pp. 38-39; June 1999, review of *Choosing Names,* p. 108.

Washington Post Book World, December 27, 1981; February 26, 1984.*

NORGAY, Jamling Tenzing 1965-

PERSONAL: Born April 23, 1965, in Darjeeling, India; son of Tenzing Norgay; married, wife's name: Soyang; children: three daughters. *Education:* Northland College, B.A. (business administration), 1989.

ADDRESSES: Home—Darjeeling, India. *Agent*—c/o Author Mail, Harper San Francisco, 353 Sacramento St., San Francisco, CA 94111.

CAREER: Author and mountain climber. Tenzing Norgay Adventures, Darjeeling, India, owner. Former black-belt instructor in karate and Tae Kwon Do.

AWARDS, HONORS: For his efforts to help save climbers trapped on Mount Everest during a severe storm, Norgay received His Holiness the Dalai Lama's Award, and the National Citizen's Award from the president of India in 1998.

WRITINGS:

(With Broughton Coburn) *Touching My Father's Soul: A Sherpa's Journey to the Top of Everest,* Harper-SanFrancisco (San Francisco, CA), 2001.

SIDELIGHTS: The son of the most famous Sherpa, or Tibetan mountain guide, in history, Jamling Tenzing Norgay had a lot to live up to. His father, Tenzing Norgay, led Sir Edmund Hillary up Mount Everest to become the first ever to stand on its summit in 1953. Norgay, the son, showed an early aptitude for mountain climbing but was encouraged by his father to pursue an education instead. So in 1985 the twenty-year-old man came to the United States to attend college, eventually earning a bachelor's degree in business administration from the same college in Wisconsin that had awarded his father an honorary degree years before. After ten years in the United States, however, and with the passing of his parents, Norgay felt compelled to return to mountain climbing in the Himalayas. After completing a five-summit solo expedition in the Himalayas, he was invited to join an American expedition to the summit of Everest. And in 1996 he was asked to guide an expedition to the summit that would be filmed in the wide-screen IMAX format.

Norgay's 1996 team, organized by filmmaker David Brashears, was at a base camp on the way to the summit when a terrible storm struck higher up the mountain, killing a number of climbers and guides in a tragedy recounted most famously by Jon Krakauer in his best-selling book *Into Thin Air.* The IMAX team participated in the rescue effort, and successfully ascended the peak in the days following the storm. Norgay writes about the experience in *Touching My Father's Soul,* a unique blend of mountaineering adventure story and family memoir in which the author interweaves stories of the late-twentieth-century expedition with little-known tales of his father's ascent nearly fifty years earlier. Some reviewers focused on the clarity with which Norgay and coauthor Broughton Coburn relate the gritty details of an Everest expedition. A reviewer in *Kirkus Reviews* remarked: "Norgay and coauthor Coburn cover the logistical details of summiting Everest with welcome precision and a clarity that opens the story to a much wider audience than merely the crampon-clad mountaineering herd." For others, the unique contribution of *Touching My Father's Soul* lies in Norgay's depiction of what climbing Everest means to one for whom it is the dwelling place of a goddess. "It is also a fascinating look into the world of climbers and their relationship to the Sherpas who risk their lives to assist them," added Eric Robbins in *Booklist.* Reviewers predicted great popularity for the book. A contributor to *Publishers Weekly* concluded that "the broad, well-established adventure audience will devour this book."

BIOGRAPHICAL AND CRITICAL SOURCES:

PERIODICALS

Booklist, April 15, 2001, Eric Robbins, review of *Touching My Father's Soul: A Sherpa's Journey to the Top of Everest,* p. 1526.
Kirkus Reviews, March 15, 2001, review of *Touching My Father's Soul,* p. 390.
Library Journal, May 1, 2001, Olga B. Wise, review of *Touching My Father's Soul,* p. 118.
Outside, May, 2001, review of *Touching My Father's Soul.*
Publishers Weekly, January 15, 2001, p. 1; April 2, 2001, review of *Touching My Father's Soul,* p. 50.
Wall Street Journal, June 4, 2001, "Two Generations and the Quest for the Summit," p. A19.
Washington Post, May 20, 2001, Ted Rose, "Heroes and High Jinks," p. T7.

OTHER

Asian Reporter, http://www.asianreporter.com/ (August 2, 2001), review of *Touching My Father's Soul.*
Backwoods, http://www.backwoods.com/ (September 6, 2001), "A Conversation with Jamling Norgay."
Mountain Hardwear, http://www.mountainhardwear.com/ (August 2, 2001), "Jamling Tenzing Norgay's Biography: 'I Feel I Am Completing a Circle.'"*

*   *   *

NORTH, Robert Carver 1914-2002

OBITUARY NOTICE—See index for CA sketch: Born November 17, 1914, in Walton, NY; died of complications from a stroke July 15, 2002, in Menlo Park, CA. Educator and author. A professor at Stanford University, North was notable for his research in international conflicts and quantitative analysis. He originally studied languages and literature, earning his bachelor's degree from Union College in 1936. After serving in the U.S. Army Air Force during World War II, he returned to college to earn his Ph.D. from Stanford University in 1957. It was while he was working as a research associate at the Hoover Institution in the early 1950s that North first gained notoriety for publishing a study blaming the rise of communism in China to the failure of not only China's nationalists but also failed U.S. foreign policy. Brave enough to criticize McCarthyism during the 1950s, North spent his entire academic career at Stanford, first as a research associate from 1950 to 1957, and then as an associate professor and professor of political science. He retired in 1985 as a professor emeritus. North was also the director of Studies in International Conflict and Integration, and through his forward-thinking leadership he insisted on the use of computers as a tool in studying international relations at the university. North was the author or coauthor of sixteen books on international politics, including *Moscow and Chinese Communists* (1953), *Chinese Communism: A History of Its Origins and Ideas* (1966), *The World That Could Be* (1976), and *War, Peace, Survival: Global Politics and Conceptual Synthesis* (1990).

OBITUARIES AND OTHER SOURCES:

BOOKS

Who's Who in America, 55th edition, Marquis (New Providence, NJ), 2001.

PERIODICALS

Los Angeles Times, August 4, 2002, p. B17.
Washington Post, August 6, 2002, p. B5.

*   *   *

NOTO, Lore(nzo) 1923-2002

OBITUARY NOTICE—See index for *CA* sketch: Born June 9, 1923, in New York, NY; died of cancer July 8, 2002, in New York, NY. Theatrical producer, actor, and playwright. Noto became a professional actor in New York City in the 1940s, but he is remembered for his work behind the scenes. It was Noto who attended a one-act college production called *The Fantasticks* in 1959 and transformed it into one of the longest-running musicals in history. When the final curtain came down on this poignant love story in 1996, after more than 17,000 performances, Noto was still at the helm. He had stayed with the production through thick and thin, using his own funds to pay the cast during lean times, for more than forty years. During many of those years, particularly in the 1970s and 1980s, Noto performed with the cast in the role of Hucklebee, the father of the male lead. Noto's other productions include *The Yearling,* a 1965 Broadway play Noto co-wrote with Herbert Martin. In 1966 he received an achievement award from the American Academy of Dramatic Art.

OBITUARIES AND OTHER SOURCES:

PERIODICALS

Chicago Tribune, July 11, 2002, section 2, p. 9.
Los Angeles Times, July 9, 2002, p. B11.
New York Times, July 10, 2002, obituary by Ari L. Goldman, p. A22.
Washington Post, July 11, 2002, p. B6.

O

OBEYESEKERE, Ranjini D. 1933-

PERSONAL: Born March 27, 1933; daughter of Gladys Panabokke and Dhanusekera Bandara Ellepola; married Gananath Obeyesekere. *Education:* University of Peradeniya, Sri Lanka, B.A. (with honors); University of Washington, Ph.D., 1968. *Religion:* Buddhist.

ADDRESSES: Home—61 West 62nd St., New York, NY 10023; and 352 B. Dharmarajaj Mawata Kandy, Sri Lanka. *Office*—100 Aaron Burr Hall, Princeton University, Princeton, NJ 08540. *E-mail*—robeyese@princeton.edu.

CAREER: Taught at University of Sri Lanka, 1966-72; University of California—San Diego, literature instructor, 1976-80; Princeton University, Princeton, NJ, lecturer in anthropology, 1988—.

AWARDS, HONORS: Fulbright Award, 1992-93; translation fellowship, National Endowment for the Humanities.

WRITINGS:

Sinhala Writing and the New Critics, M. D. Gunasena (Colombo, Sri Lanka), 1974.
(Editor, with Chitra Fernando) *An Anthology of Modern Writing from Sri Lanka,* Association for Asian Studies (Tucson, AZ), 1981.
Jewels of the Doctrine: Translations from the Saddharmaratnavaliya, State University of New York Press (New York, NY), 1998.

Sri Lankan Theater in a Time of Terror: Political Satire in a Permitted Space, Sage Publications (Thousand Oaks, CA), 1999.
Portraits of Buddhist Women: Stories from the Saddharmaratnavaliya, State University of New York Press (New York, NY), 2001.

WORK IN PROGRESS: A translation of the poem "Yasodharavata" with a critical introduction.

SIDELIGHTS: Ranjini D. Obeyesekere has published several books on Sinhala literature, the first of which, *Sinhala Writing and the New Critics,* focuses on literary criticism. Her next effort is a collection of Sinhala writing called *An Anthology of Modern Writing from Sri Lanka,* which she coedited with Chitra Fernando. In this work, Obeyesekere and Fernando present collections of poetry and prose, as well as an introduction to Sinhalese literature. *Journal of Asian Studies* reviewer Charles Hallisey noted that the "emphasis on realism will make the volume of interest to those concerned about contemporary Sri Lanka in general." And K. S. Narayana Rao commented in *World Literature Today* that although "Sri Lankan writing in English is clearly still in an evolving stage . . . the book is a worthwhile addition to the library of Asian literatures and fills a keenly felt gap."

BIOGRAPHICAL AND CRITICAL SOURCES:

PERIODICALS

Choice, January, 2000, J. L. Erdman, review of *Sri Lankan Theater in a Time of Terror: Political Satire in a Permitted Space,* p. 947.

Journal of Asian Studies, February, 1985, Charles Hallisey, review of *An Anthology of Modern Writing from Sri Lanka,* pp. 437-438.

World Literature Today, summer, 1982, K. S. Narayana Rao, review of *An Anthology of Modern Writing from Sri Lanka,* p. 576.

*   *   *

O'GARA, Geoffrey H. 1950-

PERSONAL: Born September 17, 1950, in San Francisco, CA; son of Charles O'Gara (an attorney); married Berthenia Crocker (an attorney), June 4, 1977; children: Genya Rosaleen Nicholas. *Education:* Pomona College, B.A., 1973. *Politics:* Democrat. *Religion:* Catholic.

ADDRESSES: Home—724 Washakie St., Lander, WY 82520. *Office*—Martello Tower, Inc., 339 Garfield St., Lander, WY 82520. *E-mail*—gogara@wyoming.com.

CAREER: Journalist and author. *High Country News,* Lander, WY, editor, 1979-83; *Dubois Frontier,* Dubois, WY, publisher/editor, 1985-88; *Casper Star-Tribune,* Casper, WY, bureau chief/reporter, 1989-93; Wyoming Public Television, Riverton, producer/scriptwriter, 1992. Martello Tower, Inc., Lander, president, 1998—. Fremont County District, first trustee.

AWARDS, HONORS: Kellogg fellowship in journalism, University of Michigan, 1988; Spur Award for best nonfiction, Western Writers of America, 2001, for *What You See in Clear Water.*

WRITINGS:

A Long Road Home: Journeys through America's Present in Search of America's Past, Houghton Mifflin (Boston, MA), 1989, published as *A Long Road Home: In the Footsteps of the WPA Writers,* 1990.

Great Lakes, National Geographic (Washington, DC), 1997.

Frommer's Guide to Yellowstone and Grand Teton, IDG, 2000.

(With Dan Whipple) *Frommer's Guide to Wyoming and Montana,* IDG, 2000.

What You See in Clear Water: Life on the Wind River Reservation, Knopf (New York, NY), 2000.

Far West: Guide to America's Outdoors, National Geographic (Washington, DC), 2000.

Contributor of weekly column (with Dan Whipple) to Scripps News Wire; contributor of articles to *National Geographic Traveler;* author of documentaries for Wyoming Public Television.

SIDELIGHTS: Geoffrey H. O'Gara told *CA:* "I live in a part of the country where there are many true stories that never get written—and when they do, it's often by 'parachute' writers who drop in. So there's lots to do (and so little time). I split my work between documentary television and writing books and articles. I'm making a shift now to writing some fiction—but I'll keep doing the nonfiction, with particular emphasis, in the next few years, on the energy industry."

*   *   *

O'HANLON, Michael David Peter 1950-

PERSONAL: Born July 2, 1950, in Kitale, Kenya; son of Michael Charles and Rosemary Alice (Sibbald) O'Hanlon; married Linda Helga Elizabeth Frankland, 1981; children: daughter. *Education:* Attended Plymouth College (Devon, England); Pembroke College, Cambridge University, M.A.; University of London, Ph.D., 1985.

ADDRESSES: Office—c/o Pitt Rivers Museum, University of Oxford, School of Anthropology and Museum of Ethnography, South Parks Rd., Oxford 0X1 3PP, England. *E-mail*—prm@prm.ox.ac.uk.

CAREER: Anthropologist, museum director, writer, and editor. Field researcher, Wahgi Valley, Papua New Guinea highlands, 1979-81; Pacific Collections, Ethnography Department, British Museum, curator, 1983-98; Pitt Rivers Museum, Oxford, England, director, 1998—. Linacre College, Oxford, Oxford, England, professorial fellow, 1998—.

MEMBER: Royal Anthropological Institute (member of council, 1994-97, honorary secretary, 1997—).

WRITINGS:

Reading the Skin: Adornment, Display, and Society among the Wahgi, British Museum Publications (London, England), 1989.

Paradise: Portraying the New Guinea Highlands, British Museum Press (London, England), 1993.

(Editor, with Eric Hirsch) *The Anthropology of Landscape: Perspectives on Place and Space,* Clarendon Press (Oxford, England), 1995.

(Editor, with Robert Welsch) *Hunting the Gatherers: Ethnographic Collectors, Agents, and Agency in Melanesia,* (volume 6 of Methodology and History in Anthropology series), Berghahn Books (Oxford, England), 2001.

Contributor to professional journals and anthologies, including *Protection, Power, and Display: Shields of Island Southeast Asia and Melanesia,* a catalog written in conjunction with a Boston College Museum of Art exhibition, October 6 to December 10, 1995. Reviews editor for *Man;* member of editorial boards of *Journal of Material Culture, Ethnos,* and *Journal of the Royal Anthropological Institute.*

SIDELIGHTS: Michael David Peter O'Hanlon, whose research interests include Melanesia, objectification, visual anthropology, and museology, was born in Kenya in 1950. He received his early education in that country, then went to England to complete his higher education. He holds a doctorate from the University of London in social anthropology.

He conducted his doctoral research between May 1979 and August 1981 in the Wahgi Valley of the Papua New Guinea Highlands. His book *Reading the Skin: Adornment, Display, and Society among the Wahgi* grew out of that research. Annette Lynch, reviewing the book for *African Arts,* noted, "The importance of O'Hanlon's book rests fundamentally on his recognition of how knowledge of the tradition of personal adornment and display contributes to understanding the culture of the people of Melanesia." Andrew Strathern reviewed the book for *American Ethnologist.* "Through the author's skillful handling of his theme," he wrote, "the book becomes a focused analysis of exchange occasions and the struggles which surround these as well as an account of the dance displays themselves and the criteria by which they are

evaluated." Michael Young wrote in the *Australian Journal of Anthropology:* "Reading the dustcover of this attractive book—its skin so to speak—one might be misled into thinking it belongs on the coffee table. Inside, stunning colour photographs and double columns of text encourage that impression. But don't be deceived; *Reading the Skin* is a substantial monograph, a painstakingly thorough analysis of Wahgi body decoration and a solid contribution to the ethnography of the Highlands of New Guinea."

In his book *Paradise: Portraying the New Guinea Highlands,* O'Hanlon revisits the New Guinea Highlands, focusing on the Wahgi people again through their material culture. Dan Jorgensen wrote in *American Ethnologist* that O'Hanlon "reminds us of what is commonly air-brushed out of conventional accounts. The man on the book's cover paints his face with store-bought pigments, a bride uses beer bottle rip-tops as earrings, women unravel old cloth skirts to make netbags. O'Hanlon, however, is not content to replace the bone-through-the-nose with a ballpoint pen. Instead of making a trivial point about cute appropriations of Western objects, he wants to use the material world of the Wahgi to tell us about their historical experience."

O'Hanlon co-edited *The Anthropology of Landscape: Perspective on Place and Space* with Eric Hirsch. John C. McCall wrote in *American Ethnologist* that "the quality of scholarship in this volume is excellent. The broad range of questions addressed and the scope of theoretical insights make this a stimulating and thought-provoking work. The book provides crucial insights for those intending to employ the notion of landscape in their own research. It is also an ideal text for advanced courses that review key issues relating to the problem of space in anthropology." G. W. McDonogh, reviewing the book in *Choice,* described the collection as "a provocative and engaging dialogue for interdisciplinary studies in space and time."

Hunting the Gatherers: Ethnographic Collectors, Agents, and Agency in Melanesia, which O'Hanlon co-edited with Robert Welsch, takes a critical look at the gathering of ethnographic artifacts from Melanesia and the history of the ethnographic collections in which those artifacts are preserved. Reviewer Larry Lake, in *Contemporary Pacific,* described the anthology as "a thought-provoking resource for anthropological researchers in the Pacific, for museum curators, and for serious readers of anthropology who are curious about the complex history of artifacts' changing roles in the social sciences." Writing in *Journal of Pacific History,* Vicki Lukere described the volume as "ironic, scholarly, coherent, and pleasurable" and praised it as "scholarship of quality that is also accessible to non-specialists."

BIOGRAPHICAL AND CRITICAL SOURCES:

PERIODICALS

African Arts, April, 1991, Annette Lynch, review of *Reading the Skin: Adornment, Display, and Society among the Wahgi,* p. 88.

American Anthropologist, December, 1996, Denise Lawrence-Zuniga, review of *The Anthropology of Landscape: Perspectives on Place and Space,* p. 915.

American Ethnologist, August, 1991, Andrew Strathern, review of *Reading the Skin,* p. 623; February, 1995, Dan Jorgensen, review of *Paradise: Portraying the New Guinea Highlands,* p. 208; November, 1996, Deborah B. Waite, review of *Protection, Power, and Display: Shields of Island Southeast Asia and Melanesia,* p. 915; August, 1997, John C. McCall, review of *The Anthropology of Landscape,* p. 676.

Australian Journal of Anthropology, fall, 1991, Michael W. Young, review of *Reading the Skin,* p. 327; December, 2002, James Urry, review of *Hunting the Gatherers: Ethnographic Collectors, Agents and Agency in Melanesia,* p. 364.

Choice, February, 1996, G. W. McDonogh, review of *The Anthropology of Landscape,* p. 997.

Contemporary Pacific, fall, 2002, Larry Lake, review of *Hunting the Gatherers,* p. 518.

Journal of Pacific History, June, 2002, Vicki Lukere, review of *Hunting the Gatherers,* p. 117.

Man, December, 1990, Eric Hirsch, review of *Reading the Skin,* p. 738.

OTHER

Pitt Rivers Museum Web site, http://www.prm.ox.ac.uk/ (January 27, 2003).

*   *   *

OLSEN, John Edward 1925-2002
(Jonathan Rhoades)

OBITUARY NOTICE—See index for CA sketch: Born June 7, 1925, in Indianapolis, IN; died of a heart attack July 16, 2002, on Bainbridge Island, WA. Journalist and novelist. Olsen wrote on a wide variety of subjects but is best known as an Edgar Award-winning author of true-crime books. Although he did not graduate from college, he first became interested in criminology when he took a class in the subject at the University of Pennsylvania, which he attended after serving from 1943 to 1944 in the Office of Strategic Services. Leaving college in 1946, he became a journalist, and during the 1940s and 1950s worked for several papers, including the *San Diego Union Tribune, San Diego Journal, Washington Daily News, New Orleans Item,* and *Chicago Sun-Times.* He was a correspondent for *Time* magazine from 1956 to 1958, and chief of the Midwest bureau in 1959, before joining the staff of *Sports Illustrated,* where he remained as a senior editor from 1960 to 1974. Olsen's book-writing career began while he was at *Sports Illustrated,* his first book being *The Mad World of Bridge* (1960). He would go on to write other books about bridge, as well as on other subjects, such as boxing, World War II history, and the Chappaquiddick scandal, and on one occassion published under the pseudonym Jonathan Rhoades. Olsen also wrote fiction, including the novels *Alphabet Jackson* (1974), *Night Watch* (1979), and the eco-thriller *Night of the Grizzlies* (1969), but he gained the most attention with his true-crime books. Books such as *The Man with the Candy: The Story of the Houston Mass Murders* (1974), the Edgar Award-winning works *"Son": A Psychopath and His Victims* (1983) and *"Doc": The Rape of the Town of Lovell* (1989), and the American Mystery Award winner *Predator: Rape, Madness, and Injustice in Seattle* (1991) were notable for Olsen's uncompromisingly accurate research and unwillingness to speculate on anything for which he did not have proof. His most recent true-crime work, published in 2002, is *I: The Creation of a Serial Killer.* Just before his death, he completed the first book in what was to be a three-part memoir, *The Pitcher's Kid.* In addition to his book awards, Olsen was the recipient of numerous prizes for his journalism, including the National Headliners Award, the Page One Award from the Chicago Newspaper Guild, and the Scripps-Howard Award.

OBITUARIES AND OTHER SOURCES:

PERIODICALS

Chicago Tribune, July 23, 2002, section 2, p. 9.
Independent (London, England), July 30, 2002, p. 14.

Los Angeles Times, July 19, 2002, p. B12.
New York Times, July 22, 2002, p. A15.

*   *   *

OWENS, Louis (Dean) 1948-2002

OBITUARY NOTICE—See index for *CA* sketch: Born July 18, 1948, in Lompoc, CA; committed suicide July 25, 2002, in Albuquerque, NM. Educator, author, and critic. Owens was respected equally as a scholar and a novelist. His scholarly activities focused on Native-American literature, particularly the work of mixed-blood authors, and the work of John Steinbeck, whose writing he believed deserved greater appreciation than it had received. Owens's published studies include *Mixedblood Messages: Literature, Film, Family, Place,* which earned him a writer-of-the-year award from the Wordcraft Circle in 1998; *Other Destinies: Understanding the American Indian Novel;* and *The Grapes of Wrath: Trouble in the Promised Land.* Owens, whose own ancestry was Choctaw, Cherokee, and Caucasian, also explored issues of mixed race in his novels. His characters were part-Native Americans, his themes were those of serious literature, according to critics, yet his stories were suspenseful in the manner of popular thrillers. *Wolfsong* concerns a nefarious plot to build a strip-mining operation in the Glacier Peak wilderness area, which Owens reportedly considered sacred. *Nightland,* a modern mystery blended with Native-American legend, earned the author an American Book Award from the Before Columbus Foundation in 1997. *The Sharpest Sight* involves the murder of a part-Indian Vietnam veteran and the search for his missing bones, which require traditional burial. Owens taught English literature at the University of New Mexico and various California institutions; at the time of his death he was a professor at the University of California, Davis.

OBITUARIES AND OTHER SOURCES:

PERIODICALS

Houston Chronicle, July 29, 2002.
Los Angeles Times, July 29, 2002, p. B9.
New York Times, August 3, 2002, p. B15.
Washington Post, July 28, 2002, p. C6.

P

PACKER, Miriam

PERSONAL: Born in Montreal, Quebec, Canada; daughter of Saul (a tailor) and Bella (a seamstress; maiden name, Sbriger) Packer. *Ethnicity:* "Jewish Canadian." *Education:* Sir George Williams University, B.A.; University of Montreal, M.A., Ph.D., 1978. *Politics:* Liberal. *Religion:* Jewish. *Hobbies and other interests:* Theater, African, salsa, and jazz dancing, performance reading, work on behalf of literacy, homelessness, and child abuse prevention.

ADDRESSES: Home—Montreal, Quebec, Canada. *Office*—Department of English, Dawson College, 4030 Sherbrooke St. W., Westmount, Quebec, Canada H3Z 1A4. *E-mail*—moss41211@hotmail.com.

CAREER: Sir George Williams University, Montreal, Quebec, Canada, teacher of English composition and literature until 1973; Dawson College, Montreal, professor of English literature, 1973—. Former volunteer worker with inner-city children and teenagers at community centers and summer camps for deprived children; volunteer worker with the homeless and deprived in Montreal.

MEMBER: Writers' Union of Canada, Quebec Writers Federation.

AWARDS, HONORS: Dorothy Cameron Watt Award, Canadian Playwriting Competition, 1983, for *Piece-Work;* Canada Council grants, 1983, 1986; fellow at Leighton Artist's Colony, Banff, Alberta, Canada, 1988; fellow at Yaddo Artist's Colony, 1990; Saidye Bronfman Literary Award, for *The Nest.*

WRITINGS:

Evvy's Choice (one-act play), first produced in Montreal, Quebec, Canada, at Centaur Theater, 1982.
The Nest (one-act play), first produced in Montreal, Quebec, Canada, at Centaur Theater, 1983.
Piece-Work (play), produced in one act as a staged reading, Toronto Free Theater, Toronto, Ontario, Canada, 1984, full-length version produced in Montreal, Quebec, Canada, at Collodion Theater, 1993, Guernica Editions (Toronto, Ontario, Canada), 1997.
Take Me to Coney Island (short stories), Guernica Editions (Toronto, Ontario, Canada), 1994.
Us Fools Believing (short stories), Guernica Editions (Toronto, Ontario, Canada), 2000.
Song for My Father (novel), Guernica Editions (Toronto, Ontario, Canada), 2002.

Work represented in anthologies, including *Here and Now,* edited by John Moss, N.C. Press, 1978. Contributor of short stories, plays, and articles to periodicals, including *Viewpoints, Grain, Rubicon, Quarry, Zymergy, Event, Journal of Canadian Fiction,* and *Fiddlehead.*

WORK IN PROGRESS: Knots (tentative title), a novel; research for *Creative Teaching and Student Empowerment;* research on the history of adoption in the province of Quebec.

SIDELIGHTS: Miriam Packer told *CA:* "I believe I was unconsciously preparing to be a writer, storing material in my head, and play-acting the characters' voices and feelings from the time I was a young child. I remember being very content to act out all the parts by myself. My dramatic playtime was truly a solitary activity, so much so that I remember feeling invaded one day when my siblings were secretly enjoying my performance, applauding at the end. I was horrified at the time, very much like the beginning writer hiding his or her earliest work, afraid of being exposed before he or she is ready. In any case, many of my early stories derived from my earliest experiences in the tiny, enclosed world of my childhood. Those early stories center most vividly on insensitive human behavior and reveal a concern for the fragile and more helpless members of society—the very young, the very old, the sick. I think most of that sensitivity came to me from my life in a poor immigrant area, where abuse, violence, and illness were openly evidenced on the one city block. The block was a microcosm composed of many ethnic backgrounds—Jewish, French-Canadian, Irish, African-American, and others.

"Nothing is wasted for the writer. You retain all of life's experiences, even though they may not be processed and creatively sculpted until much later. The block lived in me, its memories stored until years later. Furthermore, as a young student, I worked in a social service agency under the guidance of a very insecure and destructive senior social worker who bullied his clients; that experience surfaced in my first fictionalized story, 'The Helper.' I created an inner private life for my protagonist and completed the story which had lived in me so long.

"When I received my bachelor's degree, I had a fierce need to enter law school and was accepted in the McGill School of Law. My fantasy was to become a spokesperson and enabler for all the underclass, to speak up for the rights of those with little money, little belief, and muted voice. My vision of law practice was related to the ideal of pure justice and pure human compassion. In that vision, justice always triumphed. When I spoke to other law school registrants, I realized how naive and idealistic my concept was. I abandoned registration and turned to literature instead, the field I had majored in during undergraduate years. Happily, I found myself able to combine my love of communicating with and giving voice to my students in the classroom with my short-story writing, which gave voice to those powerless ones I had yearned to defend. I had found a double career that allowed me to fulfill my most basic professional goals.

"Later, as I became a more experienced writer, the characters in my fiction began to speak for themselves with less direction from me, it seemed. It results, I believe, from easing the writer's connection with the unconscious. The characters seem to speak for themselves more and more, often surprising their creator. One feels that strange power when looking back at an earlier work and not completely recognizing it as one's own.

"Writing, I discovered, involves surrender and a certain mystical stillness, a willingness to lighten control. At a certain point, I hear the voices, and if I am really lucky, the story begins to weave its own journey. I was startled and pleased to see this phenomenon in the second half of my novel *Song for My Father*. I did not know where the two central characters were headed until a mysterious disappearance occurred in the story, one which I had not foreseen, and I found myself 'chasing' behind my main characters in their physical and psychological game of hide and seek.

"All of this may sound entirely mystical and far too easy. Writing is not easy at all and not simply given to the writer in a vision. Writing involves commitment, hard work, and an absolutely primitive level of need to create. I write because I must do so. I find myself writing even without a pen or keyboard, in my head, and I am driven to constantly enrich and improve my work. It is never good enough or complete enough.

"Sitting down to work each day is difficult. I find it helpful to stop at a moment of suspense, to provide momentum for the next day. I have my own patterns of stalling, as most writers probably do. There are periods when the work is slow and frustrating, but there are few things as uplifting as the feeling of writing when the writing is going well. I experience that fluidity as a kind of dance, an act of pure intimacy and fulfillment—a liberating experience. Those times are not frequent, but they are worth working for.

"Finally, I think of myself as a new writer each time I begin to write. I listen to and hear my own work, to distance myself from it as much as possible and allow it to teach me to be better. I also absorb the opinions of editors and friends, then make my own decisions. My development comes from within: from staying open to life's experiences, from listening and watching, from a sense of empathy and compassion, I believe.

"I have always had an interest in the dynamics of families, those critical mini-societies which shape the lives of children so powerfully. I am particularly sensitive to the inner lives of people who may be very far removed from my own lifestyle and experience, those who are too often almost entirely invisible to the mainstream.

"As a young university student, I was immediately awed by the works of Shakespeare, Chekhov, Dostoevsky, James Joyce, and in one course, the works of Thomas Hardy. I have a continuing love for the Southern writers and many others. I continue to discover new writers who move me, or new depths in writers I have read before. In a more personal way, I search to discover new dimensions in my own creativity. In my novel in progress, I am working to unearth fresh ways of perceiving and communicating. It is an exciting process.

"Much of the response to my published work revolves around the depth of feeling and the precise crafting of fiction. That, I think, is a good start. My energy is now directed to the new work to be done, to the vision yet undiscovered."

BIOGRAPHICAL AND CRITICAL SOURCES:

PERIODICALS

Canadian Book Review Annual, December, 1994, Susan Patrick, review of *Take Me to Coney Island.*
Canadian Literature, summer, 1996, Julie E. Walchli, review of *Take Me to Coney Island.* p. 187.

*   *   *

PALMA, Michael 1945-

PERSONAL: Born September 21, 1945, in New York, NY; son of Ralph (a contractor) and Ignatia (a homemaker; maiden name, Corica) Palma; married Susan Fyfe, September 2, 1977 (divorced 1989); married Victoria Coughlin (an occupational therapist), June 6, 1992; children: (first marriage) Brian. *Ethnicity:* "Italian" *Education:* Iona College, B.A. (English),

1967; New York University, M.A. (English), 1968. *Politics:* Democrat. *Hobbies and other interests:* Book collecting, crossword puzzles, films, music.

ADDRESSES: Home—New Rochelle, NY. *Agent*—c/o Author Mail, Gradiva Publications, P.O. Box 831, Stony Brook, NY 11790. *E-mail*—vm6692@aol.com.

CAREER: Poet, translator, editor, proofreader, and critic. Blueberry Inc., Brooklyn, NY, counselor, 1968-69; Iona College, professor of English, 1969-96.

AWARDS, HONORS: Italo Calvino Award, 1989, for translation of *My Name on the Wind;* Raiziss/de Palchi Book Prize, Academy of American Poets, 1997, for translation of *The Man I Pretend to Be;* Premio Speciale, Associazione Culturale Campana (Latina, Italy), 2001, for translations of *The Man I Pretend to Be, My Name on the Wind,* and *Inferno.*

WRITINGS:

POETRY

The Egg Shape: Thirty-two Poems (chapbook), Archival Press (Cambridge, MA), 1972.
Antibodies (chapbook), Somers Rocks Press (Brooklyn, NY), 1997.
A Fortune in Gold, Gradiva Publications (Stony Brook, NY), 2000.

EDITOR

(And translator) Guido Gozzano, *The Man I Pretend To Be: The Colloquies and Poems of Guido Gozzano,* with an introductory essay by Eugenio Montale, Princeton University Press (Princeton, NJ), 1981.
(With Dana Gioia) *New Italian Poets,* Story Line Press (Brownsville, OR), 1991.
(With Alfredo de Palchi) Luciano Erba, *The Metaphysical Streetcar Conductor: Sixty Poems,* Gradiva Publications (Stony Brook, NY), 1998.
(And translator) Alfredo De Palchi, *Addictive Aversions/Le Viziose avversioni,* with an introduction by Alessandro Vettori, Xenos Books (Riverside, CA), 1999.

TRANSLATOR

Diego Valeri, *My Name on the Wind: Selected Poems of Diego Valeri,* Princeton University Press (Princeton, NY), 1989.

(With Ernest A. Menze) Johann Gottfried Herder, *Johann Gottfried Herder: Selected Early Works, 1764-1767: Early Addresses, Essays, and Drafts, Fragments on Recent German Literature,* edited by Ernest A. Menze and Karl Menges, Pennsylvania State University Press (University Park, PA), 1992.

Johann Gottfried Herder, *On World History: An Anthology,* edited by Ernest A. Menze and Hans Adler, M. E. Sharpe, Inc. (Armonk, NY), 1997.

Sergio Corazzini, *Sunday Evening: Selected Poems,* Gradiva Publications (Stony Brook, NY), 1997.

Armando Patti, *The Eye Inside the Wind: Selected Poems of Armando Patti,* with an introductory note by Andrea Zanzotto, Gradiva Publications (Stony Brook, NY), 1999.

Luigi Fontanella, *The Transparent Life and Other Poems,* introduction by Alfredo de Palchi, Xenos Books (Riverside, CA), 1999.

Ljuba Merlina Bortolani, *Siege: Poems by Ljuba Merlina Bortolani,* BOA Editions (Rochester, NY), 2002.

Dante Alighieri, *Inferno: A New Verse Translation,* W. W. Norton & Company (New York, NY), 2002.

Franco Buffoni, *The Shadow of Mount Rosa: Selected Poems,* Gradiva Publications (Stony Brook, NY), 2002.

Paolo Valesio, *Every Afternoon Can Make the World Stand Still: Thirty Sonnets, 1987-2000,* introduction by John Hollander, Gradiva Publications (Stony Brook, NY), 2002.

Ljuba Merlina Bortolani, *The Siege: A Poetic Sequence,* introduction by Alfredo de Palchi, BOA Editions (Rochester, NY), 2002.

(With Emanuel di Pasquale) Maura del Serra, *Infinite Present: Selected Poems,* Bordighera Press (Boca Raton, FL), 2002.

WORK IN PROGRESS: Translations of contemporary poets Franco Loi and Giovanni Raboni.

SIDELIGHTS: Michael Palma is a poet, translator, editor, and critic. He has written two poetry chapbooks, *The Egg Shape* and *Antibodies,* and has published one full-length collection of his poems, *A Fortune in Gold.*

His poetry collections have not received much media attention, except in reviews of works he has translated, in which critics often refer to his sensitivity to other authors' works due to his own poetic leanings. In one review of Palma's *A Fortune of Gold,* however, *America* critic Fred L. Gardaphe complimented Palma's verses, noting how they seem to have been influenced by such poets as William Carlos Williams. "Even Palma's most opaque work is accessible in ways that counter the trend of academic poetry," said Gardaphe.

Palma's award-winning translations are highly praised. In his translation of *My Name on the Wind: Selected Poems of Diego Valeri,* Palma offers both the original Italian and his English translation of Valeri's poetry. "Though adhering closely in general to the colorful, vivid Italian lines," wrote Patricia M. Gathercole in a review for *World Literature Today,* "Palma does at times offer a freer rendition to communicate the meaning of the romantic verse." Palma makes adjustments to both Valeri's words and phrasing so as to "give a more poetic version in the less melodious English language," observed Gathercole.

Palma worked with coeditor Dana Gioia on *New Italian Poets,* which introduces ten Italian poets who might otherwise have remained unknown to English-speaking readers. Works by such poets as Maria Luisa Spaziani, Luigi Fontanella, and Fabio Doplicher are presented in this collection. Penny Kaganoff, for *Publishers Weekly,* noting that Palma himself is a poet, appreciated the "highly informative introduction and critical notes." G. Singh, who reviewed this collection for *World Literature Today,* wrote that the book reads like a "labor of love as well as of critically informed intelligence."

Palma worked with Ernest A. Menze on the translation of *Johann Gottfried Herder: Selected Early Works, 1764-1767: Early Addresses, Essays, and Drafts, Fragments on Recent German Literature.* Herder, as Robert E. Norton stated in his article for the *Review of Metaphysics,* was "unquestionably one of the most productive and influential minds of the eighteenth century." He also has been "poorly served by posterity," Norton claimed, until this publication was produced. One of the reasons for a lack of attention to this great thinker, especially outside of Germany, is that Herder drew his thoughts from so many disciplines, making his complex writing difficult to translate. Herder was interested in theology, history, metaphysics, literature, art, and language. Another reason, wrote Norton, was that "Herder wrote hastily and in broad strokes, sketching the outlines of what he may have intended to color in later." After noting the tremendous challenge that the translators had to face, Norton praised Palma and Menze for having "met the challenge of transferring Herder into a foreign idiom with admirable aplomb: the translations are fluid and accurate."

J. K. Fugate, for *Choice,* also admired the translation of Herder's works, stating, "The translators have admirably accomplished the daunting task of transferring Herder's language into accurate and readable English." Hugh West, writing for *Central European History,* praised Palma for making Herder's work comprehensive in English, and for making it "especially beautiful." The translation, West said, is "thoroughly responsible."

Inferno: A New Verse Translation includes Palma's translation with facing Italian text and explanatory notes. The book's publisher has noted that Palma's translation is unique in its use of contemporary English without sacrificing Dante's original triple-rhyme scheme. Palma himself noted in an interview with Francine Stock for BBC Radio's Front Row posted online that he found the most difficult part of translating Dante's text was "to keep the rhymes of the original, to keep the terza rima form." Critics of Palma's translation were very receptive. For example, *Choice* reviewer S. Botterill said this version of Dante's work "stands comparison with the classic work of John Ciardi or Allen Mandelbaum." And Guido Waldman, writing in *Spectator,* was pleased to see that the Italian version is printed next to Palma's translation and "includes such notes as are needed to enhance the reader's understanding and enjoyment."

Palma once commented, "Through translation, I have discovered, and continue to discover, a wonderful body of literature that I am eager to share with those of my country and my language. Through translation, I have made many friends and have made many opportunities that would never have come to me otherwise."

BIOGRAPHICAL AND CRITICAL SOURCES:

PERIODICALS

America, February, 2002, Fred L. Gardaphe, review of *A Fortune in Gold.*

Central European History, fall, 1992, Hugh West, review of *Johann Gottfried Herder,* pp. 462-464.
Choice, February, 1994, J. K. Fugate, review of *Johann Gottfried Herder,* p. 938; May, 2002, S. Botterill, review of *Inferno.*
Modern Language Review, April, 1997, H. B. Nisbet, review of *Johann Gottfried Herder,* pp. 503-504.
Publishers Weekly, November 30, 1990, Penny Kaganoff, review of *New Italian Poets,* p. 66; November 19, 2001, review of *Inferno: A New Verse Translation,* p. 62.
Review of Metaphysics, June, 1995, Robert E. Norton, review of *Johann Gottfried Herder,* pp. 895-897.
Spectator, March 23, 2002, Guido Waldman, review of *Inferno.*
Virginia Quarterly Review, summer, 2002, review of *Inferno.*
World Literature Today, winter, 1982, Thomas G. Bergin, review of *The Man I Pretend to Be,* p. 204; winter, 1990, Patricia M. Gathercole, review of *My Name on the Wind,* p. 91; spring, 1992, G. Singh, review of *New Italian Poets,* p. 329; summer, 2000, Patricia M. Gathercole, review of *The Transparent Life and Other Poems,* p. 662.

OTHER

Academy of American Poets Web site, http://www.poets.org/ (February 9, 1998), "Michael Palma Receives 1997 Raiziss/de Palchi Book Prize."
BBC Radio 4 Web site, http://www.bbc.co.uk/radio4/ (April 26, 2002), Francine Stock, Front Row interview with Michael Palma.
W. W. Norton & Company Web site, http://www.wwnorton.com/ (April 20, 2002), *Inferno.*

*   *   *

PARISH, Peter J(oseph) 1929-2002

OBITUARY NOTICE—See index for *CA* sketch: Born April 24, 1929, in Barking, Essex, England; died May 16, 2002, in Cambridge, England. Historian, educator, and author. Parish was a highly regarded expert of U.S. Civil War history. He earned his B.A. at the University of London in 1950. After serving in the Royal Air Force from 1950 to 1952, he continued with graduate studies at the Institute of Historical Research from 1952 to 1954, and then as a research fellow at

Bowdoin College from 1954 to 1955. Joining the University of Manchester's library staff in 1955, he moved on to the University of Glasgow as a lecturer in 1958, becoming a senior lecturer in 1972. In 1976 Parish was promoted to Bonar Professor of Modern History at Dundee University; he served as head of the department, and was dean of the faculty of arts from 1978 to 1981. In 1982 he was hired as the director of the Institute of United States Studies at London University. The institute was at risk of being closed, however, and Parish spent much of his time trying to save it, successfully merging it with the Institute of Historical Research. In addition to this work, Parish served on numerous commissions and committees, retiring from university work in 1992. After retirement, he cofounded the British-American Nineteenth-Century Historians. As for his publications, Parish is probably best known for his comprehensive, authoritative first book, *The American Civil War* (1975), but he was also the author of *Slavery: The Many Faces of a Southern Institution* (1979); *The Divided Union: The Story of the Great American War, 1861-65,* written with Peter Batty (1987); and *Slavery: History and Historians* (1989), as well as editor of *A Reader's Guide to American History* (1997). For his work in history, Parish was given an honorary doctorate from Middlesex University in 1999.

OBITUARIES AND OTHER SOURCES:

BOOKS

Writers Directory, sixth edition, St. James Press (Detroit, MI), 1983.

PERIODICALS

Independent (London, England), June 8, 2002, p. 20.
Times (London, England), May 29, 2002, p. 31.

*   *   *

PASTOUREAU, Michel 1947-

PERSONAL: Born June 17, 1947, in Paris, France; son of Henri (an educator) and Helene (Level) Pastoureau; married Mireille Laprabande, May 19, 1971. *Education:* Lycee Michelet a Vances, Faculte des Letters et des Sciences Humaines de Paris; Ecole Nation-

ale des Chartes, Maitrise es Lettres, Archiviste Paleographe. *Hobbies and other interests:* Bridge, chess, painting.

ADDRESSES: Home—48 rue des Francs-Bourgeois, 75003 Paris, France. *Office*—Bibliotheque Nationale, 58 rue de Richelieu, 75084 Paris, Cedex 02, France.

CAREER: Archivist and historian. Bibliotheque Nationale, Paris, France, conservator, 1972—, and curator, Cabinet des Medailles, 1975—. Ecole Pratique des Hautes Etudes, Paris, director of studies.

MEMBER: International Academy of Heraldry, French Society of Heraldry, Racing Club of France, National Society of French Antiquarians, Swiss Heraldic Society, French Coin-Collectors Society.

AWARDS, HONORS: Broquette-Gonin Prize from Academic Française.

WRITINGS:

La vie quotidienne en France et en Angleterre au temps des chevaliers de la Table Ronde, 1972.
Les armoiries, Brepols (Turnhout, Belgium), 1976, second edition, 1998.
(With G. Duchet-Suchaux) *Les chateaux forts,* 1978.
Traité d'héraldique, Picard (Paris, France), 1979.
Les sceaux, Brepols (Turnhout, Belgium), 1981.
Jetons, méreaux et médailles, Brepols (Turnhout, Belgium), 1984.
(With Gaston Duchet-Suchaux) *The Bible and the Saints,* Flammarion (Paris, France), 1994.
The Devil's Cloth: A History of Stripes and Striped Fabric, translation by Jody Gladding, Columbia University Press (New York, NY), 2001.
Blue: The History of a Color, translation by Markus I. Cruse, Princeton University Press (Princeton, NJ), 2001.

SIDELIGHTS: Michel Pastoureau is a French archivist and historian who has worked at France's Bibliotheque Nationale and has served as director of studies at the Ecole Pratique des Hautes Etudes in Paris. His earlier books, scholarly works in the area of medieval studies, are not available in English translation. *La vie quotidienne en France et en Angleterre au temps des chevaliers de la Table Ronde* describes daily life in France and England in the late twelfth and early thirteenth centuries. *Les armoiries* is a research guide on coats of arms, while *Traité d'heraldique* provides an overview of the practice and study of heraldry from the twelfth century through modern times. Writing in *Speculum,* Gerard J. Brault described *Traité d'heraldique* as "the most authoritative and comprehensive introduction to heraldry available in any language today," and commented, "[Pastoureau] has rendered a great service to medievalists and provided a manual that should do much to stimulate interest in medieval heraldry."

Les sceaux is a study of medieval seals, impressions stamped in wax or metal that were used as a way of authenticating documents. The book reviews not only the history of seals, but the practice of sigillography—the collection and preservation of seals—and the ways in which information gleaned from seals can be used in historical study. In *Jetons, méreaux et médailles,* the author discusses the significance of counters and tokens used in financial transactions in the Middle Ages.

The Bible and the Saints, written with Gaston Duchet-Suchaux, is an iconographic guide to biblical figures and religious scenes that are frequently found in Western and Byzantine art. In *The Devil's Cloth: A History of Stripes and Striped Fabric,* Pastoureau examines the social history of striped fabric. The author contends that in medieval Europe, stripes were considered a symbol of moral turpitude and were often associated with social outcasts. In the eighteenth century, stripes, like those on the American flag, symbolized rebellion and revolution. Later, however, stripes were worn by American gangsters and jail prisoners. In the *New York Times Book Review,* Angeline Goreau described the book as "playful but learned," and wrote that it "gets to the heart of matters like the way we perceive color and pattern, and speculates interestingly on whether these perceptions derive from nature or nurture."

Blue: The History of a Color, looks at the history of the color blue in Western culture, from its use in pre-christian orgiastic body painting to its place as the customary color of the Virgin Mary's robes in medieval art. Later, blue became the color of royalty, as the French kings included blue in their coat of arms. Pastoureau explores the work of dyemakers, painters, and other craftspeople involved in creating and using the color blue.

BIOGRAPHICAL AND CRITICAL SOURCES:

PERIODICALS

Booklist, June 1, 2001, Barbara Jacobs, review of *The Devil's Cloth,* p. 1806.
Choice, February, 1995, G. Holloway, review of *The Bible and the Saints,* p. 914.
Forbes, April 30, 2001, p. 82.
Guardian (London, England), September 15, 2001, p. 10.
Los Angeles Times, November 11, 2001, William Gass, "On Being Blue," p. 6.
New York Times, June 9, 2001, Emily Eakin, "When Fashion Decreed Stripes a Capital Crime," p. B7; July 22, 2001, p. 30.
New York Times Book Review, July 22, 2001, Angeline Goreau, "How to Dress an Evil Dwarf," p. 30.
Speculum, October, 1982, Gerard J. Brault, review of *Traité d'héraldique,* p. 921; July, 1983, Brigitte M. Bedos Rezak, review of *Les sceaux,* p. 793; April, 1987, Alan M. Stahl, review of *Jetons, méreaux et médailles,* p. 514.*

*   *   *

PEDEN, Henry C(lint), Jr. 1946-

PERSONAL: Born November 4, 1946, in Baltimore, MD; son of Henry Clint and Mary Catherine (Frank) Peden; married Veronica Ann Clarke, July 11, 1970; children: Henry Clint III. *Ethnicity:* "Scotch-Irish." *Education:* Essex Community College, A.A., 1972; Towson State University, B.S., 1973, M.A., 1980. *Politics:* Republican. *Religion:* Presbyterian. *Hobbies and other interests:* Genealogy.

ADDRESSES: Home—707 Bedford Rd., Bel Air, MD 21014. *Agent*—Delmarva Roots, 217 Schley Ave., Lewes, DE 19958. *E-mail*—pedenroots@msn.com.

CAREER: Bethlehem Steel Corp., Baltimore, MD, workers' compensation administrator in Department of Human Resources, 1972-98; writer and genealogist,

1998—. National Board for the Certification of Genealogists, certified genealogical records searcher, 1990-2000. Genealogical Council of Maryland, Bible records chair, 1990-93; Maryland State Archives, member of Search Room advisory board, 1995-97. Past member of Historic District Committee of Harford County, MD. Bel Air Board of Zoning Appeals, chair, 1985-86; Bel Air Planning Commission, vice chair, 1986-88; Bel Air Historic District Commission, member, 1988-89. *Military service:* U.S. Air Force, 1966-70; served in Vietnam; became staff sergeant.

MEMBER: Sons of the American Revolution (chapter president, 1979-82; state historian, 1987-89; state genealogist and state archives chair, 1993—), Society of Descendants of Washington's Army at Valley Forge (life member), Sons of Confederate Veterans, Society of the War of 1812 (state genealogist, 1990—), Society of the Cincinnati of Maryland, Society of Colonial Wars of Maryland (life member), Maryland Genealogical Society (fellow; vice president, 1991-93; president, 1993-95), Maryland Historical Society, Maryland Citizen Planners Association, Virginia Genealogical Society, South Central Kentucky Genealogical and Historical Society, Harford County Historical Society (member of board of directors, 1985-87, 1999-2002), Harford County Genealogical Society (president, 1989-90), Highland Society of Harford County (historian, 1985-87; president, 1990-91), Baltimore County Genealogical Society (vice president, 1988-89), St. Andrews Society of Baltimore, American Legion (post commander, 1977; historian), Military Order of the Stars and Bars.

AWARDS, HONORS: Kenneth Hammer History Awards, Maryland chapter, American Legion, 1976, 1978, 1981; Cross of Military Service, United Daughters of the Confederacy, 1981; Sons of the American Revolution, Patriot Medal from Maryland chapter, 1984, Bronze Good Citizenship Medal from Delaware Society, 1996, for *Revolutionary Patriots of Delaware, 1775-1783;* Award of Excellence, *Maryland and Delaware Genealogist,* 1989; first prize, best genealogical source book in Maryland, Maryland Historical Society, 1993.

WRITINGS:

EDITOR

The Pedens of Southwest Virginia and South Central Kentucky, privately printed (Baltimore, MD), 1978.

William Wood and Related Families of Albemarle County, Virginia, and Barren County, Kentucky, privately printed (Baltimore, MD), 1984.

Revolutionary Patriots of Harford County, Maryland, 1775-1783, privately printed (Bel Air, MD), 1985, revised edition, 1987.

Historical Register of the Sparrows Point Police Department, 1901-1986, privately printed (Bel Air, MD), 1986.

Truman and Related Families of Early Maryland, privately printed (Bel Air, MD), 1986.

Frank Genealogy: Descendants of Henry Frank and Hannah High of Maryland, privately printed (Bel Air, MD), 1986.

Gilbert Records in Harford County, Maryland, privately printed (Bel Air, MD), 1986.

Genealogy of the Pedens of Kentucky, 1756-1986, privately printed (Bel Air, MD), 1986.

St. John's and St. George's Parish Registers, 1696-1851, Family Line Publications (Silver Spring, MD), 1987.

Heirs and Legatees of Harford County, Maryland, 1802-1846, Family Line Publications (Silver Spring, MD), 1988.

Revolutionary Patriots of Baltimore Town and Baltimore County, 1775-1783, Family Line Publications (Silver Spring, MD), 1988.

Centennial History of the Maryland Society, Sons of the American Revolution, 1889-1989, Sons of the American Revolution (Baltimore, MD), 1989.

Heirs and Legatees of Harford County, Maryland, 1774-1802, Family Line Publications (Westminster, MD), 1989.

(With others) *Abstracts of Baltimore County Land Commissions, 1727-1767,* Baltimore County Genealogical Society (Baltimore, MD), 1989.

Inhabitants of Baltimore County, 1763-1774, Family Line Publications (Westminster, MD), 1989.

Early Anglican Church Records of Cecil County, Maryland, Family Line Publications (Westminster, MD), 1990.

Revolutionary Patriots of Cecil County, Maryland, 1775-1783, Family Line Publications (Westminster, MD), 1991.

Marylanders to Kentucky, 1775-1825, Family Line Publications (Westminster, MD), 1991.

Maryland Deponents, 1634-1799 Family Line Publications (Westminster, MD), 1991.

Orphans Court Proceedings of Harford County, Maryland, 1778-1800, Family Line Publications (Westminster, MD), 1991.

Harford County Tax Records of 1870, 1872, and 1883, Harford County Genealogical Society (Aberdeen, MD), 1992.

Revolutionary Patriots of Anne Arundel County, Maryland, 1775-1783, Family Line Publications (Westminster, MD), 1992.

More Maryland Deponents, 1716-1799, Family Line Publications (Westminster, MD), 1992.

A Medical Ledger of Dr. John Archer of Harford County, 1786-1796, Harford County Genealogical Society (Aberdeen, MD), 1992.

Quaker Records of Southern Maryland, 1655-1800, Family Line Publications (Westminster, MD), 1992.

Baltimore County Overseers of Roads, 1693-1793, Family Line Publications (Westminster, MD), 1992.

Quaker Records of Northern Maryland, 1716-1800, Family Line Publications (Westminster, MD), 1993.

Early Harford Countians, 1773-1790, Family Line Publications (Westminster, MD), 1993.

Inhabitants of Cecil County, Maryland, 1649-1774, Family Line Publications (Westminster, MD), 1993.

Marylanders to Carolina: Migrations prior to 1800, Family Line Publications (Westminster, MD), 1994.

Inhabitants of Kent County, Maryland, 1637-1787, Family Line Publications (Westminster, MD), 1994.

Methodist Church Records of Baltimore City, 1799-1829, Family Line Publications (Westminster, MD), 1994.

Methodist Church Records of Baltimore City, 1830-1839, Family Line Publications (Westminster, MD), 1994.

Revolutionary Patriots of Kent and Queen Anne's Counties, 1775-1783, Family Line Publications (Westminster, MD), 1994.

Children of Harford County: Indentures and Guardianships, 1801-1830, Family Line Publications (Westminster, MD), 1994.

Colonial Delaware Soldiers and Sailors, 1638-1776, Family Line Publications (Westminster, MD), 1995.

Presbyterian Records of Baltimore City, 1765-1840, Family Line Publications (Westminster, MD), 1995.

Genealogy of the Crenshaws of Kentucky, 1800-1995, privately printed (Bel Air, MD), 1995.

Revolutionary Patriots of Frederick County, Maryland, 1775-1783, Family Line Publications (Westminster, MD), 1995.

Descendants of William and Margaret Clarke and Joseph and Stefania Papsa of Baltimore City, privately printed (Bel Air, MD), 1995.

Harford County, Maryland, Bible Records, Harford County Genealogical Society (Aberdeen, MD), Volume 4, 1996, Volume 5, 2000.

Revolutionary Patriots of Delaware, 1775-1783, Family Line Publications (Westminster, MD), 1996.

Revolutionary Patriots of Montgomery County, Maryland, 1776-1783, Family Line Publications (Westminster, MD), 1996.

Revolutionary Patriots of Calvert and St. Mary's Counties, 1775-1783, Family Line Publications (Westminster, MD), 1996.

A Collection of Maryland Church Records, 1689-1845, Family Line Publications (Westminster, MD), 1997.

Revolutionary Patriots of Prince George's County, MD, 1775-1783, Family Line Publications (Westminster, MD), 1997.

More Marylanders to Kentucky, 1778-1828, Family Line Publications (Westminster, MD), 1997.

Dr. John Archer's First Medical Ledger, 1767-1769, Harford County Genealogical Society (Aberdeen, MD), 1997.

(With others) *Church Records of Delaware County, Pennsylvania,* Family Line Publications (Westminster, MD), 1997.

Revolutionary Patriots of Charles County, Maryland, 1775-1783, Family Line Publications (Westminster, MD), 1997.

Revolutionary Patriots of Washington County, Maryland, 1775-1783, Family Line Publications (Westminster, MD), 1998.

Baltimore City Deaths and Burials, 1834-1840, Family Line Publications (Westminster, MD), 1998.

Revolutionary Patriots of Dorchester County, Maryland, 1775-1783, Family Line Publications (Westminster, MD), 1998.

Revolutionary Patriots of Caroline County, Maryland, 1775-1783, Family Line Publications (Westminster, MD), 1998.

Revolutionary Patriots of Lancaster County, Pennsylvania, 1775-1783, Family Line Publications (Westminster, MD), 1998.

Survey Book of David and William Clark of Harford County, 1770-1812, Harford County Genealogical Society (Aberdeen, MD), 1998.

Revolutionary Patriots of Talbot County, Maryland, 1775-1783, Family Line Publications (Westminster, MD), 1998.

More Marylanders to Carolina: Migrations prior to 1800, Family Line Publications (Westminster, MD), 1999.

(With others) *Colonial Families of the Eastern Shore,* Volume 5, Family Line Publications (Westminster, MD), 1999, Volumes 6-7, Willow Bend Books (Westminster, MD), 1999, Volumes 8-9, 2000, Volumes 11-12, Delmarva Roots (Lewes, DE), 2001, Volumes 13-14, 2002.

Colonial Families of Cecil County, Maryland, Family Line Publications (Westminster, MD), 1999.

Abstracts of the Bush River and Rock Run Stores, 1759-1771, Harford County Genealogical Society (Aberdeen, MD), 1999.

Revolutionary Patriots of Worcester and Somerset Counties, 1775-1783, Family Line Publications (Westminster, MD), 1999.

Supplement to Early Harford Countians, Volume 3, Willow Bend Books (Westminster, MD), 1999.

Harford County Placenames, two volumes, Historical Society of Harford County (Bel Air, MD), 1999.

Harford County Divorce Cases, 1827-1912, privately printed (Bel Air, MD), 1999.

Inhabitants of Harford County, Maryland, 1791-1800, Willow Bend Books (Westminster, MD), 1999.

Union Chapel United Methodist Church Cemetery Tombstone Inscriptions, Wilna, Harford County, Maryland, privately printed (Bel Air, MD), 1999, revised edition, 2001.

Revolutionary Patriots of Maryland, 1775-1783: A Supplement, Willow Bend Books (Westminster, MD), 2000.

Quaker Records of Baltimore and Harford Counties, Maryland, 1801-1825, Willow Bend Books (Westminster, MD), 2000.

Maryland Deponents, Volume 3: *1634-1776,* Willow Bend Books (Westminster, MD), 2000.

Colonial Maryland Soldiers and Sailors, 1634-1734, Willow Bend Books (Westminster, MD), 2001.

A Guide to Genealogical Research in Maryland, Maryland Historical Society Press (Baltimore, MD), 2001.

Bastardy Cases in Harford County, Maryland, 1774-1844, Willow Bend Books (Westminster, MD), 2001.

Joseph A. Pennington and Co., Havre de Grace, Maryland Funeral Home Records, Volume 2: *1877-1882, 1893-1900,* Harford County Genealogical Society (Bel Air, MD), 2001.

Bastardy Cases of Baltimore County, Maryland, 1673-1783, Willow Bend Books (Westminster, MD), 2001.

Our Anderson Ancestors: Descendants of William Anderson and Mary Land of Harford County, MD, privately printed (Bel Air, MD), 2001.

St. George's (Old Spesutia), Harford County, Maryland Church and Cemetery Records, 1820-1920, Willow Bend Books (Westminster, MD), 2002.

Revolutionary Patriots of Maryland, 1775-1783: Second Supplement, Willow Bend Books (Westminster, MD), 2002.

(With others) *Abstracts of Harford County, Maryland Wills, 1800-1805* Harford County Genealogical Society (Bel Air, MD), 2002.

Maryland Public Service Records, 1775-1783, Willow Bend Books (Westminster, MD), 2002.

*   *   *

PEET, Bill
See PEET, William Bartlett

*   *   *

PEET, William Bartlett 1915-2002
(Bill Peet)

OBITUARY NOTICE—See index for *CA* sketch: Born January 29, 1915, in Grandview, IN; died May 11, 2002, in Los Angeles, CA. Animator, illustrator, and author. Peet was a former animator for Walt Disney Studios who later became a popular author and illustrator of children's books under the name Bill Peet. After studying at the John Herron Art Institute from 1933 to 1936, Peet worked briefly for a greeting card company before joining Walt Disney Studios as an illustrator in 1937. While at Disney, he worked on such well-known animated features as *Fantasia* (1940), *Dumbo* (1941), *Song of the South* (1946), *Cinderella* (1950), *Alice in Wonderland* (1951), and *Sleeping Beauty* (1959). Not only was he an artist, but he also outlined many of the stories and directed the actors who voiced the characters. Peet made his first forays into writing when he adapted Dodie Smith's children's book into the 1961 animated film *101 Dalmatians,* and he later also adapted T. H. White's story of King Arthur into *The Sword in the Stone* (1963). Despite his success at Disney, Peet was not happy there because he was tired of collaborative work and because of numerous personal conflicts between himself and Walt Disney. He therefore decided to branch out into children's books on his own. Even before he left the studio in 1964, he had had several books published, including *Goliath II* (1959), *Hubert's Hair-Raising Adventure* (1959), *Huge Harold* (1961), and *The Pinkish, Purplish, Bluish Egg* (1963). Writing sometimes in verse, sometimes in prose, Peet continued to publish children's books into the 1990s, many of which won awards. Some of his many works include *Capyboppy* (1966), *How Droofus the Dragon Lost His Head* (1971), *Cyrus, the Unsinkable Serpent* (1975), *Big Bad Bruce* (1977), *Encore for Eleanor* (1981), *Cock-a-Doodle Dudley* (1990), and his last work, *Abdo and Daughters* (1996), written with J. C. Wheeler. Peet also wrote about his life experiences in *Bill Peet: An Autobiography* (1989), which was a Caldecott honor book. Some of his other honors include an International Reading Association Children's Choice award and the Annie Award for distinguished contribution to the art of animation.

OBITUARIES AND OTHER SOURCES:

BOOKS

Writers Directory, 15th edition, St. James Press (Detroit, MI), 1999.

PERIODICALS

Chicago Tribune, May 16, 2002, section 2, p. 9.
Los Angeles Times, May 14, 2002, p. B10.
New York Times, May 18, 2002, p. B15.
Times (London, England), May 15, 2002.
Washington Post, May 17, 2002, p. B6.

*   *   *

PORTER, George 1920-2002

OBITUARY NOTICE—See index for CA sketch: Born December 12, 1920, in Stainforth, West Yorkshire, England; died August 31, 2002, in Canterbury, England. Chemist, educator, and author. Porter was a Nobel Prize-winning chemist who helped develop a

way to observe chemical reactions using flashes of light. A 1941 graduate of the University of Leeds, where he earned his B.S., he was in the Royal Navy Volunteer Reserve during World War II. He then went back to school to earn his Ph.D. from Cambridge University in 1952. While at Cambridge he conducted research on free radicals in gaseous photochemical reactions with Ronald Norrish. Together, they developed a method of flash photolysis to observe these reactions using two flashes of light: one to initiate a chemical reaction and a second to observe the free radicals which briefly formed before the reaction was completed. Their methods, which were improved with the invention of the laser in 1960, proved to be applicable to many other fields of study, such as physics and biology, and for their work they won the Nobel Prize in Chemistry in 1967. Porter left Cambridge in 1954 to work for a year as assistant director of research at the British Rayon Research Association. In 1955 he joined the faculty at the University of Sheffield, where he was a professor of chemistry until 1966. During his last year at Sheffield, Porter began his work to popularize science by hosting a television show called *Laws of Disorder*. He also appeared in numerous lectures broadcast by the BBC to explain science to the general public. Joining the Royal Institution of Great Britain as its director and professor of chemistry in 1966, Porter continued his groundbreaking research using lasers to analyze chemicals while also working to educate children about science. These efforts included opening the Faraday laboratory for schoolchildren and creating the television shows *Young Scientist of the Year* (1966-81), *Time Machines* (1969-70), *Controversy* (1971-75), and *Natural History of a Sunbeam* (1976-77). He contributed to the education of children in the sciences in many other ways, including as president of the National Association for Gifted Children. Porter was also involved in trying to find a way to create an efficient process of artificial photosynthesis that would produce hydrogen for use as an energy source. However, these efforts proved futile, and he later decided that trying to improve on nature was presumptuous. In 1985 Porter was elected president of the Royal Society and the British Association for the Advancement of Science. He left the royal institution in 1988 but continued to be active into the 1990s, accepting an appointment as Gresham Professor of Astronomy at Gresham College from 1990 to 1994 and serving as the president of the National Energy Foundation from 1990 to 2000. During his career, Porter authored several books, including *Chemistry for the Modern World* (1962), *Laws of Disorder* (1965), *Time Machines* (1969), and the young-adult book *Mol-*

ecules to Man (1971). He also edited several books. For his important contributions to science, Porter was made a knight of the realm in 1972, received the Order of Merit in 1989, was elevated to the House of Lords as Baron Porter of Luddenham in 1990, and received numerous honorary doctorates.

OBITUARIES AND OTHER SOURCES:

BOOKS

Biographical Dictionary of Scientists, third edition, Oxford University Press (New York, NY), 2000.
Notable Scientists from 1900 to the Present, second edition, Gale (Detroit, MI), 2001.
Who's Who in Science and Engineering, fifth edition, Marquis (New Providence, NJ), 1999.
World of Chemistry, Gale (Detroit, MI), 2000.

PERIODICALS

Independent (London, England), September 4, 2002, p. 16.
Los Angeles Times, September 4, 2002, p. B11.
New York Times, September 4, 2002, p. A20.
Times (London, England), September 2, 2002, p. 7.
Washington Post, September 5, 2002, p. B6.

*　　*　　*

PRINCIPAL, Victoria 1945-

PERSONAL: Born Concettina Principale, January 3, 1945 (some sources cite 1946 or 1950), in Fukuoka, Japan; daughter of Victor (a U.S. Air Force officer) and Ree (Veal) Principal; married Christopher Skinner (an actor), 1978 (divorced, 1980); married Harry Glassman (a plastic surgeon), June 22, 1985. *Education:* Attended Miami-Dade Community College in the 1960s; studied at Royal Academy of Ballet in England in the early 1970s; also studied at Royal Academy of Dramatic Art, London.

ADDRESSES: Agent—Innovative Artists Talent, 1999 Avenue of the Stars, Los Angeles, CA 90067-6022.

CAREER: Actress, writer, producer, model, and talent agent. National spokesperson for Victory over Violence.

Appearances in television series include *Dallas,* CBS, 1978-87, and *Titans,* NBC, 2000. Appearances in TV miniseries include *The Burden of Proof,* ABC, 1992. Appearances in TV pilots include *Fantasy Island,* ABC, 1977. Appearances in TV movies include *Last Hours before Morning,* 1975; *The Night They Stole Miss Beautiful,* 1977; *Pleasure Palace,* 1980; *Not Just Another Affair,* 1982; *Mistress,* CBS, 1987; *Naked Lie,* CBS, 1989; *Blind Witness,* ABC, 1989; *Sparks: The Price of Passion,* CBS, 1990; *Don't Touch My Daughter,* NBC, 1991; "Sacrifice," "Temptation," and "Ecstasy," *Seduction: Three Tales from the "Inner Sanctum,"* ABC, 1992; *River of Rage: The Taking of Maggie Keene,* CBS, 1993; *Beyond Obsession,* ABC, 1994; *Dancing in the Dark,* Lifetime, 1995; *The Abduction,* Lifetime, 1996; *Love in Another Town,* CBS, 1997; and *After Dallas,* 2002; also appeared in *Delaney.* Appearances on episodic television include *Love Story,* 1973; "Fly Me—If You Can Find Me," *Banacek,* 1974; "The Year of the Horse: Part 2," *Hawaii Five-0,* 1979; *On Top All over the World,* 1985; *Conversation with Cassini,* Arts and Entertainment, 1989; "Swing Time," *Home Improvement,* ABC, 1994; "Beverly and the Prop Job," *The Larry Sanders Show,* 1995; *Tracey Takes On . . . ,* HBO, 1996; "The Other Cheek," *Chicago Hope,* CBS, 1998; "These Are the Days" and "The Awful Truth," *Jack and Jill,* The WB, 1999; "Love Is in the Air," *Just Shoot Me,* NBC, 1999; "Da Boom," *Family Guy,* Fox, 1999; "The Apartment," "Sibling Rivalry" and "Do the Right Thing," *Providence,* NBC, 2000; "Black Widows," *The Practice,* ABC, 2000; "Andy Gibb," *Behind the Music;* And in *Love, American Style,* ABC. Appearances on TV specials include *Battle of the Network Stars IV,* 1978; *Battle of the Network Stars VI,* 1979; *Celebrity Challenge of the Sexes,* 1980; *Sixty Years of Seduction,* 1981; *Women Who Rate a "10,"* 1981; *Night of 100 Stars,* ABC, 1982; *Memories Then and Now,* CBS, 1988; *Conquering Pain,* Lifetime, 1989; *Just Life,* ABC, 1990; *TV Guide: Fortieth Anniversary Special,* 1993; *Intimate Portrait: Victoria Principal,* Lifetime, 1998; and *Doing Dallas,* 2000. Appearances on awards presentation ceremonies include *The Twelfth Annual People's Choice Awards,* 1986; *The Thirteenth Annual People's Choice Awards,* 1987; *The Thirty-Ninth Annual Emmy Awards,* 1987; *The All-Star Pro Sports Awards,* ABC, 1990; *The Sixteenth Annual People's Choice Awards,* 1990; *The Forty-Third Annual Prime-*

time Emmy Awards Presentation, 1991; *The Forty-Third Annual Golden Globe Awards,* 1991; *The Forty-Fourth Annual Primetime Emmy Awards,* 1992; and *The Forty-Fifth Annual Primetime Emmy Awards,* 1993. Work on television movies includes (executive producer) *Naked Lie,* CBS, 1989; (co-executive producer) *Blind Witness,* ABC, 1989; (executive producer) *Sparks: The Price of Passion,* CBS, 1990; (executive producer) *Don't Touch My Daughter,* NBC, 1991; (executive producer) *Midnight's Child,* Lifetime, 1992; and (executive producer) *Seduction: Three Tales from the "Inner Sanctum,"* ABC, 1992.

Film appearances include *The Life and Times of Judge Roy Bean,* National General, 1972; *The Naked Ape,* Universal, 1973; *Earthquake,* Universal, 1974; *I Will, I Will . . . for Now,* Twentieth Century-Fox, 1976; *Vigilante Force,* United Artists, 1976; *Greatest Heroes of the Bible,* Sunn Classic Pictures, 1979; and *Michael Kael contre la World News Company,* Bac Films, 1998. Stage appearances include *Night of 100 Stars,* Radio City Music Hall, New York City, 1982; *Love Letters,* 1990; *Mere Mortals,* Second City, Chicago, IL, 1998; and *Time Flies,* Los Angeles Theatre Works, Los Angeles, 1998.

AWARDS, HONORS: Honored in the 1980s by President Ronald Reagan for her work on behalf of arthritis sufferers.

WRITINGS:

The Body Principal: The Exercise Program for Life, photographs by Harry Langdon, Simon & Schuster (New York, NY), 1983.
The Beauty Principal: The Beauty Program for Life, photographs by Harry Langdon, Simon & Schuster (New York, NY), 1984.
The Diet Principal, Simon & Schuster (New York, NY), 1987.
The Living Principal: Looking and Feeling Your Best at Every Age, Simon & Schuster (New York, NY), 2001.

SIDELIGHTS: Daughter of a U.S. Air Force sergeant, Victoria Principal attended seventeen different schools in her childhood, living variously in England, Florida, Puerto Rico, Massachusetts, Georgia, and other locales. She began acting at age five, when she ap-

peared in a commercial, and made her first film appearance opposite Paul Newman in *The Life and Times of Judge Roy Bean.* Despite this promising start, by 1976, twenty-nine-year-old Principal was ready to quit acting and attend law school in hopes of becoming a studio executive. Producer Aaron Spelling, however, offered her a year's tuition to appear in the pilot of his new show *Fantasy Island.* Not only did that program become an enormous success, but Principal soon afterward landed a role as Pamela Ewing on an even more successful show, *Dallas.*

Dallas aired for nearly a decade, from 1978 to 1987, but long before the show ended, Principal had put her entrepreneurial savvy to work in a number of ways: a production company, a line of skin-care products (with infomercials to support them), and a series of books on health and beauty. The first of these, published in 1983, was *The Body Principal: The Exercise Program for Life.* In it, Principal explains that a number of factors had driven her to become enthusiastic about health and exercise.

While playing football on vacation in Hawaii in 1977, she had injured her knee, and doctors told her she would have to have surgery and avoid physical activity for half a year. Instead, she embarked on an exercise program that cut her recovery time in half, and at the end of three months, she was wearing high heels again. Around the time of the leg injury, she writes, she had also become concerned because her "bottom had fallen."

Regarding Principal's claim that she had gotten fat, a reviewer in *People* wrote, "Don't kid yourself. Victoria"—widely regarded as one of the most glamorous women on television in the 1970s and 1980s—"didn't look too shabby even before she started exercising." The reviewer went on to compare *The Body Principal* favorably with similar celebrity exercise books, noting "Principal's appears to have taken more than a day to slap together, and is written with touches of self-deprecating wit."

In *The Beauty Principal: The Beauty Program for Life,* published a year later, Principal offers such secrets as how to avoid "garage door eyes"—eyes whose lids are made up with a single, solid color. She followed *The Beauty Principal* in 1987 with *The Diet Principal,* and in 2001 published *The Living Principal:*

Looking and Feeling Your Best at Every Age. The Living Principal includes advice on appearance, diet, and exercise, along with a thirty-day whole-health plan. "What distinguishes this from other mind-body tomes," maintained Barbara Jacobs in *Booklist,* "are, first, Principal's personality and willingness to reveal the bad with the good and, second, her spirituality."

BIOGRAPHICAL AND CRITICAL SOURCES:

BOOKS

Contemporary Theatre, Film, and Television, Volume 34, Gale (Detroit, MI), 2001.
Notable Hispanic American Women, Book 2, Gale (Detroit, MI), 1998.

PERIODICALS

Booklist, April 15, 2001, Barbara Jacobs, review of *The Living Principal,* p. 1519.
Cosmopolitan, September, 1987, Paul Rosenfield, "The Very Principled Victoria Principal," pp. 156-158.
Good Housekeeping, June, 1989, Vernon Scott, "Victoria Principal: The Girl Who Has Everything," pp. 112-115.
Health, January, 1984, Sally Cummings, review of *The Body Principal,* p. 59.
McCall's, August, 1992, Margy Rochlin, "I'm Having a Good Life" (interview), pp. 120-25.
New York, February 20, 1984, Mona Shangold, review of *The Body Principal,* p. 61.
People Weekly, October 10, 1983, review of *The Body Principal,* p. 22; January 7, 1985, review of *The Beauty Principal,* pp. 17-18.
Publishers Weekly, August 19, 1983, review of *The Body Principal,* p. 65; March 12, 2001, review of *The Living Principal,* p. 84.
Redbook, October, 1990, Alan W. Petrucelli, "Talking with Victoria Principal: 'I'm in Great Shape,'" pp. 72-73.
TV Guide, March 14, 1987, Michael Leahy, "She's Risen Above—But Can't Ever Forget—Her Troubled Years," pp. 34-41; October 2, 1993, Frank Swertlow, "Victoria's Secrets," pp. 8-12; July 1, 1995, Stephanie Mansfield, "Principal Player," pp. 8-12.
Washington Post, June 16, 1987, Carole Sugarman, review of *The Diet Principal,* p. WH15.

OTHER

Principal Secret, http://www.principalsecret.com (October 29, 2002).
Victoria Principal Web site, http://www.victoriaprincipal.com (October 29, 2002).*

R

RADAVICH, David (Allen) 1949-

PERSONAL: Born October 30, 1949, in Boston, MA; son of Frederick Radd (a metallurgist) and Marian Wright Martin (a mathematician); married Anne Ricketson Zahlan (a professor), January 2, 1988; children: Leila Amal Zahlan. *Education:* University of Kansas, B.A. (psychology), 1971, M.A. (English), 1974, Ph.D. (English/theater), 1979. *Politics:* Democrat. *Religion:* Episcopalian.

ADDRESSES: Home—1020 Williamsburg Drive, Charleston, IL 61920. *Office*—Eastern Illinois University, 600 Lincoln Avenue, Charleston, IL 61920. *E-mail*—cfdar@eiu.edu.

CAREER: Educator, poet, and playwright. University of Kansas, Lawrence, English instructor, 1973; University of Stuttgart, Stuttgart, Germany, Fulbright lecturer, 1979-81; Iowa State University, Ames, English instructor, 1982-84; Eastern Illinois University, Charleston, English professor, 1984—.

MEMBER: Dramatists Guild, Chicago Alliance for Playwrights, Missouri Association of Playwrights, Playwrights Express (co-founder), Modern Language Association, University Professionals of Illinois, (vice president, EIU Chapter, 1998-2000; president, 2000—), Phi Beta Kappa.

AWARDS, HONORS: Named Illinois Distinguished Author, Illinois State Library, 1995; Person of the Year, *Daily Eastern News,* 2000.

WRITINGS:

Slain Species (poetry), Court Poetry Press (London, England), 1980.
Nevertheless (drama), Aran Press, 1988.
By the Way: Poems over the Years (poetry), Buttonwood Press (Champaign, IL), 1998.
Greatest Hits (poetry), Pudding House Publications, 2000.

Contributed poetry and short drama, as well as scholarly and informal essays on poetry, drama, and contemporary writing, to journals.

WORK IN PROGRESS: On the Verge: Plays for Our Time (cycle of seven plays); a poetry collection; research on the heritage of Midwestern plays and playwrights.

SIDELIGHTS: David Radavich told *CA:* "My writing is very much concerned with social issues, albeit approached aesthetically, and I consider my role as artist to be one of public service to the larger community. In my plays, I endeavor to tackle major social conflicts and investigate possibilities for insight and resolution. In my poetry, I explore more existential questions within this larger context. My essays, both scholarly and informal, often examine neglected authors or subjects, such as the rich heritage of drama in the Midwest, as well as the changing context of contemporary writing."

RADISH, Kris 1953-

PERSONAL: Born September 18, 1953, in Milwaukee, WI; daughter of Richard (a retired bricklayer) and Pat (a retired medical worker; maiden name, Goodreau) Radish; children: Andrew Carpenter, Rachel Carpenter. *Education:* University of Wisconsin—Milwaukee, B.A. (journalism), 1975. *Politics:* "Very liberal." *Religion:* "Spiritual." *Hobbies and other interests:* Running, tennis, poetry, drinking wine, hiking, training for physically challenging events, motorcycling, raising two kids, biking, books, funky movies, sleeping once a year.

ADDRESSES: Home—747 Adams Street, Oconomowoc, WI 53066. *Agent*—Barb Doyan, Doyan Literary, Newell, IA. *E-mail*—kradish@voyager.net.

CAREER: Journalist and educator. *Deseret News,* Salt Lake City, UT, bureau chief, 1978-85; freelance writer, 1985—; University of Wisconsin- Milwaukee, reporter and journalism instructor, 1989-92. DBR Media, New York, NY, 2000—; CNI Newspapers, New Berlin, WI, managing editor, 2001—. *Daily Universe,* Brigham Young University, faculty advisor; University of Wisconsin—Milwaukee, board of directors, 1973-75; *Intermountain Catholic Newspaper,* board of advisors, 1985-87; writing volunteer, Oconomowoc school district.

MEMBER: National Organization for Women.

AWARDS, HONORS: Livingston Award finalist, for general excellence; Pulitzer Prize finalist for investigative journalism; *Deseret News* awards, for reporting; Society of Professional Journalists award, for reporting.

WRITINGS:

Run, Bambi, Run: The Beautiful Ex-Cop and Convicted Murderer Who Escaped to Freedom and Won America's Heart (true crime), Carol (New York, NY), 1992.
(With Chris Isaacson) *The Birth-Order Personality Method: How to Better Understand Yourself and Others* (psychology), Adams Media (Avon, MA), 2002.
An Elegant Gathering of White Snow (novel), Spinsters Ink (Denver, CO), 2002.

Contributor to periodicals, including *Better Homes and Gardens, Sierra, Skiikng, Islands,* and *Midwest Living.*

WORK IN PROGRESS: Whispers on the Windowsill (poetry); *What Was I Thinking?,* a guide for women exploring alternatives to traditional marriage; *Dancing with the FBI* (short nonfiction); psychological women's romance novel.

SIDELIGHTS: Kris Radish told *CA:* "I am a wild, daring, wonderful, bold woman who creates and crafts sentences that flow from my heart to my soul and out the tips of my fingers. My writing is done with great honesty and personal revelation and always with the charge that maybe I can do something for the women of the world. I am inspired by women's issues, by the causes of the female world that I have always held sacred, and I hope that I can portray the secrets and glories of a woman's life with great honesty and reverence. My stories and poetry come to me like fine gifts. I carry papers and pencils with me everywhere, and when I am naked I write on my hand. I write very quickly. I hate to edit—what is a comma?—and I adore good editors. If I can make someone feel and think—well—what a day, what a world, what a life. I say things out loud and with my words that most people only think. I charge through life and am always poised for a new adventure."

*   *   *

REGISTER, William Wood 1958-
(Woody Register)

PERSONAL: Born 1958. *Education:* Sewanee, the University of the South, B.A.; Brown University, Ph. D., 1991.

ADDRESSES: Home—Sewanee, TN. *Office*—Walsh Ellet 305, Sewanee, the University of the South, 735 University Ave., Sewanee, TN 37383. *E-mail*—wregiste@sewanee.edu.

CAREER: Sewanee, the University of the South, Sewanee, TN, associate professor of history, 1993—.

WRITINGS:

AS WOODY REGISTER

The Kid of Coney Island: Fred Thompson and the Rise of American Amusements, Oxford University Press (New York, NY), 2001.

Contributor to books, including *Inventing Times Square: Commerce and Culture at the Crossroads of the World,* edited by William R. Taylor, Johns Hopkins University Press (Baltimore, MD), 1996; and *The American Reform Tradition,* edited by Karen Halttunen. Contributor to periodicals, including *masculinities.*

SIDELIGHTS: William Wood Register, who has published under the name Woody Register, teaches American history at Sewanee, the University of the South, with an emphasis on American culture and intellectual history since the U. S. Civil War. He has written several articles in which he examines gender, popular amusements, and consumer culture in early twentieth-century America. One of his articles, "New York's Gigantic Toy," was included in the book *Inventing Times Square: Commerce and Culture at the Crossroads of the World.* This article studies the development and culture of New York's Hippodrome Theatre, a site where Houdini often played, some of Edward Albee's plays were dramatized, and RKO's first all-talking movie *Syncopation* premiered in 1929.

In his book *The Kid of Coney Island: Fred Thompson and the Rise of American Amusements* Register focuses on the man sometimes known as the "boy-wonder" of American popular amusements prior to the Walt Disney era. Thompson (1873-1919) also built New York's Hippodrome Theatre.

Thompson's career as an entertainment entrepreneur began as a "creator and promoter of carnival shows and world's fairs, including the World's Columbian Exposition in 1893," as noted at the Oxford University Press Web site. It was during the Chicago Fair in 1893 that Thompson became fascinated with the idea of building amusement parks, and, for the next eight years, he traveled around the United States in search of new ideas and of sites where he could stage them. His creations became more and more complex as he learned to employ the new technologies that were developing at the turn of the century. His use of Edison's talking cylinders, lights, and water fountains helped him create exciting fantasy worlds built for the benefit of adults.

In 1903 Thompson constructed Luna Park on Coney Island, one of his greatest creations. Luna Park was a collection of thrill rides which included a "Twenty Thousand Leagues under the Sea" attraction in which participants experienced a pseudo-submarine ride to the "North Pole," where live polar bears were kept in a refrigerated, partially frozen man-made sea. Another theme of Thompson's attractions was that of great battles and disasters. His rides would take people into the path of a devastating tornado or into the midst of a battle between make-believe warriors and defenders of the shores of New York. Thompson's Luna Park brought legitimacy to Coney Island, which had previously been known as a crude place in which respectable people would never venture.

Thompson built the Hippodrome Theater so he could produce expensive extravaganzas attracting primarily adult audiences, luring them to shows that would take them into a world of fantasy. Register explains why this fantasy world was so appealing to adults of this era, many of whom were living in an otherwise serious-minded world of business and Victorian disciplines. Thompson's entertainments encouraged adults, especially men, to forget the rigors of early twentieth-century life and go out and have fun. Though Thompson was creative, he was lacking in business expertise. He eventually lost both Luna Park and the Hippodrome to men who knew more about making money than creating fantasy.

Register's book places Thompson in the middle of a vast cultural shift at the turn of the twentieth century, a time when Victorian ethics emphasized a strict diet of educational venues. During this time, amusement for its own sake was viewed as decadent.

Register "creates a vivid and captivating biography," wrote John E. Hodgkins for *Library Journal,* who also called the book "beautifully and artfully written." *Library Journal* named *The Kid of Coney Island* one of its Best Books of 2001. A reviewer for *Publishers Weekly* stated, "This wonderfully written, entertaining and unusually perceptive look at a forefather of 20th-century American leisure culture makes delightful reading out of serious scholarship."

BIOGRAPHICAL AND CRITICAL SOURCES:

PERIODICALS

Library Journal, August, 2001, John E. Hodgkins, review of *The Kid of Coney Island,* p. 124; January, 2002, Barbara Hoffert, review of *The Kid of Coney Island*, p. 51.

Publishers Weekly, July 23, 2001, review of *The Kid of Coney Island*, p. 64.

OTHER

Oxford University Press Web site, http://www.oup-usa. org/ (April 19, 2002).

*   *   *

REGISTER, Woody
      See REGISTER, William Wood

*   *   *

RHOADES, Jonathan
      See OLSEN, John Edward

*   *   *

RICHLER, Emma

PERSONAL: Born in London, England; daughter of Mordecai (a writer) and Florence (Wood) Richler. *Education:* Degrees from University of Toronto, Universite de Provence, and Circle in the Square Theatre School.

ADDRESSES: Home—London, England. *Agent*—Zoë Waldie, Rogers, Coleridge & White Ltd., 20 Powis Mews, London W11 1JN, England.

CAREER: Worked as an actress in England in theatre, film, television drama, and on BBC radio until 1996; reader for publishers, including Chatto & Windus, Bloomsbury, and Harvill, London, England, 1995—.

WRITINGS:

Sister Crazy (novel), Pantheon Books (New York, NY), 2001.

WORK IN PROGRESS: A second novel.

SIDELIGHTS: Although writing may be in Emma Richler's genes—her father was a writer and her three brothers are journalists—Richler spent ten years training and working as an actress before publishing her debut novel, *Sister Crazy*. Born in London, England, Emma moved with her family to Canada when she was eleven years old. After studying French literature in college, she turned to studying acting in New York City at a two-year professional conservatory training program called Circle in the Square Theatre School. In 1989 she moved to London and embarked on a career in theatre, film, television, and radio, retiring from the profession to work on her first novel while also reading for several publishers and writing book reviews.

Although she has been asked numerous times if her novel *Sister Crazy* is about her life, Richler says she often wonders why the question is asked and what is behind it. "My answer to this question," she told Shelagh Rogers during an interview on CBC Radio, "is always honest and simple: the only tools available to me are my experience and my imagination . . . [and] at a certain point the story just takes off and has a life of its own." Richler went on to tell Rogers that although there are certain similarities between her life and the book, like the fact that the book is told from the perspective of a middle child of five, "had I written a novel about the First World War or polar bears on some other planet, it would have been just as true to life and untrue to life as this book." Lisa Appignanesi wrote in *Jewish Chronicle* that "Richler, like Jemima, has a writer father, the famous Mordecai Richler, who took his family of five children from Britain to Canada. But where memoir ends and fiction begins is, in a sense, irrelevant. Richler has written a deeply moving book. Her language is electric, her formal poise astonishing in a first novel."

Sister Crazy is composed of seven nonlinear, stream-of-consciousness stories or episodes as seen through the eyes of the troubled Jemima Weiss and told to her psychotherapist. The story focuses primarily on Jemima's close-knit but somewhat eccentric family, a family to which Jemima is still attached by a metaphorical umbilical cord. Although she now lives on her own, she still longs for the safe cocoon of life that her family represents. Jemima feels her idyllic life has been destroyed by events such as her siblings—and in a sense, her aging mother and father—departing for lives of their own. Her resulting psychosis includes cutting herself with a knife.

Sister Crazy has been hailed by reviewers as a promising first novel by a gifted writer. Reviewing the book for *Booklist,* Stephanie Zvirin noted, "In a lyrical, intricately woven patchwork of memory and emotion, Richler brings these characters brilliantly to life." A *Publishers Weekly* reviewer observed that Richler "captures the allure and subtle perils of a similarly intense, hothouse upbringing," as that of J. D. Salinger's Glass family stories.

Many reviewers also praised the book for its blending of pathos with humor. "As humorous as it is tense, the voice here is intelligent and hopeful," wrote reviewer Josette Kurey at the Web site *Bookreporter.com,* continuing, "The text is filled with great slang and a childlike energy." Reviewer Sienna Powers, writing for *January Magazine,* commented, "Richler consistently lightens the dark areas of *Sister Crazy* with humor and deepens humorous passages with dollops of darkness."

Although Richler has spent ten years of her life as an actor, the success of *Sister Crazy* may permanently set her on a new career path. As reviewer Nancy Schiefer noted in a *London Free Press* article featured on the *Canoe* Web site, "It is a riveting and important book, one difficult to put down and one composed in the clear and assured style of the gifted writer. It must be in the genes." And Daniel Mendelsohn, writing in *New York Magazine,* concluded that Richler goes beyond the usual clichés "and creates something striking and original."

BIOGRAPHICAL AND CRITICAL SOURCES:

PERIODICALS

Booklist, April 15, 2001, Stephanie Zvirin, review of *Sister Crazy,* p. 1537.
Globe and Mail, May 5, 2001, Gale Zoe Garnett, "The Apprenticeship of Emma Richler," p. D15.
Jewish Chronicle, September 21, 2001, Lisa Appignanesi, "Paradise Soured."
Kirkus Reviews, March 15, 2001, review of *Sister Crazy,* p. 357.

Los Angeles Times, April 29, 2001, review of *Sister Crazy,* p. 22.
Maclean's, May 14, 2001, John Bemrose, "Writing up a Storm," p. 65.
New Yorker, July 9, 2001, review of *Sister Crazy,* p. 87.
New York Magazine, June 11, 2001, pp. 55-56.
New York Times Book Review, May 6, 2001, Marcel Theroux, "Family Album," p. 7.
Publishers Weekly, April 16, 2001, review of *Sister Crazy,* p. 43.
Quill and Quire, April, 2001, Marnie Woodrow, review of *Sister Crazy.*

OTHER

Bookreporter.com, http://www.bookreporter.com/ (September 5, 2001), Josette Kurey, review of *Sister Crazy.*
Canoe, http://www.canoe.ca/ (June 2, 2001), Nancy Schiefer, "No Limit to Writing Talent in Richler Family."
CBC Radio, http://infoculture.cbc.ca/ (May 9, 2001), Shelagh Rogers, "Interview: Emma Richler on Her Debut Novel, *Sister Crazy.*"
January Magazine, http://www.januarymagazine.com/ (July, 2001), Sienna Powers, "Sister Talent."

*   *   *

RIGOULOT, Pierre 1944-

PERSONAL: Born February 12, 1944, in Paris, France; son of André and Joffrette (Girard) Rigoulot; divorced; children: Hélène, Marc, Simon, Ève. *Education:* Sorbonne, University of Paris, degree, 1968, teaching certification, 1978.

ADDRESSES: Office—Institut d'Histoire Sociale, 4 avenue Benoit Franchon, 92023 Nanterre Cedex, France. *E-mail*—rigoulotp@aol.com.

CAREER: Writer. Associated with Institute d'Histoire Sociale, France.

AWARDS, HONORS: Prix Chateaubriand, 2001, for *Les siècle des camps.*

WRITINGS:

(With Geoffroi Crunelle) *Des Français au goulag: 1917-1984,* Editions Fayard (Paris, France), 1984.

L'Yonne dans la guerre: 1939-1945, Editions Horvath (Paris, France), 1987.

(With Branko Lazitch) *The Battle for Angola, 1974-1988: A Set-back for Communism in Africa,* preface by Jean-Francois Revel, translated by Nicholas Rowe, Better Britain Society (London, England), 1989.

La tragédie des Malgré-nous, Tambor, le camp des Français, Editions Denoël (Paris, France), 1990.

Les paupières lourdes: les Français face au goulag: aveuglements et indignations, Editions Universitaires (Paris, France), 1991.

Les enfants de l'épuration, Editions Plon (Paris, France), 1993.

(With Ilios Yannakakis) *Un pavé dans l'histoire: le débat français sur Le livre noir du communisme,* Editions Laffont (Paris, France), 1998.

(With Kang Ch'or-hwan) *Les aquariums de Pyongyang: dix ans au goulag nord-coréen,* Editions Laffont (Paris, France), 2000, translated by Yair Reiner as *The Aquariums of Pyongyang: Ten Years in a North Korean Gulag,* Basic Books (New York, NY), 2001.

(With Joel Kotek) *Le siècle des camps: détention, concentration extermination: cent ans de mal radical,* Editions Lattès (Paris, France), 2000.

Also author of text selection and notes, with Branko Lazitch, for *Chronique du mensonge communiste,* Editions Plon (Paris, France), 1998. Contributor to books, including *Un échec du communisme en Afrique,* by Branko Lazitch, preface by Jean-François Revel, Editions Est & Ouest (Paris, France), 1988; and *Le Livre Noir de Communisme,* Editions Robert Laffont (Paris, France), 1997, translated as *The Black Book of Communism,* Harvard University Press (Cambridge, MA), 2000.

ADAPTATIONS: Les enfants de l'épuration was broadcast on French television, June 11, 2000.

WORK IN PROGRESS: An overview of North Korea, due in 2003; a book on anti-Americanism in France, for Editions Laffont, 2003.

SIDELIGHTS: Pierre Rigoulot was born in 1944 in Paris and came of age as a student believing that social justice could be achieved most efficiently through Marxist Leninism. During the student uprisings of May 1968, he was already a committed supporter of Chinese dictator Mao Zedong and considered Mao's Cultural Revolution a cleansing approach to Stalinism, as well as the fastest way to social reform.

During the 1970s, Rigoulot became disenchanted with Marxism and looked for another social system that would work better in Western Europe. In 1973, he first read Alexander Solzhenitzen's *Gulag Archipelago.* As Rigoulot told Ki-Hong Han, in an interview for *NK Net,* "His reintroduction of ethics in political thought helped us to break with Hegel's and Marx's views on a progressive and necessary sense of History."

Despite rising doubts regarding the Marxist model, Rigoulot went to work for *Les Temps Modernes,* the Marxist magazine of Jean Paul Sartre and Simone Beauvoir. He left *Les Temps Modernes* in 1982, convinced that its worldview of an enlightened international socialism, though coupled with a condemnation of Stalinist excesses, was an unworkable political ideal.

Since 1984, Rigoulot has worked at *Est et Ouest,* a magazine founded by Boris Souvarine, a former head of the French Communist Party, who was eventually expelled from the Party. Rigoulot divides his time between his duties as an editor for *Est et Ouest* and his research and writing.

Rigoulot also contributed to the best-selling *Black Book of Communism (Le livre noir de communisme)* by detailing the abuses of human rights in North Korea. The book has become an international bestseller and has been translated and published in more than thirty languages. Rigoulot told *NK Net,* "I am not an editor of the *Black Book.* I contributed only the North Korean chapter. But I can say that we felt, since the beginning of the nineties, that we had entered a new political and historical era. Today, communism is not any more a menace. It does not any more shape any political debate or any political struggle. This system failed to realize its goals. It even failed to give a decent life to men and women under its control."

Although Rigoulot's institute and its magazine are dedicated to the study of communism, he became interested in North Korea through a chance encounter with a woman asking for directions in Paris. Through her and her family, Rigoulot learned about the ongoing tragedy suffered by the North Korean people.

Rigoulot began a political action newsletter to make the plight of twenty-two million starving North Koreans known to the French people. His collaboration with Ch'or-hwan Kang began with an invitation to Paris and an interview with the leftwing daily, *Liberation.* This began a series of interviews on both television and radio, as well as in print.

The Aquariums of Pyongyang: Ten Years in a North Korean Gulag, grew out of this collaborative effort between Rigoulot and Ch'or-hwan Kang. It is a stark account of Kang's imprisonment on the North Korean Yodok gulag. It begins with the story of how Kang's grandparents emigrated from Japan to North Korea in the 1960s. His grandparents, who had become wealthy living in Japan, were convinced to repatriate to North Korea by the Chosen Soren, a Korean exile group in Japan. Upon arriving in North Korea, their hope for an egalitarian society quickly turned to a nightmare. One of Kang's uncles describes their arrival in these words. "It was like the city was dead—the strangest atmosphere. The people all looked so shabby and aimless in their wanderings." At first, his life was better than most—his grandfather was appointed a to a high-level government position, but that quickly changed. His grandfather was arrested for the crime of "reactionary bourgeois tendencies" and disappeared. Kang was nine years old when he was arrested along with his sister, father, and uncle for the crime of high treason. Thus began ten years of physical and emotional abuse, including twelve-hour workdays, hours of "political training," and near-starvation rations that included a supplement of rats and bugs. After his inexplicable release in 1987, Kang wrote that the only lesson his imprisonment had "pounded into me was about man's limitless capacity to be vicious."

Iris Chang, discussing Rigoulot and Kang's book in her *The Rape of Nanking,* wrote: "*The Aquariums of Pyongyang: Ten Years in a North Korean Gulag* is one of the most terrifying memoirs I have ever read. As the first such account to emerge from North Korea, it is destined to become a classic. Kang Cho'r-hwan's beloved but doomed aquarium is a microcosm of his boyhood in a North Korean prison camp: a world of constant surveillance, isolation and death."

BIOGRAPHICAL AND CRITICAL SOURCES:

BOOKS

Chang, Iris, *The Rape of Nanking,* Basic Books (New York, NY), 1997

Rigoulot, Pierre and Kang Ch'or-hwan, *The Aquariums of Pyongyang: Ten Years in a North Korean Gulag,* Basic Books (New York, NY), 2001.

PERIODICALS

l'Express International, February 7, 1992, review of *Les Francais face au goulag: aveuglements et indignations,* p. 431; December 15, 1994, Bernard Lecomte, "Il faut ouvrir le proces du goulag," p. 46.

New American, February 11, 2002, Thomas R. Eddlem, review of *The Aquariums of Pyongyang: Ten Years in a North Korean Gulag,* p. 31.

New York Review of Books, October 18, 2001, Anne Applebaum, review of *The Aquariums of Pyongyang: Ten Years in a North Korean Gulag,* p. 40.

Publishers Weekly, July 30, 2001, review of *The Aquariums of Pyongyang: Ten Years in a North Korean Gulag,* p. 72.

Russian Review, October, 1989, J. Arch Getty, review of *Les paupières lourdes: Les Français face au goulag: aveuglements et indignations,* p. 431.

Slavic Review, fall, 1989, Ruth Rischin, review of *Les Francais au goulag: 1917-1984,* p. 500; spring, 1994, Ruth Rischin, review of *Les paupières lourdes,* p. 272.

*   *   *

RILEY, Gregory J. 1947-

PERSONAL: Born 1947. *Education:* University of California, Los Angeles, B.A., M.A.; University of California, Santa Barbara, M.A.; Harvard University, M.A., Ph.D.

ADDRESSES: Office—Claremont Graduate University, School of Religion, 831 Dartmouth Avenue, Claremont, CA 91711. *E-mail*—griley@cst.edu.

CAREER: Claremont School of Theology, Claremont, CA, associate professor of religion.

WRITINGS:

Resurrection Reconsidered: Thomas and John in Controversy, Fortress Press (Minneapolis, MN), 1995.
One Jesus, Many Christs: How Jesus Inspired Not One Christianity, but Many: The Truth about Christian Origins, HarperSanFrancisco (San Francisco, CA), 1997.
The River of God: A New History of Christian Origins, HarperSanFrancisco (San Francisco, CA), 2001.

SIDELIGHTS: Gregory Riley, a highly educated professor of religion, has written three well-received books on aspects of the Bible and Christianity. He has degrees in ancient history, classics, Near-Eastern languages, the study of religion, and New Testament and Christian origins. His primary areas of research interest are the culture and religions of the Greco-Roman world and ancient Near East.

Riley's first book, *Resurrection Reconsidered: Thomas and John in Controversy,* is based on questions Riley had about the Gospel of John's emphasis on Thomas and what it was that Thomas doubted about Christ's resurrection. In order to answer his questions, Riley researched the writings and beliefs of the Semitic and Greco-Roman people, who were contemporaries of Thomas. Riley sought to learn what their beliefs about an afterlife might have been, in hopes of shedding light on Thomas. He discovered that although there were some references to life beyond the grave, most people had reservations about fully trusting in any form of existence after death. Riley's study concludes that there must have been contradictions between the opinions of the early Christian Church and doctrines that would become the foundation of Christianity as it is known in more modern times.

Although there has been some controversy concerning Riley's interpretation of the history of the early Christian Church, many reviews have praised Riley's extensive research and his writing. "This well-written and well-argued book," wrote Holly Hearon for *Interpretation,* "is a significant contribution to the study of the Thomas traditions." Although Pheme Perkins, writing for *Theological Studies,* had some issues with

Riley's explanations, Perkins stated, "the book provides a wealth of suggestive information to reinterpret the resurrection accounts."

In 1997 Riley wrote *One Jesus, Many Christs: How Jesus Inspired Not One Christianity, but Many: The Truth about Christian Origins.* In this study, Riley is interested more in the Jesus of history than the Jesus of theology. In other words, he is interested in how Jesus affected the people of his time rather than how he affected Christianity.

Riley discusses the many gods of early Greco-Roman paganism and tries to place Jesus among them. He questions what kind of god Jesus was to these early people. His conclusion is that Jesus was a hero, who preached that everyone should strive to be heroes in their own lives. However, as time went on, followers and believers in Jesus as god/hero were diverse in their doctrines. Each group held separate beliefs about Jesus' life, his death, his resurrections, and his definition as god. In reaching his conclusion, Riley then projects his findings onto modern Christianity, demonstrating that Christianity is multidimensional and pluralistic, capable of incorporating many diverse ideas.

A writer for *Kirkus Reviews* noted that Riley finds the story of Jesus similar to the stories of Achilles and Hercules in that all three heroes have a "mix of divine-human parentage," experienced a virgin birth, performed miracles, died violently, and "their deaths powerfully transformed other people's lives." Steve Schroeder, for *Booklist,* described Riley's book in a similar manner, "In Riley's account, the Gospel is a cosmic Iliad, and Jesus its Achilles." A *Publishers Weekly* reviewer also made allusions to Riley's Achilles model for Jesus, but noted that in the final chapters of his book, Riley shows how the early Christians altered the story of Jesus by emphasizing his role as martyr, "using Jesus as their model" and engaging "in martyrdom as a form of heroism . . . establishing Christianity as a religious force in the Roman Empire." Robert H. O'Connell, for *Library Journal,* found Riley's work to be "well-argued" and "richly illustrated with literary connections between biblical and Greek portrayals of heroic traits."

In *The River of God: A New History of Christian Origins,* Riley continues his research of Jesus and the early beginnings of Christianity. He argues that the true origins cannot be wholly established in the roots of Judaism but rather, as a reviewer for *Publishers Weekly* stated, in "a threefold model of genealogy," including Greek and Roman thought. Riley demonstrates how concepts of the devil, one god, the soul separate from the body, and other beliefs came to be infused in Christianity from a variety of sources. David Bourquin, for *Library Journal,* pointed out that there have been several recent studies focused on the same argument, "but Riley . . . gives us one of the best. His arguments are far more balanced and substantiated."

BIOGRAPHICAL AND CRITICAL SOURCES:

PERIODICALS

Booklist, October 1, 1997, Steve Schroeder, review of *One Jesus, Many Christs: How Jesus Inspired Not One Christianity, but Many: The Truth about Christian Origins,* pp. 289-290.

Interpretation, January, 1997, Holly Hearon, review of *Resurrection Reconsidered: Thomas and John in Controversy,* p. 98.

Journal of Religion, July, 1999, Kurt Rudolph, "The Nag Hammadi Library after Fifty Years," pp. 452-457.

Kirkus Reviews, September 15, 1997, review of *One Jesus, Many Christs,* pp. 1444-1445.

Library Journal, November 1, 1997, Robert H. O'Connell, review of *One Jesus, Many Christs,* pp. 79-80; August, 2001, David Bourquin, review of *The River of God: A New History of Christian Origins,* p. 118.

Publishers Weekly, October 27, 1997, review of *One Jesus, Many Christs,* pp. 70-71; July 23, 2001, review of *The River of God,* p. 72.

Theological Studies, March, 1996, Pheme Perkins, review of *Resurrection Reconsidered,* pp. 182-183.*

*   *   *

ROBERTS, Kenneth B. 1940-

PERSONAL: Born September 24, 1940, in Stockport, England; son of Ernest William and Nancy (Williams) Roberts; married Patricia Newton, August 8, 1964; children: Gavin, Paul, Susan, Alexis, Vanessa Jane. *Education:* London School of Economics, B.Sc., 1961, M.A. 1966.

ADDRESSES: Home—2 County Rd., Ormkirk L39 1QQ, England. *Office*—Department of Sociology, Social Policy and Social Work Studies, Eleanor Rathbone Building, University of Liverpool, Bedford Street South, Liverpool L69 7ZA, England; fax: 44 151 794 3001. *E-mail*—k.roberts@liverpool.ac.uk.

CAREER: University of Liverpool, Liverpool, England, began as assistant lecturer, 1966, became reader, professor of sociology, 1988—, head of sociology department, 1987-90, head of department of sociology, social policy and social work studies, 1990-95; visiting professor, Nottingham Trent University, 2001—. Chair of World Leisure Research Commission, 1991-96; academic fellow, Institute of Careers Guidance, 2000—.

MEMBER: International Sociological Association (president of research committee on leisure).

AWARDS, HONORS: Elected academician of Academy for Learned Societies of the Social Sciences.

WRITINGS:

Leisure, Longman (London, England) 1970, revised edition, 1981.

(With Tony Lane) *Strike at Pilkingtons,* Collins Fontana (London, England), 1971.

From School to Work: A Study of the Youth Employment Service, David & Charles (Newton Abbott, England), 1971, published as *From School to Work: A Study of the British Youth Employment Service,* Barnes & Noble (New York, NY) 1972.

(With Graham E. White and Howard J. Parker) *The Character-training Industry,* David & Charles (Newton Abbot, England), 1974.

(With F. G. Cook, S. Clark, and E. Semeonoff) *The Fragmentary Class Structure,* Heinemann (London, England), 1977, reprinted, Gregg Revivals (Aldershot, England), 1993.

The Working Class, Longman (London, England), 1978.

Contemporary Society and the Growth of Leisure, Longman (London, England), 1978.

Youth and Leisure, Allen & Unwin (London, England), 1983.

School-leavers and Their Prospects, Open University Press (Milton Keynes, England), 1984.

(Editor, with A. Olszewska) *Leisure and Lifestyle,* Sage (London, England), 1989.

(Editor, with T. J. Kamphorst) *Trends in Sports: A Multinational Perspective,* Giordano Brune (Culemborg, Netherlands), 1989.

(With others) *Careers and Identities,* Open University Press (Milton Keynes, England), 1992.

(With M. Connolly, G. Ben-Tovim, and P. Torkington) *Black Youth in Liverpool,* Giordano Brune (Culemborg, Netherlands), 1992.

(With D. A. Brodie) *Inner-City Sport: Who Plays and What Are the Benefits?,* Giordano Brune (Culemborg, Netherlands), 1992.

(With D. Brodie and K. Lamb) *Citysport Challenge,* Health Promotion Research Trust (Cambridge, England), 1992.

Youth and Employment in Modern Britain, Oxford University Press (New York, NY), 1995.

(With B. Jung) *Poland's First Post-Communist Generation,* Avebury (Aldershot, England), 1995.

(Editor) *Leisure and Social Stratification,* Leisure Studies Association (Eastbourne, England), 1995.

(Editor, with L. Machacek) *Youth Unemployment and Self-Employment in East-Central Europe,* Slovak Academy of Sciences (Bratislava, Slovakia), 1997.

Leisure in Contemporary Society, CAB International (Wallingford, England), 1999.

(With S. Clarke, C. Fagan, and J. Tholen) *Surviving Post-Communism: Young People in the Former Soviet Union,* Edward Elgar (Cheltenham, England), 2000.

Class in Modern Britain, Palgrave (Basingstoke, England), 2001.

Contributor to books, including *Penelope Hall's Social Services of England and Wales,* edited by J. B. Mays and others, Routledge, 1975; *Sport and Leisure in Contemporary Society,* edited by S. Parker and others, Polytechnic of Central London, 1975; *Concepts of Leisure,* edited by J. F. Murphy and others, Prentice-Hall, 1974; *Race, Class, and Education,* edited by L. Barton and S. Walker, Croom Helm, 1983; *Scarman and After,* edited by J. Benyon, Pergamon, 1984; *Politics and Class,* edited by N. Woodhead, Hesketh, 1985; *Sport, Culture, Society,* edited by K. Mangan and R. B. Small, Spon, 1986; *Gender Segregation at Work,* edited by S. Walby, Open University Press, 1988; *Freedom and Constraint,* edited by F. Coalter, Routledge, 1989; *Leisure and Life-Style,* edited by A. Olszewska and K. Roberts, Sage, 1989; *Trends in Sports,* edited by T. J. Kamphorst and K. Roberts,

Giordano Bruno, 1989; *Training and Its Alternatives,* edited by D. Gleeson, Open University Press, 1990; *Work and the Enterprise Culture,* edited by M. Cross and G. Payne, Falmer Press, 1991; *Sport and Physical Activity,* edited by T. Williams, L. Almond, and A. Sparkes, Spon, 1992; *Guidance and Counselling in Britain: A Twenty-Year Perspective,* edited by W. Dryden and A. G. Watts, Hobsons, 1993; *Becoming Adults in England and Germany,* edited by K. Evans and W. R. Heinz, Anglo-German Foundation, 1994; *Professional and Development Issues in Leisure, Sport, and Education,* edited by L. Lawrence, E. Murdock, and S. Parker, Leisure Studies Association, 1995; *Youth and Life Management: Research Perspectives,* edited by H. Helve and J. Bynner, Helsinki University Press, 1996; *Youth, the Underclass, and Social Exclusion,* edited by R. MacDonald, Routledge, 1997; *Social Inequalities in Coronary Heart Disease,* edited by I. Sharp, National Heart Forum, 1998; *Leisure and Human Development,* edited by I. Richter and S. Sardei-Biermann, Leske & Budrich, 2000; and *Youth on the Threshhold of the Third Millennium,* edited by V. Puuronen, Karelian Institute, University of Joensuu, 2001.

Contributor to journals and other periodicals, including *Sociological Review, New Society, British Journal of Social Work, British Journal of Guidance and Counselling,* and *Youth in Society.* Member of editorial advisory board for *Leisure Studies,* 1982—, *Society and Leisure,* 1984—, and *Leisure Sciences,* 1986-92.

SIDELIGHTS: Over the course of a distinguished career that has spanned five decades, sociologist, educator, and researcher Kenneth B. Roberts has been a prolific author of scholarly books and papers dealing with various aspects of British labor history, class distinctions, and, according to the University of Liverpool sociology department's Web site, "young people's education, training, employment and unemployment" in what Roberts himself describes as "the sociology of leisure."

A native of Stockport, an industrial center in northwest England, Roberts did his graduate studies at the prestigious London School of Economics and then joined the faculty of the sociology department at the University of Liverpool in 1966, where he has taught ever since. Roberts's first book, *Leisure,* was published in 1970. The following year, he teamed with colleague Tony Lane on *Strike at Pilkingtons,* a study of a bitter labor strike, and he also wrote a book about a subject that has been at the heart of his academic research and writing over the years: youth employment and leisure activities. *From School to Work: A Study of the Youth Employment Service* traces the history and examines the role of the Youth Employment Service (YES), a British government agency established in 1909 to help young people look for and find work. "The book is a well presented case for changes in the provisions made for vocational guidance, placement and follow-up work with young people," observed Margaret Grubb in the *Sociological Review.*

The next four books Roberts wrote or contributed to— *The Character-training Industry, The Fragmentary Class Structure, Contemporary Society and the Growth of Leisure,* and *The Working Class*—all explore issues and trends in organized labor. A reviewer for *Choice* described *Contemporary Society and the Growth of Leisure* as a "relatively brief sociological analysis of leisure as a vital element in industrialized society." David Berry, writing in the *Sociological Review,* stated that "Roberts provides useful material on the family and social networks, and notes that an important aspect of the relation between work and leisure is the extent to which work relationships provide a social basis for leisure activities."

The Working Class, an update of a work by British sociologist Gordon Rose, is a survey of the literature and studies of the British working class in the mid-1970s. *Encounter* reviewer Philip Abrams called *The Working Class* "a useful digest of British studies," while Seamus Hegarty stated in the *Times Educational Supplement* that one of the strengths of Roberts's efforts is that they help to clarify the theoretical framework within which discussions of British labor history and culture take place. According to Hegarty, Roberts displays "a genuine awareness of the imprecision surrounding class concepts."

Roberts has continued his research into aspects of the working and leisure culture of British young people into the twenty-first century. He has written several books that deal with aspects of the subject, including *Youth and Leisure, School-leavers and Their Prospects, Changing Structure of Youth Labour Markets,* and *Youth and Employment in Modern Britain.* At the same time, Roberts has cast his eyes farther afield to collaborate with three academic colleagues on the book *Surviving Post-Communism: Young People in the*

Former Soviet Union. Robert's *Class in Modern Britain* is a survey text that puts forward the theory that, despite all of the changes that occurred in the final decades of the twentieth century, Britain is still very much a class-based society.

BIOGRAPHICAL AND CRITICAL SOURCES:

PERIODICALS

British Book News, April, 1984, David Jary, review of *Youth and Leisure,* p. 210.
Choice, May, 1979, review of *The Working Class,* p. 426; April, 1980, review of *Contemporary Society and the Growth of Leisure,* p. 291; May, 1984, review of *Youth and Leisure,* p. 1386.
Encounter, Volume 51, issue 6, Philip Abrams, review of *The Working Class,* pp. 62-64.
International Labour Review, August, 1972, review of *From School to Work,* p. 291.
Journal of Economic Literature, March, 1996, review of *Youth and Employment in Modern Britain,* p. 239.
Journal of Occupational and Organizational Psychology, June, 1993, Jennifer M. Kidd, review of *Careers and Identities,* pp. 193-194.
Sociological Review, Volume 21, issue 1, 1973, Margaret Grubb, review of *From School to Work,* pp. 155-156; Volume 28, issue 1, 1980, David Berry, review of *Contemporary Society and the Growth of Leisure,* pp. 207-208; Volume 32, issue 4, 1984, Michael Brake, review of *Youth and Leisure,* pp. 799-801; Volume 33, issue 1, 1985, Paul Bagguley, review of *School-leavers and Their Prospects,* pp. 166-167.
Sociology, February, 1993, Bogusia Temple, review of *Careers and Identities,* pp. 184-188.
Times Educational Supplement, September 22, 1978, Seamus Hegarty, review of *The Working Class,* p. 25; December 14, 1984, review of *School-leavers and Their Prospects,* p. 24.
Times Literary Supplement, May 12, 1972, review of *From School to Work,* p. 557.

OTHER

University of Liverpool Web site, http://www.liv.ac.uk/ (July 13, 2002).

ROBERTS-JONES, Philippe 1924-
(Philippe Jones)

PERSONAL: Born November 8, 1924, in Brussels, Belgium; son of Robert (an attorney) and Suzanne (Goemaere) Roberts-Jones; married Françoise Popelier; children: Eric, Oliver. *Education:* Harvard University; Ph.D., University of Brussels, 1955.

ADDRESSES: Office—Musées royaux des Beaux Arts de Belgique, 9 rue de Musée, Brussels 1000, Belgium.

CAREER: Art historian, curator, and writer. Candidate, Belgian National Foundation for Scientific Research, Brussels, Belgium, 1952-54; Office of Stamps, National Library of Paris, France, attaché, 1953-54; Ministry for Public Instruction, Brussels, inspector of public libraries, 1956-58, cultural attaché, 1958-61; Université Libre de Bruxelles, Brussels, professor, 1959—, chair of departments of contemporary art history, history of engraving, and conservatorship and concepts in seventeenth- and eighteenth-century art and archaeology, became professor emeritus; Royal Museums of Fine Arts, Brussels, chief curator, 1961-84, oversaw expansion of Museum of Ancient Art and nineteenth-century collections, 1974-84, and expansion of Museum of Modern Art, 1976-84; board of directors, Higher Institute of the History of Art and Archaeology, Brussels, vice president, 1966; Association des Musées de Belgique et du Comité National Belge du Conseil International des Musées, president, 1971-73; co-director, *Journal des Poètes,* 1981. *Wartime service:* Volunteer with underground army and liaison with British Army, 1944-46; received Médaille du volontaire de guerre and Médaille commémorative de la guerre 1940-45 avec sabres.

MEMBER: Académie Royale des Sciences, des Lettres et des Beaux-Arts de Belgique (honorary permanent secretary), Académie Royale de Langue et de Littérature françaises (director, 1998), Institut de France, Académie Européenne des Sciences, des Arts et des Lettres (founding member), Académie Mallarmé, Académie Européenne de Poésie (founding member), Academie Romana (honorary member), Institut Grand-Ducal de Luxembourg (honorary member), étranger de la Hollandsche Maatschappij der Wetenschappen, Académie Royale d'Archéologie, Accademia dei Georgofili, de Florence, Commission de la Biographie Nationale, Centre International pour l'etude du XIX siècle (president), Fondation Bertrand, Union Académique Internationale (administrative secretary, 1985-990, Fondation Francqui (board of directors), Association International des Critiques d'Art, Société des Gens de Lettres, Pen Club français de Belgique (vice president), Fondation Roi Baudoin, Comité International d'Histoire de l'Art.

AWARDS, HONORS: Prix Polak, Académie Royale de Langue et de Littérature françaises de Belgique, 1957, for *Amour et autres visages;* Prix Malherbe de la Province de Brabant, 1976, for *L'Art Majeur;* Grand Prix du Rayonnement français, Académie Française, 1980, for body of work; Grand Prix de Poésie, Académie Française, 1985; awarded title of Baron from king of Belgium, 1988; Commander of Order of Leopold (Belgium), Order of Arts and Letters (France), Order of Isabel the Catholic (Spain), Order of Merit (Italian Republic), and Order of the Lion (Finland); Grand-Croix de Ordre de la Couronne (Belgium); Officier, Légion d'Honneur (France); Médaille civique de première classe (Belgium).

WRITINGS:

POEMS; AS PHILIPPE JONES

La Voyageur de la nuit (title means "The Night Traveler"), 1947.

Grande largue, La Maison du Poète (Brussels, Belgium), 1949.

Seul un arbre (title means "A Single Tree"), Les Lettres (Paris, France), 1952.

Tu caressais un bois, L'Atelier du Livre (Brussels, Belgium), 1955.

Amour et autres visages (title means "Love and Other Faces"), Les Lettres (Paris, France), 1956.

Quatre domaines visités, L'Atelier du Livre (Brussels, Belgium), 1958.

Graver au vif (title means "Engrave to the Quick"), Recontre (Lausanne, Switzerland), 1971.

Jailler saisir, Le Cormier (Brussels, Belgium), 1971.

Etre selon (title means "To Be as May Be"), Le Cormier (Brussels, Belgium), 1973.

Le sens et le fleuve, Lettera Amorosa (Braine-le-Comte, Belgium), 1974.

Racine ouverte (title means "Bare Root"), preface by René Char, Le Cormier (Brussels, Belgium), 1976.

Carré d'air, [Paris, France], 1978.

D'un epsace renoué, Le Cormier (Brussels, Belgium), 1979.

Paroles données, Le Cormier (Brussels, Belgium), 1981.

Fêtes, Ed. Biskupic (Zagreb, Yugoslavia), 1983.

Indices d'ailleurs, L'Empreinte et la Nuit (Brussels, Belgium), 1983.

Image incendie mémoire, Le Cormier (Brussels, Belgium), 1985.

Paysages (title means "Landscapes"), La Grippelotte, 1987.

Les sables souverains, Le Cormier (Brussels, Belgium), 1988.

D'encre et d'horizon: poèmes 1981-1987, La Différence (Paris, France), 1989.

Ce temps d'un rien, L'Arbre à Paroles (Amay, Belgium), 1990.

La mort éclose, Le Taillis Pré (Châtelineau, Belgium), 1991.

Passion, 1993.

Toi et le tumulte, Le Cormier (Brussels, Belgium), 1993.

Proche de Horeb, La Gripelotte, 1994.

Le temps hors le temps, Le Cormier (Brussels, Belgium), 1994.

Les noeuds du sens, Tétras Lyre (Ayeneux-Soumagne, Belgium), 1997.

Le soleil s'écrit-il soleil, Le Cormier (Brussels, Belgium), 1997.

Le miroir et le vrai (title means "The Mirror and the Truth"), PHI (Echternach, Luxembourg), 2001.

Domaines en cours, Le Cormier (Brussels, Belgium), 2001.

ESSAYS; AS PHILIPPE ROBERTS-JONES

La presse satirique illustrée entre 1860 et 1890, Université de Paris (Paris, France), 1956.

De Daumier à Lautrec: essai sur l'histoire de la caricature française entre 1860 et 1890 (title means "From Daumier to Lautrec: Essay on the History of French Caricature between 1860 and 1890"), Les Beaux-Arts (Paris, France), 1960.

Daumier: moeurs conjugales, Vilo (Paris, France), 1967, English edition, Boston Book & Art Shop, 1968.

Ramah, Meddens (Brussels, Belgium), 1968.

Du réalisme du surréalisme: la peinture en Belgique de Joseph Stevens à Paul Delvaux, Laconti (Brussels, Belgium), 1969, new edition, Cahiers du Gram (Brussels, Belgium), 1994.

Magritte, poète du visible (title means "Magritte: Poet of the Visible"), 1972.

Bruegel: la chute d'Icare (title means "Bruegel: The Fall of Icarus"), Office du Livre (Fribourg, Switzerland), 1974.

L'art majeur, Jacques Antoine (Brussels, Belgium), 1974.

Friedlaender: tableaux, bildler, paintings, Manus Press (Stuttgart, Germany), 1976.

Lismonde, Laconti (Brussels, Belgium), 1977.

La peinture irréaliste au XIX siècle, Office du Livre (Fribourg, Switzerland), 1978, English edition, Oxford University Press (Oxford, England).

L'alphabet des circonstances: essais sur l'art des XIX et XX siècles, Académie royale de Belgique (Brussels, Belgium), 1981.

Van Lint, Ministère de la Communauté française (Brussels, Belgium), 1983.

René Carcan, Les Editeurs d'Art Associés (Brussels, Belgium), 1984.

André Willequet ou la multiplicité du regard, Labor (Brussels, Belgium), 1985.

Jos Albert, Lebeer-Hossmann (Brussels, Belgium), 1986.

Image donnée, image reçue, Académie Royale de Belgique (Brussels, Belgium), 1989.

Lismonde: Conversation avec Philippe Roberts-Jones, Editions Tandem (Gerpinnes, Belgium), 1992.

Octave Landuyt: Aurum Flandriae, Roularta Art Books (Zellik, Belgium), 1994.

Bruxelles fin de siècle, Flammarion (Paris, France), 1994.

Ivan Lackovic Croata: gravures, Belus (Zagreb, Yugoslavia), 1994.

Eugène Laermans 1864-1940, Crédit Communal et Snoeck-Ducaju (Brussels, Belgium), 1995.

Histoire de la peinture en Belgique du XIV siècle à nos jours, la Renaissance du Livre (Brussels, Belgium), 1995.

La peinture abstraite en Belgique 1920-1970, Crédit Communal (Brussels, Belgium), 1996.

L'art au présent: regards sur un demi-siècle (1960-1990), La Lettre volée, 1996.

Signes ou traces: arts des XIX et XX siècles, Académie royale de Belgique (Brussels, Belgium), 1997.

(With Françoise Roberts-Jones) *Pierre Bruegel l'Ancien,* Flammarion (Paris, France), 1997.

L'art pour qui, pour quoi?, Labor (Brussels, Belgium), 1999.

Magritte ou le leçon poétique, La Renaissance du Livre (Tournai, Belgium), 2001.

FICTION; AS PHILIPPE JONES

L'embranchement des heures, Editions de la Différence (Paris, France), 1991.
Le double du calendrier, Editions de la Différence (Paris, France), 1993.
L'angle de vue, Editions de la Différence (Paris, France), 1997.
L'instant multiple, Différence (Paris, France), 1997.

Also author, as Philippe Jones, of *Formes du matin* (poems); contributor of preface to *Mélot du Dy. Poèmes choisis,* Académie Royale de Langue et de Littérature Françaises (Brussels, Belgium), 2001. Contributor of articles to scholarly publications, including *Bulletin de l'Académie Royale de Belgique, Bulletin de l'Académie Royale de Langue et de Littérature françaises, Bulletin des Musées Royaux des Beaux-Arts de Belgique, Cahiers du Sud, Combat, Esprit et Vie, Giornale de Poeti, Journal des Poètes, Marginales, Nouvelles Littéraires, Courrier du Centre International d'Etude poétiques, Revue Générale, Poésie I, Le Soir, Snythèses, Gazette des Beaux-Arts, Revue de l'Université de Bruxelles, Connaissance des Arts, L'Oeil,* and *Nota bene;* contributor of textual material to numerous national and international exhibitions.

SIDELIGHTS: Philippe Roberts-Jones is a product of mixed European ancestry—his British father, Robert Roberts-Jones, was a noted attorney who was tortured and killed by the Germans during World War II, while Roberts-Jones's mother, Suzanne Goemaere, was of Gallic background. Roberts-Jones was born in Brussels and writes in French.

While he built his first career as a museum curator—and authored such related books as *Du Realisme au surrealisme: la peinture en Belgique de J. Stevens a Paul Delvaux* (a comparative study of Belgian surrealist painting)—Roberts-Jones gained more popular attention as a poet, writing under the name Philippe Jones. He brings the sensibility of the visual artist to his verse, according to an entry in *Columbia Dictionary of Modern European Literature.* In *Racine ouverte,* for example, the poet "prolongs the questioning of visual representation" in describing something as basic as a tree. According to the *Columbia Dictionary* critic, Roberts-Jones has developed "a voice of his own that transcends diverse tendencies of contemporary poetry."

In addition to verse, Roberts-Jones has also published four books of fiction, including the novels *L'embranchement des heures* and *L'instant multiple* as well as the short-story collection, *Le double du calendrier.* Judith Greenberg, reviewing *Le double du calendrier* for *World Literature Today,* compared reading the tales to gazing through a looking-glass: "Time is telescoped, the past obtrudes, the future intrudes." In these stories of love and death, added Greenberg, "ambiguities are tested. Motives are examined; one's own are found to be hidden from oneself."

Roberts-Jones has written and lectured extensively about Belgian art, and has traveled worldwide for conferences and exhibitions. His work has been translated into several languages, including German, English, Bulgarian, Croatian, Spanish, Greek, Italian, Dutch, Portuguese, Polish, Romanian, and Japanese.

BIOGRAPHICAL AND CRITICAL SOURCES:

PERIODICALS

Courrier de Centre International d'Etudes Poetiques, July, 1996, "Le piege blance de Philippe Jones," pp. 51-54.
Revue Generale, April 1998, "Philippe Jones ou Roberts-Jones, selon l'angle de vue," pp. 19-24.
World Literature Today, spring, 1994, Judith Greenberg, review of *Le double du calendrier,* p. 337.

*   *   *

ROGERS, Joel (Edward) 1952-

PERSONAL: Born March 19, 1952, in Long Ranch, NJ; son of Edward Franklin and Ann (Flemming) Rogers; married Sarah Siskind, December 2, 1980; children: Helen, Sophia. *Education:* Yale University, B.A., 1972, J.D., 1976; Princeton University, M.A., 1978, Ph.D., 1984.

ADDRESSES: Office—University of Wisconsin Law School, 975 Bascom Mall, Madison, WI 53706.

CAREER: Called to the Bar of New York State and U.S. Court of Appeals; University of Miami, Miami, FL, associate professor of law, 1986-87; University of Wisconsin, Madison, assistant professor, 1987-88, associate professor, 1988-90; professor of law, political science, and sociology, 1991—. Institute for Research on Poverty, Madison, affiliate, 1988—; A. Eugene Havens Center, Madison, associate director, 1988—; Disputes Processing Research Program, Madison, co-director, 1988—; Center for a New Democracy, Washington, DC, board chairperson, 1992—; New Party, New York, NY, executive committee chairperson, 1992—; director, Center on Wisconsin Strategy, 1993—; executive committee chairperson, Sustainable America, Madison, 1994—.

WRITINGS:

(With Joshua Cohen) *On Democracy,* 1983.
(With Thomas Ferguson and others) *Right Turn: The Decline of the Democrats and the Future of American Politics,* 1986.
(Editor with Wolfgang Streeck, and contributor) *Works Councils: Consultation, Representation, and Cooperation in Industrial Relations,* University of Chicago Press (Chicago, IL), 1995.
(With Ruy A. Teixeira) *America's Forgotten Majority: Why the White Working Class Still Matters* Basic, 2000.

Also co-author, with Richard B. Freeman, of *What Workers Want*; and with Daniel D. Luria and Joshua Cohen, of *Metro Futures: Economic Solutions for Cities and Their Suburbs.* Author of *Divide and Conquer: Post-War U.S. Labor Policy.*

SIDELIGHTS: Joel Rogers is a law professor and writer whose publications include *Works Councils: Consultation, Representation, and Cooperation in Industrial Relations,* which Gary Herrigel described in the *American Journal of Sociology* as "a very informative book on a subject of considerable interest and debate in progressive labor circles." This book, which Rogers edited with Wolfgang Streeck, argues that the development of works councils (representative bodies of workers within individual workplaces) in the United States could prove profitable for the American economy."The bulk of the volume," wrote Jonas Pontusson in *Contemporary Sociology,* "consists of case

studies, which describe the organization and functioning of works councils in individual countries and discuss their evolution over time." In his review, Herrigel affirmed that "these arguments are very solid, well-conceived, and pragmatic," and he noted that the various contributors "genuinely believe that American workplaces, and American workers, would benefit from the diffusion of works councils." Another reviewer, Lowell Turner, declared in the *Industrial and Labor Relations Review* that *Works Councils* "offers the latest word on the subject, and will be of great interest to anyone studying works councils and related issues of workplace representation." Craig A. Olson, meanwhile, wrote in the *Journal of Economic Literature* that *Works Councils* "clearly identifies fertile opportunities for more research on . . . important industrial relations institutions."

In a *New Party* online interview, Rogers commented on American industry and workers. "You basically cannot have a functioning mass pluralistic democratic order unless you've got some significant organizations of working people as workers," he stated. In addition, he declared, "The U.S. has never had a particularly strong labor movement, but it certainly had a stronger one in the past than it has now. Anybody who is concerned about democracy . . . should be concerned about that decline."

BIOGRAPHICAL AND CRITICAL SOURCES:

PERIODICALS

American Journal of Sociology, January, 1997, Gary Herrigel, review of *Works Councils: Consultation, Representation, and Cooperation in Industrial Relations,* pp. 1205-1208.
Contemporary Sociology, May, 1997, Jonas Pontusson, review of *Works Councils,* pp. 338-339.
Industrial and Labor Relations Review, July, 1999, Lowell Turner, review of *Works Councils.*
Journal of Economic Literature, December, 1996, Craig A. Olson, review of *Works Councils,* pp. 1979-1981.

OTHER

New Party, http://newparty.org/ (March 14, 2001), "It's All about Democracy."*

ROJAS, Ricardo 1882-1957

PERSONAL: Born September 16, 1882, in Tucumán, Argentina; died July 29, 1957.

CAREER: Writer. Held administrative and faculty positions at University of Buenos Aires.

AWARDS, HONORS: Honorary doctorate, University of Buenos Aires, 1927.

WRITINGS:

IN ENGLISH TRANSLATION

El Cristo invisible, J. Roldán (Buenos Aires, Argentina), 1927, translation by Webster E. Browning published as *The Invisible Christ,* Abingdon Press (New York, NY), 1931.

El santo de la espada: Vida de San Martín (biography), Librerías Anaconda (Buenos Aires, Argentina), 1933, translation by Herschel Brickell and Carlos Videla published as *San Martín, Knight of the Andes,* Doubleday (Garden City, NY), 1945.

Latin Ode (poetry), translated by Bernardo Frichard, [Buenos Aires, Argentina], 1954.

COLLECTED WORKS

Obras de Ricardo Rojas (twenty-nine volumes), J. Roldán (Buenos Aires, Argentina), 1923-1930.

Obras completas de Ricardo Rojas (thirty volumes), Editorial Losada (Buenos Aires, Argentina), 1947-1953.

OTHER

La victoria del hombre (poetry; title means "Man's Victory"), [Buenos Aires, Argentina], 1903.

El país de la selva (short stories; title means "The Jungle Country"), Garnier Hermanos (Paris, France), 1907.

El alma española (title means "The Spanish Soul"), F. Sempere (Valencia, Spain), 1908.

Cartas de Europa, [Barcelona, Spain], 1908.

Cosmópolis (essays), Garnier Hermanos (Paris, France, 1908.

La restauración (essays; title means "Nationalist Restoration"), Ministerio de justica é instrucción pública (Buenos Aires, Argentina), 1909.

Las lises del blasón (poetry; title means "The Blazon's Fleur-de-lis"), M. García (Buenos Aires, Argentina), 1911.

Blasón de plata (title means "Silver Blazon"), Editorial Losada (Buenos Aires, Argentina), 1912.

La argentinidad (title means "Argentinehood"), J. Roldán (Buenos Aires, Argentina), 1916.

La literatura Argentina (four volumes; title means "Argentine Literature"), de Coni Hermanos (Buenos Aires, Argentina), 1917-1922.

Conciones (poetry), [Buenos Aires, Argentina], 1920.

Eurindia, J. Roldán (Buenos Aires, Argentina), 1924.

Las provincias, [Buenos Aires, Argentina], 1927.

Elelín (play), J. Roldán (Buenos Aires, Argentina), 1929.

Silabario de la decoración americana (title means "Syllabary of American Decoration"), J. Roldán (Buenos Aires, Argentina), 1930.

El radicalismo de mañana (title means "Tomorrow's Radicalism"), L. J. Rosso (Buenos Aires, Argentina, 1932.

La casa colonial (play; title means "The Colonial House"), 1932.

Cervantes, J. Roldán (Buenos Aires, Argentina), 1935.

Retablo español (title means "Spanish Alter Piece"), Editorial Losada (Buenos Aires, Argentina), 1938.

Ollantay (play), Editorial Losada (Buenos Aires, Argentina), 1939.

Archipiélago: Tierra del Fuego, Editorial Losada (Buenos Aires, Argentina), 1942.

La salamanca (play; title means "The Salamander"), Editorial Losada (Buenos Aires, Argentina), 1943.

El profeta de la pampa: Vida de Sarmiento (biography; title means "Prophet of the Pampa: The Life of Sarmiento"), [Buenos Aires, Argentina], 1945.

Un titan de las Andes, Editorial Losada (Buenos Aires, Argentina), 1949.

Ensayo de crítica história episodios de la vida internacional Argentina, [Buenos Aires, Argentina], 1951.

Work represented in anthologies, including *The Golden Land,* [New York, NY], 1948. Contributor to periodicals, including *La Nacío.*

SIDELIGHTS: Ricardo Rojas was a notable Argentine writer who produced poetry, biographies, critical essays, and short stories during a literary career that spanned the first half of the twentieth century. Rojas was born in Tucumán, where his father served as governor, in 1882. During his student years, Rojas studied law. He ultimately turned to writing, though, and in 1903 he published *La victoria del hombre,* a volume of poetry. Throughout the remaining years of the decade, Rojas issued such works as *El país de la selva,* a collection of tales on the theme of pre-Hispanic Americanism, and *Cosmópolis* and *La restauración,* two collections of essays in which he continued his analysis of pre-Hispanic—or native—South American culture, and in the 1910s he published such works as *Blasón de plata* and *La argentinidad,* two books in which he articulates his notion of Argentine ethnicity and culture.

In the ensuing three decades, Rojas produced a sizeable body of literature, some of which defies easy categorization. In 1924, for example, he published *Eurindia,* a theoretical consideration of Spain's influence on Argentine culture, and in 1927 he issued *El Cristo invisible,* an examination of Christian iconography. Other notable works include *La casa colonial* and *La salamanca,* two plays commemorating pivotal moments in Argentine history.

During the 1940s, while World War II raged in Europe and Asia, Rojas found himself increasingly alienated from Argentine society as it existed under President Ramon S. Castillo and, after a military coup, Juan D. Perón. By the mid-1940s he had significantly diminished his literary output. During the 1940s, despite his stature as an accomplished literary figure, Rojas endured imprisonment and internal exile, and in 1957 he died in poverty.

BIOGRAPHICAL AND CRITICAL SOURCES:

PERIODICALS

Hispanic American Historical Review, Volume 43, number 1, 1963, Earl T. Glauert, "Ricardo Rojas and the Emergence of Argentine Cultural Nationalism," pp. 1-13.
Revista de la Universidad de Buenos Aires, Volume 3, number 3, 1958, Nélida Salvador, "Ensayo de bibliografia de Ricardo Rojas," pp. 479-490.
Revista Iberoamericana, Volume 23, number 46, 1958, "Bibliografía de Ricardo Rojas," pp. 335-350.*

ROSEBORO, John (Jr.) 1933-2002

OBITUARY NOTICE—See index for *CA* sketch: Born May 13, 1933, in Ashland, OH; died of complications from a stroke August 16, 2002, in Los Angeles, CA. Professional baseball player, public relations executive, and author. Roseboro spent most of his active career as a starting catcher for the Los Angeles Dodgers baseball team, replacing the disabled Roy Campanella in 1958. Though he helped carry the team to three World Series victories and also played in several All-Star games for both the American League and the National League, he is remembered less for what he did than for what someone did to him. It was in 1965 that Roseboro was clubbed over the head with a baseball bat by San Francisco Giants pitcher Juan Marichel, starting a ballfield brawl that went down in history. Two years after the incident, Roseboro left the Dodgers to spend two seasons with the Minnesota Twins and an even shorter period as a player and coach for the then-Washington Senators. The title of his autobiography, however, *Glory Days with the Dodgers and Other Days with Others,* suggests that his heart remained in Los Angeles with the Dodgers. After retirement from baseball, Roseboro and his wife operated the public relations firm of Fouch-Roseboro.

OBITUARIES AND OTHER SOURCES:

BOOKS

Roseboro, John, *Glory Days with the Dodgers and Other Days with Others,* Atheneum (New York, NY), 1978.

PERIODICALS

Los Angeles Times, August 20, 2002, obituary by Gary Klein, p. B10.
New York Times, August 20, 2002, obituary by Richard Goldstein, p. C16.
Washington Post, August 24, 2002, p. B7.

*   *   *

ROTHENBERG, Robert E(dward) 1908-2002

OBITUARY NOTICE—See index for *CA* sketch: Born September 27, 1908, in New York, NY; died April 10, 2002, in New York, NY. Rothenberg was a prominent surgeon who also wrote medical books for the general public. He earned his medical degree from Cornell

University in 1932 and was certified for surgery in 1942. During World War II Rothenberg commanded the First Auxiliary Surgical Group as a lieutenant colonel near the front lines in Europe. After the war he became a clinical assistant professor of environmental medicine and community health for the State University of New York's Downstate Medical Center, remaining there from 1950 to 1960. During the early 1960s he served as a consultant surgeon for the U.S. Army at Fort Jay, New York, and then worked as an attending surgeon for several hospitals in New York City and Brooklyn through the 1970s. From 1981 to 1986 he was also a professor of surgery at New York Medical College. As a writer, Rothenberg helped explain health and medical issues to lay readers in such books as *Health in the Later Years* (1964), *What Every Patient Wants to Know* (1975), *The Complete Book of Breast Care* (1975), and the four-volume children's series "Disney's Growing up Healthy" (1976). He also wrote and edited a number of technical books for medical professionals.

OBITUARIES AND OTHER SOURCES:

BOOKS

Who's Who in America, 55th edition, Marquis (New Providence, NJ), 2001.

PERIODICALS

New York Times, April 30, 2002, p. C18.

*   *   *

ROTHSCHILD, Emma (Georgina) 1948-

PERSONAL: Born May 16, 1948, in London, England; daughter of Lord Victor and Teresa Georgia Rothschild; married Amartya Kumar Sen (a Nobel laureate economist), 1991; *Education:* Degree from Somerville College, Oxford, 1967; Massachusetts Institute of Technology, MA.

ADDRESSES: Office—Centre for History and Economics, King's College, University of Cambridge, Cambridge CB2 1ST, England. *E-mail*—amp@kings.cam.ac.uk.

CAREER: Writer and educator. Massachusetts Instutute of Technology, Cambridge, MA, associate professor of humanities, 1978-80 associate professor of science, technology, and society, 1979-88; Ecole des Hautes Etudes en Sciences Sociales, Paris, France, directeur invité, 1981-82; King's College, Cambridge, England, senior research fellow, 1988-96, director, Centre for History and Economics, 1996—. Member of OECD Group of Experts on Science and Technology in the New Socioeconomic Context, 1976-80, OECD scientific examiner, Australia, 1984-85. Distinguished fellow, Harvard Center for Population and Development Studies; member of governing board, Stockholm International Peace Research Institute, 1983-93; member of board, Olaf Palme Memorial Fund, Stockholm, 1986—, Royal Commission on Environmental Pollution, 1986-93, British Council, 1993—, and United Nations Foundation; chair, Kennedy Memorial Trust and United Nations Institute for Social Development.

WRITINGS:

Paradise Lost: The Decline of the Auto-Industrial Age, Random House (New York, NY), 1973.
Economic Sentiments: Adam Smith, Condorcet, and the Enlightenment, Harvard University Press (Cambridge, MA), 2001.

SIDELIGHTS: Emma Rothschild has written extensively on economic history and the history of economic thought. In *Paradise Lost: The Decline of the Auto-Industrial Age,* Rothschild describes difficulties in the American automobile industry, and what Richard J. Barnet described in the *New York Review of Books* as "America's fading love affair with the car." As Robin Morris summed up in the *Times Literary Supplement,* "Her argument is that, whatever they say or claim to do, contemporary American automobile executives will be incapable of developing a simple utility car." At the time the book was written, American car manufacturers were doing poorly; General Motors had closed fifteen of its twenty-two assembly plants, laid off 65,000 workers, then laid off 57,000 more, and the company's sales were down 35.7 percent. Rothschild analyzes strategies the auto industry used in the past, and shows how clinging to these strategies made it impossible for the manufacturers to successfully deal with events of the 1970s. Barnet wrote, "*Paradise Lost* is a morality play because it shows how the arrogance and insensitivity of the industry lead inexorably to its decline." In the *New York Times,* Robert Sherrill praised the "orderliness and elegance" of Rothschild's style, and noted that although the book "appears to be a sober sociological study," it is actually "richer than that, almost cinematic."

In *Economic Sentiments: Adam Smith, Condorcet, and the Enlightenment* Rothschild examines eighteenth-century economic theorist Adam Smith, who is considered the founder of modern capitalist economics, and links his ideas with those of French economic philosopher the Marquis de Condorcet. Condorcet, like Smith, linked economic freedom to other personal freedoms. In the *Sunday Telegraph,* Noel Malcolm called the book a "searching reappraisal of Smith's economic and political thought." In the *New Republic,* Peter Berkowitz wrote, "With a wealth of detail, Rothschild sketches the forgotten lineage of selected concepts that are critical to Smith's system, and reconstructs the reception of Smith's ideas, and deftly guides the reader through debates whose terms and stakes are distant and unfamiliar."

BIOGRAPHICAL AND CRITICAL SOURCES:

BOOKS

Contemporary Issues Criticism, Volume 1, Gale (Detroit, MI), 1982, pp. 530-533.

PERIODICALS

Economist, August 18, 2001, "Meeting in the Middle," p. 72.
New Republic, October 1, 2001, Peter Berkowitz, "Money and Love," p. 41.
New York Review of Books, May 2, 1974, Richard J. Barnet, "Morality Play," p. 33; July 5, 2001, p. 42.
New York Times, August 16, 2001, Alan B. Krueger, "The Many Faces of Adam Smith," p. C2.
New York Times Book Review, October 28, 1973, Robert Sherrill, review of *Paradise Lost,* pp. 1, 14; July 8, 2001, Paul Mattick, "Who Is the Real Adam Smith?," p. 25.
Spectator, September 8, 2001, Sylvana Tomaselli, review of *Economic Sentiments,* p. 44.

Sunday Telegraph (London, England), July 1, 2001, Noel Malcolm, "Adam Smith with Spin," p. 16.
Times Higher Education Supplement, June 22, 2001, William Kennedy, review of *Economic Sentiments,* p. 27.
Times Literary Supplement, May 24, 1974, Robin Morris, "End of the Road," p. 544.
Wall Street Journal, June 21, 2001, Jerry Z. Muller, "Great Minds, Imperfect Markets," p. A16.
Working Woman, December, 1982, Robert Barnett, "Running on Empty," p. 58.

OTHER

King's College, Cambridge, Web site http://www.kings. cam.ac.uk/ (December 2, 2001).
United Nations Foundation Web site, http://www. unfoundation.org/ (December 2, 2001).*

*   *   *

ROWELL, Galen 1940-2002

OBITUARY NOTICE—See index for CA sketch: Born August 23, 1940, in Berkeley, CA; died in a plane crash August 11, 2002, near Bishop, CA. Photographer and author. Sometimes called the successor to Ansel Adams, Rowell was a renowned nature photographer and adventurer. He first became excited by nature when his parents took him camping in the Sierra Mountains, and by the age of ten he was learning to climb mountains. Although he attended the University of California at Berkeley from 1958 to 1962, he dropped out of college without a degree and opened up a car-repair business. While working as a mechanic, he climbed and took photographs on the weekends, finally selling his business in 1972 to become a full-time photographer and writer. With his superior climbing skills, Rowell was able to explore almost inaccessible places throughout the world, including locations in China, Nepal, Alaska, and Africa. Still, one of his favorite subjects was nearby Yosemite National Park. Often working with his wife, photographer Barbara Rowell, he took photographs for the National Geographic Society and the Sierra Club, and had his work reproduced in magazines such as *Life, Audubon,* and *Outdoor Photographer.* Rowell also contributed photos to numerous books, many of which he wrote himself, including *The Vertical World of Yosemite* (1974),

Mountains of the Middle Kingdom: Exploring the High Peaks of China and Tibet (1983), *The Art of Adventure* (1990), and *Bay Area Wild: A Celebration of the Natural Heritage of the San Francisco Bay Area* (1997). He received the Ansel Adams Award in 1984 for his wilderness photography.

OBITUARIES AND OTHER SOURCES:

PERIODICALS

Los Angeles Times, August 13, 2002, pp. B1, B9.
New York Times, August 14, 2002, p. A18.
Times (London, England), August 20, 2002.
Washington Post, August 14, 2002, p. B6.

*   *   *

RUEHMKORF, Peter
    See RÜHMKORF, Peter

*   *   *

RUEL-MÉZIÈRES, Laurence 1957-
    (Camille Laurens)

PERSONAL: Born November 6, 1957, in Dijon, France; married Yves Mézières; children: Aube.

ADDRESSES: Agent—c/o Author Mail, P.O.L., 33, rue Saint-André-des-Arts, 75006 Paris, France.

CAREER: Educator and novelist.

AWARDS, HONORS: Prix Femina, 2000, for *Dans ces bras-la;* Prix Goncourt shortlist, 2000.

WRITINGS:

AS CAMILLE LAURENS

Index, P.O.L. (Paris, France), 1991.
Romance, P.O.L. (Paris, France), 1992.
Les travaux d'Hercule, P.O.L. (Paris, France), 1994.

Philippe, P.O.L. (Paris, France), 1995.
L'avenir, P.O.L. (Paris, France), 1998.
Quelques-uns, P.O.L. (Paris, France), 1999.
Dans ces bras-la, P.O.L. (Paris, France), 2000.

Contributor to *Mourir avant de n'être,* edited by René Frydman and Muriel Flis-Trêves, éditions Odile Jacob (Paris, France), 1997. Columnist for French newspaper, *L'Humanité.*

SIDELIGHTS: Laurence Ruel-Mézières, writing as Camille Laurens, seeks the essential meaning of words, and her writing reflects this search in its clear and pared-down language. This lucid prose style was validated by the selection of *Dans ces bras-la* for competition in the Prix Goncourt in 2000.

In *Dans ces bras-la,* the narrator tells the story of the men she has known in her life. Although Laurens maintains that the book is a novel and not an autobiography, the text shifts from the "I" to the "she" with mischievous ease. The narrator's memory brings the men of her life out of the past and into the present. The images she retains of her grandfather, her father, her son, a lover, her boss, friends and colleagues are all rendered with a loving and sympathetic eye. As Sylvia Trotter wrote in the online magazine, *Nuit Blanche,* "*Dans ces bras-la* is a novel which one tastes with slowness. . . . With Camille Laurens, one remembers the heights and lows of her men and, in particular, 'that sensitivity is the most locked up secret.'"

After winning the Prix Femina, *Dans ces bras-la* was purchased by U.S. and British publishers for English-language publication. Random House senior editor, Joy de Menil, quoted in *Publishers Weekly,* called *Dans ces bras-la* "a stylish, saucy, smart, funny novel."

Laurens' first four novels form a sort of tetralogy of the discovery of identity and are extremely personal and often painful in nature. In the first of the cycle, the autobiographical *Philippe,* Laurens tells the story of her son, who was born on February 7, 1994, but lived only two hours and ten minutes. "The next day I went with Yves, his father, to see him at the morgue." begins the first chapter. His death could have been avoided; the obstetrician did not intervene in time.

Even though "unhappiness is always a secret," Laurens started writing because it was her only means of defense. With precise prose, she recreated the exact events of the delivery, especially the record of the infant's heartbeat, which clearly indicated criminal neglect on the doctor's part. *Philippe* is not a novel at all. It is clearly an autobiographical work, yet it has gained high critical acclaim as literature as well.

Quelques-uns explores Laurens' passion for words. In the opening chapters, the author asks, "How can words, which are things, help man to live?" Through the following chapters, the author invokes Joyce, Rabelais, Miloz, Racine, and others to help bring her subject to life.

Laurens' novels and stories always convey her belief that words are more than simple messengers of plot, that, in fact, they are the means of talented inquiry into the power and beauty of language.

BIOGRAPHICAL AND CRITICAL SOURCES:

BOOKS

Laurens, Camille, *Philippe,* P.O.L. (Paris, France), 1995.

PERIODICALS

French Review, October, 2000, Marie Naudin, review of *Dans ces bras-la,* p. 193.
Publishers Weekly, December 18, 2000, John F. Baker, "French Prizewinner to Random," p. 13.

OTHER

Librarie Pantoute, http://librariepantoute.com/ (December 4, 2001), Liette Lemay, online interview with Camille Laurens.
Nuit Blanche, http://www.nuitblanche.fr/ (December 4, 2001), Sylvia Trotter, review of *Dans ces bras-la.*

*   *   *

RUFFIN, Paul D. 1941-

PERSONAL: Born May 14, 1941, in Millport, AL; son of David and Zealon (Robinson) Ruffin; married Sharon Krebs (a homemaker), June 20, 1973; children: Genevieve Baptiste, Matthew Krebs. *Education:* Mississippi State University, B.S., 1964, M.A., 1968;

University of Southern Mississippi, Ph.D., 1974. *Politics:* Republican. *Religion:* Catholic. *Hobbies and other interests:* Gardening, woodworking, shooting.

ADDRESSES: Home—Huntsville, TX. *Office*—Department of English, Sam Houston State University, Sam Houston Ave., Huntsville, TX 77341-2146. *E-mail*—eng_pdr@shsu.edu.

CAREER: Sam Houston State University, Huntsville, TX, professor of English, 1975—. *Texas Review Press,* director; *Texas Review,* editor. *Military service:* U.S. Army and National Guard, 1959-67; became staff sergeant.

MEMBER: Texas Institute of Letters, Mississippi Institute of Arts and Letters, Texas Association of Creative Writing Teachers.

WRITINGS:

The Man Who Would Be God: Stories, Southern Methodist University Press (Dallas, TX), 1993.
(Editor, with Donald V. Coers and others) *After the Grapes of Wrath: Essays on John Steinbeck in Honor of Tetsumaro Hayashi,* Ohio University Press (Athens, OH), 1995.
(Editor, with George P. Garrett) *That's What I Like about the South: And Other New Southern Stories for the Nineties* (fiction anthology), University of South Carolina Press (Columbia, SC), 1995.
(Editor, with Brooke Horvath and Irving Malin) *A Goyen Companion: Appreciation of a Writer's Writer,* University of Texas Press (Austin, TX), 1996.
Circling (poetry), Browder Springs Press (Dallas, TX), 1997.
(Editor) *So There You Are: The Selected Prose of Glenn Brown, Journalist,* Sam Houston State University Press (Huntsville, TX), 1998.
Islands, Women, and God (short stories), Browder Springs Press (Dallas, TX), 2001.
Pompeii Man (novel), Louisiana Literature Press, 2002.

Contributor of fiction, poetry, and essays to hundreds of journals, including *Southern Review, Georgia Review, Ploughshares, Michigan Quarterly Review,*

New England Review, Mississippi Review, Texas Quarterly, Alaska Quarterly Review, and *Southwestern American Literature.* Author of a regular column "Ruffin-It," which appears in several newspapers.

WORK IN PROGRESS: Growing up in Mississippi Poor and White but Not Quite Trash (memoir); *Castle in the Gloom* (novel); *The Keepers* (novel).

SIDELIGHTS: In his stories set in his native South, Paul Ruffin "paints poignant pictures of Southerners leading lives devoid of passion, engulfed by fear or haunted by apocalypse," according to a *Publishers Weekly* critic. In his collection *The Man Who Would Be God,* Ruffin looks to Texas, where the title story follows two cowboys who glimpse something unusual—a white house in the far distance—and compare it to Paradise. "A sleeping world? A cowboy's fascination with revelation? We are unbalanced by the juxtapositions," said Irving Malin in the *Review of Contemporary Fiction.* Malin went on to praise the stories in this collection as "haunting and memorable."

Reviewing *Islands, Women, and God* for the *Houston Chronicle,* Eric Miles Williamson declared that Ruffin writes so surely about Texas that this collection "is likely to define the literary territory for many years to come." The seventeen stories cover different subjects but in effect constitute "a man's book about the world of men," said Williamson. "The stories center on the conflicts inherent in the stifled, brutal and often senseless world of masculinity." He cited one story, "The Sign," which opens with a father beating his son. Forty years later the son returns and exacts his revenge "in spectacular and appropriate fashion, not by killing the father but by doing something far worse and more enduring."

In its raw imagery, *Islands, Women, and God* is "an astonishing book," Williamson concluded. "Every page is beautifully written, splendidly rendered and bold. Where weaker writers grow timid and shrivel, Ruffin burrows deep into truths we know but don't admit to knowing."

As a poet, Ruffin has produced *Circling,* a collection praised by Robert Phillips in a *Houston Chronicle* review as "full of moments of grace [and] great moments of camaraderie, too."

BIOGRAPHICAL AND CRITICAL SOURCES:

PERIODICALS

American Studies International, April, 1994, Robert Combs, review of *That's What I Like about the South: And Other New Southern Stories for the Nineties,* p. 119.

Booklist, April 1, 1993, Joe Collins, review of *That's What I Like about the South,* p. 1412; December 1, 1993, Mary Frances Wilkens, review of *The Man Who Would Be God,* p. 677.

Choice, July-August, 1997, W. B. Warde, Jr., review of *A Goyen Companion: Appreciation of a Writer's Writer,* p. 1801.

Christian Science Monitor, June 4, 1993, Mary Warner Marien, review of *That's What I Like about the South,* p. 11.

Houston Chronicle, August 11, 1996, Robert Phillips, "Poets Find Power, Grace in Rural Settings," p. 21; November 11, 2001, Eric Miles Williamson, "Fine Stories of Men's World," p. 19.

Mississippi Quarterly, spring, 1998, Helen S. Garson, review of *A Goyen Companion,* p. 407.

New York Times Book Review, December 26, 1993, Susan Lowell, review of *The Man Who Would Be God,* p. 14.

Publishers Weekly, March 8, 1993, review of *That's What I Like about the South,* p. 72; November 1, 1993, review of *The Man Who Would Be God,* p. 71.

Review of Contemporary Fiction, spring, 1994, Irving Malin, review of *The Man Who Would Be God,* p. 229.

*   *   *

RUGGIERI, Helen 1938-

PERSONAL: Born August 30, 1938, in Plainfield, NJ; daughter of James and Lily Mitchell; married Ford F. Ruggieri; children: Maria Ruggieri Moen, Ford M., Andrea. *Ethnicity:* "Scot." *Education:* Pennsylvania State University, B.A., M.F.A.; St. Bonaventure University, M.A.

ADDRESSES: Home—111 North Tenth St., Olean, NY 14760. *Office*—University of Pittsburgh, Bradford, PA 16701. *E-mail*—ruggieri@pitt.edu.

CAREER: Jamestown Community College, Cattaraugus County Campus, Olean, NY, adjunct instructor in composition, 1983; University of Pittsburgh, Bradford, PA, assistant professor of English, 1985—, acting director of writing program, 1998-99, 2000-01. Allegany Mountain Press, editor and publisher. Yokohama College of Commerce, visiting professor, 2000. Alternative Literary Programs in the Schools, poet-in-residence, 1995-2000.

MEMBER: Associated Writing Programs, Friends of the Olean Public Library.

AWARDS, HONORS: Sasakawa fellow, Nippon Foundation, 2001; Academy of American Poets Prize; Allen Ginsberg Prize, William Paterson College of New Jersey; poetry prizes from Artists Embassy International and Goose Festival, College of the Redwoods.

WRITINGS:

POETRY

Concrete Madonna, Black Rose Books, 1982.
The Poetess, Uroborus Books (Olean, NY), 1981.
Rock City Hill Exercises, Allegheny Mountain Press, 1985.
Walking the Dog, Cave Canum Chapbooks, 1986.
Small Song for Jupiter, Moonwash Press, 1987.
BeBop a Lula, Elvis Press, 1997.
Glimmer Girls, Mayapple Press, 1999.

Work represented in anthologies, including *Words of Wisdom,* H & H Press; *Place of Passage: Poems of the Spirit,* Storyline Press; *Under a Gull's Wing: Poems of the Jersey Shore,* Down the Shore Publications; *Looking for Home: Writing about Exile,* Milkweed Editions; and *Fine China: Twenty Years of Earth's Daughters,* Springhill Publications. Contributor of more than 200 poems to magazines, including *River Styx, Abraxes, Sing Heavenly Muse, Slipstream, Northern Review, Greenfield Review, Akros, New York Quarterly, Poet Lore,* and *Hawaii Pacific Review.*

OTHER

The Character for Woman, Foothills Publications, in press.

Contributor to books, including *Touching Fire,* Carroll & Graf; *The Erotic Impulse,* J. P. Tarcher; *The Environment: Essence and Issue,* Pig Iron Press; *Tested Ideas for Teaching Business Communication,* McGraw-Hill (New York, NY); and *A Poetry Therapy Sourcebook,* Puddinghouse. Contributor of short stories, feature articles, and reviews to magazines, including *Potomac Review, Buffalo Spree, Enterpreneur, Mother Earth News, Lake Effect, Boston Review, Palo Alto Review, Explicator,* and *Studies in Contemporary Satire.* Editor of woman's pages, *Olean Times Herald;* editor, *Amplifier.*

WORK IN PROGRESS: Research on Japanese literature in translation.

*   *   *

RÜHMKORF, Peter 1929-
(Leslie Meier, Leo Doletzki, Johannes Fontara)

PERSONAL: Born October 25, 1929 in Dortmund, Germany. *Education:* Attended University of Hamburg.

ADDRESSES: Office—Archiv Peter Rühmkorf, Fersenfeldtsweg 6, D-22303 Hamburg, Germany.

CAREER: Rowohlt Verlag, Hamburg, Germany, editorial reader, 1958; staff member of Literarisches Colloquium, Berlin, 1963; freelance writer, beginning 1966. Fellow of Villa Massimo, Rome, 1964-65.

WRITINGS:

(With Werner Riegel) *Heisse Lyrik,* Limes Verlag, 1956.
Irdisches Vergnugen in "g" (poems), Rowohlt (Hamburg, Germany), 1959.
Wolfgang Borchert in Selbstzeugnissen und Bilddokumenten, Rowohlt (Hamburg, Germany), 1961, reprinted, 1983.
Kunststücke: fünfzig Gedichte nebst einer Anleitung zum Widerspruch (poems), Rowohlt (Hamburg, Germany), 1962.
(Editor) *Die traurigen Geranien: und andere Geschichten aus dem Nachlass,* Rowohlt (Hamburg, Germany), 1962, reprinted, 1982.

(With Armin Schmid) *Primanerlyrik, Primanerprosa* (poetry), Rowohlt (Hamburg, Germany), 1965.

Über das Volksvermögen: Exkurse in den literarischen Untergrund, Rowohlt (Hamburg, Germany), 1967.

Was heisst hier Volsinii? Bewegte Szenen aus dem klassischen Wirtschaftsleben, Rowohlt (Hamburg, Germany), 1969.

(Editor) *Friedrich Gottlieb Klopstock: Gedichte,* Fischer-Bucherei, 1969, reprinted, Rowohlt (Hamburg, Germany), 1996.

Lombard gibt den Letzten, Wangenbach (Berlin, Germany), 1972.

Die Jahre die Ihr kennet: Anfälle und Erinnerungen, Rowohlt (Hamburg, Germany), 1972.

Die Handwerker kommen, Wagenbach (Berlin, Germany), 1974.

Walther von der Vogelweide, Klopstock und ich (criticism), Rowohlt (Hamburg, Germany), 1975.

(Editor) *Das Vergehen von Hören und Sehen* (criticism), Rowohlt (Hamburg, Germany), 1976.

Gesammelte Gedichte, Rowohlt (Hamburg, Germany), 1976.

(Editor) *131 expressionistische Gedichte,* Wagenbach (Berlin, Germany), 1976.

Phönix voran!, Pawel-Pan-Presse, 1977.

Strömungslehre (poems), Rowohlt (Hamburg, Germany), 1978.

Haltbar bis Ende 1999, Rowolht (Hamburg, Germany), 1979.

(With others) *Als Schriftsteller leben* (criticism), Rowohlt (Hamburg, Germany), 1979.

Im Fahrtwind: Gedichte und Geschichte, Reinhard Mohn, 1980.

Auf Wiedersehen in Kenilworth: ein Märchen in dreizehn Kapiteln, Fischer Taschenbuch Verlag, 1980.

Peter Rühmkorf (speech), Die Bibliothek, 1980.

Es muss doch noch einen zweiten Weg ums Gehirn rum geben, Internationale Literaturfabrik im Bund-Verlag, 1981.

Agar Agar, Zaurzaurim: zur Naturgeschichte des Reims und der menschlichen Anklangsnerven, Rowohlt (Hamburg, Germany), 1981.

Kleine Fleckendunde, Haffmans (Zurich, Switzerland), 1982.

Der Hüter des Misthaufens: aufgeklärte Märchen, Rowohlt (Hamburg, Germany), 1983.

Blieb erschütterbar und widersteh, Rowohlt (Hamburg, Germany), 1984.

Ausser der Liebe nichts (poems), Rowohlt (Hamburg, Germany), 1985.

Dintemann und Schindemann: Aufgeklärte Märchen, Reclam (Ditzingen, Germany), 1985.

(Editor) *Mein Lesebuch,* Fischer Taschenbuch, 1986.

Selbstredend und selbstreimend: Gedichte, Gedanken, Lichtblicke, Reclam (Ditzingen, Germany), 1987.

Der Hüter des Misthaufens, Rowohlt (Hamburg, Germany), 1987.

Werner Riegel, Haffmans (Zurich, Switzerland), 1988.

Lass leuchten!: Memos, Märchen, Tabu, Gedichte, Selbstporträt mit und ohne Hut, Rowohlt (Hamburg, Germany), 1989.

Dreizehn deutsche Dichter (essay), Rowohlt (Hamburg, Germany), 1989.

Einmalig wie wir alle, Rowohlt (Hamburg, Germany), 1989.

Selbst III/88 aus der Fassung, Haffmans (Zurich, Switzerland), 1989.

Komm raus!: Gesänge, Märchen, Kunststücke, Wagenbach (Berlin, Germany), 1992.

Deutschland, ein Lügenmärchen, Wallstein, 1993.

Tabu I: Tagebücher, 1989-1991, Rowohlt (Hamburg, Germany), 1995.

(With others) *StörtebeckerHolzschnittTurm,* Merlin Verlag, 1995.

Ich habe Lust, im weiten Feld, Wallstein (Göttingen, Germany), 1996.

(Editor) *Lesen ist schrecklich!: Das Arno-Schmidt-Lesebuch* (criticism and interpretation), Haffmans (Zurich, Switzerland), 1997.

Lethe mit Schuss, Suhrkamp (Frankfurt, Germany), 1998.

Ausser der Liebe nichts: Liebesgedichte, Rowohlt (Hamburg, Germany), 1998.

Wo ich gelernt habe, Wallstein (Göttingen, Germany), 1999.

Von mir zu euch für uns, Steidl (Göttingen, Germany), 1999.

Wenn, aber dann: vorletzte Gedichte (poems), Rowohlt (Hamburg, Germany), 1999.

(With Horst Janssen) *Mein lieber Freund und Kompanjunk,* Verlag Felix Jud, 1999.

Werke, Rowohlt (Hamburg, Germany), 2000.

Some of author's works published under pseudonyms Leslie Meier, Leo Doletzki, and Johannes Fontana.

SIDELIGHTS: One of Germany's leading practitioners of post-World War II avant-garde style, Peter Rühmkorf began writing his lyric poetry in the manner of Gottfried Benn and Bertoldt Brecht. Like contemporaries such as Magnus Enzensberger, Rühmkorf "made the contradictions of his generation the main subject of his work," according to *Times Literary Supplement* critic Jochen Hieber.

Rühmkorf was still a literary influence at age sixty-seven, when Christian Grawe of *World Literature Today* reviewed *Tabu I: Tagebücher 1989-1991.* This collection of diaries covers the tumultuous period of German reunification—a sore spot for the poet, an "honest and defiant leftist" as Grawe described him, loathing the Nazi Party and dedicated to socialist credos. As the Berlin Wall came down, noted Grawe, Rühmkorf seemed "defeated on all fronts . . . Socialism is in disgrace, and he abhors the German unification and hates the ruthless capitalism that set out to destroy what little dignity and vision of a better future was left in the disintegrating GDR," referring to the German Democratic Republic, or East Germany.

Grawe called *Tabu I* an important poetic work which chronicles the events, cultures, and personalities influencing this important moment in world history, concluding that Rühmkorf's "personal impressions and observations make challenging, stimulating, and pleasurable reading."

BIOGRAPHICAL AND CRITICAL SOURCES:

PERIODICALS

Times Literary Supplement, February 23, 1990, p. 7.
World Literature Today, summer, 1996, review of *Tabu I: Tagebücher 1989-1991,* p. 687.

*   *   *

RUSSELL, Thaddeus

PERSONAL: Born in Berkeley, CA; married. *Education:* Antioch College, B.A.; Columbia University, Ph.D. (history).

ADDRESSES: Home—New York, NY. *Agent*—c/o Knopf Publishing, Author Mail, 299 Park Avenue, 4th Floor, New York, NY 10171.

CAREER: Writer. Barnard College, visiting assistant professor of history.

WRITINGS:

(Editor, with Jack Salzman and Greg Robinson) *Encyclopedia of African-American Culture and History,* Macmillan Reference USA (New York, NY), 2001.
Out of the Jungle: Jimmy Hoffa and the Remaking of the American Working Class, Alfred A. Knopf (New York, NY), 2001.

SIDELIGHTS: Thaddeus Russell's *Out of the Jungle: Jimmy Hoffa and the Remaking of the American Working Class* was born out of his doctoral dissertation at Columbia University and has garnered a lot of media attention. Reviewers noted that the book tells a story about Teamster leader Jimmy Hoffa in a way it has never been told before. For some critics, such as John Gallagher in the *Detroit Free Press,* Russell's book is different because it "will spark controversy for its portrait of labor leaders motivated more by rivalry with fellow unionists than by concern for their members or fights with management." For other reviewers, such as Thomas J. Sugrue in the *Washington Post Book World,* Russell's book stands out because he "offers a provocative, if not wholly convincing, reappraisal of American labor since the New Deal."

The so-called jungle Russell refers to in his title, noted Sugrue, represents the United States during the Great Depression years, particularly the labor scene. Unions were struggling against business leaders who often fired anyone caught trying to organize workers, hired "scabs"—workers who would cross picket lines—to break strikes, and used violence "to thwart organizing campaigns." Sugrue continued, "Rather than acquiesce, Jimmy Hoffa fought fire with fire," advocating "all-out war on his opponents."

Hoffa was born in Indiana and rose to national prominence in his fight for union rights. While still a teenager, he helped organize a strike at Kroger Company where he worked as a warehouseman. Several years later, he became the business agent for Teamster Local 299 in Detroit. Teamster unions represent employees in transportation and other freight-related industries, and Hoffa was responsible for transforming the International Brotherhood of Teamsters into one of the largest and most powerful unions in the United States. With Hoffa in a leadership position, Teamster membership grew to more than two million.

In 1957 Hoffa came under government investigation. He was sentenced to prison in 1967 for jury tampering and pension-fund fraud. President Nixon later commuted his sentence, and Hoffa was released in 1971. While in prison, Hoffa refused to resign from his post as president of the Teamsters. However, "organized crime," observed Alan Miller in the *Christian Science Monitor,* "which had gained control of several Teamster locals, was not going to tolerate Hoffa's return. As the bring-back-Hoffa movement gained momentum in early 1975, he was headed for a collision."

In July of 1975, Hoffa disappeared. No trace of his body has ever been found. No one has been convicted of his possible murder. More than twenty-five years since his disappearance, Hoffa's life remained a mystery; Russell's book is an attempt to erase some of the myths that arose through the years, and to fill in precise details about Hoffa's life.

Russell does not focus on the mysterious disappearance of Hoffa; rather, "he's more concerned with charting Hoffa's ascendance as America's most dynamic labor boss," wrote Miller. As a reviewer for *Publishers Weekly* remarked, "For Russell, Hoffa is both the product and the shaper of an American working class more focused on getting a piece of the pie than on creating a new society."

Maurice Isserman, reviewed Russell's book for the *New York Times* and concluded that Russell, although somewhat tough on Hoffa, was not tough enough. "Like many such endeavors by young scholars," Isserman wrote, "this book sets out to overthrow the dominant orthodoxy in its field." Isserman stated that Russell "believes" that many modern historians have "skewed the actual history of the American labor movement to the left . . . overemphasizing the importance of the big industrial unions." Isserman further noted that Russell downplays Hoffa's, in Russell's words, "clandestine dealings with Mafia godfathers." Isserman concluded Hoffa "wasn't worthy of Nixon's presidential pardon in 1971; he isn't worthy of Russell's historical pardon in 2001." Sugrue, on the other hand, observed: "Russell amply documents Hoffa's sordid record of corruption and graft but reserves his harshest criticism for the Teamsters' opponents, both past and present."

BIOGRAPHICAL AND CRITICAL SOURCES:

PERIODICALS

Christian Science Monitor, September 6, 2001, Alan Miller, "Labor's Love Lost."
Detroit Free Press, September 9, 2001, John Gallagher, "Labor Study Is Harsh on Hoffa and Other Unionists."
New York Times, September 9, 2001, Maurice Isserman, "The Cost of Doing Business," p. 14L.
Publishers Weekly, July 23, 2001, review of *Out of the Jungle,* p. 63.
Washington Post Book World, September 2, 2001, Thomas J. Sugrue, "Teamster Spirit," p. BW06.

OTHER

Borzoi Reader, http://www.randomhouse.com/ (April 19, 2002).
USofA, http://usofa.com/ (April 21, 2002), "The Greatest American Labor Leader in History."*

*   *   *

RUY-SANCHEZ, Alberto 1951-

PERSONAL: Born December 7, 1951, in Mexico City, Mexico; son of Joaquín (a painter) and Antonieta (Lacy) Ruy-Sánchez; married Margarita de Orellana (a Mexican historian and editor), August 27, 1975; children: Andrea, Santiago. *Education:* Attended Universidad Iberoamericana, 1970-75; University of Paris VIII, Vincennes, M.A., 1977; attended École des Hautes Etudes en Sciences Sociales, 1975-80; University of Paris VIII, Jussieu, Ph.D., 1980.

ADDRESSES: Agent—c/o Author Mail, Editorial Santillana, Avenue Universidad, No. 767, Col de Valle 03100, Benito Juarez, Mexico.

CAREER: Writer. Cinemateca Nacional de México, Mexico City, researcher on film history and aesthetics, 1973-75; Dystique (publishing house), Paris, France, assistant editor of *Livraisons* (magazine), 1978-79; Promociones Editoriales Mexicanas, Paris, France, and

Mexico City, editor of special collections, 1980-84; *Vuelta* (magazine), assistant editor, 1984-86; Artes de Mexico (publishing house), Mexico City, editor of *Artes de Mexico* (magazine), 1987—, chief executive officer, 1993—.

AWARDS, HONORS: Premio Xavier Villarrutia, 1987, for *Los nombres del aire;* Guggenheim fellow, 1988; editorial awards, Unión Nacional de las Artes, annually, 1988-92, Premio Nacional de las Artes Gráficas, annually, 1989-91, and Premio México, Patronato Nacional de la Asociaciones de Diseño, 1993, all for *Artes de México;* Premio José Fuentes Mares, New Mexico State University, 1991, for *Una introducción a Octavio Paz;* named an honorary citizen of Louisville, KY, 1998; Prix des Trois Continents, 1999, for French translation of his second novel; named a Kentucky Colonel, governor of Kentucky, 1999; named Officier de l'Ordre des Artes et des Lettres, government of France, 2000.

WRITINGS:

(Translator with Margarita de Orellana) M. A. Mattelart, *Comunicación e ideologías de la seguridad,* Anagrama (Barcelona, Spain), 1978.
(Translator) Eugenio Andrade, *Brevísima antología, Cuadernos de poesía* (Mexico City, Mexico), 1981.
Mitología de un cine en crisis (essays), Premía (Mexico City, Mexico), 1981.
Los demonios de la langua, La Orquesta (Mexico City, Mexico), 1987.
Les nombres del aire (novel), Joaquín Mortiz (Mexico City, Mexico), 1987, translation published as *Mogador: The Names of the Air,* City Lights (San Fransico, CA), 1982.
Al filo de las hojas (essays), Plaza y Valdés/SEP (Mexico City, Mexico), 1988.
La inaccesible (poems), Taller Martín Pescador, Acámbaro (Michoacán, Mexico), 1990.
Una introducción a Octavio Paz, Joaquín Mortiz (Mexico City, Mexico), 1990.
Tristeza de la verdad: André Gide regresa de Rusia (essays), Joaquín Mortiz (Mexico City, Mexico), 1991.
De cuerpo entero (travelogue), Ediciones Corunda y Unam (Mexico City, Mexico), 1992.
Cuentos de Mogador, Collección Lecturas Mexicanas 89, Consejo Nacional para la Cultura y las Artes (Mexico City, Mexico), 1994.

Con la literatura en el cuerpo (essays), Editorial Taurus (Mexico City, Mexico), 1995.
En los labios del agua (novel), Editorial Alfaguara (Mexico City, Mexico), 1996.
Cuatro escritores rituales (essays), Instituto Mexiquense de Cultura, (Toluca, Mexico), 1997.
Diálogos con mis fantasmas (essays), Difusión Cultural UNAM (Mexico City, Mexico), 1997.
De agua y aire (fiction), UNAM (Mexico City, Mexico), 1999.
Aventuras de la Mirada (essay), ISSTE (Mexico City, Mexico), 1999.
La pied de la tierra o los jardines secretos de Mogador (novel), Alfaguara (Mexico City, Mexico), 2001.

Coauthor of (with Mary Ann Martin) *Alfredo Castaneda* (essays), 1989; *Mexican Art Today,* 1990; *New Moments in Mexican Art,* 1990; *Tonalá, sol de barro,* 1991; *Mito y magia en América: Los 80,* 1991; *Arturo Rivera,* 1991; *Días de Feria,* 1992; and *Recintos fugaces,* 1993. Contributor to books, including *Cine, censura y exilio en América Latina,* 1979. Contributor to periodicals.

BIOGRAPHICAL AND CRITICAL SOURCES:

BOOKS

Rosaura, Hernandez Monroy, editor, *La seduccion de la escritura: Los discursos de la cultura hoy,* [Mexico City, Mexico], pp. 50-55, 259-66.

PERIODICALS

World Literature Today, autumn, 1997, Ilan Stavans, review of *En los labios del agua,* p. 762.

OTHER

Arts History, http://www.arts-history.mx/ (August 23, 2000).

* * *

RYNNE, Xavier
See MURPHY, Francis Xavier

S

SAMUELS, Harold 1917-2002

OBITUARY NOTICE—See index for CA sketch: Born July 9, 1917, in Brooklyn, NY; died July 28, 2002, in Falmouth, MA. Businessman, art dealer, and author. Samuels was a respected expert in art pf the Old West, especially that of Frederic Remington. He received his master's degree from Ohio University in 1938 and a law degree from Harvard University in 1941. After graduation he worked for a number of companies in New York and the Midwest, including the Doehler-Jarvis Company, before starting his own company, American Leisure Products, with his wife. The company sold decorative puzzles and chess sets. However, Samuels and his wife were also greatly interested in art, and they sold their company to become art dealers and to write books about Western art. Together they published ten books, including *The Illustrated Biographical Encyclopedia of Artists of the American West* (1976), *Contemporary Western Artists* (1985), *Teddy Roosevelt at San Juan: The Making of a President* (1997), and the critically praised biography *Frederic Remington* (1982).

OBITUARIES AND OTHER SOURCES:

PERIODICALS

New York Times August 1, 2002, p. C15.

*   *   *

SANCHEZ, Alberto Ruy
See RUY-SANCHEZ, Alberto

SANDALL, Roger 1933-

PERSONAL: Born December 18, 1933, in Christchurch, New Zealand; son of Frederick Arthur (a university librarian) and Helen Beatrice (Russell) Sandall; married Philippa Margaret Norris (a book editor and publisher), May 8, 1968; children: Richard Arthur, Emma Elisabeth. *Ethnicity:* "British." *Education:* University of Auckland, B.A., 1956; Columbia University, M.F.A., 1962. *Hobbies and other interests:* Hiking, music (Bach, Haydn, Mozart), popular science, motor sports.

ADDRESSES: Home and office—98 Hall St., Bondi Beach, New South Wales 2026, Australia; fax: 02-93-00-9398. *E-mail*—rogersandall@bigpond.com.au; roger.sandall@anthropology.usyd.edu.au.

CAREER: American Museum of Natural History, New York, NY, instructor, 1959-62; Australian Institute of Aboriginal Studies, Canberra, Australia, film director, 1965-73; University of Sydney, Sydney, Australia, senior lecturer in anthropology, 1973-95; writer, 1995—. Documentary filmmaker, including a series on Aboriginal religious life, between 1968 and 1972.

AWARDS, HONORS: Venice Film Festival, first prize in documentary category, for *A Lion of St. Mark,* 1968.

WRITINGS:

The Culture Cult: Designer Tribalism and Other Essays, Westview Press (Boulder, CO), 2001.

Contributor of articles on film-making, theater, literature, art, and social philosophy to periodicals, including *Atlantic Monthly, Encounter, Commentary, Landfall, Sight and Sound, Art International, Mankind, Anthropology Today,* and *New Lugano Review.* Editor, *Quadrant,* 1987-88.

WORK IN PROGRESS: Research on "the romantic idealization of Sparta in Plutarch and others," and on "cultural factors underlying the events of September 11," 2001.

SIDELIGHTS: Roger Sandall was a professor of anthropology at the University of Sydney for more than twenty years, but it was not until after his retirement in 1995 that he published his first book. *The Culture Cult: Designer Tribalism and Other Essays* is a collection of provocative pieces that challenge prevailing academic orthodoxy about the value and importance of traditional indigenous cultures. Sandall is blunt in his dislike of programs to preserve indigenous cultures without regard to the often damaging effects of this preservation on the people who belong to that culture. One typical and oft-quoted statement from *The Culture Cult* is as follows: "Most traditional cultures feature domestic repression, economic backwardness, endemic disease, religious fanaticism, and severe artistic constraints. If you want to live a full life and die in your bed, then civilization—not romantic ethnicity—deserves your thoughtful vote."

Predictably, *The Culture Cult* drew a wide range of critical responses, all of them passionate. Critics like Roger Kimball of the *New Criterion* commended Sandall for daring to point out politically incorrect facts, like the high rates of violence toward women in Aboriginal communities and the plunge in literacy among Aborigines after well-meaning politicians privileged the preservation of local culture over the teaching of modern subjects like English to Aboriginal children. Others, like Matthew Ryan of *Arena Magazine,* decried Sandall's position as one "that strips Aboriginal people of any individual agency, any cultural resources, any political will." However, *Times Literary Supplement* reviewer Raymond Tallis attested that "Roger Sandall's brilliant, impassioned and sardonic *The Culture Cult* explains among other things how the phrase 'in our culture' has come to be used to defend behavior that would otherwise be seen as quite abhorrent."

Sandall told *CA:* "After growing up in New Zealand, I became struck by the gap between the observable facts of ethnic culture around me and the romanticized versions in *National Geographic* magazine. Much of this seemed to be promoted by idealistic middle-class folk who had taken Anthropology 101, so my first serious writing was a commentary on academic anthropology's rather rosy view of the tribal world.

"My essay 'On the Way to the Pig Festival: Dramatic Illusions,' published in *Encounter* in 1978, satirized theatrical metaphors for social life, commenting *en passant* on Richard Sennett, Kenneth Burke, Erving Goffman, and Richard Schechner. Another article, 'When I Hear the Word Culture . . . : From Arnold to Anthropology,' looked at the change from the nineteenth-century use of the word 'culture' found in Matthew Arnold and the usage found in T. S. Eliot and Raymond Williams, and concluded it was generally a change for the worse. This essay is elaborated and updated in the final chapter of *The Culture Cult: Designer Tribalism and Other Essays.*

"As I see it, the idealization of primitive societies amounts to a disorder of the moral imagination. In the West it has proceeded in leaps and bounds until today, for large numbers of middle-class people of religious temperament, the salvation of tribal cultures has replaced the salvation of souls. This is something *The Culture Cult* traces to such eighteenth-century sources as J. G. Herder and Jean-Jacques Rousseau, and to influential interpreters of Herder in the twentieth century like Isaiah Berlin. Connections are made with communitarian social philosophies, and to the commune movement, but affinities with the historic development of socialism in western thought are suggested rather than explored.

"An appendix points to the sentimental psychology underlying the transfiguration of the tribal world. In a discussion of 'The Four Stages of Noble Savagery' I argue that intellectuals, 'by a process of compensatory moral reasoning, use the misery of modern indigenes as a motive for glorifying the cultures they once had.' The logic behind this is something Bertrand Russell once described as a fallacious belief in 'the superior virtue of the oppressed.'

"What Arthur O. Lovejoy and George Boas described in 1935 as the social ideal of 'primitivism' is a fertile field for scholarship. In their words it represents a revolt of civilized people against civilization itself. It regards the historically primitive as morally superior to the socially advanced. Primitivism therefore continually presents itself as the antagonist of 'civil society,' and of modernizing tendencies more generally, and is invariably hostile to science. Karl Popper pointed to this fifty years ago in his comments on Plato in *The Open Society and Its Enemies*. At present I am investigating the ascetic idealization of Spartan culture by Plutarch and numerous later commentators (down to and including the Nazis) in contrast to the protean variety and abundance of artistic and commercial enterprise in Periclean Athens."

BIOGRAPHICAL AND CRITICAL SOURCES:

PERIODICALS

Arena Magazine, June, 2001, Matthew Ryan, "The Return of the Repressed," p. 2.
New Criterion, April, 2001, Roger Kimball, "The Perils of Designer Tribalism," p. 15.
Quadrant, January-February, 2002, Geoffrey Partington, "All Those Peaceful Happy Natives."
Prospect, October, 2001, Samuel Brittan, "The Not So Noble Savage."
Sydney Morning Herald, April 26, 2001, Bettina Arndt, "A Culture of Denial."
Times Literary Supplement, August 16, 2002, Raymond Tallis, review of *The Culture Cult: Designer Tribalism and Other Essays,* p. 6.

*   *   *

SANTORO, Gene

PERSONAL: Born in New York, NY; son of Eugenio and Anne (Kelly) Santoro; married Tesse Viola; children: Donna, Linda. *Education:* City University of New York—Queens, B.A., 1976; Stanford University, M. Phil., 1979.

ADDRESSES: Agent—c/o Oxford University Press, 198 Madison Ave., New York, NY 10016.

CAREER: Columnist for the *Pulse,* CA, 1984-93, *Nation,* New York, NY, 1986—; and writer for periodicals, including *Billboard, Downbeat, Musician, Village Voice,* and the *New York Post.*

AWARDS, HONORS: Fulbright Scholar, 1978-79.

WRITINGS:

(With Allan Koznin, Pete Welding, and Dan Forte) *The Guitar: The History, the Music, the Players,* Morrow (New York, NY), 1984.
Dancing in Your Head: Jazz, Blues, Rock, and Beyond, Oxford University Press (New York, NY), 1994.
Stir It Up: Musical Mixes from Roots to Jazz, Oxford University Press (New York, NY), 1997.
Myself When I Am Real: The Life and Music of Charles Mingus, Oxford University Press (New York, NY), 2000.

SIDELIGHTS: A music critic and columnist, Gene Santoro has also written books on jazz music as well as a biography of well-known jazz musician Charles Mingus. Santoro's very first publication, however, was a collaborative history that focused on guitar lore, and was titled *The Guitar: The History, the Music, the Players.* Divided into five chapters, the book provides an overview of different types of guitars available, as well as the playing styles and artists associated with each type.

Santoro's next book, *Dancing in Your Head: Jazz, Blues, Rock, and Beyond* draws on his own expertise and interest in music as he traces the evolution of American popular music in the twentieth century. *Kliatt*'s Jeffrey Cooper called this collection of Santoro's writings "insightful" and "almost breathtaking in both its range and its depth." Similarly, in *Stir it Up: Musical Mixes from Roots to Jazz,* Santoro once again surveys a variety of music in a collection of his own writings that were previously published in such periodicals as *Nation* and the *Atlantic Monthly.* A *Kirkus Reviews* contributor noted that a wide variety of musicians and ideas are covered in this anthology, which provides "intelligent coverage of major artists."

In 2000 Santoro published *Myself When I Am Real: The Life and Music of Charles Mingus,* a biography of the noted jazz musician. Considered one of the most innovative jazz musicians of the twentieth century, Mingus was equally famous for his high-strung temperament and tumultuous personal life. In this work, noted a *Kirkus Reviews* critic, Santoro "offers the first complete Mingus biography since the jazz legend's death in 1979." The critic also explained that while Mingus was an inspiring musician, one who infused his own music with both originality and theatricality, he was also a person who "inspired extraordinary loyalty" and Santoro's book is evidence of that.

Mingus himself wrote a third-person memoir before his death, *Beneath the Underdog,* but as Jabari Asim said in the *Washington Post Book World,* the book was a mirror image of Mingus's boisterous and sensational personal life, and it had all the "grotesque magnetism of a car wreck," discouraging all but Mingus's most dedicated fans to actually plough through the work. In contrast, said Asim, Santoro's account of Mingus's life creates a much more accurate and perceptive portrait of a man who was "a gargantuan character." Similarly, William G. Kenz remarked in *Library Journal* that "after reading this work, Mingus's fictionalized account of his life, *Beneath the Underdog . . . ,* makes much more sense." Kenz was also appreciative of Santoro's recreation of the historical setting that framed Mingus's life, saying that it provides insight into the musician's creativity. In contrast, a critic for *Publishers Weekly* felt that in recreating the details of Mingus's life, including the numerous anecdotes that Santoro has framed the narrative around, he "fails to marshal his sources into a nuanced portrait, producing a mythological figure, not the man himself." Yet, noted the critic, that when Santoro is "writing about Mingus's actual musicmaking, [he] is in his element."

BIOGRAPHICAL AND CRITICAL SOURCES:

PERIODICALS

Kirkus Reviews, May 15, 1997, review of *Stir It Up: Musical Mixes from Roots to Jazz,* p. 784; July 1, 2000, review of *Myself When I Am Real: The Life and Music of Charles Mingus,* pp. 945-946.
Kliatt, January 1996, Jeffrey Cooper, review of *Dancing in Your Head: Jazz, Blues, Rock, and Beyond,* p. 34.
Library Journal, July 2000, William G. Kenz, review of *Myself When I Am Real,* p. 98.
Publishers Weekly, May 11, 1984, review of *The Guitar: The History, the Music, the Players,* p. 270; June 26, 2000, review of *Myself When I Am Real,* p. 63.
Washington Post Book World, July 25, 2000, Jabari Asim, "Charles Mingus: Oh Yeah," p. C8.*

SAPINSLEY, Alvin 1921-2002

OBITUARY NOTICE—See index for CA sketch: Born November 23, 1921, in Providence, RI; died of complications from pneumonia July 13, 2002, in Woodland Hills, CA. Scriptwriter. Sapinsley was a prolific writer for radio and television. After graduating with a B.A. degree from Bard College in 1942, he served in the U.S. Navy as a cryptographer during World War II. Returning from the war, he began writing for radio programs and then television during the days when programs were still recorded live. Although temporarily blacklisted in the 1950s because he attended some Communist Party meetings, he managed to get his career back on track and write scripts for made-for-television movies, such as *Don Quixote, A Star Is Born,* and *The Great Gatsby,* and for television series, including *Philip Morris Playhouse, Chrysler Theatre, Night Gallery, Hawaii Five-O, Bonanza, Kojak,* and *The Man from U.N.C.L.E.,* among others. For his writing, Sapinsley was honored with an Edgar Award in 1955 for *Sting of Death* and the TV-Writers' Annual Award for the 1966-67 season of *Code Name Heraclitus.* The president of Granville Productions in Hollywood, beginning in 1978, Sapinsley also taught creative writing at the university level during the 1950s.

OBITUARIES AND OTHER SOURCES:

PERIODICALS

Los Angeles Times, July 26, 2002, p. B13.

*   *   *

SARACINO, Mary 1954-

PERSONAL: Born October 4, 1954, in Seneca Falls, NY; daughter of Frank Saracino and Margaret Vergamini Malley. *Education:* College of St. Catherine, St. Paul, MN, B.A., 1976; University of Minnesota, graduate study, 1978-80.

ADDRESSES: Home—Denver, CO. *Agent*—c/o Publicity Director, Spinsters Ink, P. O. Box 22005, Denver, CO 80222. *E-mail*—marysar@aol.com.

CAREER: Writer.

MEMBER: PEN American Center, National Writer's Union, Colorado Authors' League, Collective of Italian-American Women.

AWARDS, HONORS: Minnesota Book Award finalist, Minnesota Center for the Book, for *No Matter What,* 1994; Book of the Year finalist, *ForeWord* magazine, for *Finding Grace,* 1999; Top Hand Award, Colorado Authors' League, for *Finding Grace,* 1999; Salvator and Margaret Bonomo Memorial Prize for Literature, *Italian Americana,* for "Valentino, Puglia, and Seneca Falls," 2000.

WRITINGS:

No Matter What (novel), Spinsters Ink (Denver, CO), 1993.
Finding Grace (novel), Spinsters Ink (Denver, CO), 1999.
Voices of the Soft-bellied Warrior: A Memoir, Spinsters Ink (Denver, CO), 2001.

Contributor to periodicals, including *Tuttestorie, Italian Americana, Voices in Italian Americana,* and *Sinister Wisdom.* Work represented in anthologies and other volumes, including *The Penguin Book of Italian American Writing,* edited by Regina Barreca, Penguin Books, 2002; *The Milk of Almonds: Italian-American Women Write about Ethnicity, Identity, and Sustenance,* edited by Edvige Giunta and Louise DeSalvo, Feminist Press, 2002; and *Writers Who Cook: An Anthology of Recipes, Prose, and Poetry,* Herringbone Press, 1995.

WORK IN PROGRESS: "A Talk with the Moon," a memoir of personal narratives and essays about class, gender, and ethnicity; a novel about Italian and Italian-American women and their families; a novel about the life of a Sicilian priestess of the Black Madonna. Researching pre-Christian Sicily, the Black Madonna and the Dark Mother, and the lives of southern Italians' pre-diaspora and post-immigration to America.

SIDELIGHTS: Mary Saracino's *Finding Grace,* a sequel to her young adult novel *No Matter What,* "stands on its own," said Carol DeAngelo in a *School Library Journal* review. In *Finding Grace,* set in 1967,

eleven-year-old Regina "Peanut" Giovanni is facing the breakup of her family after her mother leaves home with her lover, a fallen priest, taking her daughters with her. The man is given to drink and violence, however, and Peanut and her sisters are forced to seek refuge in a bus shelter. The plot of this story "may sound crudely melodramatic," said *Booklist's* Whitney Scott, "but it rises above its elements to become a compelling account of grace and redemption." A similar view was expressed by a *Publishers Weekly* contributor, who praised the young protagonist's "valiant innocence, her heartbreaking loyalty and vulnerability and her clear unassailable voice."

Saracino told *CA:* "My primary motivation for writing is to tell a compelling story that uncovers the emotional truth of my characters' lives. I write to give voice to what has long been silenced in our collective culture, especially with regards to the lives of girls and women. The writers who have most influenced my work include Toni Morrison, Audre Lorde, Virginia Woolf, and William Faulkner."

BIOGRAPHICAL AND CRITICAL SOURCES:

BOOKS

Giunta, Edvige, *Writing with an Accent: Contemporary Italian-American Women Authors,* Palgrave, 2002.

PERIODICALS

Booklist, October 1, 1999, Whitney Scott, review of *Finding Grace,* p. 344.
Denver Rocky Mountain News, October 5, 2001, Jean Hinkemeyer, review of *Voices of the Soft-bellied Warrior,* p. D30.
Minneapolis Star Tribune, June 12, 1994, Dave Wood, review of *No Matter What,* p. F16.
Publishers Weekly, September 27, 1999, review of *Finding Grace,* p. 68.
School Library Journal, May, 2000, Carol DeAngelo, review of *Finding Grace,* p. 193.
Voice of Youth Advocates, April, 1994, Barbara Flottmeier, review of *No Matter What.*

*   *   *

SCAPERLANDA, Maria (de Lourdes) Ruiz 1960-

PERSONAL: Born August 13, 1960, in Pinar del Río, Cuba; daughter of Ignacio M. Ruiz (a writer) and Maria de Jesus Paez (a Spanish professor); married Michael A. Scaperlanda (a law professor), December

27, 1981; children: Christopher Michael, Anamaria, Rebekah Elizabeth, Michelle Josefa. *Ethnicity:* Hispanic/Cuban. *Education:* University of Texas, B.A., 1981; University of Oklahoma, M.A., 1997. *Politics:* Independent. *Religion:* Roman Catholic. *Hobbies and other interests:* Photography, reading, music.

ADDRESSES: Home and office—3816 Waverly Ct., Norman, OK 73072. *E-mail*—mscaperlanda@ mmcable.com.

CAREER: Freelance writer and author, 1981—. *Daily Texan,* news assistant, 1979-80; Austin Parks and Recreation Summer Neighborhood Park Program, public information specialist, 1980-81; Catholic Diocese of Austin Religious Education Center, media coordinator, 1983-84; *Texas Catholic Press,* Austin, TX, state correspondent, 1990-94; *Our Sunday Visitor,* Huntington, IN, senior correspondent, 1997-2000. Former member, Sooner Catholic Review Board, Oklahoma City, OK.

MEMBER: International Women's Writing Guild, American Society of Journalists and Authors, Society of Professional Journalists, Catholic Press Association.

AWARDS, HONORS: Excellence in Public Service Journalism, second place, Society of Professional Journalists, 2000, for feature on Neve Shalom, Israel; Catholic Press Association, Best Personality Profile, second place, 2001, for interview with Vatican astronomer and for interview with Madeleine L'Engle, and Best Regular Column, 2001, for "Heartland."

WRITINGS:

Their Faith Has Touched Us: The Legacies of Three Young Oklahoma City Bombing Victims, Sheed & Ward (Kansas City, MO), 1997.
Edith Stein: Teresa Benedicta of the Cross, Our Sunday Visitor Books (Huntington, IN), 2001.
Seeker's Guide to Mary, Loyola Press (Chicago, IL), 2002.
Pilgrimage: A Way of Travel, a Way of Life, Loyola Press (Chicago, IL), 2002.

Contributor to periodicals, including *U.S. Catholic Magazine, Catholic Digest, Columbia, Vision, Catholic Parent, National Catholic Register, Family, Lutheran,* and *St. Anthony Messenger. Catholic Parent,* columnist, 1997—; *Catholic Practice,* e-zine columnist, 1998-2000.

WORK IN PROGRESS: Cuba Perdida, a novel.

SIDELIGHTS: Maria Ruiz Scaperlanda told *CA:* "Writing is, for me, a spiritual experience. It is in and through writing that I fully open myself to God's work in my life—and in so doing, I open myself to God in the world. I believe that in choosing our calling, our profession, the reality is not that 'you are what you do' as much as 'you do what you are'! Even when I don't understand the why in it, I know I am a writer in my heart. One of my goals as a writer is to take events, people, and concepts that may be ordinary or perhaps even difficult to understand—such as the Oklahoma City bombing—and to offer a new perspective on it, a new vision, which brings hope to the reader. My hope is that my writing not only stretches and nourishes me as author, but that it also touches the reader in surprising and unexpected ways. That is the meaning of God's hand at work in the world!"

In 1997 Scaperlanda wrote about an domestic terrorist attack from a spiritual point of view in her book *Their Faith Has Touched Us: The Legacies of Three Young Oklahoma City Bombing Victims.* "The world knows that 168 people died . . . and hundreds of others were maimed and injured in the blast that ripped through the cool air that spring morning," she writes. "And, while it is difficult to use the word 'blessing' [to describe the] healing process, the stories of faith in this city community are also ingrained in America's memory: stories of devoted volunteers, of tireless rescue workers . . . , of still-hopeful survivors and of faithful victims' families." The force of the blast, she reported, sent thousands of bills from the Federal Employees Credit Union into the streets. And yet, "there was no looting in this wrecked downtown. . . . And when all the money was gathered and counted, the Credit Union ended up with more money than it originally held in the vault."

Scaperlanda wrote *The Seeker's Guide to Mary* as "an introduction to Mary of Nazareth, the mother of Jesus," as she told *CA.* "My hope is that it opens up for readers a new understanding of this wonderful woman—and that it invites every Christian, not just Catholics, to examine and define their personal relationship to Mary. Anyone who is a follower of Jesus should get to know his mother better! As a Hispanic. Mary was a natural and prominent part of my growing up," she continued. "We celebrated Marian feasts and we remembered Mary as a family, but more importantly, we saw Mary as an important and natural part of our Catholic faith experience. The Hispanic sense of family, and the beautiful role of mothers and grandmothers within that cultural and ethnic community, are important elements in my approach to writing about Mary."

Born in Cuba, Scaperlanda was raised in Puerto Rico, "so I am truly a Caribbean, 'island girl'!" she said. "My place of birth and the way that my culture weaves itself within a Catholic reference is an essential basis of all my writing—whether news or feature stories, essays, columns, or fiction. But perhaps what colors my writing the most is not my sense of 'place,' but my sense of 'home,' in a spiritual and physical sense— and how that understanding and that reality was shaped by the fact that I am a refugee, an immigrant. That reality will always be at the heart of who I am."

When asked about how she became a writer, Scaperlanda said, "For the first thirteen years of my life, Spanish was my first language. I still have the 'books' that I would put together as a young child, filling them up with my own poems and thoughts, essays and pictures—quite often relating to what it felt to be a Cuban living in Puerto Rico or to some of the religious events that our family participated in. I honestly don't know when I actually 'defined' myself as a writer, but I think my heart, my spirit, always knew it. I heard somewhere that it's not so much that we are what we do, but that we DO what we ARE. I truly believe that."

BIOGRAPHICAL AND CRITICAL SOURCES:

BOOKS

Scaperlanda, Maria Ruiz, *Their Faith Has Touched Us: The Legacies of Three Young Oklahoma City Bombing Victims,* Sheed & Ward (Kansas City, MO), 1997.

PERIODICALS

National Catholic Reporter, December 12, 1997, Maria Ruiz Scaperlanda, "Book Tells Redeeming Stories from Oklahoma City Tragedy: Excerpt from *Their Faith Has Touched Us,*" p. 2.

SCOTT, Alicia Anne 1810-1900

PERSONAL: Born in 1810, in Berwickshire, Scotland; died of influenza, March 12, 1900; buried at Westruther Kirk; daughter of John and Helen Wauchope Spottiswood; married Lord John Douglas Montague Scott, 1836.

CAREER: Poet.

WRITINGS:

Songs and Verses, David Douglas (Edinburgh, Scotland), 1904, revised and enlarged edition (including biographical sketch), 1911.

SIDELIGHTS: The little that is known about Scottish poet Alicia Anne Scott is revealed in a biographical sketch written by her grandniece Margaret Warrender and included in the 1911 edition of *Songs and Verses.* Some of Scott's poems, notably "Ettrick," "The Comin' o' the Spring," and "Durisdeer," are familiar to people versed in Scottish literature and music, but it is her singular accomplishment, the ballad "Annie Laurie," for which she is remembered.

Scott was born Alicia Anne Spottiswood, the eldest of four children of one of the oldest families in Berwickshire, Scotland. Scott was educated in literature, the arts, and languages and was trained to play the harp. She created her own songs and sang as she played for hours at a time. She preferred to walk and ride in the country that she loved and dreaded the family's yearly trips to London. She was interested in geology, archeology, and botany, traits she inherited from her father. Her grandfather, Andrew Wauchope, fostered her love of history with his stories of the Stuart cause.

In 1834 Scott's sister, Margaret, married her childhood friend Sir Hugh Hume Campbell and moved to his estate, Marchmont, which was only ten miles from Spottiswood. The sisters visited often, and it was during one of these visits that "Annie Laurie" was written. Scott made alterations to a poem attributed to William Douglas and published in Allan Cunningham's *The Songs of Scotland, Ancient and Modern,* and combined it with a tune she had made up years before. The poem is about a man's love of a beautiful woman. It was published without her permission in 1838, having been copied when she sent her music book to be bound. It was also attributed to various authors and appeared anonymously as sheet music before the true author was discovered sometime after the Crimean War (1854-1856), at which time she requested that all profits from its publication be given to the widows and orphans of fallen British soldiers.

Scott's husband, Lord John Douglas Montague Scott, was the brother of Walter Francis Scott, duke of Buccleuch and Queensbury, and the nephew of Lady Caroline Scott. They spent most of their time at Cawston, his estate in Warwickshire. Scott was homesick for Scotland, and many of her poems were inspired by her absence. In "Ettrick," for instance, the speaker's observations of nature are colored by her emotional states, which become more depressed as the poem develops. When Margaret died of scarlet fever in 1839, Scott wrote two poems of grief. Susannah Clements noted in *Dictionary of Literary Biography* that the latter, written three years after Margaret's death, "expresses Scott's despair and sense of isolation. She is the only person still grieving for her sister, while everyone else talks, laughs, and enjoys the spring." Scott never recovered from her sister's death or from the death of her eldest brother John seven years later. "The two poems Scott wrote on his death continue to express her absorption with death and isolation," noted Clements.

Most of Scott's work was unpublished, but her only book, *Songs and Verses,* reflects her Victorian themes of death and isolation and her interest in history, geography, and politics. From the early 1840s until his death in 1851, she corresponded with Scottish folklorist Charles Kirkpatrick Sharpe, which further piqued her interest in her native Scotland. Her 1858 poem "The Bounds of Cheviot" reflects her desire to see Scotland and her regret at being away from home. Lord John died suddenly in 1859, and Scott took his death very hard. According to Warrender, Scott wrote journal letters to him regularly during her remaining forty years and her poems increasingly reflected remorse and the pain of loss. Clements noted that the poem "Written at Thurso," composed after her husband's death, "depicts nature as an inadequate mediator between the living and the dead."

Scott enjoyed good health until late in the 1890s, when it became necessary for her to use two canes to walk after she suffered a sprained ankle. Her last poem "I See Them Not" was written in November 1899. The next year Spottiswood experienced an epidemic of influenza, which Scott contracted, and she died of the illness. After Scott's death, a memorial poem signed "G. N. N.," the original version of "Annie Laurie," and a facsimile of her October 17, 1899 letter that describes its composition were published in a pamphlet. Clements wrote that the poem, "The Burial of Lady John Scott, Authoress of 'Annie Laurie,' 16th March 1900," "possesses little literary merit, but it reveals the extent to which Scott's renown rests on the composition of 'Annie Laurie.'"

BIOGRAPHICAL AND CRITICAL SOURCES:

BOOKS

Dictionary of Literary Biography, Volume 240: *Late Nineteenth- and Early Twentieth-Century British Women Poets,* Gale (Detroit, MI), 2001.*

*   *   *

SEARLES, John 1968(?)-

PERSONAL: Born c. 1968. *Education:* Connecticut State University, graduate; New York University, master's degree.

ADDRESSES: Agent—c/o Author Mail, William Morrow, 1350 Avenue of the Americas, New York, NY 10019.

CAREER: Cosmopolitan, New York, NY, senior book editor; also read fiction submissions for *Redbook;* worked as a factory worker, stock boy, and telemarketer before attending college and waited on tables after graduate school.

WRITINGS:

Cosmopolitan Bedside Quiz Book: Get the Real Deal on the Inner You, the Secret Him, the Truth about Your Friends, and Everything Else You Ever Wanted to Know about Love, Life, and Lust, Hearst Books (New York, NY), 1999.
Boy Still Missing (novel), Morrow (New York, NY), 2001.

Contributor to periodicals, including *Mademoiselle* and *Out*.

ADAPTATIONS: Boy Still Missing has been optioned for a film.

WORK IN PROGRESS: A second novel.

SIDELIGHTS: As a senior book editor for *Cosmopolitan* magazine, John Searles is very familiar with current literary trends. This knowledge undoubtedly contributed to the success of his novel *Boy Still Missing*. The book attracted considerable attention before it even reached bookstore shelves. Advance publicity included praise by novelists Wally Lamb and Frank McCourt, and the book's movie rights had already been purchased. The story is about a teenage boy struggling to deal with his father's alcoholism and promiscuity, his mother's death following an attempt to give herself an abortion, and his own first sexual and romantic experiences. The book was widely reviewed and received a wide range of responses from critics. With its treatment of complex social issues and quickly shifting plot, it struck some reviewers as a failed attempt at serious literature, while others called it entertaining and thought-provoking.

Searles studied writing as an undergraduate, having dropped business studies after the diabetes-related death of one of his younger sisters. After earning a master's degree at New York University, he worked as a waiter before freelancing as a fiction reader for *Redbook* and then *Cosmopolitan*. According to Searles, who is quoted in a *Washington Post* article by Lydia Millet, he at first felt out of place among the glamorous "Cosmo girls" who were his co-workers and was unfamiliar with the reputation of publisher Helen Gurley Brown, his new boss. However, he was soon enamored of Brown, whom he met when she was a sexy seventy-something, and was impressed by her clothes, energy, and interest in her employees. Searles wrote that it took some time to adjust to working and writing according to her guidelines, but that he ultimately discovered "there is a Cosmo girl inside everybody. Even a boy like me."

Boy Still Missing was penned while Searles worked at *Cosmopolitan*; he used a four-month leave of absence to complete the work. The author told *BookSense.com*

interviewer Linda M. Castellitto that his job had given him a new appreciation for the "commercial thriller" after having looked down on such books. "It taught me the value of keeping the reader entertained, not just writing for myself with all my pretty descriptions," he explained. He also credits two mentors with encouraging him to continue writing after his first novel was rejected. College professor Ann Hood continued to guide him and was instrumental in his meeting novelist Wally Lamb, who offered to read his work and then recommended Searles to his agent.

Publisher William Morrow accepted *Boy Still Missing* on the strength of Searles's first 120 pages, which introduce sixteen-year-old Dominick Pindle and his dramatic coming-of-age story. Set in the 1970s in a dull New England town, the novel opens with Dominick and his mother on their habitual Saturday night search for his father in the local bars. On one of these nights, Dominick meets his father's current mistress and develops a crush on the beautiful woman. The father ends the relationship even though the woman is pregnant with his child, prompting Dominick to steal his mother's life savings for her. When his mother also discovers herself to be pregnant—not by Dominick's father—she does not have enough money for a safe, if illegal, abortion. She tries to terminate the pregnancy herself and dies in the attempt. Guilt-ridden, Dominick travels to New York City in search of his half-brother. He decides to hold the child hostage in a motel room, hoping to persuade the news media to investigate his mother's death. During this attempt, he meets and falls in love with a girl named Jeanny.

Reviews of *Boy Still Missing* ranged from decidedly negative to strongly positive. In an article for *Library Journal*, Nancy Pearl considered the plot to be "overly complicated" and warned that "the book ends as it begins, in a flurry of unconvincing events." Jana Siciliano wrote for *Bookreporter.com*, "If you're interested in hackneyed stories about drunken dads, mistresses, and the sons who sleep with them, then *Boy Still Missing* is right up your alley." Critical of overdone "stage directions and commercial-fiction painting," Walter Kirn described the novel in *Time* as "an action-packed tale but light in every other way, although its tone can be very, very heavy."

For several reviewers *Boy Still Missing* had considerable appeal, even when it was not considered a total success. *Entertainment Weekly* critic Daniel Fierman was dazzled by the first part of the novel and disappointed by the plot's development after the mother's death. He commented, "As the plot spins into absurdity . . . you'll feel so betrayed you'll almost want to skip his next book. Almost." In the *Washington Post,* Lydia Millet judged that "fans of easy-to-read, bestselling dramas about families in the grips of crises . . . will probably enjoy it." She further felt that Searles' novel falls short of "literary" status, but credited it with a "carefully constructed narrative arc" and "the odd moment of welcome grittiness." A *Publishers Weekly* reviewer predicted that some readers will object to the author's pro-choice stance, but that "many more . . . will find his story of hard choices, bleak times and unwilling kidnappers captivating indeed."

More enthusiastic reviewers valued Searles's ability to involve the reader in Dominick's troubles. In the *New York Times Book Review,* Peter Khoury praised Searles's evocation of "quotidian details of an adolescent boy's life." Khoury remarked, "Although sometimes far-fetched, the narrative is often riveting and is laced with insight about choice, fate and luck." Convinced that Searles is "clearly talented," *Booklist* contributor John Green said that the new novelist "builds suspense and excitement with surprising turns of plot weaving back into one another." And in a review for *People,* Laura Jamison called Searles "an impressively assured new voice" and advised that while "the story line is straight out of a thriller . . . the novel always stays centered on a decent kid's struggle to understand himself and his own ever expanding heart."

BIOGRAPHICAL AND CRITICAL SOURCES:

PERIODICALS

Booklist, January 1, 2001, John Green, review of *Boy Still Missing,* p. 921.
Entertainment Weekly, March 9, 2001, Daniel Fierman, review of *Boy Still Missing,* p. 76.
Library Journal, April 1, 2001, Nancy Pearl, review of *Boy Still Missing,* p. 134.
New York Times Book Review, March 18, 2001, Peter Khoury, review of *Boy Still Missing,* p. 16.
People, March 12, 2001, Laura Jamison, review of *Boy Still Missing,* p. 43.

Publishers Weekly, January 29, 2001, review of *Boy Still Missing,* p. 62.
Time, February 12, 2001, Walter Kirn, "Seven New Voices," p. 88.
Washington Post, March 18, 2001, Lydia Millet, "A Family Affair," p. T13.

OTHER

Bookreporter.com, http://www.bookreporter.com/ (October 7, 2001), Jana Siciliano, review of *Boy Still Missing.*
BookSense.com, http://www.booksense.com/ (October 7, 2001), Linda M. Castelitto, "John Searles."*

*   *   *

SEGEV, Tom 1945-

PERSONAL: Born 1945, in Jerusalem, Israel. *Education:* Boston University, Ph.D. (history).

ADDRESSES: Home—Jerusalem, Israel. *Office*—21 Schocken St., Tel Aviv, Israel 61001.

CAREER: Haaretz, Tel Aviv, Israel, journalist.

AWARDS, HONORS: Best book, *New York Times,* 2000, for *One Palestine, Complete: Jews and Arabs under the British Mandate.*

WRITINGS:

1949, the First Israelis, Henry Holt (New York, NY), 1986.
Soldiers of Evil: The Commandants of the Nazi Concentration Camps, McGraw-Hill (New York, NY), 1987.
The Seventh Million: The Israelis and the Holocaust, Hill and Wang (New York, NY), 1993.
One Palestine, Complete: Jews and Arabs under the Mandate, Metropolitan Books (New York, NY), 2000.
Elvis in Jerusalem: Post-Zionism and the Americanization of Israel, translated by Haim Watzman, Metropolitan Books (New York, NY), 2002.

SIDELIGHTS: Tom Segev was born in Jerusalem, the son of German Jewish parents. He earned a doctorate in history from Boston University, but now lives in Israel, where he is a journalist for the daily newspaper *Haaretz.* He has written several books about Israel and Jewish history. In the *New Republic,* Anita Shapira called Segev "one of Israel's most prominent and most controversial journalists. Gifted with a sharp eye and a barbed tongue, he presents himself as the ironic, even cynical critic of Israeli reality."

Segev's *1949: The First Israelis* describes the experiences of the first immigrants to the new state of Israel, and also describes what the Arab people of the region went through during the same time period. In the *New York Times Book Review,* Elmore Jackson wrote, "This book should be required reading for all who want to understand the Arab-Israeli conflict."

The Soldiers of Evil: The Commandants of the Nazi Concentration Camps is a collective portrait of the commandants of these death camps. Drawing on interviews with the commandants and their families, Segev portrays the origins of these men, their identification with the Nazi party, and their identity as soldiers. In *Kirkus Reviews,* a writer commented, "Overall, a skillfully presented and chilling look at one of history's most blood-curdling events."

In *The Seventh Million: The Israelis and the Holocaust,* Segev contends that the Zionist leadership preferentially chose only committed Zionists to save from the Nazi Holocaust, and left the rest of the European Jews at the mercy of Hitler and Stalin. However, he leaves the question open: perhaps they really did all they could. In the *New Republic,* Anita Shapira wrote, "This ambiguous formulation infuriated readers, who interpreted it as an unforgivable innuendo on a matter of the utmost sensitivity." In the *Journal of Palestine Studies,* though, Milton Viorst wrote that Segev "has written a brilliant study of the impact of the Holocaust on his countrymen" and commented that the book, "though simply written, even anecdotal, is subtle and complex."

In *One Palestine, Complete: Jews and Arabs under the Mandate* Segev tells the story of Israel and Palestine, beginning with the British conquest of the Ottoman Empire during World War I. Both Palestinians and Jews welcomed the British, believing the

British would give them independence. By 1947, the British had left the region after the United Nations resolved to divide the country into two separate states; this resolution led to a bloody war that ended in the establishment of the state of Israel and the expulsion of over 700,000 Palestinians. Segev tells this story through the actual experiences of people from all sides of the conflict, filling the book with material gathered from letter, diaries, and archives. In the *Guardian,* Colin Schindler wrote, "It is a kind of literary theatre rather than history, and Segev moves his actors on and off stage with great skill." *Washington Post* reviewer Haim Watzman called the work "a book of pressing relevance," and wrote that it is "an antidote to myths" about the history of the region. Omer Bartov wrote in the *New York Times,* "Instead of telling his story through the loud pronouncements of political leaders, he has woven a fine tapestry of individual portraits, curious anecdotes and penetrating insights." Bartov also wrote, "Segev has written an enormously important book, perhaps the best single account of Palestine under the British mandate. For the first time . . . the story of the [British] mandate has been told from all three perspectives—the Zionist, the Arab and the British."

In the *Middle East Journal,* Lawrence Davidson wrote that Segev's presentation of Palestinians is not as balanced as it initially appears to be. Davidson wrote that Segev "persistently describes Arab resistance to colonialism as 'terrorism,' and repeatedly reminds readers that, beginning in the 1930s, the Palestinians became 'Nazi sympathizers.'" However, he also noted, "When all is said and done, however, Segev's presentation is broad enough and rich enough to allow the reader to see beyond the standard pro-Zionist viewpoint, and that is the great virtue of *One Palestine, Complete.*"

In 2002 Segev published *Elvis in Jerusalem: Post-Zionism and the Americanization of Israel.* With this book Segev moves away from the study of Israel's past and focuses on its present. He sites many examples of how the collective identity of Zionism has slowly given way to the American notions of individualism and consumerism, and, in his opinion, that is a good thing. Many Israelites do not agree; the subject of post-Zionism is very sensitive in Israel but, according to a reviewer from *Publishers Weekly,* Segev "makes a powerful case for it in reasoned and measured tones."

BIOGRAPHICAL AND CRITICAL SOURCES:

PERIODICALS

Asian Affairs, June, 2000, Ivor Lucas, review of *One Palestine, Complete: Jews and Arabs under the Mandate,* p. 203.

Booklist, March 15, 1993, p. 1295; September 1, 2000, Vanessa Bush, review of *One Palestine, Complete,* p. 5.

Commentary, November, 1999, Hillel Halkin, "Was Zionism Unjust?," p. 29.

Daily Telegraph (London), January 20, 2001, John Simpson, "Gleams of Decency," p. 4.

Economist, January 20, 2001, review of *One Palestine, Complete,* p. 4.

Foreign Affairs, March-April, 2001, p. 162.

Guardian (London, England), February 3, 2001, Colin Shindler, "Saturday Review," p. 8.

International Affairs, October, 1994, p. 793.

Journal of Palestine Studies, winter, 1995, Milton Viorst, review of *The Seventh Million: The Israelis and the Holocaust,* p. 94.

Library Journal, February 1, 1986, p. 81; April 15, 1993, p. 111; September 15, 2000, Nader Entessar, review of *One Palestine, Complete,* p. 94.

Middle East Journal, spring, 2001, Lawrence Davidson, review of *One Palestine, Complete,* p. 335.

Middle East Quarterly, summer, 2001, p. 90.

Nation, July 26, 1993, Norman Birnbaum, review of *The Seventh Million,* p. 142.

National Review, March 19, 2001, Amos Perlmutter, "Bad Tidings to Zion."

New Republic, October 18, 1993, Moshe Halbertal, review of *The Seventh Million,* p. 40; December 11, 2000, Anita Shapira, "Eyeless in Zion—When Palestine first Exploded," p. 26.

New Statesman, January 22, 2001, Philip Ziegler, "This Monstrous Canker," p. 51.

New York Review of Books, September 26, 1985, Avishai Margalit, "Passage to Palestine," p. 23; September 28, 1989, Istvan Deak, "The Commandants," p. 63; February 17, 1994, p. 7.

New York Times, April 18, 1993, p. 3; May 5, 1993, p. B5; August 14, 2001, "Mideast Nationalism, with Nowhere to Go," p. A16.

New York Times Book Review, February 2, 1986, Elmore Jackson, "The Past as Prologue," p. 13; November 12, 2000, Omer Bartov, "The Promised Land," p. 12; December 3, 2000, p. 9.

Publishers Weekly, January 10, 1986, p. 81; August 19, 1988, review of *Soldiers of Evil: The Commandants of the Nazi Concentration Camps,* p. 64; February 8, 1993, review of *The Seventh Million,* p. 62; October 23, 2000, review of *One Palestine, Complete,* p. 66; April, 2002, review of *Elvis in Jerusalem: Post-Zionism and the Americanization of Israel.*

Sunday Telegraph (London, England), January 14, 2001, David Pryce-Jones, "Was Zionism just a British ploy?"

Sunday Times (London, England), January 14, 2001, Geoffrey Wheatcroft, "When the British ruled Palestine," p. 36.

Tikkun, January, 2001, "An Interview with Tom Segev," p. 27.

Wall Street Journal, July 15, 1993, Amy Dockser Marcus, review of *The Seventh Million,* p. A12.

Washington Post, November 5, 2000, Gershom Gorenberg, "Foundation Myths," p. X02.

OTHER

Metropolitan Books Web site, http://www.holtzbrinkpublishers.com/ (February 17, 2003), synopsis of *Elvis in Jerusalem: Post-Zionism and the Americanization of Israel.**

*   *   *

SHAPIRO, Gilbert 1926-

PERSONAL: Born July 1, 1926, in New York, NY; married Marion Herman (deceased); children: Laura and Amy. *Education:* Cornell University, B.A., 1947, M.A., 1951, Ph.D., 1954.

ADDRESSES: Home—4625 5th Ave., Apt. 503, Pittsburgh, PA 15213. *E-mail*—gns@vms.cis.pitt.edu.

CAREER: Oberlin College, Oberlin, OH, instructor, assistant professor, 1955- 59; Wayne State University, Detroit, MI, assistant professor, 1959-61; Washington University, St. Louis, MO, associate professor, director Social Science Institute, 1961-65; Boston College, Boston, MA, research associate professor, 1965-68; University of Pittsburgh, Pittsburgh, PA, professor, 1968-88. *Military service:* United States Army, sergeant, 1945-47.

AWARDS, HONORS: Pinckney Award for *Revolutionary Demands: A Content Analysis of the Cahiers de Doléances of 1789,* Society for French Historical Studies, 1999.

WRITINGS:

(With John Markoff) *Revolutionary Demands: A Content Analysis of the "Cahiers de Doléances" of 1789,* Stanford University Press (Stanford, CA), 1998.

Contributor to books, including *The Dimensions of Quantitative Research in History,* edited by William O. Aydelotte, Allan G. Bogue, and Robert W. Fogel, Princeton University Press (Princeton, NJ), 1972, *Sociological Methodology,* edited by David R. Heise, Jossey-Bass (San Francisco, CA), 1974, and *Text Analysis for the Social Sciences: Methods for Drawing Statistical Inferences from Texts and Transcripts,* edited by Carl W. Roberts, Lawrence Erlbaum Associates (Mahweh, NJ), 1997.

SIDELIGHTS: Gilbert Shapiro's book *Revolutionary Demands: A Content Analysis of the Cahiers de Doléances of 1789,* which he wrote with John Markoff and the help of numerous contributors, was published in 1998 when Shapiro was seventy-two years old. He had spent almost forty years working on the book, which "attempts to apply the methods of social science to a specific historical problem—the state of public opinion on the eve of the French Revolution," explained Jeff Horn in the *Journal of Interdisciplinary History.* In addition to the book, the authors have created a huge database "relating to," in Horn's words, "social life and social problems at the outbreak of" the French Revolution.

The *cahiers de doléances* consist of more than 40,000 lists of demands made by "royal subjects from all quarters of France and from all walks of life" that were drafted in 1789 just prior to the start of the French Revolution, according to Michael Kwass in the *Journal of Modern History.* Because the *cahiers* are, as Kwass noted, "such a well-exploited source," he questioned whether "this lengthy new study . . . is really necessary," and answered with an "emphatic 'yes,'" for both methodological and analytical reasons." Kwass went on to say, "The scientific rigor with which Shapiro and Markoff have compiled data on the *cahiers* is simply unprecedented."

The book is "neatly divided into two parts," wrote D. M. G. Sutherland in *The Historian,* "a theoretical discussion of content analysis and a second section showing the application of the procedure as applied to the *cahiers de doléances* of France in 1789." Horn wrote in the *Journal of Interdisciplinary History,* "Shapiro and Markoff have made an important, and explicitly interdisciplinary, contribution to the study of history." "The genuine contribution of this book," Horn continued later, "is that it helps the hard-science side of the social sciences to communicate with the mainstream of the historical profession." Horn further complimented the authors for using "clear prose with a minimum of jargon."

Jack R. Censer in the *Journal of Social History* observed that *Revolutionary Demands* contains "some 200,000 words, 100 pages of appendices, and 80 pages of notes," and said, "this volume is more a report than a conventional book." Censer stated that through the combination of the database with the book the authors "raise the study of the cahiers to a new, higher level and make a major contribution to the study of the French Revolution."

Perhaps the highest compliment made to the book was by John A. Hall in the *American Journal of Sociology.* He wrote, "this is an awesome and path-breaking achievement of which sociology as a whole should be proud: every angle of a key historical data source has been teased out and made available to systematic use, and in a way that for once really does immeasurably improve upon prior work of historians."

BIOGRAPHICAL AND CRITICAL SOURCES:

PERIODICALS

American Journal of Sociology, November, 1999, John A. Hall, review of *Revolutionary Demands: A Content Analysis of the Cahiers de Doléances of 1789,* p. 846.
English Historical Review, April, 2000, Colin Jones, review of *Revolutionary Demands,* p. 474.
Historian, spring, 2000, D. M. G. Sutherland, review of *Revolutionary Demands,* p. 699.
Journal of Interdisciplinary History, winter, 2001, Jeff Horn, review of *Revolutionary Demands,* p. 453.

Journal of Modern History, September, 2000, Michael Kwass, review of *Revolutionary Demands,* p. 801.
Journal of Social History, winter, 2000, Jack R. Censer, review of *Revolutionary Demands,* p. 443.

* * *

SHELLY, Adrienne 1966-

PERSONAL: Born 1966, in Queens, NY. *Education:* Attended Boston University.

ADDRESSES: Agent—c/o Magic Lantern Inc., 250 West 57th St., New York, NY 10107.

CAREER: Actress, director, and writer. Previously associated with Workhouse Theatre, Ltd., New York, NY.

Film appearances include *The Unbelievable Truth,* Miramax, 1990; *Trust,* Republic Pictures, 1990; *Lonely in America,* 1990; *Big Girls Don't Cry . . . They Get Even,* 1991; *Hold Me, Thrill Me, Kiss Me,* Live Video, 1992; *Hexed,* Columbia TriStar Films de Espana, S.A., 1993; *The Road Killers,* Miramax, 1994; *Teresa's Tattoo,* Trimark Pictures, 1994; *Sleeping with Strangers,* 1994; *Sleep with Me,* Metro-Goldwyn-Mayer, 1994; *Opera No. 1,* 1994; *Kalamazoo,* 1994; *Sudden Manhattan,* Phaedra Cinema, 1997; *Grind,* Fox Lorber, 1997; *The Regulars,* 1997; *Wrestling with Alligators,* 1998; *I'll Take You There,* 1999; *Dead Dog,* 2000; *Revolution #9,* 2001; and *Searching for Debra Winger,* 2002. Work as film director includes *Urban Legend,* 1994; *Sudden Manhattan,* Phaedra Cinema, 1997; and *I'll Take You There,* 1999.

Appearances on episodic television include "A Many Splendored Thing," *Homicide: Life on the Street,* NBC, 1994; "Phantom at the Opera," *Early Edition,* CBS, 1997; "Ancient Tribes," *Oz,* HBO, 1998; and "High & Low," *Law & Order,* NBC, 2000. Other television appearances include *Rock the Boat,* 2000. Work as television director includes *Lois Lives a Little,* CBS, 1997.

AWARDS, HONORS: Best Independent Feature Film Award, Trola Film Festival, Portugal, 1997, for *Sudden Manhattan;* Film Showcase Jury Award, U.S. Comedy Arts Festival, best director, 2000, for *I'll Take You There.*

WRITINGS:

Sudden Manhattan (screenplay), Phaedra Cinema, 1997.
Lois Lives a Little (TV special), CBS, 1997.
Francis Ford Coppola and the Dream of Spring (play), Westbeth Theatre (New York, NY), 1997.
I'll Take You There (screenplay), Stark Productions, 1999.

Other screenplays include *Urban Legend,* 1994.

SIDELIGHTS: Describing Adrienne Shelly as a "little heart-faced red-headed charmer," Michael Wilmington of the *Chicago Tribune* wrote that after seeing her in a 1992 film, "I was sure that, with the right role, she'd be a big star within a year." However, "The right roles didn't come," but with her first feature-length film as writer and director, 1997's *Sudden Manhattan,* "she surprises us in a different way."

Sudden Manhattan grew out of a difficult time in Shelly's life, when a series of misfortunes struck her. As David Daley wrote in the *Hartford Courant,* "Directing came easy, Shelly said, especially considering everything else that happened at the same time: breaking up with [two boyfriends in a row], the burglary of her apartment, and a viral disease that left her dehydrated and hooked up to an IV machine." No wonder, then, that she could effectively present the beleaguered protagonist Donna, described by Justine Elias in the *Village Voice* as "a bright woman caught up in a stream of continual apologies." The film earned Shelly comparisons to Woody Allen, but Elias maintained that unlike Allen and "other solipsistic filmmakers . . . Shelly is as fascinated by other people's peculiarities as she is by the little earthquakes in her own head."

With *I'll Take You There* in 1999, Shelly's character plays matchmaker to her brother Bill, who has just been deserted by his wife, fixing him up with former classmate Bernice (played by Ally Sheedy). Bill takes out his hurts on Bernice, treating her rudely, but Bernice does not take this lying down. Instead, she kidnaps him at gunpoint and takes him to her grandmother's house. Calling the film "a semi-engaging, semi-irritating New York indie about a semi-deranged woman who bullies a semi-depressed man into a semi-romance," Todd McCarthy in *Variety* maintained that *I'll Take You There* is a "brightly mounted low-budgeter [that] possesses enough charm to please sympathetic viewers looking for a quirky offbeater."

BIOGRAPHICAL AND CRITICAL SOURCES:

BOOKS

Contemporary Theatre, Film, and Television, Volume 32, Gale (Detroit, MI), 2000.

PERIODICALS

Chicago Tribune, August 1, 1997, Michael Wilmington, review of *Sudden Manhattan,* p. H7.
Connoisseur, August, 1991, Jean Nathan, "In Adrienne We Trust," pp. 23-24.
Hartford Courant (Hartford, CT), June 1, 1997, David Daley, "The Unbelievable Truth," p. G7.
Interview, August, 1991, Henry Cabot Beck and Pamela Hanson, "I'm Absolutely This Way," pp. 66-69.
New York Times, May 8, 1996, Stephen Holden, review of *Urban Legend,* p. C15; March 7, 1997, Stephen Holden, review of *Sudden Manhattan,* p. B12.
Premiere, September, 1991, Alex Patterson, "Adrienne Shelly" (interview), p. 56.
Variety, October 18, 1999, Todd McCarthy, review of *I'll Take You There,* p. 43.
Village Voice, March 11, 1997, Justine Elias, review of *Sudden Manhattan,* p. 74.*

*   *   *

SHYNNAGH, Frank
See WILL, Frederic

*   *   *

SIBLEY, William Jack 1952-

PERSONAL: Born November 13, 1952, in Corpus Christi, TX. *Education:* University of Texas at Austin, B.S. (communications), 1975. *Hobbies and other interests:* Historical building restoration, ranching, growing olive trees.

ADDRESSES: Home—Los Angeles, CA, and Corpus Christi, TX. *Agent*—Lisa FitzGerald, FitzGerald Literary Management, 84 Monte Alto Rd., Santa Fe, NM 87505. *E-mail*—WJ894@aol.com.

CAREER: Writer. Worked as a dialogue writer for daytime television drama *The Guiding Light;* former playwright-in-residence at Humboldt University; guest playwright at Tennessee Williams Festival, Key West, FL, and Texas Playwright's Festival, Houston; Circle Repertory Theater, New York, NY, assistant to managing director, 1983.

MEMBER: PEN International, Dramatist Guild, Writers Guild of America.

AWARDS, HONORS: Winner, Southwest Regional Playwright's Competition, 1978, for *Governor's Mansion;* Blue Mountain Writer's Colony fellow.

WRITINGS:

Governor's Mansion (play), produced in Austin, TX, at Center State, 1978.
Mortally Fine (play), produced Off-Broadway at Chelsea Ensemble Theatre, November, 1985.
Lock the Doors (play), produced Off-Broadway at 29th Street Repertory Theater, 1990.
It Happened in Santa Fe (play), produced in Santa Fe, NM, at Railyard Performance Center, fall, 1994.
Any Kind of Luck (novel), Kensington (New York, NY), 2001.

Also author of screenplays *Where All the Rattlesnakes Are Born, Amor, December Story, White on Rice,* and *Dead Giveaway;* author, with Diane Ladd, of *Hot Water Biscuits, High Maintenance,* and *Last of the Bad Girls.* Author of plays *The Bird Girl of Menlo Park* produced Off-Broadway; *Mr. and Mrs. Coffee,* produced in Arcata, CA, at Humboldt University, *If You Loved Me,* produced in Key West, FL, at Tennessee Williams Playwright Festival; *Kitten and Princess* and *Two Men, Two Women, and a Bird.* Former contributing editor to *Interview* and *Flying Colors.*

WORK IN PROGRESS: Completing a second novel, *Faded Love,* expected 2003.

SIDELIGHTS: William Jack Sibley has done all kinds of writing, including dialogue for *The Guiding Light,* plays, screenplays, and a novel; two of his plays, *Lock the Doors* and *The Bird Girl of Menlo Park,* have been produced Off-Broadway. After working for eight years in New York City, the native Texan now divides his time between Los Angeles and San Antonio. His debut novel, *Any Kind of Luck,* draws upon his experience of returning to his tiny Texas hometown with his male lover.

In a review for *Backstage,* Michael Sommers reported on the 29th Street Repertory Theater's 1990 production of *Lock the Doors.* The play was part of the third annual "New Voices in the American Theater" festival. Sommers described *Lock the Doors* as a comic play-within-a-play that shows the backstage actions of cast and crew when threatened by a crazed killer. The critic regretted that Sibley put in a few too many plot twists, which he felt "eventually snarl into exasperation," but enjoyed the funny, if mean, scene in which the director coaches the female understudy while she struggles with the knife-wielding killer.

Sibley's novel *Any Kind of Luck* is also a comic piece. It takes its cues from the author's own Texas homecoming after having become accustomed to the freedom and sophistication of Manhattan. The central characters in *Any Kind of Luck* include the returning Clu and his lover, Chris. Clu has been working as an actor, director, and hand model, but now must go home to help his ailing mother, Bettie Jean. He is immediately immersed in a variety of family problems, including Bettie Jean's engagement to a clergyman and resuming contact with his redneck brother and usually pregnant sister. Clu is repeatedly pressed to defend his lifestyle to townsfolk, but he also renews some ties with family and friends. Meanwhile, he becomes the director for the local production of *Agamemnon Ya'll: A Country and Western Musical,* and Chris is befriended by a handsome young resident.

A reviewer for *Publishers Weekly* warned that *Any Kind of Luck* is akin to much of contemporary gay fiction, calling it "giddy, clichéd fluff." Within that context, the critic attended to the strengths of Sibley's offering to the genre, calling it a "light, humorous beach book shot through with campy one-liners and the sweet syrup of happy endings." Noting that Sibley has given Clu an excess of angry "gay-rights soapbox" speeches, the reviewer judged that the storyline

"recovers gracefully" when it focuses on the relationship between Chris and Clu and their inclination to return to New York City.

BIOGRAPHICAL AND CRITICAL SOURCES:

PERIODICALS

Backstage, August 3, 1990, Michael Sommers, "New Voices in American Theatre," p. 40.
Publishers Weekly, July 30, 2001, review of *Any Kind of Luck,* p. 63.

OTHER

William Jack Sibley Home Page, http://hometown.aol.com/wjsibley/index.html (December 4, 2002).

*   *   *

SISTER WENDY
  See BECKETT, Wendy

*   *   *

SIVULKA, Juliann 1950-

PERSONAL: Born December 28, 1950, in St. Joseph, MI; daughter of John and Julia Sivulka. *Education:* Attended University of Michigan, 1969-75; Michigan State University, B.A., 1975; Academy of Art College, San Francisco, CA, B.F.A., 1989, M.F.A., 1995; Bowling Green State University, M.A., 1997, Ph.D., 2000.

ADDRESSES: Home—2502 Monroe St., Columbia, SC 29205. *Office*—College of Mass Communications and Information Studies, University of South Carolina, Carolina Coliseum, Columbia, SC 29208; fax: 803-777-4103. *E-mail*—juliann.sivulka@usc.jour.sc.edu.

CAREER: Worked for Nurseryman's Exchange, Inc., and Pacific Mutual, both San Francisco, CA, 1975-82; Hotel Information Systems, Concord, CA, marketing communications manager, 1982-84; Academy of Art College, San Francisco, CA, instructor in advertising,

1984-96; Bowling Green State University, Bowling Green, OH, instructor in marketing, 1997-99, instructor in popular culture, 1999-2000; University of South Carolina, Columbia, assistant professor of mass communication and information studies, 2000—. ProMark, Inc., founder and president, 1984-90; Borland International, marketing communications manager, 1990-91; Downtown Business Association, Bowling Green, intern, 1999. Fulbright lecturer at University of Tokyo and Japan Women's University, 2001-02; guest lecturer at schools, including Josai International University, Doshisha University, Tohoku University, University of Louisiana, Queen's University, Kingston, Ontario, Canada, and St. Mary's College, San Rafael, CA. Appeared in television documentaries, including *Sell and Spin: A History of Advertising,* History Channel, 1999; and *American Classics,* History Channel, 2001; guest on other media programs, including *Carolina Minute,* National Public Radio.

MEMBER: American Studies Association, Popular Culture Association, Association of Educators in Journalism and Mass Communication, Association of Historical Research in Marketing, Fulbright Alumni Association.

AWARDS, HONORS: Margaret Storrs Grierson scholar-in-residence fellow, Sophia Smith Collection and Smith College Archives, 2001.

WRITINGS:

Soap, Sex, and Cigarettes: A Cultural History of American Advertising, Wadsworth Group (Belmont, CA), 1998.
Stronger than Dirt: A Cultural History of Advertising Personal Hygiene in America, 1875 to 1940, Humanity Books (Amherst, NY), 2001.

Contributor to books, including *Sex in Advertising,* edited by Jacques Lambaise and Tom Reichert, Erlbaum (New Jersey), 2002. Contributor to periodicals, including *Journal of American Culture.*

Author's writings have been published in Chinese, Russian, and Greek.

WORK IN PROGRESS: A bilingual handbook on American culture, for International Language Laboratory, Tokyo, Japan, and local authorities of Nagasaki prefecture, Japan; research for a book on gender and consumption from a historical perspective.

SIDELIGHTS: Juliann Sivulka told *CA*: "I grew up in the small town of St. Joseph, Michigan. After graduation from Michigan State University in 1975 with a bachelor's degree in marketing, I moved to San Francisco rather than endure another Midwest winter.

"While working in various marketing positions, I completed a second bachelor's degree in advertising, which opened up new opportunities for me in the field of marketing communications. I worked as a marketing communications manager and, for six years, I owned my own business. I provided marketing, advertising, and communications consulting services to diverse clients. At the same time I taught advertising and marketing courses part-time. From 1990-91 I returned to the corporate world, working as a marketing communications manager for Borland International, yet I still continued to teach a course in advertising history.

"In my forties, I left the corporate world to pursue a full-time career in higher education. I also decided to write a book. I then went out and bought ten books on how to write a book, studying everything from how to write a book proposal and marketing your manuscript to writing techniques and strategies to overcoming writer's block. It worked. I published *Soap, Sex, and Cigarettes: A Cultural History of American Advertising*, positioning the book as a supplementary text for both the academic market as well as the trade. I so enjoyed the process of research, writing, and developing the book manuscript that I was encouraged to go on for my doctorate.

"My primary motivation for writing is the joy of research and discovery. It is encouraging people to realize that mundane, everyday objects deserve serious study. As a cultural historian, I bring an interdisciplinary approach to my studies. With professional experience and a doctoral degree in American studies, I am prepared to move beyond the narrow confines of compartmentalized disciplines and draw on the fields of history, English, anthropology, sociology, and communications, as well as popular culture studies.

"When I wrote *Soap, Sex, and Cigarettes* I was influenced by my students. I taught a course titled 'History of American Advertising' for more than ten years in San Francisco. I would show my students slides, tell anecdotes, and display artifacts. When I'd talk to my students, they'd often say, 'How could we be so stupid as to believe this advertising?' I realized you could not teach this topic without teaching the cultural context of the time. Thus I started distributing handouts each with, with images of the ads, brief history of the period, notes on major agencies, and discussion of the art styles. My students than said I should write a book. My colleagues said I should write a book. The chair of the advertising department said the same. And so I did.

"My second book, *Stronger than Dirt: A Cultural History of Advertising Personal Hygiene in America, 1875 to 1940,* came from my first book. When I was writing the chapter on the 1920s, I found myself fascinated. It was a decade obsessed with bodily hygiene, and in the new liberated era, ad-makers dared to mention the unmentionable. Ads appeared for products like deodorant, sanitary napkins, mouthwash, among others. Bathing and washing hands and taking a daily bath became the norm. I set out to tell the story of how soap was transformed from a luxury to a necessity.

"In my writing process, I bring an experiential, experimental, and interpretive approach to my work. I start out with an overall research question. Then I collect information, artifacts, and background information from both primary and secondary sources. I go through an exhaustive collection process. Over the course of the project, I also become a collector of advertising history. I now am the owner of thirty bars of soap, more than 2,000 ad tear-sheets, 1,000 slides, and two dozen detergent boxes from the 1890s to the 1940s.

"Then the material shapes the narrative. What I find tells the story. What makes the writing really interesting is the curious anecdotes about products we take for granted in everyday life. For example, what did people use before toilet paper was invented? Or there are the ads for La Perle Obesity Soap Company, which promised 'a perfectly formed woman to order' by taking ten pounds of fat off any part of the body.

"My books go through three or four drafts. I approach writing like an artist. First I put my ideas into thumbnail sketches, outlining chapter ideas on index cards. Next I sort out the research material into boxes by chapter. From this material I develop a chapter-by-chapter outline in narrative form, writing one or two pages per chapter. On the outline, I note the additional

research material needed and obtain the material. I then write a rough draft and again note the additional research material needed to support the concepts. After I have completed my research and incorporated the new material, I refine the draft two or three times. Finally I give it to colleagues for review and incorporate their comments into a final draft. How long does it take me to write a book? The collection process takes two or three years, the writing another two years.

"My writing is inspired by an interest in gender, material culture—that is, objects of our everyday life, and how changes in consumption represent larger cultural shifts.

"Cultural shifts did not evolve at a steady, predictable rate, but rather at an uneven one with new developments interacting in complex ways and exhibiting many ambiguities and contradictions. Some of these ambiguities and contradictions of American society were expressed in objects of everyday American life. Even an everyday object such as soap embodied many of the central issues that occupied American society at the turn of the twentieth century: issues of power and power relations, the distribution of wealth and resources, gender roles and expectations, and enforcement of appropriate beliefs and behaviors, as well as continuity and change. Cleanliness had become an indicator that some individuals were morally superior, of better character, or more civilized than others. It also served to differentiate larger numbers of Americans, especially as society increasingly became more middle class and white collar. Gender was also a vital part of the production of cleanliness, particularly since cleanliness came to be modeled as women's role.

"In any case, consumption choices simply cannot be understood without considering the cultural context. Culture is the lens through which people view the world of goods and which determines the overall priorities and meanings people attach to activities and products. In particular, women's continuous association with consumption calls attention to the fact that important evidence of changes in consumer behaviors and attitudes occurring throughout the twentieth century is likely to be found in sources relating to women's everyday lives. And perhaps this is most notable in materials associated with popular culture. Those sources need to be examined more closely by all researchers who are interested in the role of consumption in American life."

BIOGRAPHICAL AND CRITICAL SOURCES:

PERIODICALS

Choice, May, 2002, J. Sochren, review of *Stronger than Dirt: A Cultural History of Advertising Personal Hygiene in America, 1875-1940,* p. 1650.

Library Journal, August, 2001, Lawrence R. Maxted, review of *Stronger than Dirt,* p. 133.

Publishers Weekly, August 13, 2001, review of *Stronger than Dirt,* p. 247.

* * *

SKOUEN, Arne 1913-

PERSONAL: Born 1913, in Oslo, Norway; married Kari Oksnevad. *Education:* Attended University of Oslo.

ADDRESSES: Agent—International Creative Management, 40 West 57th St., New York, NY 10019.

CAREER: Journalist, author, screenwriter, and film director. Norwegian Embassy, press attaché in the United States, 1945-46; *Verdens Gang Oslo,* member of editorial staff, beginning 1947. Founder of a film production company.

AWARDS, HONORS: Academy Award nomination, best foreign picture, Academy of Motion Picture Arts and Sciences, for *Ni liv.*

WRITINGS:

SCREENPLAYS; ALSO DIRECTOR

Gategutter (title means "Street Urchins"), 1949, published by Aschehoug (Oslo, Norway), 1948.

Nødlanding (title means "Emergency Landing"), 1952.

Cirkus Fandango (title means "Circus Fandango"), 1954, published as *Cirkus Fandango: En filmfortelling,* Aschehoug (Oslo, Norway), 1953.

Det brenner i natt! (title means "Burning Nigh"), 1955.

Barn av solen (title means "Children of the Sun"), 1955.

Ni liv (title means "Nine Lives"), 1957, broadcast as an episode of the television series *Omnibus,* NBC-TV, 1958.

Pastor Jarman kommer hjem (title means "The Return of Pastor Jarmann"), 1958.

Herren og hans tjenere (title means "The Master and His Servants"), 1959.

Omringet (title means "Surrounded"), 1960.

Bussen (title means "The Bus"), 1961.

Kalde spor (title means "Cold Tracks"), 1962.

Om Tilla (title means "About Tilla"), 1963.

Pappa tar gull (title means "Daddy's Success"), 1964.

Vaktpostene (title means "The Guards"), 1965.

Reisen til havet (title means "A Journey to the Sea"), 1966.

Musikanter (title means "Musicians"), 1967.

An-Magritt, 1969.

OTHER

Ansikt til ansikt (play), produced in Oslo, Norway, at Søilen Teater, 1939.

Barn av solen (play; title means "Children of the Sun"; produced in Oslo, Norway, at Nye Teater, 1941), published as *Barn av solen: Et sommerdøgn i 10 billeder,* Aschehoug (Oslo, Norway), 1941.

Seks og seksti skinnbrev fra Oslo, G. Lindström (Stockholm, Sweden), 1943, reprinted, 1994.

Gullstolen (play; produced in Oslo, Norway, at Nye Teater, 1943), published as *Gullstolen: Komedie i 6 billeder,* Aschehoug (Oslo, Norway), 1943.

Fest i Port des Galets, Aschehoug (Oslo, Norway), 1947, translation by Joran Birkeland published as *Stokers' Mess,* Knopf (New York, NY), 1948.

Leirplassen (play; produced in Norway, at Nationaltheatret, 1950), published as *Leirplassen: Skuespill i 2 akter,* Aschehoug (Oslo, Norway), 1950.

Pappa tar gull (play; produced in Oslo, Norway, at Nye Theater, 1964), published by Aschehoug (Oslo, Norway), 1962, published as *Pappa tar gull: Et lystspill,* 1963.

Pappas dans, Aschehoug (Oslo, Norway), 1964.

Rettferd for de handicappede: Et foreldresynspunkt på velferdsstat og samfunnsmoral, Aschehoug (Oslo, Norway), 1966.

Pappa blir voksen, Aschehoug (Oslo, Norway), 1966.

Bare om barn, Aschehoug (Oslo, Norway), 1969.

De veldedige politikerne: Nye synspunkter, Aschehoug (Oslo, Norway), 1969.

Tusen kyss fra Bagdad (play; produced in Oslo, Norway, at Nye Teater, 1970), published as *Tusen kyss fra Bagdad: Et svart lystspill,* Aschehoug (Oslo, Norway), 1970.

Alle elsket enken, Aschehoug (Oslo, Norway), 1970.

Sir Williams bohémer, Aschehoug (Oslo, Norway), 1972.

Ytringer (collected newspaper columns), Gyldendal (Oslo, Norway), 1973.

Nye ytringer (collected newspaper columns), Gyldendal (Oslo, Norway), 1976.

Ballerina (play; produced in Norway at Nationaltheatret, 1976; produced in England, Canada, the United States, New Zealand, and elsewhere), published as *Ballerina: Skuespill i 2 akter,* Gyldendal (Oslo, Norway), 1976, translation by Skouen published as *Ballerina: A Play,* Samuel French (New York, NY), 1985.

(Editor) Hans Heiberg, *Mest om teater: Artikler, gjennom 40 år; Til forfatterens 75-årsdag 28. januar 1979,* Aschehoug (Oslo, Norway), 1979.

Flere ytringer, Gyldendal (Oslo, Norway), 1980.

(With Sigrid Undset) *Sigrid Undset skriver hjem: En vandring gjennom emigrantårene i Amerika* (correspondence), Aschehoug (Oslo, Norway), 1982.

Bess (play; produced in Norway, at Nationaltheatret, 1983), published as *Bess: Et skuespill i to akter,* Aschehoug (Oslo, Norway), 1983, translation published by Samuel French (London, England), 1985, Theatre Communication Group (New York, NY), 1988.

Roller: Tre filmer og to skuespill (plays and screenplays; contains *Gategutter, Det brenner i natt, Kalde spor, Ballerina,* and *Bess*), Aschehoug (Oslo, Norway), 1993.

En journalists erindringer, Aschehoug (Oslo, Norway), 1996.

Other writings include *Naaskulde Ruth sett mig.* Columnist for newspaper *Dagbladet.*

BIOGRAPHICAL AND CRITICAL SOURCES:

BOOKS

Det forste halvsekel: Bilder fra norsk barndom, Gyldendal (Oslo, Norway), 1974.

PERIODICALS

Filmtidsskrift, Volume 8, number 2, 1990, Gunnar Iversen, "Oslo—apen by: Arne Skouens Gategutter og neorealismen," pp. 32-37; Volume 9, number 3, 1991, Gunnar Iversen, "En ekspresjonistisk idefilm: Om Arne Skouens *Det brennet i natt!,*" pp. 28-34; Volume 1, number 43, 1993, Gunnar Iversen, "Om Arne Skouens film *Ni liv: En indre kamp,*" pp. 46-51.

Samtiden, Volume 77, 1968, Arne Skouen, "'An-Magritt' som film-drama," pp. 569-579.

Vinduet, Volume 33, number 1, Erna Ofstad and Harald Ofstad, "Samspillet mellem svake identiteter: *Ballerinas* bidrag til synet pa autentiske barn," pp. 65-71.

*   *   *

SLOAN, Bill
See SLOAN, William E., III

*   *   *

SLOAN, William E., III 1935-
(Bill Sloan)

PERSONAL: Born September 8, 1935, in Dallas, TX; son of William E. (a service manager) and Linnie (Fisher) Sloan; married Jane Everett (divorced, June, 1975); married Lana Henderson, January 30, 1976; children: Sheri, Suzanne. *Ethnicity:* "Scotch-Irish." *Education:* University of North Texas, Dallas, TX, B.A., 1957. *Politics:* Independent. *Religion:* Methodist. *Hobbies and other interests:* Travel, gardening, painting, classic cars.

ADDRESSES: Home—3603 Urban Ave., Dallas, TX 75227. *Agent*—Jim Donovan, Jim Donovan Literary, 4515 Prentice St., Suite 109, Dallas, TX 75206. *E-mail*—bsloan@flash.net.

CAREER: Dallas Times Herald, Dallas, TX, feature writer, journalist, and investigative reporter, 1961-68, 1971-72; chief writer, *National Enquirer,* 1968-70; Southern Methodist University, adjunct professor of journalism, 1981-98.

AWARDS, HONORS: Pulitzer Prize nominee, 1971; Sweepstakes Award, Texas Associated Press Managing Editors, 1971.

WRITINGS:

The Other Assassin, Tudor Publishing (New York, NY), 1989.

(With Jean Hill) *JFK: The Last Dissenting Witness,* Pelican Publishing (Gretna, LA), 1992.

JFK: Breaking the Silence, Taylor Publishing (Dallas, TX), 1993.

The Mafia Candidate, SPI Books (New York, NY), 1993.

(With Horace Logan) *Elvis, Hank, and Me,* St. Martin's (New York, NY), 1998.

I Watched a Wild Hog Eat My Baby, Prometheus Press (Amherst, NY), 2001.

Given up for Dead: America's Heroic Stand and Unwarranted Surrender at Wake Island, Bantam (New York, NY), 2003.

Former editor, *Country Rambler* magazine.

SIDELIGHTS: Bill Sloan was a young reporter for the *Dallas Times Herald* the day president John F. Kennedy was assassinated a few blocks away from his office. As Sloan told *CA,* "Later, I covered the aftermath of the case intensively for years, which inspired me to write three books on the subject." Sloan co-authored *JFK: The Last Dissenting Witness,* with Jean Hill, the famous "lady in red" who was standing only fifteen feet away from the presidential car when the president was shot. She testified and insisted through years of discouragement, disbelief, and distortion on the part of the official investigation that she saw an unidentified man firing from the grassy knoll, and later a person who looked exactly like Jack Ruby running toward that man. Hill, in her own words, tells how she decided not to go to Washington to testify in front of the Warren Commission, having been intimidated by frequent phone threats, the sabotage of her car, and an alarming move against one of her children. A reviewer for *Publishers Weekly* said, "Her tale is often engaging, sometimes infuriating; the feisty schoolteacher emerges as something of a folk heroine."

Sloan has published many of the stories he has collected in the thirty years since the assassination as *JFK: Breaking the Silence.* He focuses primarily on lesser-known characters, such as deaf and dumb Ed Hoffman, who saw a man shoot from the grassy knoll but could not communicate what he witnessed. The next chapter is the story of Jim Tagrue, who was nicked by a splinter sent flying by a bullet that the Warren Commission concluded did not exist, and the Newmans, who heard shots from behind them on the knoll and were never asked about them. A *Publishers Weekly* contributor wrote that "Sloan offers food for thought."

Elvis, Hank, and Me is the story of the *Louisiana Hayride,* a CBS radio network show out of Shreveport, Louisiana, that was springboard for characters in the country-music business in the late 1950s hoping to make the move to Nashville or Los Angeles. Kitty Wells, Hank Williams, Johnny Cash, and Webb Pierce, as well as Elvis himself, "took a ride on the *Hayride.*" On Elvis's first visit to the *Hayride* in 1954, Logan lent a dramatic touch to proceedings by sporting about the stage in a ten-gallon hat and six-shooters. The emcee, Ray Bartlett, spiced his act with somersaults and back flips. The *Hayride* became the foundation of Elvis's early rise to stardom. A *Publishers Weekly* contributor said the book "reads like the best country music songs, filled with just the right combination of sorrow and swing."

From 1968 to 1970 Sloan was the chief writer for the *National Inquirer.* In his book *I Watched a Wild Hog Eat My Baby,* he reviews the history of the *Enquirer* from mainstream publication in the early 1960s to its current tabloid format. Citing several tabloid headlines, Sloan asserts his belief that the line between mainstream and tabloid journalism is blurred. His approach is to trace the history of the supermarket papers by profiling both the men who created and ran them and the journalists who did the legwork and wrote the stories. "My hope," Sloan said in *Publishers Weekly,* "is that it will help Americans—even those who never bought a supermarket tabloid—to understand what vast impact these papers have had on today's mainstream media, our approach to 'news' and our entire population."

The tabloids got their start in the United States in 1952, when Generoso Pope, Jr., bought the struggling *New York Enquirer.* Pope renamed the paper the *National Inquirer* and filled it with crime stories so lurid that many distributors refused to carry it. The paper's circulation grew to 250,000 despite the distributors, but Pope wanted more. In the late 1960s he decided to "clean up" the paper so it would be more suitable for sale at supermarket checkout counters. As Sloan relates, Pope had an unlikely ally in Jackie Kennedy who, in 1968, married Greek shipping magnate Aristotle Onassis, creating an atmosphere that promoted celebrity gossip. "As Sloan leads readers along the curve that took tabloids from outrageous silliness to slick cynicism, it's hard not to yearn for the long-gone days when space aliens and abominable snow-babies filled tabloids' covers. By the time readers arrive in the '90's, all six major tabloids are owned by a single conglomerate, and their once rich universe of far-fetched themes and subjects has been narrowed to almost nothing but celebrity diets and celebrity weddings," wrote Tom Maurstad, in the *Dallas Morning News.*

BIOGRAPHICAL AND CRITICAL SOURCES:

PERIODICALS

Australian, November 1, 2001, Kerrie Murphy, review of *I Watched a Wild Hog Eat My Baby,* p. M14.
Booklist, June 1, 1998, Mike Tribby, review of *Elvis, Hank, and Me,* p. 211; April 1, 2001, Ilene Cooper, review of *I Watched a Wild Hog Eat My Baby,* p. 1430.
Buffalo News, March 18, 2001, Lee Coppola, review of *I Watched a Wild Hog Eat My Baby,* p. F6.
Dallas Morning News, April 29, 2001, Tom Maurstad, review of *I Watched a Wild Hog Eat My Baby,* p. 12C.
Library Journal, February 1, 2001, Susan M. Colowick, review of *I Watched a Wild Hog Eat My Baby,* p. 104.
Palm Beach Post, June 17, 2001, Scott Eyman, review of *I Watched a Wild Hog Eat My Baby,* p. 8J.
Publishers Weekly, March 16, 1992, review of *JFK: The Last Dissenting Witness,* p. 71; August 9, 1993, review of *JFK: Breaking the Silence,* p. 428; March 25, 1998, review of *Elvis, Hank, and Me,* p. 21; January 22, 2001, review of *I Watched a Wild Hog Eat My Baby,* p. 211; February 12, 2001, review of *I Watched a Wild Hog Eat My Baby,* p. 198.
Record (Bergen County, NJ), Bill Ervolino, review of *I Watched a Wild Hog Eat My Baby,* p. E3. DOGG,

SNOOP DOGGY DOGG 1972-
(Calvin Broadus, Coravar Varnado)

PERSONAL: Born Calvin Broadus (some sources say Cordavar Varnado), October 20, 1972, in Long Beach, CA; son of Vernell Varnado (a singer and postal worker) and Beverly Tate; married Shantay Taylor, 1997; children: Spanky (son), ChordT (daughter).

CAREER: Actor and musician, 1990—. Film appearances include *Murder Was the Case,* 1994; contributor to film soundtracks as follows: *Deep Cover* (soundtrack), Death Row, 1992; *Dr. Dre: The Chronic,* Death Row, 1992; *Snoop Doggy Dogg: Doggystyle,* Death Row, 1993; *Above the Rim* (soundtrack), Death Row, 1993; *Murder Was the Case* (soundtrack), Death Row, 1996; *Tha Dogg Pound: Dogg Food,* Death Row 1995; *One Million Strong,* Death Row, 1995; *2Pac: All Eyez on Me,* Death Row, 1996; *Snoop Doggy Dogg: Tha Doggfather,* Death Row, 1996; *Christmas on Death Row,* Death Row, 1996; *Gridlock'd* (soundtrack), Death Row, 1997; *The Lady of Rage: Necessary Roughness,* Death Row, 1998; *Men in Black* (soundtrack), Death Row, 1997; *Gang Related* (soundtrack), Death Row 1997; *Snoop Dogg: Smokefest Underground,* Death Row, 1998; *Snoop Dogg: Da Game Is to Be Sold, Not to Be Told,* No Limits, 1998; *Snoop Dogg: No Limit Top Dogg,* No Limits, 1999; *Snoop Dogg Presents Tha Eastsidaz,* No Limits, 2000; *Snoop Dogg: Dead Man Walking,* No Limits, 2000; *Doggy's Angels: Pleezbaleevit,* No Limits, 2000; *Snoop Dogg: Tha Last Meal,* No Limits, 2000.

AWARDS, HONORS: Platinum record, 1994 for *Doggystyle,* 1994; MTV Video Music Award for best rap video, 1994, for "Doggy Dogg World"; voted best rapper in Rolling Stone readers' and critics' polls, 1994.

WRITINGS:

(With David Seay) *The Doggfather: The Times, Trials, and Hardcore Truths of Snoop Dogg,* Morrow/ HarperCollins (New York, NY), 1999.

SIDELIGHTS: As the symbol of '90s gangsta rap, Snoop Doggy Dogg blended the lines between reality and fiction. Introduced to the world through Dr. Dre's landmark *The Chronic,* Snoop Dogg quickly became the most famous star in rap, partially because of his drawled, laconic rhyming and partially because the violence that his lyrics portrayed seemed real, especially after he was arrested on charges of being a murder accomplice. The arrest certainly strengthened his myth, and it helped his debut album, *Doggystyle,* become the first debut album to enter the charts at number one. But in the long run, it hurt his career. Dogg had to fight charges throughout 1994 and 1995, and while he was eventually cleared, it hurt his momentum. The *Doggfather,* his second album, wasn't released until November of 1996, and by that time, pop and hip-hop had burned itself out on gangsta-rap. *The Doggfather* sold half as well as its predecessor, so while Snoop would remain a star, he no longer had the influence he had just two years before.

Nicknamed "Snoop" by his mother because he looked like Snoopy, the cartoon character, Dogg was born Calvin Broadus and raised in Long Beach, California, where he excelled in sports and in school. But he frequently ran into trouble with the law. Not long after his high school graduation with above average grades and basketball scholarship offers, he was arrested for possession of cocaine, beginning a period of three years where he was often imprisoned. He found an escape from a life of crime through music. Dogg began recording homemade tapes with his friend Warren G, who happened to be the stepbrother of N.W.A.'s Dr. Dre. Warren G gave a tape to Dre, who was immediately impressed with Snoop's style and began collaborating with the rapper.

When Dr. Dre decided to make his tentative first stab at a solo career in 1992 with the theme song for the film *Deep Cover,* he had Dogg rap with him. "Deep Cover" started a buzz about Dogg that escalated into full-fledged mania when Dr. Dre released his debut album, *The Chronic,* on Death Row Records late in 1992. Dogg rapped on *The Chronic* as much as Dr. Dre, and his drawled vocals were as important to the record's success as its P-Funk bass grooves. Dr. Dre's singles "Nuthin' but a 'G' Thang" and "Dre Day," which prominently featured Snoop, became Top-ten pop crossover hits in the spring of 1993, setting the stage for Snoop Doggy Dogg's much-anticipated debut album, *Doggystyle.* While he was recording the album with producer Dr. Dre in August, Dogg was arrested in connection with the drive-by-shooting death of Phil-

lip Woldermarian. According to the charges, the rapper's bodyguard, McKinley Lee shot Phillip Woldermarian as Snoop drove the vehicle; the rapper claimed it was self-defense, alleging that the victim was stalking Snoop. Following a performance at the MTV Music Awards in September 1993, he turned himself in to authorities.

After many delays, *Doggystyle* was finally released on Death Row in November of 1993, and it became the first debut album to enter the charts at number one. Despite reviews that claimed the album was a carbon copy of *The Chronic,* the Top-ten singles "What's My Name?" and "Gin & Juice" kept *Doggystyle* at the top of the charts during early 1994, as did the considerable controversy over Dogg's arrest and his lyrics, which were accused of being exceedingly violent and sexist. During an English tour in the spring of 1994, tabloids and a Tory minister pleaded for the government to kick the rapper out of the country, largely based on his arrest. Dogg exploited his impending trial by shooting a short film based on the Doggystyle song "Murder Was the Case," and releasing an accompanying soundtrack which debuted at number one in 1994. By that time, *Doggystyle* had gone quadruple platinum.

Dogg spent much of 1995 preparing for the case, which finally went to trial late in the year. In February of 1996, he was cleared of all charges and he began working on his second album, this time without Dr. Dre as producer. Nevertheless, when *The Doggfather* was finally released in November 1996, it bore all the evidence of a Dr. Dre-produced, G-funk record. The album was greeted with mixed reviews, and it initially sold well, but it failed to produce a hit along the lines of "What's My Name?" and "Gin & Juice." Part of the reason of the moderate success of *The Doggfather* was the decline of gangsta rap. 2pac Shakur, who had become a friend of Snoop Dogg during 1996, died weeks before the release of *The Doggfather,* Dr. Dre had left Death Row to his partner Suge Knight, who was indicted on racketeering charges by the end of 1996. Consequently, Dogg's second album got lost in the shuffle, stalling at sales of two million, which was disappointing for a superstar.

Perhaps sensing something was wrong, Dogg began to revamp his public image, moving away from his gangsta roots towards a calmer lyrical aesthetic. He also began making gestures toward the rock community, signing up to tour with Lollapalooza 1997 and talking about two separate collaborations with Beck and Marilyn Manson.

Following on the heels of his move to Master P's No Limit Records in Baton Rouge, Dogg decided to complete the move away from Death Row with by writing his autobiography. The book, told in the streetwise, laconic style of his rapping, enjoyed critical success. A critic from *Kirkus Reviews* praised the book and noted that "a surprisingly humanistic portrait of the rapper emerges: Dogg explains how his religion, a passion for honesty, and the fierce love of his mother and brothers sustained him from his childhood, an evocatively rendered portrait of tarnishing ghetto innocence." Ray Olson, writing in *Booklist* gave Dogg's autobiography high marks, calling it "absolutely vital for pop culture collections. But be careful: too much exposure to Dogg's ambience and 40-ouncers and blunts might replace Chablis and brie at one's social functions."

BIOGRAPHICAL AND CRITICAL SOURCES:

BOOKS

Billboard Illustrated Encyclopedia of Rock Stars, Billboard Books (New York, NY), 1998, p.302.
Encyclopedia of Rock Stars, DK Publishing (New York, NY), 1996, pp. 798-99.

PERIODICALS

Billboard, November 1, 1997, Bill Holland, "VA Promoter Sues Snoop & Co." p. 6; February 7, 1998, Chris Morris, "Snoop Sues Accounting Firms, Ex Staffer," p. 38.
Booklist, February 1, 2000, Ray Olson, review of *The Doggfather: The Times, Trials, and Hardcore Truths of Snoop Dogg,* p. 1003.
Entertainment Weekly, September 24, 1993, Nisid Hajari, "Gansta Rap,", p. 9; February 3, 1995, David Browne, movie review of *Murder Was the Case,* p. 62; January 23, 1998, David Browne, "MTV Party to Go 1998,", p. 61; July 17, 1998, p. 82; August 14, 1998, review of "Da Game Is to Be Sold, Not to Be Told," p. 80; May 14, 1999, Tom Sinclair, review of *The Doggfather: The Times, Trials, and Hardcore Truths of Snoop Dogg,* p. 74.
Interview, December, 1996, Eric Berman, interview with Snoop Dogg, p. 106-07; September, 1999, Dimitri Ehrlich, interview with Snoop Dogg, p. 138-44.
Jet, March 11, 1996, p. 21; February 2, 1998, "Rapper Snoop Doggy Dog Leaves Death Row Records; Fears For His Life," p. 15; May 3, 1999, p. 72.
Library Journal, January, 2000, Dan Bogey and Ray Olson, review of *The Doggfather: The Times, Trials, and Hardcore Truths of Snoop Dogg,* p. 116.
National Review, January 24, 1994, David Klinghoffer, "See No Evil," p. 73.
Newsweek, March 4, 1996, Allison Samuels, "Snoop Doggy Dogg Acquitted of Murder," p. 54; October 28, 1996, Allison Samuels, review of *The Doggfather,* p. 80; May 24, 1999, review of *No Limit Top Dogg,* p. 74.
New York Times Magazine, January 14, 1996, Lynn Hirschberg, "Does a Sugar Bear Bite? Suger Knight and His Posse," p. 24.
People Weekly, July 21, 1997, Amy Linden, *Men in Black—The Album,* p. 21.
Playboy, May, 1995, Nelson George, review of *Murder Was the Case,* p. 18.
Publishers Weekly, November 29, 1999, review of *The Doggfather: The Times, Trials, and Hardcore Truths of Snoop Dogg,* p. 61; December 13, 1999, review of *The Doggfather: The Times, Trials, and Hardcore Truths of Snoop Dogg,* p. 47.
Rolling Stone, January 27, 1994, review of *Doggystyle,* p. 51; April 4, 1996, Dave Wienga, "The Dogg Walks," p. 545; January 23, 1997, Kevin Powell, review of *The Doggfather,* p. 67; December 11, 1997, p. 80; August 20, 1998, p. 47; June 19, 1999, Kevin Powell, review of *No Limit Top Dogg,* p. 120.
Time, November 29, 1993, John Farley, sound recording review of *Doggystyle,* p. 73; November 25, 1996, John Farley, review of *The Doggfather,* p. 102; March 4, 1996, "Snoop Doggy Dogg Acquitted of Murder," p. 21; August 10, 1998, Christopher John Farley, "New Leash on Life: Rapper Snoop Dogg Is on the Comeback Trail, but at What Price," p. 84.
Variety, March 2, 1998, Leonard Klady, "Caught Up," p. 84.

OTHER

Wall of Sound, http://wallofsound.go.com/ (November 9, 1998)*

*   *   *

SOLNIT, Albert J(ay) 1919-2002

OBITUARY NOTICE—See index for *CA* sketch: Born August 26, 1919, in Los Angeles, CA; died after a car crash June 21, 2002, in Bethlehem, CT. Psychiatrist, psychoanalyst, educator, and author. Solnit was respected above all as a tireless advocate for children. As a child psychiatrist and psychoanalyst at the Child Study Center at Yale University, Solnit became increasingly aware that legal proceedings related to issues of family law often overlooked the interests of the very children they were intended to protect. He and his colleagues broke new ground in 1973 when they published *Beyond the Best Interests of the Child.* At a time when minors had little or no legal voice, the book stirred controversy with the suggestion that custody disputes should focus on children's needs rather than what was best for the parents or the courts. Solnit and his team followed up with *Before the Best Interests of the Child* and *In the Best Interests of the Child.* The trilogy has been cited in hundreds of court cases and credited with transforming family law across America. Solnit's other writings include a 1996 book, *The Best Interests of the Child: Least Detrimental Alternative,* the subtitle of which summarizes the author's convictions. He believed that child placement decisions should be made as expeditiously as possible, adoptive parents providing daily nurture should have priority over biological parents who provided none, and, in the event that termination of parental rights was determined to be necessary, the cases of children in foster care should be decided quickly to facilitate the process of permanent adoption. Solnit taught at Yale University for nearly forty years and directed the Child Study Center from 1966 to 1983. After formal retirement in 1990, he spent nearly ten years as a commissioner of the Connecticut Department of Mental Health and Addiction Services. He was active throughout his career in child advocacy organizations and regulatory bodies, as an advisor to academic research institutes, and as a trainer of future psychoanalysts.

OBITUARIES AND OTHER SOURCES:

PERIODICALS

Los Angeles Times, July 2, 2002, obituary by Elaine Woo, p. B11.
New York Times, June 27, 2002, obituary by Anahad O'Connor, p. C23.
Washington Post, June 29, 2002, p. B6.

*   *   *

SONIAT, Katherine (Thompson) 1942-

PERSONAL: Born January 11, 1942, in WA; daughter of Raymond Webb and Katherine Lenox Hayward Thompson; married Robert Upshur Soniat, 1964; children: Shelton, Ashton. *Education:* Newcomb College, B.A. (history), 1964; Tulane University, Ph.D. (English), 1983. *Hobbies and other interests:* Second Harvest Food Bank, Share Our Strength, outreach programs for communities and schools.

ADDRESSES: Home—300 Fincastle Dr., Blacksburg, VA 24060. *Office*—Virginia Polytechnic Institute and State University, English Department, Blacksburg, VA 24061-0112. *E-mail*—KSoniat@vt.edu.

CAREER: Poet. Hollins University, assistant professor of English, 1989-91; Virginia Polytechnic Institute and State University, Blacksburg, VA, associate professor of English, 1991—.

MEMBER: Poetry Society of America, Academy of American Poets, Associated Writing Programs, Wilderness Society.

AWARDS, HONORS: Camden (New Jersey) Poetry Award, Walt Whitman Center for Arts, 1984, for *Notes of Departure;* Prize for Poetry, Virginia Council for the Arts, 1989; Iowa Prize and Edwin Ford Piper Award, University of Iowa Press, both 1993, both for *A Shared Life;* several Ann Stanford Prizes, University of Southern California—Los Angeles, beginning 1996; Library of Virginia Prize finalist, 2001, for *Alluvial.*

WRITINGS:

Notes of Departure, Walt Whitman Center (Camden, NJ), 1984.
Cracking Eggs, University Press of Florida (Gainesville, FL), 1990.

A Shared Life, University of Iowa Press (Iowa City, IA), 1993.

Alluvial, Bucknell University Press (Lewisburg, PA), 2001.

Contributor of poetry to journals, including *Amicus, TriQuarterly, Southern Review,* and *Witness.*

WORK IN PROGRESS: *Ghost Laundry,* a poetry collection.

SIDELIGHTS: Katherine Soniat's *Notes of Departure* is filled with images of Soniat's childhood, which, a *Booklist* reviewer wrote, are "pointed to and made possible by the complex sensibility these poems record." The reviewer praised Soniat's "freshness," and noted that the collection is "quite special and un-like what we've seen before." In *Choice,* B. Almon remarked that the poems display "simple excellence, without schools or isms," and that the book "deserves a place on everybody's shelf." Anne C. Bromley wrote in *Prairie Schooner* that the book marks "the welcome debut of a new voice in American poetry." The collection won the Camden Poetry Award in 1984.

In *A Shared Life,* which won the Edwin Ford Piper Award in 1993, Soniat explores relationships, longing, and desire. Laurel Blossom wrote in *American Book Review,* "One poem follows another, crafted, musical, the eye and ear slide over one, then the next one. . . . This is a well-written book." A *Library Journal* reviewer wrote that the poems show Soniat's "willing-ness to present and engage in some of the complexi-ties and difficulties that come with the territory" of the subjects Soniat explores.

Alluvial, Soniat's 2001 poetry collection, is set in the Chesapeake Bay, the largest estuary in the world, and in Louisiana, the most tributaried land in the United States. According to the *Bucknell University Press Web site,* the collection "charts the course of individual and collective histories influenced by the rich alluvium of culture and geography, ecology and autobiography." In *American Poet,* David St. John noted that the poems "reflect how lives lived by water articulate both intimate and historically charged fluctuations."

Soniat told *CA:* "I am most interested in how place and region intersect with private lives and history, forming a synchronicity of lasting value. This territory offers the rich complexity where the mystic and arche-typed form beside the personal."

BIOGRAPHICAL AND CRITICAL SOURCES:

PERIODICALS

American Book Review, March, 1995, Laurel Blossom, "Less Is More," p. 25.

American Poet, spring, 2001, David St. John, review of *Alluvial,* p. 60.

Booklist, April 1, 1986, Joseph Parisi, review of *Notes of Departure,* p. 1112.

Choice, September, 1986, B. Almon, review of *Notes of Departure,* p. 125.

Library Journal, January, 1994, Jessica Grim, review of *A Shared Life,* pp. 119-120.

Prairie Schooner, winter, 1986, Anne C. Bromley, review of *Notes of Departure,* p. 114.

Southern Review, autumn, 1994, David Kirby, "Is There a Southern Poetry?," p. 869.

OTHER

Bucknell University Press Web site, http://www.departments.bucknell.edu/univ_press/ (September 16, 2001).

*   *   *

STAINCLIFFE, Cath 1956-

PERSONAL: Born 1956, in Leeds, England; daughter of M. J. Cullen and Evelyn Ryan; adopted by David (a businessman) and Margarett (a homemaker; maiden name, Lund) Staincliffe; partner of Tim Preston (an arts worker); children: three. *Ethnicity:* "Irish by birth." *Education:* Birmingham University, degree in Drama and Theatre Arts, 1978. *Hobbies and other interests:* Reading crime fiction and gardening.

ADDRESSES: *Agent*—c/o Author Mail, Allison & Busby Ltd., Suite 111, Bon Marche Centre, 241-251 Ferndale Rd., Brixton, London SW9 8BJ, England. *E-mail*—all@allisonbusby.co.uk.

CAREER: Community artist and novelist, 1980—. Founding member of Murder Squad, a crime fiction writers group that promotes members' books and the genre through readings, workshops, residencies, and other projects.

MEMBER: Crime Writers Association, Mystery Women.

WRITINGS:

Looking for Trouble (mystery novel), Crocus Books (Winona, MN), 1994.
Go Not Gently (mystery novel), Headline (London, England), 1997.
Dead Wrong (mystery novel), Headline (London, England), 1998.
Stone Cold Red Hot (mystery novel), Allison & Busby (London, England), 2001.
Towers of Silence (mystery novel), Allison & Busby (London, England), 2002.
Trio (novel), Severn House (London, England), 2002.

Poetry and short stories included in anthologies.

ADAPTATIONS: Looking for Trouble was serialized on *Woman's Hour,* BBC Radio 4.

WORK IN PROGRESS: Adapting crime thriller *Cry Me a River* for Granada Television; another novel featuring Sal Kilkenny, expected in 2003.

SIDELIGHTS: Cath Staincliffe has created a series of mystery novels following the adventures of Sal Kilkenny, a single mother turned private eye living in the city of Manchester, England. Some of Sal's experiences are based on Staincliffe's own life. Like her character, the author knows the challenge of balancing a career with raising children. The mother of three, she has combined childcare with work as a freelance community artist. Having earned a drama and theater degree from Birmingham University, Staincliffe had almost stopped writing when her first maternity leave gave her the opportunity to return to creating fiction and poetry. Staincliffe is also familiar with the streets of Manchester, which feature prominently in Sal's work. Having moved to Manchester for a job, Staincliffe has turned the large northern city into a multi-faceted setting for her fiction.

The first "Sal Kilkenny" novel is *Looking for Trouble,* in which Staincliffe introduces the detective and her battle to manage both personal and professional troubles. Accustomed to following adulterous hus-

bands, she takes on a more difficult and dangerous case when asked to find a runaway teen. The assignment takes her into wealthy homes in the suburbs where she finds evidence of pederasty, as well as into squatters' holes where drugs and crime abound. Two murders prove that Sal is putting herself and her daughter in danger's way.

Reviewing the book for its interest to young adult readers, Patricia Peacock commented in *School Librarian* that *Looking for Trouble* contained strong language and realistic characters. She described Manchester as a dynamic part of the novel and noted that a local arts council had supported Staincliffe's work on the book. Calling Sal a "tough, compassionate, determined and yet vulnerable" character, Peacock said that she was eager to read the further adventures of this thoroughly contemporary protagonist.

Two cases are central to the action in the second "Sal Kilkenny" novel, *Go Not Gently.* Hired by Jimmy Achebe to confirm that his wife is having an affair, Sal finds that her client has since become a widower and that her case now involves a possible murder. At the same time, Sal is looking into the Alzheimer's diagnosis of an elderly woman's friend. Hoping to simply give client Agnes Donlan a better understanding of the situation, she discovers that there may in fact be criminal action involved in the woman's hospitalization.

The next installment in the series, *Dead Wrong,* is also dominated by two cases. Sal is working for divorcee Debbie Gosforth in pursuit of a stalker and helping teen Luke Wallace determine if he murdered a friend during an evening blacked out by Ecstasy-and-alcohol amnesia. During these investigations, an IRA bomb explodes in Manchester's Arndale Center shopping district, introducing a real-life event into the mystery's plot.

Stone Cold Red Hot is the fourth "Sal Kilkenny" novel, in which Sal and her daughter still reside with another single parent and his child. The arrangement allows Sal to take a job for the Neighborhood Nuisance Unit, spending nights videotaping evidence of racial tension in a low-income housing development. Arson erupts when fascist youths terrorize a Muslim family from Somalia. Another case has Sal searching for Jennifer Pickering, a woman who was disinherited by her family twenty years earlier when she was pregnant and unwed. Pickering's brother wants to find her, despite the disapproval of their mother, who is gravely ill.

The novel earned good reviews for its deft writing and appealing protagonist. Writing for *Library Journal*, Rex Klett advised that *Stone Cold Red Hot* was "Traditional fare, ably handled and strongly recommended." A *Publishers Weekly* critic enjoyed Sal and the way her home life was threaded throughout the book. Staincliffe was described as being an evident admirer of Manchester, which was called a "principal character" in the book. The reviewer concluded, "This fine piece of craftsmanship is a very pleasant, well-paced read."

Staincliffe's more recent novels are *Towers of Silence* and *Trio*. The former story concerns a grieving family whose members are unhappy about the suicide verdict on their mother's death. Although she was afraid of heights, she died falling off a high-rise building, so her family suspects foul play and seeks out Sal's help. In the meantime, Sal is also involved in a case to uncover the reasons behind a schoolboy's lapse into depression and truancy. A critic for the *Literary Review* called *Towers of Silence* "unmistakably [Staincliffe's] best, with writing that gives Britcrime its heart, mind and soul. Accept no substitute; this is the real thing."

With *Trio* the author decided to leave Sal behind and write a mainstream fiction work. *Trio* traces the stories of three babies given up for adoption in 1960. As an adoptee herself, Staincliffe has used fiction to explore the complex issues surrounding adoption from the perspectives of all involved. *Trio* also covers the fascinating social history of Britain from 1960 through the new millennium.

Staincliffe told *CA:* "I'm delighted at the success of the 'Sal Kilkenny' series and the positive feedback I get from readers. I still find it hard to believe I've written six novels and seen a dream come true. And I'm looking forward to the next one . . . and the next."

BIOGRAPHICAL AND CRITICAL SOURCES:

PERIODICALS

Library Journal, August, 2001, Rex Klett, review of *Stone Cold Red Hot*, p. 169.

Literary Review, May, 2002, review of *Towers of Silence*, p. 58.
Publishers Weekly, July 23, 2001, review of *Stone Cold Red Hot*, p. 53.
School Librarian, February, 1995, Patricia Peacock, review of *Looking for Trouble*, p. 34.

*   *   *

STRATTON, Jon 1950-

PERSONAL: Born 1950, in London, England; immigrated to Australia, 1981. *Education:* Bradford University, B.Sc. (with honors), 1973; Essex University, M.A., 1974, Ph.D., 1978.

ADDRESSES: Office—Curtin University of Technology, G.P.O. Box U1987, Perth 6845, Australia. *E-mail*—J.Stratton@curtin.edu.au

CAREER: Affiliated with Colchester Institute of Higher Education, England, 1973-74, 1974-76, and University of Essex, England, 1976-81; University of Maryland, lecturer in sociology, 1979-82; Open University, tutor-counselor, 1981; University of Queensland, Australia, part-time tutor in sociology, 1983, lecturer in English, 1986-88; Darwin Institute of Technology, Australia, lecturer in sociology, 1988-91; Curtin University of Technology, Perth, Australia, senior lecturer, 1991-97, associate professor, 1997-99, professor of cultural studies, 1999—. Griffith University, Brisbane, Australia, visiting fellow, 1981-82, temporary lecturer, 1983-85; University of New England, visiting lecturer, 1985; Queensland University of Technology, visiting senior lecturer, 1990; Murdoch University, visiting associate professor, 1995.

WRITINGS:

The Virgin Text: Fiction, Sexuality, and Ideology, Oklahoma University Press (Norman, OK), 1987.
Writing Sites: A Genealogy of the Postmodern World, University of Michigan Press (Ann Arbor, MI), 1990.
The Young Ones: Working-Class Culture, Consumption and the Category of Youth, Black Swan Press (Chicago, IL), 1992.

The Desirable Body: Cultural Fetishism and the Erotics of Consumption, Manchester University Press (Manchester, England), 1996.

Race Daze: Australia in Identity Crisis, Pluto Press (Amandale, New South Wales, Australia), 1998.

Coming out Jewish: Constructing Ambivalent Identities, Routledge (New York, NY), 2000.

Contributor to numerous books on sociology, including *The Subcultures Reader,* Routledge, 1997; *Sport-Cult,* University of Minnesota Press, 1999; and *The Cybercultures Reader,* edited by David Bell, Routledge, 2000. Contributor to scholarly journals, including *European Journal of Cultural Studies, Diaspora of Transnational Studies,* and *Australian Humanities Review.*

SIDELIGHTS: Jon Stratton, a transplanted Englishman who teaches culture studies at Curtin University of Technology in Perth, Australia, is the author of a number of critical treatises on various issues in contemporary sociology. Stratton earned a doctorate from Essex University before relocating to Australia, and authored his first book, 1987's *The Virgin Text: Fiction, Sexuality, and Ideology,* while teaching at the University of Queensland. The book's focus lies in a "sexualization of the text and of the reading process" according to *Novel* critic Patrick McGee. More concisely, Stratton sees links between a highly literate society, the commodification of sexuality, novel-reading, and the treatment of women in fiction. He writes about author Samuel Richardson and his innovative 1740 novel, *Pamela; or, Virtue Rewarded,* as well as subsequent works from Richardson's pen that were renowned for their modern, feminist spirit; he also investigates Bram Stoker's *Dracula.* In other sections, Stratton examines the perceived role of women in a bourgeois society, and he links the growth of a modern consumer culture with changing attitudes toward sexuality. He draws upon theories from Karl Marx, Jacques Derrida, and others to support his arguments. Robert D. Hume, writing in *Studies in English Literature 1500-1900,* noted that the author "writes with verve" and termed the work "genuinely provocative and highly entertaining."

Stratton's two subsequent works were *Writing Sites: A Genealogy of the Postmodern World,* published in 1990, and *The Young Ones: Working-Class Culture, Consumption, and the Category of Youth,* which fol-

lowed two years later. His *The Desirable Body: Cultural Fetishism and the Erotics of Consumption,* was published in 1996. Again, Stratton discusses cultural fetishism and the impact of capitalism upon representations of and attitudes toward the human body, and draws upon writings from Karl Marx and Sigmund Freud to support his assertions. Capitalism, he argues, instills desire in its participants, and commodities fulfill some of that yearning. J. L. Croissant, reviewing *The Desirable Body* for *Choice,* found it presents a "provocative argument."

Stratton's next book, *Race Daze: Australia in Identity Crisis,* was published in 1998. He cites as its impetus the 1997 launch of a "One Nation" political movement by Pauline Hanson, an Australian who objected to government policies establishing a more egalitarian society for the country's Asian immigrants and native Aboriginal populace. Excoriated as racist, Hanson denied the charges, and Stratton saw the need "that somebody should write about the meaning of 'race' in multicultural Australia," as he explained in his introduction. *Race Daze* dissects the semantics behind Hanson's assertions of national identity and inclusion politics. In the end, Australia's official policies are found wanting genuine tolerance and the spirit of inclusion in Stratton's judgment, and in some ways only reinforce exclusionary tendencies amongst the country's core Anglo-Celtic citizenry. To corroborate his theories, Stratton examines images of national identity in contemporary Australian films such as *Strictly Ballroom.* "*Race Daze* is not so much a critique of the Hanson phenomenon as an incisive analysis of certain discourses and circumstances that may have contributed to its existence," noted *Meanjin* reviewer Wenche Ommundsen.

BIOGRAPHICAL AND CRITICAL SOURCES:

PERIODICALS

Alternatives Journal, summer, 2001, review of *The Desirable Body,* p. 27.

Arena, February, 2000, Nadine Dolby, review of *Race Daze,* p. 48.

Australian Journal of Political Science, November, 1999, Ken Gelder, review of *Race Daze,* p. 433.

Choice, December, 1987, R. R. Warhol, review of *The Virgin Text,* p. 626; February, 1997. J. L. Croissant, review of *The Desirable Body,* p. 1004.

Meanjin, Number 2, 1999, Wenche Ommundsen, review of *Race Daze,* pp. 191-195.

Novel, winter, 1989, Patrick McGee, review of *The Virgin Text,* pp. 244-246.

Studies in English Literature 1500-1900, summer, 1988, Robert D. Hume, review of *The Virgin Text,* pp. 532-533.

OTHER

Australian Book Review, http://home.vicnet.au/ (April, 1999), Foong Ling Kong, review of *Race Daze.*

M/C Review, http://www.uq.edu.au/ (October 24, 1999), Paul McCormack, review of *Race Daze.*

*   *   *

STRYDOM, (Barend) Piet(er) 1946-

PERSONAL: Born April 6, 1946, in Pretoria, South Africa; son of Johannes Jacobus (a civil servant) and Maria (a teacher; maiden name, Marais) Strydom; married Sunette H. Paulsen, March 23, 1972; children: Hanno, Maria. *Ethnicity:* "Caucasian." *Education:* University of Stellenbosch, B.A. (cum laude), 1968; University of South Africa, M.A. (cum laude), 1972. *Politics:* "Deliberative Democrat." *Hobbies and other interests:* Human rights activities, international affairs, music.

ADDRESSES: Home—County Cork, Ireland. *Office*— Department of Sociology, University College—Cork, National University of Ireland, Cork, Ireland; fax: 00-353-21-4902-72004. *E-mail*—p.strydom@ucc.ie.

CAREER: University College of the Western Cape, Bellville, South Africa, assistant lecturer, 1969-70; *National Press,* Cape Town, South Africa, court and general reporter, 1970-71; Human Sciences Research Council, Pretoria, South Africa, researcher, 1971-72; University of South Africa, Pretoria, South Africa, lecturer, 1972-74; National University of Ireland, University College—Cork, Cork, Ireland, lecturer in sociology, 1976—, director of Centre for European Social Research, 1991-96.

MEMBER: Irish Sociological Association, Amnesty International.

AWARDS, HONORS: Scholar, Human Sciences Research Council; grants from European Union and Irish Higher Education Authority.

WRITINGS:

Discourse and Knowledge: The Making of Enlightenment Sociology, Liverpool University Press (Liverpool, England), 2000.

Risk, Environment, and Society, Open University Press (Philadelphia, PA), 2002.

(Editor, with Gerard Delanty) *Philosophies of Social Science: The Classic and Contemporary Readings,* Open University Press (Philadelphia, PA), 2003.

Contributor to books, including *Learning Technology in the European Communities,* edited by S. A. Cerri and J. Whiting, Kluwer Academic Publishers (Boston, MA), 1992; and *Nature, Risk, and Responsibility: Discourses of Biotechnology,* edited by P. O'Mahoney, Macmillan (London, England), 1999. Contributor of articles and reviews to periodicals, including *Sociological Theory, Philosophy and Social Criticism, Current Sociology, Praxis International, Theory, Culture, and Society, Political Studies,* and *European Journal of Social Theory.* Some early writings were published in Afrikaans.

WORK IN PROGRESS: Sociology and Cognitive Science; Toward a New Cognitive Sociology; research on technological citizenship and on responsibility in the "risk society."

SIDELIGHTS: Piet Strydom told *CA:* "My consciousness and identity as a sociologist, educator, and author were formed under the impact of a number of forces: politically, a negative experience of apartheid in South Africa; philosophically and scientifically, the internationally significant epistemological, methodological, and theoretical debate of the late 1960s known as the 'Positivist Dispute in German sociology'—in this respect influenced in particular by Jürgen Habermas and Karl-Otto Apel, two of the most important philosophers of the late twentieth century. I stumbled upon them in 1967 and in the late 1960s was able to absorb their early writings. Intellectually I understand myself as belonging to and creatively continuing the tradition of critical theory of which Habermas and Apel are the two leading second-generation figures, but it should be said that I have a wide background in the philosophy, theory, and history of the social sciences.

"My motivation for writing is threefold. Substantively, I wish to make a contribution to my discipline, sociology, and more broadly to the social sciences. Educationally, I seek to produce materials with at least some pedagogical value. Perhaps my primary motivation is political and ethical, in that I am committed to the advancement of human rights and a democratic society and form of global governance.

"The particular context within which I choose my specific themes is provided by current developments in the social sciences and philosophy, research projects I am conducting at the time, and finally political-ethical problems in contemporary society."

*   *   *

SU, Louis
  See KAUFMAN, Lloyd

T

TAYLOR, James A(llan) 1925-2002

OBITUARY NOTICE—See index for CA sketch: Born June 20, 1925, in St. Helens, Lancashire, England; died April 21, 2002. Geographer, educator, and author. Taylor was interested in how geography and climate influence flora and fauna. A graduate of the University of Liverpool, where he earned a master's degree in 1949, he spent his academic career at the University College of Wales, where he was first hired as a lecturer in 1950 and retired as a professor emeritus of geography in 1991. As a consultant, Taylor was widely sought after by the British government and media for his opinions on environmental and weather issues. He was the author of *British Weather in Maps* (1958), written with R. A. Yates, *Weather and Agriculture* (1967), and the textbook *Integrated Physical Geography* (1994) as well as being editor of several other books on climatology, the environment, and biogeography. Several of his last works focused on bracken control in England, including his last book, *Bracken Fern: Toxicity, Biology, and Control* (1999).

OBITUARIES AND OTHER SOURCES:

BOOKS

Writers Directory, St. James Press (Detroit, MI), 2001.

PERIODICALS

Times (London, England), August 7, 2002.

TERSTALL, Eddy 1964-

PERSONAL: Born 1964 in Amsterdam, Netherlands. *Education:* Studied sociology and political science at University of Amsterdam.

ADDRESSES: Agent—Jeroen van de Noort, Agents After All, P.O. Box 10175, 1001 ED Amsterdam, Netherlands.

CAREER: Actor, director, and writer. Film work as director includes *Transit,* Shooting Star Film, 1995; *Walhalla,* 1995; *HUFTERS & hofdames,* Concorde, 1997; *Babylon, the Movies,* 1998; *De boekverfilming,* RCV Film, 1999; *Rent a Friend,* A-FILM, 2000; and *Die belangwekkende documentaire over overspel gemaakt door een vrouw,* 2001. Film appearances include *HUFTERS & hofdames,* Concorde, 1997; *Siberia,* Warner Bros., 1998; and *De boekverfilming,* RCV Film, 1999.

WRITINGS:

Transit, Shooting Star Film, 1995.
(With Rolf Engelsma) *HUFTERS & hofdames* (also known as *Bastards and Bridesmaids*), Concorde, 1997.
De boekverfilming (also known as *Based on the Novel*), RCV Film, 1999.
Rent a Friend, A-FILM, 2000.

Other screenplays include *Walhalla,* 1995; *Transit,* 1995; *Babylon, the Movies,* 1998; and *Die belangwekkende documentaire over overspel gemaakt door een vrouw,* 2001. Also wrote screenplay for *Island of the Porno People.*

SIDELIGHTS: Dutch independent filmmaker Eddy Terstall is known as the director and writer or cowriter of humorous films he has made on a shoestring budget—although such is not the case with his 2000 offering, *Rent a Friend.* Terstall's *Based on the Novel* is a look at the art of independent filmmaking itself, presented through the character of a bad filmmaker whose principal interest is bedding one of three women. In *HUFTERS & hofdames,* released to English-speaking audiences as *Bastards and Brides- maids,* protagonist Dimitri pursues and is rejected by his friend Esther, but on the rebound he comes together with another young lady, Susan. The story is told from the contrasting viewpoints of both Dimitri and Susan.

Rejection and rebounding are also themes in *Rent a Friend,* which, thanks to Terstall's successes with earlier works, was made for a considerably higher budget than its predecessors. This time around, an art- ist named Alfred leaves his girlfriend, Monique, when he realizes that she will not be faithful to him. Her taunt that he is incapable of commercial success spurs him to prove her wrong, and the result is the establish- ment of a business suggested in the film's title: a service that provides "friends" for any occasion at a price. According to David Rooney in *Variety,* "The rent-a-friend idea is amusingly developed and gives rise to some nifty comic scenes."

BIOGRAPHICAL AND CRITICAL SOURCES:

BOOKS

Contemporary Theatre, Film, and Television, Volume 34, Gale (Detroit, MI), 2001.

PERIODICALS

Variety, February 24, 1997, David Rooney, review of *Bastards and Bridesmaids, p. 94;* March 6, 2000, David Rooney, review of *Rent a Friend,* p. 44.*

*   *   *

THOMPSON, John (Anderson) 1918-2002

OBITUARY NOTICE—See index for *CA* sketch: Born June 14, 1918, in Grand Rapids, MI; died June 24, 2002, in New York, NY. Educator, poet, critic, and author. Thompson was nominated for a National Book Award in 1968 for his single volume of poetry, *The*

Talking Girl, and Other Poems. Most of his writings were scholarly works that emerged from his career as a professor of English literature at the State University of New York at Stony Brook. These include the histori- cal works *The Founding of English Meter* and *Histori- cal Guide to English Prosody.* Thompson also contrib- uted articles and reviews to literary journals and popular magazines, including *Commentary, Harper's, Kenyon Review, Hudson Review,* and the *New York Review of Books.* During his years at Stony Brook, Thompson served as the executive director of the Farfield Foundation, a patron of literary and cultural events in Europe and the developing countries of Africa.

OBITUARIES AND OTHER SOURCES:

PERIODICALS

New York Times, July 6, 2002, p. A11.

*   *   *

THOMPSON, Sue Ellen 1948-

PERSONAL: Born July 19, 1948, in Glen Ridge, NJ; daughter of Elliott (a businessman) and Eleanor (a homemaker; maiden name, Bromley) Thompson; mar- ried Stuart Parnes (a museum director), November 15, 1979; children: Thomasin. *Education:* Middlebury College, B.A. (English), 1970; Bread Loaf School of English, M.A. (English), 1974. *Hobbies and other interests:* Biking, cross-country skiing.

ADDRESSES: Home—P.O. Box 326, Mystic, CT 06355. *E-mail*—Iambic@aol.com.

CAREER: Poet and editor. Prentice-Hall, Waterford, CT, editor, 1971-79; freelance writer/editor, 1979—.

MEMBER: Associated Writing Programs; American Academy of Poets.

AWARDS, HONORS: Samuel French Morse prize, Northeastern University Press, 1986, for *This Body of Silk;* Robert Frost fellow, Bread Loaf Writers' Confer- ence, 1987; individual artist's grant, Connecticut Com- mission on the Arts, 1993; poet-in-residence, The Frost Place, 1998.

WRITINGS:

POETRY

This Body of Silk, Northeastern University Press (Boston, MA), 1986.
The Wedding Boat, Owl Creek Press, 1995.
The Leaving: New and Selected Poems, Autumn House Press (Pittsburgh, PA), 2001.

Contributor to *Touchstones: American Poets on a Favorite Poem, Introspections: American Poets on One of Their Own Poems,* and *Contemporary Poetry of New England.*

OTHER

(Editor, with others) *The Personnel Manager's Encyclopedia of Prewritten Personnel Policies,* three volumes, Business and Legal Reports (Madison, CT), 1987, revised edition, 1998.
(Editor) *Holiday Symbols,* Omnigraphics (Detroit, MI), 1998, third edition published as *Holiday Symbols and Customs,* 2002.
(Compiler with Barbara W. Carlson) *Holidays, Festivals, and Celebrations of the World Dictionary,* Omnigraphics (Detroit, MI), 1994, 2nd edition (with Helene Henderson), 1997.
Halloween Program Sourcebook, illustrated by Mary Ann Stavros-Lanning, Omnigraphics (Detroit, MI), 2000.

WORK IN PROGRESS: A fourth volume of poetry.

SIDELIGHTS: Sue Ellen Thompson told *CA:* "I am particularly interested in writing about long-term human relationships, including the bonds between mothers and daughters, husbands and wives, and aging parents and their adult offspring. In recent years I have been writing more about the aging process, particularly as it affects female sexuality and self-awareness."

*   *   *

TOMSON, Graham R.
   See WATSON, Rosamund Marriott

TRASK, Larry, 1944-
   (R. L. Trask)

PERSONAL: Born November 10, 1944, in Olean, NY. *Education:* Rensselaer Polytechnic Institute, B.S. (chemistry); Brandeis University, M.S. (chemistry); School of Oriental and African Studies, University of London, Ph.D. (linguistics).

ADDRESSES: Office—School of Cognitive and Computing Sciences, University of Sussex, Falmer, Brighton BN1 9QII, England. *Agent*—c/o Author Mail, Penguin Books Ltd., 27 Wright Lane, London W8 5TZ, England. *E-mail*—larryt@cogs.susx.ac.uk.

CAREER: Writer and educator. Polytechnic of Central London (now University of Westminster), London, England, instructor; University of Liverpool, Liverpool, England, instructor; University of Sussex, Brighton, England, professor of linguistics.

AWARDS, HONORS: Leverhulme fellowship.

WRITINGS:

AS R. L. TRASK

A Textbook of Syntax, University of Sussex Cognitive Science Research Report (Brighton, England), 1991.
A Dictionary of Grammatical Terms in Linguistics, Routledge (London, NY), 1993.
Language Change, Routledge (London, England), 1994.
Language: The Basics, Routledge (London, England), 1995.
(Coeditor with J. I. Hualde and J. Lakarra) *Toward a History of the Basque Language,* John Benjamins Publishing Company (Amsterdam, Netherlands), 1995.
A Dictionary of Phonetics and Phonology, Routledge (London, NY), 1996.
Historical Linguistics, Arnold (London, England), 1996.
The History of Basque, Routledge (London, England), 1997.
A Student's Dictionary of Language and Linguistics, Arnold (London, England), 1997.

Key Concepts in Language and Linguistics, Routledge (London, NY), 1999.

The Penguin Guide to Punctuation, Penguin (London, England), 1999.

The Dictionary of Historical and Comparative Linguistics, Fitzroy Dearborn (London, England), 2000.

Introducing Linguistics, illustrated by Bill Mayblin, Totem Books (New York, NY), 2001.

Mind the Gaffe: The Penguin Guide to Common Errors in English, Penguin (New York, NY), 2001.

Contributor to numerous books and scholarly journals.

WORK IN PROGRESS: Recently completed a large reference grammar of Basque; compiling an etymological dictionary of Basque; writing a book on the origin and evolution of language.

SIDELIGHTS: Larry Trask, who publishes as R. L. Trask, notes at his Web site that his primary interest is the Basque language, particularly "its history and prehistory." "I'm largely a historical linguist," he says, "and I work chiefly on historical morphology and syntax, occasionally on phonology. My other interests are grammar, typology and universals." While his initial studies were in chemistry, in 1970 he moved from the United States to London, England, where he developed an interest in linguistics and began studying the Basque language.

A Dictionary of Grammatical Terms in Linguistics affords readers what Lev I. Soudek, writing in *American Reference Books Annual,* called "generous coverage of traditional and modern terms." Soudek summarized the dictionary as "an instrument that alleviates . . . problems with grammatical terms and their meanings."

Language: The Basics likewise impressed reviewers as a useful contribution to the field of linguistics. Colette van Kerckvoorde, writing in *Language,* described this work as "the perfect book for anybody who indicates an interest in learning about languages but who does not have the need . . . to take a linguistics course." Barbara Gonzalez Pino, in a *Modern Language Journal* assessment, commented that *Language* "would serve well as an introductory linguistics text." Pino noted that the "examples and anecdotes are interesting, relevant, and helpful, making [Trask's] presentation readable as well as informative."

In *A Dictionary of Phonetics and Phonology,* Trask provides definitions for more than two thousand terms, including some he considers obsolete. Writing in *Choice,* J. R. Luttrell called Trask's book a "comprehensive and up-to-date dictionary," and he concluded that "this work is unique in its combination of phonetics and phonology in one thoroughly executed reference source." Bruce A. Shuman observed in *American Reference Books Annual* that "there is much to admire in this work." Frances Ingemann wrote in *Language* of the book's "comprehensiveness and clarity," stating that *A Dictionary of Phonetics and Phonology* "should be recommended to all beginning linguistics students."

The History of Basque was described by Alan R. King in *Modern Language Journal* as "a compendium of what is currently known or believed about the evolution of the Basque language based on available data and theoretical analysis." King called Trask's book "a worthy contribution to the field," adding that "it definitely should be read." Similarly, José Ignacio Hualde wrote in *Anthropological Linguistics* that *The History of Basque* "comes close to being 'everything you ever wanted to know about Basque.'" Hualde further observed that "this book offers a wealth of information . . . and constitutes a major contribution to Basque linguistics." John D. Bengtson noted in *Romance Philology* that "Trask's book finally makes a substantial amount of Basque data . . . available in English."

The same year he issued *The History of Basque,* Trask also published *A Student's Dictionary of Language and Linguistics,* which John B. Romeiser, writing in *American Reference Books Annual,* referred to as a "useful guide" and "a nice reference tool for people who are fascinated by how language works." J. M. Alexander, writing in *Choice,* also recommended the book, deeming it "a lifesaver for readers who do not need the scholarly analysis of more expansive dictionaries."

According to *Booklist* reviewer Deborah Rollins, *Key Concepts in Language and Linguistics* deals with "important key concepts that every beginning student is likely to encounter from every area of language study." *Choice* critic P. Crossman found the book "well arranged and thoughtfully researched." *American Reference Books Annual* reviewer Romeiser considered it "an accessible text for the layperson as well as the specialist." Another critic, Christiane Laeufer, wrote in

Modern Language Journal that Trask "is to be commended for undertaking a project of this scope and nature."

Trask's ensuing publications include *The Dictionary of Historical and Comparative Linguistics,* which *Choice* reviewer J. M. Alexander called "the first dictionary devoted to historical linguistics." Marianne Orme observed in *Library Journal,* however, that the book "will best serve those already knowledgeable about linguistics." Another book, *Mind the Gaffe: The Penguin Guide to Common Errors in English,* prompted D. J. Enright to comment in the *Times Literary Supplement* that Trask takes "a dim view of . . . lazy laxities and arrogant liberties." Enright added that Trask is "right and helpful . . . in pointing out the errors of our ways."

BIOGRAPHICAL AND CRITICAL SOURCES:

PERIODICALS

American Reference Books Annual, 1995, Lev I. Soudek, review of *A Dictionary of Grammatical Terms in Linguistics,* p. 454; 1997, Bruce A. Shuman, review of *A Dictionary of Phonetics and Phonology,* p. 377; 1998, John B. Romeiser, review of *A Student's Dictionary of Language and Linguistics,* pp. 426-427; 2000, John B. Romeiser, review of *Key Concepts in Language and Linguistics,* pp. 413-414.

Anthropological Linguistics, fall, 1997, José Ignacio Hualde, review of *The History of Basque,* pp. 475-482.

Booklist, May 1, 1999, Deborah Rollins, review of *Key Concepts in Language and Linguistics,* p. 1630.

Choice, May, 1996, J. R. Luttrell, review of *A Dictionary of Phonetics and Phonology,* p. 1458; January, 1998, J. M. Alexander, review of *A Student's Dictionary of Language and Linguistics,* p. 797; September, 1999, P. Crossman, review of *Key Concepts in Language and Linguistics,* p. 114; January, 2001, J. M. Alexander, review of *The Dictionary of Historical and Comparative Linguistics,* p. 878.

Language, March, 1997, Colette van Kerckvoorde, review of *Language: The Basics,* p. 202; December, 1997, Frances Ingemann, review of *A Dictionary of Phonetics and Phonology,* p. 904.

Library Journal, September 15, 2000, Marianne Orme, review of *The Dictionary of Historical and Comparative Linguistics,* p. 62.

Modern Language Journal, winter, 1999, Alan R. King, review of *The History of Basque,* pp. 600-601; fall, 2000, Barbara Gonzalez Pino, review of *Language: The Basics,* pp. 461-462; winter, 2000, Christiane Laeufer, review of *Key Concepts in Language and Linguistics,* pp. 596-597.

Romance Philology, spring, 1999, John D. Bengtson, review of *The History of Basque,* pp. 219-223.

Studies in Language, fall, 1998, Werner Abraham, review of *Historical Linguistics,* pp. 522-523.

Times Literary Supplement, September 21, 2001, D. J. Enright, "Albeit in Limbo," p. 11.

OTHER

Larry Trask's Home Page, http://www.cogs.susx.uk/ users/larryt/ (August 23, 1996).

Cognitive and Computing Sciences, http://www.cogs. sussex.ac.uk/ (May 28, 2002), "Larry Trask."*

* * *

TRASK, R. L.
　　See TRASK, Larry

* * *

TROELL, Jan (Gustaf) 1931-

PERSONAL: Born July 23, 1931, in Limhamn, Sweden.

ADDRESSES: Agent—c/o AB Svensk Filmindustri, SE-169 86 Stockholm, Sweden.

CAREER: Teacher, Sorgenfri primary school, Malmo, Sweden, for nine years; director, cinematographer, film editor, screenwriter. Film work includes (director and cinematographer, except where indicated) *Stad,* 1960; *Baten,* 1961; *Sommartag,* 1961; *Nyarsafton pa skanska slatten,* 1961; *De kom tillbaka,* 1962; *Pojken och draken,* 1962; (co-director only) *Var i Dalby hage,* 1962; (cinematographer only) *Barnvagnen,* 1962; *De gamla kvarnen,* 1964; *Johan Ekberg,* 1964; *Trakom,*

1964; "Uppehaall i myrlandet" in *4 x 4,* 1965; *Haer har du ditt liv,* Brandon, 1966; *Ole dole doff,* 1967; *Utvandrarna,* Warner Bros., 1970; *Nybyggarna,* Warner Bros., 1972; (director only) *Zandy's Bride,* Warner Bros., 1974; (and editor) *Bang!,* Svenska Filminstitutet, 1977; (director only) *Hurricane,* Paramount, 1979; (and editor) *Ingenjoer Andrees luftfaerd,* Svenska Filminstitutet, 1982; (and editor) *Sagolandet,* Svenska Filminstitutet, 1986; (and editor, producer) *Il Capitano,* 1991; (and editor) *Hamsun,* First Run, 1996; (and editor) *En Frusen droem,* 1997; *92,8 MHz—droemmar i soeder,* 2000; and *Saa vit som snoe,* 2000. Film appearances include *Sagolandet,* Svenska Filminstitutet, 1986; *Liv till varje pris,* 1998; and *Ljuset haaller mig saellskap,* 2000.

AWARDS, HONORS: Berlin International Film Festival C.I.C.A.E. Award, C.I.D.A.L.C. Award, Interfilm Award, and Guldbagge Award, all 1967, all for *Haer har du ditt liv;* Berlin International Film Festival Golden Berlin Bear, IWG Golden Plaque, Interfilm Award—Otto Dibelius Film Award, OCIC Award, and UNICRIT Award, all 1968, all for *Ole dole dorff;* Bodil Award, 1973, and Western Heritage Bronze Wrangler Award, 1974, both for *Nybyggarna;* Berlin International Film Festival Interfilm Award honorable mention, for *Sagolandet,* 1988; Guldbagge Creative Achievement Award, 1989; Berlin International Film Festival Silver Berlin Bear and Norwegian International Film Festival Amanda Award for Best Foreign Feature Film, both 1992, both for *Il Capitano;* Montreal World Film Festival Prize of the Ecumenical Jury, 1996, and Rouen Nordic Film Festival Grand Jury Prize, 1997, both for *Hamsun;* Valladolid International Film Festival Best Documentary Award, 1998, and San Francisco International Film Festival Certificate of Merit, 1999, both for *En frusen droem;* Guldbagge Award for Best Cinematography, 2002, for *Sas vit som snoe.*

WRITINGS:

(With Bengt Forslund) *Haer har du ditt liv* (also known as *Here's Your Life* and *This Is Your Life*), Brandon, 1966.

(With Forslund) *Utvandrarna* (also known as *The Emigrants*), Warner Bros., 1970.

(With Forslund) *Nybyggarna* (also known as *The New Land*), Warner Bros., 1972.

(With Sven Christer Swahn) *Bang!,* Svenska Filminstitutet, 1977.

(With Georg Oddner, Ian Rakoff, and Klaus Rifbjerg) *Ingenjoer Andrees luftfaerd* (also known as *The Flight of the Eagle*), Svenska Filminstitutet, 1982.

Sagolandet (also known as *Land of Dreams*), Svenska Filminstitutet, 1986.

Il Capitano (also known as *Il Capitano: A Swedish Requiem*), Svenska Filminstitutet, 1991.

Hamsun, First Run Features, 1996.

En frusen droem (also known as *A Frozen Dream*), Svenska Filminstitutet, 1997.

Saa vit som snoe (also known as *As White as in Snow*), Svensk Filmindustri, 2000.

Other screenplays include *Pojken och draken* (television), 1962; *Barnvagnen* (also known as *The Baby Carriage* and *Pram*), 1963; (cowriter) "Uppehaall i myrlandet" in *4 x 4* (also known as *Nordisk Kvadrille*), 1965; *Ole dole doff* (also known as *Who Saw Him Die?*), 1967.

Contributor to periodicals and journals.

SIDELIGHTS: Like his better-known countryman and colleague Ingmar Bergman, Swedish filmmaker Jan Troell creates films that exude a coldness that is strangely inviting. In the case of Troell's films, the cold may be literal, as with that experienced by the characters in *The Flight of the Eagle;* or it may be the figurative coldness of *Hamsun*'s protagonist. Then, of course, there is *As White as in Snow,* with the cold permeating even the title.

In *Haer har du ditt liv* (*Here's Your Life*), based on a four-volume autobiographical novel by Eyvind Johnson, protagonist Olof leaves home in search of adventure, of which he finds plenty. Much darker is *Ole dole doff* (*Who Saw Him Die?*), the tale of a teacher and his deep depression and loneliness. (Troell himself was once a teacher, and the film was shot at the school where he worked.) Many of Troell's films star Max von Sydow, including such works as *The Emigrants* and *The New Land,* in which von Sydow and Liv Ullmann appear as Swedish farmers who attempt to eke out a better life in Minnesota.

Troell's films often concern real-life figures from Scandinavian history, an example being *The Flight of the Eagle,* the story of Swedish adventurer S. A.

Andree. Andree, who was either foolhardy or brave, depending on whose opinion one consults, set sail for the North Pole in a hydrogen balloon called the *Ornen* ("Eagle") in 1896. Thirty-four years later, explorers found the bodies of Andree and his two companions, whose disastrous expedition is recounted in the film.

A reviewer in *People Weekly* complained that *The Flight of the Eagle* is too long, and the "the boredom of being marooned at the North Pole is conveyed all too realistically," but John Simon of the *National Review* called it "a deep and noble film of great and subtle artistry." No longer, Simon maintained, should critics say that Troell is "second only to Ingmar Bergman": *Flight* shows him to be Bergman's equal. Michael Sragow in *Rolling Stone* likewise praised what he called "an engrossing, eye-popping action epic."

Von Sydow plays the title character in *Hamsun*, Norwegian novelist and 1920 Nobel Prize winner Knut Hamsun, whose legacy was forever marred by his support for Hitler and the Nazis. "The movie ends up being a tough, tragic assessment of the consequences of ill-considered political endorsements that seem almost inseparable from senility," wrote John Hartl in the *Seattle Times*. Its story begins in 1935, when Hamsun, already in his seventies and well past his prime as a writer, becomes enamored of Nazism. Ironically, he believes that to embrace Nazism is to embrace Norwegian nationalism, and he continues to believe this even after the Germans take over his country.

Particularly noteworthy, in the view of many critics, is a scene depicting Hamsun's one meeting with Hitler—who Hamsun, with egotism bordering on mania, had believed to be a Napoleon to the author's Goethe. In fact, the meeting was a disaster, and Hitler (played by Ernst Jacobi) becomes so disgusted with Hamsun's pro-Norwegian stance that he storms out of the room. Elliott Stein of the *Village Voice* called Hamsun "a rambling affair," but Kevin Thomas in the *Los Angeles Times* described it as "remarkably compelling."

As White as in Snow depicts another real person, but one much more admirable than either Andree or Hamsun: Swedish aviator Elsa Andersson. Gunnar Rehlin in *Variety* pronounced the film, whose title comes from an old song, "as beautiful and evocative as a poem."

BIOGRAPHICAL AND CRITICAL SOURCES:

BOOKS

Contemporary Theatre, Film, and Television, Volume 34, Gale (Detroit, MI), 2001.
International Dictionary of Films and Filmmakers, Volume 2: *Directors,* St. James Press (Detroit, MI), 1996.

PERIODICALS

American Spectator, December, 1997, James Bowman, review of *Hamsun,* p. 73.
Boston Globe, September 3, 1997, Jay Carr, review of *Hamsun,* p. C2.
Library Journal, August, 1998, Jeff T. Dick, review of *Hamsun,* p. 148.
Los Angeles Times, November 21, 1997, Kevin Thomas, review of *Hamsun,* p. F10.
Nation, May 14, 1983, Robert Hatch, review of *The Flight of the Eagle,* pp. 617-618.
National Review, June 10, 1983, John Simon, review of *The Flight of the Eagle,* pp. 702-704.
New Republic, May 16, 1983, Stanley Kauffmann, review of *The Flight of the Eagle,* pp. 24-25; May 19, 1997, Stanley Kauffmann, review of *Hamsun,* pp. 26-27.
Newsweek, April 25, 1983, Jack Kroll, review of *The Flight of the Eagle,* p. 50.
New York, April 25, 1983, David Denby, review of *The Flight of the Eagle,* p. 69.
New Yorker, May 16, 1983, Pauline Kael, review of *The Flight of the Eagle,* pp. 112-116.
New York Times, May 31, 1981, Peter Cowie, "Intrepid Filmmakers Re-create an Arctic Tragedy," p. D15; April 8, 1983, Vincent Canby, review of *The Flight of the Eagle,* p. 22; August 8, 1997, Stephen Holden, review of *Hamsun,* p. B5.
People Weekly, May 2, 1983, review of *The Flight of the Eagle,* p. 12.
Rolling Stone, April 28, 1983, Michael Sragow, review of *The Flight of the Eagle,* p. 51; June 9, 1983, Michael Sragow, "Jan Troell: Hypnotist on a Grand Scale" (interview), p. 50.
Saturday Review, May-June, 1983, Judith Crist, review of *The Flight of the Eagle,* p. 42.

Seattle Times, August 7, 1998, John Hartl, review of *Hamsun,* p. G1.

Smithsonian, May, 1983, R. T. Kahn, review of *The Flight of the Eagle,* pp. 122-132.

Variety, February 26, 2001, Gunnar Rehlin, review of *As White as in Snow,* p. 43.

Village Voice, August 12, 1997, Elliott Stein, review of *Hamsun,* p. 67.*

*   *   *

TRUE, (Phaedra) Alianor 1975-

PERSONAL: Born May 26, 1975, in Atlanta, GA; daughter of Walter Edwin (a wine consultant) and Leamarie (a teacher) True. *Ethnicity:* "Caucasian." *Education:* Cornell University, B.A., 1997; University of Michigan, M.S., 2001. *Hobbies and other interests:* Running, hiking, reading, environmental advocacy.

ADDRESSES: Home—Prineville, OR. *Agent*—c/o Author Mail, Island Press, 1718 Connecticut Ave. NW, Suite 300, Washington, DC 20009.

CAREER: National Park Service, Washington, DC, wild-land firefighter at Grand Canyon National Park, 1996-97, and at Big Cypress National Preserve and Sequoia National Park, both 1998; Bureau of Land Management, Washington, DC, wild-land firefighter in Las Vegas, NV, 1999, and Prineville, OR, 2001—.

MEMBER: Sierra Club.

WRITINGS:

(Editor) *Wildfire: A Reader,* Island Press (Washington, DC), 2001.

Contributor to books, including *American Nature Writing,* edited by John Murray, Sierra Club Books, 1998.

WORK IN PROGRESS: A collection of essays about her wild-land firefighting career, completion expected in 2003.

U

ULIVI, Ferruccio 1912-

PERSONAL: Born September 10, 1912, in Borgo San Lorenzo, Italy; son of Francesco Giovanni and Cantini Direa; married, 1941; children: two. *Education:* Graduated from University of Florence, 1934. *Religion:* Catholic. *Hobbies and other interests:* Italian literature.

ADDRESSES: Home—Via Zara 16, Roma, Italy.

CAREER: University of Bari, Bari, Italy, professor of Italian literature, beginning 1954; has also taught at the University of Perugia and University of Rome.

MEMBER: Varie accademie.

WRITINGS:

Federigo Tozzi Morcelliana, [Brescia, Italy], 1946, revised edition, 1973.

Il romanticismo di Ippolito Nievo, A.V.E. (Rome, Italy), 1947.

Il Manzoni lirico e la poetica del Rinnovamento, Gismondi (Rome, Italy), 1950.

Galleria di scrittori d'arte, Sansoni (Florence, Italy), 1953.

Settecento neoclassico, Nistri-Lischi (Pisa, Italy), 1957.

Il primo Carducci, Le Monnier (Florence, Italy), 1957.

L'imitazione nella poetic del Rinascimento, Marzorati (Milan, Italy), 1957.

Gian Vincenzo Gravina: I Minori, Marzorati (Milan, Italy), 1958.

Dal Manzoni ai decadenti, Caltanissetta (Rome, Italy), 1963.

Il Canto XX del "Purgatorio," Marzorati (Milan, Italy), 1964.

Il romanticismo e Alessandro Manzoni, Capelli (Bologna, Italy), 1965.

Il manierismo del Tasso e altri studi (title means "Tasso's Mannerism and Other Studies"), Olschki (Florence, Italy), 1966.

Figure e protagonisti dei "Promessi Sposi," ERI-RAI (Turin, Italy), 1967.

La lirica del Manzoni, Adriatica (Bari, Italy), 1967.

La lirica del Carducci dai primi versi a "Levia gravia"; saggio e antologia, Adriatica (Bari, Italy), 1968.

Poesia come pittura (title means "Poetry as Painting"), Adriatica (Bari, Italy), 1969.

Stile e critica: Avviamento allo studio della letteratura italiana, Adriatica (Bari, Italy), 1969.

(With Rodolfo Macchioni Jodi) *Le origini e il Duecento,* D'Anna (Florence-Messina, Italy), 1971.

(With Rodolfo Macchioni Jodi) *Prospettive e problemi: antologia della critica letteraria e della civiltà italiana,* D'Anna (Florence-Messina, Italy), 1971.

(With Rodolfo Macchioni Jodi) *La civiltà comunale,* D'Anna (Florence-Messina, Italy), 1971.

(With Rodolfo Macchioni Jodi) *L'umanesimo,* D'Anna (Florence-Messina, Italy), 1971.

(With Rodolfo Macchioni Jodi) *Rinascimento e manierismo,* D'Anna (Florence-Messina, Italy), 1971.

(With Rodolfo Macchioni Jodi) *Il barocco,* D'Anna (Florence-Messina, Italy), 1971.

(With Rodolfo Macchioni Jodi) *Dall'Arcadia al neo-classicismo,* D'Anna (Florence-Messina, Italy), 1971.

(With Rodolfo Macchioni Jodi) *Dal romanticismo al verismo,* D'Anna (Florence-Messina, Italy), 1971.

(With Rodolfo Macchioni Jodi) *Dal decadentismo alla esperienze contemporancee,* D'Anna (Florence-Messina, Italy), 1971.

La letteratura verista, Eri (Turin, Italy), 1972.

La letteratura artistica dal manierismo al classicismo secentesco, Elia (Rome, Italy), 1972.

Acquarelli di Marino, Sciascia (Caltanisetta, Italy), 1972.

Alberto Chiari, Paideia (Brescia, Italy), 1973.

Manzoni: Storia e Provvidenza, Bonacci (Rome, Italy), 1974.

Racconto siciliano di Carpinteri, Sciascia (Caltanisetta, Italy), 1974.

Salvator Rosa: pittore e poeta, Accademia Nazionale (Rome, Italy), 1975.

E le ceneri al vento (fiction; title means "Ashes in the Wind"), Mondadori (Milan, Italy), 1977.

Il visibile parlare: saggi sui rapporti fra lettere e arti, Sciascia (Caltanissetta, Italy), 1978.

Le mani pure (title means "Pure Hands"), Rizzoli (Milan, Italy), 1979.

Le mura del cielo (title means "The Boundary Walls of Heaven"), Rizzoli (Milan, Italy), 1981.

L'alba del terzo giorno, Edizioni del Tornese (Rome, Italy), 1982.

La notte di Toledo (title means "Toledo Night"), Rusconi (Milan, Italy), 1983.

Manzoni, Rusconi (Milan, Italy), 1984.

Trenta denari (title means "Thirty Pieces of Silver"), Rusconi (Milan, Italy), 1986.

D'Annunzio, Rusconi (Milan, Italy), 1988.

Linee per un ritratto di Manzoni, Edizioni Scientifiche Italiane (Naples, Italy), 1988.

La maschera senza il volto, Edizioni Scientifiche Italiane (Naples, Italy), 1989.

L'anello, Rusconi (Milan, Italy), 1990.

La parola pittorica, Sciascia (Caltanissetta, Italy), 1990.

Storie bibliche d'amore e di morte, Edizioni Paoline (Cinisello Balsamo, Italy), 1990.

Vita e opere di Gabriele D'Annunzio, Mucchi (Modena, Italy), 1990.

(With P. Paganuzzi and P. Rabuzzi) *Da Leopardi a Montale: aggiornamenti di letteratura ottonove-centesca e testimonianze di scrittori contemporani,* Grafo (Brescia, Italy), 1990.

La straniera (novel; title means "The Foreigner"), Mondadori (Milan, Italy), 1991.

L'angelo rosso (title means "The Red Angel"), Piemme (Casale Monferrato, Italy), 1992.

Tempesta di marzo (novel; title means "March Storm"), Piemme (Casale Monferrato, Italy), 1993.

Torquato Tasso: l'anima e l'avventura, Piemme (Casale Monferrato, Italy), 1995.

Come il tragitto di una stella: Giuseppe di Nazareth, sogno, amore e solitudine (title means "As the Journey of a Star: Joseph of Nazarath, Dream, Love and Solitude), Paoline (Cinisello Balsamo, Italy), 1997.

EDITOR

Eugenio Cirese, *Poesie mosane,* Sciascia (Caltanisetta, Italy), 1955.

I poeti della Scuola Romana dell'Ottocento, Cappelli (Bologna, Italy), 1964.

Il conte di Carmagnola, [Rome, Italy], 1966.

(With Elio Filippo Accrocca) *Lirici pugliesi del Novecento,* Adriatica (Bari, Italy), 1967.

Gianna Manzini, *Un'altra cosa; con una scelta di prose,* Mondadori (Milan, Italy), 1969.

Alessandro Manzoni, *I promessi sposi,* RADAR (Padua, Italy), 1969.

(With Elio Filippo Acrocca) *Prosatori e narratori pugliesi,* Adriatica (Bari, Italy), 1969.

Pompeo Bettini, *Poesie e prose,* Cappelli (Bologna, Italy), 1970.

Gaetano Giangrandi, *Giangrandi, i gatti, il surreale,* Sciascia (Caltanissetta, Italy), 1971.

Alessandro Manzoni, *Poesie: Inni sacri, odi, poesie non approvate o postume,* Mondadori (Milan, Italy), 1985.

Matteo Maria Boiardo, *Opere,* Mursia (Milan, Italy), 1986.

Francesco Petrarca, *Poesie d'amore,* Newton Comption (Rome, Italy), 1989.

(With Marta Savini) *Le più belle poesie d'amore della letteratura italiana: dalle origini all novecento,* Newton Comption (Rome, Italy), 1990.

(And author of introduction) Alessandro Manzoni, *Storia della Colonna infame,* TEN (Rome, Italy), 1993.

(With Marta Savini) *Poesia religiosa italiana: dalle Origini al '900,* Piemme (Casale Monferrato, Italy), 1994.

(And author of introduction) *Gli scrittori d'arte,* Istituto Poligrafico e Zecca dello Stato (Rome, Italy), 1995.

WORK IN PROGRESS: Raccolta di racconti; Raccolta di raggi critici.

SIDELIGHTS: A native of Borge San Lorenzo near Florence, Italy, Ferruccio Ulivi has lived in Rome since 1941. He has served as a literature professor at several of Italy's top universities. As a respected literary scholar, Ulivi established himself during the course of six decades as an expert on Alessandro Manzoni, the Renaissance, and the eighteenth century. These topics have been covered frequently in the dozens of volumes he has produced since the 1940s.

The eighteenth-century poet Manzoni, in particular, "has held a privileged place in Ulivi's professional life," according to Salvatore Cappelletti, writing in *Dictionary of Literary Biography.* The scholar has written major studies, biographies, short stories, and novels based on Manzoni's works; "moreover, through Manzoni, Ulivi discovered several minor Italian writers of the nineteenth century," Cappelletti noted. Through Manzoni, Ulivi once wrote in a passage quoted by Cappelletti in the *Dictionary of Literary Bioography,* "I learned how to recognize the most delicate fibers in the poetic and literary texture of an historical period. Ever since, I have been keenly interested in questions of taste, cultural relationships, the relationship between aesthetic and poetic theories, and the connections among the arts."

In 1977, at age sixty-five, Ulivi made his first foray into fiction with *E le cenari al vento,* a work described by Cappelletti as four novellas inspired by four major writers: Oscar Wilde, Manzoni, Giacomo Leopard, and Torquato Tasso. "The unifying link of the stories is the theme of solitude, which reveals the temperament and the folds of the characters' inner lives," Cappelletti continued. "In this collection, as well as in the works that follow, Ulivi brings the reader close to the mysterious truths and tragedies that lie at the core of the human condition." A 1992 novel, *La staniera,* deals with the private life of Manzoni. In particular, Ulivi "successfully studies the reasons for Manzoni's odd behavior toward his legitimate father," as Michela Montante wrote in a *World Literature Today* review. Ulivi's novel, she summarized, "combines the rigorous

historical research of literary criticism with the engaging prose of a novelist. The style recalls the limpid prose of Manzoni's classic, *The Betrothed.*"

Another biography-in-fiction, *Trenta denari,* explores the inner emotional struggles of Judas. In Ulivi's interpretation, Cappelletti said, the biblical figure "acquires depth and ambiguity as a result of doubts that slowly seem to change the way he feels and thinks." Struggling over his fateful role as the betrayer of Christ, Judas reaches epiphany at Gethesmane. As he looks at the crucified Christ, "he is moved by anguish and overwhelmed with mixed feelings of retaliation, suffering, and affection," as Cappelletti noted. Other New Testament characters covered in Ulivi's fiction include Pontius Pilate, in *L'angelo rosso,* and Joseph of Nazareth, in *Come il tragitto di una stella.* In Cappelletti's view, the latter work finds Joseph "exploring his innermost silences, shadows, dreams, desires, and dilemmas. . . . As Joseph gains awareness of his ontological relationship with Christ (toward and from whom he would often feel concurrently close and distant), he also finds in Christ the source and stimulus of the search for truth."

Ulivi explored the life of Gabriele d'Annunzio in a volume released in commemoration of the fiftieth anniversary of the poet's death. In Ulivi's hands, *D'Annunzio* "is much more than a biography," declared *Times Literary Supplement* contributor Filippo Donini. The author charts the life of his subject from D'Annunzio's humble beginnings in Abruzzi to his seclusion under Mussolini, "with close and impartial attention, but [the subject's] adventures are never allowed to obscure his literary oeuvre. Each of the poet's main books is carefully examined and judged exclusively by its aesthetic value. Indeed the distinctive feature of Ulivi's contribution to the understanding and appreciation of D'Annunzio is the conviction that he was above all else an artist." In the opinion of *Modern Language Review* writer J. R. Woodhouse, *D'Annunzio* "is almost Manzonian in its beauty of construction; it reads as fluently as a popular historical novel and is a most palatable introduction for the non-academic."

BIOGRAPHICAL AND CRITICAL SOURCES:

BOOKS

Dictionary of Literary Biography, Volume 196: *Italian Novelists since World War II, 1965-1995,* Gale (Detroit, MI), 1999.

PERIODICALS

Comparative Literature, winter, 1969, Lienhard Bergel, review of *Il manierismo del Tasso e altri studi,* p. 93.

Humanities, December, 1997, p. 931.

Modern Language Review, July, 1991, J. R. Woodhouse, review of *D'Annunzio,* p. 755.

Otto Novecento, January-February, 1991, pp. 103-108.

Stampa, July 2, 1968, p. 4.

Studium, November-December, 1982, pp. 737-746.

Times Literary Supplement, March 10, 1989, Filippo Donini, review of *D'Annunzio,* p. 254.

World Literature Today, autumn, 1992, review of *La staniera,* p. 705.

*   *   *

UMRIGAR, Thrity 1961-

PERSONAL: Born 1961, in Bombay (now Mumbai), India. *Ethnicity:* "Parsi". *Education:* Ohio State University, M.A. (journalism), 1983; Kent State University, Ph.D. (English), 1997. *Politics:* Liberal.

ADDRESSES: Office—Case Western University, Guilford Hall, Cleveland, OH 44106. *E-mail*—thrity@ umrigar.com.

CAREER: Journalist, author, and critic, 1985—. *Lorain Journal,* journalist, 1985-87; *Akron Beacon,* journalist, 1987-2002. Visiting professor, Case Western Reserve University, Cleveland, OH, 2002-03.

AWARDS, HONORS: Nieman fellowship, Harvard University, 1999; awards from the Society of Professional Journalists and the Press Club of Cleveland.

WRITINGS:

Bombay Time, Picador (New York, NY), 2001.

WORK IN PROGRESS: A memoir about growing up in Mumbai, India.

SIDELIGHTS: Thrity Umrigar was born in India, but moved to the United States when she was twenty-one to study journalism at Ohio State University. Since then, she has worked as a journalist in Ohio. Umrigar was an only child, but grew up in a large extended family with several aunts and an uncle, as well as her parents. She told *Indya.com,* "I never felt I belonged only to my parents but to this larger group of people." The experience, she said, taught her to get along with many different kinds of people, and it also gave her an expanded definition of family. "So," she said, "I keep 'adopting' new family members along the way."

In an interview on her Web site, Umrigar said that she came to the United States because she realized that if she remained in India, "I would never be totally independent and would never discover who exactly I was as a person. I wanted to live in a place where I would rise or fall based on my own efforts and talents." Her father encouraged her to follow her dream. She chose Ohio State University because, as she explained it, "I was sitting in my living room in Bombay, checking off a list of American universities that offered an M.A. in journalism when my eyes fell on 'Ohio State University.' There was a Joan Baez record playing . . . her song, 'Banks of the Ohio,' came on. I looked up and thought, 'It's a sign,' and decided to apply there."

Umrigar writes every day. She told *Indya.com,* "It helps to take the mystique out of fiction writing—which I think is a healthy thing—and to approach it as a job, with a more roll-up-your-sleeves-and-get-to-work kind of attitude." She has always been interested in stories "that buck the trend, that take the minority position. And for fiction to be startling and fresh, I think that posture—of telling the unpopular truth—is almost essential."

Umrigar's novel *Bombay Time* depicts the lives of people in the closely knit Parsi community of Wadia Baug. The Parsis, a minority in India, are the descendants of people who fled from Persia a thousand years ago. Set at a wedding, the book allows the reader to observe each of the guests arriving and hear their disparate stories of love, loss, and betrayal. In the *Washington Post,* Helen C. Wan wrote, "Umrigar is at her best when imagining each character's colorful history and circumstances, and vividly portraying jealousies, passion and unfulfilled ambitions," and that she "displays an impressive talent for conceiving multidimensional, sympathetic characters with life-like emotional quandaries and psychological stumbling blocks." A *Publishers Weekly* reviewer called the book "an impressive debut offering a glimpse into a cultural world . . . that most Westerners know only in its barest outlines." In *Booklist,* Bonnie Johnston described the book as "sweet, frightening, poignant, and chaotic." *Library Journal* reviewer Michelle Reale wrote that the novel "poignantly explicates" the Parsi community in a "startling contemporary portrait."

Umrigar told *CA:* "Indian-American writers have a wonderful canvas to draw on. A larger-than-life city like Bombay is a fiction writer's dream come true because the city throbs with drama and pathos and humanity and passion and tragedy and comedy. There are stories around every corner in a place like that. And we are lucky enough to live in an age where at last there is an interest in hearing the stories of people living on the other side of the globe. My purpose in writing *Bombay Time* was to make sense of the lives of the people I grew up with because, like the main character Rusi, many of them believe that their lives have ended in failure. And I refuse to believe that. So I saw the book as the act of gathering in all their stories like flowers, and turning them into art, into a bouquet, if you will, and handing it back to them."

BIOGRAPHICAL AND CRITICAL SOURCES:

PERIODICALS

Booklist, May 15, 2001, Bonnie Johnston, review of *Bombay Time,* p. 1734.
Library Journal, June 1, 2001, Michelle Reale, review of *Bombay Time,* p. 219.
Publishers Weekly, July 2, 2001, review of *Bombay Time,* p. 51.
Washington Post Book World, July 22, 2001, Helen C. Wan, review of *Bombay Time,* p. T05.

OTHER

Indya.com, http://www.indya.com/ (December 2, 2001), Nitish S. Rele, "Diaspora."
Thrity Umrigar Web site, http://www.umrigar.com/ (October 2, 2001).

UPADHYAY, Samrat

PERSONAL: Born in Kathmandu, Nepal; married; wife's name, Babita; children: Shahzadi. *Education:* College of Wooster, B.A.; Ohio University, M.A.; University of Hawaii, Ph.D.

ADDRESSES: Office—Baldwin-Wallace College, 275 Eastland Rd., Berea, OH 44017-2088.

CAREER: Baldwin-Wallace College, Berea, OH, professor of English. Also taught English in Saudi Arabia and at Kathmandu University; was assistant editor at Travellers' Nepal; fiction editor for *Hawaii Review.*

AWARDS, HONORS: Fiction prize, Ohioana Library Association; Stryker award, University of Hawaii; Academy of American Poets prize; Whiting Award, 2001.

WRITINGS:

Arresting God in Kathmandu (short stories), Houghton Mifflin (Boston, MA), 2001.
The Guru of Love (novel), Houghton Mifflin (Boston, MA), 2003.

Contributor of stories to anthologies, including *Best American Short Stories 1999,* edited by Amy Tan; *Scribner's Best of the Fiction Workshops 1999;* and *Writing in the Stepmother Tongue,* edited by Josip Novakovich and Robert Shapard. Also contributor of stories, poems, book reviews, and essays to *Kathmandu Post, North Dakota Quarterly, Chelsea, Indiana Review, Green Mountains Review,* and *Confrontation.* Editor of a special issue on contemporary Nepali literature for *Manoa.*

SIDELIGHTS: With his first collection of short stories, *Arresting God in Kathmandu,* Samrat Upadhyay gained notice as a skilled commentator on the universal human condition and as the first Nepali author writing in English to be published in the West. Critics were impressed by the subtle manner with which he presents the troubles of ordinary people who live in a place perceived to be extraordinary by outsiders. Upadhyay almost exclusively writes about his homeland of Nepal, but he now lives and works in the United States, having come to the country to attend college. As a professor at Baldwin-Wallace College, he teaches creative writing and English literature. As Upadhyay has pointed out, English is not widely known in Nepal, and whereas writers from former British colonies such as India often write in English, he was exceptionally privileged to study the language at a Jesuit school and to attend college abroad. Upadhyay has said that he cannot imagine setting his stories anywhere else. He also hopes to help familiarize Western readers with the work of other Nepali writers.

The nine stories collected in *Arresting God in Kathmandu* were written over a period of ten years. The tale "The Man with Long Hair" was originally written for an Ohio University class. In an interview with Nitish S. Rele for *indya.com,* Upadhyay said, "The book reflects my obsession with the intimate lives of the inhabitants of Kathmandu, a city that's mostly exoticized in Western literature and popular media. . . . I am interested in deconstructing the myth that surrounds the people of Kathmandu, and by extension, the people of Nepal." Thus, while cultural elements such as arranged marriages and the caste system may be foreign to Western readers, the subjects of marital infidelity and parents trying to control adult children will be familiar. The stories also show how global cultural influences—in the form of foreigners entering Nepali society, Nepalis traveling around the world, and the media—are impacting modern life in Kathmandu.

Marriages new and old are central to Upadhyay's stories. Some address the convention of arranged marriages, including "The Limping Bride." In this story, a widower hopes to reform his alcoholic son, but instead creates a tangled situation where his son is humiliated by his wife's hobbling, he finds himself attracted to the woman, and the young wife takes charge of them both. Infidelity is treated in stories such as "Deepak Misra's Secretary," in which an accountant who is estranged from his American wife seeks to seduce his homely secretary. Two unsatisfactory marriages are viewed in "The Room Next Door," a tale about a mother who is ashamed of her unwed and pregnant daughter. Conventions are upheld when the daughter marries an unemployed simpleton, but the mother ends up reluctantly returning to her husband's bed so that room can be made in her house for her daughter and son-in-law.

Reviewers repeatedly praised Upadhyay's work in *Arresting God in Kathmandu.* He is credited with presenting a rich mix of ideas in a seemingly simple fashion. In a review for the *San Francisco Chronicle,* Tamara Straus said that Upadhyay's "startlingly good" stories feature a style that reminded her of Anton Chekhov. "Like Chekhov, he constructs an ordinary incident and sends his characters on a kaleidoscopic journey of emotions through it, with the result that their inner and outer worlds are exposed," she explained. Noting that while the collection's title might create other expectations, Elizabeth Roca commented in the *Washington Post* that the book's "primary themes are secular and ruefully familiar." Roca admired the way in which Upadhyay "combines exact details of plot and setting with a reflective tone . . . his stories have been burnished until they glow with visual and emotional precision."

In an article for the *Los Angeles Times Book Review,* Susan Salter Reynolds found that the collection "provides an insight into Nepalese culture at home and abroad," especially the issue of social classes. Other reviewers found it notable that such subjects do not overshadow more familiar elements. A *Publishers Weekly* critic said, "Those seeking the exoticism so often found in contemporary Indian fiction won't find it here. . . . In an assured and subtle manner, Upadhyay anchors small yet potent epiphanies." In a review for *Booklist,* Donna Seaman judged that "it's really the universal inner realm and the mysterious state of marriage that [Upadhyay] illuminates so marvelously" in his "polished, transfixing stories."

Still other reviewers were impressed by the complexity of Upadhyay's stories. Writing for *Library Journal,* Shirley N. Quan touched on the author's deft portrayal of Nepali culture, individual personalities, and the universal human condition. She concluded that all the stories "leave the reader with much food for thought." Critic Richard Bernstein wrote in the *New York Times* that the stories manage to "bring us into contact with a world that is somehow both very far away and very familiar." Bernstein described the stories as showing that the people of Kathmandu are beset by the same temptations and weaknesses found in other places, despite its idealized image. "There is a deceptive simplicity to all of these stories, just as there is a deceptive simplicity to Katmandu, whose appearance of traditional piety is . . . a mask behind which all manner of complications flourish," he noted. Bernstein advised that the author's gentle touch merit careful reading, because "interior events occur like tumblers falling in a lock, so quietly and inconspicuously that we almost don't notice them."

BIOGRAPHICAL AND CRITICAL SOURCES:

PERIODICALS

Booklist, August, 2001, Donna Seaman, review of *Arresting God in Kathmandu,* p. 2093.
Library Journal, July, 2001, Shirley N. Quan, review of *Arresting God in Kathmandu,* p. 128.
Los Angeles Times Book Review, August 12, 2001, Susan Salter Reynolds, "Discoveries," p. 11.

New York Times, August 24, 2001, Richard Bernstein, "In Nepal, Too, Desire Defies Modern Times," p. E37.
Publishers Weekly, July 30, 2001, review of *Arresting God in Kathmandu,* p. 62.
San Francisco Chronicle, August 26, 2001, Tamara Straus, "Nepali Writer's Stories of Life and Love Speak to Common Truths."
Washington Post, August 26, 2001, Elizabeth Roca, "From Kathmandu to Kenya, International Tales of Tradition, Upheaval and Loss," p. BW09.

OTHER

Indya.com, http://news.indya.com/ (August 14, 2001), Nitish S. Rele, "Samrat Upadhyay: Arresting God and Readers in Kathmandu."

V-W

VALLE, Rafael Heliodoro 1891-1959

PERSONAL: Born July 3, 1891, in Tegucigalpa, Honduras; immigrated to Mexico, 1907; died July 29, 1959, in Mexico City, Mexico; married Laura Alvarez, 1938 (died); married Emilia Romero (a poet), 1941. *Education:* Attended Tacuba Normal School; National Autonomous University, Ph.D., 1948.

CAREER: Journalist and writer. Worked as Honduran consul, Mobile, AL, 1913; member of Mexican Ministry of Education, 1920s; Honduran ambassador to United States, 1949-55. Consultant, National Museum of Mexico City; teacher, San Jacinto Military College.

AWARDS, HONORS: Maria Moors Cabot Prize for Journalism, Columbia University, 1940; honorary doctorate, San Carlos University, 1945.

WRITINGS:

El rosal de ermitaño (poetry; title means "The Hermit's Rosebush"), [Tegucigalpa, Honduras], 1911.
Cómo la luz del día (poetry; title means "Just as the Light of Day"), [Tegucigalpa, Honduras], 1913.
Anecdotario de mi abuelo (essays; title means "Grandfather's Anecdotes"), [Tegucigalpa, Honduras], 1915.
El perfume de la tierra natal (poetry; title means "The Sweet Scent of Fatherhood"), [Tegucigalpa, Honduras], 1917.

Anfora sedienta (poetry; title means "The Thirsty Urn"), [Mexico City, Mexico], 1922.
Cómo era Iturbide (title means "The Real Iturbide"), [Mexico City, Mexico], 1922.
La nueva poesía de América (title means "Spanish America's New Poetry"), [Mexico City, Mexico], 1923.
El convento de Tepotzotlán (history; title means "The Tepotzotlán Convent"), [Mexico City, Mexico], 1924.
Rusticatio mexicana, 1924.
(Editor) *La anexión de Centroamérica a México* (six-volume history; title means "Central America's Annexation to Mexico"), 1924-1949.
San Bartolomé de las Casas (history), [Mexico City, Mexico], 1926.
Indice de escritores (bibliography), [Mexico City, Mexico], 1928.
Bibliographic Cooperation between Mexico and the United States, [Chicago, IL], 1929.
Bibliografía mexicana, [Mexico City, Mexico], 1930.
Bibliografía de don José Cecilio del Valle, 1934.
Policarpo Bonilla: Algunos spuntes biográficos, [Mexico City, Mexico], 1936.
Bibliografía maya, [Mexico City, Mexico], 1937-41.
Bibliografía de historia de América, [Mexico City, Mexico], 1938.
Tierras de pan llevar, [Santiago, Chile], 1939.
Cronología de la cultura, [Monterey, Mexico], 1939.
Bibliografía de Manuel Ignacio Altamirano, [Mexico City, Mexico], 1939.
La bibliografía del periodismo en la América española, [Cambridge, MA], 1942.
Cartas de Bentham a José Cecilio del Valle, [Mexico City, Mexico], 1942.

La cirugía mexicana de siglo XIX (bibliography), [Mexico City, Mexico], 1942.

Contigo, [Mexico City, Mexico], 1943.

Visión de Perú, [Mexico City, Mexico], 1943.

Iturbide, varón de Dios, [Mexico City, Mexico], 1944.

Imaginación de México, [Buenos Aires, Argentina], 1945.

Cartas hispanomericanas, [Mexico City, Mexico], 1945.

Bolívar en México, [Mexico City, Mexico], 1946.

Oradores americanos (bibliography), [Mexico City, Mexico], 1946.

Tres pensadores de América: Bolívar, Bello, Martí, [Mexico City, Mexico], 1946.

Animales de la América antígua, [Mexico City, Mexico], 1947.

Semblanza de Honduras, [Tegucigalpa, Honduras], 1947.

Cristóbal de Olid, [Mexico City, Mexico], 1948.

(Editor) *Un diplomático mexicano en París,* [Mexico City, Mexico], 1948.

Bibliografía cervantina de la América española, [Mexico City, Mexico], 1950.

La sandalia de fuego [Managua, Nicaragua], 1952.

(With Salvador Toscano) *Cuauhtémoc,* [Mexico City, Mexico], 1953.

Bibliografía de Hernán Cortés, [Mexico City, Mexico], 1953.

Flor de Mesoamérica, [San Salvador, El Salvador], 1955.

Jesuítas de Tepotzotlán, [Bogotá, Colombia], 1955.

Viajero feliz, [San Salvador, El Salvador], 1959.

Historia de las ideas contemporáneas en Centro-América (history; title means "History of Contemporary Thought in Central America"), 1960.

El periodismo en Honduras: Notas para su historia (history), [Mexico City, Mexico], 1960.

Bibliografía de Porfirio Barba-Jacob, [Bogotá, Colombia], 1961.

La rosa intemporal: Antología poética, 1908-1957, [Mexico City, Mexico], 1964.

Work represented in anthologies. Contributor to periodicals, including *Diario de la Marina, El Universal, Excélsior,* and *La Prensa.*

SIDELIGHTS: Rafael Heliodoro Valle was a notable Honduran journalist and writer whose career covered five decades and included more than thirty books. Valle was born in Honduras, but he received his education in Mexico City, Mexico, where he studied at the Tacuba Normal School. His earliest publications include the poetry collections *El rosal de ermitaño,* which appeared in 1911, and *Cómo la luz del día,* which followed two years later. These works, which proved successful, were followed by the essay collection *Anecdotario de m abuelo* and the poetry volume *El perfume de la tierra natal.* During this period, in addition to establishing his literary career, Valle began serving the Honduran government as a diplomat. In 1913 he traveled to the United States to work in Mobile, Alabama, and in 1919 he served in Washington, D.C. After returning to Mexico in the early 1920s, Valle began contributing articles to various publications, including *El Universal* and *Excélsior.* He also worked as a museum consultant and taught at a military college.

In the 1920s Valle commenced work on *La anexión de Centroamérica a México,* a collection of papers—ultimately filling six volumes—documenting the annexation of Central America in the early 1820s, and he published works ranging from *Anfora sedienta,* another poetry collection, to *El convento de Tepotzotlán,* a history of the Tepotzotlán convent. In the 1930s he concentrated on journalism, and in the 1940s he became active in Honduran politics, successfully lobbying for the resignation of President Andino and the election of Manuel Gálvez. After Gálvez assumed the presidency in 1949, he named Valle ambassador to the United States. Valle served in that capacity until 1955, when he was recalled by Julio Lozano, who had recently replaced Gálvez as the Honduran president. Valle eventually returned to Mexico City, where he died in 1959. The next year saw the appearance of another key publication, *Historia de las ideas contemporáneas en Centro-América,* in which Valle had chronicled developments in Central American politics, religion, and culture.

BIOGRAPHICAL AND CRITICAL SOURCES:

BOOKS

Latin American Writers, edited by Carlos A. Sole and Marialsabel Abreu, Scribner's (New York, NY), 1989.

Oxford Companion to Spanish Literature, Clarendon Press (Oxford, England), 1978.*

VAN TIGHEM, Patricia 1959(?)-

PERSONAL: Born c. 1959, in Calgary, Alberta, Canada; married Trevor Janz (a doctor); children: four.

ADDRESSES: Home—British Columbia, Canada. *Agent*—c/o Author Mail, Pantheon Books, 201 East 50th St., New York, NY 10022.

CAREER: Writer and public speaker. Previously worked as a nurse.

AWARDS, HONORS: Canada Permanent Trust short-story competition winner.

WRITINGS:

The Bear's Embrace: A Story of Survival, Pantheon (New York, NY), 2001.

SIDELIGHTS: Canadian author Patricia Van Tighem is a former nurse who was severely injured during a grizzly bear attack in 1983. The experience and many years of recovery are the subject of her book *The Bear's Embrace: A Story of Survival.* Critics have called the account painful and inspiring, and have commended her skill as an author as well as her bravery. Van Tighem's story has been treated in television programs produced by National Geographic and the BBC. She won a Canada Permanent Trust short-story competition and also received a creative writing scholarship to the Banff School of Fine Arts. Van Tighem has also become a public speaker, talking to audiences about the attack and health care.

The dramatic interest of *The Bear's Embrace* is made up of two horrific components. The first is the attack on Van Tighem and her husband, Trevor Janz, during a hiking trip in the Canadian Rockies. The aggressive animal broke Janz's nose, tore at his face, and displaced his jaw. Van Tighem, sadly, suffered far greater injuries. Nearly half of her face was destroyed, including her left eye. While both were lucky to survive the attack, Van Tighem still faced a terrible physical and psychological ordeal. The numerous surgeries that were undertaken to treat her disfigurement included unsuccessful bone grafts and left Van Tighem with intense, chronic pain. Her emotional problems were also complex, and included a fear of being seen in public, turmoil at home, and depression, which led to repeated stays at a psychiatric hospital. Some fifteen years passed before Van Tighem came to terms with her new existence, after a healing process that culminated with the effort to write *The Bear's Embrace.*

Critics agreed that Van Tighem's harrowing history is effectively mirrored in the book, making the reader appreciate her difficult and agonizingly long process of recovery. As a result, *The Bear's Embrace* was discovered to be a sometimes difficult reading experience. "Her writing is candid—at times painfully so," a *Publishers Weekly* reviewer noted, adding that the author's nightmares about the attack are perhaps the most frightening aspect of the book. The critic judged that Van Tighem addressed "questions of random events and meaning, the bravery of surviving an attack and the fortitude of facing life with a facial disfigurement." Moreover, the writer believed that the book show how the act of recounting and "owning" the story aided in Van Tighem's healing.

Booklist critic Elsa Gaztambide also recommended *The Bear's Embrace.* She advised readers not be put off by the slow, grim nature of the account and said, "[Van Tighem] is courageous to share her darkest moments on the path to healing." *Chatelaine*'s Bonnie Schiedel remarked on the book's advantage over other "bear stories," noting, "Van Tighem's . . . is the most compelling by far because of her tough honesty and graceful writing."

BIOGRAPHICAL AND CRITICAL SOURCES:

PERIODICALS

Booklist, September 1, 2001, Elsa Gaztambide, review of *The Bear's Embrace,* p. 30.
Chatelaine, November, 2000, Bonnie Schiedel, "After the Bear," p. 17.
Publishers Weekly, July 23, 2001, review of *The Bear's Embrace,* p. 62.*

*   *   *

VARNADO, Coravar
See SNOOP DOGGY DOGG

VELASQUEZ, Mary Marden 1954-

PERSONAL: Born August 10, 1954, in Fitchburg, MA; daughter of Edward W. (a real estate developer) and Helena (a homemaker; maiden name, Philips) Marden; married Jerry Velasquez (an operations manager), October 21, 1972; children: Keith E., Daniel A. *Education:* University of Houston—Clear Lake, B.S. (summa cum laude), 1986, M.A. (with highest honors), 1988; University of Texas—Houston School of Public Health, Ph.D., 1997.

ADDRESSES: Office—Department of Family Practice and Community Medicine, University of Texas—Medical School at Houston, 6431 Fannin St., JJL324, Houston, TX 77030. *E-mail*—mvelasquez@uth.tmc. edu.

CAREER: University of Texas Health Science Center, Houston, instructor in public health, 1994-97, adjunct faulty in behavioral sciences, 1997—, investigator for Center for Health Promotion and Development, 1999—; University of Texas Medical School, Houston, associate professor of family practice and community medicine and faculty member at Center for Clinical Research and Evidence-based Medicine, 2000—. University of Houston, assistant professor, 1995-99, associate professor, 1999-2000, adjunct associate professor, 2000—; University of Texas School of Public Health, Houston, associate professor, 2001—; lecturer at Texas Women's University; workshop presenter. Gathering Place, member of board of directors, 1994—, chair of program committee, 1998—; Homeless Healthcare Research Coalition, member, 2001—.

MEMBER: International Association of Motivational Interviewing Trainers, Society for Behavioral Medicine, American Public Health Association, Research Society on Alcoholism, Texas Public Health Association, Texas Alliance for the Mentally Ill, Houston Alliance for the Mentally Ill.

AWARDS, HONORS: New Investigator Award, National Institute on Alcohol Abuse and Alcoholism, 1994; grants from National Institute on Alcohol Abuse and Alcoholism, Centers for Disease Control and Prevention, Robert Wood Johnson Foundation, National Institute on Allergies and Infectious Disease, National Institute for Drug Abuse, National Institute for Dental and Craniofacial Research, National Cancer Institute, U.S. Department of Health and Human Services, National Institute on Child Health and Human Development, National Institutes of Justice, and National Heart, Lung, and Blood Institute.

WRITINGS:

(With G. Gaddy-Maurer, C. Crouch, and C. C. DiClemente) *Group Treatment for Substance Abuse: A Stage-of-Change Treatment Manual,* Guilford Press (New York, NY), 2001.

Contributor to books, including *Treatment of Drug and Alcohol Abuse,* edited by R. R. Watson, Humana Press (Totowa, NJ), 1992; *The Change Book,* U.S. Department of Health and Human Services (Rockville, MD), 2000; and *Motivational Interviewing,* edited by W. R. Miller and S. Rollnick, Guilford Press (New York, NY), 2nd edition, 2001. Contributor of articles and reviews to professional journals, including *Family Medicine, American Journal of Preventive Medicine, Tobacco Control, Drug and Alcohol Dependence, Addictive Behaviors, Journal of Substance Abuse Treatment, Journal of Studies on Alcohol,* and *Journal of Consulting and Clinical Psychology.*

*   *   *

WACKER, Grant 1945-

PERSONAL: Born 1945. *Education:* Stanford University, B.A., Harvard University, Ph.D. *Religion:* Evangelical Christian.

ADDRESSES: Office—c/o Duke University Divinity School, 304 Old Divinity, Box 90967, Durham, NC 27708. *E-mail*—gwacker@div.duke.edu.

CAREER: University of North Carolina at Chapel Hill, taught in department of religious studies, 1977-92; Duke University, Durham, NC, associate professor of the history of religion in America, 1992—.

AWARDS, HONORS: Foreword Magazine Book of the Year (Religion), 2001, American Academy of Religion, Award for Excellence in History, 2002, and *Christianity Today* Outstanding Book Award, 2002, all for *Heaven Below: Pentecostals and American Culture.*

WRITINGS:

Augustus H. Strong and the Dilemma of Historical Consciousness, Mercer University Press (Macon, GA), 1985.

(Co-editor with Edith L. Blumhofer and Russell P. Spittler) *Pentecostal Currents in American Protestantism,* University of Illinois Press (Urbana, IL), 1999.

Religion in Nineteenth-Century America, Oxford University Press (New York, NY), 2000.

Heaven Below: Early Pentecostals and American Culture, Harvard University Press (Cambridge, MA), 2001.

(With Jon Butler and Randall Balmer) *Religion in American Life: A Short History,* Oxford University Press (New York, NY), 2002.

(Co-editor with James R. Goff, Jr.) *Portraits of a Generation: Early Pentecostal Leaders,* University of Arkansas Press (Fayetteville, AR), 2002.

(Co-editor with Daniel H. Bays) *The Foreign Missionary Enterprise at Home: Explorations in American Cultural History,* University of Alabama Press (Tuscaloosa, AL), 2003.

WORK IN PROGRESS: A survey of religion in U.S. history with Randall Balmer and Harry S. Stout, and a biography of Billy Graham.

SIDELIGHTS: A professor of religious history, Grant Wacker has written or edited a number of books on both the intellectual strivings and emotional currents in American Protestantism. Wacker's first book concerns a leading nineteenth-century figure in the history of the American Baptists. In *Augustus H. Strong and the Dilemma of Historical Consciousness,* "Wacker chronicles the thought of an influential Baptist leader who had the courage to face paradoxes, and his sympathetic portrait shows him to be essentially a victim of his times," wrote Henry Warner Bowden in *Church History.* Those "paradoxes" involved Strong's attempt to defend traditional Christian doctrines without rejecting the growing scholarship questioning the timelessness of certain Christian claims and seeking to put them in historical context. This question of historical consciousness sharply divided Fundamentalists and liberals. "Wacker argues that Augustus H. Strong stood firmly with a foot in each camp," wrote Donald White in *Religious Studies Review.* His struggle to reconcile these

contradictions culminated in Strong's influential book, *Systematic Theology,* but ultimately even he felt dissatisfied with the results. "In the end Strong's story is important because his personal crisis was typical of that experienced by many late-nineteenth-century Protestants. . . . Nor has the dilemma been neatly resolved in the twentieth century," wrote David Edwin Harrell, Jr. in the *Journal of American History.*

This question of historical growth plays a big part in Wacker's *Religion in Nineteenth-Century America,* which was designed for young adults. "In this brief book, Wacker offers an objective and yet compelling overview of the 'ever-shifting landscape of the United States in the nineteenth century,'" wrote Pamela Robinson Durso in the *Journal of Church and State.* Jonathan Betz-Zall noted in the *School Library Journal* that Wacker's "style is clear and fairly lively, and does not oversimplify complex events like the vicissitudes of the Mormons."

In two other books Wacker confronts the "vicissitudes" of another religious movement, Pentecostalism. *Pentecostal Currents in American Protestantism,* co-edited by Wacker, is an anthology of case studies and sociological essays exploring "the complexity and often troubled nature of the relationship between 'spirit-filled' Christians and the dominant Protestant community," as put by J. C. Hanges in *Choice.* Wacker's own essay "analyzes the sibling rivalry within the 'radical evangelical' subculture, as he calls it, from which Pentecostalism emerged and in which the most direct tensions were felt," wrote Jeffrey Gros in the *Christian Century.*

Wacker further explores the emergence of Pentecostalism in *Heaven Below: Early Pentecostals and American Culture.* "The genius of the Pentecostal movement, Wacker states, lies in its ability to hold two seemingly incompatible impulses—the primitive and the pragmatic—in productive tension," wrote George Westerlund in *Library Journal.* These "primitive" impulses include speaking in tongues, faith healing, and the body convulsions that have given Pentecostals their reputation as "holy rollers." But the pragmatic is very real, too, including the organizational skills of the early Pentecostal leaders and the upwardly mobile tastes of numerous Pentecostals. As Alan Wolfe wrote in the *New Republic,* "*Heaven Below* is an informative and fascinating account of a religion that has not so much been misunderstood—Pentecostals did much of the holy rolling associated with them—as underestimated. If you want to understand how John Ashcroft, a product of this sometimes otherworldly tradition, became attorney general in this world, then this is the book that you should read." For a reviewer in *Publishers Weekly,* "It is difficult to imagine a more judicious treatment of the subject; meticulously researched, lyrically written and continuously illuminating, Wacker's book is essential reading for anyone who wishes to understand the origins of this influential current in American culture."

BIOGRAPHICAL AND CRITICAL SOURCES:

PERIODICALS

Choice, February, 2000, J. C. Hanges, review of *Pentecostal Currents in American Protestantism,* p. 1118.
Christian Century, February 2, 2000, Jeffrey Gros, review of *Pentecostal Currents in American Protestantism,* p. 152.
Church History, September, 1986, Henry Warner Bowden, review of *Augustus H. Strong and the Dilemma of Historical Consciousness,* p. 391.
Journal of American History, September, 1986, David Edwin Harrell, Jr., review of *Augustus H. Strong and the Dilemma of Historical Consciousness,* pp. 484-485.
Journal of Church and State, winter, 2001, Pamela Robinson Durso, review of *Religion in Nineteenth-Century America,* p. 158.
Library Journal, May 15, 2001, George Westerlund, review of *Heaven Below,* p. 129.
New Republic, August 27, 2001, Alan Wolfe, "Holy Realists," p. 59.
Publishers Weekly, April 23, 2001, review of *Heaven Below,* p. 70.
Religious Studies Review, April, 1986, Donald White, review of *Augustus H. Strong and the Dilemma of Historical Consciousness,* pp. 183-184.
School Library Journal, August, 2000, Jonathan Betz-Zall, review of *Religion in Nineteenth-Century America,* p. 210.*

*   *   *

WAIT, Lea 1946-

PERSONAL: Born May 26, 1946, in Boston, MA; daughter of George (an accountant) and Sally (an artist and antiques dealer; maiden name, Smart) Wait; children: Caroline Wait Childs, Alicia Wait Gutschen-

ritter, Rebecca Wait Wynne, Elizabeth Wait. *Education:* Chatham College, B.A., 1968; New York University, M.A., 1974, doctoral studies, 1974-77.

ADDRESSES: Home—P.O. Box 225, Edgecomb, ME 04556. *E-mail*—leawait@clinic.net.

CAREER: Author and antiques dealer. A. T. & T., New York, NY, and New Jersey, public relations manager, 1968-98; M. A. H. Antiques, owner, 1977—. Adoptive Single Parents of New Jersey, president, 1978-92.

MEMBER: Authors Guild, Mystery Writers of America, Sisters in Crime, Society of Children's Book Writers and Illustrators, Maine Writers and Publishers Alliance (Board of Trustees), National Council for Single Adoptive Parents (Board of Trustees).

AWARDS, HONORS: Notable Children's Book designation, *Smithsonian* magazine, and Best Children's Books selection, Bank Street College of Education, both 2001, both for *Stopping to Home.*

WRITINGS:

FOR CHILDREN

Stopping to Home, Simon & Schuster (New York, NY), 2001.
Seaward Born, Simon & Schuster (New York, NY), 2003.
Wintering Well, Simon & Schuster (New York, NY), 2004.

OTHER

Shadows at the Fair: An Antique Print Mystery, Scribner (New York, NY), 2002.
Shadows on the Coast of Maine: An Antique Print Mystery, Scribner (New York, NY), 2003.

WORK IN PROGRESS: An historical novel about two young Scottish immigrants who face a moral dilemma in 1850s New England.

SIDELIGHTS: Lea Wait has drawn on her love of New England and its history to author a number of books for young readers. In novels such as *Stopping to Home* and *Seaward Born,* she focuses on self-reliant young people living in the early nineteenth century who overcome difficult circumstances and gain knowledge and maturity. A search for family and security runs through each of Wait's novels, as well as a strong sense of the past. Reviewing *Stopping to Home* in *Publishers Weekly,* a reviewer praised Wait for "effectively" evoking the past by weaving in the "customs . . ., language and geography that capture" life in a coastal town in Maine.

Wait was born in Boston, Massachusetts, in 1946, and spent winters at her home in suburban New Jersey and summers in Maine with her grandparents. "My grandmother was the first person to take me to a library, or encourage me to read," Wait once told *CA.* "She had me read Shakespeare's plays out loud to her and encouraged me to read and talk about adult books when I was just in grade school. Many of the books she suggested I read were nineteenth-century novels about brave women or girls, many of them without families, who succeeded through hard work and gumption. She taught me that possibilities were unlimited and that books could lead you to them."

Wait's grandmother was an antique dealer as well as an avid reader; as Wait grew up she decided that she wanted to follow the same path and be a writer too. She served as editor of her high school newspaper, and then studied English and drama at Chatham College in Pittsburgh, Pennsylvania. Following college, she got a job with A. T. & T., and worked in their public relations department for many years. "I did start an antique print business," she added, "but my mother ran it, since my life quickly became very busy." Wait also decided to adopt several children; as she noted, "Ever since I had read those nineteenth-century novels about abandoned children, I had planned to adopt, and when I was in my late twenties I decided it was the right time." She soon found herself the single mother of four older girls, and her experiences as a single adoptive parent prompted her involvement in adoption advocacy.

In the late 1990s, Wait left her corporate job to attend to her lifelong dreams of following her grandmother's lead. Moving to Maine, she became active in her antique print business and started writing. Her first published book for young readers was *Stopping to Home,* published in 2001. Taking place in Wiscasset, Maine, during the first decade of the nineteenth century, the novel finds eleven-year-old Abigail Chambers taking care of her four-year-old brother after her mother dies of smallpox. With her father, a sailor, likely lost at sea, Abigail must bring in enough money to keep the children out of the orphanage, but as the smallpox epidemic lingers on, work becomes more difficult to find. Fortunately, a pregnant teen widow opens her home to the two Chambers children, and a bond develops that creates a new family, in a novel that *Horn Book* contributor Martha V. Parravano called "quietly compelling" and Hazel Rochman praised in a *Booklist* review as "a moving first novel that finds drama in ordinary life."

Other novels for young readers include *Seaward Born,* which finds thirteen-year-old slave Michael Lautrec working on the docks in Charleston and dreaming of freedom. The year is 1805, and when the opportunity to take the chance and run away comes, Michael bravely takes flight, realizing that it is a risk worth taking. Wait's *Wintering Well* returns readers to Maine, as Will Ames must deal with life as a cripple after he loses a leg in a farming accident. With dreams of a future as a farmer now dashed, the young man determines to deal with life on his own rather than stay in the care of his parents. In addition to her works for children, Wait is the author of a series of adult mystery novels focusing on the antiques business.

BIOGRAPHICAL AND CRITICAL SOURCES:

PERIODICALS

Book, March-April, 2001, review of *Stopping to Home,* p. 81.

Booklist, November 15, 2001, Hazel Rochman, review of *Stopping to Home,* p. 567; June 1, 2002, Sue O'Brien, review of *Shadows at the Fair,* p. 1692.

Horn Book, January-February, 2002, Martha V. Parravano, review of *Stopping to Home,* p. 85.

Kirkus Reviews, September 15, 2001, review of *Stopping to Home,* p. 1371; May 1, 2002, review of *Shadows at the Fair,* p. 623.

Library Journal, June 1, 2002, Rex E. Klett, review of *Shadows at the Fair,* p. 200.

Publishers Weekly, November 5, 2001, review of *Stopping to Home,* p. 69; June 24, 2002, review of *Shadows at the Fair,* p. 42.

School Library Journal, October, 2001, Sue Sherif, review of *Stopping to Home,* p. 174.

OTHER

Lea Wait Home Page, http://www.leawait.com (May 24, 2002).

*   *   *

WAITZKIN, Fred

PERSONAL: Son of Abe (a lighting fixtures salesman) and Stella (a painter) Waitzkin; married; wife's name, Bonnie (a teacher); children: Josh, Katya. *Education:* Graduated from Kenyon College, 1965; New York University, M.A. *Hobbies and other interests:* Fishing.

ADDRESSES: Home—New York, NY and Martha's Vineyard, MA. *Agent*—c/o Penguin Putnam, Attn: Viking Author Mail, 375 Hudson St., New York, NY 10014.

CAREER: Journalist and nonfiction writer. Taught literature at College of the Virgin Islands.

WRITINGS:

Searching for Bobby Fischer: The Father of a Prodigy Observes the World of Chess, Penguin (New York, NY), 1989.

Mortal Games: The Turbulent Genius of Garry Kasparov, Putnam (New York, NY), 1993.

The Last Marlin: The Story of a Family at Sea, Viking (New York, NY), 2000.

Writings have appeared in *New York Times Magazine, New York, Esquire, Sports Illustrated,* and *Motorboating and Sailing.*

ADAPTATIONS: A film based on *Searching for Bobby Fischer* was released by Paramount Pictures in 1992.

SIDELIGHTS: With the 1992 film adaptation of his memoir *Searching for Bobby Fischer: The World of Chess Observed by the Father of a Child Prodigy,* Fred Waitzkin experienced the fame he had long dreamed of attaining. But the media attention did more than generate new readers for Waitzkin; it also turned the journalist into an interviewee rather than interviewer. "Not only am I answering the questions, I'm developing a shtick," he told Jeff Bell of the *Kenyon College Alumni Bulletin;* "I'm answering the questions the same way and starting to sound rather cliched to myself. And the writing is not coming. I'm worrying about how I came across in the last interview." Waitzkin told himself that it was time to get back to work. His next book, *Mortal Games: The Turbulent Genius of Garry Kasparov,* showed that the author was still engrossed by the world of chess. He finally broke with the subject to write an autobiographical book about his own childhood, *The Last Marlin: The Story of a Family at Sea.*

Waitzin's nonfiction stories are born of a narrative urge that their author once hoped to use as a fiction writer. After earning a master's degree at New York University, he started teaching literature at the College of the Virgin Islands; however, Waitzkin soon discovered that the job robbed him of the creative energy he needed to write. He returned to New York City to work on novels and short stories, and was published in the *Transatlantic Review* and *Yale Literary Magazine.* It was in the 1980s that Waitzkin turned to feature journalism, hoping to find greater artistic satisfaction as well as a bigger paycheck. Generating plots had once been a problem for the writer, but now he saw writing opportunities all around him, including stories where he was a character. "I discovered the same kind of literary impulses I felt with fictional stories could be used in nonfiction. . . . That was amazing to me, and instead of two hundred people reading my stories, I had a very large audience and could make a living at my writing," he told Bell. Those audiences included readers of the *New York Times Magazine, New York,* and *Esquire.*

The article "The Grungy World of Big-Time Chess," written for *New York,* started Waitzkin on the path leading to *Searching for Bobby Fischer.* He had also discovered his six-year-old son's remarkable aptitude for the game, which led to regular matches with adult players in Washington Square Park and then to Josh Waitzkin studying chess with Bruce Pandolfini. During the initial stages of writing a book on chess, Waitzkin's agent urged him to focus the book on Josh. The resulting story follows Josh into the world of chess, among impoverished fanatics in the park, pushy parents of other prodigies, and even to Russia to see a championship match between Anatoly Karpov and Garry Kasparov. Soon Josh was the No.1-ranked eight year old in the United States. These experiences would prompt his father to search for the American chess genius Bobby Fischer, who went into hiding after winning a world championship match against Boris Spassky in 1972. Waitzkin maintains that public interest in Fischer's career might have made chess a popular sport in the United States, if Fischer had not succumbed to paranoia and other personal problems.

Searching for Bobby Fischer was praised by book reviewers for its simultaneous pursuit of personal and global themes. The story of father and son generated great interest, as did the surprising picture of serious chess playing. "In the United States, where there is virtually no state or commercial support for the game, chess is more likely to be a way of getting yourself *into* the gutter," reflected *New Statesman & Society* reviewer Sean French; "Waitzkin gives vivid accounts of the bizarre milieux that he and his son pass through. . . . [He] keeps asking the questions [about the perils and opportunities faced by chess prodigies] but neither he nor anyone else can answer them. This is a fascinating and moving memoir." In the *Times Literary Supplement,* Martin Amis called the memoir "a vivid, passionate and disquieting book." Amis advised that "Throughout, it runs a light fever of anxious pride and anxious love. As a 'chess parent,' a journalist, and a sane man, Fred Waitzkin is articulately aware of what he is doing. And what he is doing isn't always pretty. . . . The book hinges on this kind of contrast: the purity and otherworldliness of the game, and the human mess and wreckage that almost always surrounds it."

In the late 1980s, Waitzkin met Armenian chess champion Garry Kasparov at a party, more than a year after the chess champion had simultaneously played chess against Josh and fifty-eight other school children. Kasparov remembered Josh and the moves he had used to achieve one of two draws in the event. A friendship developed and an agreement that Waitzkin would write a book about Kasparov based on interviews that would include dinners with the chess master following each of his matches. The resulting publica-

tion was *Mortal Games: The Turbulent Genius of Garry Kasparov,* a volume covering personal, professional, and political developments from 1990 to 1993. It details Kasparov's chess matches, including a narrow victory over rival Anatoly Karpov, as well as his response to the 1990 Azerbaijani pogrom against Armenians in Baku and his resulting resettlement in Moscow.

The book won praise as a tantalizing introduction to chess and the game's reigning champion. In *Tribune Books* Laurel Bauer noticed that "fathers and sons appear in the book as a kind of sub-obsession," including Kasparov's relationship with his father, who decided that it would be better for his son not to see him while he died of a terminal illness. Lauding the author's writing skills, Bauer said, "A journalist, Waitzkin gives that profession a rare-enough good name. His skillful use of physical detail in capturing the least physical of sports . . . is matched by muscular descriptions of [games]. . . . On the human side, he is able to tell us quite a lot about Kasparov, his family and a large cast of supporting characters without recourse to prurience or, for the most part, banality."

A *Publishers Weekly* reviewer asserted that *Mortal Games* "catches readers up in the frenzy of grandmasters for whom chess is life itself, the ultimate challenge to ego." The article described Waitzkin as "clearly a Kasparov partisan" and suggested that the author "doesn't altogether succeed in making the haughty, relentless, volatile champ sympathetic." A similar observation came from *American Spectator* reviewer Craig S. Lerner: "He strains to show Kasparov as more human, and humane, than the caricature of the monomaniacal chess wizard . . . but the champion's smiling mask occasionally slips." In *Kirkus Reviews* a critic reflected that readers might find that "high-level chess outdoes Hollywood for daffiness." The reviewer also noted that the specter of Fischer reappeared in *Mortal Games:* "While suggesting that Fischer is mentally ill, Waitzkin also implies that he remains a chess genius and, in the eyes of the public, Kasparov's real rival."

Waitzkin's extended immersion in competitive chess came to an end after he promised his son that he would drop the subject for five years. He now chose to write about his own childhood in *The Last Marlin: The Story of a Family at Sea.* The book, sub-titled "A Father-Son Memoir," reflects its focus on the relationship between Waitzkin and his own father. It recounts family fishing trips to the island of Bimini in the Bahamas, a favorite distraction amidst family infighting. Waitzkin shows his father, Abe, to be a brilliant, sometimes ruthless lighting salesman, whom the boy credits with the glory of the Manhattan skyline at night. His mother, Stella, no longer loves or respects Abe, having turned to the artistic circles in Greenwich Village for companionship and intellectual stimulation. A love of music is a tenuous link between mother and son, something that is also stimulated by the trips to Bimini.

Among the reviews of *The Last Marlin,* Michelle Kaske commented in *Booklist* that "a love or even a like for fishing is not necessary to enjoy this work, because Waitzkin's passionate words will lure you in and stay with you." The difficulty of relating to Abe had a strong impact on other critics. In *Library Journal* Marty Soven called the book "a well-done father-son tale of bonding" but he cautioned that "Fred allows the big fish to get away by not developing the characters of his mother, Stella, and free-spirited brother more." A *Publishers Weekly* reviewer considered the book to be "largely an homage to Waitzkin's dad" and advised that readers might well find "Waitzkin's clear, resonant writing" an insufficient distraction from the problem of why Waitzkin is obsessed with his father's skill as a salesman. Conversely, *New York Times Book Review* writer Bruce Barcott complimented Waitzkin's "moving portrayal of his father, a man of singularly unsympathetic character." Barcott placed Abe Waitzkin in "the contemporary literary pantheon of flawed fathers whose sons yearn to understand them" and called *The Last Marlin* "a remarkably ambitious and satisfying memoir."

BIOGRAPHICAL AND CRITICAL SOURCES:

PERIODICALS

American Spectator, December, 1993, Craig S. Lerner, review of *Mortal Games,* p. 83.
Booklist, March 15, 2000, Michelle Kaske, review of *The Last Marlin,* p. 1312.
Kirkus Reviews, July 1, 1993, review of *Mortal Games,* p. 850.
Library Journal, April 1, 2000, Marty Soven, review of *The Last Marlin,* p. 108.

Maclean's, August 16, 1993, Brian D. Johnson, review of the film *Searching for Bobby Fischer,* p. 48.
New Statesman and Society, March 31, 1989, Sean French, "The Prodigious Son," p. 33.
New York Times Book Review, April 16, 2000, Bruce Barcott, "Fishing for Answers," p. 7.
Publishers Weekly, June 28, 1993, review of *Mortal Games,* p. 63; March 13, 2000, review of *The Last Marlin,* p. 72.
Times Literary Supplement, June 30, 1989, Martin Amis, "The Winners Who Are Losers," p. 709.
Tribune Books (Chicago, IL), September 12, 1993, Laurel Bauer, "The Moves of a Mental Matador," p. 6.

OTHER

Chicago Sun-Times, http://www.suntimes.com/ (August 11, 1993), Roger Ebert, review of film *Searching for Bobby Fischer.*
Kenyon College Alumni Bulletin, http://circle.kenyon.edu/publications/bulletin/ (spring/summer, 1998), Jeff Bell, "The Question of Genius."*

*   *   *

WALD, Elijah 1959-

PERSONAL: Born March 24, 1959, in Boston, MA; son of Ruth Hubbard (a professor of biology at Harvard University). *Education:* Studied music under Dave Van Ronk and Jean-Bosco Mwenda.

ADDRESSES: Home—21 Lakeview Ave., Cambridge, MA 02138. *E-mail*—elijah@elijahwald.com.

CAREER: Writer and musician. Toured internationally and in the United States as a singer and guitarist. Wrote on folk roots and international music for various magazines in the early 1980s. *Boston Globe,* Boston, MA, freelance world music critic, 1984-2000.

WRITINGS:

(With Ruth Hubbard) *Exploding the Gene Myth: How Genetic Information Is Produced and Manipulated by Scientists, Physicians, Employers, Insurance Companies, Educators, and Law Enforcers,* Beacon Press (Boston, MA), 1993, third edition, 1999.

(With John Junkerman) *River of Song: A Musical Journey down the Mississippi,* St. Martin's Press (New York, NY), 1998.

Josh White: Society Blues (biography), University of Massachusetts Press (Amherst, MA), 2000.

Narcocorrido: A Journey into the Music of Drugs, Guns, and Guerrillas, HarperCollins (New York, NY), 2001.

Contributor to periodicals, including the *Boston Globe.*

SIDELIGHTS: Elijah Wald is a musician and writer who has published several books and hundreds of articles, mainly on music-related topics. He began his career touring internationally as a guitarist and singer and has been writing since the early 1980s. Wald's main musical influences are Dave Van Ronk, his mentor and former guitar teacher, and Congolese musician Jean-Bosco Mwenda, with whom he studied for several months in Zaire. He is most well known for his freelance articles contributed to the *Boston Globe,* where he worked as the newspaper's world music critic for over fifteen years.

Wald's first book, *Exploding the Gene Myth: How Genetic Information Is Produced and Manipulated by Scientists, Physicians, Employers, Insurance Companies, Educators, and Law Enforcers,* is coauthored with his mother, Ruth Hubbard, and first published in 1993. Hubbard, a biochemist and former Harvard professor, supplies the theories and scientific data for the book, while Wald serves as writer and collaborator. The two authors discredit the belief that there is a simple correlation between genes and traits, creating a solid argument against genetic reductionism. Wald and Hubbard insist that "The myth of the all-powerful gene is based on flawed science that discounts the environmental context in which we and our genes exist," and have succeeded in writing a scientific and technical book which is accessible to the average reader. Neil A. Holtzman of the *New England Journal of Medicine* called *Exploding the Gene Myth* "good reading for anyone who wants to learn more about the science underlying the quest for human genes and the political, social, and ethical implications."

Wald's next book, *River of Song: A Musical Journey down the Mississippi,* returns him to his area of expertise—music. This book is a companion to a PBS television series highlighting the origins of American music and was written along with the documentary's director, John Junkerman. The two men traveled to nearly seventy locations along the Mississippi and interviewed over five hundred musicians, who tell their stories through music and biographical vignettes. The music profiled in the book includes everything from jazz, blues, and gospel, to punk rock, Ojibwe Indian songs, and hip-hop brass band fusion. A reviewer from *Kirkus Reviews* reported, "the book offers both an engaging overview of modern American music . . . and a fascinating glimpse of the ways in which American music continues to reflect and to shape American life." There is also a thirty-six song, two-CD soundtrack that accompanies the book and documentary.

Wald also wrote the first major biography of renowned folk-blues artist Josh White titled *Josh White: Society Blues,* which was published in 2000. In this work, Wald chronicles the life of the musician whose contribution to the folk music revivals of the mid-twentieth century had been largely overlooked until now, following him from his childhood of leading blind singers around the south, to the 1940s and 1950s when he became a celebrated blues recording star. Wald also writes about White's commitment to social activism and his lifelong struggle against discrimination, which often came through in his folk songs.

Other works by Wald include various political commentary pieces, album liner notes for a number of compact discs, and a fourth book, *Narcocorrido: A Journey into the Music of Drugs, Guns, and Guerillas,* which was published in both English and Spanish by HarperCollins.

BIOGRAPHICAL AND CRITICAL SOURCES:

PERIODICALS

Booklist, January 1, 1999, Mike Tribby, review of *River of Song: A Musical Journey down the Mississippi,* p. 118.

Kirkus Reviews, December 15, 1998, review of *River of Song,* p. 1790.

Lancet, August 28, 1993, Ian N. M. Day, review of *Exploding the Gene Myth: How Genetic Information Is Produced and Manipulated by Scientists, Physicians, Employers, Insurance Companies, Educators, and Law Enforcers,* p. 540.

Library Journal, January, 1999, Michael Colby, review of *River of Song,* p. 102.

New Scientist, October 23, 1993, Lynda Burke, review of *Exploding the Gene Myth,* p. 38.

New Statesman, September 9, 1994, Marek Kohn, review of *Exploding the Gene Myth,* p. 40.

New York Times Book Review, September 12, 1993, Daniel Callahan, review of *Exploding the Gene Myth,* p. 26.

Publishers Weekly, March 8, 1993, review of *Exploding the Gene Myth,* p. 58; November 23, 1998, review of *Exploding the Gene Myth,* p. 52.

Time, January 11, 1999, Christopher John Farley and John Junkerman, "*Sounding the Waters: PBS Explores the Music along the Mississippi,*" p. 95.

Variety, February 1, 1999, Phil Gallo, review of *River of Song,* p. 30.

OTHER

Beacon Press, http://www.beacon.org/ (January 9, 2002).

Elijah Wald Web site, http://www.elijahwald.com/ (December 18, 2001).

Fayetteville Online, http://www.fayettevilleobserver.com/ (April 18, 1999), Jim Washington, "Josh White, Jr., Follows in His Father's Footsteps."

Keysound, http://www.keysound.com/ (January 9, 2002).

New England Journal of Medicine, http://www.nejm.org/ (January 9, 2002).

Powells.com, http://www.powells.com/ (January 9, 2002).

Public Broadcasting Service Web site, http://www.pbs.org/riverofsong/ (January 9, 2002), review of *River of Song.*

*   *   *

WALDNER, Liz

PERSONAL: Born in Cleveland, OH. *Education:* St. John's College, B.A.; University of Iowa, M.F.A.

ADDRESSES: Agent—c/o University of Georgia Press, 330 Research Dr., Athens GA 30602-4901.

CAREER: Cornell College, Mt. Vernon, IA, director of creative writing; Tufts University, Boston, MA, instructor.

AWARDS, HONORS: Barbara Deming Memorial Award; Gertrude Stein Award; Lannan Foundation Award, 1998; Robert Winner Memorial Prize, Poetry Society of America, 1999; Iowa Poetry Prize, 1999, and Academy of American Poets Laughlin Award, 2000, both for *A Point Is That Which Has No Part;* Beatrice Hawley Prize, Alice James Books, 2001, for *Self and Simulacra.*

WRITINGS:

Homing Devices, O Books (Oakland, CA), 1998.

A Point Is That Which Has No Part, University of Iowa Press (Iowa City, IA), 2000.

Self and Simulacra, Alice James Books (Farmington, ME), 2001.

Etym(Bi)Ology, Omnidawn (Richmond, CA), 2002.

Dark Would: (The Missing Person), University of Georgia Press (Athens, GA), 2002.

SIDELIGHTS: Liz Waldner's poetry has often been compared to that of experimental writer Gertrude Stein (1874-1946) for its innovative voice and style, which has been described as audacious, witty, intelligent, and sarcastic. Waldner is said to push the edge in terms of meaning and language.

Waldner's most celebrated publication is *A Point Is That Which Has No Part* (2000), a collection of poems that mix math and science with modern poetics. Whether she is discussing sex, time, or death, the subjects of her poems are colored with emotions that express longing and loss. This is a book that a reviewer for *American Poet* described as "deliberately unpredictable in its forms and subjects," referring to Waldner's ability to write as if her words were coming straight from her unconscious onto the page. This excerpt from "Wednesday Morning Pray Time" provides an example:

"Thumb, plum sex in a nutshell, plumb line, heart line, throw out the live line (phone sex) I mean lifeline, Jesus is coming for me. When he washed oh when he washed when my Jesus washed he washed my sins away. O happy day with thunder clouds, O dunderhead, O Donner, O Blitzen, all alone (a sorry pass) in the wrack of the roof of history."

In this passage, Waldner wanders through nursery rhymes, Biblical stories, lines from hymns, and finally historical events and pop culture. A reviewer for the

American Poet quoted Waldner's description of her method of writing, in which, she says, there is "no transition from 'out of it' to 'right back in.'"

Although Waldner does not define her writing as such, her poetic style calls to mind the stream-of-consciousness writing that James Joyce (1882-1941) first popularized, a process through which the author tries to capture meaning by exploring his own random thought processes. That is why Waldner's poems read as if she is flowing through snatches of her memories, stopping only briefly at one image, which quickly reminds her of a somewhat related but different one. In the words of the *American Poet* reviewer, Waldner's writing is similar to observing "an animator drawing the hand of an animator drawing a bridge as the mouse crosses over it. Waldner seems to compose a line from moment to moment as we watch."

The poetry in Waldner's writing resides mostly in the sounds of, her choices of, and her combinations of words. The sounds rush out as the words cross the page, "not in nonsense," though, as Cole Swensen, for the *Boston Review,* pointed out, "for in part what Waldner demonstrates is that nonsense doesn't exist—where sense is not, something else is." And that something else, Swensen believes, is "a deep engagement with sound."

For a reviewer in *Publishers Weekly,* that something else in Waldner's work is deeply felt emotion. This reviewer appreciated Waldner's poetry for the fact that she "mixes sassiness, smarts and lyricism, intellectual querulousness with personal bitterness, vigor and exasperation."

Waldner's work elicits a variety of effects on her readers. Some critics attempt to understand her work on an intellectual level, trying to comprehend all her allusions, puns, and hidden meanings. Others enjoy the linguistic challenge that she offers in presenting words in unusual patterns and forms; while still others relinquish the need to understand her words and instead simply enjoy the musicality of her poetry.

Waldner has released additional collections, including *Self and Simulacra,* in 2001. In this volume, she more precisely addressed the issues of women as she explored the influences that help create female identity. Her most recent work includes *Dark Would: (The Missing Person)* and *Etym(Bi)Ology,* both published in 2002.

BIOGRAPHICAL AND CRITICAL SOURCES:

PERIODICALS

American Poet, winter, 2000, "James Laughlin Award," pp. 33-38.
Boston Review, December, 2000, Cole Swensen, review of *A Point Is That Which Has No Part.*
Publishers Weekly, February 7, 2000, review of *A Point Is That Which Has No Part,* p. 69.

OTHER

Academy of American Poets, http://www.poets.org/ (September 16, 2001), "Liz Waldner."
Electronic Poetry Review, http://www.poetry.org/ (March 2, 2002), "Liz Waldner."
Ploughshares, http://www.pshares.org/ (March 2, 2002), "Liz Waldner."
Poetry Daily, http://www.poems.com/ (March 2, 2002), "Feature: Liz Waldner."
University of Iowa Press, http://www.uiowa.edu/ (March 2, 2002), "Winner of the 2000 Iowa Poetry Prize."*

*   *   *

WALL, Geoffrey
    See CHADWICK, Geoffrey

*   *   *

WARSHAWSKI, Morrie

PERSONAL: Male.

ADDRESSES: Home—Ann Arbor, MI. *Agent*—c/o Author Mail, National Assembly of State Arts Agencies, 1029 Vermont Ave. N.W., 2nd Floor, Washington, DC 20005. *E-mail*—morriewar@aol.com.

CAREER: Independent arts consultant, facilitator, and writer, Ann Arbor, MI, 1986—.

WRITINGS:

Shaking the Money Tree: How to Get Grants and Donations for Film and Video Projects, Michael Wiese Production, 1994.

(Editor) *The Next Step: Distributing Independent Films and Videos,* AIVF/FIVF, 1996.

A State Arts Agency Strategic Planning Toolkit, National Assembly of State Arts Agencies, 2000.

The Fundraising Houseparty: How to Get Donations from Individuals in a Houseparty Setting, privately printed, 2002.

Contributor of articles, essays, and poetry to periodicals, including *Ford Times, Foundation News, Los Angeles Times, Modern Poetry Studies, Parenting, Rolling Stone, St. Louis Post-Dispatch,* and *San Francisco Examiner.*

BIOGRAPHICAL AND CRITICAL SOURCES:

PERIODICALS

Booklist, March 15, 1994, Mike Tribby, review of *Shaking the Money Tree: How to Get Grants and Donations for Film and Video Projects,* p. 1317.

*   *   *

WATSON, Rosamund Marriott 1860-1911
(Graham R. Tomson, R. Armytage)

PERSONAL: Born October 6, 1860, in Hackney, England; died of uterine cancer, December 29, 1911; buried in St. James Churchyard, Shere, England; daughter of Benjamin Williams (an accountant) and Sylvia (Good) Ball; married George Francis Armytage, September 9, 1879 (divorced, 1887); married Arthur Graham Tomson (an artist), September 21, 1887 (divorced, 1895); companion to H. B. Marriott Watson (a writer), 1894-1911; children: (first marriage) Eulalie Georgina, Daphne; (second marriage) Graham; (with Watson) Richard Marriott.

CAREER: Poet, author, and editor. *Sylvia's Journal,* London, England, editor, 1892-94; *Atheneum,* London, England, reviewer; columnist with the *Scots Observer, Pall Mall Gazette, Daily Mail,* and *New Liberal Review,* all London, England.

WRITINGS:

(Published anonymously) *Tares,* Kegan Paul, Trench (London, England), 1884, published under name Rosamund Marriott Watson as *Tares: A Book of Verses,* Mosher (Portland, ME), 1898.

(Editor, under pseudonym Graham R. Tomson) *Ballads of the North Countrie,* White and Allen (New York, NY), 1888, abridged edition published as *Border Ballads,* White and Allen (New York, NY), 1888.

(Under pseudonym Graham R. Tomson) *The Bird-Bride: A Volume of Ballads and Sonnets,* Longmans, Green (London, England), 1889.

(Editor, under pseudonym Graham R. Tomson) *Selections from the Greek Anthology,* Gage (New York, NY), 1889.

(Under pseudonym Graham R. Tomson) *The Patch-Work Quilt,* Dutton (New York, NY), 1891.

(Under pseudonym Graham R. Tomson) *A Summer Night, and Other Poems,* Methuen (London, England), 1891, published under her own name as *A Summer Night, and Other Poems,* Way and Williams (Chicago, IL), 1895.

(Editor, under pseudonym Graham R. Tomson) *Concerning Cats: A Book of Poems by Many Authors,* Unwin (London, England), 1892.

Vespertilia, and Other Verses, Way and Williams (Chicago, IL), 1895.

The Art of the House, Macmillan (New York, NY), 1897.

(Under pseudonym Graham R. Tomson) *Old Books, Fresh Flowers,* Adirondack Press (Gouverneur, NY), 1899.

An Island Rose, Nister (London, England), 1900.

After Sunset, John Lane (New York, NY), 1904.

The Heart of a Garden, Jacobs (Philadelphia, PA), 1906.

(Editor) *Wells for Every Day in the Year,* Palmer (London, England), 1911, published as *Great Thoughts from H. G. Wells,* Dodge (New York, NY), 1912.

The Poems of Rosamund Marriott Watson, John Lane (London, England), 1912.

Work represented in collections, including *Ballades and Rondeaus, Chants Royal, Sestinas, Villanelles, Etc.,* edited by Gleeson White, Walter Scott (New York, NY), 1887; *Daisy Days,* Dutton (New York, NY), 1888; *Ballads of Books,* edited by Andrew Lang, Longmans, Green (New York, NY), 1888; *Sea-Music: An Anthology of Poems and Passages Descriptive of the Sea,* edited by Elizabeth A. Sharp, Walter Scott (London, England), 1888; *Mother Goose Nursery Tales,* Nister (London, England), 1898; and *Victorian Anthology,* edited by Edmund Clarence Stedman, 1895. Contributor to periodicals, including the *Yellow Book,*

Independent, Daily Mail, New Liberal Review, Fortnightly Review, Woman's World, Harper's, Scribner's, Illustrated London, Magazine of Art, Atlantic Monthly, Art Weekly, Pall Mall Gazette, and *National Observer.*

The John Lane papers at the Harry Ransom Humanities Research Center, University of Texas, Austin, comprise the principal archive of Rosamund Marriott Watson's correspondence and also include letters of Arthur Thomson and H. B. Marriott Watson. The Louis Chandler Moulton and Pennell papers at the Library of Congress and the Gordon Ray papers at the Pierpont Morgan Library in New York City also include significant materials.

SIDELIGHTS: Rosamund Marriott Watson was a prolific poet, author, and editor who wrote under the surnames of two husbands and a companion. Watson's poetry contains aspects of women's modernism, impressionism, myth, and includes poems that express female desire. Linda K. Hughes wrote in *Dictionary of Literary Biography* that Watson's "admission of broken marriage and divorce as subjects of poetry and her unstable nom de plume also illuminate the role of gender in poetic careers and anticipate twentieth-century feminist issues."

Watson was born Rosamund Ball. Little is known about her childhood, but in a 1905 letter to Nora Hopper, she described herself as lonely. She was one of five siblings, but none was close to her in age. During her early years, she was happiest in her accountant father's extensive library with the authors she discovered there, such as Jean Ingelow, Algernon Swinburne, Dante Gabriel Rossetti, Christina Rossetti, and William Morris, all of whom influenced her work. Ball was thirteen when her mother died of uterine cancer, isolating her even further. Her father was an amateur poet, and her brother Wilfred, also an accountant, attended art school in the evening. His watercolors were praised by James McNeill Whistler in the early 1880s, but his chosen field did not please his father, who cut him from his will. His young sister considered art but decided it would not be practical.

After Benjamin Ball achieved the position of secretary at a bank, he relocated his family to Wandsworth, a more prestigious address than their former home in Hackney. His daughter, now able to mingle with the social elite, met George Francis Armytage, an independently wealthy man seven years her senior. They married in 1879 and moved to Surbiton. Rosamund Armytage, who soon became the mother of two daughters, continued to write her poetry and articles under the name "Mrs. G. Armytage." She would later write a fashion column in the *Scots Observer.*

Her debut volume, a slim book of fifteen poems, was published anonymously. Hughes noted that "*Tares* might derive its title from Sir Thomas Browne's *Religio Medici* (1643): 'Not picked from the leaves of any author, but bred amongst the weeds and tares of mine own brain'—boastful and modest at once, a coupling that characterized her dealings in the literary marketplace all her life. *Tares* reflects wide reading (writers such as Horace, François Villon, John Milton, and Johann Wolfgang von Goethe) and—despite what may be the title's boast—direct borrowing from Robert Browning, Alfred Tennyson, and Ingelow." Not yet developed as a poet, she showed a tendency to break rules and engage in experimentation.

A theme throughout *Tares* is disillusionment and dissolution. This may be related to the deterioration of relations between Watson and her husband. They separated in 1885, and Armytage agreed to provide his wife with an allowance of 500 pounds a year. She moved in with Sylvia Lewis, a married sister, and continued to write as R. Armytage. At the same time, she was involved in a relationship with Arthur Graham Tomson, an artist who had studied in Germany and was exhibiting at the Royal Academy and Grosvenor Gallery, and who became affiliated with the new English Art Club. George Armytage filed for divorce. By the time the matter was settled and he had gained custody of the couple's two daughters, Rosamund was seven months pregnant. A month later she and Tomson married, and their son was born at the end of October.

By that time, however, she had already begun to publish in an American periodical, using the name Graham R. Tomson. Other American periodicals which regularly ran her work included the *Atlantic Monthly, Harper's,* and *Scribner's,* and it was her initial acceptance in the United States that opened doors to her in England. Andrew Lang, who was the British editor for *Harper's,* hailed the new poet in *Longman's.* Almost immediately, twelve of her poems were chosen for Gleeson White's collection *Ballades and Rondeaus, Chants Royal, Sestinas, Villanelles, Etc.* White, like Lang, however, noted her as being "Mr. Graham R.

Tomson," which for her purposes was preferable until the details of her divorce were no longer news. Lang was the first to learn her gender when she invited him to dinner, and by that time, she had become firmly entrenched in literary society.

Lang was a great influence on Tomson, correcting her poems and helping her with projects like *Border Ballads,* for which he wrote the notes. He advised her on *The Bird-Bride: A Volume of Ballads and Sonnets.* He was not, however, enthusiastic about the heavy social schedule kept by Tomson and Arthur. They moved to a new home with a studio where they entertained their many literary, artistic, and feminist friends. In 1889 Thomas Hardy nominated Tomson for membership in the Society of Authors, and she also attended the first meeting of the Literary Ladies. Tomson also began writing her fashion column for W. E. Henley in the *Scots Observer* at this time.

Amid all this activity, Tomson's second collection, *The Bird-Bride,* was published. Divided into five sections, it contains ballads, sonnets, verses, translations, and fixed French verse forms, with most of the latter being reprinted from White's collection. Hughes wrote that "the emotional register ranges from violent passion to wistful yearning to the hard-edged skepticism of 'The Smile of All-Wisdom' (which sees precisely nothing behind the veil of death) or humor of 'The Optimist.'" The volume sold only a few hundred copies but enhanced Tomson's reputation within the writing community.

The Bird-Bride was followed by *Selections from the Greek Anthology, A Summer Night, and Other Poems,* and *Concerning Cats: A Book of Poems by Many Authors.* The frontispiece of *A Summer Night* was Arthur's impressionistic painting of Tomson in their garden, and he also illustrated *Concerning Cats.* She did not include her mythological poems that had appeared in *Universal Review,* and she placed the seven supernatural poems at the back of the book. She "emphasized impressionist landscapes and urban lyrics as well as other decadent material akin to that of Rhymers' Club poets," noted Hughes. The volume received many favorable reviews.

Tomson accepted the position of editor of the women's magazine *Sylvia's Journal* in 1892. As editor, Tomson became even more visible and used her position to promote writers (particularly women writers) whom she believed in. She introduced a gardening column, provided more extensive coverage of books and poetry, and wrote articles about women's colleges. Katharine Tynan wrote a series about women's history, and the new visuals for the periodical included the work of such female artists as black-and-white artist R. Anning Bell. Tomson also contributed one column each Thursday to the *Pall Mall Gazette,* and her articles on interior decorating were later collected and published as *The Art of the House.*

Tomson had brief flirtations with T. Fisher Unwin and John Lane in their correspondences and with Hardy, whose advances she then rebuffed. But she did succumb to temptation in the form of H. B. Marriott Watson, an Australian scholar, who moved within her own social circle. Watson was very different from her quiet husband; he had published stories of illicit love in the *National Observer,* and was credited for jump-starting the career of Wells. Tomson apparently made the first move and left Arthur and their young son (then seven) and moved in with Watson. She left *Sylvia's Journal* and lost some of the prestige she had earned by changing her name yet again, to Rosamund Marriott Watson. Arthur did not file for divorce for another year.

As Watson she published *Vespertilia, and Other Verses,* which like *Tares,* is heavily weighted with poems about death, disillusionment, and failed love, with a few that celebrate desire and love, themes with which Watson was very familiar. The collection received positive reviews, but only one critic noted that Watson had written other work under another name.

The surviving letters of Watson reveal nothing of her first three children but do mention Richard, the son she had with H. B., and her poems after his birth reflect a new maternal affection. Watson and H. B. had a volatile relationship at the beginning, but they settled down into a loving and peaceful life, although they never married. In 1895 they moved into Heathfield Cottage in Chiswick, the garden of which Watson had planted with 6,000 bulbs by 1898. They were close enough to London that they continued meeting with their friends, including James, Arthur Symons, and Charlotte Mew. Watson continued to have her poems published by periodicals in the United States and the *Yellow Book* and *Pall Mall Gazette* in England. She wrote *An Island Rose,* a novel for children, and gardening columns for the *Daily Mail* and *New Liberal*

Review. These meditations were collected with poems and published as *The Heart of a Garden.*

By the time Watson's *After Sunset* was published, the poet was already showing symptoms of the illness that would claim her in another decade, and she suffered a nervous breakdown. Because of her poor health, the family moved in 1904, to Orchard Cottage in Shere in the Surrey Downs, where Watson tended a more modest garden than her creation at Chiswick. She gave up most of her writing, now concentrating on children's literature, poetry, interior decoration, and furniture. She collected her gardening essays and poems and took the photographs for *The Heart of a Garden,* but she continued to decline. Her cancerous uterus was removed in 1910. H. B. felt publishing her collected poems might give Watson the will to live, but she died two months before their publication.

The Poems of Rosamund Marriott Watson contains the works from all her previous volumes and new poems, including those dedicated to friends. In this last collection, Hughes felt, "she recovered much of the grace and charm of her 1890s volumes, with their glancing rhythms and mellifluous diction; if it includes little experimentation and some poems that fall below her general average, several demonstrate her continuing vitality as a poet. . . . [Many] of these poems seem expressive, even confessional, dealing with everything from lost beauty and youth or continuing friendships to her literary fame."

In an *Athenaeum* obituary, Vernon Rendall praised Watson for combining "gifts of technique which mark the scrupulous artist" with "a sense of passion and wistfulness that are all her own." In H. B.'s novel *Rosalind in Arden,* he quotes from her verse. Hughes concluded by saying that "Watson is an important figure for her sheer command of poetic craft; for her anticipation of modernist work by women; for the boldness of her lyrics and ballads; for her verve as 'Graham R. Tomson' in negotiating the literary marketplace; and for the price in reputation she paid when 'Graham R. Tomson' became Rosamund Marriott Watson."

BIOGRAPHICAL AND CRITICAL SOURCES:

BOOKS

Archer, William, *Poets of the Younger Generation,* John Lane (New York, NY), 1902, pp. 469-480.

Dictionary of Literary Biography, Volume 240: *Late Nineteenth- and Early Twentieth-Century British Women Poets,* Gale (Detroit, MI), 2001.

Mix, Katherine Lyon, *A Study in Yellow: The Yellow Book and Its Contributors,* University of Kansas Press (Lawrence, KS), 1960.

Pennell, Elizabeth Robins, *Nights: Rome and Venice in the Aesthetic Eighties, London and Paris in the Fighting Nineties,* second edition, Lippincott (Philadelphia, PA), 1916.

Schaffer, Talia, *The Forgotten Female Aesthetes: Literary Culture in Late-Victorian England,* University Press of Virginia (Charlottesville, VA), 2000.

Schaffer, Talia, and Kathy Alexis Psomiades, editors, *Women and British Aestheticism,* University Press of Virginia (Charlottesville, VA), 1999, pp. 119-138.

Scott, Cyril, *My Years of Indiscretion,* Mills and Boon (London, England), 1924, pp. 74-77.

PERIODICALS

English Illustrated Magazine, April, 1894, Richard Le Gallienne, "Woman-Poets of the Day," pp. 649-657.

News of the World, February 6, 1887.

Notes & Queries, July, 1973, Michael Millgate, "Thomas Hardy and Rosamund Tomson," pp. 253-255.

Tulsa Studies in Women's Literature, spring, 1995, Linda K. Hughes, "A Fin-de-Siècle Beauty and the Beast: Configuring the Body in Works by Graham R. Tomson (Rosamund Marriott Watson)," pp. 95-121.

Victorian Periodicals Review, summer, 1996, Linda K. Hughes, "A Female Aesthete at the Helm: *Sylvia's Journal* and 'Graham R. Tomson,' 1893-1894," p. 173-192.

OBITUARIES:

PERIODICALS

Atheneum, January 6, 1912, obituary by Vernon Rendall.

Times (London, England), January 2, 1912.*

WAUTISCHER, Helmut 1954-

PERSONAL: Born June 15, 1954, in Klagenfurt, Austria; *Education:* Bundeshandelsakademie Klagenfurt, B.A., 1974; Karl-Franzens Universitat Graz, Ph. D., 1985.

ADDRESSES: Office—Department of Philosophy, Sonoma State University, 1801 East Cotati Ave., Rohnert Park, CA 94928-3609. *E-mail*—wautisch@ sonoma.edu.

CAREER: San Diego State University, San Diego, CA, lecturer in philosophy, 1988-91; California State University, Long Beach, lecture in philosophy, 1989-92; Humboldt State University, Arcata, CA, visiting assistant professor of philosophy, 1992-94; California State University, Hayward, lecturer in philosophy, 1996; Sonoma State University, Rohnert Park, CA, senior lecturer in philosophy, 1995—. Universitat Klagenfurt, universitatslektor, 1995-97. Organizer, coordinator, and presenter at numerous professional conferences.

MEMBER: Karl Jaspers Society of North America, American Philosophical Association (Pacific division), American Anthropological Association, Society for the Anthropology of Consciousness (secretary/treasurer, 1994-96, executive board, 1991-99), Council of Philosophical Societies (executive board, 1997—), Osterreichische Gesellschaft für Philosophie.

AWARDS, HONORS: Fulbright scholar, Austrian-American Educational Commission, 1981.

WRITINGS:

(Editor) *Tribal Epistemologies: Essays in the Philosophy of Anthropology,* Ashgate, 1998.

Contributor of essays to books, including *Bachtin and the Problem of Methodology for Humanitarian Knowledge,* edited by V. N. Pivojev; and to periodicals, including *Anthropology of Consciousness, Dialogue and Humanism,* and *Social Neuroscience Bulletin.* Contributor of book reviews to periodicals, including *Anthropology of Consciousness.* Guest editor, *Anthropology of Consciousness,* 1994; editorial review board,

Yearbook of Cross-Cultural Medicine and Psychotherapy, 1991-95, *Anthropology of Consciousness,* 1992-98, *Mind, Brain, and Social Organization,* 1995—, and *Noetic Journal,* 1999—; textbook reviewer for Blackwell Publishing Company, Mayfield Publishing Company, and Broadview Press.

WORK IN PROGRESS: Editor, *Ontology of Consciousness: A Modern Synthesis.*

*   *   *

WEBB, Nancy Boyd 1932-

PERSONAL: Born 1932, in Massachusetts; daughter of Earl G. (a professor of mathematics) and Angie P. Boyd; married Kempton E. Webb. *Education:* Harvard University, A.B. (cum laude); Smith College, M.S.S.; Columbia University, D.S.W.

ADDRESSES: Office—Graduate School of Social Service, Fordham University at Westchester, Neperan Ave., Tarrytown, NY. *E-mail*—nancyboydwebb@aol. com.

CAREER: Fordham University, New York, NY, university distinguished professor of social work, 1979—, and James R. Dumpson Chair of Child Welfare Studies. American Board of Examiners in Clinical Social Work, diplomate; private practice of social work with children and families; presenter of workshops. Westchester Task Force on Children and Loss, member.

MEMBER: Council on Social Work Education, National Association of Social Workers, Association for Play Therapy, Association for Death Education and Counseling, Ortho, New York Association for Play Therapy (member of board of directors).

WRITINGS:

Techniques of Play Therapy: A Clinical Demonstration (videotape), with manual, Guilford Press (New York, NY), 1994.
Social Work Practice with Children, Guilford Press (New York, NY), 1996.

(Editor) *Play Therapy with Children in Crisis: Individual, Group, and Family Treatment,* Guilford Press (New York, NY), 2nd edition, 1999.

(Editor) *Culturally Diverse Parent-Child and Family Relationships,* Columbia University Press (New York, NY), 2001.

(Editor) *Helping Bereaved Children: A Handbook for Practitioners,* Guilford Press (New York, NY), 2nd edition, 2002.

Contributor to books, including *Living with Grief: Helping Children and Adolescents Adapt to Loss,* edited by K. Doka, Hospice Foundation of America (Washington, DC), 2000; and *Handbook of Social Work Practice with Vulnerable and Resilient Populations,* edited by A. Gitterman, Columbia University Press (New York, NY), 2nd edition, 2001. Contributor to periodicals, including *Crisis Intervention* and *American Journal of Orthopsychiatry.* Consulting editor, *Children and Schools.*

Some of Webb's writings have been translated into Chinese.

WORK IN PROGRESS: Revising *Social Work Practice with Children,* completion expected in 2003.

*   *   *

WEBLING, Lucy 1877-1952
(Lucy Betty MacRaye)

PERSONAL: Born August 30, 1877; daughter of Robert James (a retailer) and Maria Webling; married Walter Jackson McRea (an actor); children: Lucy, Louis Drummond.

CAREER: Actress and writer. Actress in stage productions, including *Little Lord Fauntleroy,* 1886, *Nixie,* 1890, and *Uncle Mike,* 1892.

WRITINGS:

(With sister, Peggy Webling) *Poems and Stories,* McLean (Toronto, Canada), c. 1896.

(Under pseudonym Lucy Betty MacRaye) *One Way Street* (novel), Hutchinson (London, England), 1933.

(Under pseudonym Lucy Betty MacRaye) *Centre Stage* (novel), Hutchinson (London, England), 1938.

SIDELIGHTS: Lucy Webling was an English actress and writer who produced two novels in the 1930s. As a child, she appeared in stage productions of works such as *Little Lord Fauntleroy* and *Nixie,* and in her teens she joined sisters Peggy Webling and Rosalind Webling in performing Shakespearean scenes during a tour of Canada. About this time, the mid-1890s, she also collaborated with her sister Peggy in producing *Poems and Stories,* which features poetry by Lucy and fiction by Peggy. Jeanie Grant Moore, writing in the *Dictionary of Literary Biography,* described Webling's poems as "rhythmic and romantic" but added that they are "not distinguished by striking language or images." According to Moore, Webling's poems "paint an idyllic picture of Canadian beauty, and . . . they express a longing for Britain."

While her sister pursued a literary career, ultimately issuing more than twenty publications, Webling continued to act on the stage. In 1909, however, she married a fellow performer, Walter Jackson McRea, and settled in Canada. She gave birth to a daughter, who died, and a son, before leaving her husband and returning—with her son—to England. In 1933, writing as Lucy Betty MacRaye, she published *One Way Street,* a novel in which—as Moore noted in the *Dictionary of Literary Biography*she "abjured the social judgment placed on unwed mothers." Webling, still writing as MacRaye, produced a second novel, *Centre Stage,* in 1938. Moore wrote that Webling's novels "demonstrate at least a potential for more sophisticated writing than that of her sister." Despite showing literary promise, Webling abandoned her writing career after issuing *Centre Stage.* She died in 1952.

BIOGRAPHICAL AND CRITICAL SOURCES:

BOOKS

Dictionary of Literary Biography, Volume 240: *Late Nineteenth- and Early Twentieth-Century British Women Poets,* Gale (Detroit, MI), 2001.*

*   *   *

WEIL, Samuel
See KAUFMAN, Lloyd

*   *   *

WEIL, Samuel L.
See KAUFMAN, Lloyd

WEIR, Robert E. 1952-

PERSONAL: Born March 11, 1952, in Chambersburg, PA; son of Archie E. and Sarah M. (Kessinger) Weir; married Emily B. Harrison (a writer and editor), May 13, 1978. *Ethnicity:* "Caucasian." *Education:* Shippensburg University, B.S., 1974, M.A., 1980; University of Massachusetts—Amherst, Ph.D., 1990. *Politics:* "Democratic Socialist." *Religion:* Society of Friends (Quakers). *Hobbies and other interests:* Photography, Celtic music, travel.

ADDRESSES: Home—15 Woods Rd., Florence, MA 01062. *Office*—Bay Path College, Longmeadow, MA 01106. *E-mail*—rweir@mtholyoke.edu.

CAREER: Smith College, Northampton, MA, assistant professor of history, 1989-93; Bay Path College, Longmeadow, MA, associate professor of liberal studies, 1993—.

MEMBER: New England Historical Society (member of executive board), North East Popular Culture Association (member of executive board).

AWARDS, HONORS: Senior Fulbright fellow in New Zealand, 2001.

WRITINGS:

Beyond Labor's Veil: The Culture of the Knights of Labor, Pennsylvania State University Press (University Park, PA), 1996.
(With John T. Cumbler) *The Changing Landscape of Labor: American Workers and Workplaces,* photographs by Michael Jacobson-Hardy, University of Massachusetts Press (Amherst, MA), 1996.
Knights Unhorsed: Internal Conflict in a Gilded Age Social Movement, Wayne State University Press (Detroit, MI), 2000.

Contributor of essays and music reviews to periodicals.

WORK IN PROGRESS: Encyclopedia of American Labor, for Greenwood Press (Westport, CT).

SIDELIGHTS: Robert E. Weir told *CA*: "I am a professional historian specializing in American social, labor, and sports history, especially that of the late nineteenth century. My work is informed mainly by social class, race, ethnicity, and gender. In addition I am a freelance journalist with a part-time career in music reviewing (Celtic, folk, world), and in political 'op-ed' articles."

BIOGRAPHICAL AND CRITICAL SOURCES:

PERIODICALS

American Historical Review, April, 1998, Eric Arnesen, review of *Beyond Labor's Veil: The Culture of the Knights of Labor,* p. 612.
Historian, summer, 1997, Thomas Winter, review of *Beyond Labor's Veil,* p. 889.
History, winter, 1997, Robert Whaples, review of *Beyond Labor's Veil,* p. 58.
Journal of American History, March, 1997, Paul Buhle, review of *Beyond Labor's Veil,* p. 1427.
Journal of Economic History, March, 1997, David Witwer, review of *Beyond Labor's Veil,* p. 245.
Labor History, fall, 1996, Susan Levine, review of *Beyond Labor's Veil,* p. 551; November, 1999, Jeffrey Ryan Suzik, review of *The Changing Landscape of Labor: American Workers and Workplaces,* p. 563; November, 2001, Ken Fones-Wolf, review of *Knights Unhorsed: Internal Conflict in a Gilded Age Social Movement,* p. 430.

*   *   *

WEISBERG, Harold 1913-2002

OBITUARY NOTICE—See index for *CA* sketch: Born April 8, 1913, in Philadelphia, PA; died of cardiovascular disease February 21, 2002, in Frederick, MD. Researcher, intelligence analyst, farmer, journalist, and author. Weisberg was a poultry farmer in Maryland when President John F. Kennedy was assassinated and the Warren Commission issued its controversial report on the event. The report launched him on a quest for the truth that lasted for the rest of his life. Weisberg had worked as a journalist in the 1930s and as a State Department intelligence analyst in the 1940s. Using his past experience, he began to gather information about the assassination and the accused killer, Lee

Harvey Oswald. Weisberg filed dozens of lawsuits under the Freedom of Information Act and accumulated a vast collection of government papers, which he began to publish, often at his own expense and in the face of increasing financial hardship. In time, he also began to research the assassination of Martin Luther King, Jr. on behalf of convicted murderer James Earl Ray. Weisberg became convinced that neither Oswald nor Ray had committed the crimes of which they were accused, but he never offered to identify the actual perpetrators. Weisberg's work on the Kennedy assassination was indirectly corroborated in 1979, when the House Select Committee on Assassinations cited the Warren Commission for inadequate investigation and the primary American intelligence agencies for withholding their cooperation in the matter, concluding that the assassination was "probably" the result of a conspiracy. Weisberg's books include *Whitewash: The Report on the Warren Report, Photographic Whitewash: Suppressed Kennedy Assassination Pictures, Martin Luther King: The Assassination,* and *Frame-up: The Martin Luther King-James Earl Ray Case.*

OBITUARIES AND OTHER SOURCES:

PERIODICALS

Los Angeles Times, February 25, 2002, obituary by Adam Bernstein, p. B9.
New York Times, March 4, 2002, obituary by Stuart Lavietes, p. A25.

* * *

WETTERHAHN, Ralph (Francis) 1942-

PERSONAL: Born April 20, 1942, in New York, NY; son of John William and Marie Bernadette (Hackenberg) Wetterhahn; married Mary Ann Bowers, June 26, 1963 (divorced, June, 1985); married Carol L. Leviton, May 28, 1986; children: Scott Gerald, Thomas Michael, Michael David. *Education:* United States Air Force Academy, B.S., 1963; Auburn University, M.B.A., 1973; University of Southern California Professional Writing Program.

ADDRESSES: Home—Long Beach, CA. *Agent*—c/o Carroll & Graf Publishers, 161 William St., 16th Floor, New York, NY 10038. *E-mail*—wcadence@aol.com.

CAREER: U.S. Air Force 1963-92; R & R Aviation Service Ltd., Bangkok, Thailand, chairman, 1992-93; freelance writer, 1993—. *Military service:* U.S. Air Force, 1963-92; fighter pilot; became colonel; received Silver Star and Distinguished Flying Cross.

MEMBER: Air Force Association, Long Beach Writers Group.

WRITINGS:

The Last Battle: The Mayaguez Incident and the End of the Vietnam War, Carroll & Graf (New York, NY), 2001.
Shadowmakers (fiction), Carroll & Graf (New York, NY), 2002.

Contributor to periodicals, including *Air & Space, Smithsonian, Popular Science, Bangkok Post, Soldier of Fortune, U.S. Air Force Academy Checkpoints Magazine, Retired Officers Magazine, Retired Officer, VFW,* and *Vietnam Magazine.*

WORK IN PROGRESS: Two nonfiction books for Carroll & Graf: *Riding the Empire Express,* which is about World War II bombing missions launched from the Aleutian Islands to attack the Northern Kuriles, due in 2003, and *Secret War, Stolen Hardware, Vanished Warriors,* which is about Russia's involvement in the Korean War, the technology the Russians copied, and the American POWs they executed, due in 2004.

SIDELIGHTS: A decorated fighter pilot who flew 180 combat missions in Vietnam, Ralph Wetterhahn went on to serve nearly thirty years in the U.S. Air Force. A few years after his retirement he began to look into the events surrounding the S.S. *Mayaguez,* a U.S. cargo ship seized by Cambodian rebels a few weeks after the fall of Saigon. When the United States responded with a military rescue operation, the captives were released. At least that is the official version. In *The Last Battle: The Mayaguez Incident and the End of the Vietnam War,* Wetterhahn "clearly shows that the rescue operation was botched terribly," wrote a reviewer in *Publishers Weekly.* Marines were sent to the wrong island, forty-one American troops were killed (to rescue forty crew members), and three marines were actually left behind to be caught and executed by the Khmer Rouge. "Far worse, none of it had to happen, because the Khmer Rouge had already let the crew go," wrote Marlene Chamberlain in *Booklist.* Wetterhahn did a great deal of interviewing and other research, including literally digging in the beaches of Cambodia, to put together his book, "which is written in a strong, hard-to-put down narrative style," according to Mark Ellis in *Library Journal.* Christopher Hitchens, writing in *Nation,* called *The Last Battle* "extraordinary," and added that Wetterhahn's "book deserves the highest praise and widest circulation."

BIOGRAPHICAL AND CRITICAL SOURCES:

PERIODICALS

Booklist, June 1, 2001, Marlene Chamberlain, review of *The Last Battle,* p. 1834.
Library Journal, May 1, 2001, Mark Ellis, review of *The Last Battle.*
Nation, April 30, 2001, Christopher Hitchens, "The Kiss of Henry," p. 9.
Publishers Weekly, April 16, 2001, review of *The Last Battle.*

*   *   *

WILL, Frederic 1928-
(Frank Shynnagh)

PERSONAL: Born December 4, 1928, in New Haven, CT; son of Samuel (a university professor) and Constance (Bickwell) Will; married Julia Ogaga, 1994; children: Alex, Barbara, Jennifer Will Onamado, Christopher, Carson, Kyle. *Ethnicity:* "White." *Education:* Indiana University, B.A., 1949; Yale University, Ph.D., 1953. *Politics:* "Tory." *Religion:* Roman Catholic. *Hobbies and other interests:* "Wide-arc conversation, outrageous humor, sexuality."

ADDRESSES: Home—617 Seventh St. NW, Mount Vernon, IA 52314; fax: 319-895-6399. *Agent*—Malaga Baldi, Malaga Baldi Literary Agency, 204 84th St., Suite 3C, New York, NY 10024. *E-mail*—samuelw981@aol.com.

CAREER: Poet, scholar, and educator. Dartmouth College, Hanover, NH, assistant professor of classics, 1952-54; Pennsylvania State University, University Park, teacher of classics, 1955-60; University of Texas—Austin, associate professor of classics, 1960-65; University of Iowa, Iowa City, professor of English, 1965-70, fellow of Institute for Advanced Studies, 1983-91; University of Massachusetts—Amherst, professor of comparative literature, 1970-82; Mellen University, Mount Vernon, IA, president, 1993-2000; Chinese Academy of Social Sciences, visiting research associate at Chinese Institute of Sociology, 2002—. Gives lectures and readings from his works at educational institutions and on media programs.

AWARDS, HONORS: Fulbright fellow in Greece, 1950-51, Germany, 1956-57, Tunisia, 1975-76, and Ivory Coast, 2000-02; fellow of Bollingen Foundation, Ford Foundation, and American Council of Learned Societies; awards from Texas Institute of Letters and *New York Quarterly* for poetry, prose, and translation; grants from Coordinating Council of Literary Magazines and National Endowment for the Arts.

WRITINGS:

Intelligible Beauty in Aesthetic Thought, Niemeyer (Tübingen, Germany), 1958.
Mosaic and Other Poems, Pennsylvania State University Press (University Park, PA), 1959.
A Wedge of Words (poetry), University of Texas Press (Austin, TX), 1963.
(Translator from Greek and author of introduction) Kōstēs Palamas, *The Twelve Words of the Gypsy,* University of Nebraska Press (Lincoln, NE), 1964.
(Editor and author of introduction) *Metaphrasis: An Anthology from the University of Iowa Translation Workshop, 1964-1965,* Verb (Denver, CO), 1964.
(Editor and author of introduction) *Hereditas: Seven Essays on the Modern Experience of the Classical,* University of Texas Press (Austin, TX), 1965.
Flumen Historicum: Victor Cousin's Aesthetic and Its Sources, University of North Carolina Press (Chapel Hill, NC), 1965.
(Translator from Greek and author of introduction) Kōstēs Palamas, *The King's Flute* (poetry), University of Nebraska Press (Lincoln, NE), 1966.
Literature Inside Out: Ten Speculative Essays, Press of Western Reserve University (Cleveland, OH), 1966.
From a Year in Greece, illustrated by John Guerin, University of Texas Press (Austin, TX), 1967.

Planets (poetry), Golden Quill Press (Francestown, NH), 1968.

Archilochus, Twayne Publishers (New York, NY), 1969.

Herondas, Twayne Publishers (New York, NY), 1972.

Brandy in the Snow: Poems, 1966-1970, New Rivers Press (New York, NY), 1972.

The Jargon of Authenticity, Northwestern University Press (Evanston, IL), 1973.

The Fact of Literature: Three Essays on Public Material, Rodopi (Amsterdam, Netherlands), 1973.

The Knife in the Stone: Essays in Literary Theory, Mouton (The Hague, Netherlands), 1973.

Guatemala, Bellevue (Binghamton, NY), 1973.

Botulism, Micromegas (Amherst, MA), 1975.

The Generic Demands of Greek Literature, Rodopi (Amsterdam, Netherlands), 1976.

Belphagor: Six Essays in Imaginative Space, Rodopi (Amsterdam, Netherlands), 1977.

The Gross National Product: Fifty Epics of America, Panache Books (Sunderland, MA), 1977.

Our Thousand-Year-Old Bodies: Selected Poems, 1956-1976, University of Massachusetts Press (Amherst, MA), 1980.

The Sliced Dog, L'Epervier Press (Seattle, WA), 1984.

Shamans in Turtlenecks, Rodopi (Amsterdam, Netherlands), 1984.

Thresholds and Testimonies: Recovering Order in Literature and Criticism, Wayne State University Press (Detroit, MI), 1988.

Entering the Open Hole, L'Epervier Press (Seattle, WA), 1989.

A Portrait of John: The Midwest and the World, 1928-1984, Wayne State University Press (Detroit, MI), 1990.

Founding the Lasting, Wayne State University Press (Detroit, MI), 1991.

Big Rig Souls, A & M Publishers (Detroit, MI), 1991.

Translation Theory and Practice: Reassembling the Tower, Edwin Mellen Press (Lewiston, NY), 1993.

Recoveries, 1975-1986 (poetry), Edwin Mellen Press (Lewiston, NY), 1993.

Trips of the Psyche, Edwin Mellen Press (Lewiston, NY), 1993.

Textures, Spaces, Wonders, Edwin Mellen Press (Lewiston, NY), 1993.

Literature as Sheltering the Human, Edwin Mellen Press (Lewiston, NY), 1993.

Singing with Whitman's Thrush: Itineraries of the Aesthetic, Edwin Mellen Press (Lewiston, NY), 1993.

Social Reflections on Work, Edwin Mellen Press (Lewiston, NY), 2002.

(With Rick Molz) *Field Research in North American Agricultural Communities: Products and Profiles from the North American Family,* Edwin Mellen Press (Lewiston, NY), 2003.

Where the Beard Grows (novel trilogy), Fourth Dimension Press (Enugu, Nigeria), 2003.

Bananas, Corn, and Cheese, Edwin Mellen Press (Lewiston, NY), 2003.

By the Sweat of Thy Brow, Edwin Mellen Press (Lewiston, NY), 2003.

Miroirs d'eternité: Une saison au sahel, Puci (Abidjan, Ivory Coast), 2003

Flesh and the Color of Love, Puci (Abidjan, Ivory Coast), 2003.

Work represented in anthologies, including *Best Poems of 1963.* Contributor of articles and poetry to periodicals, including *Paris Review, Massachusetts Review, Ploughshares, Poetry Northwest, Philosophical Quarterly, Comparative Literature, Personalist, Carleton Miscellany, Modern Language Notes,* and *Journal of Philosophy and Phenomenological Research.* Founding coeditor, *Arion,* 1962; founder and editor, *Micromegas,* 1965-84. Some writings appear under pseudonym Frank Shynnagh.

Will's papers are collected at the Humanities Research Center Archives, University of Texas—Austin.

WORK IN PROGRESS: Mellen University: The Early Years, for Edwin Mellen Press.

SIDELIGHTS: Frederic Will told *CA:* "My primary purpose in writing is to complete many unexpressed thoughts and to formulate new ones. I am influenced by texts which make my life truer: *Bhagavad Gita,* meditations of Marcus Aurelius, Walter Pater's *The Renaissance,* Jaeger's *Paideia.* I am also touched by African animism.

"I have written about love, sex, despair, silliness, and finally about growing up, doing only one thing at a time and only believing in that, but really believing in it. Living my life inspired me to write on these matters."

Will is fluent in French, German, Spanish, Greek, Latin, Italian, Icelandic, Manx, and Sanskrit.

WILLETT, John (William Mills) 1917-2002

OBITUARY NOTICE—See index for CA sketch: Born June 24, 1917, in Hampstead, England; died August 20, 2002, in Le This, Normandy, France. Editor, translator, and author. Willett was a leading expert on German author Bertolt Brecht and is credited by many for helping to bring Brecht to the attention of the international community. He studied at Winchester and Christ Church, Oxford, where he earned his master's degree in 1939, as well as at the Ruskin School of Art and the Manchester Municipal College of Art before going to Vienna to study the cello and stage design. With the onset of World War II, Willett enlisted in the British Army, serving as an intelligence officer in the Eighth Army. He saw action in North Africa and Italy, reaching the rank of lieutenant colonel and receiving the Order of the British Empire for his service. After the war he returned to England as a newspaperman. He was a writer for the *Manchester Guardian* from 1948 to 1951 and an assistant editor at the *Times Literary Supplement* during the 1960s, but he left the paper to move to France and become a freelance writer and editor. Willett's interest in theater and German culture led him to Brecht, about whom he conducted extensive research and at one point even met and befriended before the author's death in 1956. Sometimes collaborating with Ralph Manheim, Willett wrote about, translated, and edited many volumes about Brecht, including *The Theatre of Bertolt Brecht: A Study from Eight Aspects* (1959; fourth edition, 1977) and *Bertolt Brecht: Bad Time for Poetry: Was It? Is It?: One Hundred Fifty Poems and Songs* (1995). He also edited *The Brecht Yearbook,* published by the International Brecht Society in 1995. Willett was also interested in other topics that often were the subject of his writing, such as the history of the Weimar Republic, art, Russian politics, typography, and design.

OBITUARIES AND OTHER SOURCES:

BOOKS

Writers Directory, 16th edition, St. James Press (Detroit, MI), 2001.

PERIODICALS

Independent (London, England), August 26, 2002, p. 14; September 17, 2002, p. 18.
New York Times, August 24, 2002, p. A13.
Times (London, England), August 22, 2002, p. 30.

WILLIAMS, Craig A(rthur) 1965-

PERSONAL: Born July 1, 1965, in Albany, NY; son of Danny C. and Patricia M. (O'Donnell) Williams. *Education:* Yale University, B.A. (summa cum laude), 1986, Ph.D., 1992.

ADDRESSES: Office—Brooklyn College, Department of Classics, 2900 Bedford Ave., Brooklyn, NY 11210. *E-mail*—cawbc@cunyvm.cuny.edu.

CAREER: City University of New York, Brooklyn College, assistant professor, 1992-97, associate professor of classics, 1998—.

MEMBER: American Philological Association, Phi Beta Kappa.

AWARDS, HONORS: Outstanding Academic Title, *Choice,* 1999; Ethyle R. Wolfe Institute for the Humanities fellow, 1999-2000; research fellow, Alexander von Humboldt Foundation, Freie Universität, Berlin, Germany, 2001-02.

WRITINGS:

Roman Homosexuality: Ideologies of Masculinity in Classical Antiquity, Oxford University Press (New York, NY), 1999.

Contributor to books, including *Classical Homoeroticism: Configuration of Age-graded Homosexuality in Culture and History,* edited by Gilbert Herdt. Contributor to periodicals, including *Philologus* and *Arethusa.*

WORK IN PROGRESS: The Second Book of Martial's Epigrams: Introduction, Text, Translation, and Commentary, for Oxford University Press, expected 2003.

SIDELIGHTS: In his career as a professor of classics, Craig A. Williams has focused on issues of gender roles and sexuality, particularly male homosexuality, in ancient Rome; he is currently adding a specialization in the Latin epigrammatist martial. In 1999, he published *Roman Homosexuality: Ideologies of Masculinity in Classical Antiquity,* which draws on a wide range of sources, including love poems, legal records, philosophical tracts, and even graffiti, to discover what a typical ancient Roman might consider a "real man," and how homosexual acts might affect that opinion. "In the hands of a queer theorist," wrote Jay Weiser in the *Harvard Gay & Lesbian Review,* "this difficult material would read as though the author were speaking in tongues." Instead, Williams "provides a readable, convincing account of how Roman men perceived sex," added Weiser.

For the ancient Romans, according to Williams, the crucial distinction was not between "homosexuals" or "heterosexuals," but between active or passive sex roles, and between free citizens and slaves. As Williams puts it, if a freeborn Roman male "played the insertive role, he might do so with either male or female partners, or both, as he pleased: the sex of his partner had no bearing on his own status as a man." There was one other consideration, however: "Were his sexual partners slaves or free?" As W. V. Harris, reviewing the work for *Times Literary Supplement,* put it: "With extraordinary clarity and persuasiveness, Williams shows that in the upper class, at least, the normal adult male was expected to desire insertive sex with young males, but that the social code permitted him such pleasures only with his own slaves." Harris added that Williams' book "may do more for the understanding of classical sexuality than any since Kenneth Dover's *Greek Homosexuality* of twenty years ago."

Williams of course goes beyond purely sexual activities in asking, "What exactly did it mean to act like a man?" Clothing, lifestyle, and mannerisms also affected a Roman's reputation for masculinity or effeminacy, and *Roman Homosexuality* explores all of these. Other considerations include the differences between Greek and Roman attitudes toward sexuality and the rise of asceticism in the later centuries of the Roman Empire. Some questions are left unanswered, including "the consequences of the charge of being the sexually penetrated partner," according to *Choice* reviewer C. M. C. Green. "It is characteristic of Williams' thoroughness, however, that such questions can now arise."

BIOGRAPHICAL AND CRITICAL SOURCES:

PERIODICALS

American Journal of Philology, spring, 2001, Nikolai Endres, review of *Roman Homosexuality: Ideologies of Masculinity in Classical Antiquity,* pp. 143-147.

Choice, December, 1999, C. M. C. Green, review of *Roman Homosexuality,* p. 776.
Classical World, spring, 2001, Kirk Ormand, review of *Roman Homosexuality,* pp. 295-297.
Harvard Gay & Lesbian Review, summer, 1999, Jay Weiser, "Roman Masters," p. 62.
Journal of Homosexuality, Volume 40, issue 1, 2000, David D. Leitao, review of *Roman Homosexuality,* pp. 163-168; Volume 41, issue 2, 2001, Beert Verstraete, review of *Roman Homosexuality,* pp. 167-170.
Times Literary Supplement, April 28, 2000, W.V. Harris, "They Weren't like Us," p. 6.

*   *   *

WIMSATT, William Upski 1972-

PERSONAL: Born November 18, 1972, in Chicago, IL; son of William (a professor) and Barbara (maiden name, Horberg) Wimsatt. *Education:* Attended Oberlin College.

ADDRESSES: Office—226 West 135th St., 4th floor, New York, NY 10030. *Agent*—c/o Publicity Director, Soft Skull Press, 100 Suffolk St., Basement, New York, NY 10002. *E-mail*—www.nomoreprisons.com.

CAREER: Writer, journalist, artist, philanthropist, social activist.

MEMBER: Active Element Foundation (trustee); Adventure Philanthropy (director).

AWARDS, HONORS: Firecracker Book Award, 1999.

WRITINGS:

Bomb the Suburbs, Subway and Elevated Press (Chicago, IL), 1994, 3rd edition, Soft Skull Press (New York, NY), 2001.
No More Prisons, Soft Skull Press (New York, NY), 1999.
The Future 500, New Mouth from the Dirty South (New Orleans, LA), 2002.

WORK IN PROGRESS: The Passion Brokers.

SIDELIGHTS: William Upski Wimsatt was raised in an upper-middle class Jewish family in Chicago's Hyde Park neighborhood; his father was a philosophy of science professor at the University of Chicago. Wimsatt was only eleven when he became absorbed with graffiti. "I was this cerebral, bratty kid of intellectuals," Wimsatt told Marcia Froelke Coburn of *Chicago* magazine.

By the time Wimsatt was fourteen he had been arrested eight times. Fascinated with black culture and hip-hop, he became well known throughout the city for his graffiti. About that time his parents took him out of Kenwood High School and enrolled him at the University of Chicago Lab School, one of the city's most prestigious private high schools. "My parents have liberal pretensions," Wimsatt told Coburn. "My mom even liked me doing graffiti at first; she thought it was cute. That lasted about a year. Then once I started getting arrested and staying out all night, it became bad. They tried to stop me. They did the usual: giving me punishments and yelling at me. Some other parents would send their kid to the army; mine sent me to counseling and the Lab School." He went on to Oberlin College in Ohio but dropped out after two years.

Wimsatt called his first book *Bomb the Suburbs,* published when he was just twenty-one, "the literary culmination of what I'm trying to do—in other words, it's my manifesto." He prided himself on entering the world of black culture as few white people could. "Bomb" is the word for spray painting used by "taggers," the colloquial term given to graffiti painters. In a *Horizon* review of Wimsatt's second book, *No More Prisons,* Neal Pollack recalled an "especially witty essay" from *Bomb the Suburbs* in which Wimsatt mocks his own "Wigger" (white boy) persona: "Sporting their rap gear and attitude serves to disguise White kids' often bland, underdeveloped personalities."

No More Prisons, published in 1999, is a collection of essays, many of which were previously published in periodicals, including the *Utne Reader* and the *New Haven Advocate.* According to *Publishers Weekly,* "in some of his most lucid writing, the self-proclaimed 'cool rich kid' takes on the American penal system and its emphasis on punishment at the expense of hope

and rehabilitation." In reviewing the book for *Library Journal,* Chogollah Maroufi noted that Wimsatt's "zany writing is a refreshing voice for Generation X-style activism." *No More Prisons* was released with a CD of the same title, and it has since generated a Web site devoted to the cause. Jennifer Gonnerman reported in the *Village Voice* that the slogan "No More Prisons"—spray-painted by Wimsatt himself—has appeared in cities from New York to Washington, Cleveland, Chicago, Minneapolis, and as far away as Vancouver. Gonnerman wrote: "Wimsatt insists his sidewalk scribblings are not just a clever marketing strategy, but an effort to raise public awareness." He said, "We're trying to get people to question the insane build-up of the prison industry." Pollack noted in his review that "Wimsatt attacks the public-school system with wit and ardor." He quotes the author: "School is like a drug. Okay when used in moderation but too much of it can cause damaging side effects, including passivity, dullness, emotional dependency, rebelliousness, anti-social behavior, mood swings, disorientation, impaired judgment, eating disorders, depression, self-hatred, and dislike of learning." Wimsatt's "version of self-education has little to do with popular conceptions of home schooling," Pollack pointed out. He advocates living in a different city every year, playing a different sport every day of the week, and attending a different place of worship every Sunday. In conclusion, Pollack speculated that "Wimsatt is either a lunatic snake-oil salesman unleashed upon the nonprofit world, or the Saul Alinsky of his generation. Either way, he shouldn't be dismissed."

Ben Diamond reported in the *Yale Daily News* that Wimsatt, delivering one of the many university lectures he has given throughout the country, challenged his audience with these remarks: "The question is not, do you have black friends? But rather, what do you do and what do you not do with them? . . . Who has the upper hand in the friendship? If you find it easy to be friends with someone of a different culture than you, it's probably because they're working twice as hard."

Wimsatt was the youngest person named a "visionary" by the *Utne Reader* in 1996. He is a founding member of the Active Element Foundation in New York City, the Self-Education Foundation, based in Philadelphia, and he serves as director of Adventure Philanthropy, also based in New York.

BIOGRAPHICAL AND CRITICAL SOURCES:

PERIODICALS

Chicago, August, 1994, Marcia Froelke Coburn, "Getting down with Upski: A Young Graffiti Tagger Publishes a Hip-hop Manifesto about His Late-Night Walk on the Wild Side," p. 27.

Library Journal, November 1, 1999, Chogollah Maroufi, review of *No More Prisons,* p. 113.

Publishers Weekly, January 31, 2000, review of *No More Prisons,* p. 96.

Village Voice, November 24, 1999, Jennifer Gonnerman, "Sidewalk Politics: Graffiti Campaign Demands 'No More Prisons.'"

Yale Daily News, November 19, 1996, Ben Diamond, "Wimsatt Lets Loose on Race, Rape, Money."

OTHER

Horizon, http://www.horizonmag.com/ (March 7, 2002), Neal Pollack, review of *No More Prisons.*

In Context, http://www.context.org/ (March 7, 2002), William Upski Wimsatt, "Hip-Hoppers and Do-Gooders: An Essay in Two Worlds," winter, 1993.

No More Prisons, http://www.nomoreprisons.net/ (March 7, 2002).

Riseup.net, http://www.riseup.net/ (March 7, 2002).

Self Education Foundation, http://www.selfeducation. org/ (March 7, 2002).*

*   *   *

WIRTH, John D(avis) 1936-2002

OBITUARY NOTICE—See index for *CA* sketch: Born June 17, 1936, in Dawson, NM; died of a heart aneurysm June 20, 2002, in Toronto, Ontario, Canada. Historian, educator, administrator, and author. In 1988 Wirth founded the North American Institute to foster understanding and cooperation among the three major nations of North America: Canada, the United States, and Mexico. His vision was aimed at a seamless North American community that would work to build business, political, and social partnerships for the benefit of all. He contributed to the establishment of the North American Community Service Project, a volunteer youth program related to conservation, preservation,

and community enrichment, and the Alliance for Higher Education and Enterprise in North America. After the North American Free Trade Agreement was enacted, Wirth was appointed to the Commission for Environmental Cooperation, a government agency that had emerged from the agreement. Wirth taught history at Stanford University from 1966 through 2002, becoming the Gildred Professor of Latin American Studies in 1991. In addition to his ongoing interest in Canada and Mexico, Wirth also took pride in his involvement with Brazilian studies. His writings on North America include *Smelter Smoke in North America: The Politics of Transborder Pollution* and the edited volumes *Identities in North America: The Search for Community, Environmental Management on North America's Borders,* and *The Oil Business in Latin America: The Early Years.* Among his works on Brazil, *The Politics of Brazilian Development, 1930-1954* was awarded the Bolton Memorial Prize of the Conference on Latin American History and was later translated into Portuguese.

OBITUARIES AND OTHER SOURCES:

PERIODICALS

Albuquerque Journal, July 15, 2002, obituary by Jerry Pacheco, p. 5.

New York Times, June 27, 2002, obituary by Anthony DePalma, p. C23.

San Francisco Chronicle, June 30, 2002, obituary by Jim Herron Zamora, p. A29.

*   *   *

WYATT, Richard Jed 1939-2002

OBITUARY NOTICE—See index for *CA* sketch: Born June 5, 1939, in Los Angeles, CA; died of lung cancer June 7, 2002, in Washington, DC. Neuropsychiatrist, institutional administrator, educator, and author. A pioneer in research on the biology and biochemistry of schizophrenia, Wyatt is credited with training the world's leading researchers in that field. After earning his medical degree at Johns Hopkins University in 1967, Wyatt joined the National Institutes of Health as a researcher and founded one of the earliest scientific teams dedicated to the study of schizophrenia. He also studied other neurological diseases, such as Alzheimer's and Parkinson's, as well as sleep disorders. Wyatt was appointed chief of the Neuropsychiatry Branch of the National Institute of Mental Health in 1972. He was also active as a professor at the nation's leading universities, from Harvard to Stanford. Among many honors, Wyatt received the Stanley R. Dean Research Award of the American College of Psychiatrists, the McAlpin Mental Health Research Achievement Award from the National Mental Health Association, and the Daniel Efron Award of the American College of Neuropsychopharmacology. With his wife, psychologist Kay Redfield Jamison, Wyatt worked on the television specials *To Paint the Stars* and *Moods in Music*. He wrote hundreds of articles for scientific journals and published a half-dozen books, including (as coauthor) *Dementia in the Presenium, Human Sleep and Its Disorders,* and *Understanding and Treating Tardive Dyskinesia;* he was the sole author of *After Middle Age: A Physician's Guide to Staying Healthy while Growing Older.* Wyatt was one of the earliest researchers to document the biological causes of schizophrenia, in contrast to a prevailing notion that the disease was the result of early childhood experiences and other external factors. At the time of his death Wyatt was reportedly working to identify risk factors for schizophrenia.

OBITUARIES AND OTHER SOURCES:

PERIODICALS

Los Angeles Times, June 15, 2002, p. B18.
New York Times, June 12, 2002, obituary by Anahad O'Connor, p. A25.
Washington Post, June 12, 2002, obituary by Graeme Zielinski, p. B6.

Y-Z

YATSKO, Pamela

PERSONAL: Female. *Education:* Johns Hopkins Center for Chinese Studies and International Economics, graduate degree.

ADDRESSES: Office—c/o Wiley Publishers, 605 Third Ave., New York, NY 10158-0012.

CAREER: Writer. Managing editor, Economist Group's *Business China,* Hong Kong; Shanghai bureau chief, *Far Eastern Economic Review,* 1995-98.

WRITINGS:

The New Shanghai: The Rocky Rebirth of China's Legendary City, Wiley (New York, NY), 2001.

SIDELIGHTS: Pamela Yatsko is the former bureau chief of the *Far Eastern Economic Review*'s Shanghai office, and the author of *New Shanghai: The Rocky Rebirth of China's Legendary City.* Yatsko grew up in a middle-class American family in New Bedford, Massachusetts, but was always fascinated with international affairs. In 1986 she went on a backpacking trip through China and visited Shanghai for the first time. As Lisa Movius wrote in *China Now,* "She fell in love with Shanghai's persisting beauty, the old city's ubiquitous legacy, and its very 'Chineseness' shining through all the foreign trappings." Yatsko earned a graduate degree at the Johns Hopkins Center for Chinese Studies and International Economics, with a semester abroad in Nanjing, China. After graduating, she went to Hong Kong to become managing editor for the Economist Group's *Business China.*

In 1994 Yatsko was asked to open a bureau for the *Far Eastern Economic Review* in Shanghai, China, and become the first bureau chief for the publication in that city since 1949. She told a reporter for the *Correspondent,* "It seemed at the time that everyone was opening up offices and bureaus in Shanghai . . . and I was lucky enough to be part of the first wave of foreign correspondents." As bureau chief for the periodical from 1995 through 1998, Yatsko spent much of her time interviewing a wide variety of people in Shanghai and elsewhere in China for numerous articles. She carried her interest in people and the city of Shanghai, as well as her interview skills, into her research for *The New Shanghai: The Rocky Rebirth of China's Legendary City.*

The New Shanghai explores the twentieth-century history of Shanghai, its glamour as "Old Shanghai," a hive of trade, adventure, vast wealth, and grinding poverty; its death after the Chinese Communist victory of 1949, and its rebirth in the 1990s as an international business hub. In writing the book, Yatsko interviewed Shanghainese from all social classes and many walks of life to provide a sense of the city's past and present, as well as glimpses of its future. In a profile in the Hong Kong Women in Publishing Society's *Women at Work Archive,* Yatsko described her explorations of the city to gain background material, and commented that despite these trips, "Mostly what I do all day is tap away at my computer, trying to organize reams of research into a readable book. Sometimes the writing goes well. Other days I struggle over the accuracy of an analytical paragraph, the most effective way to fit my material together, or the realization that I'm missing some needed information."

Yatsko also commented that her goal in writing the book was to mix interesting anecdotes with narrative chapters depicting the city's rebirth. She wrote, "Since the issues facing Shanghai are much the same as those facing the rest of urban China, I see my market as anyone interested in China or communist societies in transformation." In the *Age,* John Schauble wrote, *The New Shanghai* "is likely to become . . . a much cited and referred to text in the absence of other accessible and clear portrayals of the city's recent history." A *China Detective* writer commented that the book is "a work of exceptional richness and observation," and that it is "beautifully constructed and written."

BIOGRAPHICAL AND CRITICAL SOURCES:

PERIODICALS

Far Eastern Economic Review, February 15, 2001, Derek Parker, "City of Dreams and Illusion"; March 1, 2001, Jonathan Mirsky, "Great Companion."

OTHER

Age, http://www.theage.com/ (January 15, 2002), John Shauble, "Something's Lacking in an Old Whore's Story."
China Detective, http://www.c007.com/English/cc/ (January 15, 2002), "New Shanghai."
China Now, http://www.chinanow.com/ (March 8, 2002), Lisa Movius, "A Conversation with Pam Yatsko."
Correspondent, http://www.fcchk.org/ (January 15, 2002), "Shanghai: The Rebirth of China's Legendary City."
Women at Work Archive, http://www.hkwips.org/ (January 15, 2002), "Pamela Yatsko."*

*   *   *

YEH, Michelle (Mi-Hsi) 1955-

PERSONAL: Born January 6, 1955, in Taipei, Taiwan; daughter of Hsing-chu Sun and Shu-chuang Hsi; married Kwang Yeh, June 15, 1980; children: Jonathan. *Education:* National Taiwan University, Taipei, B.A.

(English), 1976; University of Southern California, M.A. (comparative literature), 1978, Ph.D. (comparative literature), 1983.

ADDRESSES: Office—Department of Chinese and Japanese, University of California, Davis, Davis, CA 95616. *E-mail*—mmyeh@ucdavis.edu.

CAREER: California State University, Long Beach, assistant professor of Chinese and comparative literature, 1983-88; University of California, Davis, assistant professor, 1988-90, associate professor of Chinese, 1990—. Member of Fulbright Awards Committee.

MEMBER: Association for Asian Studies, Council for International Exchange of Scholars, American Association of Chinese Comparative Literature (member of executive board).

AWARDS, HONORS: Writing grant, Pacific Cultural Foundation (Taiwan), 1991; translation grant, Council for Cultural Planning and Development (Taiwan), 1991-92; research grant, Chiang Ching-kuo Foundation for International Scholarly Exchange, 1993-95.

WRITINGS:

Modern Chinese Poetry: Theory and Practice since 1917, Yale University Press (New Haven, CT), 1991.
(Editor and translator) *Anthology of Modern Chinese Poetry,* Yale University Press (New Haven, CT), 1992.
(Cotranslator) *No Trace of the Gardener: Poems of Yang Mu,* Yale University Press (New Haven, CT), 1998.
Xian Dang Dai Shi Wen Lu (title means "Essays on Modern Chinese Poetry"), Taibei Shi, 1998.
(Coeditor with N. G. D. Malmquist) *Frontier Taiwan: An Anthology of Modern Chinese Poetry,* Columbia University Press (New York, NY), 2001.

SIDELIGHTS: A Taiwanese-American with a strong background in traditional Chinese literature, Michelle Yeh turned to a more contemporary literature with her publication of *Modern Chinese Poetry: Theory and Practice since 1917.* "In a disarming preface, Michelle

Yeh admits that her interest in modern Chinese poetry is of fairly recent vintage. Indeed, her study displays a fresh enthusiasm for the subject that is altogether winning," wrote Eugene Eoyang in the *Journal of Asian Studies.* The book incorporates mainland Chinese poetry between 1917 and 1949 and post-1978, with Taiwanese poetry from 1949 to the present. "Throughout the book, she unapologetically compares twentieth-century works with well-known examples of premodern poetry," wrote Marston Anderson in the *Harvard Journal of Asiatic Studies.* According to Russell McLeod in *World Literature Today,* "Yeh finds that in imagery and metaphor modern Chinese poetry has a closer affinity with Western 'Modernist' poetics than with traditional Chinese poetics." Such things as analogy, irony, and metaphor play a much greater role for the modern poets than their classical predecessors. However, Anderson noted, Yeh makes clear that "Western influences succeeded in China . . . only when internal conditions paved the way for their assimilation."

In a natural follow-up, Yeh published an *Anthology of Modern Chinese Poetry* the next year. "Yeh's selection is, happily, exhausting," wrote Simon Patton in *World Literature Today.* The anthology, including over three hundred poems by sixty-seven poets born between 1891 and 1963, draws from both Taiwanese and Chinese communist poetry, tearing down an old and artificial barrier. Patton added that "The rationale behind the translations—'to give readers a sense of [the poetry's] original form, rhythm, diction, and ever-elusive style without sacrificing readability'—yields consistent results and provides Yeh with ample opportunities to demonstrate her ingenuity."

Reviewing the anthology, Pat Monaghan wrote simply in *Booklist:* "Its scope is enormous, its range impressive." The collection spans the troubled twentieth century, and there is a fair amount of political and intellectual ferment in the poetry. Stephen Owen wrote in the *New Republic,* "There are readers who may come to this anthology out of an interest more in modern China than in modern poetry. . . . Yeh's volume is a rich testimony to the experience of Chinese intellectuals in the twentieth century." But there is a great deal more than that, from the somewhat sentimental poets who first confronted modernism, through a growing mastery and comfort with this European import, combined with traditional forms, and on to the postmodernist poets emerging in Taiwan and on the mainland today.

Joseph R. Allen commented in the *Journal of the American Oriental Society* that "With this volume, especially combined with her companion book of essays, *Modern Chinese Poetry: Theory and Practice since 1917,* Professor Yeh has become the new 'czar' of modern Chinese Poetry. . . . In a time of highly theoretical speculations on the nature of Chinese classical poetry and modern fiction, Yeh offers a relatively straightforward reassessment of Chinese poetry in terms of late twentieth-century thought, especially as reflected in the debates on modernism."

Yeh's next book considers the special case of Taiwan, with its close cultural links and sharp political differences with the mainland. In *Frontier Taiwan: An Anthology of Modern Chinese Poetry,* she discusses the various influences on the island's modern poets, revealing for instance that its first modernist poets wrote in Japanese. In doing so, she brings U.S. readers together with Taiwanese poets. A *Publishers Weekly* reviewer, highlighting this role, felt "the main impact of this book will be sociopolitical, allowing connections between writers who might have had difficulty finding each other without this judicious letter of introduction."

BIOGRAPHICAL AND CRITICAL SOURCES:

PERIODICALS

Booklist, November 15, 1992, Pat Monaghan, review of *Anthology of Modern Chinese Poetry,* p. 575.
Harvard Journal of Asiatic Studies, June, 1993, Marston Anderson, review of *Modern Chinese Poetry,* pp. 169-174.
Journal of Asian Studies, February, 1994, Eugene Eoyang, review of *Modern Chinese Poetry* and *Anthology of Modern Chinese Poetry,* pp. 186-188.
Journal of the American Oriental Society, April-June, 1994, Joseph R. Allen, review of *Anthology of Modern Chinese Poetry,* p. 324.
New Republic, February 22, 1993, Stephen Owen, review of *Anthology of Modern Chinese Poetry,* p. 38.
Publishers Weekly, April 23, 2001, review of *Frontier Taiwan,* p. 74.
World Literature Today, summer, 1992, Russell McLeod, review of *Modern Chinese Poetry,* pp. 579-580; autumn, 1993, Simon Patton, review of *Anthology of Modern Chinese Poetry,* p. 888.

YORK, Neil Longley 1951-

PERSONAL: Born April 21, 1951, in San Luis Obispo, CA; son of Eric K. and Joel B. York; married Carole Mikita (a television reporter and anchor), August 29, 1981; children: Jennifer, Caitlin. *Education:* Brigham Young University, B.A., 1973, M.A., 1975; University of California—Santa Barbara, Ph.D., 1978. *Politics:* Democrat. *Religion:* Church of Jesus Christ of Latter-day Saints (Mormons).

ADDRESSES: Home—2519 Cliff Swallow Dr., Sandy, UT 84093. *Office*—Department of History, Brigham Young University, Provo, UT 84602; fax: 801-422-5784. *E-mail*—neil_york@byu.edu.

CAREER: Brigham Young University, Provo, UT, instructor, 1977-79, assistant professor, 1979-84, associate professor, 1984-94, professor of history, 1994—, Karl G. Maeser Professor of General Education, 2000-02, coordinator of American studies program, 1980-85, 1994-98. University of California—Davis, visiting assistant professor, summers, 1980, 1981; Duquesne University, guest lecturer, 1982, 1984; University of Utah, visiting associate professor, 1989.

MEMBER: Institute of Early American History and Culture (associate), Colonial Society of Massachusetts, Phi Kappa Phi, Phi Alpha Theta (member of international council, 1984-86).

WRITINGS:

Mechanical Metamorphosis: Technological Change in Revolutionary America, Greenwood Press (Westport, CT), 1985.
(Editor) *Toward a More Perfect Union: Six Essays on the Constitution,* Brigham Young University Press (Provo, UT), 1988.
Neither Kingdom nor Nation: The Irish Quest for Constitutional Rights, 1698-1800, Catholic University of America Press (Washington, DC), 1994.
Fiction as Fact: "The Horse Soldiers" and Popular Memory, Kent State University Press (Ashland, OH), 2001.
Maxims for a Patriot: Josiah Quincy Junior and His Commonplace Book, University Press of Virginia (Charlottesville, VA), in press.

Author of pamphlet "Burning the Dockyard: 'John the Painter' and the American Revolution," City of Portsmouth Publications (Portsmouth, England), 2001. Contributor to books, including *The New American Nation, 1775-1820,* Volume 2, edited by Peter Onuf, Garland Publishing (New York, NY), 1990; *Great Britain and the American Revolution,* edited by H. T. Dickinson, Longman (London, England), 1998; and *Liberty and Justice,* edited by Patrick T. Conley, Rhode Island Publications Society (Providence, RI), 1998. Contributor of articles and reviews to periodicals, including *Quaker History, History, Pennsylvania Magazine of History and Biography, Hamlet Studies, Rhode Island History, Eire-Ireland, Journal of American Culture, Military Affairs,* and *Peace and Change.*

WORK IN PROGRESS: Turning the World upside Down: The War of American Independence and the Problem of Empire, for Praeger Publishers (Westport, CT).

BIOGRAPHICAL AND CRITICAL SOURCES:

PERIODICALS

American Historical Review, June, 1986, Diane Lindstrom, review of *Mechanical Metamorphosis: Technological Change in Revolutionary America,* p. 731; April, 1996, John D. Fair, review of *Neither Kingdom nor Nation: The Irish Quest for Constitutional Rights, 1698-1800,* p. 498.
Annals of the American Academy of Political and Social Science, May, 1987, H. A. Gemery, review of *Mechanical Metamorphosis,* p. 224.
Business History Review, autumn, 1986, Chandos Brown, review of *Mechanical Metamorphosis,* p. 495.
English Historical Review, September, 1996, Thomas Bartlett, review of *Neither Kingdom nor Nation,* p. 993.
Historian, winter, 1996, Lawrence W. McBride, review of *Neither Kingdom nor Nation,* p. 455.
Journal of American History, March, 1986, Hugo A. Meier, review of *Mechanical Metamorphosis,* p. 940; December, 1989, John W. Larner, review of *Toward a More Perfect Union: Six Essays on the Constitution,* p. 923.
Science, January 17, 1986, Paul F. Paskoff, review of *Mechanical Metamorphosis,* p. 278.

YORK, Sarah

PERSONAL: Daughter of Dick (a cartoonist) and Gretchen (a concert pianist and sculptor) Moores; married Chuck Campbell (an antique dealer). *Education:* Harvard University, M.Div. *Religion:* Unitarian Universalist.

ADDRESSES: Home—North Carolina. *Agent*—c/o Jossey-Bass, 989 Market St., San Francisco, CA 94103-1741.

CAREER: Worked for twenty years as a Unitarian Universalist minister in California, New York, Maryland, and London, England; Reynolds High School, Reynolds, NC, former English teacher.

MEMBER: Unitarian Universalist Ministers Association (vice president).

WRITINGS:

Into the Wilderness, Apollo Ranch Institute Press, 2000.
Remembering Well: Rituals for Celebrating Life and Mourning Death, Jossey-Bass (San Francisco, CA), 2000.
Pilgrim Heart: The Inner Journey Home, Jossey-Bass (San Francisco, CA), 2001.
The Holy Intimacy of Strangers, Jossey-Bass (San Francisco, CA), 2002.

SIDELIGHTS: After publishing *Into the Wilderness,* a short, largely autobiographical piece about finding spiritual truths in everyday life, Sarah York turned to the big question that all faiths must deal with: death. As a longtime Unitarian Universalist minister, York has presided over many funerals and dealt with the grief of many families. *In Remembering Well: Rituals for Celebrating Life and Mourning Death,* she provides both spiritual counsel and practical advice on how to plan a fitting memorial when a loved one dies. "She speaks eloquently of the need to give authentic expression to grief," a *Publishers Weekly* reviewer commented. "Dozens of stories of individual rituals serve as inspiring examples of how a uniquely fitting memorial . . . may be crafted," wrote a *Booklist* contributor. "One might think this would be a sad

book, but it is not," wrote reviewer Reese Danley-Kilgo in the *Huntsville Times,* adding that York "quotes from Shakespeare, 'Give sorrow words,' and provides the help needed to plan meaningful and personal rituals."

In 2001's *Pilgrim Heart: The Inner Journey Home,* York turns from departures to arrivals and the longing people feel for a spiritual home in this life. "Spiritual readers of all stripes will enjoy this meditation on the meaning of home and journey," wrote a reviewer for *Publishers Weekly.* Using her own travels through Thailand and Nepal and the Scottish island of Iona, York illustrates the ways in which physical journeys can mirror spiritual searching. Frederic and Mary Ann Brussat, reviewing the book for *Spirituality & Health,* wrote, "When you finish this heartfelt work, you'll agree with York that 'the goal of any sacred journey . . . is to feel more at home at home.'"

BIOGRAPHICAL AND CRITICAL SOURCES:

PERIODICALS

Booklist, October 1, 2000, Patricia Monaghan, review of *Remembering Well.*
Huntsville Times (Huntsville, AL), December 10, 2000, Reese Danley-Kilgo, "Book Helps Families to Celebrate Life."
Publishers Weekly, September 25, 2000, review of *Remembering Well,* p. 110; April 23, 2001, review of *Pilgrim Heart,* p. 72.

OTHER

Spirituality & Health, http://spiritualityhealth.com/ (December 31, 2001), Frederic and Mary Ann Brussat, review of *Pilgrim Heart.*

*   *   *

YOUNG, A. S. "Doc"
See YOUNG, Andrew Spurgeon Nash

*   *   *

YOUNG, Andrew Spurgeon Nash 1919-1996
(A. S. "Doc" Young)

PERSONAL: Born October 29, 1919, in Dunbrooke, VA; died of pneumonia, September 6, 1996; son of Andrew (a teacher) and Gertrude (a homemaker and piano teacher) Young; married Hazel Jackson, October 28, 1945; children: Norman Gregory, Brenda. *Education:* Hampton Institute (now Hampton University), B.A. (with honors), 1941.

CAREER: Sportswriter, author, historian, and publicist. Hampton Institute, Hampton, VA, accounting clerk, 1942; *Los Angeles Sentinel,* Los Angeles, CA, sportswriter, 1944-46; *Cleveland Call and Post,* Cleveland, OH, 1946-47, sportswriter, 1947-48, sports editor and columnist, 1948-49; *Los Angeles Sentinel,* Los Angeles, CA, sports editor, 1949-86, contributor, 1986-96; *Ebony,* Chicago, IL, associate editor, 1950s, also served as sports editor, assistant managing editor, and managing editor; *Jet,* Chicago, IL, sports editor, 1950s; *California Eagle,* Los Angeles, CA, co-owner, 1964-66; Pepperdine University, Los Angeles, CA, public relations officer, 1972-73; oversaw special editions of various publications, including the *Chicago Defender* and *New York Amsterdam News;* served briefly as managing editor of the West Coast edition of the *Defender.*

AWARDS, HONORS: American Library Association award, 1963, for *Negro Firsts in Sports;* President's Anniversary Sports Award, 1970, Best Sports Column award, and Best Sports Section award, National Newspaper Publishers Association; National Service Award, *Los Angeles Sentinel,* 1993.

WRITINGS:

AS A. S. "DOC" YOUNG

Great Negro Baseball Stars, and How They Made the Major Leagues, A. S. Barnes (New York, NY), 1953.
Negro Firsts in Sports, Johnson Publishing (Chicago, IL), 1963.
Sonny Liston: The Champ Nobody Wanted, Johnson Publishing (Chicago, IL), 1963.
(Editor) *The Incomparable Nat King Cole,* Sepia Publishing (Fort Worth, TX), 1965.
Black Champions of the Gridiron: Leroy Keyes and O. J. Simpson (juvenile), Harcourt (New York, NY), 1969.
The Mets from Mobile: Tommie Agee and Cleon Jones, Harcourt (New York, NY), 1970.

Contributor to periodicals, including *Sporting News, Saturday Evening Post, New York Post, Parent's Digest, Saga, Negro Digest, Las Vegas Sun, Los Angeles Mirror-News, Chicago American, Sepia, Chicago Defender, New York Times, Big Blue Review,* and *Dodger* magazine. Wrote column "Sportivanting" for *Cleveland Call and Post.*

ADAPTATIONS: Sonny Liston: The Champ Nobody Wanted was used as background for the documentary movie *Sonny Liston: The Mysterious Life and Death of a Champion,* HBO, 1995.

SIDELIGHTS: Andrew Spurgeon Nash Young, who wrote as A. S. "Doc" Young, was a top editor and sportswriter. More than that, he covered the social issues, politics, entertainment, and business of the black community. Young contributed to the major black and general interest publications and was one of the first black members of the Baseball Writers Association of America. As a book author, he was a historian of black accomplishment.

Young was born in Virginia, the elder of two children. His father was a high school teacher with postgraduate training in divinity. His mother had graduated from Hampton Institute (now Hampton University) and earned a graduate degree in music at Columbia University's Barnard College. She taught piano in their home (Young himself played piano, saxophone, and clarinet). A jazz fan from an early age, as an adult his friends included the musicians Lionel Hampton and Nat King Cole.

Young enjoyed sports, both as a participant and as a collector of statistics, but in his junior year of high school he dislocated his left hip while playing football. He stopped walking for more than a year and, because the injured leg became shorter than the right leg, he walked with a limp for the rest of his life. With the help of a tutor he graduated at the top of his class at Union High School in Bowling Green. He had always been a good student, which led his friends to give him the nickname "Doc" when he was younger. He then attended Hampton Institute, where he began his career in journalism as a reporter and as the business manager of the campus newspaper. Following graduation, he worked for a year in the school comptroller's office, then moved to Los Angeles, where he was a sportswriter with the *Los Angeles Sentinel,* an African-

American weekly. He also worked as the assistant manager of a grocery store, where he met his future wife, Hazel Jackson. They married in 1945 and had a son and a daughter, both of whom earned degrees in law.

The family moved to Cleveland, Ohio, the next year, where Young took a spot with the *Cleveland Call and Post,* a black weekly. He began as a sportswriter but soon became the sports editor and wrote about baseball, football, and boxing in his column "Sportivanting." He covered outfielder Larry Doby, the first black player in the American League, after he joined the Cleveland Indians in 1947, and Satchel Paige, the first black American League pitcher, when he arrived in 1948. The two players were often guests of the Youngs.

Young ghostwrote "What's Wrong with Negro Baseball," Jackie Robinson's *Ebony* article in which he spoke out for players in the Negro leagues, about the lack of contracts, poor accommodations, and substandard officiating of the games. Young went back to the *Los Angeles Sentinel* as sports editor and sold what he claimed was the first article by a black writer to a major sports magazine. Although Young stayed with the *Sentinel* until his retirement, and even then continued to write occasional articles, he also served variously as associate editor, assistant managing editor, managing editor, and sports editor for *Ebony,* as well as for *Jet,* where he was sports editor. Michael Marsh noted in *Dictionary of Literary Biography* that "a longtime friend, former *Ebony* editor Herbert Nipson, said Young was valuable because he had established relationships with top athletes and considered the needs of readers when he wrote his stories. When the company wanted to run an article about a sports figure, Young was often able to locate the person quickly and write a piece that told readers 'what he thought they wanted to know. When you read Doc Young, you came away with a better understanding of why the athlete was the way he was.'"

Great Negro Baseball Stars, and How They Made the Major Leagues, Young's first book, is a history of black athletes who had become major league players during the six years prior to the book's 1953 publication. In addition to including lists of facts about honors won by the men, Young wrote from his observations, including a comparison of Robinson and Doby. In his memoir, William Veeck, owner of the

Indians during the late 1940s, wrote that Young had helped him when he sought to buy the Philadelphia Phillies in 1942 and hire players from the Negro leagues.

In the civil rights era of the 1960s, Young published *Negro Firsts in Sports,* in which he profiled black athletes in a variety of sports. Young was following in the footsteps of Edwin Henderson, who had written extensively about black athletes and published the history *The Negro in Sports.* Later, in 1988, tennis great Arthur Ashe interviewed Young for his three-volume *Hard Road to Glory* and used Young's books as sources.

Sonny Liston: The Champ Nobody Wanted is Young's profile of the heavyweight boxer who knocked out champion Floyd Patterson in 1962. Liston fought his way up from poverty in Arkansas, served time in prison, and was rumored to have ties to organized crime. In the ring, however, he conducted himself professionally, and Young criticized the hypocrisy of the fans who booed him and yet placed their bets on Liston to win.

Baseball player Willie Mays was a favorite of Young. Young also admired Jackie Robinson for his manners, business acumen, and civil rights activism; Ashe for his social activism; and Joe Black, a pitcher for the Dodgers who became a Greyhound executive. Young predicted in a *Sepia* article that Robinson and former Los Angeles Dodgers star Maury Wills were the blacks most likely to become major league managers. Robinson was named a player-manager in 1974, and Wills became the third black manager in the major leagues when he managed the Seattle Mariners in the 1980 and 1981 seasons. Both had first managed winter league teams, and Wills won a pennant his first year with a Mexican team.

Young was quick to write about blacks who he felt gave a negative impression of the community. In a column for the *Chicago Defender,* he addressed boxer Mike Tyson's problems with his wife, Robin Givens, and with his promoter, Don King. In another *Defender* column, he criticized college basketball coaches John Chaney and John Thompson for being against Proposition 42, a rule of the National Collegiate Athletic Association that raised admissions standards for athletes. In *Black Champions of the Gridiron: Leroy Keyes and*

O. J. Simpson, an illustrated book for younger readers, Young portrays the two athletes as honest and hard-working; years later, when Simpson was charged with the murder of Nicole Brown Simpson and Ronald Goldman, he changed his opinion. Young was upset that people cheered for Simpson as he fled from police and by allegations that the star had beaten his wife during their marriage. In a column in the *Sentinel,* Young contrasted Keyes's and Simpson's post-football careers, praising Keyes for his work with disadvantaged children.

Young was also sympathetic toward black sportswriters who struggled to succeed as journalists. He mentored such young writers as Dan Burley, who worked with him at *Ebony.* Young also penned articles about other subjects and people, including politician Adam Clayton Powell and singer Nancy Wilson. He wrote an article for the *New York Times,* defending *The Bill Cosby Show* after a critic wrote that it was an inaccurate representation of black family life. He wrote about social issues, such as the increasing violence in black neighborhoods, and praised Andrew Young's *A Way Out of No Way* and the book's argument in favor of nonviolence and spirituality.

Young received many honors during his life and many tributes after his death. Libby Clark, who worked with him at the *Los Angeles Sentinel,* called him "a deep thinker, argumentative, a visionary, a great writer, profoundly loyal to those he liked, a master with the printed word, and a 'loner.' One never knew what made Doc tick. He could be warm and engaging at times and as 'cold' as last year's mashed potatoes at other times. Cross him and you had hell on your hands."

BIOGRAPHICAL AND CRITICAL SOURCES:

BOOKS

Burns, Ben, *Nitty Gritty: A White Editor in Black Journalism,* University Press of Mississippi (Jackson, MS), 1996.
Dictionary of Literary Biography, Volume 241: *American Sportswriters and Writers on Sport,* Gale (Detroit, MI), 2001.
Murray, James P., *To Find an Image: Black Films from Uncle Tom to Super Fly,* Bobbs-Merrill (Indianapolis, IN), 1973.

Veeck, William and Ed Linn, *Veeck—As in Wreck,* Putnam (New York, NY), 1962.
Wilson, Clint, *Black Journalists in Paradox: Historical Perspectives and Current Dilemmas,* Greenwood Press (New York, NY), 1991.

PERIODICALS

Chicago Defender, January 30, 1989; February 9, 1989.
Los Angeles Sentinel, September 27, 1973; June 30, 1994; September 24, 1994.

OBITUARIES:

PERIODICALS

Los Angeles Sentinel, October 31, 1996, Jim Cleaver; November 7, 1996, obituary by Libby Clark.*

*   *   *

YOUNG, David M. 1940-

PERSONAL: Born September 22, 1940, in Evanston, IL; son of Robert A. (a fire protection engineer) and Elizabeth (a homemaker; maiden name, Morehead) Young; married Mary Dene Davis (a school administrator), September 20, 1969; children: Darienne Young Zamis, Darcee, Denise. *Education:* Attended University of Illinois, 1958-63. *Religion:* Protestant. *Hobbies and other interests:* Gardening, vertebrate paleontology.

ADDRESSES: Home and office—710 Howard St., Wheaton, IL 60187; fax: 630-665-5801. *E-mail*—dxyoung@msn.com.

CAREER: Chicago Tribune, Chicago, IL, writer and transportation editor, 1963-99; freelance writer, 1999—. *Military service:* U.S. Army, 1964-66.

WRITINGS:

Fill the Heavens with Commerce, Chicago Review Press (Chicago, IL), 1981.
Chicago Transit: An Illustrated History, Northern Illinois University Press (DeKalb, IL), 1998.

Chicago Maritime, Northern Illinois University Press (DeKalb, IL), 1998.

The Illinois Story, Illinois Publishing Group, 2002.

Chicago Aviation: An Illustrated History, Northern Illinois University Press (DeKalb, IL), 1993.

WORK IN PROGRESS: Lone Stranger, a work of humor; research for *Chicago Railroads* for Northern Illinois University Press (DeKalb, IL).

SIDELIGHTS: David M. Young told *CA:* "My motivation for writing is to fill holes in the historical literature. I was transportation editor of the *Chicago Tribune* for a number of years and wanted to document the role of that industry in the development of Chicago and the Midwest."

BIOGRAPHICAL AND CRITICAL SOURCES:

PERIODICALS

Transportation Journal, winter, 1998, George M. Smerk, review of *Chicago Transit: An Illustrated History,* p. 48.

*   *   *

YOUNG, Fay
    See YOUNG, Frank A.

*   *   *

YOUNG, Frank A. 1884-1957
    (Fay Young)

PERSONAL: Born October 2, 1884, in Williamsport, PA; died of an intestinal obstruction, October 27, 1957; wife's name, Cora; children: Louise, Frank, Jr.

CAREER: Sportswriter. Chicago and Northwestern Railroad, dining car waiter, early 1900s-1915; *Chicago Defender,* Chicago, IL, contributor, 1907-15, reporter, 1915-16, managing editor, 1916, became city editor, sports editor, managing editor, 1929-34; Negro National League, Kansas City, MO, official statistician, 1920-31; *Kansas City Call,* Kansas City, MO,

managing editor, 1934-37; *Chicago Defender,* Chicago, IL, sports editor and columnist, 1937-49, contributor 1949-57; Negro American League, Chicago, IL, director of publicity, secretary, 1939-48; *Abbott's Monthly,* managing editor, 1930s; WSBC-AM, Chicago, IL, broadcaster, 1940s; worked variously as a postal clerk, waiter, manager of the Lincoln Athletic Club (semi-pro football team), and timekeeper and referee for the Illinois Athletic Commission; cofounder of Everybody's Church, Chicago, IL, 1952.

AWARDS, HONORS: Frank A. Young Poultry Research Plant, named in Young's honor, Tennessee A & I State University (now Tennessee State University), 1953.

WRITINGS:

Author of columns, including "It's All in the Game," "Just Confidential," "Fay Says," "The Stuff Is Here," and "Through the Years Past Present Future," all for the *Chicago Defender.*

SIDELIGHTS: Frank A. "Fay" Young was the first full-time black sportswriter in the United States and also the first to cover black college sports. He wrote his stories for more than fifty years, contributed to many firsts in black sports, and acted as an advocate for racial justice. He was a writer, a manager, an editor, and an unpaid contributor for many years before he was hired to his first regular staff position.

Young was orphaned at age eight, and little has been recorded about his early life. He finished one year of high school in Massachusetts and a second in Illinois. At sixteen he was selling newspapers on the South Side of Chicago. The *Chicago Defender,* a black newspaper, was established in 1905 by Robert S. Abbott, working out of a friend's kitchen. Two years later Young began to point out factual errors to Abbott, who had no sportswriter at the time. Young worked as a dining car waiter for the Chicago and Northwestern Railroad, and his ability to glean news from black porters, waiters, and barbers and to collect various newspapers as he made the run from Chicago to Milwaukee gave him access to news about black athletes, which he could then turn into stories for the *Defender.* He worked nights for the railroad and spent his days and his two days off at the newspaper. He made a good salary working for the railroad and paid all of the expenses he accrued while working for the paper out of his own pocket. He sometimes even paid Abbott's expenses.

The only person at the *Defender* who was being paid was J. Hockley Smiley, the managing editor, and Young worked unpaid for years, even when he was producing the paper's first sports page. Finally Abbott asked him to leave the railroad and join the paper for fifteen dollars a week. This was a difficult decision, because as Roi Ottley pointed out in *The Lonely Warrior: The Life and Times of Robert S. Abbott,* "railroad men were among the sought-after figures in Negro society, and newspapermen were considered merely hustlers." Ottley also noted that even though their wages were low, "the staff regarded themselves as adequately paid, as no one then thought of Negro journalism as professional work."

Young joined the *Defender* full-time, but like his coworkers, he took other jobs in order to survive. He worked at the post office during the Christmas rush and as a waiter at Chicago's Palmer House and Edgewater Beach Hotel. In 1915 he managed a semipro football team, the Lincoln Athletic Club. The *Defender* was so underfunded that, until Abbott agreed to take over the payments on a typewriter Young had purchased for himself, stories were written in longhand. Young contributed to every aspect of publishing the *Defender* and even cooked for the night crew as they proofread galleys. When Booker T. Washington died in 1915, Young put out a special edition, a single-page tribute to Washington's life, and personally distributed copies to the ministers at black churches in the area. The next year he was named managing editor at a salary of twenty-five dollars a week. He quickly changed jobs to become city editor and then sports editor.

Now sports editor for both the weekly and national editions of the *Defender,* Young often traveled by train to cover black college sports in the South, made difficult by poor accommodations. Joel Sternberg noted in the *Dictionary of Literary Biography* that "during his fifty years as a columnist-reporter-editor, he reacted quickly and angrily to racial slights, abuses, and indignities. Along with other notable black journalists such as Wendell Smith of the *Pittsburgh Courier,* Sam Lucy of the *Baltimore Afro-American,* and Joe Bostic of the *Harlem People's Voice,* Young's reputation was that of a man who fought consistently against segregation." As the official scorer and statistician for

the Negro National League from its inception in 1920 until its dissolution in 1931, Young advocated the inclusion of blacks in the major leagues. He also criticized the Baseball Umpires Association for the bad umpiring by white officials at games played by black teams and called for the hiring of black umpires.

During the 1920s, Young covered nearly every type of sporting event, including the World Series, heavyweight boxing championships, and national track competitions. He was instrumental in expanding the athletic programs on black campuses—particularly at Tuskegee Institute, where he established the school's annual Thanksgiving game with Alabama State. In 1929, he was a founder of the Prairie View Bowl game, held annually in Houston, Texas, the second oldest post-season bowl game in the country and the first black post-season bowl game in history.

From 1929 until 1934, Young was again managing editor of the *Defender.* For a short time during that period, he was also managing editor of *Abbott's Weekly,* a black magazine that published fiction, nonfiction, editorials, and romance. Young wrote about black athletes, including one of his favorites, Rube Foster, a star pitcher who became a team owner and then president of the Negro National League. Foster developed dementia before the age of fifty, however, and Young scolded black club owners and officials for failing to play benefit games for the man who had selflessly given his own health and money to the sport. Foster died shortly after the article was published, and the National Negro League dissolved in 1931, unable to survive the financial hardships of the Great Depression.

The economic downturn of the 1930s also hit Young, who was asked by Abbott to leave in 1934 when the paper lost money due to decreased circulation. Young worked for three years as managing editor of the *Kansas City Call* and then returned to the *Defender* as sports editor. He became involved in a controversial incident in 1938 involving Jake Powell, a white infielder for the New York Yankees. During a radio interview with Chicago commentator Bob Elson, Powell said he stayed fit during the winter by beating up blacks. Elson cut him off, but not soon enough. His remarks outraged not only blacks, but whites as well, and Young's anger was intensified by the fact that baseball commissioner Judge Kenesaw Mountain Landis gave Powell only a slap-on-the-wrist ten-day suspension. Young warned that Powell's safety might be in jeopardy and began a boycott of the brewery of Yankee owner Colonel Jacob Ruppert. Under pressure, the Yankees forced Powell to make formal apologies, which he did at Harlem bars and through a printed statement in the *Defender*. The black community, which wanted Powell's suspension extended to one year, was not happy when Landis refused to go further, and the boycott of Ruppert's beer went on for the whole period. Powell remained with the Yankees through the 1940 season, but his playing time was cut. He was often the target of verbal abuse and bottles thrown by black fans.

A new Negro American League was formed in 1937, and Young served as its secretary from 1939 to 1948. During World War II he often wrote about blacks in the military. In May 1942 pitcher Satchel Paige led his Kansas City Monarchs to a win over Dizzy Dean's All-Stars at Wrigley Field. The game benefited the Navy Relief Fund and was the first in which black teams played in a National League park. Young used the occasion to berate the major leagues for refusing to hire black players. Brooklyn Dodgers manager Leo Durocher made a comment that he had been forbidden from hiring blacks, a statement he later retracted. Landis stated that black players had never been barred from the majors during his twenty-one years as commissioner. But the unwritten rule had always been that they were not hired. Young objected to the practice, noting that George S. Mays of the Professional Golfers Association saw to it that blacks played in the Tam O'Shanter Open.

Young used the pages of the *Defender* to showcase outstanding black athletes and integrated teams such as the *Chicago Tribune*'s 1942 All-Star football squad. When boxer Joe Louis fought, he added pages to the *Defender*, sold papers on the street, and made the actual broadcast available with loudspeakers to people who stood outside the newspaper's offices. He published a special World War II edition of the *Defender* with the banner headline "Victory through Unity," in which he focused on integrating major league ball. Young also used his columns to denounce trends he saw as detracting from his highly-idealized conception of sports, including black players who conducted themselves improperly in public. He spoke out against a promotional event in Louisville, Kentucky, in which Jesse Owens was to run against a racehorse. He felt that Owens would be demeaning his accomplishments as a world record holder, university graduate, and role model.

When Brooklyn Dodgers owner Branch Rickey announced that he was creating a Brooklyn Brown Dodgers team that would also play at Ebbets Field, Young, said Sternberg, wrote in the *Defender* that Rickey was "trying to assume the role of an Abraham Lincoln in Negro baseball." There was speculation that Rickey actually had no such plan but had put it out there to make it easier for him to look for black players. Jackie Robinson was signed to the Montreal minor league team of the Dodgers in 1945, and when, in 1949, he was transferred to the Brooklyn team, Young used it as an opportunity to chide the Chicago Cubs and White Sox for not yet signing black players. He was an advocate of black players considered too old to play on white teams and suggested that farm clubs could be established through Negro League teams, so that players would not have to play in the South.

In 1949 Young suffered a ruptured appendix and peritonitis. For several weeks, as he endured several operations and daily blood transfusions, his column appeared under his byline without pause, with the writing contributed by friends—writers, coaches, and others in the field of physical education. He was now officially retired but contributed regularly. He also acted as an official and timekeeper in 1951 for the Jake La Motta vs. Sugar Ray Robinson middleweight title match. His interests also ran to areas other than sports. Young helped establish Tennessee A & I State University's poultry program. He was honored when the school named its new poultry building after him on Thanksgiving Day, 1953. Young also was involved with other agricultural projects in horticulture and stock breeding.

On the day Young died he brought his last column, a tribute to the success of the Harlem Globetrotters, to the office in person. His death was attributed to intestinal obstruction, possibly caused by the shock of the death of his sister two days earlier. Young's funeral was held at Everybody's Church, which he had helped establish in 1952. His pallbearers included Owens, Ralph Metcalfe, Russ Cowans, reporter Wendell Smith, and *Defender* publisher John Sengstacke. In an obituary published in the *Defender*, Cowans wrote of Young, "Oh, he would grumble and one would believe he was the meanest fellow in he world, but deep down in his heart there was a soft spot, and it could be reached by anyone with a heart-touching story." In an article in *Ebony*, journalist and colleague A. S. Young called Young the "patron saint of black college athletics."

BIOGRAPHICAL AND CRITICAL SOURCES:

BOOKS

Chalk, Ocania, *Pioneers of Black Sport,* Dodd, Mead (New York, NY), 1975.

Dictionary of Literary Biography, Volume 241: *American Sportswriters and Writers on Sport,* Gale (Detroit, MI), 2001.

Henderson, Edwin Bancroft, *The Negro in Sports,* Associated Publishers (Washington, DC), 1939.

McNary, Kyle P., *Ted "Double Duty" Radcliffe: Thirty-Six Years of Pitching and Catching in Baseball's Negro Leagues,* McNary (Minneapolis, MN), 1994.

Ottley, Roi, *The Lonely Warrior: The Life and Times of Robert S. Abbott,* Regnery (Chicago, IL), 1955.

Peterson, Robert, *Only the Ball Was White: A History of Legendary Black Players and All-Black Professional Teams,* Oxford University Press (New York, NY), 1970.

Rampersad, Arnold, *Jackie Robinson: A Biography,* Knopf (New York, NY), 1997.

Reisler, Jim, *Black Writers/Black Baseball: An Anthology of Articles from Black Sportswriters Who Covered the Negro Leagues,* McFarland (Jefferson, NC), 1994.

Ribowsky, Mark, *A Complete History of the Negro Leagues, 1884 to 1955,* Citadel (Secaucus, NJ), 1995.

Tygiel, Jules, *Baseball's Greatest Experiment: Jackie Robinson and His Legacy,* Oxford University Press (New York, NY), 1997.

Waters, Enoch P., *American Diary: A Personal History of the Black Press,* Path (Chicago, IL), 1987.

PERIODICALS

Chicago Defender, December 20, 1941, "West Virginia State Quits Mid-West Conference: Fay Young Is Given Award," p. 23; November 28, 1953, Russ J. Cowans, "He's Worthy of Tribute," p. 24; December 5, 1953, "Tenn U. Honors Fay Young," p. 1.

Ebony, June, 1955, Clotye Murdock, "Robert Abbott: Defender of His Race," pp. 69-75; October, 1970, A. S. Young, "Black Athletes in Golden Age of Sports: The Black Sportswriter," pp. 56-58, 60-62, 64.

OBITUARIES:

PERIODICALS

Chicago Defender, November 2, 1957, Russ J. Cowans, "Frank 'Fay' Young, Ex-Sports Editor, Dies," pp. 1-2; November 9, 1957, Russ J. Cowans, "Fabulous 'Fay': Defender's Frank Young Has Long, Well-rounded and Colorful Career," p. 11, "The End of a Great Career," p. 24.*

*   *   *

YOUNG, Noel (B.) 1922-2002
(Leon Elder)

OBITUARY NOTICE—See index for *CA* sketch: Born December 25, 1922, in San Francisco, CA; died from complications of Alzheimer's disease May 31, 2002, in Santa Barbara, CA. Publisher, printer, and author. As the founder and publisher of Capra Press, Young presented the work of dozens of authors from 1969 through the late 1990s. He published short and relatively minor works by celebrated authors, such as Anaïs Nin and mystery author Ross Macdonald, and introduced the work of newer, lesser-known ones, including short-story writer Raymond Carver and poet Kenneth Patchen. The initial publication of Capra Press was a volume of poems by Young's friend, Gordon Grant. His modest beginning was soon aided by contributions from his Santa Barbara neighbors, most notably his longtime friend, author Henry Miller. One of the highlights of Capra Press was a highly respected chapbook series through which Young offered short works that might otherwise never see the light of day: a short story by novelist Laurence Durrell, an essay or two from Miller or science-fiction writer Ray Bradbury, a selection of poetry by Carver. In another series, Young promoted the work of an emerging author by packaging it back-to-back with a title by a recognized literary figure. He financed the small, independent press by publishing his own writings under the pseudonym Leon Elder. The most commercially successful of these efforts was the nonfiction work *Hot Tubs: How to Build and Install and Enjoy Your Own.* Young balanced the literary output of Capra Press, which was of high merit but not necessarily profitable, with nonfiction works he believed would offer practical benefits to his readers, whether the subject was hot tubs, yoga, or heart health. Young began his career after World War II as a printer. He designed and printed books for several independent or avant-garde publishers, including Black Sparrow Press, for some twenty years before striking out on his own. He also wrote short stories.

OBITUARIES AND OTHER SOURCES:

PERIODICALS

Los Angeles Times, July 4, 2002, obituary by Dennis McLellan, p. B15.
San Francisco Chronicle, June 29, 2002, obituary by David Kipen, p. D3.

* * *

ZAUNDERS, Bo 1939-

PERSONAL: Born June 5, 1939, in Sweden; son of Erik Johansson (a farmer and banker) and Thea (a milliner) Zaunders; married Anna-Stina Erhardt, 1962 (divorced, 1963); married Roxie Munro (an artist), 1986. *Education:* Attended Folkhögskola in Sweden; studied with surrealist painter Waldemar Lorentzon. *Hobbies and other interests:* Travel, literature, cooking.

ADDRESSES: Home and office—20 Park Ave., New York, NY 10016. *E-mail*—zaundersnyc@aol.com.

CAREER: Art director, photographer, illustrator, and author. Young & Rubicam (advertising agency), art director in Stockholm, Sweden, Madrid, Spain, Paris, France, London, England, and New York, NY, 1965-79; freelance illustrator, 1980—; freelance photographer and writer, 1985—; art director and creative director in advertising for New York agencies, beginning 1989. *Military service:* Swedish Navy; served as medic.

MEMBER: Players Club (New York, NY).

AWARDS, HONORS: Georgia Children's Picture Storybook Award, 1988, for *Max, the Bad-talking Parrot* by Patricia B. Demuth; Children's Book Council Outstanding Book of the Year, National Council for

the Social Studies, 1999, for *Crocodiles, Camels, and Dugout Canoes: Eight Adventurous Episodes;* Best Book of the Year designation, *School Library Journal,* and Best Book of the Year List, *Center for Children's Books,* both 2002, both for *Feathers, Flaps, and Flops: Fabulous Early Fliers.*

WRITINGS:

Crocodiles, Camels, and Dugout Canoes: Eight Adventurous Episodes, illustrated by Roxie Munro, Dutton (New York, NY), 1998.
Feathers, Flaps, and Flops: Fabulous Early Fliers, illustrated by Roxie Munro, Dutton (New York, NY), 2001.

ILLUSTRATOR

Patricia B. Demuth, *Max, the Bad-talking Parrot,* Dodd, Mead (New York, NY), 1986.
Joanne Oppenheimer, adaptor, *One Gift Deserves Another,* Dutton (New York, NY), 1992.

WORK IN PROGRESS: Two children's books: *Gargoyles, Girders, and Glass Houses,* a book about architecture, and *Ule,* a book about a Swedish troll.

SIDELIGHTS: On the heels of a long career in advertising that took him from his native Sweden to New York City and many other places in between, Bo Zaunders began a second career as a children's book writer in the late 1990s. Working with his illustrator wife Roxie Munro, Zaunders has published two nonfiction titles that showcase the daring of men and women from history and benefit from what a *Horn Book* contributor called his "fast-paced descriptive narration and an innate sense of history." *Crocodiles, Camels, and Dugout Canoes: Eight Adventurous Episodes* and its follow-up, *Feathers, Flaps, and Flops: Fabulous Early Fliers* contain brief biographical portraits that place each of Zaunders' subjects into their technological and historic context.

Crocodiles, Camels, and Dugout Canoes introduces readers to such people as nineteenth-century British explorer Richard Burton, mid-twentieth-century cross-

Europe cyclist Dervla Murphy, and early-twentieth-century mountaineer Annie Smith Peck. Beginning each section with what *Booklist* contributor Susan Dove Lempke characterized as "a particularly thrilling moment," Zaunders relates the career of these amateur explorers, revealing their motives to be intense curiosity rather than a quest for fame or riches. According to a *Publishers Weekly* reviewer, the enthusiasm of the husband-and-wife team—"and their subjects' own intrepid spirits—shine through the pages of this absorbing picture book." Calling *Crocodiles, Camels, and Dugout Canoes* "informative and supremely entertaining," the *Publishers Weekly* contributor concluded that Zaunders "demonstrates that reading can be a great adventure, too."

A new batch of adventurers take to the air in *Feathers, Flaps, and Flops,* as Zaunders and Munro once more tantalize young readers with their stylish nonfiction. Early-twentieth-century African-American pilot Bessie Coleman, the Montgofier brothers and their development of the hot-air balloon, dirigible innovator and pilot Alberto Santos-Dumont, and "Wrong-Way" Corrigan and his memorable 1938 flight to Ireland are among the airborne luminaries whose life stories are "told in a lively manner," according to Louise L. Sherman in her *School Library Journal* review. In addition to citing Munro's water color and ink drawings, *Booklist* contributor Carolyn Phelan praised *Feathers, Flaps, and Flops* as "an eclectic and appealing introduction to early fliers" while in *Horn Book,* Zaunders was praised for including a thorough biography and an introduction that "highlights the span of aviation history."

In addition to his work as an author, Zaunders has also illustrated several books for other authors. Reviewing his illustrations for Patricia B. Demuth's *Max, the Bad-talking Parrot,* a *Publishers Weekly* reviewer praised Zaunders for his "expressive" and "quirky" contribution to the humorous picture book, while the watercolor cartoon illustrations he contributed to Joanne Oppenheim's adaptation of *One Gift Deserves Another* were praised by a *Publishers Weekly* reviewer. Noting that the illustrations "heighten the humor, by comically exaggerating" story elements, the reviewer remarked upon Zaunders' use of bright color and "engaging peripheral touches."

"I've always loved books," Zaunders told *CA.* "By age eleven I had read every single one in my father's library—some with a flashlight, long after I was sup-posed to be asleep. Now, being involved with actually creating books is tremendously exciting. I can think of nothing more satisfying."

BIOGRAPHICAL AND CRITICAL SOURCES:

PERIODICALS

Booklist, October 15, 1998, Susan Dove Lempke, review of *Crocodiles, Camels, and Dugout Canoes: Eight Adventurous Episodes,* p. 420; August, 2001, review of *Feathers, Flaps, and Flops: Fabulous Early Fliers,* p. 2118.

Horn Book, January, 1999, review of *Crocodiles, Camels, and Dugout Canoes,* p. 85; July, 2001, review of *Feathers, Flaps, and Flops,* p. 480.

Publishers Weekly, April 25, 1986, review of *Max, the Bad-talking Parrot,* p. 73; October 5, 1992, review of *One Gift Deserves Another,* p. 69; August 31, 1998, review of *Crocodiles, Camels, and Dugout Canoes,* p. 76.

School Library Journal, November 1, 1998, Patricia Manning, review of *Crocodiles, Camels, and Dugout Canoes,* p. 144; July, 2001, Louise L. Sherman, review of *Feathers, Flaps, and Flops,* p. 101.

*   *   *

ZERBE, Richard O., Jr. 1938-

PERSONAL: Born October 2, 1938, in Nitro, WV; son of Richard (a patent agent) and Fanny (a teacher; maiden name, Carter) Zerbe; married Evelyn Ashe, 1966 (marriage ended, 1969); married Diane Husband, 1971; children: Robert Riley, Richard Alexander. *Education:* University of Oklahoma, A.B., 1960; Duke University, Ph.D., 1964. *Hobbies and other interests:* Track, cross-country skiing, history.

ADDRESSES: Home—939 21st Ave. E., Seattle, WA 98112. *Office*—Daniel J. Evans School of Public Affairs, University of Washington, Seattle, WA 98195. *E-mail*—zerbe@u.washington.edu.

CAREER: Educator and author. University of Chicago, Chicago, IL, research fellow in law and economics, 1969-71; Roosevelt University, Chicago, IL, associate professor of economics, 1971-76; University of Washington, Seattle, professor of public affairs, 1981—, adjunct professor of civil engineering, 1980-95, economics, 1990, and law, 1990—. American Bar Foundation, scholar-in-residence, 1971-72, affiliated scholar, 1972-74; University of Chicago, research associate, 1972-76; Northwestern University, visiting associate professor, 1972-76. Regional Taxicab Commission, member; European Law and Economics Project, member of scientific committee; consultant to Federal Trade Commission, U.S. Department of Justice, and Regional Commission for Airline Affairs.

MEMBER: American Law and Economics Association (founding member; past member of board of directors), American Economic Association, Association for Economic Research and Education, Law and Society Association, American Bar Association (associate member), Western Economic Association (member of executive committee, 1994-98).

AWARDS, HONORS: Grants from Ontario Department of Public Health, 1968, and Ford Foundation, 1969; award from Council of Law-related Studies, Harvard University, 1971; sea grant, 1977-78; award from National Bureau of Economic Research, 1978; Olin fellow, Yale University Law School, 1990; grant from RAND Corp., 1995; grants from National Science Foundation and Pacific Earthquake Engineering Research Center, 1999, 2000, 2001.

WRITINGS:

(With K. Croke) *Urban Transportation for the Environment,* Ballinger Press, 1975.
(With D. Dively) *Benefit-Cost Analysis in Theory and Practice,* HarperCollins (New York, NY), 1994, revised edition, 2002.
(With Jonathan Lesser and Daniel Dodds) *Environmental Economics,* Addison-Wesley, 1997.
Economic Efficiency in Law and Economics, Edward Elgar Publishing (Northampton, MA), 2001.

Contributor to books, including *Energy versus the Environment,* edited by Holleb and Alexander, University of Chicago Press (Chicago, IL), 1976; *Environmental Pollutants and the Urban Economy,* edited by George Tolley, Ballinger Press, 1981; *Coasean*

Economics: Law and Economics and the New Institutional Economics, edited by Steven G. Medema, Kluwer Academic Publishers (Boston, MA), 1997; *The Encyclopedia of Law and Economics,* Volume 1, edited by Bouckaert and DeGeest, Edward Elgar (Aldershot, England), 2000; and *Improving Regulation: Cases in Environment, Health, and Safety,* edited by Paul Fischbeck and R. Scott Farrow, Resources for the Future, 2001. Contributor of articles and reviews to periodicals, including *Regulation, Journal of Economic History, Journal of Policy Analysis and Management, Risk Analysis, Contemporary Economic Policy, Asian Economic Journal, Social Justice Research, Energy, Journal of Agriculture History,* and *Antitrust Bulletin.* Senior editor, *Research in Law and Economics Research Annual,* 1979—.

WORK IN PROGRESS: A textbook on benefit and cost analysis; a novel.

BIOGRAPHICAL AND CRITICAL SOURCES:

PERIODICALS

Economic Record, June, 2002, Megan Richardson, review of *Economic Efficiency in Law and Economics,* p. 232.

*   *   *

ZILBERGELD, Bernie 1939-2002

OBITUARY NOTICE—See index for *CA* sketch: Born June 28, 1939, in Freehold, NJ; died of complications from diabetes June 12, 2002, in Oakland, CA. Psychologist, psychotherapist, educator, and author. Zilbergeld was one of the first clinical psychologists to specialize in the area of male sexuality. At the University of California in San Francisco during the 1970s, he codirected clinical training for the school's human sexuality program. In 1978 he published *Male Sexuality: A Guide to Sexual Fulfillment;* at the time it stood almost alone as a counterpart to the proliferation of books on female sexuality. This practical book and its update, *The New Male Sexuality,* offered a self-help format complete with exercises and quizzes that contributed to their bestseller status. Zilbergeld discussed topics rarely seen in print at the time and countered the prevailing consensus of opinion that male sexuality was a simple and unproblematic function. This was not the only controversial view Zilbergeld espoused. He was a vocal critic of the popular sex therapists Masters and Johnson whose research, he claimed, could not even meet their own standards for quality and accuracy. Soon afterward, he challenged the entire discipline of psychotherapy in *The Shrinking of America: Myths of Psychological Change.* Zilbergeld argued that therapy is rarely successful in changing behavior and sometimes exacerbates a patient's problems, partly by focusing on his faults and shortcomings and partly by offering cures which, by virtue of its own flaws, it cannot achieve. His own books, conversely, were praised for the reassurance they offered, along with practical tips and advice for self-improvement. Zilbergeld maintained a private practice of psychotherapy near Berkeley, California, from 1972. He also lectured widely, appeared in media interviews, and contributed to the *San Francisco Chronicle.* At the time of his death, he had reportedly completed a book on sexuality and aging.

OBITUARIES AND OTHER SOURCES:

PERIODICALS

Los Angeles Times, July 21, 2002, p. B17.
New York Times, June 21, 2002, obituary by Anahad O'Connor, p. A23.
San Francisco Chronicle, June 20, 2002, obituary by Kelly St. John, p. A20.

ZIMMERMANN, Matilde 1943-

PERSONAL: Born 1943, in Washington, DC. *Education:* Harvard University, A.B. (magna cum laude), 1964; University of Wisconsin—Madison, M.A., 1967; University of Pittsburgh, Ph.D., 1998.

ADDRESSES: Office—Department of History, Sarah Lawrence College, 1 Mead Way, Bronxville, NY 10708. *E-mail*—mzimmermann@slc.edu.

CAREER: Vassar College, Poughkeepsie, NY, assistant professor of history, 1998-99; Marist College, Poughkeepsie, assistant professor of history, 1999-2000; Bridgewater State College, Bridgewater, MA, assistant professor of history, 2000-02; Sarah Lawrence College, Bronxville, NY, professor of history, 2002—.

WRITINGS:

Sandinista: Carlos Fonseca and the Nicaraguan Revolution, Duke University Press (Durham, NC), 2001.

BIOGRAPHICAL AND CRITICAL SOURCES:

PERIODICALS

Perspectives on Political Science, fall, 2001, Edward S. Mihalkanin, review of *Sandinista: Carlos Fonseca and the Nicaraguan Revolution,* p. 240.